BIOLOGICAL
ANTHROPOLOGY

BIOLOGICAL ANTHROPOLOGY

A Synthetic Approach to Human Evolution

Second Edition

Noel T. Boaz

International Institute for Human Evolutionary Research

Alan J. Almquist

California State University–Hayward

Prentice Hall

Upper Saddle River, New Jersey 07458

Library of Congress Cataloging-in-Publication Data

Boaz, Noel Thomas.
   Biological anthropology : a synthetic approach to human evolution / Noel T. Boaz,
Alan J. Almquist.—2nd ed.
      p. cm.
   Includes bibliographical references and index.
   ISBN 0-13-090819-3
   1. Physical anthropology. 2. Human evolution. I. Almquist, Alan J. II. Title.

GN60 .B67 2002
599.9—dc21
                                                                    2001051150

AVP/Publisher: *Nancy Roberts*
Editorial Assistant: *Lee Peterson*
Developmental Editor: *Elaine Silverstein*
VP, Director of Manufacturing and Production:
   Barbara Kittle
Executive Managing Editor: *Ann Marie McCarthy*
Production Liaison: *Fran Russello*
Project Manager: *Linda B. Pawelchak*
Manufacturing Manager: *Nick Sklitsis*
Prepress and Manufacturing Buyer: *Ben Smith*
Creative Design Director: *Leslie Osher*
Art Director: *Nancy Wells*

Interior and Cover Design: *C2K, Inc.*
Cover Art: *John Gurche Studios*
Director, Image Resource Center: *Melinda Lee Reo*
Interior Image Specialist: *Beth Boyd*
Manager, Rights and Permissions: *Kay Dellosa*
Photo Researcher: *Sheila Norman*
Manager, Art Formatting: *Guy Ruggiero*
Line Art Coordinator: *Mirella Signoretto*
Marketing Manager: *Chris Barker*
Copy Editing: *Katherine Evancie*
Proofreading: *Ann-Marie WongSam*

Acknowledgments begin on page 496, which constitutes
a continuation of this copyright page.

This book was set in 10/12 Sabon by Interactive Composition
Corp. and was printed and bound by Banta Book Group.
The cover was printed by Phoenix Color Corp.

Printed in the United States of America
10 9 8 7 6 5 4 3 2 1

ISBN 0-13-090819-3

Pearson Education LTD., *London*
Pearson Education Australia PTY, Limited, *Sydney*
Pearson Education Singapore, Pte. Ltd
Pearson Education North Asia Ltd, *Hong Kong*
Pearson Education Canada, Ltd, *Toronto*
Pearson Educación de Mexico, S.A. de C.V.
Pearson Education—Japan, *Tokyo*
Pearson Education Malaysia, Pte. Ltd
Pearson Education, Upper Saddle River, New Jersey

To Our Children

Lydia, Peter, and Alexander
Christopher and Emily

Brief Contents

CONTENTS

8 PRIMATES: PATTERNS IN SOCIAL BEHAVIOR   194

9 INTRODUCTION TO THE HOMINOIDS   224

10 THE AUSTRALOPITHECINES   244

11 THE GENUS HOMO   277

16 HUMANS IN EVOLUTIONARY PERSPECTIVE: APPLIED BIOLOGICAL ANTHROPOLOGY   439

BOXED FEATURES

FRONTIER BOXES

RESEARCH HIGHLIGHTS BOXES

The first edition of *Biological Anthropology* appeared in 1997. Since that time, a significant number of new discoveries in all of the subfields have been made that have altered to a greater or lesser extent our understanding of ourselves. Perhaps the most rapidly changing subfield of biological anthropology is that of paleoanthropology, or the study of our origins and evolution. During 2000 and 2001, two new genera of fossil hominids were announced based on discoveries that, in one instance, exceeded 5 million years of age. We were able to report on this discovery of a new fossil genus called *Orrorin* in this edition. We were not able to report on one new subspecies of another hominid genus, *Ardipithecus,* a fossil hominid that, up to this point, we believed was only 4.5 million years of age because of publication deadlines. We will take the opportunity here to say that this new subspecies, called *Ardipithecus ramidus kadabba,* is represented by cranial, dental, and postcranial fragments, including a toe bone. This is enough to establish this new 5.5–million-year-old fossil from a site in the Middle Awash region of Ethiopia as the earliest upright walking biped thus far known.

Such discoveries, while not what one should consider commonplace, do set the field of biological anthropology off as different from many others because change, not quiescence, is its hallmark. This alone makes it nearly impossible to write a textbook that is completely up-to-date with new discoveries and the interpretations of those discoveries that follow by researchers who study them. It also makes this field one of the most fascinating, perhaps imponderable, likening itself to a mystery story whose plot not only thickens but is continually altered by a never-ending stream of new facts. Realizing our limitations to elucidate, we can only hope that we have passed on the sense of the fascination that will spark our readers to seek out answers to the many questions that remain about the human condition.

ABOUT THE BOOK

We believe *Biological Anthropology, Second Edition,* represents both a useful approach to the teaching of biological anthropology at the introductory college and university level and a restatement of the coherency and fundamental compatibility of the many subfields that contribute to its makeup. Throughout the book, the reader will find the unifying thread of evolution by natural selection that forms the basic paradigm of the discipline. As scientists, we believe that every question should remain open to the possibility of a new answer; however, Charles Darwin's formulations of evolution and its later modifications continue to be our best explanation for life on earth and the world around us.

This work remains organized along lines of increasing complexity of living forms, beginning from prebiotic replicating molecules through to modern *Homo sapiens*. Since this book is devoted to issues that revolve around us, we have devoted considerable space in the text to considering our past and present situation and, in an educated fashion, to speculating about our future. We have used available paleo-ecological data to set the stage and provide the context of the morphological and behavioral adaptations that have characterized our ancestors during each phase of our evolution. We believe that this organization serves to build students' understanding of the biological, genetic, and anatomical basics of biological anthropology so that complex questions of human relatedness to other life forms, behavior, variability, and modern-day adaptation to our increasingly demanding environments can be approached in more meaningful ways.

In a field as fast paced as biological anthropology, we welcome the opportunity to revise and update the original text. New insights into old problems, new fossil finds, new people working in the field, and, sadly, people who have made their contribution and passed on—all require comment. Of the many contributors who have died since we first began this project, we note the death of our mentor, Professor Sherwood L. Washburn, whose influence continues to be felt throughout much of this new text, and Professor Jean de Heinzelin, whose contributions to African geochronology will remain the benchmark for others for years to come. A large part of the fascination that we have for this field came from knowing and working with these individuals.

HIGHLIGHTS OF THE SECOND EDITION

Every chapter in the second edition has been revised, and several new chapters have been added when it appeared that greater detail was necessary to explain some parts of the field more clearly. These revisions were the outcome of the combined efforts of reviewers, students who have used the original text, and our second look at what we had done in the first edition.

An expanded section on genetics, which includes Chapters 2 and 3, provides a clearer emphasis on Mendelian genetics and gives new emerging data on genetics and natural selection.

A new chapter on the living nonhuman primates highlights their distribution and anatomical adaptations.

The section on human evolution has been expanded to accommodate the growing fossil evidence and now includes a full chapter on *Homo sapiens sapiens*.

A new chapter comparing and contrasting ape and human behavior provides a more coherent picture of the evolution and development of hominoid social behavior.

The unique chapter on applied biological anthropology now includes a discussion of evolutionary medicine and provides the guidelines as to how to relate the accumulated data of biological anthropology to problems that modern urban humans face.

An expanded box series allows students to explore important concepts in each chapter.

Frontiers *Frontiers* boxes look at new research and the direction this research might take in the future. For example, in the final chapter a Frontiers box looks at the subject of nanotechnology, a new field whose products are atom-sized self-replicating machines capable of doing work of nearly infinite variety. The potential for harm, however, is predicted by evolutionary theory—if rogue machines created by "mutation" begin to self-replicate in directions not foreseen by their creators.

Research Highlights New research and how this research has affected our understanding of current problems are featured in *Research Highlights*. For example, a recent hominid fossil discovery made by Meave Leakey and her team on the western shores of Lake Turkana, Kenya, holds promise of altering our ideas about early human evolution. This discovery, which the Leakey team has called *Kenyanthropus*, is dated to about 3.5 million years ago and is contemporaneous with the well-known fossil group *Australopithecus afarensis*, of which "Lucy" is a member. Many paleoanthropologists believe that more than one taxon of bipeds evolved during the early phases of hominid evolution. *Kenyanthropus* may be just the discovery to help prove that point. The human family tree at its trunk may be a lot more "bushy" than we thought.

A running glossary has been added to each chapter. The definitions of key terms have been placed in the margins so that students will be able to find them more quickly and efficiently. The full glossary is also located at the end of the book.

INTEGRATING MEDIA AND TECHNOLOGY

We have made this edition more user friendly by taking advantage of the advanced technology of the Internet.

Expanded Internet exercises are found at the end of each chapter, allowing students to take full advantage of incredible resources of this new powerful databank. A *Critical Thinking Exercise* and a *Writing Assignment* are included; a complete listing of Internet resources to help students complete the exercises is located on the Companion Website™ that accompanies this book.

New to this edition, a *MediaLab* is located at the end of every chapter. The topics were carefully chosen not only for student interest but also because they highlight information that students may very well encounter in their daily lives. All of the necessary information is included in the text; the static becomes dynamic once the student accesses the Companion Website™ for animations or videos to illustrate the topic. As a summation, students are asked to communicate the results of their explorations.

SUPPLEMENTS FOR THE STUDENT

Companion Website In tandem with the text, students can now take full advantage of the World Wide Web to enrich their study of biological anthropology through the Boaz Companion Website™. This resource correlates the text with related material available on the Internet. Features include chapter objectives, study questions, research projects, animations, and links to additional material that can reinforce and enhance the content of each chapter. **Address: www.prenhall.com/boaz**

Anthropology on the Internet: Evaluating Online Resources, 2001 This guide focuses on developing the critical thinking skills necessary to evaluate and use online sources effectively. The guide also provides a brief introduction to navigating the Internet, along with complete references related specifically to the anthropology discipline and how to use the Companion Websites™ available for many Prentice Hall textbooks. This brief supplementary book is free to students when shrink wrapped as a package with *Biological Anthropology, Second Edition.*

The New York Times/Prentice Hall Themes of the Times The *New York Times* and Prentice Hall are sponsoring *Themes of the Times*, a program designed to enhance student access to current information relevant to the classroom. Through this program, the core subject matter provided in the text is supplemented by a collection of timely articles from one of the world's most distinguished newspapers, the *New York Times*. These articles demonstrate the vital, ongoing connection between what is learned in the classroom and what is happening in the world around us. To enjoy a wealth of information provided by the *New York Times* daily, a reduced subscription rate is available. For information, call toll-free: 1-800-631-1222.

Prentice Hall and the *New York Times* are proud to co-sponsor *Themes of the Times*. We hope it will make the reading of both textbooks and newspapers a more dynamic, involving process.

SUPPLEMENTS FOR THE INSTRUCTOR

Instructor's Resource Manual with Tests This essential instructor's tool includes chapter outlines, resources for discussion, discussion questions, paper topics and research projects, Web resources, and film resources. In addition, the test portion of the manual includes 1,600 questions in multiple-choice, true/false, and essay formats. All test questions are page referenced to the text. The test questions are available in both **Windows** and **Macintosh** computerized formats. Contact your Prentice Hall representative for more details.

Distance Learning Solutions Prentice Hall is committed to providing our anthropology content to the growing number of courses being delivered over the Internet by developing relationships with the leading platforms, as well as Course Compass, Prentice Hall's own easy-to-use course management system powered by Blackboard™. Please visit our technology solutions Website at http://www. prenhall. com/demo for more information or contact your local Prentice Hall sales representative.

The second edition of *Biological Anthropology* continues to present the field as an exciting, challenging, and ever changing one. Above all else, though, we continue to believe that the importance of this book lies in our efforts to present many different ideas to be discussed and, as warranted, challenged by the reader.

ACKNOWLEDGMENTS

Many individuals have shaped this book now and in the past. The late Sherwood Washburn and Jane Lancaster were instrumental in developing our ideas of a text that brought together fossils and behavior. The late Joe Birdsell was an important influence in our incorporation of ecology and population perspectives. John Cronin deserves credit for contributing the concept of a textbook that fully integrates molecular and fossil approaches, and we are grateful for his continuing interest in this text. We are indebted to the authors of the text's Research Highlights and Frontiers boxes, who agreed to share their perspectives and insights: Lloyd H. Burckle, Linda D.Wolfe, David R. Begun, Alan Walker, Craig B. Stanford, and S. Boyd Eaton.

Biological Anthropology continues to be a reality because one individual at Prentice Hall makes it so. We are indebted to Nancy Roberts, who has spearheaded this edition through the publishing process. She has always believed in this book and encouraged us onward. Within the scope of Nancy's vision came the other creative people we worked with on a day-to-day basis. We continue to recognize past efforts of one of our former editors, Sabina Johnson. A sentence cannot be written without feeling the guidance of her wit and good humor. We will miss her.

For this edition, as it was for our companion volume, *Essentials of Biological Anthropology,* the careful and painstaking work of Elaine Silverstein, developmental editor for Prentice Hall is gratefully acknowledged. Elaine's patience and perseverance should be a model for all developmental editors to come. Our production editor, Linda Pawelchak, must also be given a large measure of credit and thanks for bringing the manuscript through this process and into publication. This, too, was no mean feat. All of these talented individuals, along with those who obtained the necessary permissions, and the artists at Prentice Hall, who created new art often from nothing more than our crudely drawn sketches, did a truly magnificent job. We gratefully thank all of you for your efforts.

As in the past, readers and reviewers have helped immensely in refining passages of the text and helping us rephrase muddled text. We particularly wish to acknowledge and thank Dr. Katherine Dettwyler of Texas A&M University for an exhaustive review of the manuscript, along with her help and assistance in the collegial way it was offered. In addition, the following people provided extensive feedback for this revision:

John A. Williams	University of North Dakota
Peer H. Moore-Jansen	Wichita State University
R. D. McCall	Univ. of North Carolina–Wilmington
John R. Baker	Moorpark College
Lorena Madrigal	University of South Florida
Della Collins Cook	Indiana University
Paul J. Bybee	Utah Valley State College
Timi L. Barone	University of Nebraska—Omaha
Leonard Greenfield	Temple University
Mark Fleischman	Syracuse University
Robert Shanafelt	Florida State University
Lawrence Kuznar	Indiana-Purdue at Fort Wayne
Edward A. Wheeler	Butte College

Students at California State University, Hayward, also contributed to the development of the text by their many questions and careful reading, pointing out places where improvement might be warranted. We thank all of you. We offer, however, no excuses for omissions or errors that may still be found in the text. Despite the fine work of our reviewers, that final call was ours.

For much of the research in biological anthropology that has been conducted and reported on in this edition, we wish to thank the L.S.B. Leakey Foundation of San Francisco, California, for its program of grants and awards and its untiring efforts to fund scientific endeavors. We especially would like to thank Kay Woods, president of the foundation, and the members of the board of trustees who have furthered knowledge in this field through their most generous financial support of scientists in the field. Toward our own support of new research (and, thus, assuring that we will have something to write about in the future), a portion of the royalties from the sale of this book is being donated to the L.S.B. Leakey Foundation.

Finally, once again, the forbearance, support, and encouragement of Barbara Almquist and Meleisa McDonell ensured that the second edition of *Biological Anthropology* did not take the decade, though it seemed like that at times, to complete that the first edition did. For that we are all most grateful.

Noel Boaz
Alan Almquist

Noel T. Boaz is founder of the International Institute for Human Evolutionary Research in Oregon and Professor of Anatomy at Ross University School of Medicine. Dr. Boaz received his Ph.D. in biological anthropology at the University of California at Berkeley in 1977 and is currently working on his M.D. degree. A paleoanthropologist with many years of field experience in Africa, his most recent research has been on Chinese *Homo erectus*. Other research interests include earliest hominid origins, paleoecology, evolutionary medicine, and forensic anthropology. In 1999, Dr. Boaz was scientific planning director in Bosnia for Physicians for Human Rights. His most recent publications include *Eco Homo* (1997), an ecological history of the human species, and *Evolving Health* (2002), an application of human evolutionary biology to preventive medicine.

Alan J. Almquist is Professor of Anthropology at California State University, Hayward. Dr. Almquist received his Ph.D. in Anthropology in 1974 at the University of California, Berkeley. A dedicated teacher, he has also headed the Clarence Smith Museum of Anthropology at Hayward and has undertaken fieldwork at early hominid sites in the Middle Awash, Ethiopia. Current research interests include the evolution of human sexual behavior and paleoanthropology. Publications include *Milestones in Human Evolution* (1993) edited with Ann Manyak; a reader, *Human Sexuality* (1995) with Andrei Simic and Patricia Omidian; and *Contemporary Readings in Physical Anthropology* (2000), a collection of articles from the *New York Times*, edited by Dr. Almquist and published by Prentice Hall.

EVOLUTIONARY PERSPECTIVES ON HUMAN BIOLOGY AND BEHAVIOR

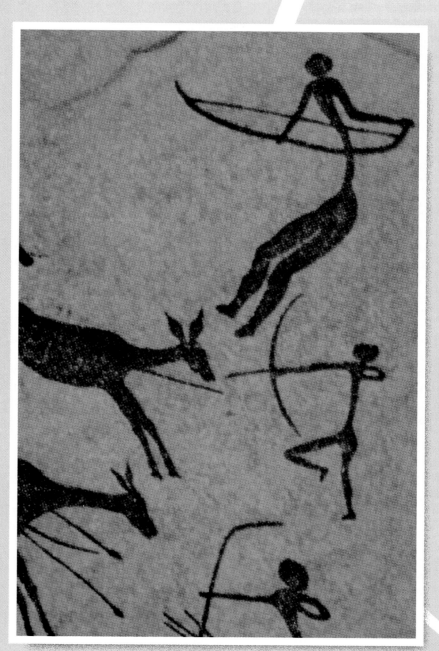

OUTLINE

After reading this chapter, you should be able to discuss the following questions:

1. What fields of study are included within anthropology? Within biological anthropology?
2. What are the steps in the scientific method, and how do biological anthropologists use the scientific method to study human and primate differences?
3. What subjects do biological anthropologists study?
4. What bases do scientists use for classifying organisms? How are scientific names assigned to organisms?
5. What tools do biological anthropologists use to reconstruct the evolutionary relationships between species?
6. What can the perspective of human evolution teach us about the human condition, both today and in the past?

biological anthropology: the study of human evolution, biology, variation, and adaptation (also known as physical anthropology).

FIGURE 1–1 The survival of early human ancestors on the African savanna 3 million years ago, as depicted by a contemporary French artist. We are still quick-witted, omnivorous opportunists.

Biological anthropology is about humankind's place in nature, how we came to be, how and why our bodies and brains are built the way they are, and why we behave as we do. Portions of these subjects are studied by scientists in many diverse disciplines, but the general, or holistic, study of them is the domain of biological anthropology. This broad-based understanding of the human organism is the strength of biological anthropology, and in today's increasingly specialized world of science, it is an important perspective.

The basic scientific framework of modern biological anthropology is *evolution by natural selection,* the theory that explains the origin and diversity of species on earth. This theory provides scientists with a way to make predictions about human evolution, biology, and behavior and to test their predictions against observations made in nature. These observations may involve laboratory experiments, field studies of our living primate relatives in remote rain forests, or excavations of fossils millions of years old. To give our readers an overall appreciation of human adaptation, anatomy, behavior, and evolution, this book integrates the advances that biological anthropologists have made in understanding human evolution and biology. We draw on many different lines of evidence to demonstrate both the uniqueness of the human condition and those continuities that make humans part of nature.

Human beings evolved out of and are still today intimately connected with the natural world. Our ancestors lived as gatherers and hunters for the past several million years. We have lived in permanent structures packed into villages, towns, and cities, growing food plants, tending domesticated animals, and using metal tools for the past few thousand years. This period is less than one-half of 1 percent of the length of time since our ancestors became stone tool-using, larger brained early humans—approximately 2.5 million years ago. Our biology is still that of hunter-gatherers, quick-witted opportunists who can eat almost anything and who can survive under conditions of great hardship as well as prosperity (Figure 1–1).

ANTHROPOLOGY AND BIOLOGICAL ANTHROPOLOGY

Anthropology is the science that studies humans, their biology, behavior, and variations. Anthropologists study humans within the context of a specialized **adaptation** of learned social behavior called **culture**. Anthropologists study such broad-ranging phenomena as physical and cultural differences among human groups, the structure of the many human languages, the adaptability of human groups to different environmental conditions, the patterns of growth, and the changing patterns of culture over time. This broad scientific agenda makes anthropology a discipline with many specialists and many subdisciplines. For this reason, anthropological research is frequently described as *multidisciplinary*. One characteristic of all anthropologists is a commitment to understanding humanity in its entirety as a functioning whole. For this reason anthropology is also termed *holistic*.

Anthropology in the United States consists of four fields: biological or physical anthropology, **cultural anthropology** or ethnology, **archaeology**, and **linguistics** (Figure 1–2). Biological anthropologists study the physical makeup, evolution, and variations of human populations; the relationships of humanity with the natural world; and the biological bases of human behavior. Cultural anthropologists study living societies of people, their customs, their myths, their kinship systems, their rituals, and all aspects of their social behavior within the uniquely human adaptation of culture. Archaeologists examine how human culture has adapted and evolved over time through the study of artifacts and sites. Linguists study language: its many varieties, the forces governing how languages change, the relationships between language and the brain, and the interactions between language and cultural concepts. The four disciplines are joined, sometimes loosely, by their shared focus on human adaptation within culture—that set of learned behaviors that, shared by all members of a society, mediates all social interactions.

Biological anthropology, the subject of this book, is closely related to the branch of biology known as **human biology**. Biological anthropologists strive to accurately describe human physical structure, both in the present and in the past. They seek to understand how human structure functions in real life and how human individuals

anthropology: the study of humankind.

adaptation: biological change effected by evolution to accommodate populations to different environmental conditions.

culture: learned aspects of behavior passed on from one generation to the next in human societies.

cultural anthropology: the anthropological study of human societies, their belief systems, their cultural adaptations, and their social behavior.

archaeology: the anthropological study of past cultures, their social adaptations, and their lifeways by use of preserved artifacts and features.

linguistics: the anthropological study of languages, their diversity and connections, and the interaction of language and culture in society.

human biology: the branch of biological anthropology that studies human physiology and adaptation.

FIGURE 1–2   The four fields of anthropology, and the related fields that contribute to the knowledge base of biological anthropology.

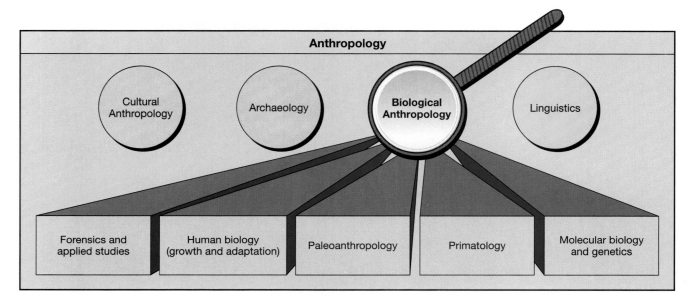

with that structure behave. In addition, biological anthropologists investigate how function and behavior are integrated into the environment in which human beings live. Because they want to understand the origins of structures, biological anthropologists also explore human genetics, growth and development, and evolutionary history.

There are some strong connections between biological anthropology and other anthropological subdisciplines. For example, biological anthropologists may associate with archaeologists in the interdisciplinary area of **paleoanthropology,** the study of human evolution through fossils and artifacts (Figure 1–3). Biological anthropologists may find it essential to put together their knowledge of skeletal biology with that of the cultural contexts that the archaeologist has discovered in order to better understand a past human population.

Many of the subject areas relevant to understanding human evolution and biology discussed in this book are taught not only in anthropology departments but also within departments of biology, genetics, biochemistry, anatomy, geology, geography, environmental sciences, and psychology. Researchers in human evolution may call themselves biological anthropologists, biologists, geneticists, biochemists, geologists, anatomists, paleontologists, or psychologists, depending on their research specialty. We use *biological anthropology* and *biological anthropologists* as the most inclusive terms to refer to this broad, interdisciplinary field. Our goal in this book is to provide a synthetic, or unified, treatment of these diverse facets of biological anthropology.

paleoanthropology:
the study of the physical characteristics, evolution, and behavior of fossil humans and their relatives, incorporating parts of biological anthropology and archaeology.

FIGURE 1–3
Paleoanthropologists and archaeologists at work in the field laying out a grid before beginning a surface excavation in Kenya.

✦ FRONTIERS

Forensic Anthropology in Investigations of Genocide

One of the most visible of the applied fields of biological anthropology today is forensic anthropology. Forensic anthropologists study human skeletal remains to determine victims' age, sex, stature, race or population affinities, personal characteristics, history of injuries, and time since death. They work closely with forensic pathologists, with police, and with international human rights organizations in solving crimes.

A growing area of forensic anthropological work is in the realm of international human rights. The Balkans, particularly Bosnia and Kosovo, have been the sites of horrendous genocidal wars in recent years. By the end of 1999, working under contract with such nongovernmental organizations as the U.S.-based Physicians for Human Rights and the International Court of Justice in The Hague, the Netherlands, forensic anthropologists have assisted local authorities and forensic pathologists

in exhuming and analyzing some 5,000 bodies in Bosnia. An estimated minimum of 19,000 bodies of missing persons in Bosnia remain to be found, exhumed, identified, and returned to their families for burial.

New approaches for finding clandestine graves or skeletal remains left on the surface of the ground have been developed. "Cadaver dogs" specially trained to detect the scent of decaying bodies or skeletons have become very useful. With the help of a soil probe to punch into the ground at suspected locations of buried remains, cadaver dogs can materially help in finding bodies of long-dead victims. In Bosnia, where the war ended in 1995, almost all bodies not buried in airtight coffins, immersed in water, or wrapped in plastic are now skeletonized (Figure 1–4). Ground-penetrating radar can also help in locating deeper graves. But witnesses willing to come forward are still the best source for locating grave sites for missing persons.

Once graves are located, forensic anthropologists must ensure that the remains are excavated with as much

care as has traditionally been given to rare and very ancient fossil remains. Sometimes these excavators are called "forensic archaeologists." But in Bosnia there are so many bodies that are waiting to be exhumed that the process needs to be rapid and efficient. Excavation teams frequently use heavy machinery, such as backhoes, to excavate down to near the bodies and then proceed through the last centimeters using shovels and trowels. New techniques that include the use of precision backhoes mounted on four-wheel drive vehicles, mobile autopsy labs, and portable forensic DNA analysis units are being developed to help the process.

There are two primary uses for the results of forensic anthropological investigations: to prosecute and seek convictions of perpetrators of crimes, be they crimes against individuals or crimes against humanity; and to provide identifications of missing persons to family members and loved ones, an increasingly important humanitarian application of biological anthropology.

FIGURE 1–4 Forensic anthropologists at work at a mass grave in Bosnia.

The Science of Biological Anthropology

Anthropology, biology, and other branches of science use a *hypothetico-deductive* scientific method, which requires the framing of ideas in the form of hypotheses. A **hypothesis** is a preliminary explanation of observations phrased as a proposition, for example, if X is true, then Y is true. The most significant characteristic of a hypothesis is that it must be falsifiable; that is, we must be able to *disprove* it. Testing and experimentation determine whether a given hypothesis explains or conforms with an observation. If it does not, it is rejected or modified. A **theory** is a hypothesis or a series of hypotheses that has stood the test of time and numerous attempts at falsification.

Deductive reasoning is the process whereby observed facts are gathered and then explained by a plausible hypothesis. It is distinguished from inductive reasoning, in which principles are inferred only after facts have been gathered. Modern scientists generate hypotheses to guide their investigations. The hypothetico-deductive method distinguishes science from the humanities.

The most widely understood application of the scientific method is the *experiment*. Scientists formulate a question that they want to answer, devise a test in which the variables are all held constant except those being tested, run the experiment while varying the conditions of interest, and compare the results to a *control* condition in which all the variables are held constant. This is the standard mode of operation in experimental sciences such as physics and chemistry.

In the science of biological anthropology, investigators often interview, observe, measure, and analyze in an attempt to develop explanations that fit the known facts. Biological anthropologists may then generate hypotheses and afterward go back to the data (or gather new data) to test these hypotheses. For example, a researcher might propose testing the hypothesis that a male langur monkey, when he displaces the dominant male in the social group, tends to kill infants that have been fathered by the previous dominant male. This is a testable hypothesis. Either the males kill the infants most of the time or they do not (Figure 1–5).

Biological anthropology is also a historical science concerned with reconstructing past events. Hypotheses relating to events that happened millions of years ago in the human evolutionary past may seem to be beyond the scope of experiment. But experiments have been designed that re-create the conditions of the past in order to test various hypotheses. Paleoanthropological studies, for example, may be designed to discover how and under what circumstances fossils or artifacts were buried in sediments. In attempting to answer these questions, scientists conduct experiments to see what sorts of changes occur in bones in modern environments. They may observe hyenas at a kill, collect the bones after the hyenas are finished,

hypothesis: an explanation of a set of observations that can be disproved or falsified by additional observations or facts.

theory: usually a set of hypotheses that withstands attempts at disproof and continues to successfully explain observations as they are made, thus gaining scientific support over time.

deductive reasoning: the process whereby observed facts are gathered and then explained by a plausible hypothesis.

FIGURE 1–5 The steps in the scientific method include formulating a hypothesis, making observations, and drawing a conclusion based on those observations.

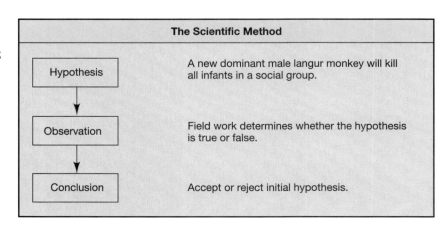

and look at the bones under a microscope. They may examine the scratches on bone after trampling by a herd of cattle. Or they may examine the cut marks made when meat is cut off bones using stone tools. These sorts of experiments may tell researchers whether a particular scratch pattern found at a fossil site was made by the teeth of predators, by trampling under hooves, or by the hands of ancient humans while obtaining meat for food.

In the natural sciences the concept of experiment has been broadened to encompass the comparative study of animals and plants in different habitats, environments, or time periods. In a real sense these natural scientists are doing experiments, but instead of varying experimental conditions themselves, they allow nature to vary the conditions. For example, Charles Darwin undertook these sorts of studies in the Galápagos Islands off South America (see Chapter 2) when he compared the animal species on various islands to determine how they had responded biologically to different environmental conditions.

For both ethical and practical reasons, biological anthropologists cannot perform controlled laboratory experiments on human beings. Therefore, they undertake comparative studies of human groups to test alternative hypotheses for human biological differences. For example, anthropologists interested in the causes of the unique, physical attributes of people living high in the Andes Mountains (see Chapter 15) can compare the anatomy of members of the group who moved to the lowlands as children with that of relatives who stayed at home. In this way, the researchers can test whether environment or inheritance was the main cause of the mountain group's physical characteristics.

The Paradigms of Biological Anthropology

Like other fields of science, biological anthropology has a method of inquiry and an associated set of questions that serve as an organizing framework of inquiry, or a **paradigm.** Observations that are made and tests or experiments that are undertaken are grounded in these paradigms. For example, if we observe that different peoples around the world have different colors of skin, we must explain how these differences are caused, how they originated in the past, and how they are affected by today's world. The paradigms that biological anthropologists use to explain such human diversity have changed significantly over the years. We examine these changes in the following paragraphs.

Typology. In the early years of biological anthropology, when scientific interest lay in putting the vast array of new information about human diversity into some sort of order, the paradigm of biological anthropology was typology. **Typology** is the designation of one individual, drawn from a larger group, as typical of that group. It is defined as the *type*. Typology attempts to define a clear set of criteria that can be used to characterize any given species and to classify individuals within that group. For example, if a typologist was interested in studying dogs, he or she might choose a type, say an individual German shepherd, to exemplify the concept of dog (species *Canis familiaris*). Although the researcher might be aware that there is quite a bit of variation in dogs, from Chihuahuas to Great Danes, typologists deemphasize individual variation from the type, because the goal is to classify the diversity of life. There is nothing wrong with typology, which is still the first step in biological investigations, because we must know and define the species with which we are working. But other paradigms have come into play that are important.

Typology was the first organized approach to studying the human species. The founder of biological anthropology, German scientist Johann Friedrich Blumenbach (1752–1840), whose interest lay in chronicling the worldwide diversity of modern human beings, used typology to define different human "races," or biological

paradigm: a framework for understanding and interpreting observations.

typology: idealist definition of an entire group by reference to a type that tends to ignore variation from that ideal.

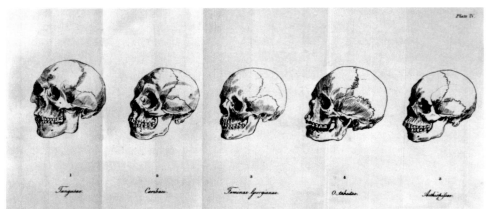

FIGURE 1–6 Johann Friedrich Blumenbach, the founder of biological anthropology, and his classification of human "races": Mongolian, or "yellow" (*Tungusae*); American, or "red" (*Caribaei*); Caucasian, or "white" (*Georgianae*); Malayan, or "brown" (*Taheitae*); and Ethiopian, or "black" (*Aethiopilsae*). This arbitrary division of the human species has been rejected by modern biological anthropologists.

groups (Figure 1–6). He established types that were ideals of whole groups of people. Blumenbach divided the human species into five major divisions based on physical characteristics and geography. This grouping became the accepted formulation for many years. Today's biological anthropologists have much more data on modern human biological variation than were available to Blumenbach, and we now know that all human beings are much more alike than different (see Chapter 14 for a detailed discussion of human variation). Yet Blumenbach's pioneering work was important in establishing the groundwork for the later development of biological anthropology.

Culture.   Culture, the human adaptation of learned social behavior, became a second important paradigm in biological anthropology. In the early phases of the history of anthropology, many human attributes were considered innate characteristics—that is, inherited and not affected by environment, for example, the large canine teeth found in many monkeys and apes. Early anthropologists might describe a group of South Sea Islanders, previously unknown to Westerners, by the color of their skin, the color and curl of their hair, the clothes they wore, their marriage customs, the language spoken by the group, and even individuals' psychological attributes, all in the same context of innate characteristics. But as indigenous peoples began to migrate to Europe, it became apparent that specific cultural patterns were not innate to a particular human group and could be changed. A young Australian aborigine or a Maasai from Kenya could be transplanted to England; attend Eton and Oxford; and end up speaking, acting, dressing, and thinking just like someone of similar educational background who was a native of England. However, nothing changed the essential physical characteristics of the Australian or the Maasai, even if he or she did speak with an "Oxbridge" accent. Clearly, physical and cultural traits were controlled by different laws.

Cultural anthropologists, archaeologists, and linguists study how and why cultures differ one from another and how a particular culture meshes with its environment. A question that an anthropologist studying culture might ask, for example, is why a Polynesian tribe would have elaborate prayers, ceremonies, and gear for dangerous fishing on the open sea, and simple and few cultural attributes for relatively safe fishing in lagoons. One possible answer is that magic and religion, along with material culture, help humans cope with the environment. Culture, then, is one of the primary ways that humans adapt to their environment.

FIGURE 1–7 A mother chimpanzee in the Tai Forest, Ivory Coast, uses a stone hammer to crack open a nut while her offspring watches. Chimpanzees in neighboring areas, despite the availability of nuts and stones, do not use this technology. This is evidence for the existence of culture among chimpanzee groups.

Biological anthropologists have also contributed to the concept of culture. Primatologists studying the behavior of chimpanzees, for example, maintain that a number of behaviors seen in the wild are learned and passed on by learning within the social group (Figure 1–7). Many of our colleagues, as we discuss later in this book, argue that chimpanzees can invent new customs and technologies, and that these behaviors are passed on socially rather than genetically.

Evolution by natural selection.   The third paradigm of importance to biological anthropology is **evolution by natural selection**. This theory holds that nature will favor the fittest individuals, those that possess traits that allow them to survive and to have more offspring. The process of passing on these traits leads to biological differentiation over time, and eventually it may result in the formation of new species (see Chapter 2). Biological anthropologists use evolution by natural selection as the basis for many research projects. Biological anthropologists study human biological variability. Some of this variability is associated with the geographic location of human groups. Other variability is caused by the biological and physical adaptation to particular environments. The evolutionary paradigm (one of a number of other explanations that we discuss later in this book) helps explain the biological variability seen in human groups, and it provides a means to make predictions and to test hypotheses. Chapters 2, 3, and 4 deal at length with evolution by natural selection, and they provide the organizing framework for succeeding chapters.

SUBJECTS THAT BIOLOGICAL ANTHROPOLOGISTS STUDY

Biological anthropologists study how and why groups of people differ physically and genetically from one another, how they adapt biologically to their environments, how they grow and develop, and how the human species ultimately originated in the animal world. These questions can be framed broadly as questions relating to human evolution, that is, the laws that underlie human variation, adaptation, and patterns of physical change through space and time.

evolution by natural selection: Darwin and Wallace's theory that inherited variability results in the differential survival of individuals and in their ability to contribute to offspring in succeeding generations.

Human Differences

Biological anthropologists study human **variation** and ask questions about human differences. One such question is, "How and why do people around the world look different?" Human beings throughout the world look different partly because they have adapted to different environmental conditions (for example, the majority of people who live in the sunny tropics have dark skin color) and partly because each population has a different history of migrations and infusions of peoples from elsewhere. Untangling the causes of variation can be complex. Humans have adapted successfully to different habitats throughout the world today. How and under what conditions adaptability is expressed in growth patterns, physiology, or anatomical traits is an area of ongoing research in biological anthropology.

How Human Populations Adapt

Biological change over time to accommodate environmental conditions is called *adaptation.* The long-term adaptation of humans and other populations of living organisms to the varied habitats into which they have spread over time is a focus of evolutionary studies. This adaptation occurs by anatomical change and is little modified by environment during individuals' lifetimes.

Changes that might occur within the lifetimes of individuals reflect what is known as **adaptability** (we consider this topic in detail in Chapter 14). Such short-term reversible responses to immediate environmental challenges are part of everyone's biological heritage. For example, people who live high in the mountains have larger lungs that extract more oxygen from the air than the smaller lungs of lowland-dwelling people.

Origins

One of the most interesting and controversial issues that biological anthropologists have pursued, both today and in the past, is the origin of humans. Such questions as "What living animals are most closely related to humans?" and "What was the ancestral form of the living relatives like?" are still issues today, as they have been for more than a century in one form or another. The time of appearance of the unique human lineage has been a topic of lively debate, and estimates span a range of more than 30 million years. Paleontologist Bjorn Kurtén (1972), for example, suggested that the human lineage appeared very early, approximately 30 million years ago, whereas molecular anthropologists Vincent Sarich and Allan Wilson suggested that the human lineage separated from that leading to the African apes much later, not much more than 5 million years ago (Sarich and Wilson, 1967) (Figure 1–8; see also Chapter 9). The consensus is now for a late or recent divergence, that is, 5 million to 10 million years ago. Many tests of the various hypotheses of human origins have been carried out over the past century. We discuss them in Chapters 10 through 12.

Phylogeny, from the Greek word for "originating from branches," refers to the lineage relationships of fossil humans and other **primates,** which include monkeys, apes, and prosimians (a group of animals that includes lemurs, lorises, and tarsiers). Determining these relationships has been a primary consideration of biological anthropologists since fossil specimens were first found and recognized. The German naturalist Ernst Haeckel (1834–1919) produced the first phylogenetic tree for the human species by making use of comparative anatomy (Figure 1–9, p. 12), because no fossil humans were recognized at the time.

Traditionally, phylogenetic studies were *vertical* in their orientation, because they extended back into history. They sought to determine the ancestors "below" and the descendants "above" a given species. In contrast, studies of the ecology and behavior of fossil species, now gaining much research attention, are more *horizontal*

variation: the range of differences in physical or genetic makeup across, within, and between populations of individuals of the same species.

adaptability: the range of physiological and behavioral responses that an individual can make to adjust to environmental changes.

phylogeny: the study of evolutionary relationships of organisms.

primates: the zoological order of mammals that includes living and extinct monkeys, apes, and humans, as well as more primitive taxa.

Sarich and Wilson (1967)

Kurtén (1972)

FIGURE 1–8 Two widely varying hypotheses on the timing of evolutionary divergences of the apes and hominids. Contemporary views favor the Sarich and Wilson late-divergence hypothesis, shown on the left. We discuss this topic more fully in Chapter 9.

in design. Biological anthropologists are no longer satisfied with hypothesizing only evolutionary relationships between fossils. They want to know how early people and their primate ancestors adapted to their environments, to their diets, and to their social living arrangements and behavior.

Molecular Biology

A number of problems in human evolution are now addressed using the methods of molecular biology. Molecular evidence concerning the actual biological relationships of humans to the other primates is rapidly accumulating. The data show that humans are most closely related to the African great apes, the chimpanzee and gorilla (see Chapter 9). In fact, humans and chimpanzees are so closely related that they differ by only 1 to 2 percent of their DNA sequences (Figure 1–10, p. 13). Molecular data have also played important roles in interpreting the evolutionary history of modern *Homo sapiens* (see Chapter 12). New molecular data are now forcing an entirely new view of human population variability, very different from Blumenbach's original ideas (Chapter 14).

Behavior

Behavior, the patterning of animal activity over time, and how it relates to evolution and adaptation, has become an important research focus in biological anthropology. Today's scientists want to know what animals did (not simply what they were), in what period of time they lived, and to what other animals they were related. Contemporary human behavior is the evolutionary result of the behaviors

behavior: patterns of animal activity over time.

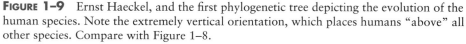

FIGURE 1–9   Ernst Haeckel, and the first phylogenetic tree depicting the evolution of the human species. Note the extremely vertical orientation, which places humans "above" all other species. Compare with Figure 1–8.

in our ancestors that led to reproductive success—that is, successfully reproducing offspring in worlds long vanished and in ways of life quite different from today's. With a fuller knowledge of the behavior of our own closest living relatives, we can better understand how modern human behavior came to be. This comparative approach works because the early social and environmental situations to which the hominid lineage adapted in times past are similar to those of many nonhuman primates today. One of the keys, then, to understanding human evolution is a full appreciation of nonhuman primate social systems, and how and under what conditions they developed.

primatologists: scientists who study primates, usually primate behavior and ecology.

naturalistic fieldwork: the study of primates in their natural environment.

Biological anthropologists known as **primatologists** study primates, usually nonhuman primates. Primatologists often engage in studies of primate behavior in the wild. Such studies are called **naturalistic fieldwork.** Primatologists are interested in

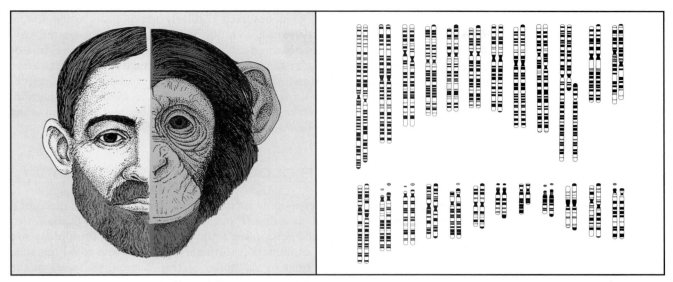

FIGURE 1-10 Chromosomes of human and chimpanzee compared. Within each pair of chromosomes, the human chromosome appears on the left, the chimpanzee chromosome on the right. With minor exceptions, the matches are extremely close.

questions such as, "How and why do primate species behave differently from one another?" and "What can an understanding of this behavior tell us about the behavior of early humans?"

Most of our knowledge of the behavior of the nonhuman primates is derived from recent fieldwork and new controlled laboratory experiments (Figure 1–11). These studies, especially long-term fieldwork, have clarified many misconceptions of how different primate species behave in the wild and what their true behavioral capabilities are. For example, Jane Goodall's 30-year field study among the chimpanzees at Gombe, Tanzania, has resulted in fundamental changes in how we view the human condition. We no longer think of ourselves as the only tool-using

FIGURE 1-11 Naturalistic field research in primate behavior. Jane Goodall observing chimpanzees at her research site, Gombe Stream Reserve, Tanzania.

animals, because chimps have been observed regularly making and using simple tools. We no longer consider meat eating as uniquely human (among primates, anyway), because chimps have been observed catching and eating animal prey. Primatological studies now seek to understand nonhuman primates based on fact rather than folklore. As previously stated, living primates help anthropologists interpret the fossil remains of our ancestors, as well as provide case studies of evolution. These studies in turn help in our understanding of fossil bones and evolution when we consider the fact that these bones were once parts of living animals.

THE LANGUAGE OF BIOLOGICAL ANTHROPOLOGY

The language of biological anthropology is composed of the specialized jargons of a number of scientific disciplines, as well as some jargon unique to biological anthropology itself. Many of the basic descriptive terms in biological anthropology are anatomical. In our discussions of human evolutionary anatomy and fossil remains, we use a number of terms to refer to the bones of the skeleton, the parts of the brain, and the teeth. Appendix 1 lists some of the anatomical terms used.

A number of geological terms are used in biological anthropology based on the work of paleoanthropologists, who extract fossils from the ground and thus have much in common with earth scientists. The interaction of evolution with climate change, the drifting of continents over time (Figure 1–12), and the reconstruction of the ancient environments in which our ancestors lived keep this a lively area of research. Appendix 2 discusses basic geological terminology and illustrates the geological time scale. Appendix 4 describes the methods biological anthropologists use to date fossil remains.

A large component of the terms making up the biological anthropological lexicon comes from biology. The proliferating terms used in the rapidly developing fields of genetics and molecular biology make their way into biological anthropology, as do the terms used in ecology, evolutionary biology, zoology, and behavioral biology. Perhaps the largest source of new terms for the beginning

FIGURE 1–12 The earth's present-day landmasses evolved over millions of years, by means of continental drift, from a supercontinent called Pangaea. Pangaea started to break apart more than 225 million years ago, first forming the northern continent of Laurasia and the southern continent of Gondwanaland.

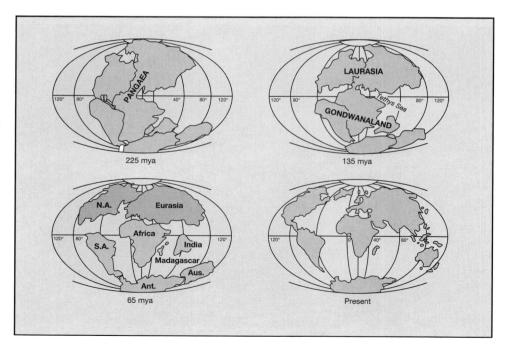

TABLE 1–1	Taxonomy of the Human Species

Kingdom Animalia
   Phylum Chordata
      Class Mammalia
         Order Primates
            Infraorder Anthropoidea
               Superfamily Hominoidea
                  Family Hominidae
                     Genus *Homo*
                        Species *Homo sapiens*

student is the **taxonomy,** or scientific classification and naming of different animals. We provide the English translations of the names of animals when they are first mentioned, and they can also be looked up in the Glossary. There is an order to the organization of these names, appropriately termed **systematics,** which is based on the closeness of relationship among the animals. Appendix 3 provides the taxonomy and systematics of the primates, that order of mammals to which human beings belong. The taxonomic classification of the human species is presented in Table 1–1.

In this book we discuss many different kinds of animals, and taxonomy gives us a clear-cut and unambiguous way to refer to them. Taxonomy begins with the species, originally a term that simply meant "kind" but now indicates a formal taxonomic unit basic to biological classification. A **species** is defined as a group or population of organisms, the individuals of which naturally interbreed and produce fertile offspring (see also Chapters 3 and 4). Species are designated scientifically by a system of *binomial* ("two-named") terms. Our species designation is *Homo sapiens* (Latin for "human the wise"). When only the first part of the binomial name is used, it refers to the level above the species in the taxonomic hierarchy, the genus. A **genus** groups species that are similar in adaptation. We are classified in the genus *Homo*.

Genera (the plural of genus) are placed within **families.** Our zoological family, the **Hominidae,** is defined on the basis of our mode of movement, or *locomotion;* hominids walk on two legs. How two-legged walking, or *bipedalism,* evolved and what type of locomotion preceded it are among the oldest unsolved questions in biological anthropology (see Chapter 9). But bipedalism serves as a useful defining feature for all the known members of the hominid family.

A zoological family is nested within a *superfamily,* which is nested within an *order,* which is nested within a *class,* and so on, up to a *kingdom.* In this book, we recognize five kingdoms that include all organisms on earth (see Chapter 2).

Species

The concept of the biological species is important because we rely on it for purposes of constructing biological and evolutionary relationships among organisms. Ernst Mayr (1963:19) defined species as "actually or potentially interbreeding populations which are reproductively isolated from other such populations." We discuss the concept of populations in greater depth in Chapter 4, but for now it is sufficient to realize that a **population** is a group of related individuals of one species that live together in one place. For example, all the people in a Chicago neighborhood make up a population, as do all the chimpanzees, *Pan troglodytes,* in the Ishasha Forest in the Democratic Republic of Congo.

taxonomy: the science of naming different organisms.

systematics: the science of classifying and organizing organisms.

species: an actually or potentially interbreeding group of organisms in nature.

genus: a taxonomic grouping of similar species.

family: a taxonomic grouping of similar genera.

Hominidae: the zoological family to which living humans and their bipedal relatives, all now extinct, belong.

population: a geographically localized group of individuals in a species that more likely share a common gene pool among themselves than with other individuals in the species.

holotype: the single specimen on which a taxonomic name is based.

paratypes: a group of specimens on which a taxonomic name is based.

morphology: the study of the form and anatomy of physical structures in the bodies of living or once living organisms.

Only within a species are male and female animals able to mate and produce offspring capable of reproducing. Sometimes animals in different species can mate and produce offspring—a horse and donkey can produce a mule—but the offspring will usually be infertile and incapable of having offspring. These cases present special problems in defining species on the basis of reproductive isolation.

Mayr's definition works well for living species, but it poses special problems for interpreting the fossil records. For example, we cannot determine whether animals that we know only from their bones and teeth could or did interbreed. Instead, we must use a concept of anatomical distance: how distant in physical form species are in the modern world. That is, we compare extinct and living species and extrapolate this into the past. For example, most anthropologists accept that Neandertal people could have interbred with anatomically modern people, and they classify them within our species, *Homo sapiens*. However, "Java Man" people are considered so different anatomically that they are classified in a different species, *Homo erectus*.

We can ascertain whether the anatomical differences between two fossils are about the same as, less than, or greater than, those between two known living species that cannot mate and produce fertile offspring. Because species possess their own unique adaptations, understanding the functional anatomy of fossils also helps in deciding whether they were truly separate species in the past. Species determined from the fossil record are known as *paleospecies* (*paleo* means "old").

Species, whether living or extinct, are defined in taxonomic use by reference to a type (see the previous discussion of typology). This may be a single specimen (a **holotype;** Figure 1–13) or a series of specimens (**paratypes**). **Morphology** is the study of form and structure in organisms. Morphological characteristics of the type, such as the shape and size of the teeth, are described and used to define an entire population of organisms, a species. However, because individuals vary one from another in all biological populations, adequate allowance must be made for slight differences. Suppose we have a type specimen and an unknown specimen that may possibly be tagged with a new species designation. Before a species designation is made, the difference between the type and the unknown specimen must be seen as greater than would be expected between any two individuals within a normal population. In the past, variation within populations was seldom recognized and, consequently, every new fossil discovery was given the name of a new species. Today, biological

FIGURE 1–13 The holotype specimen of the gelada baboon, *Theropithecus gelada*, as displayed in the Senckenburg Museum, Frankfurt, Germany. What information can biological anthropologists obtain from studying holotypes?

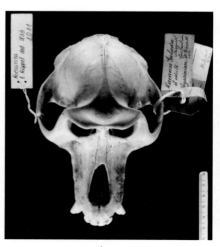

top

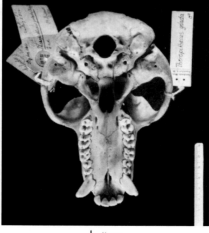

bottom

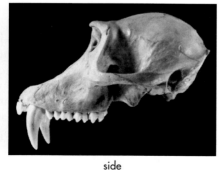

side

anthropologists study anatomical difference to discover at what point observed differences between two specimens are within the species limits or are large enough to place them in two different species.

Subspecies

Subspecies, also known as races, are populations within a species that are usually geographically distinct from one another, and may be distinguishable from other subspecies by morphology and by genetic and behavioral differences. Members of subspecies may interbreed and frequently do so at the fringes of their distribution. This pattern of interbreeding creates geographic gradients of physical or biological variations that are called **clines.** They sometimes make clear-cut distinctions between population centers in a species difficult to discern. Modern human beings may be one such species (see Chapter 12). In contrast, numerous species of African and Asian monkeys form well-defined subspecies over their geographic ranges. The gorilla is well known for its three subspecies: two lowland subspecies in central and West Africa, and the well-studied mountain gorilla in the east. In taxonomy, a species name is a binomial, but a subspecies name is a trinomial. Thus, the mountain gorilla is taxonomically *Gorilla gorilla beringei,* and the Neandertals are *Homo sapiens neanderthalensis.* No subspecies, or races, appear in the modern species of *Homo sapiens.* As we shall see later, geographically differentiated groups of a species form the bases of future species.

RECONSTRUCTING THE EVOLUTIONARY HISTORY OF SPECIES

Classification of any set of organisms should be based on an easily understood and reproducible set of criteria so that scientists may communicate effectively about the organisms. In biological theory, the ideal is to classify species together that are closely related to each other. *Phylogenetic* relationships are those that link species through their evolutionary history: a "family tree" through which species B is related to species C through an earlier common ancestor A (Figure 1–14). Classification schemes, then, should reflect our current knowledge of evolutionary history. This means that as further discoveries improve our knowledge of this history, they may change our classification schemes (see Figure 1–15 for an example).

Higher levels of classification above the species (the levels of genus and family) should reflect true evolutionary groupings; in other words, there should be successive levels of more distantly related species as one goes up the hierarchy. For example, here we use Hominidae (a taxonomic family) to refer only to bipedal primates closely related to modern humans (see Chapter 10), a position also adopted by Fleagle (1999). There is controversy, however. In one scheme, chimps, gorillas, and orangutans could be placed in a separate family. Figure 1–15 shows the two different ways of classifying the great apes and hominids. These names become important in debates on the evolutionary origins and relationships among hominids and their primate relatives.

Cladistics

For the purposes of classification, scientists need to determine the important defining characteristics of a species. For example, if we wish to classify horses and cows, it hardly does any good to note that they both have four feet. Why? Because many other animals do as well. Thus, the morphological characteristic of having four feet does not serve to distinguish horses and cows from each other.

subspecies: a geographically defined population within a species, the individuals of which tend to share certain physical and genetic traits but who are nevertheless infertile with other members of the species; a race.

cline: a gradient of genotypes or phenotypes over a geographic range.

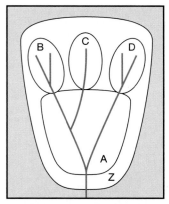

FIGURE 1–14 Phylogenetic relationships: How a species evolves determines how it is classified. In this example, species A is ancestral to species B, C, and D, as indicated by the red line, which shows evolutionary descent through time. All four species are grouped together in a higher taxonomic category (family Z), because they share a common descent.

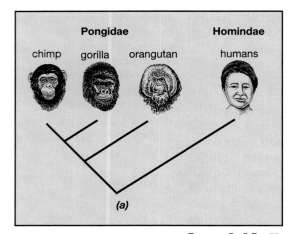
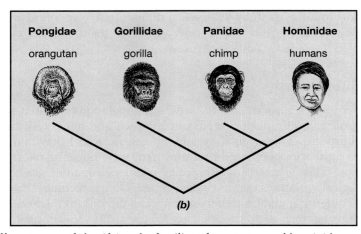

FIGURE 1–15 Two different ways of classifying the families of great apes and hominids. In this text we use the classification in (*a*), although not all biological anthropologists agree. Some taxonomists use the term *hominid* to include all the clades shown in (*b*). In this usage, humans are termed *hominins*.

cladistics: the common term for the study of the phylogenetic relationships among a group of related animals by reference to only derived traits shared in common.

apomorphy: in cladistic terminology, a newly arisen or derived trait used in systematics.

cladogram: branching diagram showing relative relationships among taxonomic groups of animals; not to be confused with a phylogenetic tree, which postulates ancestor–descendant relationships.

The German biologist Willi Hennig (1966) instituted the field termed **cladistics** (Greek, meaning "splitting apart") during the 1950s. Cladistics is a way of analyzing relationships among animals in the fossil record by using only newly arisen, or *derived,* traits or characters. It offers a clear method for determining which characters to use in classification. Characters that have been inherited from ancient, primitive ancestors are thrown out, and only the derived characters, also called **apomorphies,** that are new and unique to the group are used for classification. In the example of horses and cows previously mentioned, a derived character of cows might be the presence of horns, whereas four-footedness is discarded for purposes of this classification because it is a primitive character. Once derived characters are determined for a group of organisms, it is possible to draw a diagram of relatedness, or a **cladogram** (Figure 1–16). The cladogram can then be used to construct a

FIGURE 1–16 A cladogram showing the relationships among four species. Traits in complex A define a human–cow–horse group, or clade, as distinct from a larger grouping of animals that includes chickens. Such traits could include presence of fur, teeth, and amniotic egg. Traits in complex B define a cow–horse clade as distinct from humans. These could include quadripedal locomotion and eyes on the side, rather than in the front of the head. Note that a cladogram simply groups organisms with similar traits. It does not imply time relationships or imply that one organism is descended from another.

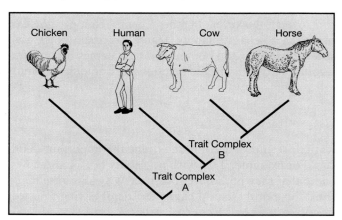

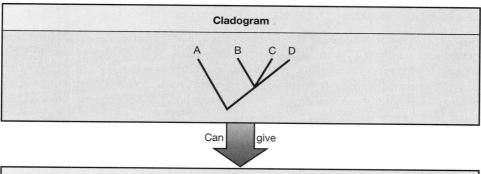

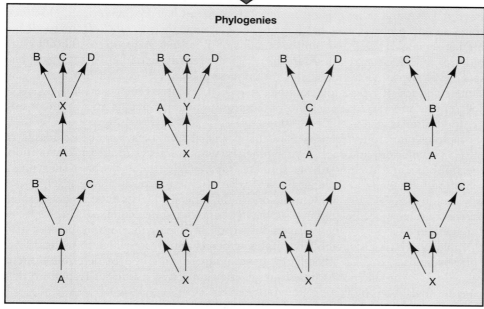

FIGURE 1-17 A cladogram, and the number of different phylogenies, or evolutionary relationships, it can yield. Note that a cladogram does not imply specific evolutionary relationships, only shared traits.

series of phylogenies, or possible evolutionary relationships, which hypothesize ancestor–descendant relationships (Figure 1–17).

Scientists can reconstruct the phylogenetic history of a species using a basic principle of evolutionary biology: Descendants resemble their ancestors because they are related genetically; that is, they share a large number of genes. A corollary to this principle is that descendants far removed in time from an ancestral population will be more dissimilar than descendants not so distant in time from each other. The key assumption here is that anatomical similarity reflects closeness of relationship. The fact that virtually every anatomical structure of a human body can be matched in the chimpanzee body led Thomas Henry Huxley (1825–1895), for example, to hypothesize a close relationship between the African apes and humans. Sometimes, however, overall anatomical similarity may be misleading. Species that are unrelated or distantly related may adapt to similar environments and end up looking very similar (see Chapter 4). This phenomenon results either from **parallelism** (similar traits in closely related organisms) or **convergence** (similar traits in distantly related organisms).

Some species evolve very slowly, and a modern descendant species, or "living fossil," can closely resemble an ancestor. For this reason evolutionists use the geological record to determine the age of fossils. Armed with data on anatomical similarity and geological age, they can then assemble a phylogenetic tree for the fossil forms under study.

parallelism: the evolution of similar traits in two closely related species, such as elongated hind legs for jumping in two small rodent species.

convergence: the evolution of similar traits in two distantly related animals, such as similar streamlined body form for swimming in dolphins and sharks.

Gene Lineages and Organismal Lineages

Molecular biologists have devised an alternative way of investigating the phylogenetic history of living forms. If the goal of evolutionary research is to discover the genetic relatedness of organisms in order to reconstruct their phylogenetic histories, why not measure genetics itself? By using techniques to determine the actual structure of the DNA molecule that makes up genes, researchers are able to assess the genetic relatedness of species directly.

Molecular approaches to phylogeny are much more recent than those that use fossils only, and the relationship between the two approaches has sometimes been rocky. Two major areas of difference have separated the two disciplines. First, extracting DNA and other organic material from fossils has proven difficult. However, some recent progress has been made in isolating ancient DNA from fossilized human remains as well as from the remains of other mammals up to 100,000 years old. Second, a close relationship does not necessarily exist between genetic distances, as measured by molecular techniques, and morphological distance. Quite similar species of frogs, for example, may be very divergent genetically, whereas species that are very different morphologically, such as humans and chimpanzees, are quite similar genetically (see Chapter 4).

Despite numerous recent debates between paleontologists, who use fossils to measure evolution, and molecular biologists, who use genes to measure evolution, their approaches attempt to measure the same phylogenetic history. They must, therefore, ultimately be compatible. However, the two groups of scientists do not rely on identical sets of data. On the one hand, paleontologists have access to some species that have become extinct and have left no living descendants. Those species can contain clues about the twists and turns of phylogeny that cannot be discerned by molecular biologists, who have no living descendant from which to work. Molecular biologists, on the other hand, have a superior method of determining true relatedness between species based on genetic similarity—a level of resolution that paleontologists can only approximate.

When molecular biologists reconstruct phylogeny, they are actually reconstructing gene lineages—specific sequences of DNA that descend from ancestor to offspring. When paleontologists reconstruct phylogeny, they are attempting to reconstruct population lineages of whole organisms. These two measures of phylogenetic change may not always coincide. Genes may evolve faster, more slowly, or stay the same, depending on selection, as organisms evolve within populations. But often the two measures will coincide. When they do not, the challenge will be to determine which of the many evolutionary forces have been at work to put the molecular and paleontological assessments at variance with one another. A better and more complete view of evolutionary history will ultimately emerge from a successful interaction between the two disciplines.

Ecology and Evolution

Ecology (from the Greek, meaning "study of habitation") integrates study of the habitat in which a population lives with that population's genetic, morphological, and behavioral adaptations. Each species is part of a complex *ecosystem* made up of a community of plants and animals. Within this ecosystem a species occupies its own **ecological niche**, a unique way of life to which it alone is adapted. A species' niche is defined by where it lives, what it eats, and how it goes about its daily life. For example, some prosimians are insect eaters, and some are fruit eaters. Even if two such species live in the same ecosystem, they occupy different niches.

ecology: the science that studies the biological relationships between species and their environment.

ecological niche: the ecological space to which a species is adapted, including its habitat, diet, and behavior.

The Human Genome Diversity Project

The Human Genome Project (Figure 1–18) is the now-famous, multibillion-dollar effort of genetics laboratories worldwide that has recently revealed "the" human DNA sequence, using a few people (mainly the U.S. scientists themselves) as subjects. A much less well-known but related research initiative is the Human Genome Diversity Project (HGDP). This essentially anthropological project is aimed at obtaining good genetic information from as wide a sampling of worldwide human populations as possible. Many laboratories are participating in the coordinated research, making the HGDP perhaps the biggest cooperative research venture ever undertaken by biological anthropologists. It will yield data of use to scientists from many disciplines who study

humans, including biological anthropologists and human biologists who study human variation, the evolution of human populations, and how they are related; biomedical scientists and physicians, who research the evolution of disease, and the interaction of genetics and environment in maintaining healthy human populations; and even anthropological linguists, who are interested in how languages and the genetics of populations covary.

Despite its great research potential, the HGDP has not been without its critics. Selection of the populations to be included in the HGDP initially caused controversy. Scientists inevitably had many more potential groups targeted than could be included because of funding constraints. There were issues of privacy. Were the HGDP scientists getting prior authorization from the subjects to include their personal data? (What could be more personal than

one's own genetic blueprint?) Were the same safeguards that were in place for Westernized populations being observed for non-Western and tribal populations? Some anthropologists charged the HGDP with exploitation of tribal peoples. And when the genetic sequence data of the entire population of Iceland went to the highest bidder, a pharmaceutical company interested in developing new drugs for genetically mediated disease, alarm cries went up worldwide.

The disputes surrounding the HGDP have helped to focus research and to prevent infringement on individuals' rights to privacy. The project holds great promise for increasing the store of anthropological knowledge about the world's human populations. For example, one very important fact is that Africa contains more genetic variation in its human populations than the rest of the world combined.

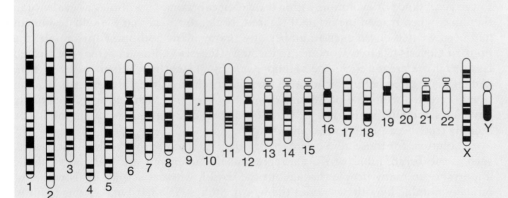

FIGURE 1-18 The human genome, arranged from the largest chromosome, Chromosome 1 (left), to the smallest nonsex chromosomes (21 and 22, right), and the two sex chromosomes, X and Y.

Change in the environment in which a species lives is a major driving force behind evolutionary change in populations. If the environment stays the same over eons, there may be very little morphological change observed in some species. But earth scientists have accumulated more and more evidence to show that our planet has undergone many episodic and sometimes rapid climatic and environmental changes. For example, the widely fluctuating climates of the Pleistocene had an important role in the evolution of anatomically modern *Homo sapiens*.

A dynamic interplay has existed between ecology and evolution. Evolutionists are now looking at the geological record of climatic change, at molecular phylogeny, and at the paleontological record of species to piece together how the forces of evolution have formed the species that have existed on earth.

Evolution Versus Creationism

Early in the development of biological anthropology the subject of the evolution of the human species began to be considered. The earliest ideas on human origins were derived from studies of the anatomy of many different kinds of animals, compared with human anatomy. Human beings share many traits with apes, fewer traits with monkeys, fewer with cats, and fewer still with birds, reptiles, fish, and insects, respectively. The existence of fossil forms that bridged the gaps between the living animals was debated. Particular attention was focused on the hypothetical common ancestor of humans and apes, which was given the popular nickname of the "missing link" (see Eldredge, 2000).

Two of the primary methods of investigation of human evolution used by modern biological anthropologists involve the use of **fossils,** usually bones that have been mineralized over time, and the analysis of molecules in the body. But early evidence for the great antiquity of human beings came first in the form of stone tools discovered in France in the late 1700s. Later, fossilized bones of people were found associated with those of extinct animals. Actual evidence of a form of human so different that it would fit into no known living human group was not recognized until 1856, when the Neandertal "caveman" was discovered in Germany (see Chapter 12).

Even before scientists began to delve into human origins, religious scholars had questioned the status quo. As one of the founders of the scientific method, Sir Francis Bacon (1561–1626) pronounced, in the early seventeenth century, that scholars should look to nature, not to books, for enlightenment. During the next century—the Age of Enlightenment—a movement known as Biblical Criticism led to the acceptance of evolution within a theological framework. Internal evidence in the Bible, when read in the original Hebrew, began to reveal that the Old Testament had been written down over a number of years by many authors. For example, the book of Genesis has two accounts: In the first (Genesis 1), human beings are created last of all the creatures; in the second (Genesis 2), the first human being, a man (Adam), is created before the animals and names them as they are created. Woman (Eve) is created from one of Adam's ribs in this version. (Men and women actually have the same number of ribs, 12 pairs for a total of 24.) Both accounts cannot be literally true, because they are contradictory.

A solution, for those who desire to seek one, is to accept that religious Scripture, such as the Torah, Bible, or Koran, represents documents of spiritual and symbolic importance to many people throughout the world, whereas science deals with empirically testable hypotheses about the world. Stokes (1988:16) makes this point in his restatement of the creation passages in Genesis, a version with which many scientists could agree:

> All known matter appeared in the simplest, elemental form through a single, unique event called the "big bang." With time, as things quieted down, heavier elements and compounds including watery mixtures of gas and dust appeared. The gathering, and compression of matter into galaxies produced light, nuclear reactions, and massive explosions (supernovas). Eventually all elements were produced and dispersed. From enriched mixtures of gas and dust came suns with attendant systems of planets. In one case, at least, a body (our earth) unusually rich in water was produced. A copious supply of water came from within and remained attached to its surface as liquid oceans and seas. Life as we know it emerged from water; and the oceans, as shown by fossils, were well populated by varied species before land life was in existence. On land, a great variety of bony vertebrate animals appeared and eventually occupied all continents and islands. Man was one of the last creatures to

fossils: remains of animals and plants preserved in the ground.

appear; his unique physical and mental attributes allow him to dominate all forms of life.

Evolutionary science, like all sciences, is neutral in one sense regarding theological beliefs. Supernatural events cannot be explained by science, because science seeks the simplest possible natural explanations to understand observations. Religion, however, deals with the spiritual, symbolic, and moral spheres of human life. Science deals with falsifiable hypotheses, ideas that can be disproved, and gives precedence to material causes over supernatural ones; religion depends on faith, which is not subject to scientific proof.

In upholding the teaching of evolution in the public schools, U.S. courts have reasserted the division between church and state. Yet science and religion can coexist, and both responsible scientists and theologians resist efforts to bring the two into unnecessary conflict. Most major Western religions accept evolution as part of the process of creation (Lieberman and Kirk, 1996). In the Anglican Church, evolution has been formally accepted since the 1890s; the Roman Catholic Church has officially accepted evolution as "an open question" since the 1950s. More recently, Pope John Paul II announced he believed that "fresh knowledge leads to recognition of the theory of evolution as more than just a hypothesis." Other major denominations have followed suit.

THE PERSPECTIVE OF HUMAN EVOLUTION

The study of human evolution has much to contribute to a general understanding of human beings, their origins, adaptations, and way of life. The popular interest that surrounds biological anthropology is derived to a large extent from high-visibility discoveries of fossils. Initially, the fossils themselves were considered of paramount interest, but increasingly the contexts in which the fossils are found have become of equal, if not of more, importance. The context can tell how old the fossil is, what the climate was like when the species was alive, what other animals and plants were in the environment, what the species may have eaten, what other species may have eaten it, and many other aspects of its evolutionary history not discernible from its bones or teeth alone (Figure 1–19). In short, the total contexts of fossil discoveries have become important because we now want to understand how early humans lived and behaved, as well as how they are related to other life forms, including today's humans. In this way, we seek to understand the natural history of our ancestors and of ourselves.

What an individual does during his or her lifetime affects the passing on of his or her hereditary characteristics. Behaviors that contribute to a longer childbearing or reproductive life and increase the number of offspring will tend to become more prevalent as evolution proceeds. Our behavior today is the result of millions of years and hundreds of thousands of generations of evolution. If we understand how our ancestors behaved and the conditions under which their behavior evolved, we will have a much better insight into our behavior today.

The increasingly well-documented human fossil record now demonstrates that for the longest part of our history we have evolved to social and technological conditions that no longer exist. Most of human evolution took place before even the advent of agriculture, some 10,000 years ago. Throughout our evolutionary history, humans have lived in small social groups. During this immense span of time, humans "evolved to feel strongly about a few people, short distances, and relatively brief intervals of time" (Washburn and Harding, 1975:11). The final chapter in this book discusses how a species with such an evolutionary heritage has coped with such issues as crowding and overpopulation, international conflict, pollution, health, and education.

FIGURE 1–19 Reconstruction of an event in the human evolutionary past: butchering of a dead animal by a group of hominids at Olduvai Gorge, Tanzania. The setting is reconstructed using many different lines of evidence, such as fossil bones of hominids and other animals, cut marks on bones, and climate and pollen evidence. Such reconstructions allow us to visualize the entire context of key events in human evolution.

◖ SUMMARY

1. What fields of study are included within anthropology? Within biological anthropology?

Anthropology is a four-field discipline that includes biological (physical) anthropology, cultural anthropology, archaeology, and anthropological linguistics. Anthropology is united not only by the concept of culture, a unique human adaptation, but by the shared paradigm of evolution by natural selection. A synthetic treatment of human evolution, that is, one that integrates biological makeup, physical structure, genetics, behavior, and culture, is the basis of this textbook. Biological anthropologists practice many subspecialties, including primatology, paleoanthropology, forensic anthropology, and molecular anthropology, among others.

2. **What are the steps in the scientific method, and how do biological anthropologists use the scientific method to study human and primate differences?**

   Biological anthropology is a science with one foot in the natural sciences and one in the social sciences. Research in biological anthropology uses the scientific method—gathering data, formulating hypotheses, and testing the hypotheses. If a hypothesis is disproved by testing, an alternative hypothesis is then generated.

3. **What subjects do biological anthropologists study?**

   Biological anthropologists study the wide and fascinating varieties of human beings worldwide and how they have biologically adapted to their environment. They study how humans grow and develop, as well as how, when, and where the species as a whole has evolved. The study of nonhuman primates is an important comparative basis for understanding the evolution of human behavior.

4. **What bases do scientists use for classifying organisms? How are scientific names assigned to organisms?**

   Biological anthropologists use zoological classification in order to precisely define the species of animals, usually primates, that they study. A species is based on a type specimen that scientists may always use as a reference. Humans are the species *Homo sapiens,* and they are placed in the zoological family Hominidae.

5. **What tools do biological anthropologists use to reconstruct the evolutionary relationships between species?**

   Biological anthropologists use anatomy of living and fossil animals interpreted in the form of cladograms and phylogenies to reconstruct the relationships among the many living and extinct species of primates. Molecular evidence is now also an important aspect of understanding evolutionary relationships among species, and it has been very important in recent advances in researching human evolution.

6. **What can the perspective of human evolution teach us about the human condition, both today and in the past?**

   Human evolution provides a unique, long-range perspective on the human condition, and in a world in which the behavior of human beings can be so perplexing, disturbing, and even horrific, biological anthropology may provide our most important tools for understanding ourselves.

CRITICAL THINKING QUESTIONS

1. Biological anthropologists ask questions that are wide ranging and require information from many different scientific disciplines. What are some of the possible fields of science that a biological anthropologist studying human adaptation in the weightlessness of space might need to investigate? Of what other fields would a forensic anthropologist investigating crimes need to be aware? Of what fields would a paleoanthropologist interested in hominids' adaptation to past climate conditions need to know? What fields would a biomedical anthropologist interested in the evolutionary history of AIDS need to consult?

2. You are embarking on a study of human evolution, yet there are many people, in American society at least, who believe that you should be denied that right. What drives creationists in their quest to undermine the teaching of evolution in

schools? Who would benefit if evolutionary science were not taught? What are some of the practical consequences of subjugating scientific inquiry to dogma? What is the official doctrine on evolution that is taught by your religion? Do you think that science and religion are mutually compatible?

◄ INTERNET EXERCISES

Critical Thinking Exercise

Evolution Versus Creationism. This chapter provides an overview of the creationism versus evolution debate, which has existed for more than 100 years and still occasionally is mentioned on the evening news. After reading this chapter, construct your own answers to these questions:

1. Is this a real debate with equivalent, comparable evidence on both sides? Or are the two sides based on different kinds of evidence and different kinds of arguments?
2. How do creationists attempt to refute the theory of evolution? Why is this debate necessary from their point of view?
3. What arguments would you use to refute the creationist point of view?

Writing Assignment

Taxonomy. Write a brief paper that explains the rationales that biologists use to classify things. Your paper should answer the following questions:

1. How do biologists classify living things?
2. Why do biologists classify living things?

See Companion Web site for Internet links.

The Human Genome Project, the biological equivalent of the 1960s Apollo space program in scale and ambition, was begun in the mid-1980s and completed in 2000. Its goal was to sequence—to determine the sequence of bases in—the entire human genome. It used as samples the genetic material of only a few individuals, primarily that of scientists working on the project. In the text of this chapter, we compare the Human Genome Project with the Human Genome Diversity Project, an anthropological project that is aimed at obtaining genetic information from as wide a sampling of human populations as possible.

In the Web Activity for this chapter, you will view an interview with a scientist involved with the project and see footage of lab work actually taking place.

WEB ACTIVITY

The Human Genome Project is an international research program designed to construct detailed genetic and physical maps of the human genome, to determine the complete nucleotide sequence of human DNA, to localize the individual genes, and to perform similar analyses on the genomes of several other organisms used extensively in research laboratories as model systems, such as mice and dogs. The first report of the entire human genome sequence was issued in 2000, and among the surprises was the discovery that the human genome contains only about 30,000 genes, not the 50,000 to 100,000 expected. Work is ongoing to fill in the blanks in the genome and, especially, to map out variations.

Activity

1. View the video. Why was the project undertaken? How long did it take to complete?
2. In what ways might the information obtained affect human health?
3. Compare the Human Genome Project with the Human Genome Diversity Project, which is discussed in Chapter 1. How are the projects' goals and methods different? How do they complement each other?

The MediaLab can be found in Chapter 1 on your Companion Web site http://www.prenhall.com/boaz

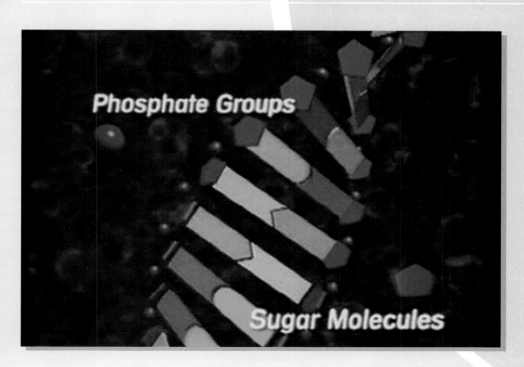

2

DARWIN'S THEORY OF EVOLUTION BY NATURAL SELECTION

After reading this chapter, you should be able to discuss the following questions:

1. What is the scientific revolution? In what way did it lead to the discovery of evolution by natural selection?
2. How did Darwin and Wallace formulate their theories? What were their major principles?
3. What is sexual selection? How can genes influence behavior?
4. What were the limitations of the theory of natural selection at the time it was developed?

We turn now to a discussion of the development of the theory that explains the many known facts about the origins and diversity of species of organisms on earth: the theory of evolution by natural selection, conceived of and developed by Charles Darwin (1809–82) and Alfred Russel Wallace (1823–1913). Darwin and Wallace's theory successfully explained the observable diversity and adaptations of animals and plants, but not inheritance of characteristics, because they lacked the knowledge of genetic mechanisms and the genetic basis of variability. Later, in Chapter 3, we discuss the synthesis of the laws of genetic inheritance, developed by Gregor Mendel (1822–84), and the integration of modern cell biology and molecular genetics. We will see how our knowledge of the molecular basis of inheritance contributed to a more complete understanding of the intricate workings of the **DNA** molecule and the process of mutation. Together, molecular genetics and the theory of natural selection form the basis for the modern synthesis of evolutionary theory. How this synthesis itself evolved is the topic of this chapter and Chapter 3.

INFLUENCES ON DARWIN

In 1830 the English astronomer Sir John Herschel (1792–1871) wrote that "[T]o ascend to the origin of things, and to speculate on the creation, is not the business of the natural philosopher" (Herschel, 1831:29). Yet one undergraduate at Cambridge University who read those words in 1831 was not dissuaded from a career that eventually led him to investigate the origin of biological species, "that mystery of mysteries" (Darwin, 1859:141). The student's name was Charles Darwin (Figure 2–1).

Darwin prided himself on his **inductive scientific method,** defined as the collection of data without preconceived notions or hypotheses (Hull, 1973:9–10). Nevertheless, the work of several influential scientists profoundly affected his later thoughts and views of his data, and they contributed to the **deductive** framework for his theory of evolution by natural selection.

The Enlightenment and the Scientific Revolution

John Ray (1627–1705) was an English natural historian and Anglican priest whose early classification of plants and animals was instrumental in allowing scientists to organize the diversity of life and begin to develop hypotheses to explain that diversity. Ray developed the philosophy of "natural theology," the idea that the study of the natural world, which was created by God, would lead to a greater understanding

DNA: double-chain molecule that contains the genetic code.

inductive scientific method: inferring a generalized conclusion from particular instances.

deduction: inferring conclusions about particular instances from general or universal premises.

FIGURE 2–1 Charles Darwin as a young man.

of God. Natural theology was a powerful influence in England and affected Charles Darwin and the overall acceptance of his work by the Church of England. Ray widely encouraged the study of natural history and wrote in 1691 in his book *The Wisdom of God as Manifested in the Works of the Creation*, "Let it not suffice to be book-learned, to read what others have written and to take upon trust more false-hood than truth, but let us ourselves examine things as we have opportunity, and converse with Nature as well as with books."

Malthus's Theory of Populations

In his *Essay on the Principles of Population* (1798), English economist Thomas Malthus (1766–1834) observed that human population numbers increase geometri-cally (multiplication by a constant factor), whereas food resources increase only arithmetically (addition by a constant factor). He put forward the idea that the world always tends to have more people in it than it has food to feed them. Popula-tion checks such as famine, disease, and war were to Malthus unavoidable facts of society. In 1838 the young Charles Darwin read Malthus's book "for amusement" (Darwin, 1859:1), anticipating a parallel between his observations on plants and animals and Malthus's "struggle for existence" theory about human beings. Instead, Darwin hit on a crucial ingredient that he would later incorporate into his theory of natural selection:

> [I]t at once struck me that under these circumstances favorable variations would tend to be preserved, and unfavorable ones to be destroyed. The result of this would be the formation of a new species. Here, then, I had at last got a theory by which to work. (DARWIN, 1859:1)

At the same time that Malthus was making his observations on factors that contributed to the size of populations, Jean-Baptiste de Lamarck (1744–1829; Figure 2–2), an important French natural scientist, was working, first as a botanist and later as the first curator of invertebrates at the national Natural History Mu-seum in Paris, on some new ideas about the evolution of living species. Between 1801 and 1809, Lamarck published his theory of evolution, which posited that changes in the environment created needs in organisms, which altered behavior, which in turn caused bodily changes. For example, eyes that were no longer used by a cave salamander became reduced and nonfunctional, and the neck of a giraffe became longer by stretching for leaves on branches of tall trees. Lamarck codified these ideas as his first law.

Lamarck's second law was that the changes that an organism underwent during life were inherited by the organism's offspring. In this way organisms slowly changed through time to become well adapted to their environments. Lamarck ac-cepted the immensity of geological time, but he did not believe in the possibility of extinction, except insofar as species evolved into other species. Darwin recognized Lamarck's pioneering influence as an early evolutionist and his importance in at-tempting to explain changes in the organic and inorganic worlds by recourse to nat-ural laws and not "miraculous interposition." Darwin's own grandfather, the physician and scientist Erasmus Darwin (1731–1802), was a contemporary of Lamarck and espoused very similar evolutionary views in England. Figure 2–3 com-pares Lamarck's theory of inheritance of acquired characteristics with the younger Darwin's theory of evolution by natural selection.

Comparative anatomist and paleontologist Georges Cuvier (1769–1832) worked alongside Lamarck in the Natural History Museum, but he was Lamarck's bitter adversary. Lamarck believed that evolution was unilinear: primitive life forms gave rise to more complicated ones along a single pathway. Cuvier opposed Lamarck's evolutionary ideas. On the basis of his studies of comparative anatomy, Cuvier

FIGURE 2–2   Jean-Baptiste de Lamarck.

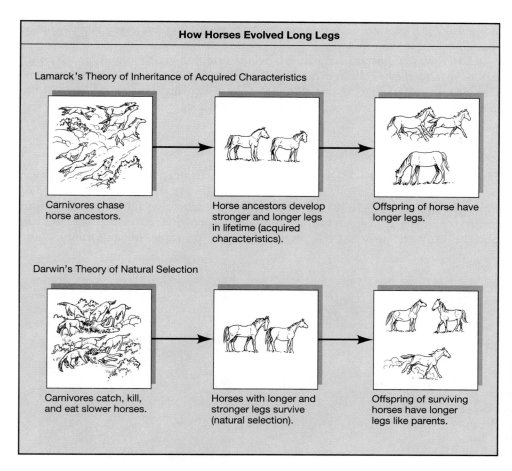

How Horses Evolved Long Legs

Lamarck's Theory of Inheritance of Acquired Characteristics

Carnivores chase horse ancestors.

Horse ancestors develop stronger and longer legs in lifetime (acquired characteristics).

Offspring of horse have longer legs.

Darwin's Theory of Natural Selection

Carnivores catch, kill, and eat slower horses.

Horses with longer and stronger legs survive (natural selection).

Offspring of surviving horses have longer legs like parents.

FIGURE 2-3 Lamarck's theory of evolution by inheritance of acquired characteristics (above), contrasted with Darwin's theory of evolution by natural selection (below).

believed that life forms belong to many divergent evolutionary paths that could not be fit into a single lineage. Because of this, Cuvier rejected not only Lamarck's evolutionary ideas but also the concept of evolution itself.

Cuvier, along with some other earth scientists of the time, put forward instead the case for the fixity of species. He believed, on the basis of the fossil record, that past catastrophes had caused extinctions of species, first making in 1796 a persuasive case for extinctions among elephants. Cuvier and his contemporaries did not believe that small changes observable at work today could account for observed geological phenomena. They suspected that large-scale catastrophes, such as floods, earthquakes, or volcanic eruptions, were the primary forces that molded earth history.

The theory of **catastrophism,** which holds that earth history is explicable in terms of violent and sudden cataclysms that destroyed most living species, after which a new set of creations established new species, was popularized by Cuvier. It accounted for change within a relatively short, and, at that time, generally accepted, time frame. This presented a large obstacle for Darwin, because he could not reconcile the idea of a short geologic time scale with his idea of gradual morphological change in evolution.

Connected with catastrophism was **special creation,** an idea proposed to account for the repopulation of the flora and fauna after a catastrophe had wiped out previous species. "Special creation" was distinguished from the original "creation" because it had presumably occurred numerous times in earth history. Both these explanations were of the miraculous type and, therefore, nonscientific. Although special creation could explain a number of observations relating to the geological and

catastrophism: theory that earth history is explicable in terms of violent and sudden cataclysms that destroyed most living species, after which a new set of creations established new species.

special creation: the nonevolutionary theory associated with catastrophism that held that totally new species, unrelated to prior species, were created after extinctions.

FIGURE 2–4   Sir Charles Lyell.

paleontological changes seen in earth history, it was an assumption, and as such it was impossible to test directly.

Cuvier was important because he helped establish paleontology as a science based on rigorously collected facts and integrated it with comparative anatomy. Darwin's theory of natural selection was able to explain Cuvier's evidence of the extinctions of species, whereas Lamarck's earlier theory could not.

Lyell's Theory of Uniformitarianism

Sir Charles Lyell (1797–1875; Figure 2–4), a Scot trained at Oxford as a lawyer, became one of the most influential geologists of the day. His landmark work, *The Principles of Geology* (1830–33), propounded the view that the earth's geological history could be explained entirely by heat and erosion, processes that we can observe at work today. Lyell appealed to a "principle of uniformity," and

Two Valleys: Uniformitarianism and Catastrophism

Charles Lyell and the Niagara

The prevailing model of geology (and of biology) before the mid-nineteenth century was biblical. The belief that there had been a large-scale, single flood was widespread. Such geographic features as the Grand Canyon in the United States and the European river valleys were assumed to have been formed by rushing floodwaters. Charles Lyell showed, by meticulous analysis of sediments, that gradual erosion over long periods of time accounted for the cutting of valleys by rivers. In his *Principles of Geology,* he discussed Niagara Falls as a "magnificent example of the progressive excavation of a deep valley in solid rock" (Figure 2–5). Lyell showed that Niagara Falls had migrated from a former position near Queenstown inch by inch, "slowly eating its way backwards through the rocks for the distance of seven miles." Lyell's interpretations were persuasive, and his uniformitarian approach was widely adopted by younger geologists.

J. Harlan Bretz and the Channeled Scablands of Eastern Washington

Geologist J. Harlan Bretz of the U.S. Geological Survey studied the unusual

FIGURE 2–5   The Falls of Niagara, from Lyell's *Principles of Geology.* Lyell used Niagara as an example of uniformitarianism.

topography of eastern Washington state in the 1920s. Here isolated hills and low mountains, connected by a generally smooth and regular plain, dot the landscape. The topography is rather graphically termed the "scablands." Uniformitarian models had long been accepted in geology, and Bretz's apparently catastrophic interpretation of the scablands was at first rejected. Bretz believed that a major ice dam had burst at the end of the last Pleistocene Ice Age,

FIGURE 2–6   The scablands of eastern Washington state, which J. Harlan Bretz used to demonstrate that catastrophic events can dramatically alter the landscape, within a general context of uniformitarianism.

releasing massive amounts of water from the paleo-Lake Missoula in Montana, flooding Washington and Oregon to the Pacific Ocean, and causing catastrophic erosion (Figure 2–6). A wall of water 2,000 feet high would have engulfed the site of modern-day Spokane, Washington, and would still have been 400 feet high at Portland, Oregon. His evidence included massive boulders that could only have been moved by huge floodwaters, dry waterfalls, and very sharp erosional boundaries in the sediments, all differences from Lyell's examples of uniformitarian erosion. Bretz's interpretation is now widely accepted, and his work shows how catastrophic past events can be understood within Lyell's uniformitarian paradigm.

William Whewell, a reviewer of *The Principles,* coined the term **uniformitarianism** for Lyell's theory. Uniformitarianism is the principle that processes observable today can account for past events in geological history.

Charles Darwin first read Lyell's book on the round-the-world voyage of the British ship H.M.S. *Beagle* when he was employed as the ship's naturalist. In 1836, on his return to England, Darwin states in his *Autobiography* (1958:32–33) that he "saw a great deal of Lyell" and that "his advice and example had much influence on me." Uniformitarianism became one of the founding principles of modern geology, and, through Darwin, a major influence in biology. Lyell's uniformitarian theory provided the long time periods necessary for the slow and gradual change that Darwin envisioned. It also provided the basis for Darwin's notion of gradualism, the slow, constant change in life forms over time that he incorporated into his theory of evolution.

DARWIN DEVELOPS HIS THEORY

Collecting Evidence for Evolution

As we have already noted, much of the data that Darwin used to construct his theory came from his experiences as ship's naturalist aboard the H.M.S. *Beagle,* which circumnavigated the globe from 1833 to 1836 on a mission to map the South American coast for British shipping interests. When Darwin sailed from England on the H.M.S. *Beagle,* he carried with him the idea of evolution advanced by Lamarck.

In South America Darwin found evidence of evolution, but his observations forced him to question Lamarck's idea of the inheritance of acquired characteristics. If Lamarck's explanation of the mechanism for evolution was correct, similar environments would produce similar species. For example, if finches on the mainland occupied very similar habitats of the same latitude as their island relatives, they should be very similar. However, Darwin found that they were in fact very different.

uniformitarianism: principle that processes observable today can account for past events in geological history.

FRONTIERS

The Galápagos Revisited

Darwin referred to the process of speciation as "that mystery of mysteries," yet had he known something about the geological history of his Galápagos Islands he might have been able to contribute even more to the solution of the mystery than he did. The present-day Galápagos Islands are estimated to be only about 3 million years old, relative newcomers to a chain of islands that began to form more than 10 million years ago. The oldest drowned island, or seamount, now lies about 2,500 meters (7,500 feet) under the ocean surface. The entire chain sits above the Nazca tectonic plate, which drifts in an westwardly direction away from continental South America. The recent uncovering of this geological history helps explain one of the mysteries of the evolution of the unique Galápagos fauna. Molecular studies have demonstrated that different species of the Galápagos fauna diverged from one another at substantially different times in the past. However, if speciation occurred as Darwin thought it did—gradually—should not the molecular studies show that all speciation events occurred at the same time?

Oceanic islands such as the Galápagos begin as sterile masses of cooled lava, and the substantial distance of these islands from the continent makes colonization by life forms a rare event. If colonization does occur, however, the unique species cannot be any older than the island itself. If the date of divergence is greater than the island's geological age, one assumes that the species divergence must have occurred before the formation of the island.

Molecular studies of the 12 diverse species of Darwin's finches fit well with the recent geological age of the islands. In contrast, a much longer genetic distance has been determined for the marine and land iguanas, whose date of divergence is estimated to be between 15 million and 20 million years ago. The discovery of submerged islands that are considerably older than those above water today helps to solve this quandary. The apparent problem of a simultaneous presence of old and new lineages of the finches and the iguanas is no longer such a mystery, if one conjectures that the older iguana lineages diverged on islands that are now submerged.

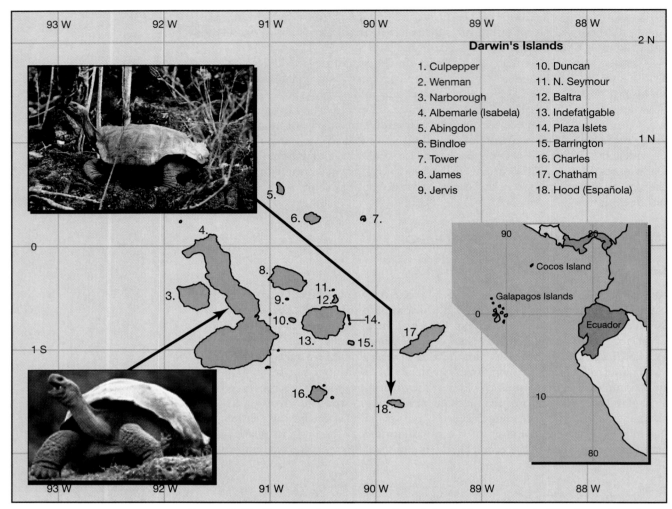

FIGURE 2–7 Natural selection in tortoises of the Galápagos Islands. The dome-shaped tortoise from the large and well-watered island of Isabela (formerly Albemarle Island) differs markedly in shell shape from the saddle-backed tortoise on the smaller and more arid Isla Española (formerly Hood Island). Because of natural selection, saddle-backed tortoises can reach higher leaves while feeding on the less abundant plants in their dry habitats.

When Darwin arrived at the Galápagos Islands, off the northwest coast of South America, in September of 1835, he discovered several important facts. The Galápagos are volcanic islands, much more recent in origin than the neighboring mainland. Darwin immediately set to work collecting animal and plant specimens from the many closely spaced islands (Figure 2–7). In accordance with Lamarck's ideas, he expected the fauna and flora of the various islands to be quite similar to one another, because the islands were close together and shared the same climate. He found, in fact, quite a unique spectrum of species of birds, lizards, and tortoises on the islands. They were related to, but also quite distinct from, mainland South American forms.

As work progressed, Darwin became aware of a strange and unexpected fact—the tortoises from each island differed from the tortoises of other islands. In fact, people could tell what island a tortoise came from by looking at the shell alone. He later found this to be also true among his collection of birds, the famous Galápagos

FIGURE 2–8 Five of the famous Darwin finches from the Galápagos Islands. Darwin's observations and collection of these birds during his visit to the islands were crucial to his later formulation of the idea of the origin of species by natural selection.

finches (Figure 2–8). How could this be so if species were adapted to the same environment?

Darwin began to think that because all the types of island tortoises were in most ways similar, they must have all descended from a common ancestral tortoise and had diverged over time by adapting to the various island environments. He concluded that geographic isolation was crucial to an understanding of evolution. Geographical variations were not separate "special creations" of species, but rather, they were local modifications of a single species.

Darwin found fossil evidence in South America that showed that evolution had occurred. He discovered in an ancient geological formation a fossil glyptodont, an extinct giant relative of the modern armadillo (Figure 2–9). An extinct llama skeleton discovered in Patagonia showed a clear connection to living South American llamas. In his *Journal of Researches* (1839), Darwin noted that "the most important result of this discovery is the confirmation of the law that existing animals have a close relation in form with extinct species." Darwin termed this "the law of the

FIGURE 2–9 Comparison of a modern armadillo (top) and a fossil glyptodont (bottom), a representative of an extinct group of South American land animals.

succession of types," an idea that formed the theoretical basis for connecting the fossil record with the diversity of living animals.

Investigating Differential Reproduction

Darwin returned home in 1836 and devoted the remaining years of his life to the study of natural history. He began to study domesticated animals and to breed pigeons. He also wrote a number of classic studies on organisms such as the barnacle and on the evolution of behavior (see Chapter 11). He observed that, through the process of artificial breeding, or selection, one could obtain populations or strains of animals that were quite different from each other and from the original parental form.

Almost all the pieces of the puzzle of evolution were in place: Individuals vary and forms could be artificially selected to breed so that change could come about, and these differences were heritable from generation to generation. What Darwin lacked was knowledge of how this inherited variability could be connected to his deduction that animals could change over time to adapt to their natural environments. Part of the answer, of course, came from Malthus's essay.

Malthus wrote in his essay that not all individuals born reached maturity. Many die from one cause or another before adulthood. A species does not continue to reproduce until it completely covers the earth with its offspring. Rather, there is

FIGURE 2–10 Darwin based his theory on two crucial observations: that individuals vary from one another and that variability is inherited.

some upper limit to population growth, and populations maintain a stable number of individuals.

Darwin's argument started with the observation that individuals within a species vary one from another (Figure 2–10). A second observation was that this variability could be inherited. Because of variability, some individuals were better suited to survive in their environments than others. Invoking Malthus's ideas that species produce more offspring than can survive, Darwin reasoned that those individuals best adapted to their environment would survive longer and, on average, produce more offspring than those less well adapted. He called the new theory **natural selection** to distinguish it from the artificial selection practiced on domestic animals by breeders.

In 1859, Darwin published *On the Origin of Species by Means of Natural Selection*. He reasoned that differential survival occurred because individuals had different abilities (fitnesses) to cope with their environments. Differential reproduction would be the result of the survival of those individuals who were better adapted. Over the generations there would be selection among the various individuals in response to environmental conditions, with the better adapted individuals producing more offspring. Those individuals disfavored by selection might not reproduce at all or would have relatively fewer offspring than the more fit animals.

natural selection: the process of differential reproduction whereby individuals who are well adapted to their environment will be "favored," that is, they will pass on more of their heritable attributes to the next generation than other, less well-adapted individuals.

Wallace's Independent Discovery of Natural Selection

Alfred Russel Wallace (Figure 2–11) was a surveyor and schoolteacher in Leicester, England, when, in 1848, he and a naturalist colleague set out for the Amazon to collect samples of various plants and animals. Unlike Darwin, Wallace set out in order to investigate the question of species' origins. Also unlike Darwin, he was not supported in his scientific endeavors by family wealth. Instead, he supported his research by collecting specimens and sending them back to England for sale.

Wallace stayed in the interior of Brazil for five years and during that time made extensive collections. He wrote in 1854 the first paper on the geographic distributions of monkey species in the Amazonian forests. Wallace was interested in where

FIGURE 2–11 Alfred Russel Wallace.

FIGURE 2-12 Wallace's line. This illustration shows the approximate distribution of land and water during the Pleistocene glaciation. Sundaland and Sahulland formed as sea levels lowered. Compare with Figure 2–13, which shows the current geography of the same area.

species were found and how they got there. He noticed in the case of the monkeys that distinct species were separated geographically by major rivers. The following year Wallace published a paper that drew on his extensive observations in South America and hypothesized that every new species that comes into existence is associated with a similar species nearby. This observation began to erode the idea of special creation, because it suggested that similar species in a region might be similar because of shared origins, not because of a certain set of environmental conditions.

During the 1850s, Wallace, who had now relocated to the Far East, studied the natural history of the islands in the Malay Archipelago, now part of Indonesia. It was here that he made his discovery of evolution by natural selection, independent of Charles Darwin. On the island of Aru he discovered a surprising discontinuity with the rest of the fauna and flora of the neighboring islands. Aru shared species with New Guinea, a large marsupial-containing island allied with Australia and New Zealand, whereas the islands to the north and west shared species with each other and the Southeast Asian mainland (Figures 2–12 and 2–13). Wallace correctly deduced that the deep sea between Aru and the other Indonesian islands prevented species from crossing to Aru, whereas the shallow seas between Aru and New Guinea and between islands to the north and west and Indonesia had at times dried up to allow dispersal of species when sea levels dropped in the geological past. This important biological boundary is still known as "Wallace's Line." As Darwin had done, Wallace drew on Malthus's theory of competition in populations, and he put this idea together with his observations that geographical barriers and isolation

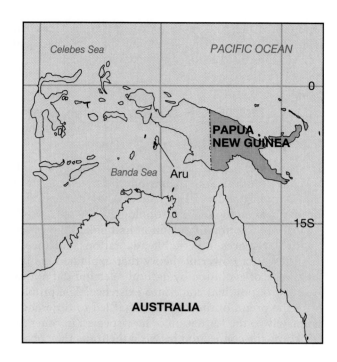

FIGURE 2-13 Aru, New Guinea, and Indonesia. Wallace spent several years studying the animals of Aru, which are different from those of the neighboring islands.

of breeding groups had important effects on the formation of new species. It was not the environmental circumstances of a place alone that determined what plants and animals live there; rather, chance, biogeography (a term that he coined), and natural selection work together as determining factors. Otherwise, Aru's fauna would have looked very similar to that of the islands near it.

Implications of Natural Selection

Darwin included only one diagram in the *Origin of Species*. It showed his conception of *phylogeny*—how evolving lineages of organisms would continue through time. Recall from Chapter 1 how a phylogeny differs from a cladogram. Darwin plotted on the vertical axis 14 hypothetical time horizons (labeled I to XIV), which he discussed in terms of generations. He used 1,000 generations as illustrative. The horizontal axis of his figure represented degrees of similarity among species labeled "A" to "L." Similar species were shown close together; very different species were further apart. Some lineages would become extinct at varying times after their separation from their ancestral species. Others would diversify and radiate into different varieties, which in turn would continue to differentiate into new species. Other species would continue and survive but would be little changed from their ancestral types. Today we call these kinds of species "living fossils."

Darwin's phylogenetic diagram also underscored his idea of the connection between the small degrees of variation seen between recent descendants of a common ancestor and the eventual large-scale differences seen between species or genera descended from them. In modern terminology, small-scale, within-species evolutionary change is called **microevolution,** and large-scale change at the level of new species, genera, and higher-level taxa is called **macroevolution.** Darwin argued that microevolution leads to macroevolution. He wrote in the *Origin of Species* that "I see no reason to limit the process of modification, as now explained, to the formation of genera alone." Referring again to his diagram, he pointed out that the two clusters of species seen at level XIV, descended from species I, would form one

microevolution: small-scale, within-species evolutionary change.

macroevolution: large-scale change at the level of new species, genera, and higher-level taxa.

family or order, and those four genera descended from species A would form another family or order, depending on how divergent in form they had become. Darwin thus tied phylogeny to classification as well.

LIMITATIONS OF DARWIN'S AND WALLACE'S THEORY

The Problem of Inherited Variation

The theory of natural selection successfully explained a biological fact—that evolution has occurred. Although evolutionary biologists debate many details of the theory, Darwin's and Wallace's theory has become the foundation for both modern biology and biological anthropology.

Darwin's notion of evolution had linked the concepts of excess reproductive capacity, differences in heritable adaptations, enhanced survival, and reproduction of the fittest in a powerful theory that explained many observations in nature. What the theory of evolution by natural selection did not explain was the mechanisms by which variation had come into existence. The problem for Darwin was how to explain the origin of the variation that led to differential success in reproduction and ultimately to the formation of new species. In other words, Darwin and Wallace did not know the connection between the traits they observed in living species and what we now call "genetics."

How variation was maintained in populations was the second profound problem that Darwin and other evolutionists considered. Darwin believed that most traits, when combined in an offspring, were blends of the parental types. For example, the mating of a tall person and a short person would produce an offspring that was intermediate in height. Two intermediate-height individuals would produce an intermediate-height offspring. The consequence of this **blending inheritance**, however, would be a *loss* of variation and an *increase* in homogeneity in the population. If inheritance by blending did occur, then after only nine generations one would have less than 0.1 percent of original variation left. This fact was noted by a Scottish engineer, Fleeming Jenkin, who criticized Darwin's hypothesis of blending inheritance. How, he asked, could a single favorable change, a heritable mutation arising in one member of a population, ever come to predominate if at each successive reproduction its benefit was halved by blending with an individual lacking the trait?

Jenkin's criticisms of blending inheritance presented Darwin with a dilemma. If this model was incorrect, then there must be some other mechanism at work that could provide the enormous quantity of variation that Darwin observed. While Darwin, to no avail, pondered this question, unbeknownst to him the finishing touches to a new theory of inheritance were being applied by a Moravian monk who studied pea plants: Gregor Mendel (see Chapter 3).

The third problem that Darwin dealt with and incorporated into his view of evolution involved the rate of evolutionary change. Based on Lyell's earlier work, as we have seen, Darwin developed his model of evolutionary gradualism. The idea of gradualism was contentious, and Darwin's friend and spokesperson on many occasions, Thomas Huxley, warned Darwin against tieing gradualism into his overall theory of evolution because he believed this rate model could not be supported by the geological and fossil evidence at hand. Later on, twentieth-century evolutionists, such as paleontologist George Gaylord Simpson, focused attention on how fast or slow phylogenetic change occurred (its tempo), as well as its pattern or mode. He maintained that evolutionary change through time was, as Darwin had postulated, gradual. In the 1970s, paleontologists Stephen Jay Gould and Niles Eldredge proposed a new mode of evolutionary change that they termed *punctuated equilibrium*. From their reading of the fossil record, Gould and Eldredge believed that the

blending inheritance: the mixing in equal halves of the contributions of parents in their offspring.

primary pattern of evolutionary change consisted of long periods of bradytely, which they termed *stasis,* interrupted by short bursts of tachytely, which they termed *punctuational events.* Gould and Eldredge suggested that punctuated equilibrium would replace the older Darwinian model of gradualism, but most evolutionary scientists remain skeptical of the general applicability of the pattern.

SEXUAL SELECTION

In response to his critics, and based on his own observations, Darwin also attempted to explain the evolution of characteristics that were apparently maladaptive. Why, for example, would a male peacock evolve such a gaudy, useless plumage that served only to make him more visible to predators (Figure 2–14)? How could such plumage evolve if birds that had it were preferentially eaten for lunch?

Darwin's explanation of traits such as the male peacock's plumage was **sexual selection,** an extension of natural selection independently developed by Ernst Haeckel in 1868. Observations of the behavior of male peacocks showed that they competed among themselves for the attentions of females during the mating season. A female then selected the most impressive male with which to mate. The male's plumage is indeed intended to be noticed, but by females of the same species rather than by predators. The brilliance and fullness of a male's plumage is likely to correspond to his general state of health and value as a breeding partner, so there is some evolutionary logic to the female's preference.

Darwin noted that sexual selection can result in the evolution of two sexes whose adult members can differ from one another substantially in their external morphology, a condition known as **sexual dimorphism** (Latin, meaning "two-bodied"; Figure 2–15). Sexually dimorphic secondary sex characteristics, such as large body size or bright-colored plumage, may be simultaneously threatening to rivals and attractive to potential mates. Darwin also noted the paradoxical situation in which characteristics that are advantageous in competition with one's rival may be very disadvantageous when it comes to the basic issues of survival. For example, male–male aggression, which occurs during the mating season in many species of prosimian primates, such as lemurs, often results in the severe wounding of both

sexual selection: selection through male–male competition or female choice in which certain characteristics evolve that confer a reproductive advantage on the individual that possesses them.

sexual dimorphism: the evolution of two sexes whose adult members can differ from one another substantially in their external morphology.

FIGURE 2-14 The theory of sexual selection explains such apparently useless, if not harmful, traits as the peacock's tail.

FIGURE 2-15 Sexual dimorphism in mandrills and in humans.

contestants (Figure 2–16). But because the chance, however small, of a male's mating with a receptive female is overpoweringly attractive, virtually all of the males engage in this sort of combat. Larger body size and elaborate coloration usually differentiate males from females in primates as well as in many other kinds of animals, because much of male–male competition depends on aggressive display.

As Helena Cronin (1992:286) describes the situation,

> If you were asked to invent an irksome challenge to Darwinian theory, you could get a long way with a peacock's tail. And if you were asked to think up a solution to the challenge that would disconcert Darwinians, you would need to go no further than Charles Darwin's own theory of sexual selection. . . . [Natural selection] should abhor the peacock's tail—gaudy, ornamental, a burden to its bearer. Darwin took the view that natural selection would indeed frown upon such flamboyance. It had been concocted, he decided, by female preference.

Thus, the "good taste" theory of female choice was born; females choose their mates on aesthetic grounds; male ornamentation developed to charm the females and "for no other purpose" (Darwin, 1871:92). Reactions to this idea developed into two different viewpoints. First was the idea that sexual selection was, in reality, unimportant and that gaudy ornamentation could be explained in terms of natural selection, having significance in warning, territorial, or threat display.

The second viewpoint involved the "good sense" of female choice. In this view females choose their mates on the basis of male vigor, good health, and territory size; in other words, these were sensible choices to make. The fact that one characteristic is chosen and embellished over another is arbitrary. The characteristic, itself, is unimportant. What is important is that at one time a preference for some characteristic was made and it became reinforced and elaborated in a positive feedback loop. Once preference for, let us say, gaudy-colored tails was established, then it was "good sense" for females to continue to make choices for mates on that basis, as all other females would be doing the same.

Sexual selection can lead to the evolution of both behavioral responses, or strategies, and physical traits. Trivers (1972) has argued that differences in male and female reproductive strategies may be accounted for by the investment each parent makes in their offspring. Females usually invest more of their time and energy in a smaller number of offspring and are more selective in their choice of mates. Males, conversely, increase their reproductive success by producing more offspring by mating with as many females as they can. The female reproductive strategy has the

FIGURE 2-16 Ring-tailed lemur males fighting during the mating season.

primary goal of protecting her offspring. It may include prolonging the period of sexual receptivity; aggression against competitors, which may involve the harassment and killing of the offspring of others; and the suppression of sexual receptivity in subordinate females. Females may also compete directly for resources necessary for producing and nurturing their offspring, and for attracting the highest ranking males that they can. Males, in contrast, may compete through a variety of behaviors that include guarding territory, dominating other animals, and guarding females.

Darwin thought that sexual selection was particularly important in human evolution, and in 1871 he published *The Descent of Man and Selection in Relation to Sex.* In this book, Darwin wrote that he considered it "highly probable that sexual selection has played an important part in differentiating the races of man." Darwin reviewed evidence from all known categories of animals, from invertebrates through primates, and he noted two types of sexual selection. The first was selection for successful male–male competition for females. Darwin wrote (1871:863) that "[m]ost naturalists will admit that the greater size, strength, courage, and pugnacity of the male, his special weapons of offence, as well as his special means of defence, have been acquired through that form of selection which I have called sexual."

In humans Darwin considered the larger body size, more heavily built skull, and beard of adult males to be products of sexual selection. He compared the well-developed beards of certain male monkeys with the beards of human males, noting that in both, beard color was lighter than body or head hair color. Chapter 19 in the *Descent of Man,* in which Darwin discusses human sexual selection, is among the most provocative of all his writings. Darwin observes that the larger body size and more pugnacious personality of human males were the products of sexual selection. He speculates that musical ability, hairlessness (which he considers to be a major disadvantage to human ancestors), and physical beauty first evolved in human females by means of sexual selection.

It is important to interject at this point that because of the inherent differences in reproductive strategies between males and females, the outcome of sexual selection appears mostly on males rather than females. For example, if relative reproductive fitness is measured in terms of number of offspring, then the greatest difference between human females is from zero to 15 or so, whereas the difference between males could range from zero to hundreds of offspring from numerous mates. Because sexual selection works through either male–male competition or female choice, it is usually the male whose characteristics allow him to mate and produce more surviving offspring. One of the few physical characteristics that may be sexually selected for in the human female as a result of male choice is the preference for a smaller waist than hips (regardless of whether both are relatively small or large as long as the waist is smaller). This feature can be directly related to success in childbirth (Dettwyler, personal comm.).

Darwin believed that sexual selection and natural selection had worked together to form the human species. Larger and stronger males, for example, would also have been favored by natural selection because they would have been able to defend the group against predators. Darwin believed that the decreased size of the canine teeth in human males, quite different from the vicious canines of nonhuman primates, resulted from the evolution of tool and weapon use. And Darwin's views about the natural superiority and higher intelligence of human males versus human females have sparked spirited debate for more than a century. We discuss the evolution of human behavior, including sexual strategies, in Chapter 14.

EVOLUTION OF BEHAVIOR

Darwin was well aware that behavior is a major component of individual fitness. For example, an animal that uses its cunning is just as likely (perhaps more so) to acquire a mate as an animal whose large size is its only advantage. Adaptive behaviors have a positive selective value and, to the extent that any behavior or set of behaviors has a genetic component, it is subject to all the same evolutionary forces that affect all genes. Thus, a genetically based or genetically influenced behavior that contributes to relative reproductive success is more likely to be passed on to future generations and spread more widely than is a behavior that detracts from relative reproductive success. As we have seen, Darwin is also responsible for placing animal behavior in an evolutionary context. In his book *The Expression of the Emotions in Man and Animals* (1872:12), Darwin showed that there were continuities between animal and human behavior, implying a common inherited basis. He concluded that behavioral traits as well as physical traits were subject to evolution.

A *behavior* can be defined as a pattern of activity that continues through time. This definition allows scientists to measure and compare behavior between individuals in different species. Understanding how animals interact in social groups is also an important aspect of the study of behavior, because humans and most other primates are highly social species.

Ethology

Ethology as a field began with Darwin, who first treated behavior in the same evolutionary context as anatomical structure and physiology. He stated that "the chief expressive actions, exhibited by man and the lower animals, are now innate or inherited—that is, have not been learnt by the individual—is admitted by every one" (1872:350). Although this tenet may have been generally accepted during Darwin's time, the rise of experimental psychology, with its emphasis on learned behavior, did not allow ethology to progress much until well into the twentieth century.

Scientists have realized that behavior evolves to allow a species to adapt effectively to a particular ecological niche. Behavioral adaptations of a particular species should be studied in animals' natural habitats. **Ethology** is the biological study of animal behavior that deals with species-specific or genetically linked behavior (Lorenz, 1965). Ethologists recognize the value of observing behavior in its entirety within an environmental context, because only under these circumstances can the evolution of behavior patterns be fully comprehended (Eibl-Eibesfeldt, 1989).

ethology: the biological study of animal behavior that deals with species-specific or genetically linked behavior.

A species' characteristic physical features develop within certain limits, through an interaction of the genotype with the environment. In a similar manner, a species' behavior—how individuals acquire food, how they interact with other members of the species, how they avoid danger, how they reproduce, and how they raise their young—is also a result of genetic development within a range of appropriate environments. As the ethologist Konrad Lorenz (1965b:xii; Figure 2–17) has noted, "behavior patterns are just as conservatively and reliably characters of species as are the forms of bones, teeth, or any other bodily structures." However, the scientific study of behavior and its evolution is a relatively new field, and many of the interactions of behavior, genetics, and environment are yet to be investigated.

Much of human ethology deals with the nonverbal, nonlearned, and noncultural behavior we share with other animals. Anthropologist Sherwood Washburn once suggested that human ethology might be defined as the science that pretends humans cannot speak. Although he intended it as a critique, because much of human behavior is mediated, expressed, and even caused by linguistic cues, it is an apt description of a science that intends to study human behavior within an evolutionary context. To understand the roots of human behavior, one must look at the nonverbal behavioral commonalities that humans share with the animal world.

Ethologists seek to establish a behavioral profile, or *ethogram* of a species—a catalog of all the behavioral patterns of an animal. In practice this is difficult. What is a "behavior pattern"? What are the basic units of behavior to be cataloged? If ethology is indeed a comparative science, what behaviors could be compared from one species to another? The first answer to these queries is behavior that is closely tied to genetics.

FIGURE 2–17 Konrad Lorenz and his geese.

Fixed Action Patterns

Ethologist Konrad Lorenz (1965b) described what he termed *inherited coordination*. In more recent literature, the term *fixed action pattern* (FAP) has replaced the earlier term. **Fixed action patterns** are behaviors that (1) are form-constant—each instance that they are expressed, the same muscles contract and the animal moves in the same sequence; (2) appear spontaneously during development, requiring no learning; (3) are characteristic of all members of the species; (4) cannot be unlearned; and (5) are released or caused by a particular stimulus, external environmental condition or internal physiological environment, of the animal. Numerous cases of FAPs are now known from observations of insects, birds, fish, and other vertebrates (Figure 2–18).

fixed action pattern (FAP): behaviors that are form-constant; appear spontaneously during development; are characteristic of all members of the species; cannot be unlearned; and are released or caused by a particular stimulus, external environmental condition or internal physiological environment, of the animal.

FIGURE 2–18 Fixed action patterns can be observed in a chameleon's unerring capture of a flying insect; in a mother wren's placement of food in the open mouths of her nestlings; and in the vocal alarm calls of a group of ring-tailed lemurs, elicited by aerial movements of a bird of prey.

A curious attribute of the FAP is that, once started, an FAP must be completed, in computerlike fashion, regardless of any further environmental information. A greylag goose mother, for example, once she has seen a loose egg away from the nest and has gone to retrieve it, will always make the same beak movements along the ground to roll the egg back to the nest even if an ethologist surreptitiously takes the egg away before the goose gets to it! Because an egg almost never disappears from under the nose of a goose under normal circumstances, natural selection has produced this FAP in the species and it functions quite successfully. The development of an FAP may, however, be affected by environmental conditions. For example, a rat mother seemingly is endowed with an FAP to groom and care for her pup, for she will do so even when she has been raised in isolation. However, if the mother is reared in isolation under the additional condition of wearing a collar that prevents her from grooming herself, then she will neglect and even abuse her offspring.

The disadvantage of FAPs for solving behavioral problems is their lack of flexibility. An FAP may be ineffective as a behavioral strategy when a species is confronted with changing environmental conditions. Undoubtedly, this is one of the strong selective reasons for behavioral evolution leading to a preponderance of learned behavioral responses in mammals. Later, in Chapter 11, we discuss fixed action patterns as they are identified in humans.

Evolution Beyond Darwin

Although Darwin and other scientists at the time investigated the intricacies of evolution, including the evolution of physical characteristics as well as complex behavioral patterns, they lacked, as we have seen, any real understanding of the mechanisms for change, in other words, a workable theory of inheritance. In the next chapter we consider the laws of inheritance as they were first worked out by Gregor Mendel. One of the great ironies in the history of biological science is that if Darwin had only heard of (and, of course, understood) Mendel's work, he might have solved many of the problems of inheritance that he pondered. But Darwin died before the remarkable work of Mendel had been "rediscovered" by other scientists, and Mendel died before what he was due was finally bestowed on him. From Mendel we go on to explore the molecular basis of Mendel's laws, as it elegantly unfolded with the discovery of DNA and modern molecular genetics.

◀ SUMMARY

1. **What is the scientific revolution? In what way did it lead to the discovery of evolution by natural selection?**
   The theory of natural selection, discovered independently by Charles Darwin and Alfred Russel Wallace, was an outgrowth of the scientific revolution. It incorporated important ideas of population dynamics postulated by Thomas Malthus and the principle of uniformitarianism put forth by geologist Charles Lyell.

2. **How did Darwin and Wallace formulate their theories? What were their major principles?**
   Darwin's evidence for evolution was gathered on a three-year, round-the-world ocean voyage, especially in South America and the Galápagos Islands, and from many published sources, as well as from breeding experiments (artificial selection) in England. Wallace's evidence for evolution came also from South America, but particularly from islands in Southeast Asia, where he observed distinct differences in fauna on islands separated from one another by deep expanses of water, a boundary later referred to as Wallace's Line. Darwin's and Wallace's argument

was that (a) individuals within a species vary; (b) at least some of this variability is inherited; (c) because of variability some individuals are better suited to survive than others; (d) those individuals best adapted to their environments survive longer and produce more offspring; and (e) evolution occurs and new species are formed as natural selection acts over time and across geography. Phylogenetic trees depict the hypothesized course of evolution and its mode, which can be slow or rapid, gradual or punctuated. Darwin and Ernst Haeckel independently proposed the mechanism of sexual selection, a type of natural selection in which mate choice within the species plays a major role. Darwin thought that sexual selection had been particularly important to human evolution.

3. **What is sexual selection? How can genes influence behavior?**

Sexual selection is the form of natural selection whereby certain males who possess physical or behavioral traits that allow them to mate more successfully and have more surviving offspring contribute more of their genes to future generations. Thus, whatever genetically based traits they had that allowed them better reproductive success—whether through male–male competition or because of female mate choice—will become more common in future generations. To the extent that behaviors are the result of genetic influences, they can be affected by evolutionary forces including natural selection. Thus, a genetically based behavior that contributes to reproductive success will become more common in future generations.

4. **What were the limitations of the theory of natural selection at the time it was developed?**

Because the laws of heredity were unknown at the time, the means by which evolutionary change occurred was unknown when Darwin and Wallace developed their ideas.

CRITICAL THINKING QUESTIONS

1. The social philosopher Herbert Spencer first applied the term *survival of the fittest* to Darwinian natural selection. Explain why this term is not entirely accurate.

2. Paleontologist Niles Eldredge suggested in his recent book *The Pattern of Evolution* that Darwin should not have used the word *selection,* borrowed from the human process of breeding domestic animals and plants, to refer to the natural process whereby some individuals have more offspring and preferentially pass on their traits to the next generation. He suggests that the term *filtration* is better. Do you agree? Explain.

3. Evolutionary change may vary in rate. What ecological conditions might be associated with slow evolutions in a species over time, and what conditions might tend to bring on rapid evolutionary change?

4. Both Darwin and Wallace arrived at their independent discoveries of natural selection by considering species' diversity and geography, specifically island geography. Could two species originate in the same area without a geographic barrier between them? Why or why not?

INTERNET EXERCISES

Critical Thinking

Island Biogeography. Darwin and Wallace independently developed the theory of evolution after studying animals on isolated islands. Is this a coincidence? Or is there something unique about the biogeography of islands? Find out more about the

Galápagos, Aru, or other isolated islands, such as Madagascar, the Hawaiian Islands, or the Seychelles. Try to answer the following questions:

1. Why do islands tend to harbor unique species?
2. Why are species more likely to become extinct on islands than on continents?
3. Why was the theory of evolution developed by naturalists who studied island biogeography?

Writing

Alfred Russel Wallace. The events of Charles Darwin's life and his development of the theory of natural selection are well known. Wallace, however, remains obscure. Research the life of this fascinating Victorian and write a brief biography. Focus on the following questions:

1. What circumstances brought Wallace to Aru and the independent development of the theory of natural selection?
2. Wallace lived until 1913. What did he do with himself after he returned to England?
3. Why is Darwin so much more famous than Wallace?

See Companion Web site for Internet links.

MEDIALAB   Evolution in Action: Galápagos Finches

Charles Darwin developed the theory of evolution by natural selection after noticing that different islands in the Galápagos archipelago had different species, especially of tortoises and finches. Although Darwin did not know the mechanism by which evolution occurred, he speculated that species differentiate in response to differences in environment.

In the Web Activity for this chapter, you will see evolution in action: morphological changes in a population of Galápagos finches that are taking place today in response to environmental change. You will see how the distribution of beak types changed over a short period of time and speculate on the cause of this change.

WEB ACTIVITY

In any population, organisms vary, and this natural variation is the basis for natural selection. In a population

of finches, for example, beak depth may vary greatly. When the climate changes, and the food supply changes as a result, some birds may have an advantage in gathering food in the changed circumstances. This animation shows you the results that biologist Peter Grant obtained when he measured the beaks of a population of finches on a small island in the Galápagos.

Activity

1. View the animation. Why did Grant base his study on the average beak depth over the entire population?
2. Speculate about the reason for the change in average beak depth after the drought. Why did the overall population of *G. fortis* decline?
3. What might have happened if the island had experienced flooding instead of drought? If a foreign seed-eating bird had been introduced from another island?

The MediaLab can be found in Chapter 2 on your Companion Web site http://www.prenhall.com/boaz

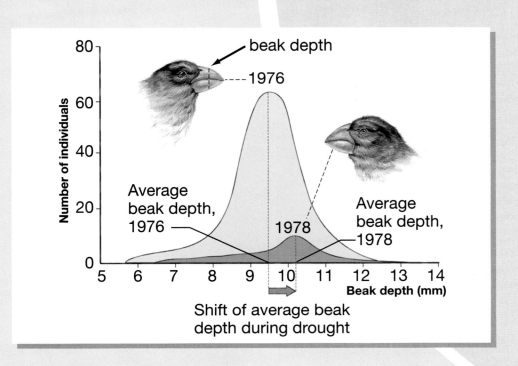

3

GENETICS

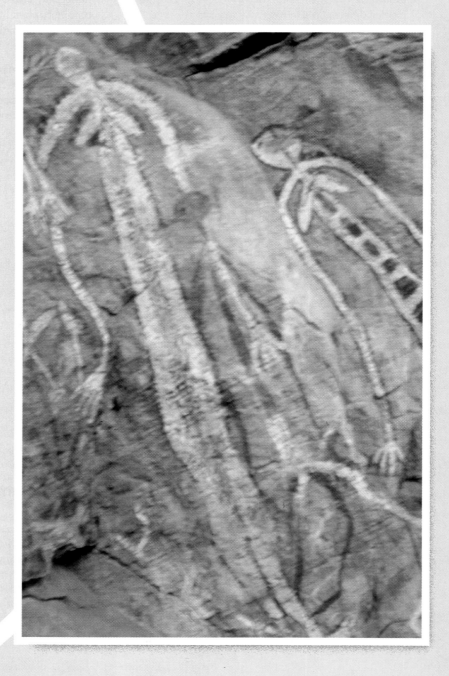

After reading this chapter, you should be able to discuss the following questions:

1. What nineteenth- and early twentieth-century discoveries led to the development of a theory of heredity?
2. What are the structures and mechanisms of heredity at a biochemical and cellular level?
3. What is the significance of sexual reproduction for the emergence of variation?
4. What are mutations, and how do they occur?

We human beings are literally part of the universe in which we live. The chemical elements, such as hydrogen, carbon, and iron, that make up our bodies are the same elements that make up the planets and stars: They differ only in proportions. These basic building blocks of physical matter on earth are constantly being recycled. Thus, our bodies may contain elements that were once parts of ancient sea algae, trees, dinosaurs, or mammoths. Each form of life has this basic bond to the earth and uses the elements found in nature to carry on its daily life functions and to reproduce more of its own kind.

The evolution of human beings, like that of other species that exist or have existed on earth, ultimately begins at the earliest appearance of life. The shared characteristics of all living things—the fact that the same basic chemicals are used in the same ways for reproducing and carrying on life—is a monumental testimony to the shared ancestry of all life. We all go back to one primordial ancestor. Although it may stretch the imagination to realize that you and the salad that you ate for lunch share distant relatives, this is in fact the case.

Much of modern biology has become focused on the molecular level of organization. These exciting new advances in genetics and molecular biology are the focus of this chapter, which explores the common genetic and evolutionary heritage of all life on earth.

DEVELOPMENT OF A THEORY OF INHERITANCE

As we saw in Chapter 2, Darwin and his contemporaries lacked any real understanding of the laws of inheritance. In attempts to develop some logical ideas about inheritance, they hypothesized a sort of blending mechanism to account for the variations they observed in the natural world. However, experimentation did not support this hypothesis. Many scientists of the day believed that the units of heredity could be found in blood. Based on this idea Sir Francis Galton (1822–1911) transfused the blood of rabbits with different fur colors and then inbred the resulting strains, crossing offspring from the same parents. He found no mixing of fur colors. The German biologist August Weismann (1834–1914) came the closest to discovering the truth when he hypothesized that all hereditary information resides in the reproductive cells, the "germ plasm," and that no changes in the body cells resulting from the environment could affect these germ cells. The nature of the units of heredity was still unknown, but Weismann's hypothesis formed one of the

FIGURE 3–1 Gregor Mendel, whose experiments with garden peas established the quantum theory of heredity.

genetics: the study of heredity and variation.

neo-Darwinism: the combined theory of evolution by natural selection and modern genetics.

quantum theory of heredity: passing of traits as clear-cut quantifiable units not subject to subdivision; characteristic of Mendelian genetics.

genes: units of the material of inheritance, now known to be sequences of DNA.

allele: alternate form of a gene.

homozygous: bearing two identical alleles at a genetic locus.

heterozygous: bearing two different alleles at a genetic locus.

genotype: the genetic composition of an organism, as compared to phenotype, the manifestation of its genes.

phenotype: an organism's appearance, a result of genetic and environmental factors.

bases for modern genetics. **Genetics** is the science that studies the mechanisms of heredity; the term was coined by the English biologist William Bateson in 1900. In rejecting the inheritance of acquired characteristics and embracing the modern concepts of genetics, Weismann's theory is also referred to as **neo-Darwinism** (Grant, 1991:17).

In 1889 Sir Hugo de Vries developed a modified hypothesis called "intracellular pangenesis," which took into account recent discoveries about the cell. De Vries's experiments, along with those of two other workers, Correns and Tschermak, led to the rediscovery in 1900 of elementary principles of inheritance. Unknown at the time to these scientists, this research and conclusions similar to their own had been completed and published 34 years earlier.

The Laws of Heredity

Many scientists and historians have pondered the idea that had Darwin known of the work of the then-scientifically obscure monk Gregor Mendel (1822–84; Figure 3–1), he would not have needed to make many of the compromises, such as his incorporation of the inheritance of acquired characteristics, that he was forced to by criticisms leveled at his work, the *Origin of Species*. Unfortunately, Mendel's work was either ignored by or unknown to most of the scientific world until 1900, because Mendel was considered by scientists that he did contact and with whom he shared his ideas to be a person with little scientific credibility, an amateur in the ways of science.

In 1856 Mendel began a series of breeding experiments involving crosses of individual edible peas, *Pisum sativum*. His goal was to investigate why certain plant hybrids all looked alike in the first descendant generation (called first filial or F1 generation) but had a tendency to revert to their original states in the second generation (second filial or F2 generation).

Mendel's results are important, because they established a **quantum theory of heredity,** distinguished from Darwin's blending theory of inheritance because it had clearly defined units that remained discrete, generation after generation. A trait, such as seed color or shape, in *Pisum* was caused by two irreducible "factors," now known to be genes. The Danish biologist Wilhelm Johannsen proposed the term *gene* in 1909 to refer to Mendel's factors.

Mendel found that for each trait of his pea plants, one factor or **gene** was *dominant* over the other, which was *recessive*. Each trait that Mendel studied in his pea plant experiments, such as seed color or seed shape, is controlled by two alternative versions of a gene. These paired genes, which may be termed "A" for a dominant gene and "a" for a recessive gene, are called **alleles.** Individuals who have two of the same alleles for a trait, either the dominant alleles, AA, or the recessive alleles, aa, are called **homozygous** for that trait (Latin, for "similar yoking together"). Individuals who have two different alleles for a trait, Aa, are called **heterozygous** (Latin for "different yoking together"). The combination of genes, which may be AA, Aa, or aa, is referred to as the individual's **genotype.** Genes do not blend together in the heterozygote but remain as two different alleles (Figure 3–2). The genotype thus expresses the individual's genetic inheritance. In contrast, the **phenotype** is the organism's appearance. Mendel's experiments showed that different genotypes, such as YY or Yy, could produce the same phenotype, such as yellow seeds.

The Principle of Segregation

Mendel's experiments disproved the early evolutionist's notion of blending inheritance once and for all. Equally important, they showed that, in the specific circumstances he was working with, even recessive alleles maintain their integrity, even

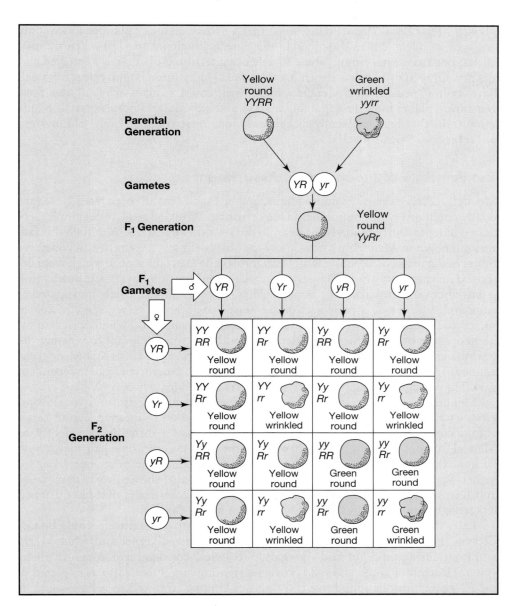

FIGURE 3–2 The results of Mendel's breeding experiments with *Pisum sativum*. Two genes were responsible for each trait, they sorted out (segregated and assorted) independently, and the numbers of each type of plant resulting from the crosses were predictable. Alleles Y and y code in combination for seed color (yellow or green), and Y allele is dominant over y allele. Alleles R and r code in combination for seed shape (round or wrinkled), and R is dominant over r.

when they don't express themselves in heterozygous combinations. In other words, a recessive allele may not be expressed, but it is not "lost." Mendel observed when crossing two "purebred" (or homozygous) strains of his pea plants that the hybrids in the F1 generation exhibited only one form of the parents' traits. For example, if purebred plants that produced only green peas were crossed with purebred plants that produced only yellow peas, invariably the F1 hybrid offspring produced only yellow peas. If later crossed together, F1 plants would give rise to offspring whose seed pods typically appeared in a ratio of three yellow-pea-producing plants to one green-pea-producing plant, regardless of the number of plants involved. These results clearly did not support the idea of the mixing or blending of equal parts of the parents' inheritance in their offspring. The peas were never greenish yellow.

Mendel discovered that the alleles, Y and y, which in different combinations were responsible for pea color, split apart independently during the production of sex cells. This important principle is called **segregation,** and sometimes also called

segregation: the separation of recessive and dominant alleles during reproduction, allowing maintenance of their separate identities and later full expression of their traits; sometimes referred to as Mendel's First Law of Segregation.

Mendel's First Law. Mendel determined that a "true-breeding" plant produces only one type of allele, either Y or y. Y in this case is dominant to y, so when the two alleles, one from each parent, come together in a fertilized plant, Y is expressed and y is not. Only in yy plants is the trait y expressed—only those homozygous for y will have yellow peas. Thus, Mendel's hypothesis could explain why all the first-generation plants look the same (all are Yy) and why the second-generation plants show traits that had apparently disappeared (one-quarter are yy). The old mystery of "reversions" was solved.

The Principle of Independent Assortment

Mendel studied seven traits in pea plants, and he found that all seven traits were randomly combined with one another in the offspring. Wrinkled peas, for example, separated independently from yellow peas, as did the other five traits. Although this fact was unknown to Mendel, we now know that Mendel's seven traits are all coded for by genes that exist on separate larger structures called chromosomes, which were described independently in 1903 by two researchers, Sutton and Boveri. **Chromosomes,** it was discovered, usually exist as pairs. Thus, whereas alleles, which are situated at comparable places on a paired set of chromosomes, are said to segregate, chromosomes and the genes they carry are said to **assort** independently. Whether a plant inherited a pair of alleles for a wrinkled or smooth pea was irrelevant to whether the pea was green or yellow, and so on with each of the other five traits that Mendel examined. The different traits were all scrambled up each generation in an independent way. The principle of independent assortment is called *Mendel's Second Law.*

Mendel's dramatic results were, to some extent, fortuitous for two reasons. First, each of the seven traits he studied was situated on a different one of seven chromosomes. Had they not been, they would not have assorted independently, as Mendel found, because if two traits were on the same chromosome pair they would be linked and, therefore, would have been transmitted to the next generation together. Second, the traits that Mendel chose to study also showed clear dominance and recessiveness. Mendel could have studied many other traits that have a much less straightforward heritability, as we see later in this chapter.

Later the Swedish botanist Herman Nilsson-Ehle proved that traits could be carried on the same chromosome pair when he crossed red-kernel and white-kernel wheat strains and did not find segregation in a clear-cut dominant–recessive allelic system. Instead of white and red kernels segregating in a 3 to 1 ratio as expected in the F2 generation, he found five color classes grading from red to yellow-white. It was clear from these results that one externally observable phenotype—the external appearance caused by the genetic complement, the genotype—could be under the control of more than one set of genes. These genes could be located at more than one place or **locus** on the chromosome, or on different chromosomes. Furthermore, these genes, when combined in offspring, did not necessarily follow a dominant–recessive relationship. The cases described earlier are examples of **polygenic** inheritance that may result in a gradational or quantitative set of phenotypes. **Epistasis** is a term used to describe the dominance of one gene on one chromosome over that of another on a different chromosome. When genes are clearly dominant or recessive, as in human eye color, ratios of phenotypes can be calculated. On the other hand, in most cases when genes are co-dominant, that is, where they are both expressed to some degree, or when many genes determine a trait, such as height or skin color, Mendelian ratios do not appear.

Mendelian Genetics and DNA

In 1869, three years after Mendel published the first results from his pea experiments, a young biochemical researcher named Johann Friedrich Miescher (1844–95)

chromosomes: structures composed of folded DNA found in the nuclei of the cells of eukaryotic organisms.

assort: the independent separation of pairs of genes on one chromosome from pairs of genes on other chromosomes; also known as Mendel's Second Law of Independent Assortment.

locus: a "place" on a chromosome or segment of DNA where a gene is located.

polygenic: a trait controlled by the interaction of genes at more than one locus.

epistasis: gene masking the effect of a nonallelic gene.

discovered a phosphorus-rich chemical in the nucleus of human cells. Miescher named the substance "nuclein," but it was in fact what we know today as deoxyribonucleic acid, or DNA, the chemical that makes up the genes that Mendel discovered.

Miescher studied lymphoid (white blood) cells in pus from hospital patients. He wanted to identify the chemical constituents of the nucleus of the cell. Miescher's method involved separating the nucleus from the rest of the cell by using hydrochloric acid to digest away the cell membrane and the cytoplasm, but he lost most of the cells in this drastic process. Later, he discovered that the digestive enzyme pepsin, obtained from pigs' stomachs, did a better job of separating out the nuclei. Because chemical techniques of the day could not separate all cellular protein from nucleic acid, Miescher and his colleagues were unable to confirm the exact chemical composition of nuclein. Miescher believed that the substance that he had discovered served as a reservoir for phosphorus in the body. He later went on to study the nuclei of salmon sperm, never knowing that he had discovered the molecule of heredity—DNA.

DNA remained a mysterious molecule well into the twentieth century. Scientists knew that it was found in the nucleus of cells. They gradually began to appreciate the fact that the nucleus was somehow responsible for such important activities as cell division and that it held the units of heredity (genes), but they did not know the details. A group of geneticists with a strong physics background, led by Max Delbruck of Rockefeller University in New York, carried forward the search for DNA. Delbruck reasoned that a virus, the simplest living thing known, would be a good place to start investigations of heredity. Delbruck's research team became known as the "Phage Group" ("phage" is shorthand for "bacteriophage," a virus that literally eats bacteria).

The Phage Group developed some important approaches to studying DNA. One was x-ray crystallography, a technique that shot x-rays through a crystal of a substance to determine its three-dimensional arrangement of atoms. An x-ray crystallographer named Rosalind Franklin took a landmark x-ray photo of DNA in 1952 (Figure 3–3). This milestone allowed two members of the Phage Group to work out the structure of DNA, which they referred to as the "double helix." The two researchers were James Watson and Francis Crick.

With the discovery of DNA as the genetic material by Watson and Crick in 1953, the era of molecular genetics began. Although the relationship between

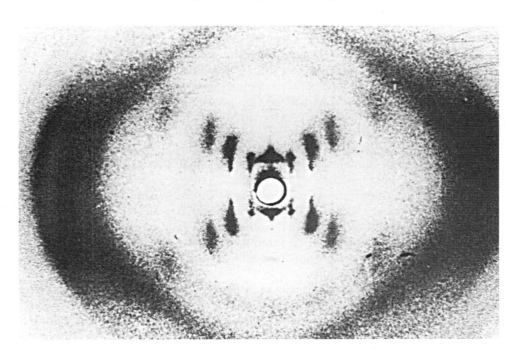

FIGURE 3–3 Rosalind Franklin's 1952 x-ray photo of the DNA molecule. Using this photo, James Watson and Francis Crick worked out the chemical structure of DNA.

segments of DNA and genes, together with their relationship to observable traits (phenotypes), still is a major question in biology, most geneticists and historians of science agree that the principles and findings of Mendelian genetics are now translatable into molecular terms (Sober, 1984).

Today it is estimated that there are some one hundred thousand billion (10^{14} or 100,000,000,000,000) cells in the human body. Almost all of these, except for the red blood cells and the mature sex cells, carry exactly the same kind and amount of DNA. All of these cells result from the one-celled embryo created at fertilization. During development, these cells become progressively different, depending on which genes are turned on or off and at what time. Cells proliferate into the different tissues of the body, such as gut, brain, kidney, and eye. Although nerve cells, for example, carry the same DNA as skin cells or as kidney cells, they all differ in function.

The DNA, or more specifically the segments of the DNA molecule that we speak of as the genes, is responsible for all of the cell's basic life functions, including (1) carrying the instructions necessary for the organism's development from its origin at fertilization to maturity, (2) the cell's ability to metabolize (use energy) or catabolize (break down products of metabolism), (3) carrying the essential genetic information for the next generation, and (4) coding for substances that act to repair injury to the body and fight disease. Using the workings of a machine as an analogy, we might say that the genes provide the blueprint for how to build the machine, the operating instructions for how to run the machine, and the repair manual for how to fix the machine.

Chromosomal Theory of Heredity

Humans have 23 pairs of chromosomes in each body cell. This number varies from species to species. For example, our closest relatives, the African apes, chimpanzees, and gorillas, have 24 pairs of chromosomes in each cell. Human females have 23 homologous pairs of chromosomes (the two chromosomes in each pair are identical to one another), including the sex chromosomes (two X chromosomes). Human males have 22 pairs of homologous chromosomes (called **autosomes**) and one pair that is different: the sex chromosomes. In males, the sex chromosomes consist of one X chromosome, inherited from the mother, and one Y chromosome, inherited from the father. The 23 pairs of chromosomes are called the full **diploid** (*diplo*, meaning two) set. **Haploid** (*haplo*, meaning one) refers to the chromosome number in the sex cells or gametes produced by meiosis.

Chromosomes consist of very long strands of DNA, folded in a complex manner and twisted. Genes, as we have seen, are sequences of the DNA found at particular *loci* on the chromosomes. In human beings, a chromosome is composed of about 1 meter (3 feet) of DNA coiled on itself many times. Therefore, in each human cell that contains the 23 pairs of chromosomes, there are about 46 meters (138 feet) of DNA (Margulis and Sagan, 1986b:279).

Traditionally, the human set of chromosomes is labeled 1 to 22, with number 1 being the largest, number 21 being the smallest, and the sex chromosomes, X and Y, constituting the twenty-third pair. A picture of chromosomes arranged in order is known as a **karyotype** (Figure 3–4). Advances in staining chromosomes, known as "banding techniques," allow us to see more structure in chromosomes. These techniques involve the use of enzymes or fluorescent stains to reveal consistent patterns of chromosomal structure. Geneticists are able to identify each human chromosome by its different band morphology.

Chromosome number by itself tells us little about genetic organization, because some mammals have as few as six or eight chromosomes, flies have four or six, and some plants have hundreds of chromosomes. Even within the higher primates,

autosomes: referring to chromosomes other than the sex (X and Y) chromosomes.

diploid: having two sets of chromosomes, as normally found in the somatic cells of higher organisms.

haploid: having a single set of chromosomes, as found in the sex cells or gametes of higher organisms.

karyotype: identified and numbered arrangement of chromosomes.

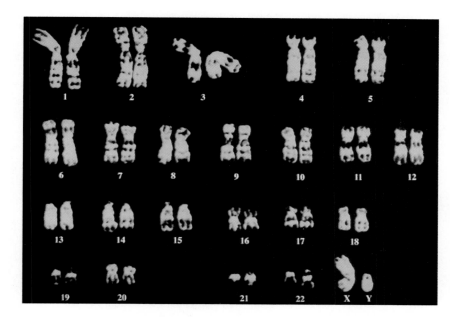

FIGURE 3–4 A human karyotype, or full set of 23 chromosomes. Note the XY pair, which indicates that these are the chromosomes of a male. Banding techniques show the chromosomes' intricate structure.

chromosome counts vary from eight to numbers in the seventies. What is important is that each individual has a full set. Individuals who lack complete sets, or who have extra chromosomes, may not survive to birth or may develop abnormally if they survive and may have anatomical abnormalities.

Gene Linkage and Crossing-Over

As they studied the inheritance of more traits caused by single genes, researchers found that some genes do not follow Mendel's law of independent assortment. Remember that Mendel's Second Law, which holds that genes assort independently, holds only for genes that are located on separate chromosomes. Groups of specific genes found on closely associated loci on the same chromosome are usually passed on together and, thus, they are said to be linked. In humans, one example of linkage is found between two blood group genes, Rh and Duffy, both of which are located on chromosome 1.

Linkage of genes was found to vary from nearly complete to about 50 percent. In other words, in up to 50 percent of the cases, linked genes on chromosomes were not passed on together. This observation was explained by a hypothesis of the Belgian biologist F. A. Janssens. He suggested that paired homologous chromosomes would become tangled up during cell division, and, as they were pulled apart, they would break. Because they were lined up, the homologous sections of the paired chromosomes would get traded by hooking on to the broken ends of the other member of the homologous pair. The process is called **crossing-over** (Figure 3–5). Genes that were close together on the chromosome rarely had a break occur between them. They were thus closely linked, that is, nearly 100 percent linkage. Genes that were more distant on the chromosome had a higher probability of intervening breaks or crossing-over, hooking up with another chromosome, thus being distantly linked.

Early in the twentieth century, T. H. Morgan of Columbia University used Janssens's hypothesis to "map" genes. The more often two traits caused by single genes were inherited together, the closer they were on the chromosome. By quantifying all known genes in fruit flies (*Drosophila*), Morgan was able to discover on which chromosomes and in what sequence genes occurred. Human geneticists

linkage: the tendency of genes to be inherited together because of their location and proximity to one another on one chromosome.

crossing-over: the exchange of genes between paired chromosomes during cell duplication.

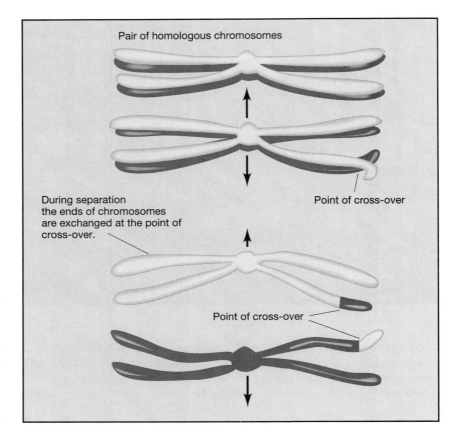

Pair of homologous chromosomes

During separation the ends of chromosomes are exchanged at the point of cross-over.

Point of cross-over

Point of cross-over

FIGURE 3–5 The mechanism of crossing-over in chromosomes. The ends of chromosomes are traded by hooking onto the other member of the homologous pair.

have now constructed maps of all 23 pairs of human chromosomes (Figure 3–6). Discovering the entire DNA sequence of the human genome was the goal of the Human Genome Project, and the results of this effort were published in the summer of 2000. Much work remains to be done, however, in decoding this sequence into functional (as well as nonfunctional) units. However, since the publication of the entire genome sequence, several groups of researchers now believe that each human may only have about 40,000 genes, considerably fewer than the earlier estimates of 140,000 genes.

DNA: THE BLUEPRINT FOR THE CELL'S REPRODUCTION AND METABOLISM

All life today uses a variant of the same molecule, DNA. This indicates that DNA's role in the life of the cell is an ancient one.

The molecular structure of DNA is the key to understanding how this molecule can accomplish all that it does in the cell. DNA's primary structure is similar to that of a rope ladder. The rungs of the ladder are *polymer* (Latin for "many-bodied") chains composed of only four types of chemical bases: adenine (A), guanine (G), thymine (T), and cytosine (C). The sides of the ladder are strong, because the bases, in any sequence, are linked together by strong (covalent) bonds. The rungs of the ladder are weak, formed by intermolecular (hydrogen) bonds. These bonds form only between A and T and between C and G. The rungs, therefore, break apart more easily than do the sides of the ladder (Figure 3–7).

The foundation of molecular biology, its so-called Central Dogma, involves three substances—DNA, **RNA,** and polypeptides—and three processes—replication,

RNA: ribonucleic acid, a molecule similar to DNA except that uracil (U) replaces thymine (T) as one of its four bases; the hereditary material in some viruses, but in most organisms a molecule that helps translate the structure of DNA into the structure of protein molecules.

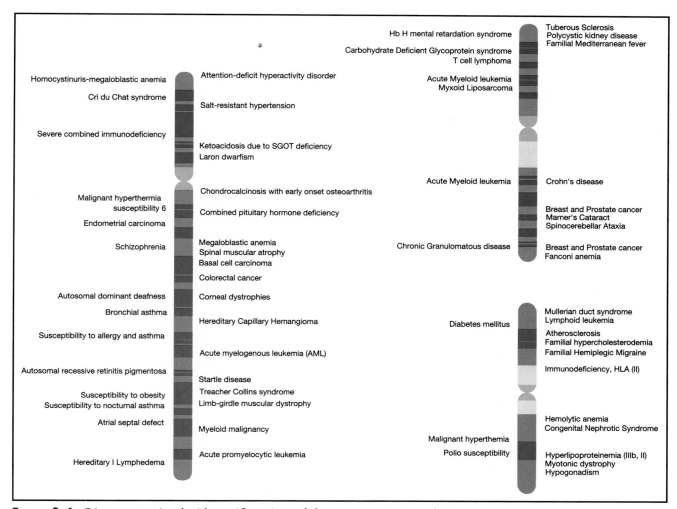

FIGURE 3-6 Diseases associated with specific regions of chromosomes 5, 16, and 19. As a result of the Human Genome Project, a similar map has been constructed for each of our 23 chromosomes.

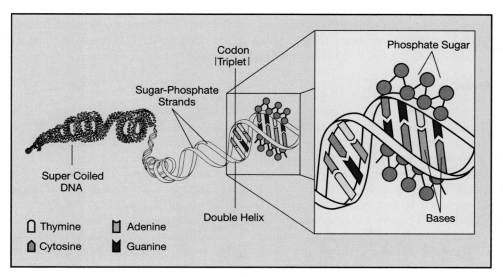

FIGURE 3-7 The structure of DNA. DNA is composed of two sugar-phosphate strands linked together by hydrogen bonds. The hydrogen bonds hold together bases A and T, and C and G. The sequence of these base pairs forms the actual genetic code. The sugar-phosphate strands wind around each other to form the famous double-helix shape. The strands are supercoiled and condensed within the chromosomes.

Why the Y? Unraveling the Secrets of the Y Chromosome

Until recently, the human Y chromosome has been a mystery waiting to be solved. It is unique among the 46 chromosomes in a number of ways. Females and males both have X chromosomes, but females do not have a Y chromosome. Because the Y chromosome rarely recombines with the X chromosome (recombination occurs only at the tips of the chromosomes), it is passed down through the male lineage mostly unchanged. The Y chromosome is only one-third the size of the X chromosome, making it the smallest chromosome. It has the fewest genes, perhaps as few as 20. (The next lowest number is found on chromosome 21, which contains fewer than 300 discernible genes.)

Although we have known for some time that the Y chromosome is in some way concerned with maleness, only recently have we more completely understood how this is so. The main function of the Y chromosome is to alter the path of the growing embryo from a female direction to a male direction. This shift is accomplished through the formation of testes—male sex organs—which in turn produce fetal testosterone, which then directs the embryological

development of a boy. The one gene on the Y chromosome that is most responsible for testes formation was discovered in 1990. The action of this gene is complicated and indirect. The gene apparently suppresses the action of another gene, one that, in the absence of the former, suppresses testes development. Once the suppresser gene is itself suppressed, testes develop.

By 1997 some additional 19 genes on the Y chromosome were identified, 11 of which have something to do with testicular function and fertility, proving that the Y chromosome is not the genetic desert that so many researchers in the past had come to believe. Out of a total of 20 genes, 9 have counterparts on the X chromosome. This makes it almost certain that earlier in our evolutionary history the X and the Y chromosomes were identical and probably had little to do with sex determination. This is still the case in many reptiles today.

This conclusion was recently explored by geneticists Bruce Lahn and David Page (1997), who identified areas of the X and Y chromosomes that had been reshuffled, apparently at different times in the past. They estimated that the X chromosome diverged from the Y chromosome in four stages, beginning somewhere between 320 million

and 240 million years ago, shortly after birds and mammals split from the common ancestor they shared with the reptiles. The most recent divergence occurred between 30 million and 50 million years ago in the primates, after anthropoids, the "higher primates" (monkeys, apes, and humans), had separated from the prosimians, the "lower primates."

The modern X and Y chromosomes represent the end product of this reshuffling, but the interactions between the two chromosomes are still complicated. As a female embryo develops, most of the matching genes on one of her two X chromosomes are shut off. However, those nine genes that have counterparts on the Y chromosome in the male remain activated as pairs. Recent research (Disteche, 1999) suggests that at least 34 genes stay activated on both X chromosomes. Female babies can live if they receive only one X chromosome, although they will have a condition known as Turner's syndrome. People with Turner's syndrome are usually shorter than average, and some, but not all, are mildly mentally retarded. Male babies need the X chromosome genes plus the 9 gene pairs that match up on the X and Y for normal development. Single Y babies do not survive.

transcription, and translation (Watson, 1970:331). These three processes control both how the genetic material passes on its inherited message and how it operates the cell, directing cell and tissue growth (Figure 3–8).

DNA Replication

A key feature of the DNA molecule is its ability to **replicate,** or make copies of itself. Replication allows all the genetic information in a cell to be reproduced in all of a the cell's daughter cells (see the discussion of mitosis later in the chapter). When DNA begins to replicate, the two strands of the DNA begin to unwind from each other. The cell machinery carries new bases, sugars, and phosphates into the nucleus. These attach themselves in sequence so that a T attracts a new A to bond with it. On the opposite strand, its former partner A attracts a new T, along with its sugar and phosphate. The new bases as they are added are linked by enzymes, and a new chain is fashioned alongside the old chain. After replication there are two double strands, each composed of one entirely new strand and one entirely old strand. Because each half of the DNA directs a new complementary sequence to be formed, cell division results in each daughter cell receiving a faithful copy of the parent's DNA.

replication: a duplication process requiring copying from a template, in this case the DNA molecule.

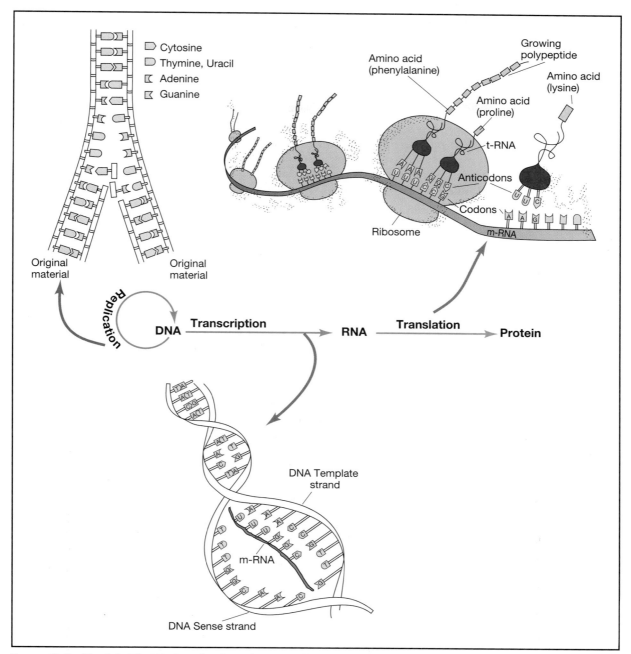

FIGURE 3–8 Top left: The DNA molecule replicates itself by splitting hydrogen bonds and separating into two strands, each of which attracts new bases in the same sequence as the original molecule. Bottom: In transcription, one side of the DNA molecule is copied to make a coded message, messenger RNA. Top right: The message encoded in the messenger RNA sequence is translated within the ribosome of the cell, and a new polypeptide chain is formed. Polypeptide chains are linked to form proteins.

DNA and Polypeptide Synthesis

Besides reproducing itself, DNA produces polypeptides in the cell. Our bodies are made primarily of polypeptides, so all biological processes depend on the manufacture and delivery of the "right" polypeptide from the "right" cells. One DNA sequence (the "gene") specifies the number, sequence, and types of amino acids in a linear fashion in what later will be assembled into a **polypeptide chain.**

polypeptide chain: a molecule consisting of a long chain of amino acids joined together by peptide bonds.

A protein, one kind of polypeptide, is a large complex molecule composed of one or more polypeptide chains, each chain having its origin (or set of instructions for its synthesis) on a different sequence of DNA. Geneticists have now modified the earlier hypothesis of "one-gene-one-protein" to the more accurate hypothesis of "one-gene-one-polypeptide." Some proteins, such as albumin, a blood protein, are composed of and function with only one polypeptide chain. Other proteins, such as hemoglobin, a protein in the red blood cells that carries and releases oxygen, are composed of several polypeptide chains. Hemoglobin has four polypeptide chains, and the molecule functions only when all are combined. Proteins can perform many of the body's functions. For example, proteins are involved in making up the structure of the body, as in the case of collagen (which helps to form the hard substance in bones); other proteins have transport properties, such as a transferrin (which carries iron in the blood). **Enzymes** are proteins that catalyze (speed up) chemical reactions. Carbonic anhydrase is an important enzyme. It catalyzes the reaction in the lungs of $H_2O + CO_2$ to H_2CO_3 (bicarbonate), an important acid/base buffer in the body. There are thousands of different proteins in our bodies.

Other proteins in the body act as chemical messengers called **hormones** (Greek, meaning "to excite or set in motion"). Hormones can be released from the brain or other organs. They travel through the bloodstream and act on distinct target organs such as the breast, inducing it to produce milk; the testis, to make sperm; or the kidney tubules, to reabsorb water. Hormones also have important functions in moderating behavior (see Chapter 12).

The production of polypeptide molecules on a consistent basis requires some kind of code. As we have seen, the double strands of DNA are joined together in the bonding of the paired bases (see Figure 3–8) A and T (adenine and thymine) or C and G (cytosine and guanine). The bases function as units of three, known as **codons.** Each codon chemically recognizes a particular amino acid (Figure 3–9). A

enzymes: polypeptides that catalyze or accelerate chemical reactions.

hormone: a chemical substance produced by an organ or structure of the body that acts on or affects another distinct organ or structure.

codons: three-unit bases of DNA that code for one of 20 amino acids or that code for a stop or termination of translation of that particular segment of DNA.

FIGURE 3–9 The genetic code uses four nucleotide bases, arranged in groups of three, to code for 20 amino acids. In this illustration, the first letter of each codon is located in the central ring, the second letter is in the second ring, and the third letter is in the third ring. The names of the amino acids are outside the circle. Thus, the codon for the amino acid tryptophan is U-G-G, and the codon for "Stop" is U-G-A. Some amino acids, such as lysine, can be "spelled" several different ways. Lysine can be coded as either A-A-A or A-A-G.

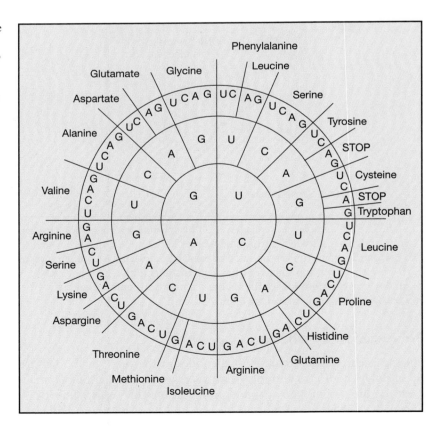

codon consists of three base positions in a row; at any one of those positions one of the four bases can be inserted. Consequently, we have a potential of 4^3, or 64, different codons that, in turn, specify the 20 different amino acids used to construct polypeptides. Because there are more codon combinations than amino acids, more than one codon combination may specify the same amino acid.

All life forms on earth share the same DNA code. This deceptively simple system codes for the stunning amount of variety that we see in organisms. Species' body forms, internal chemical makeup, and behavioral capabilities are all derived ultimately from DNA sequences. The only difference between a human being and a virus is the different sequence of the bases that make up the two organisms' DNAs.

Because of the simplicity of the code, only two types of changes are important in the evolution of life. The first is an *increase* or *decrease* in the amount of DNA in the cell. The second is a *change* in the base sequence of the DNA. Before we consider these two types of changes, we describe how the DNA molecule directs the synthesis of polypeptides within living cells.

How Polypeptide Synthesis Works

The genetic code specifies chains of amino acids that are ultimately combined to make up a polypeptide chain. Each amino acid consists of a basic chemical structure, which is similar for all amino acids, and a unique side chain. The information that the three-base DNA codon carries is converted into a polypeptide molecule by an involved sequence of interactions among DNA, enzymes, and RNA. In **transcription**, the DNA molecule unwinds, the hydrogen bonds that hold the molecular backbones together are broken, and the two sides fall apart (see Figure 3–8, bottom). New bases are brought to the DNA and are combined until the end of the DNA message is read, much as in DNA replication. However, here only one side of the DNA is copied to make a coded message, called *messenger RNA* (or m-RNA). Within the polypeptide-coding message in m-RNA, and unlike DNA itself, thymine (T) is replaced by a chemically similar base, uracil (U), which pairs with adenine (A). After the DNA message has been transcribed into RNA, the RNA molecule carries the genetic information necessary to make the required polypeptide.

When the messenger RNA molecule has been completely transcribed, it slips off the DNA and exits from the cell nucleus. Messenger RNA is a necessary intermediary because DNA cannot travel to the ribosome, where the polypeptides are actually constructed. On the surface of the ribosomes another type of RNA, called *ribosomal RNA* or r-RNA, is found, to which the m-RNA binds. The m-RNA message is "read" as it travels along a ribosome, and the message is translated into a chain of amino acids. This **translation** of the message is the second step in polypeptide synthesis.

Amino acids, which float freely in the cell cytoplasm, are attached to a third type of RNA molecule, called *transfer RNA* (t-RNA). t-RNA has a three-letter sequence of bases that recognizes a specific three-letter sequence on the m-RNA and binds to the m-RNA, carrying with it its specific amino acid. When the base sequence of the m-RNA is matched to the complementary base sequences of the t-RNA, the t-RNA sequences are aligned on the m-RNA, and the genetic message is translated again down the chain. Because the amino acids are positioned on the m-RNA, they are linked together by enzymes that form the peptide bonds and create the polypeptides (see Figure 3–8, top right). If more polypeptides are needed, the m-RNA may be read again to make another copy, or it may be destroyed and its parts reused.

Gene Structure

We have seen that what we refer to as a gene is actually a section of DNA code that carries instructions for assembling a particular polypeptide chain. Genes themselves

transcription: transfer of genetic information encoded in a DNA sequence to an RNA message.

translation: synthesis of a polypeptide chain from an RNA genetic message.

Figure 3–10 One of the earliest eukaryotic cells, larger than its prokaryotic ancestors. This fossil cell comes from 590-million-year-old sediments in the Doushantuo formation in China.

are composed of segments called introns and exons. **Exons** are parts of the gene that actually code for the amino acid sequence of the functioning protein. **Introns** are segments of DNA that are found between the exons, but their DNA sequences do not affect the amino acid chain in the protein. Introns are spliced, or edited out, of the genetic message during protein synthesis so that only the exons remain in the message.

Within the structure of the gene, certain regions act as switches, turning on or off other functional parts of the gene. These are called *regulators*. In embryological and fetal development, the process of regulating the genetic material directs the cells to different destinies. When it becomes necessary for cells to produce a polypeptide, the regulator region turns on the gene (or genes) that is specified to make the needed polypeptide. Usually, many genes are turned off, because it is beneficial for the cell to make polypeptides only when necessary and not to have the whole polypeptide-making machinery on all the time. Gene regulation is important in conceptualizing how two species that are genetically very similar (such as humans and chimpanzees) may differ in their external appearance. Because gene regulation determines when and for how long certain genes are active, it has a major effect on determining body structure, appearance, and behavior.

THE CELL NUCLEUS EVOLVES

The Earliest Organisms

The earliest organisms possessed a cell wall composed of proteins, with a double strand of DNA inside, and they reproduced by splitting in two. The earliest of these organisms metabolized *anaerobically*—without using oxygen—but some later ones began to use oxygen as an energy source. These early organisms were either stationary, attached to the shallow sea bottom, or moved around with a simple tail made up of protein. Called **prokaryotes**, they were the sole life on earth for some 2 billion years. Prokaryotes have a cell membrane but no nucleus. The DNA inside the cell floats about with all the other chemicals in the cell. In prokaryotes, cell size and the diversity of tasks that can be performed are limited.

The first **eukaryotes**, cells with true nuclei, appeared between 1.5 billion and 1 billion years ago (Figure 3–10). In these cells, the DNA was separated by a membrane from the rest of the cell into a structure called a *nucleus*. Scientists have deduced that these cells not only were capable of tolerating oxygen but also used it to produce more energy than prokaryotes could. Consequently, eukaryotes were able to grow larger and move faster. The cells in our bodies have nuclei, a feature we inherited from the early eukaryotes.

The early eukaryotes were predatory. They could eat and digest large particles and even other cells. In contrast, prokaryotes can ingest only particles of molecular size that can diffuse through their cellular membranes. Eukaryotes also had a much more efficient energy use system. Each cell contained structures, or organelles, called **mitochondria**. These structures provided the energy for cellular functions by extracting energy from the nutrients and oxygen that the cell absorbed. In addition, the chromosomes of the eukaryotes held much more genetic information than did those of the prokaryotes.

The Origin of the Mitochondria

Today no life forms between simple prokaryotic bacteria and complex eukaryotic organisms exist. This fact, and the relative rapidity of the appearance of eukaryotic multicellular organisms in the fossil record, have suggested to some microbiologists a new theory: symbiosis (Greek, meaning "living together"). **Symbiosis** is defined as

exon: the expressed segment of a gene, separated from other exons by introns.

intron: noncoding sequence of DNA that is not transcribed by the m-RNA.

prokaryotes: organisms such as bacteria that lack a differentiated cell nucleus.

eukaryotes: organisms that have a nucleus containing DNA in their cells.

mitochondria: organelles within the cell with their own DNA that carry on energy metabolism for the cell.

symbiosis: the theory that formerly free living primitive organisms came together to form a single organism capable of metabolism and reproduction as a unit.

Homeobox Genes: Connecting Genes to Body Form

For a century, scientists have generally understood that genes somehow direct the formation of an animal's entire body from only one cell. But it was not until Edward Lewis discovered homeobox genes that the exact mechanism began to be understood. In 1984 Lewis showed that a series of genes, duplicated from one ancestral gene and arranged in a row along a chromosome, controlled the development of fruit fly body segments in order from the front end to the back end of the fly. He named these duplicated genes that control body segments "homeobox" genes (Figure 3–11). A number of important discoveries followed.

Homeobox genes were found to have a wide distribution among many different organisms, indicating that they are basic building blocks of the anatomy of multicellular organisms. Homeobox genes in mammals, called *Hox* genes, were discovered to be only slightly changed descendants of more primitive homeobox genes, homologues of which exist in lower vertebrates and invertebrates. For the first time, a direct biological continuity could be established between the invertebrates and the vertebrates (see Chapter 5), a connection that had resisted anatomical research since the time of Lamarck. An exciting new era of human anatomy and embryology, developing from research on discretely controlled body segments, is on the horizon.

The entire human body, even the brain, is derived from body segments that specialize, take on new functions, and modify their structure during development and growth. The recognition of human homeobox genes has significant medical implications, particularly in understanding, preventing, and treating birth defects. Some of the most in-depth research has been on heart malformations. Specific homeobox genes control specific parts of the developing heart chambers and aorta, for example, and mutations in one or more of these genes lead to defects in these structures in the developing embryo and fetus. Research has also provided insight into previously confusing associations of birth defects. For example, because the same homeobox genes control the development of the lower limbs, reproductive organs, and kidneys, mutations may cause defects in both the feet and the kidneys.

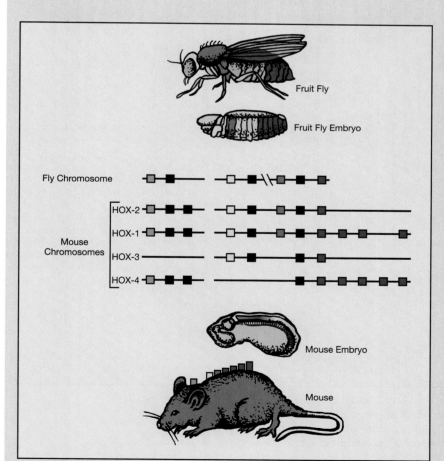

FIGURE 3–11 Homeobox genes in fruit flies and mammals. Homeobox genes, which encode for body structure, are the first genetic indication of biological continuity between invertebrates and vertebrates. Note the similar sequence of genes that encode for body parts in the fruit fly (top) and the mouse (bottom). The similarity exists in both the embryo and the adult stage of development.

mitochondrial DNA: the DNA within the mitochondria, abbreviated as mtDNA; mtDNA evolves approximately 10 times faster than the DNA in the cell nucleus.

"the merging of organisms into new collectives" (Margulis and Sagan, 1985:18). According to this view, the eukaryotic cell consists of two primitive bacterial cells with disparate parts and functions that began to live as one unit. The ancestral mitochondrion, one type of bacterium that could use oxygen, combined with other micro-organisms in a symbiotic relationship. The bacterium obtained food and shelter from this new arrangement, while simultaneously providing its host with energy from absorbed oxygen and removing cellular waste products. Because each of the two cells derived benefits from the association, eventually both cells coevolved so that one could not survive without other.

Figure 3–12 shows the major parts of a typical animal cell. It shows the relationship between the nucleus and the mitochondria. **Mitochondrial DNA (mtDNA)** is

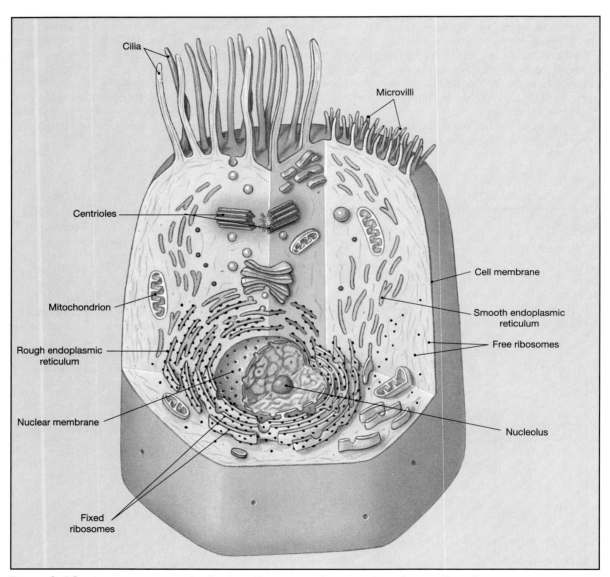

FIGURE 3–12 A composite animal cell. The cell contains a large number of organelles. The nucleus contains the nucleolus, which in turn contains the genetic material; the ribosomes synthesize proteins; the mitochondria produce energy for the cell; the centrioles move chromosomes during cell division; and the endoplasmic reticulum carries out intracellular transport.

separate from the DNA of the cell nucleus, and, like bacteria, mitochondria reproduce by simple division. As we discuss in the next section, most animals evolved a more complex method of reproduction: sexual reproduction.

SEXUAL REPRODUCTION

Sexual reproduction is the production of new cells through the contribution of genetic material from two parents. How does this happen, and why did this form of reproduction first evolve?

Several potential disadvantages to sexual reproduction made its evolution problematic. One major problem is the potential doubling of the amount of DNA in every generation when two cells fuse. This excess DNA could cause confusion in the cell, because there would be two competing sets of genetic instructions. It would also pose a potential storage problem, because accumulating DNA would take up space needed for cellular organelles and the cytoplasm. The first sexually reproducing cells solved this problem by evolving a new method of cell division in which only half of the DNA of each parent is passed on to offspring. To understand how this happened we must discover how the earliest cells began reproducing.

Mitosis

When the earliest cells grew too large, they spontaneously divided. All of the parent's original DNA, enzymes, and metabolic activity passed on to two new daughter cells. But this process could be haphazard: If important parts of the DNA molecule and important cellular chemicals did not reach a daughter cell, the cell would die. The process of cellular reproduction, subsequently, became more organized so that the same amount of DNA as was originally in the parent was passed on to the new cells. The efficient parceling out of the parent cell's DNA to offspring cells is accomplished by the process of **mitosis** (Greek, meaning "threading"). During mitosis, the DNA in a cell is replicated, and each set of genetic instructions migrates to an opposite pole of the cell. Finally, the cell divides into two new cells, each containing a complete and identical set of genetic instructions (Figure 3–13). The new cells can then carry on the same metabolic functions as the parent, because each daughter cell has exact copies of the parent's DNA.

Meiosis

The cell and its functioning became more complex in the eukaryotes. Eukaryotic sexual reproduction originated at least 850 million years ago, at which time eukaryotes with complex morphology became abundant and diverse in the fossil record.

In the eukaryotes, the DNA in the nucleus was folded up into thick threadlike structures, the chromosomes. The eukaryotes produced sex cells, or cells with half the number of chromosomes (haploid number) contained in the body cells of each parent. Human egg and sperm cells are sex cells.

During meiosis, before a cell divides, its chromosomes replicate and line up along the cell midline in their homologous pairs. During the first cell division, the members of each homologous pair split apart, and one chromosome of each pair goes to each daughter cell. During the second cell division, doubling takes place again, but each doubled chromosome splits apart, leaving only a single chromosome, one of each of the homologous pairs, in each daughter cell resulting

sexual reproduction: reproduction resulting from the exchange of genetic material between two parent organisms.

mitosis: the replication of the DNA during splitting of a cell and migration of each duplicated portion to a new cell.

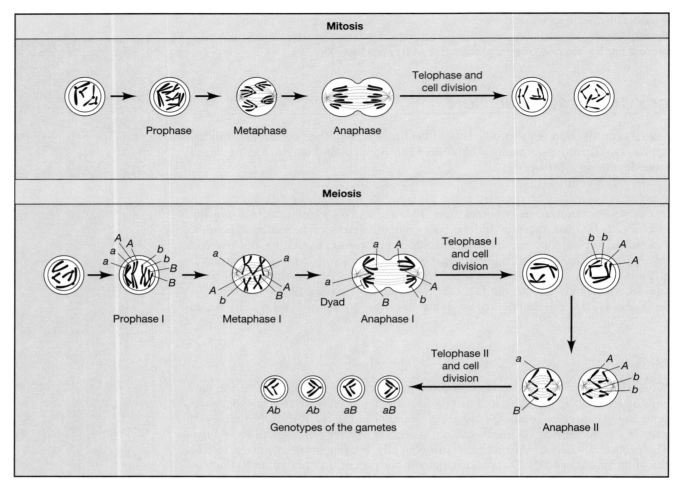

FIGURE 3–13 The cellular processes and different stages of mitosis and meiosis. Note that meiosis contains an additional step, telophase II, which results in the production of gametes with half the original number of chromosomes.

meiosis: the process whereby eukaryote sex cells halve their DNA for combination with the sex cells of another individual.

from that division. This process is known as **meiosis** (Greek for "lessening," referring to the splitting in half of the homologous pairs of chromosomes). This second division of the cell produces sex cells that later may combine through sexual activity with their counterparts from the opposite-sex parent. The union of the two sex cells produces a new cell in which the pairs of homologous chromosomes are once again combined.

Sexual reproduction, widespread among eukaryotes, thus combines the DNA from two parents in the offspring. For example, in humans, the egg and the sperm each contain 23 chromosomes, one set from the mother and one from the father. In the fertilized egg, the two haploid sets of chromosomes recombine into a single diploid set. The recombination of the homologous chromosomes in the offspring is a matter of chance.

The fact that chromosomes recombine by chance is the second significant problem of sexual reproduction. As organisms adapt to their environments, selection favors genes that maximize the organism's successful adaptation. That is, over time, selection favors genes that anatomically, physiologically, and behaviorally promote an individual's survival and ability to reproduce. Under these circumstances, it is logical that evolution would favor individuals that are well suited to their environment and who would pass on their genetic package with as little modification as possible. This helps ensure that successful adaptations are maintained throughout later generations. This method of passing on one's genetic package would by necessity be asexual, to prevent the recombinations and random changes that result from sexual reproduction. For example, a form of asexual reproduction in which a cell divides to form two identical daughter cells is called *cloning*. However, cloning only exists today among single-cell organisms, some plants, several insect species, and some fish and amphibians. Why, given the problems of sexual reproduction, do most plants and animals reproduce sexually?

The Success of Sexual Reproduction

Sex and its overwhelming success as a form of reproduction in the vast majority of living organisms remains to be explained. Darwin viewed sexual reproduction as critical to the maintenance of genetic variability in populations. This variability was the grist on which natural selection operated to produce individuals better adapted to a slowly changing environment. In other words, because the earth's environment is not static, organisms must change continually in order to adapt. That is an important reason for the success of sexual reproduction.

However, as we have noted, sexual reproduction also scrambles up perfectly good existing combinations of genes and undoes every good recombination it had created in the previous generation (Smith, 1978; Margulis and Sagan, 1986b). The logical evolutionary outcome for reproduction should be a mechanism that reverts from sex to cloning once a successfully adapted gene combination has been produced, so that the combination remains intact generation after generation. The question is, "Why did sex become the predominant form of reproduction, rather than appearing only sporadically?"

From many observations, it appears that sexually reproducing organisms have an advantage over clones if both live side by side in stable environments where competition between many different forms of life is intense. For example, results of a two-year study of sweet vernal grass by Steven Kelley of Washington State University suggests that sexually reproducing variants of these plants outreproduced the clone variant by about 1.5 times. Kelley (1994) believes that the sexually reproducing grass variants flourished because they were less prone to attack by pathogens that could cause disease, and, perhaps, early death. The idea that all living organisms must evolve mechanisms to protect themselves from pathogens that generally reproduce and mutate more rapidly than their hosts may well explain the success of sexual reproduction. Through sexual reproduction, organisms have a better chance of survival in the face of disease by creating genetic barriers to pathogen attacks by means of a continual reshuffling of their genotypes. We pursue this idea further in Chapter 12.

One further question remains to be addressed, "Why did the exchange of DNA between ancient micro-organisms come into practice in the first place?" Part of the answer may lie in the nature of the earth's primitive environment. We are descended from ancient bacteria that moved out of the airless mud to the sunlit near-surface water. But in the early earth's atmosphere, there was no shielding layer of ozone to block out ultraviolet radiation from the sun. This radiation harms DNA, rendering it inactive and unable to function. DNA repair systems no doubt originally evolved to repair this ultraviolet light damage by creating enzymes—specialized proteins that promote chemical reactions in cells—to eliminate a damaged part of the DNA.

The idea for the origin of sexual reproduction through DNA repair is credited to Richard Michod (1997) of the University of Arizona, Tucson. In his view, gene exchange between individuals originated as a mechanism to repair damaged strands of DNA. For example, a new undamaged section of DNA was borrowed from either another bacterium or a virus and then reinserted into the DNA by enzymes that "cut and paste" sections of DNA. The bacterium *Bacillus subtilis* uses a mechanism of DNA capture called **transformation,** in which independent bits of free-floating DNA from dead bacteria of the same species are captured and used to repair damaged DNA in live bacteria. Experiments show that damaged bacteria incorporate more free-floating DNA than do undamaged bacteria. Undamaged bacteria also replicate more successfully than those damaged in laboratory situations by excessive ultraviolet light or excessive oxygen.

Transformation might be considered a form of proto-sex, a behavior that has obvious short-term individual benefits. But, according to Rosemary Redfield of the University of British Columbia, it is not the only possible explanation for the origin of sex (Gutin, 1992). Redfield contends that hunger is the driving motivation behind DNA capture. She notes that the molecular spine of DNA is made up of alternating sugar and phosphate molecules and that when DNA is broken down ("digested"), an organism can use the sugars and the attached base for energy. For example, when a bacterium runs out of internal sugars, it might find and capture external DNA as a new food source. Quite by accident, undigested DNA, if it matches a bit of the organism's own DNA, might be incorporated into the organism's genetic code. Thus, what started out as a feeding strategy might have been the origin of sexual reproduction and subsequent genetic exchange (Gutin, 1992).

transformation: incorporation of another cell's DNA into a cell's own DNA structure.

Why Are There Only Two Sexes, Anyway?

Human sex chromosomes differentiated themselves from one another over a period of time that extends back to the divergence of mammals from reptiles more than 240 million years ago. The so-called sex chromosomes at that time probably had little to do with sex determination, because the X and Y chromosomes were then identical. These chromosomes still are identical in many reptiles in whom sex is determined by environmental conditions not by genetics. Thus, XX reptiles can be either male or female, depending on the external temperature when they are incubating. With turtles, for instance, more females are born when the temperature is warmer, and more males are born when it turns colder. In crocodiles it is just the opposite.

Whatever the cause of sex determination, in most life forms only two sexes are ever produced. There are some interesting exceptions to this rule, however, that lead to a question that has puzzled researchers for years, "Why do we have (usually) only two sexes?" Mushrooms, for example, have as many as 36,000 sexes, and slime molds have at least 13. And considering the diversity of life in general, having only two of anything is unusual.

Laurence Hurst (1999) of Bath University, England, believes that he has the answer to this evolutionary mystery. Hurst suggests that if there were more than two sexes, and an individual of any sex could mate with an individual of any other, the chances of finding a mate would greatly increase: the more sexes there were, the better the chance of finding a mate among any given number of individuals. If, for example, there were 100 sexes, your chance of finding a partner would be 99 percent. In contrast, having only two sexes reduces this possibility to 50 percent.

So why only two sexes? Hurst believes that it has to do with mitochondrial DNA. As we have seen, mitochondria represent an ancient symbiotic relationship that began when bacteria invaded the cells of our earliest single-cell ancestors, ultimately becoming a functional unit within the cell. The downside of this mostly beneficial relationship has to do with mitochondrial DNA's ability to reproduce very quickly, and potentially, as a consequence, to spread deleterious mutations far and wide. Greater numbers of sexes would mean that harmful mutations of the mtDNA could spread through a population at greater speed, with catastrophic results. With only two sexes, and with inheritance of mtDNA only through the maternal line, the flow of deleterious mutations is slowed. Mushrooms have solved this problem by avoiding the exchange of mtDNA when they reproduce.

MUTATION: THE SOURCE OF GENETIC VARIATION

In Chapter 2, we saw how Darwin's theory of natural selection required "inherited variability" in organisms as the raw material with which evolution worked. In this chapter, we have seen how Mendel's findings provided a mechanism for transmittal of genetic material from one generation to another. Darwin called attention to what animal breeders termed *sports*—novel forms of animals, such as short-legged sheep or tailless cats. Sometimes breeders could trace the lineage of such a breed to a single animal. For Darwin, such heritable changes could be of great importance if natural selection were to produce new species. But what was the real nature of these heritable changes?

Hugo de Vries, in his attempt to answer this question, believed that if Mendel's system worked perfectly, no new genes would ever be produced. Parents' genes would simply be passed on to offspring, shuffled up a bit, but still remain basically the same. De Vries focused attention on the evidence for heritable genetic changes, changes that he termed *mutations,* as the source of genetic novelty.

Types of Mutations

Mutation is an occasional error in DNA replication that increases the genetic variation in a group of organisms. All the differences at the genetic level we see today in human beings result from mutations in a sperm or egg somewhere in our evolutionary history. Probably the most important cause of gene mutation involves mistakes in DNA replication in which the wrong base is substituted. Changes can also occur on a larger scale and may affect the number or structure of chromosomes. Figure 3–14 illustrates both types of mutations.

Mutations are important to evolution only if they can be inherited. **Genetic mutations** occur in the sex cell lineage and can be passed on. **Somatic mutations** occur in nonsex-cell tissue, such as skin or neurons. These cannot be inherited by offspring, but they can be passed on to direct products of mitotic divisions of these cells, such as new growth of skin or epithelial tissue.

Because we have many thousands of genes, each of us has a high likelihood of carrying a new mutation in our genes. New genetic input into a population by a mutation can be beneficial, detrimental, or neutral to the organism that possesses it. The mutation may help the individual adapt better to its surroundings. For example, a new gene can make an enzyme work faster, at a different temperature, or on a different molecule. This may result in an organism that can better respond to the varying demands of its environment.

Much more frequently, however, a new mutation may result in a defective enzyme or even no enzyme at all. Such a mutation might lead to infertility, or perhaps even to death. In the case of infertility, *genetic death* is the result: even though the individual does not die, he or she does not pass on his or her genes, including the mutation, to offspring.

Neutral mutations at the biochemical level, by definition, have no effect on function or fitness of the molecule that possess them. In this case it does not matter if a codon substitution in the DNA sequence results in a different amino acid substitution at a certain position in a polypeptide chain. The protein, which has incorporated the mutated polypeptide chain, continues to function as if the substitution had not occurred.

Causes of Mutations

Mutations can be caused by many agents, ranging from x-rays to ultraviolet light to chemicals, such as caffeine commonly found in coffee and tea. Some food additives

mutation: any novel genetic change that may affect both genes and chromosomes. Such changes are spontaneous and random in occurrence. Mutations are the source of all variability in populations, and, if they occur in the sex cells usually during the formation of gametes, they hold the possibility of altering the phenotypes in succeeding generations.

genetic mutation: heritable change in the genetic material, located in the sex cells, that brings about a change in phenotype.

somatic mutation: nonheritable change in the genetic material of the cells of the body.

neutral mutation: mutation that is not acted on by selection; it does not affect the fitness of an organism in a particular environment. Neutral mutations accumulate at a more or less constant rate over time.

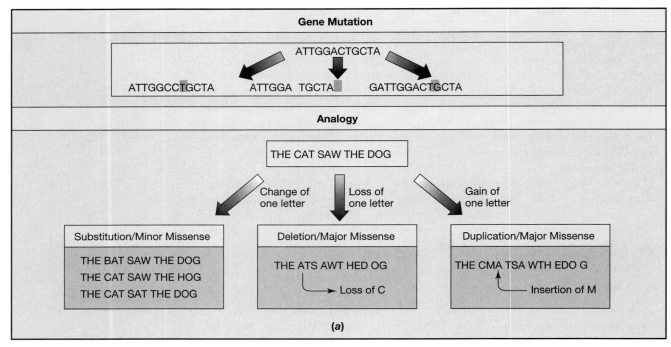

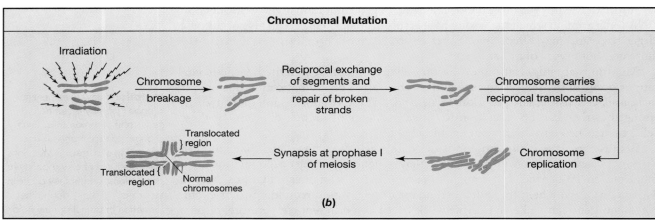

FIGURE 3–14   (a) Gene mutation, in which a single base is changed. Gene mutation may result in either major or minor changes. (b) Large-scale chromosomal mutation, resulting from chromosomal breakage and reciprocal exchange.

have been shown to cause mutations in bacteria. Some chemicals in our environment, including cigarettes, air pollution, and chemical waste, may cause mutations in genes. When they are altered, specific genes, called *oncogenes,* may be responsible for the unregulated cell growth that characterizes cancer.

Mutations are constantly recurring phenomena in biological populations, and they create genetic diversity that, as the opportunity presents itself, can be used by natural selection. For example, some bacteria have evolved in response to the challenges that antibiotic medicines present to them. Certain random mutations of a bacterium called *Gonococcus,* responsible for the venereal disease gonorrhea, have now made it difficult for the antibiotic penicillin to kill them. This particular mutation, which, not surprisingly, is rapidly spreading, produces a new bacterial enzyme called *penicillinase.* This enzyme breaks up penicillin, rendering it inactive, thus allowing these resistant bacterium to survive and replicate.

Chance, not necessity, dictates the occurrence of new mutations. Exposure to a new drug to inhibit bacterial growth does not cause a new mutation. Instead, the changed conditions allow those individual bacteria with a preexisting mutation a better chance to survive, whereas "old type" bacteria are killed. Mutations, even though they occur randomly, are produced at a consistently high rate, and as a result, enough new genetic material is produced for evolution to work. Thus, mutations are continually being inserted into the gene pool of populations. How mutations affect the genetics of populations is one of the topics of Chapter 4.

◖ SUMMARY

1. **What nineteenth- and early twentieth-century discoveries led to the development of a theory of heredity?**

   All life on earth shares a common evolutionary heritage—a genetic system based on the molecule DNA. Experiments in the late nineteenth century disproved ideas of blending inheritance and led to the rediscovery of Gregor Mendel's two principles of genetics: independent segregation (of alleles at the same locus) and independent assortment (of genes on separate chromosomes).

2. **What are the structures and mechanisms of heredity at a biochemical and cellular level?**

   What Mendel termed factors in his breeding experiments with pea plants are now known to be genes made up of DNA, a nucleic acid of the cell nucleus. James Watson and Francis Crick discovered the structure of DNA and worked out the genetic code in 1953. The central dogma of molecular biology relates this code to the replication of DNA from one generation to the next, transcription of the code into RNA messages, and translations of the messages into proteins. Proteins constitute the structural elements of our bodies as well as many biochemical components necessary for life.

3. **What is the significance of sexual reproduction for the emergence of variation?**

   Sexual reproduction evolved in the eukaryotes and is an important source of reshuffling of genes and thus of variability in offspring.

4. **What are mutations, and how do they occur?**

   Mutations are changes in DNA, and they are the ultimate source of new variations in organisms. They occur as a result of random changes in the genetic code, either at the gene or the chromosomal level.

◖ CRITICAL THINKING QUESTIONS

1. If Lamarckian evolution (inheritance of acquired characteristics) were true, what would be different about the way in which genetic information is passed from one generation to the next? Is this possible?

2. If the bacterial (symbiotic) origin of the mitochondrion is true and two primitive cells fused to become the eukaryotic cell, why doesn't this process seem to happen today?

3. The genetic code is "degenerate," that is, some amino acids are coded for by more than one triplet of three DNA bases. What might be some reasons that there are not only 20 discrete codons for the 20 amino acids?

4. Some of the eukaryotic cells developed a communal contract and began to live as multicellular organisms, giving them feeding, defense, and longevity advantages. Why couldn't or why didn't prokaryotic cells do the same?

5. How would you explain to the ghost of Gregor Mendel how a child of a tall father and a short mother grows up to be of intermediate height?

◀ INTERNET EXERCISES

Critical Thinking

Protein Synthesis. The text of this chapter states that RNA codes for polypeptides, not for proteins. What is the difference? In other words, what is a protein, and why is protein synthesis a major function of our genetic code? In this exercise, discover more about the nature of proteins by answering the following questions:

1. What is a protein? What is a polypeptide? What is the difference between them?
2. If DNA is the basis for all life on earth, how did DNA, an extremely complex molecule, evolve? Were there simpler forms before DNA-based life forms?
3. Is the process of protein synthesis simple or complicated? Explain your answer.

Writing Assignment

The Story of DNA. The story of the discovery of the structure of DNA is a fascinating episode in the history of science, but it is only one of many interesting events in the saga of genetic research. In addition to Watson and Crick and Mendel, other pioneers include Rosalind Franklin and Barbara McClintock. Research the life of one of the pioneers of genetic research, and write a paper that answers the following questions:

1. What earlier discoveries did the pioneer's work build on? How did he or she find out about the earlier work?
2. What role did technological innovations, such as X-ray photography and electron microscopy, play in the research?
3. What is the most interesting aspect of this person's discoveries?

See Companion Web site for Internet links.

Transcription and Translation

This activity gives you a detailed view of the two stages of protein synthesis: transcription and translation. Because DNA remains inside the cell nucleus, it cannot work directly within the ribosome to direct protein synthesis. The intermediate step of transcription results in the formation of messenger RNA. This molecule then exits the nucleus and directs the translation stage of protein synthesis, which takes place in the cytoplasm.

This MediaLab gives you a close look at protein synthesis and asks you to consider both what is known about this process and what is at present only speculation.

WEB ACTIVITY

The animation shows the process of protein synthesis: First, a section of DNA unwinds, and in a process called transcription, its message is copied on to a molecule of messenger RNA (m-RNA). The m-RNA leaves the cell nucleus. It heads for a ribosome, a structure in which the message and the raw materials (amino acids) are brought together to make a protein. The animation shows how, as the m-RNA message is read, a growing chain of amino acids is formed (translation).

Activity

1. View the animation. Explain in your own words why two steps are necessary for protein synthesis.
2. In what kinds of living organisms are these two steps necessary? Bacteria? Plant cells? Animal cells?
3. At what stage in the evolution of life did a two-stage process of protein synthesis become necessary?
4. Consult a basic biology text to find out where ribosomes are located in the cytoplasm. Are they found in more than one location? If so, is there a difference between the proteins manufactured by the ribosomes in the different locations?

The MediaLab can be found in Chapter 3 on your Companion Web site http://www.prenhall.com/boaz

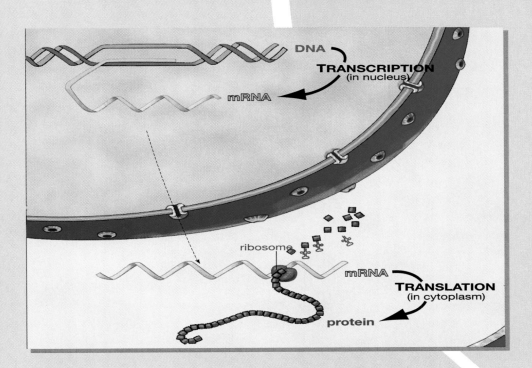

4

POPULATIONS, SPECIES, AND EVOLUTION

After reading this chapter, you should be able to discuss the following questions:

1. What two schools of thought about heredity arose in the early twentieth century? How did their disagreement lead to the development of population genetics?
2. What is the significance of the Hardy–Weinberg model of equilibrium for population studies, and what factors cause a population to fall out of equilibrium?
3. What forces of evolution affect population allele frequencies in a species?

In the preceding chapters, we described the development of Darwin's and Wallace's theory of natural selection (Chapter 2) and of genetics (Chapter 3), the two most important ideas in modern biological thought. It immediately became obvious to biologists that these two ideas had to fit together in some way—that genetics was the means by which the principles of natural selection were carried out in nature. But by the beginning of the twentieth century, because the molecular basis of heredity was still unknown, scientists were still unsure of how to make the connection.

Following Darwin's publication of the *Origin of Species* and the rediscovery of Mendel's principles of genetics, evolutionary scientists began to think in terms of populations. In this chapter, we trace the discovery of the relationship between genetics and evolutionary theory through the rise of the new science of population genetics and the development of the Synthetic Theory of Evolution. We examine how biological anthropologists apply the principles of population genetics in order to understand the dynamics of the evolutionary process as it operates in populations of organisms.

THE SCIENCE OF POPULATION GENETICS

Two schools of thought about heredity emerged in the early twentieth century. One school was composed of the Mendelians, who, as we saw in Chapter 3, held that inheritance of traits occurred through discrete, quantum units that did not blend or get mixed up with one another during reproduction. The Mendelians had a lot of experimental data on their side, mostly from plants and simple organisms.

The other school was the biometricians, who measured traits, such as height or body size, that *did* blend from parents to offspring. They believed that statistics on large numbers of individuals should be studied to arrive at a true understanding of inheritance. The biometricians believed that natural selection influenced small-scale variations between individuals in populations, and they also had a lot of data on their side. Their data came from looking at complex traits, such as height—traits that we now know result from the interaction of several genes. Thus, the biometricians were studying outward manifestations, or phenotypes, even though the exact genes that caused the anatomical or physiological traits were unknown to them.

In 1918, R. A. Fisher, a British geneticist, pointed out that the two perspectives were not at variance. Mendelians were considering characteristics that resulted from individual genes, whereas biometricians were studying phenotypic traits that were affected by many genes. By averaging the combined effects of many genes, one could reach an apparent "blending" of many discrete gene effects. Thus, the Mendelians and the biometricians were studying the same phenomena, but they were working from opposite ends of a continuum of single gene effects. Fisher's important paper set the stage for the Synthetic Theory of Evolution, which finally merged genetics and evolution by natural selection into a unified theory, and which was fully developed by the 1940s.

Before and after World War II, a number of prominent evolutionary biologists began to synthesize and incorporate their own special areas of expertise with the broader view of Darwinian natural selection and genetics. An integration of mathematics, begun by Hardy and Weinberg, was continued by R. A. Fisher and J. B. S. Haldane in Great Britain and by Sewall Wright in the United States. Theodosius Dobzhansky, a geneticist who studied fruit flies; Ernst Mayr, an ornithologist; G. Ledyard Stebbins, a botanist; and George Gaylord Simpson, a vertebrate paleontologist, all contributed to this effort.

One tool that the Mendelians and biometricians shared was their use of quantitative methods—numbers and mathematics. This aspect of genetics tends to mystify many students, but it is really rather straightforward. For example, as we saw in Chapter 3, Mendelian geneticists count genes and compare the ratios among the simple phenotypic traits that these genes cause. Similarly, with the discovery of the Hardy–Weinberg model, population geneticists learned to count alleles. This led to enormous breakthroughs in the study of populations and species.

THE HARDY–WEINBERG EQUILIBRIUM

In 1908, 10 years before Fisher's paper was published, the breakthrough in understanding how genes behave in populations occurred. Two papers were published independently by two different researchers: British mathematician Godfrey Harold Hardy and German physician Wilhelm Weinberg. Their work provided an important basis for melding Darwinian natural selection with Mendelian genetics. The apparent simplicity of their observations belies how important their insights were to all later studies of the biological evolution of populations.

Before 1908, no one really knew how genes behaved in populations of organisms. Would the dominant alleles swamp the recessive alleles? How many descendants would be heterozygous for a given trait, and how many would be homozygous? These questions were theoretically important, because their answers could predict how species could be expected to change over time. They had also begun to assume a practical importance: Certain medical conditions were discovered that were caused by recessive genes when they appeared in homozygotes. Weinberg, along with the other physicians of the time, needed to know how many patients or their offspring might be affected by genetic diseases.

Hardy and Weinberg applied a simple mathematical principle to genes: They assigned a frequency to an allele. A *frequency* is a number from zero to one that indicates how common an item is within a group. For example, suppose you have a group of 10 jellybeans. If four of the jellybeans are red, the frequency of red jellybeans in this group is four divided by the total number of jellybeans (10), or 0.4.

In diploid organisms, many different alleles might exist at specific loci in the genotype (in other words, a heterozygous state would exist). Although within a population many alleles might be present for any given locus, Hardy and Weinberg considered a two-allele system, composed of A, a dominant allele, and a, a recessive allele. They used p to refer to the frequency of the first allele and q to refer to the frequency of the second allele. Because there were only two alleles and their frequencies add up to 1, then, $p + q = 1$.

The next step in the Hardy–Weinberg model is a mathematical expression of the frequency of alleles in the production of gametes. One parent will produce sex cells, or *gametes* (for example, sperm), through meiosis, which have half the normal chromosome number (the haploid number). If the male parent is heterozygous for the particular trait, each sperm will have a 50/50 probability of having one allele or the other (*A* or *a*). A *probability* is the chance, expressed as a number from zero to one, of something occurring, with zero being no chance and one being certainty. If the female parent is also heterozygous, she will produce sex cells (the eggs) that will also have one allele or the other (*A* or *a*). When a sperm fertilizes an egg, the two combine to form a new individual (a *zygote*), whose genotype will be *AA, Aa,* or *aa,* depending on the makeup of each gamete. Note that the probability of the offspring inheriting any given genotype depends on the allele that each gamete possesses.

Of course, biologists were aware of this because knowledge of Mendel's discoveries became widespread. But Hardy and Weinberg extended this knowledge to *populations*. They showed how to determine *how many* alleles of each type were present in any given *population* and *how many* individuals of each genotype were produced as a consequence of random mating.

Hardy and Weinberg wanted to see what would happen to allele frequencies when males and females mated—in other words, when the mother's genes and the father's genes assorted independently to produce gametes. Because the probability of two independent events happening at once is the product of their individual probabilities, Hardy and Weinberg multiplied probabilities. This is simply common sense. Take, for example, the probability of your picking a red jellybean when you reach into two side-by-side jars, both of which have yellow jellybeans mixed in (Figure 4–1). In the first jar, 9 of the 10 jellybeans are red, and in the second jar, only 3 of 10 jellybeans are red. To figure out the probability of getting red jellybeans if you dipped your hands into both jars without looking, you would multiply 0.9 by 0.3 (and get 0.27, or roughly one chance in four).

FIGURE 4–1 Jar A contains 9 red jellybeans and 1 yellow jellybean. Jar B contains 3 red jellybeans and 7 yellow jellybeans. What is the probability that you select red jellybeans if you dip your hands into both jars at the same time without looking?

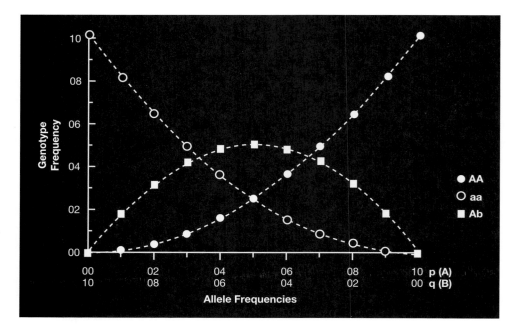

FIGURE 4–2 Graph of the frequencies of genotypes, in relation to allele frequencies, according to the Hardy–Weinberg equilibrium. For example, if the frequency of each allele is 0.50, the frequency of each genotype in the population will be $AA = 0.25$, $aa = 0.25$, and $Aa = 0.5$.

Hardy–Weinberg equilibrium: hypothetical condition in which there is no selection or other forces of evolution acting on a population and in which gene and genotype frequencies stay the same from one generation to the next. For two alleles at one locus, alleles p + alleles q = 100%.

To calculate how genotype frequencies would change from one generation to the next, Hardy and Weinberg just multiplied allele frequencies (probabilities): the frequencies of allele A and a $(p + q)$ in a population, times the same frequencies $(p + q)$. Expressed mathematically, we have

$$(p + q)(p + q) = p^2 + 2pq + q^2$$

As Figure 4–2 shows, p^2 is the frequency in the next generation of the AA homozygotes and q^2 is the frequency of the aa homozygotes. The frequency of the heterozygotes, Aa, is $2pq$. Actual numbers can be inserted into this equation to calculate the allele and genotype frequencies in a real human population.

For example, the disease cystic fibrosis (CF) affects 1 in 2,500 babies of European ancestry. Because this disease is caused by a recessive gene when in the homozygous state, the frequency of the recessive homozygous genotype (aa) is 1/2,500. This value is q^2 in the Hardy–Weinberg equation $(1 = p^2 + 2pq + q^2)$. Taking the square root of 1/2,500, we obtain q, the frequency of the CF gene in the population $(q = 0.02)$. If the CF gene frequency is 0.02, then the frequency of the normal gene is 0.98 (because $p + q = 1$). Using these numbers we can then calculate that 1 out of 25 people $(2pq)$ of European ancestry are carriers (heterozygotes) for the cystic fibrosis gene.

The theoretical results of this simple equation are astounding. First of all, for any given loci, calculations for multiple generations show that allele frequencies and genotype frequencies *do not change*. They stay the same and reach an equilibrium if evolutionary forces (which we describe in greater detail later in this chapter) are not operating on these loci. By implication, only evolutionary forces can change this equilibrium and result in changes in allele and genotype frequencies.

The equilibrium is known as the **Hardy–Weinberg equilibrium**. Figure 4–2 is a graph showing all possible allele frequencies at equilibrium. It shows that when allele frequencies are between one-third and two-thirds, heterozygotes are the most common genotypes in the population. The importance of this for a population is discussed shortly.

The Hardy–Weinberg principle of constancy of allele and genotype frequencies in a population is a powerful model for describing theoretical expectations for allele frequency in populations and, thus, for explaining phenotypes for given traits. In the ideal model, a number of assumptions are required about those evolutionary forces that might affect the Hardy–Weinberg equilibrium.

1. The organism is diploid, and reproduction is sexual. In addition, the generations of individuals in the population do not overlap.
2. Mating is random.
3. Population size is very large.
4. Migration is negligible.
5. Mutation rates can be ignored.
6. Natural selection does not affect the gene under consideration.

In most cases, these assumptions are not met in the real world, where, for example, natural selection does operate and mutations cannot be ignored. Assumption 1 is taken for granted when we are discussing humans. But when any of the other assumptions are not met, evolution happens. We thus use the Hardy–Weinberg equilibrium to study evolution in action. By examining how observed genotype frequencies vary from those calculated on the basis of allele frequencies, we can investigate the workings of evolution: the effects of mutation, population size, mating, migration, random changes in allele frequency (genetic drift), and natural selection. We examine each of these forces of evolution in turn.

Mutation

When considered gene by gene, mutations are rare in human populations. It is estimated that new mutations occur at the rate of 1 in 10,000 (1×10^{-4}) to 1 in 1,000,000 (1×10^{-6}) alleles per generation. In the entire population between 1 percent and 2 percent of births may show genetic abnormalities that result from new mutations in the egg or sperm. One such example of this is achondroplastic dwarfism. Individuals with this dominant allele have limbs and vertebral columns that are deformed, making walking difficult. The incidence of this heterozygous condition is approximately 1 in 100,000 live births. Homozygous achondroplastic offspring die in utero. This allele has an extremely low calculated fitness value of only 0.2×10^{-7}; in other words, it is extremely detrimental. If there were no recurring mutations to keep this allele in the population, it would eventually be eliminated by natural selection.

Achondroplastic dwarfism is a *dominant mutation:* Individuals who inherit only one abnormal gene exhibit the condition. In contrast, *recessive mutations* cause conditions that only become apparent when they are in the homozygous state (when an individual carries both recessive alleles).

Table 4–1 lists some common human diseases caused by mutations and their estimated mutation rates. Today some 2,000 different genetic diseases have been cataloged. Given the number of human genes, many of us probably are born with new mutations, all of which contribute to population genetic variability.

Gene (or point) mutations, as opposed to chromosomal mutations, are changes in the DNA base sequence. If a mutation is lethal, causing the death of its carrier before it has a chance of being passed on, then it never increases in frequency in the population. However, not all mutations are lethal. They range from lethal to detrimental to neutral to, in rare cases, beneficial. Mutations as a force in evolution are the ultimate source of new genetic material, and they alter the Hardy–Weinberg equilibrium by automatically changing gene frequencies as new alleles are created.

Mutations that are "invisible" to selection are known as *neutral mutations.* Even when selection favors neither allele (that is, when the fitness values for the two alleles are equivalent), new mutations can, over time, replace original alleles simply by chance.

TABLE 4–1	Mutant Traits Caused by Single Gene Mutations	
Mutant Trait	**Appears Once in Each**	**Mutation Frequency per Million**
Dominant		
Pelger anomaly (abnormal white blood cells; reduces resistance to disease)	12,500 gametes	80
Chondrodystrophic dwarfism (shortened and deformed legs and arms)	23,000 gametes	42
Retinoblastoma (tumors on retina of eye)	43,500 gametes	23
Anirida (absence of iris)	200,000 gametes	5
Epiloia (red lesions on face; later tumors in brain, kidney, heart, etc.)	83,000 gametes	12
Recessive Autosomal		
Albinism (melanin does not form in skin, hair, and iris)	37,700 gametes	28
Amaurotic idiocy (Infantile) (deterioration of mental ability during first months of life)	90,900 gametes	11
Total color blindness	35,700 gametes	28
Recessive X-linked		
Hemophilia	31,250 gametes	32

SOURCE: Winchester (1972).

In trying to understand how neutral mutations affect the genetics of populations, it is important to understand the difference between the rate of substitution and the rate of fixation. The replacement of one allele by another is called the rate of fixation. The *rate of substitution,* termed K, is defined as the long-term average number of mutations that are substituted in a population, per gene locus, per unit of time. The rate of substitution of neutral mutations within a population appears to be fairly uniform. For the hemoglobin molecule, the observed rate of amino acid substitution (a result of a neutral mutation affecting a codon sequence on the DNA) is close to 10 amino acid sites per year. K is independent of the size of the population involved. It is simply a function of the rate of occurrence of the mutation.

The *rate of fixation* is defined as the rate at which a single mutation increases its frequency in a population, or the amount of time that it actually takes for one mutation to fix itself (that is, completely replace another allele) by chance. This rate depends on population size. Replacement of one allele by another always occurs more slowly in neutral situations than it would if natural selection intervened to give one allele a higher fitness than the other. Having more than one mutation present in a population increases the odds that the newly mutated allele will ultimately become fixed.

The equation $K = 4N_e$ describes this situation (Figure 4–3). In a population of 10,000 (N_e) it will take 40,000 generations to fix a neutral mutation. In contrast, if the rate of mutant substitution is affected by natural selection, then fixing a mutation with a selective advantage may be expressed by $K = 4(\mu)(S)(N_e)$, where μ is the mutation rate and S is the selective advantage. For the same population of 10,000 individuals, given a mutation rate of 10^{-7} and a selection advantage of 0.2, $K = 0.8 \times 10^{-3}$ substitutions per generation. In this case, the mutation would be fixed in only about 1,000 generations.

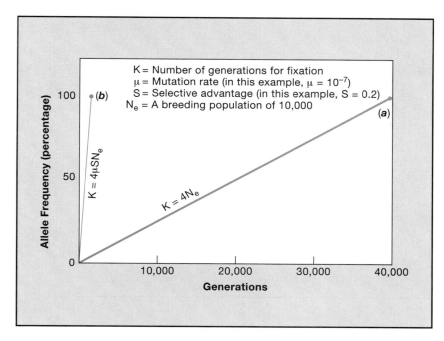

K = Number of generations for fixation
μ = Mutation rate (in this example, $\mu = 10^{-7}$)
S = Selective advantage (in this example, S = 0.2)
N_e = A breeding population of 10,000

(b)

(a)

$K = 4\mu SN_e$

$K = 4N_e$

Allele Frequency (percentage)

100

50

0

10,000   20,000   30,000   40,000

Generations

FIGURE 4–3 (*a*) Fixation of a neutral mutation depends on effective population size, in this case 10,000 breeding individuals. It takes approximately 40,000 generations. (*b*) Fixation of a mutation that carries a selective advantage occurs much more rapidly, in this case, over only 1,000 generations.

Population Size

The Hardy–Weinberg equilibrium assumes a very large population. What happens when this assumption is not met—that is, when a population is small and reproductively isolated? Certainly, one thing to consider is *sampling error,* a concept familiar from basic statistics, which may alter allele frequencies from one generation to another. The extent of sampling error depends on the size of the population and the frequency of a particular allele at the start of a generation. Sampling error increases as population size decreases. Genetic drift and the founder effect, concepts that are discussed later in this chapter, become more important as effective population size diminishes. Effective population size is determined by a number of real-world factors: Real populations include individuals of a number of generations, individuals who do not reproduce for one reason or another, and individuals who by chance belong to families of variable size. These factors must be considered in determining the actual breeding population, or the **effective population size.** Another consequence of small population size is the greater chance that one will find a mate who is closely related to oneself—a situation that results in inbreeding.

Inbreeding and Assortative Mating

The Hardy–Weinberg equilibrium assumes random mating, or *panmixis.* **Random mating** occurs when any individual of one sex has an equal probability of mating with any other individual of the opposite sex in the population. Two factors may prevent random mating and thus alter Hardy–Weinberg allele frequencies: inbreeding and assortative mating. Mating between individuals who are genetically related is called **inbreeding.** The important result of inbreeding is an increase in the level of homozygosity in the population and the subsequent loss of variability (Figure 4–4). Because inbreeding is a form of nonrandom mating, it alters genotype frequencies and affects the Hardy–Weinberg equilibrium.

How the level of homozygosity (one of the consequences of inbreeding as well as of nonrandom mating) can be increased is shown by the following simple example. We would, however, qualify this example by pointing out that inbreeding, mating

effective population size: a measure of the number of individuals of reproductive age in a population and the variance in the number of gametes that each individual produces.

random mating: mate choice among individuals in a population without regard to phenotype or genotype (also known as panmixis).

inbreeding: the increased incidence of mating within a population that results in an increase in homozygosity within the population.

FIGURE 4–4 Nonrandom mating changes allele frequency by increasing the percentage of homozygosity over time, thus affecting the Hardy–Weinberg equilibrium. The number of generations required to change allele frequencies from 50 percent is shown for mating systems that involve (a) self-fertilization, (b) siblings, (c) double first cousins, (d) single first cousins, and (e) second cousins.

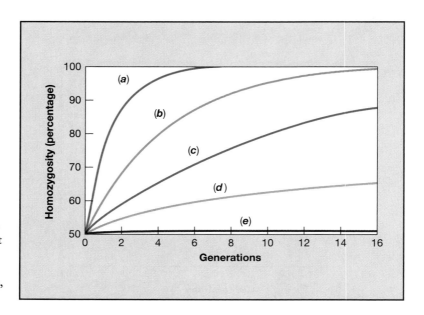

among individuals who share a common ancestor, only assumes that those individuals are more closely genetically similar than unrelated individuals in the general population. Inbreeding does not assume that people who mate are genotypically identical.

Initially, let two alleles be present in equal frequency (A and a both = 0.50). At Hardy–Weinberg equilibrium, one expects 0.25 AA, 0.5 Aa, and 0.25 aa in the population. After one generation of mating involving only those individuals who share the same genotype (AA × AA, Aa × Aa, and aa × aa), the frequency of genotypes becomes 0.375 AA, 0.25 Aa, and 0.375 aa, a decrease of 50 percent in the number of heterozygotes (Aa). In the second generation, the frequency of heterozygotes decreases to 0.125, one-half of the previous generation. For each succeeding generation the frequency of the heterozygotes decreases by one-half. Allele frequencies have not changed, however, remaining at 0.50 for both A and a alleles.

Increased homozygosity in and of itself is not a particular concern. Inbreeding can contribute to a problem, such as decreased fitness, when a recessive deleterious allele is present in both parents. In individuals who are closely related, the chance that each parent will carry a deleterious mutation is much higher than if the parents are unrelated, because each parent inherits genes from the same ancestor. If each parent has a deleterious mutation, then each of their offspring has a one in four chance of inheriting two recessive alleles and of contracting a disease caused by the homozygous recessive condition. In contrast, in a randomly mating populations the chance that a combination of recessive homozygotes will occur is usually very low, perhaps about 1 in 10,000.

The rate of human inbreeding varies from one population to another but is generally very low. The effects of inbreeding are more noticeable in populations that are geographically remote or are isolated within a surrounding large population because of religious or cultural practices. Ellen Groce in her book *Everyone Here Spoke Sign Language* (1985) has provided us with a touching example of the way in which gene flow, migration, inbreeding, and the cultural definition of a handicap were all intertwined in the story of a group of settlers on Martha's Vineyard in the 1800s and early 1900s. Her book documents the rise of hereditary deafness caused by inbreeding among members of settlers, who carried the recessive allele that caused deafness in the homozygous state. After many generations, almost every family on the island had one or more members who were deaf. As it turned out, everyone on the island learned to speak sign language, so the members who were deaf had no real disability in this small society.

Among the Dunkers and the settlers on Martha's Vineyard, the *average inbreeding coefficients,* defined as the probability that an individual will inherit at a given locus two alleles that are identical as a consequence of the descent from common ancestors, are high. In contrast, Arctic Eskimo populations, though remote and having small population sizes, have maintained a low level of population inbreeding because of cultural practices that prohibit marriage between closely related individuals, an example of outbreeding. In *outbreeding,* or lineage exogamy, individuals are required to marry outside of the kin group.

Most people in the United States today tend not to marry their relatives. In humans, many cultural and social customs, such as incest rules or taboos, restrict inbreeding. In other cultures around the world there may be very specific nonrandom preferential mating patterns that result in inbreeding: In one society, for example, the preferred marriage for a son is to a mother's brother's daughter, if there is one. Some human groups have even sanctioned inbreeding as a method of maintaining the "purity" of a particular lineage. For example, in dynastic Egypt, inbreeding in the royal family, even between brother and sister, was encouraged in an attempt to preserve "pure" bloodlines. Obviously, if you live in a small endogamous group (one whose rules prescribe marriages only within the group, such as the American gypsies), chances are great that you will marry a close relative, someone with whom you might share a common allele, because you both inherited it from a grandmother or a grandfather. But what is the chance of this happening?

The following example shows how the inbreeding coefficient is determined for a child of first cousins, who share two common grandparents (Figure 4–5). Each grandparent is heterozygous at one locus (*Aa*). The probability that either grandparent will

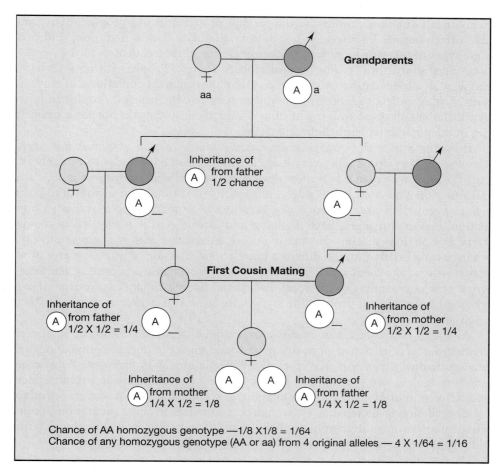

FIGURE 4–5 Calculation of the inbreeding coefficient for first-cousin mating. The chance of any homozygous genotype in the offspring of a first-cousin mating is 1/16.

contribute either one of the two alleles to an offspring is 0.50. The probability that the same allele will in turn be passed on to a grandchild is 0.25. An offspring of two first cousins has a one-eighth chance (0.125) that the allele will show up in its genotype. However, because we originally considered the four alleles in the two grandparents, each of which can be transmitted in the same fashion, the inbreeding coefficient is actually $4 \times 1/64$, or $1/16$. This is the probability that a child of a first-cousin mating will be homozygous for any two alleles by descent.

Increased homozygosity can occur as a result of nonrandom mating practices that are not related to inbreeding. For example, people tend to mate with others who generally look like themselves, such as those who share the same skin color or similar facial features. This type of nonrandom mating is called **positive assortative mating,** and it may involve many variables, some of which, such as similarity in ear lobe length (which is highly correlated with mate preference), would not at first glance appear to be significant. At the same time, red-haired people tend to avoid other red-haired people as mates, which is called **negative assortative mating.** Tall women tend to marry tall men (positive assortative), whereas short women marry men of all heights (negative assortative). Short men tend to marry only short women (positive assortative), whereas tall men marry women of all heights (negative assortative). We can also observe nonrandom mating for many social variables that may carry genetic consequences, such as mating within one's ethnic group, one's religion, and even one's socioeconomic class.

Migration

The movement of people between different populations affects the Hardy–Weinberg equilibrium. **Migration** is the movement of people, hence their genes, from one area to another. Gene flow can involve the permanent movement of people into a population from outside (in-migration) or out of a population (out-migration). Either of these types of migration can lead to changes in the allele frequencies in the population under study, thus leading to evolutionary change. People with new alleles or people with alleles in different frequencies than the original population can move in, both of which affect the combined population's allele frequencies. People can move out, including all those who might carry a rare allele, and again the allele frequencies in the population left behind will change.

In addition to such permanent migrations, people may be responsible for gene flow even if they do not stay very long. It is much easier for males to be agents of gene flow this way than it is for females, because males tend to be more mobile and transitory than females. For example, it is much less common for a women to be an agent of gene flow in a transitory way, because she would have to move into a population, become pregnant, have the baby, and leave the baby behind when she departs. For obvious reasons this rarely occurs. In warfare men may engage in rape while passing briefly through different populations. Outside of warfare men's occupations often take them away from their homes for extended periods. Ellen Groce wrote of whalers sailing to the South Pacific and finding children on remote islands who had been named, presumably by whaler-fathers of earlier voyages, for their neighbors back home.

Although migrations may continue over time, if gene flow diminishes between the migrant and its parent population, at some point the migrant population will become distinct genetically from the parent population. With little gene flow occurring between the two populations, genetic differences accumulate as a result of new and different mutations in each population, and natural selection operates to adapt each population to its separate environment. Consequently, over generations, populations may become different not only in terms of gene frequencies but also in terms of morphological characteristics (such as height, weight, and hair color).

positive assortative mating: positive correlation between partners in some character. Individuals who resemble one another mate more frequently than would be expected by chance.

negative assortative mating: individuals who bear little resemblance to one another mate more frequently than would be expected by chance.

migration: the movement of a reproductively active individual into a population from a distant population, thus bringing new genes into that population.

✳ FRONTIERS

Migration, Natural Selection, and Tay-Sachs Disease

Tay-Sachs is a fatal and incurable disease that results from a homozygous recessive allele combination. Infants who inherit two copies of the Tay-Sachs allele (one from each parent) usually appear normal for the first few months of life. An exaggerated "startle" reaction to sounds is the first sign of the onset of the disease; this is followed, at about six months of age, by stages of decreasing motor control: First the infant loses motor control of the head, then she or he cannot roll over or sit up without support, and finally the baby becomes blind. Most affected children die before they reach age four. The worldwide average for occurrences of Tay-Sachs disease is about 1 in 400,000 births, but it appears in about 1 in 3,600 births among specific populations, especially those who trace their descent from eastern European Jews, people known as Ashkenazim. By calculation, the number of carriers for the allele among this group reaches as high as 1 in 30.

What is it about these people who produce such a high risk of Tay-Sachs and, as it turns out, of nine other genetic diseases? As Jared Diamond (1991:61) put it, "finding the answer to this question concerns us all as through the afflictions of one group of people we gain a window on how our genes [may] simultaneously curse and bless us all."

Tay-Sachs disease was identified independently in the 1880s by two physicians, one British and one American. In 1962 researchers discovered that this disease is caused by an excessive accumulation in nerve cells of a fatty substance, Gm2 ganglioside, that is normally present at harmless levels in cell membranes and that is broken down by an enzyme, hexosaminidase A. In Tay-Sachs individuals this enzyme is not produced in the body, and with-

out it, Gm2 ganglioside rapidly accumulates to lethal levels.

A brief history of the Ashkenazim is important in understanding what is suspected to be the reason for their high frequency of Tay-Sachs disease. Jews who originally settled in France and Germany during the eighth and ninth centuries were later persecuted during the period of the Crusades. Fleeing eastward into Lithuania and western Russia, they remained there until the nineteenth century, when anti-Semitic attacks drove millions of them out of eastern Europe, most heading for the United States.

In the United States geneticists attempted to unravel the mystery of why high allele frequencies resulting in 10 different genetic diseases plagued these people. Researchers questioned whether founder effect and genetic drift (discussed later) could provide the simple explanation for this anomaly. But a number of facts worked against this hypothesis, at least as the full answer. First, founder effect and genetic drift only become significant in small populations, and the founding populations of Ashkenazim were probably quite large. Second, more or less isolated Ashkenazy populations were found throughout eastern Europe. The chance process of genetic drift would be expected to produce random allele frequencies in these communities, not higher frequencies in all of them. Third, even if in some odd fashion genetic drift could be held accountable for these high mutant frequencies among the Ashkenazim, natural selection over many generations would have restored allele frequencies to those observed among other peoples.

Jared Diamond believed that even though the homozygous recessive condition is lethal, these alleles carried some advantage in the heterozygous state. (As we discuss shortly, this is similar to the case of sickle-cell anemia, where the heterozygous state carries a distinct survival advantage in people

who live in malaria-prone areas.) But what is the advantage for ganglioside accumulation in eastern European Jews? Diamond believed that the answer could be found in a clue that was uncovered in 1972 when medical researchers conducted a survey asking American Ashkenazim what their parents had died of in Europe. It became strikingly apparent that many fewer Jews than expected had died of tuberculosis, a disease that in the general population at the time caused up to 20 percent of all deaths. Jews, as it turned out, had only about one-half of this mortality rate.

The question now seemed to turn to natural selection for an explanation of high allele frequencies for Tay-Sachs and other diseases of the Ashkenazim. But this story still had some unexplained twists. The pattern of Ashkenazy migration played a role, because although eastern European Jews were widespread, they all basically migrated into similar situations. For more than 1,000 years these people were confined to towns, because most were forbidden to own land. Living in crowded ghetto conditions where tuberculosis thrived, Ashkenazim survived the ravages of some diseases with a greater genetic resistance than other people. Why weren't non-Jews affected by natural selection in the same way Diamond thinks the Jews were? The answer is that as non-Jews died in the cities, their numbers were replaced by non-Jews who migrated in from the countryside. No such replacement occurred in the Jewish community; thus selection would have been intense for them but not for non-Jews.

Diamond concedes that we still have no idea what biochemical mechanisms cause ganglioside accumulation in cells to confer resistance to tuberculosis infection—if indeed it does. But the facts of the case make this a plausible hypothesis and argue in favor of some heterozygote advantage that someday may be understood.

When two populations come into contact, the usual result is eventual homogenization. Let us suppose that two populations originally differ in allele frequencies. As one population migrates into the geographical range of the other and mating takes place between individuals of the two groups, genes are shared between groups and the gene pools of each population become less different. When mating becomes completely random, the populations eventually fuse into one group.

An example of homogenization in progress is evident in the United States between Americans of European ancestry and Americans of African ancestry. Mainly between the years 1619 and 1808, Africans were brought to America as indentured servants and slaves. The genetic composition of the present-day African American population is different from that of the ancestral African populations as a result of admixture, some consensual and some not, with European Americans, Native Americans, and, later, Asian Americans that has occurred over more than 350 years.

One notable genetic marker in many West African populations is the presence of a mutant allele, *s,* which in the homozygous recessive state causes a disease known as sickle-cell anemia, usually a fatal childhood condition in these regions. In the homozygous state, *ss,* the normal red blood cell becomes distorted into an elongated "sickle," or curved, shape (Figure 4–6), and the serious and painful disease of sickle-cell anemia results. The heterozygous state, *As,* affords some protection from severe malarial infection, and under conditions of endemic malaria, as has always been prevalent in tropical Africa, this genotype confers an advantage.

Today, the heterozygote frequency of the sickle-cell trait among African Americans is about 10 percent, compared with an estimated average frequency of 15 to 20 percent among individuals in many African populations. Differences in the frequency of this trait can be partly accounted for by gene flow from other groups of Americans. In addition, with the absence of endemic malaria, natural selection has worked to eliminate this gene in America through selection against the mutant allele as it appears in different genotypes.

It is also true that in West Africa, where malaria is still prevalent, selection acts against the homozygous *AA* normal hemoglobin genotype, because these individuals are differentially infected by the malarial parasite. In the United States in the absence of malaria, there is almost complete relaxation of selection pressure against *AA* individuals. Thus, in the United States more African Americans who are *AA* survive and reproduce than do their counterparts in West Africa, who have a greater chance of dying as a result of malaria. The effect of this differential survival increases the frequency of the *A* allele in the United States relative to the *A* allele in West African populations. We examine more closely the sickle-cell trait and other examples of balanced polymorphisms (the presence of two or more genetic variants in a population) in Chapter 14.

FIGURE 4–6 Normal (left) and sickle-shaped (right) red blood cells.

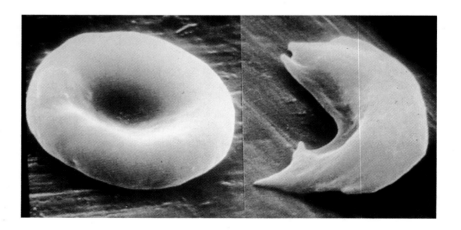

Random Genetic Drift

Sometimes change in the frequency of alleles occurs by chance in a process called **genetic drift.** There are many reasons for genetic drift, including random death, nonreproduction among individuals, differences in gamete production (especially in populations, such as the industrial Western countries, where people have fewer than two children on average), and founder effect. As we have seen, how rapidly such changes occur depends on population size. The chance that an allele will become fixed in a population, rather than lost through chance, is related to how frequently that allele occurs in the population. The rarer the allele, the more likely that it will become lost. Given an original population with two alleles in equal frequency, the chance that one will replace the other is 50 percent. If the original frequencies of the alleles are not equal, their chances of becoming fixed in the population are the same as their frequencies. For example, if A is at 90 percent and a is at 10 percent, then A has a 90 percent chance of becoming fixed in the population and a has a 10 percent chance. The rate of genetic drift is not consistent from generation to generation; it fluctuates, producing higher frequencies in one generation and lower frequencies in a succeeding one. Change, in other words, is erratic.

One special case of genetic drift is the **founder effect,** in which colonization of an isolated area by a small number of individuals determines the genetic characteristics of a new population. Small founding populations usually possess allele frequencies that are quite different from those of the parent population. The cause of this difference is twofold. First, imagine a small group setting out to inhabit an isolated South Pacific atoll or an isolated African valley (Figure 4–7). The small group of founders—perhaps 25 individuals—would not by chance exactly represent the genetic complement of the larger population from which they split off. They would not have the same frequencies of alleles, and whole alleles might even be absent. The 25 individuals thus represent only a sampling of the larger group.

To understand the second way in which genetic drift can occur, suppose that 100 couples found a population, but that 1 of the 100 men happens, for one reason or another, to have many more children than the other 99. If, for example, the one man fathers 10 percent of the next generation, their genes will disproportionately reflect that of their father, and the gene frequencies will have drifted between the first and second generation simply as a function of who fathered the most children. For example, this sort of accident accounts for the very high gene frequency of occurrence of Tay-Sachs disease among a small group of Pennsylvania Dutch, among whom 98 out of 333 individuals were determined to be carriers of this lethal allele.

genetic drift: allele frequency changes caused by chance effects, not affected by selection; most common in small population sizes.

founder effect: type of genetic drift caused by sampling a small amount of genetic variation from the original population in a group of individuals colonizing a new area.

FIGURE 4–7 An example of founder effect: syndactyly, a genetically inherited deformity frequently found in this isolated African population near the Mozambique–Zimbabwe border. This condition is traceable to one group of immigrant ancestors.

Members of the small Pennsylvania Dutch population were all descendants of one couple who came to the United States in the 1800s and had 13 children.

Another example concerns a rare dominant trait, Huntington's disease, which is associated with the degeneration of the central nervous system. The allele for this trait has been located on chromosome 4, and apparently the disease is caused by excessive replication of one area of the DNA, rather than by a change in the DNA sequence. The inheritance of the disease is interesting: If the allele comes from the mother, the same number of replications as the mother had are passed on to the offspring. If inheritance comes through the father, however, offspring receive more replications with each generation. The more replications, the earlier the onset of symptoms. In populations around Lake Maracaibo, Venezuela, children as young as two or three years of age show symptoms of this disease.

The identification of the area on chromosome 4 allows for early detection in individuals who carry it. Previously, the only way to detect the gene was to observe the onset of symptoms, which usually occurred, within a wide range of variation, at about 30 years of age. The first symptoms include *chorea,* dancelike jerking motions of the limbs, leading to early death. The last decade or two of the person's life is spent in slow, steady decline of physical and mental functions. In many populations around the world, the frequency of the heterozygote through which the dominant allele expresses itself is about 1/10,000. However, in Tasmania, an Australian state of 350,000 people, there are 120 cases of this disease, or about 1/3,000. The dominant allele for Huntington's chorea was brought to Tasmania by one woman who immigrated there in 1848, a dramatic example of genetic drift and founder effect.

Study of the genetic disease phenylketonuria (PKU) provides us with yet another example of founder effect. People who inherit two recessive alleles (homozygous) have a deficiency of the enzyme phenylalanine hydroxylase. As a consequence, the amino acid phenylalanine accumulates in the bloodstream and ultimately causes mental retardation. A diet low in phenylalanine can prevent the brain damage that leads to the symptoms.

The incidence of PKU varies among populations. The Japanese reportedly have the lowest rate (1 in every 60,000 newborns), whereas 1 in 15,000 Europeans is affected. The highest incidence of PKU, about 1 in 5,000, occurs in Ireland, western Scotland, and among Jews of Yemenite origin living in Israel. Although about 20 different mutations can cause PKU, probably only one mutation was responsible for the cases involving the Yemenite Jews, because their population of only 250,000 was so small. By retracing Jewish history, genealogist Yosef Shiloh of Tel Aviv University (Wright, 1990) was able to determine that all of the present carriers of the allele descended from individuals who had lived in a single village, San'a in Yemen, until at least the late seventeenth century. This mutation must have arisen in a single individual sometime before that time and was later spread in other parts of Yemen and finally to Israel (Figure 4–8).

Selection

The last evolutionary force that changes Hardy–Weinberg equilibrium is selection. As we saw in Chapter 2, natural selection is the mechanism by which a population becomes better adapted to its environment over time. For natural selection to work, the adaptations must occur at the genetic level so that they can be passed on to offspring. Those individuals who are more fit leave more offspring on average than do less fit individuals. **Fitness** is, therefore, defined as the percentage of offspring an individual has, relative to the number of offspring of the maximally fit individuals in the population. Fitness values for individuals relate to a specific point in time for a specified environment. Fitness may change over time as the environment changes. Following are some examples of how fitness can change, as well as explanations of the mechanisms involved.

fitness: the extent to which the genes of an individual survive in its descendants.

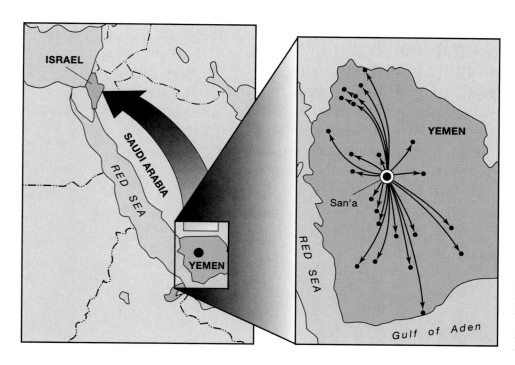

FIGURE 4-8 The spread of PKU by migration from Yemen to Israel. The mutation probably occurred before the late seventeenth century.

Directional selection. Directional selection provides a typical example of natural selection. In directional selection, the homozygote for one allele is favored rather than the heterozygote. One of the best examples of directional selection was witnessed in a population of the English peppered moth, *Biston betularia* (Figure 4–9). In the early nineteenth century, all of the individuals in the population were colored in a light gray variegated pattern. However, in 1848 a dark-colored form of the moth appeared, which over time gradually increased in frequency to greater than 90 percent and spread throughout England. Biologist H. Kettlewell (1973) studied this phenomenally rapid change in the moth population. He noted that the first dark-colored moths appeared at about the same time that major environmental effects of the British Industrial Revolution were being felt. He found that the lighter color of the original moths blended in with the lichen-covered tree trunks they rested on and provided an effective camouflage from bird predators. However, with the sooty pollution from coal-burning factories covering tree trunks, the lighter moths stood out against the darker background. Further work demonstrated that the new dark moth phenotype was caused by a mutation that was dominant over the gray color allele, and under the conditions of a polluted, sooty environment, it quickly became favored.

Experimenting with this hypothesis, Kettlewell released different-colored moths in polluted and unpolluted areas and then recaptured as many of them as possible at a later time. He demonstrated that the lighter gray moths in sooty polluted conditions were more vulnerable to predation by birds than were the darker moths. Today, however, because of decreased levels of industrial pollution, the proportion of gray moths is once again increasing.

FIGURE 4-9 The English peppered moth, *Biston betularia*, shown in light gray and dark gray variants.

directional selection: selection that acts to move the mean of a population in one particular direction.

genetic polymorphism: the existence of two or more genetic variants within a population; can be a **balanced polymorphism** when selection favors the heterozygotes, as in sickle-cell anemia.

Balanced selection and genetic polymorphism. Sometimes selection favors alleles only when they occur in certain combinations. This tends to maintain genetic diversity in the population. This balancing of selection both for and against certain alleles results in **genetic polymorphisms**, also called *balanced polymorphisms*. For example, in sickle-cell anemia, individuals who are heterozygous for the

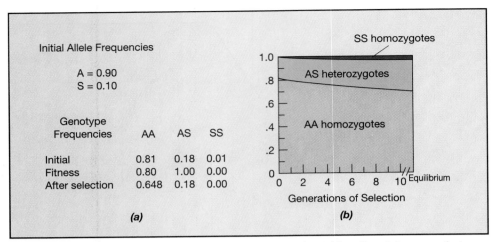

FIGURE 4-10   Diagram showing how selection acts on the sickle-cell trait in a population living in a malarial environment. (*a*) Calculation of allele frequencies *A* and *s* after one generation of selection. Note the slightly reduced fitness resulting from the *AA* genotype. (*b*) Graph of allele frequencies *A* and *s* carried out to 10 generations, when equilibrium is reached. Because the *As* genotype results in increased fitness, it gradually increases in frequency over time.

sickle-cell trait (genotype *As*) are less likely to be affected by malaria. If individuals move away from this environment or if the environment is changed through the eradication of mosquitoes that carry the malarial parasite, *As* individuals lose their selective advantage. In Figure 4–10 we show how the sickle-cell allele is maintained over time in a malarial environment. Although some people die of malaria, more of the people with the sickle-cell trait live than would be expected. We must remember, however, that people with the sickle-cell trait do still die or have miscarriages because of the malaria—the *s* allele provides protection but not 100 percent protection.

Everything else being equal, in a balanced polymorphic situation, allele frequencies would not change from generation to generation. What does change is the total number of people in the population. With malaria, more people survive when the *s* gene is in the population. If the population was living in a malarial environment and *s* alleles were not present, fewer people would survive, because the fitness of the *AA* individuals is lowered as disproportionately more of them die of malaria. So the *population* as a whole is better off with the sickle-cell gene than without it, even though the *ss* genotype is lethal to *individuals* who possess it. The net result of this system is to keep both alleles present in the population as long as environmental conditions do not change.

Average population fitness.   Natural selection may operate either for or against a specific genotype in a population, but the net outcome is always the removal of unfavorable alleles. If this process continues long enough, the environment does not change, and the heterozygote genotype in the population is not the best adapted, then homozygosity in the population increases to the point that all individuals become homozygous for the loci favored by selection. However, although unfavored alleles are never completely eliminated from a population (because some of them are replaced by new mutations), the average fitness of the population does increase as the number of unfavored alleles decreases (Figure 4–11).

In some cases, such as with balanced polymorphisms, selection acts to maintain heterozygosity. Although the effect of this heterozygosity may be to lower the overall fitness of the population, it also increases the genetic variability of the population. This variation may be important to the future of a population when environmental

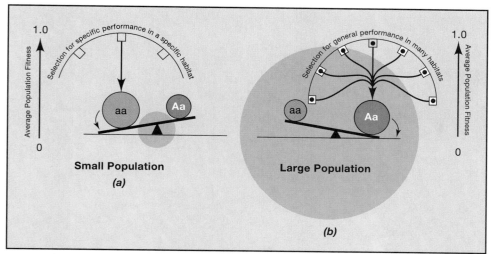

FIGURE 4–11   The relationship between population fitness and homozygosity. In general, heterozygosity *decreases* average population fitness but *increases* the population's variability. This in turn increases the population's future ability to respond to new selection pressures. (*a*) In small, marginal populations, selection favors the homozygote and leads to the fixation of specific adaptive traits. (*b*) In large populations, the scale usually tips in favor of the heterozygote. This leads to decreased average population fitness, however, because homozygotes, which are less fit than heterozygotes, are continually produced.

conditions change and new selection pressures come into play. Under these circumstances a population with little genetic variation to call on faces the possibility of extinction.

HOW MICROEVOLUTION LEADS TO MACROEVOLUTION

Evolution is defined as genetic change in a population over time. As we saw in Chapter 3, *microevolution* refers to small-scale genetic changes, ones that occur over a few generations. Microevolutionary change occurs within the confines of a single species, resulting in a shift in percentages of alleles and of morphological characters. We have seen many examples of this in this chapter so far: The change in coloration of the English peppered moth is an example of microevolutionary change. Microevolutionary change begins the process by which populations diverge from one another, which can ultimately lead to the formation of new species, or *macroevolution*. Macroevolution is long term, producing changes that result in the formation of new species over time.

How New Species Are Formed

Macroevolutionary change results in **speciation,** the process by which new biological species form. Darwin's model of speciation begins with members of a species spreading out over a large area. Environmental variation within this area brings selective pressure to bear on individuals, and this pressure results, generations later, in the production of variation. As variation increases, new species may arise.

Since Darwin's time the model of speciation that is most popular among population biologists is the one proposed by Ernst Mayr, which he called geographic or **allopatric speciation.** According to this model, geographic barriers that may divide a population are essential to speciation. After a population has divided, gene flow between the two new populations ceases. Over time, as each population evolves independently, differences accumulate, until members of one population cannot

speciation: the splitting of one species into two or more species over time (cladogenesis) or the change of an earlier species in a lineage to a new, later one.

allopatric speciation: formation of new species over time as a result of geographic isolation between members of an original single species.

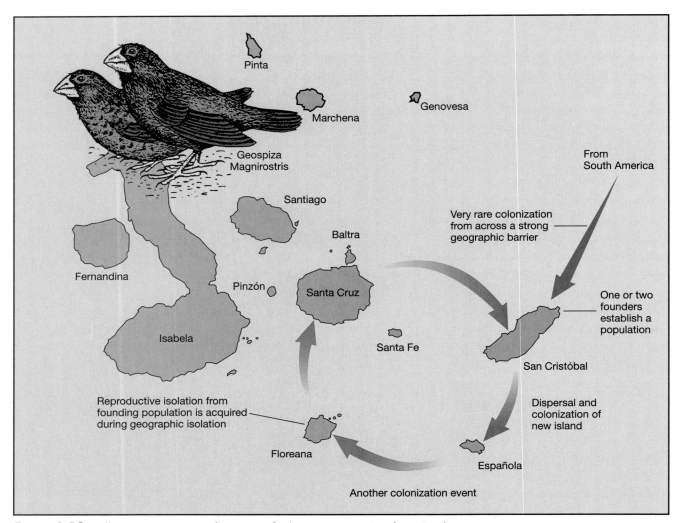

FIGURE 4-12 Allopatric speciation of Darwin's finches. One migration from South America eventually results in many different species, because offspring of the original migrants adapt to conditions on specific islands over many generations.

interbreed with members of the other. This phenomena is also known as cladogenesis. At this point reproductive isolation is established (Figure 4–12). The Galápagos finches, one example Darwin used to promote his theory of evolution by natural selection, are a case in point. Because the width of the ocean between mainland South America and the Galápagos Islands is large, it represents an effective geographic barrier that made colonization events on the Galápagos rare. Figure 4–12 shows how one species of South American finch originally colonized the Galápagos. Formation of new species, "Darwin's finches," resulted from the subsequent colonization of each island in turn.

Estimating the required time for complete reproductive isolation to occur is difficult, yet from molecular and DNA studies of modern animals some guidelines can be established. For example, the time over which such a process occurred, using modern apes and humans as an example, is somewhere between 4 million and 6 million years. Likewise, matings between chimpanzees and gorillas cannot produce offspring. These groups are completely reproductively isolated from one another. In contrast, bonobos and common chimpanzees, which are separated from each other

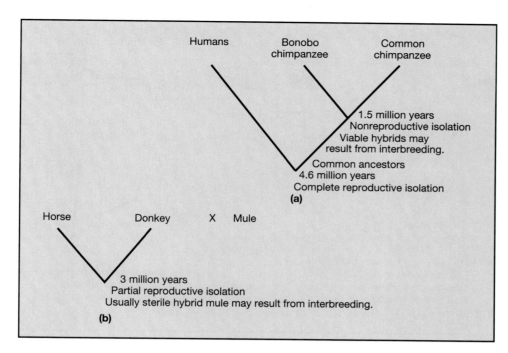

FIGURE 4-13 Time required for reproductive isolation in mammalian groups. (*a*) Humans and chimpanzees, who last shared a common ancestor 4 million to 6 million years ago, are reproductively isolated; bonobos and common chimpanzees, whose last common ancestor lived about 1.5 million years ago, can produce viable hybrid offspring. (*b*) Horses and donkeys, whose last common ancestor lived approximately 3 million years ago, are partially isolated. Matings usually result in the production of sterile offspring.

by some 1.5 million years (Ruvolo, 1997) can interbreed and produce viable off-spring. Outside of the primate order, horses and donkeys are separated by about 3 million years, yet these two "species" often reproduce, matings that result in mules, hybrid animals that are often, but not always, sterile. This situation indicates partial but not complete reproductive isolation (Figure 4–13).

Mayr also described an alternative mode of speciation, which involved the evo-lution of new species within a single locality. He defined this **sympatric speciation model** as "the establishment of new populations of a species in different ecological niches within the normal cruising range of the individuals of the parental popula-tion" (Mayr, 1963:449). As populations that occupy the different specialized niches differentiate from one another, a rapid development of reproductive isolation fol-lows and, again, new species arise. An example is the many species of lemurs that occupy different ecological niches in the rain forests of Madagascar, most of which separated from a common ancestor.

The Tempo of Speciation

There are essentially three competing theories for what has been described as the tempo and mode of speciation (Figure 4–14). First, Darwin clearly believed that macroevolution is essentially microevolution extended over long periods of geologic time. Small changes over time gradually accumulate to constitute the large changes that ultimately distinguish new species from older ones. From this basic pattern, two general predictions emerge. First, the fossil record for the origin of a new species should consist of a long sequence of continuous intermediate types from the parental type to the new species. Second, any discontinuities, or "gaps," in the fossil record are the result of an inadequate record of fossils that have simply not yet been discovered. This process, known as **phyletic gradualism**, was criticized by scientists who saw what they considered to be too many "gaps" in the fossil record.

The concept of sudden "jumps" or "leaps" in evolution is the essence of the sec-ond theory, which was outlined by the geneticist Richard Goldschmidt (1940) in an

sympatric speciation: formation of new species over time as a result of ecological isolation between members of an original single species who occupied the same ecosystem within their geographic range.

phyletic gradualism: term used to characterize Darwin's idea of evolutionary rate; slow, gradual change over long periods of time.

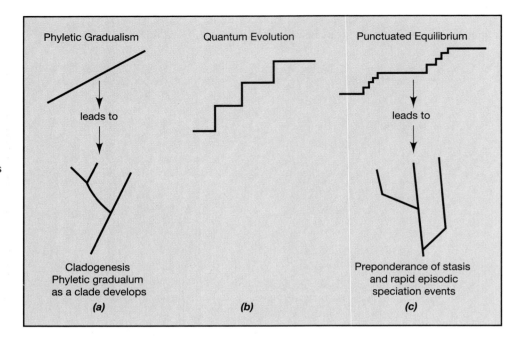

FIGURE 4–14 Three theories of how evolution leads to the formation of new species. (*a*) Darwin's idea of gradualism, or phyletic change. (*b*) Quantum evolution, or the idea that evolutionary change appears suddenly. (*c*) Punctuated equilibrium, or long periods of stasis followed by a burst of evolutionary activity.

quantum evolution: term coined by George Gaylord Simpson to describe stepwise evolutionary change.

punctuated equilibrium: term coined by Stephen J. Gould and Niles Eldredge to characterize evolution typified by long periods of little or no change (stasis) interrupted by bursts of rapid change (punctuational events).

attempt to reconcile a sporadic fossil record with modern genetic theory. He suggested that large-scale mutations could cause such jumps in evolution. Paleontologist George Gaylord Simpson in one of his major contributions to the modern synthesis, *Tempo and Mode in Evolution* (1944), argued that gaps at the level of the species could probably be accounted for as byproducts of incomplete or poor fossil preservation. Yet he was concerned about the gaps that existed between the higher taxa. As a consequence, he developed the concept of **quantum evolution,** or stepwise evolutionary change, which could explain how some populations rapidly shift in their adaptations. Later, in his book *The Major Features of Evolution* (1953) he defined quantum evolution as rapid evolutionary changes of adaptive zones, changes so rapid that transitional forms between the old zone and the new zone would be nearly nonexistent. In other words, in terms of geologic time, such leaps could be so rapid that the chance of finding an intermediate fossil form that reflected these shifts would be quite slim.

Though the predominant viewpoint concerning the rate of evolutionary change leaned toward the gradualistic model, the idea of rapid leaps continued. Stephen J. Gould and Niles Eldredge (1993) promoted a third idea: **punctuated equilibrium,** in which short bursts of change might periodically occur. They argued that most species exhibit little or no change throughout most of their evolutionary history (stasis) and that adaptive change (punctuation) is a relatively rare, rapid event, rather than a gradual process. New species would arise by the splitting of a lineage when a small local population became isolated at the margin of their geographic range. Gaps in the fossil record under this theory are explained by the fact that new fossil species do not arise in the same place their ancestors lived so it is unlikely that paleontologists can trace their divergence from parental stock. A sharp break between ancestral and derived forms is, therefore, to be expected.

It is also quite possible that evolution—at some times and for some traits—proceeds by phyletic gradualism primarily because of natural selection. At other times, and for other traits, evolution probably proceeds by rapid punctuated equilibrium as a result of mutation, isolation, and genetic drift. The tempo and mode of evolutionary change are not necessarily either/or choices. Different modes of evolutionary change can occur under different circumstances.

In the first four chapters of this book, we have discussed the theories and tools that biological anthropologists use to study the origins of humankind—the theory of evolution by natural selection, genetics, and population genetics. We now go on to study the fascinating process by which mammals, primates, and, eventually, humans, evolved.

◀ SUMMARY

1. **What two schools of thought about heredity arose in the early twentieth century? How did their disagreement lead to the development of population genetics?**

Two schools of thought arose concerning the evolution of populations among biological anthropologists and other evolutionary scientists in the late nineteenth and early twentieth centuries. The biometricians measured complex traits, such as height, that tended to show "blending" types of inheritance, whereas the Mendelians studied discrete traits that conformed to expectations of Mendelian genetics. Ultimately, in 1918 R. A. Fisher brought both approaches together into a unified Synthetic Theory of Evolution.

2. **What is the significance of the Hardy–Weinberg model of equilibrium for population studies, and what factors cause a population to fall out of equilibrium?**

Work by G. H. Hardy, a mathematician, and Wilhelm Weinberg, a physician, was instrumental in bringing about the rapprochement of biometricians and Mendelians. Hardy and Weinberg showed that genes in populations would stay the same, generation to generation, in what is termed Hardy–Weinberg equilibrium, unless forces of evolution act on them. Factors that cause a population to fall out of equilibrium include a higher-than-expected rate of mutation; population size; nonrandom mating practices; various patterns of migration; genetic drift, which includes a number of chance processes; and natural selection, which creates a situation of differential fitness.

3. **What forces of evolution affect population allele frequencies in a species?**

Directional selection occurs in a population when natural selection acts to remove certain phenotypes (and consequently their genotypes) from a breeding population. Evolution of melanism in the peppered moth is a good example of directional selection. Balanced selection occurs in a population when only certain combinations of alleles are favored. Sickle-cell anemia is an example of balanced selection in human populations in which heterozygote *AS* individuals have a selective advantage over *AA* individuals, who are unprotected from malaria, and *SS* individuals, who suffer sickle-cell anemia. Evolution is defined as genetic change in a population over time. Small-scale, or microevolutionary, changes lead to divergence of populations and start the process of speciation, which can in turn lead to large-scale, or macroevolutionary, changes, such as higher-order differences at the genus, family, and order taxonomic levels. Most evolutionary change occurred either at a more or less regular or constant rate over time (phyletic gradualism) or was concentrated in bursts of evolutionary activity interspersed between long periods of little or no change (punctuated equilibrium).

◖ CRITICAL THINKING QUESTIONS

1. Are rare genetic diseases caused by recessive genes likely to die out in a population in a few generations because of their rarity?

2. Under which specific conditions would inbreeding lead to an increase in genetically caused abnormalities?

3. In simulations of the Hardy–Weinberg equilibrium that you can carry out using three decks of cards (with 52 cards each) and using 500 M&M candies (see Internet Exercise 2), the departures from expected genotype frequencies that you see each generation are greater in the card simulations than in the M&M's. Why?

4. Describe the forces of evolution that might explain how a beneficial mutation arising in a population could spread through the population and become common over time.

5. What do you think is more common in evolution—the accumulation of many small-scale mutations over time or change by rare, large-scale mutations?

◖ INTERNET EXERCISES

Critical Thinking

Punctuated Equilibrium. Since the theory of punctuated equilibrium was first proposed, it has attracted a great deal of attention, both pro and con. In this exercise, form your own assessment of the value of this theory for understanding the fossil record by answering the following questions:

1. What are the major components of the theory of punctuated equilibrium? Do they all seem equally reasonable?

2. What evidence do proponents of the theory give? What evidence seems to work against the theory?

3. What does it mean to say that punctuated equilibrium seems to work in some situations, whereas gradualism works in others?

Writing Assignment

Hardy–Weinberg. Write your own evolutionary scenario, based on the Hardy–Weinberg equilibrium. Create a situation in an imaginary population based on the variables in the Hardy–Weinberg model. Manipulate the variables you have created in order to show what evolutionary changes would result. In your finished essay, be sure to state which Hardy– Weinberg variables result in disequilibrium.

See Companion Web site for Internet links.

Population Genetics

As we saw in this chapter, Darwin's publication of *Origin of Species* and the rediscovery of Mendel's principles of genetics caused evolutionary scientists to think in terms of populations. The new science of population genetics and the development of the Synthetic Theory of Evolution linked the principles of evolution with the rules of heredity. This allows biological anthropologists to understand the dynamics of the evolutionary process as it operates in populations of organisms.

In the Web Activity for this chapter, you will see how different types of selection cause populations to change in different ways. Different environmental conditions, and different combinations of alleles within a population's gene pool, can have very different results in terms of change within a species and the formation of new species.

WEB ACTIVITY

The ultimate cause of evolutionary change is variation within a population. In addition, certain traits will be

beneficial and others will be harmful within a given environment. Organisms that possess beneficial traits, such as protective coloration, will be more likely to survive to reproduce and pass their genes on to the next generation. Over many generations, that beneficial trait is likely to appear in more and more of the individuals in the population.

Activity

1. View the animation. What are the key features of the three types of selection depicted?
2. Give an example of how directional selection might operate in a population. What would happen if the environment remained constant? If it changed suddenly?
3. Give an example of disruptive selection. What conditions are likely to result in this type of selection?

The MediaLab can be found in Chapter 4 on your Companion Web site http://www.prenhall.com/boaz

If natural selection acts against one extreme of the population, those individuals will not be as likely to survive and reproduce as will individuals on the other extreme or the average. This produces a descendant population that has an average value skewed (or pushed) in one direction.

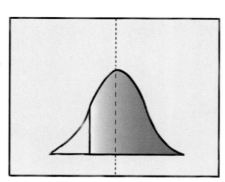

5

STAGES OF VERTEBRATE EVOLUTION

After reading this chapter, you should be able to discuss the following questions:

1. What structural and paleontological clues do biological anthropologists use to reconstruct human and nonhuman primate evolution?
2. What characteristics distinguish all chordates, including humans?
3. What adaptations occurred in the evolution of bony fishes?
4. What major adaptations led to the evolution of amphibians, reptiles, and therapsids?
5. What major adaptations occurred in the early evolution of mammals, and what was their significance?
6. What were the major steps in the evolution of the human brain?
7. What does it mean to say that no predetermined trends led inevitably toward the present human condition?

Humans are animals, only one of many species that inhabit the planet. Humans are an intimate part of the natural world linked by a network of ecological relationships with the environment and with species that are alive today, as well as with a unique and unbroken series of ancestors extending back to the primordial seas, to the beginnings of life itself (Figure 5–1). The very early stages of vertebrate evolution, from fish, amphibians, and reptiles to the primitive mammals constitute the subject of this chapter (Figure 5–2). How do we trace this ancestry?

FIGURE 5–1 One possible way in which life might have originated on earth. According to one model, the so-called temperate view, the runoff that collects in small basins is the most likely way of achieving the required concentration of ingredients to form RNA. Two other models about the origin of life are the so-called freezing and steamy scenarios. In the freezing scenario, early earth was cold. The colder the temperature, the more stable the organic compounds would be. The steamy scenario envisions early earth as a ball of fiery magma. The gases released from molten lava would have seeped to the surface, leaching out vital ingredients for RNA synthesis.

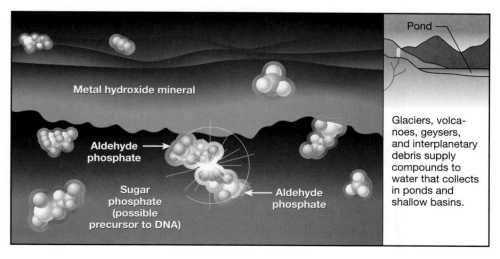

Pond

Metal hydroxide mineral

Aldehyde phosphate

Sugar phosphate (possible precursor to DNA)

Aldehyde phosphate

Glaciers, volcanoes, geysers, and interplanetary debris supply compounds to water that collects in ponds and shallow basins.

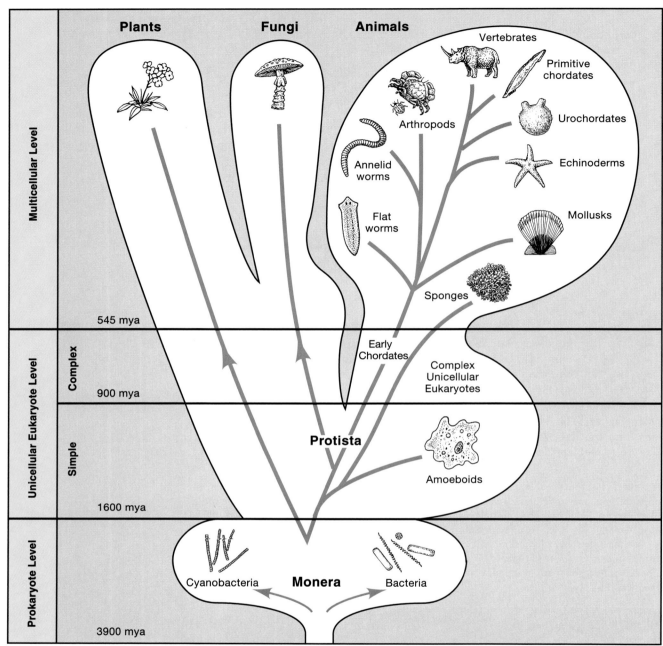

FIGURE 5–2 Evolutionary relationships among the five kingdoms of the living world: monerans, protists, plants, fungi, and animals. The earliest living forms, the monerans, are represented today by eubacteria and archaebacteria. They contain no nuclear membrane or complex organelles and divide by simple fusion. Gradually, some of the monerans evolved into early eukaryotes, represented by the protists. These forms are generally aerobic and complex, containing cell organelles, such as chloroplasts in plant cells and mitochondria, which are remnants of ancient symbiotic relationships with formerly independent cells. The protists, in turn, split into the lines that led to plants, fungi, amoeboids, sponges, and all animals. We still do not know how changes in complex unicellular eukaryotes led to the appearance of multicellular eukaryotes, but by the beginning of the Cambrian period, 545 million years ago, a widespread radiation of these organisms occurred. This marked the emergence of the largest number of distinct species that ever appeared in the fossil record.

RECONSTRUCTING EVOLUTIONARY RELATIONSHIPS

Homologous Structures

There are no tombstones marking the graves of our long-lost mammal-like reptile forebears and no family genealogies of ancestral amphibians with which we can piece together our early family tree. Instead, we compare anatomical characteristics of living and fossil animals to discover ancestor–descendant relationships. Studies of molecular evolution also provide important data on relationships between animal species and their common ancestors, but only comparative anatomy and paleontology can fill in what the actual ancestral species may have looked like.

All anatomical traits that scientists use for studying the comparative evolutionary relationships of animals must be based on a common genetic blueprint. In other words, they must be **homologous**. Evolutionary scientists determine whether structures are homologous by tracing their origins, both through the fossil record and through the embryological history of structures in modern species. Our front limbs, for example, are homologous to the front wings of modern birds. Their underlying structures are parallel, although their appearance and function are quite different (Figure 5–3a).

The term *homology* was first defined by the British anatomist Richard Owen in 1843. Owen was a conservative creationist. Ironically, by describing this concept Owen greatly assisted Charles Darwin in writing his *Origin of Species,* because homology is a key concept in phyletic reconstructions. Although Owen defined homology as "the same organ in different animals under every variety of form and function," he did not consider it a result of common ancestry and evolutionary, or *phyletic,* continuity, as our modern definition requires. Take, for example, characteristics such as the horse's hoof and the human fingernail. If these diverse features are to be considered homologous, they must be derived from structures found in the common ancestor of both.

Further discussion is necessary before this concept can be completely understood. When we observe two similar structures, such as the wing of a bat and the wing of a bird, we must ask, "Are these features homologous or not?" The answer is, "It depends." In one sense these structures are homologous if we consider them as derivatives of the forelimb of the common ancestor of birds and bats (Figure 5–3a). However, these structures are not homologous *as wings,* because the fossil record shows that bats and birds evolved independently from a common *wingless* ancestor. It is, therefore, necessary in making statements about homology to be specific about the structures being compared.

Another complicating factor is the fact that structural similarity can occur in divergent lineages as a result of similar adaptive responses to similar environmental pressures, rather than from inheritance from a common ancestor. In this case we must use another term to describe the similarity: **homoplasy**. Using our example of bird and bat wings, these features are homoplastic as wings, not homologous. They evolved independently (they are two different lineages of vertebrates) in response to similar environmental pressures.

As was discussed in Chapter 1, two different mechanisms can result in homoplastic characteristics: convergence and parallelism. *Convergence* results in similar structures in two living species that are only remotely related, whereas *parallelism* produces the same effects in animals that more recently diverged from their common ancestor. For example, some of the similarities in form and behavior between the New World and Old World monkeys may be described as parallelisms, whereas the nocturnal adaptations observed in many prosimians and in the nocturnal South American monkey, the *Aotus,* may be described as convergences (see Chapter 6).

homologous: similar because of common descent or common inheritance.

homoplasy: similarity of two characters because of parallel evolution (adaptation to similar environments) without a common ancestor.

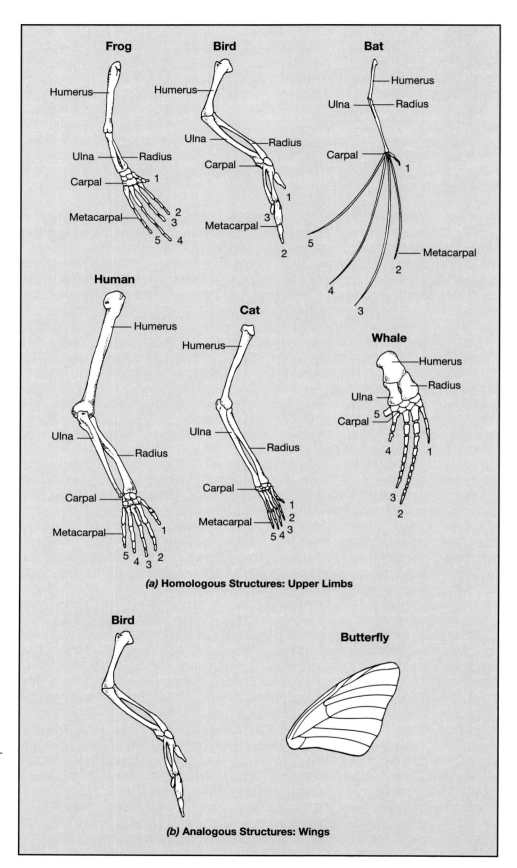

(a) Homologous Structures: Upper Limbs

(b) Analogous Structures: Wings

FIGURE 5–3 (*a*) Homologous forelimb structures of several diverse vertebrates. Although the limbs may function as arms, front legs, flippers, or wings, their structural similarities are clear. (*b*) Analogous bird's wing and butterfly forewing. These structures share a common function (flight), but their structural and evolutionary differences are clear.

Finally, features that have different structure, phyletic origin, and embryological origin may have similar functions, in which case the term **analogy** is used. Structures such as butterfly wings and bird wings, which serve the same function as organs of flight, are clearly analogous, not homologous, by this definition (Figure 5–3b). Among the primates, the prehensile tail possessed by many New World monkeys, and the grasping hands of humans and apes, are neither derived from common ancestral characters nor are they embryologically related. They are analogous, however, as organs that serve to manipulate objects in their environments.

Morphology, Embryology, and Paleontology

As we saw in the preceding chapters, individual cells of all eukaryotic organisms function and reproduce in the same way; that is, all eukaryotic organisms are alike on a cellular level. In more complex organisms, with more complex structural organization, different types of cells come together to form structures with specialized functions. For example, anatomical structures, such as limbs or eyes, are formed by the proliferation of cells that have become specialized by evolution to perform certain functions in the body.

When cells of similar type proliferate, they form **tissues,** groupings of cells of the same type, such as bone or muscle, that we can see with the naked eye. The morphology of tissues provides one of the most important, and traditionally the only, basis for taxonomic classification and evolutionary study of animal species. Although it is difficult to reconstruct exactly what an animal looked like while it was alive from its bony remains, a great deal can be determined by comparing bones of unknown origin to bones that are known to belong to specific animals.

Through such comparisons, morphological patterns can be deduced by studying the origin and insertion (the attachment areas) of muscles and the shape of the bone itself, which may reflect the way a particular animal moved. Long gracile (slender) limb bones, for example, in primates reflect a fast, leaping arboreal form of locomotion. In modern classification, genetics and behavioral characteristics can also be used. Fossils provide paleontological evidence of change through time. Fossils allow us to reconstruct the evolutionary history of animals by studying and interpreting the changes in homologous structures.

Another approach to this study is based on what the German naturalist Ernst Haeckel (1834–1919) first articulated as the "law" that *ontogeny recapitulates phylogeny,* or that growth and development mirror evolutionary history. Generally speaking, developmental stages of the embryo are similar to major evolutionary steps through which a species passed. For example, during an early phase in embryological development, dogs, pigs, and humans all resemble fish in form and shape. They have slits in the head homologous to the gill slits of a fish. These structures then develop into other, different structures in the mature fetus. This clear developmental sequence of homologous structures, and the fact that it is shared by dogs, pigs, and humans, are strong testimony to the ancient fish ancestry of all three species.

However, Haeckel's law is only a suggestion of common evolutionary descent. In living animals, selection may alter and even eliminate certain developmental stages, so that the developing embryo may not replicate exactly the evolutionary stages of its species' ancestors. It may, however, provide important clues to those stages. This embryological view into the past is possible because new species evolving from more primitive forms start out with the adaptations evolved in their ancestors, which form the bases for novel adaptations. Thus, we can use embryology, in conjunction with morphology and paleontology, to piece together the major stages of evolution.

analogy: two characters are similar because of adaptation for similar functions.

tissue: literally meaning "woven"; in anatomy referring to an aggregate of cells of the same type, which form a structural unit of the body.

Although biological anthropology focuses on primates generally, and hominids specifically, there is little in the paleontological record to support an *anthropocentric* (Greek, meaning "human-centered") view of evolution. Many animal groups now extinct, such as the dinosaurs, were larger, fleeter, more numerous, and ecologically dominant for much longer periods of time than people have been in existence. More often than not, early hominids were far from the dominant animals in the ecosystems of which they formed a part. The mistaken view that evolution has been a steady progression leading to our own species is termed **orthogenesis** (Greek, meaning "straight beginning"). On the contrary, a long and frequently tortuous chain of evolutionary events led to our being here now.

THE CHORDATES

To understand our own anatomy, we must understand the anatomy of our earliest vertebrate ancestors. The first actively moving organisms—the first animals—appeared in the earth's seas sometime more than 700 million years ago. Because these animals' bodies were soft, their remains were easily destroyed before they could become fossilized. The indications of animal life from this time consist of burrow trails left in the mud of shallow sea floors. Among the animals that made these tracks were the common ancestors of all other living and extinct animals. The first **chordates** must have evolved in the late Precambrian era, about 580 million years ago, but the fossil record of this ancient time is of little help in deciphering chordate beginnings.

Chordates are animals that share the characteristic of a stiffened rod of cartilage, the *notochord* (Greek, meaning "back string") running down the middle of their backs. They also have nearby a *dorsal nerve cord* and a series of *branchial arches*. (In fish, the homologous structures are the gill arches, or the walls of tissue that separate gill clefts or slits.) These characteristics are not necessarily found in adult chordates, but they do appear at some stage of an individual's development. We are chordates, and our most basic patterns of morphological organization have come down to us from our ancient chordate ancestors.

During the late Precambrian era, the dominant animal groups were nonchordates that evolved the first skeletal elements, which were body coverings with a protective function, probably for defense against attack by predators or parasites. Hard parts external to the body cavity, known as the **exoskeleton** (Latin, meaning "outside bony framework"), served as an anchor for muscles as well. Although an exoskeleton is an efficient adaptation for powerful movement, as we can observe today in such living arthropods as insects and crabs, it limits the size of a species. As the animal grows it must "molt," or split out of its old exoskeleton and grow another one. If an arthropod is larger than a lobster or a large crab, its body cannot retain its integrity during the molting period when there is no support for internal structures.

Other groups of animals, including the ancestors of chordates, did not evolve hard outer coverings. Instead, these prechordates were dome-shaped, soft-bodied animals attached to rocks at the bottom of shallow seas (Figure 5–4). They fed on micro-organisms, which they filtered out of the water. Embryological and life-cycle studies of the living sea squirt, which in many ways is similar to these early prechordates, have suggested how our phylum arose.

Although the adult sea squirt is an immobile species that stays attached to the shallow seabed, its immature, or *larval*, form is an active swimmer. In the swimming stage, the sea squirt has clearly defined head and tail regions, and the tail has a notochord running through it, like chordates and unlike the adult sea squirt. A nerve cord on the dorsal (back) side of the notochord transmits impulses that activate

orthogenesis: mistaken view of evolutionary change always proceeding in a "straight-line," directed course.

chordates: animals with a notochord and a dorsal nerve cord.

exoskeleton: hard and inflexible outer covering of the body of invertebrate animals, such as insects and crustaceans.

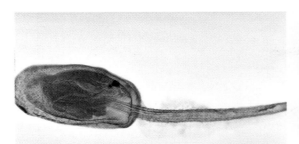

FIGURE 5-4 The adult sea squirt (right) is a sedentary animal that lives attached to the sea floor. In its larval stage (left), however, it is free swimming and possesses the defining traits of all chordates. Evolutionary differentiation of the chordates most likely took place when free-moving larval forms became able to reproduce.

muscles. All these traits seen in the larva of the sea squirt are found in adult chordates.

As natural selection began to favor animals that could move about in their environments and search for food, rather than having to rely on chance encounters and the ocean's currents to bring food to them, a whole new group of animals appeared. The larval free swimmers developed their own ability to reproduce. This process, called *pedogenesis,* refers to the retention in adult animals of some characteristics of their immature stages, in this case, the ability to swim freely. As mobility was achieved in some lineages, the adult immobile (sessile) stage was eliminated from the life cycle of these ancestors of later vertebrate species.

As chordates, we share at some phase of our development all of the following characteristics with other members of the phylum:

- a solid notochord
- a dorsal nerve cord
- one or more pairs of branchial arches (Figure 5–5)

We share other characteristics with other chordates and with some nonchordates: *bilateral symmetry* (similar right and left sides of the body); *cephalization* (development of a specialized head region); a tail at some stage of development; a true *endoskeleton* (a bony or cartilaginous framework overlaid by muscle); *segmentation of the body* (similar structural units throughout part or all of the body); and a three-layered structure of *ectoderm, mesoderm,* and *endoderm* (Latin, meaning "outside," "middle," and "inside skin") during development.

Humans have now lost the solid notochord, but its remnants persist as the semi-liquid *nucleus pulposus* (Latin, meaning "pulpy center") of the intervertebral discs of our backbones. When we have a "slipped disc," it is this evolutionarily ancient structure that oozes out to press against a spinal nerve and cause pain. The early chordate dorsal nerve cord, greatly enlarged and specialized, has become our spinal cord.

Branchial arches, homologous to gill slits in fish, are present in the developing human embryo, but they become substantially modified in the mature condition (see Figure 5–5). For example, the auditory ("eustachian") tube (running between the throat and the middle ear) and the ear canal (running between the middle ear and the outside of the head) form the remnants of the cleft between our first and second pharyngeal arches, the tissue divisions between the clefts. That is why we "pop our ears" when undergoing changes in altitude and hear through a canal originally evolved by our ancient ancestors to filter micro-organisms out of seawater.

We retain the bilateral symmetry that separates us from the *radially symmetrical* (able to be cut up into equal-size parts from a central point fanning outward)

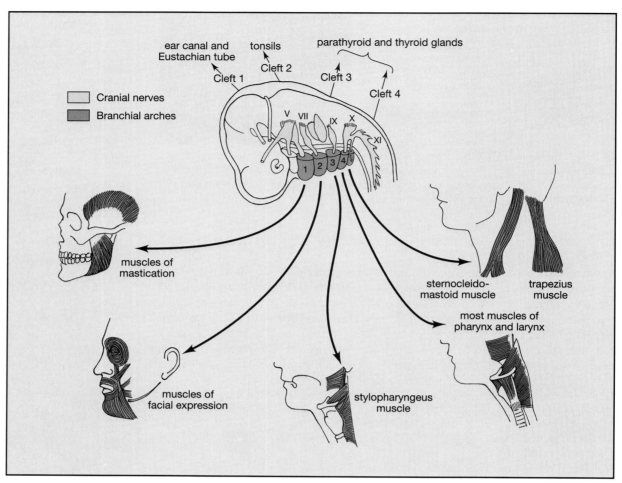

FIGURE 5–5 The pharyngeal arches of the human embryo, and the structures that develop from them. Branchial arches are a defining feature of all chordates.

starfish group (the coelenterates) and the differentiation of head region and the internal skeleton of our early chordate ancestors. Much of body segmentation has been lost, but our vertebrae, ribs, sensory nerve distribution, and patterns of certain muscles, such as the rectus abdominis, show this heritage. Furthermore, we have a tail until the eighth week of embryonic development.

THE FIRST VERTEBRATES: OUR FISH HERITAGE

When environmental conditions change so significantly that major ecological niches open up, species rapidly evolve to fill those niches. "Fanning out" of species in *adaptive radiations,* resulting in the occupation of new niches and the formation of new species (see Chapter 1), has occurred numerous times throughout the history of life. These radiations seem to follow periods of significant environmental change and large-scale extinctions. Adaptive radiations may also be related to new adaptations that appear in a species.

At the beginning of the Paleozoic era, during the so-called Age of Fish (some 545 million to 245 million years ago), there was a major adaptive radiation of animals. This explosion of new forms may have been the result of increasingly high levels of oxygen in the environment. Gill-feeding, gill-breathing, free-swimming chordates that appear in the fossil record earlier were the ancestors of these vertebrates.

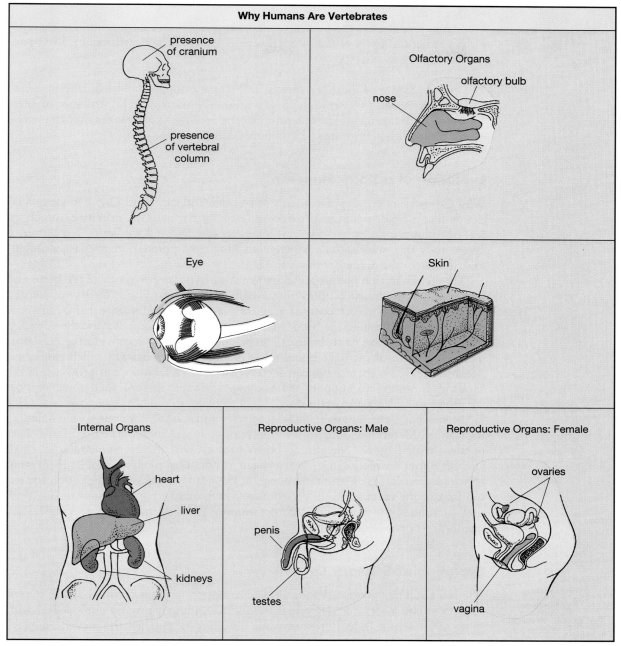

FIGURE 5–6 Traits shared by all vertebrates, and their appearance in humans.

The first **vertebrates** (animals that have "vertebrae" or backbone segments) in the fossil record are small, primitive, jawless fish. Collectively often referred to as the *ostracoderms* (bony skins), they had a large muscular pharynx (throat) that allowed them to rapidly suck up and process large quantities of food-laden water. These animals were vertebrates, chordate animals that share the following characteristics (Smith, 1960; Figure 5–6):

- a bony vertebral column
- a cranium (skull)
- a brain of three primary parts, or vesicles
- olfactory organs, for sense of smell

vertebrates: animals with backbones and segmented body plans.

- true eyes
- a true skin, consisting of dermis and epidermis
- the structural basis of the internal organs (such as the heart, kidney, liver, pancreas, ear, and pharynx)

The co-occurrence of these features is found first among small ostracoderm fish of the Silurian Period (440 million to 410 million years ago). The structure of these earliest vertebrates forms the blueprint for the evolutionary changes that characterize the many different groups of backboned animals.

Evolution of a Bony Skeleton

Why did ostracoderms evolve skeletons of bone and **cartilage?** One likely explanation is that a rigid backbone provided a frame firmer than the primitive notochord for swimming movements. Skeletal support also allowed the animal to attain a larger body size, which was advantageous in avoiding predation: the larger an animal, the fewer the predators that can eat it.

The bones in our bodies are classified into two categories: **cartilage bone** and **membrane bone**, based on how they *ossify,* or turn into bone. We have inherited both types from our ostracoderm ancestors. Vertebrae and most other *postcranial* (Latin, meaning "behind the head") bones are cartilage bones, because they develop from a cartilage base, with bone cells replacing the cartilage cells during bone formation. Growth of cartilage bones takes place at lines of growth called *epiphyses.* Because the bones themselves can increase in size, vertebrates can grow while the skeleton continues to support the body—vertebrates do not shed their support structure, as lobsters and crabs do.

Membrane bone, however, lacks epiphyses and instead develops within a netlike membrane. Membrane bone forms with bone cells replacing the cells within a sheet of mesodermal tissue. Membrane bones first evolved in the ostracoderms, small animals about six inches in length, as head armor, most likely to protect them from attacks by predators. Membrane bones in the head provide the foundation for the top part of the cranium in all vertebrates. The bones forming the part of our skull that surrounds the brain, the **neurocranium** (Latin, meaning "brain skull"), are membrane bones (see Chapter 2).

Evolution of Sensory Organs

cartilage: supporting tissue more elastic and flexible than bone (e.g., the "gristle" in meat).

cartilage bone: bone formed by development from cartilage and growth at epiphyses, characteristic of vertebrate limb bones.

membrane bone: bone formed by development from a connective tissue membrane, characteristic of vertebrate skull bones.

neurocranium: that part of the skull holding the brain.

placoderms: early fish with biting jaws.

The ostracoderms possessed an improved sensory apparatus compared with that of their chordate ancestors. They had brains that, though tiny by comparison with those of modern fish, had three separate divisions (or *vesicles,* the prosen-, mesen-, and rhombencephalon) that developed embryonically into a structure that is common to all of the more complex vertebrate brains. They had true eyes that were not only sensitive to light but also able to discern form and movement. They also had a sense of smell. Their increased efficiency in sensing environmental stimuli and processing this information probably helped them obtain food and avoid predators.

Evolution of Biting Jaws

Fish with biting jaws, called **placoderms** (Latin, meaning "plate-skinned"), first appeared in the Devonian period (about 410 million to 360 million years ago). How and why did their jaws evolve? Using an embryological model, both the upper and lower jaws of placoderms were derived from the first two branchial arches, the ancestral strucures originally used to filter food from sea water.

The evolution of biting jaws and sharp teeth indicates that placoderms had become predatory, feeding on other fish and invertebrates. Predation allows a species to take advantage of "prepackaged" food of higher quality (other animals) but in smaller quantities, rather than eating widely scattered, lower quality but usually more abundant food (such as plant food) in larger quantities. It also creates changes in body shape. For example, to prevent placoderms from rotating in the water, pairs of laterally placed fins evolved from flaps of skin and muscle from the body wall. Two pairs of fins, one in front and one behind, represent the structural change, or *preadaptation,* that later fish were to employ to conquer the land. These fins evolved into limbs.

Evolution of Limbs and Lungs

During the Devonian period, the first modern fish evolved. They are called the lobe-finned fish, the **sarcopterygians** (Greek, meaning "fleshy appendage"). They had thick and fleshy lateral fins, which were an effective and important part of their adaptation to a fresh-water environment. According to one hypothesis (Romer, 1971), some lived in ponds and streams subjected to periodic drought, a situation common in semiarid parts of the tropics today (Figure 5–7). Their stout fins, composed of heavy bone, allowed them to support their bodies on land and to slither from a drying pond to one with more water. Some modern fish, such as the "walking" catfish of Florida, have this ability.

As part of the adaptation to periodic drought, lobe-finned fish evolved an *air bladder,* an outpocketing of the pharynx into which air was gulped. The air bladder

sarcopterygians: lobe-finned fish capable of some support of the body on land.

FIGURE 5–7 Reconstruction of the late Devonian environment in Pennsylvania showing a recently discovered tetrapod (*Hynerpeton*). Many researchers believe that limbs that could be used on land evolved in swamplike environments as a means of escaping large predatory fish.

extracted oxygen from the air and allowed the fish to make the overland trek necessary for it to reach its normal environment—water. With relatively little modification in basic plan, the lobe-fin air bladder became the air-breathing lung of the land vertebrates. The anatomy of these fish forms the basic plan on which all later land *tetrapod* (four-limbed) vertebrate limbs evolved.

AMPHIBIANS AND REPTILES

First Forays onto Dry Land: The Amphibians

The vertebrate class called **Amphibia** (Greek, meaning "dual life") comprises animals that are essentially land-living fish, inexorably tied to water because of their mode of reproduction. Most amphibians lay eggs in water, and their larvae are swimming, gill-breathing forms that die if exposed to air. Most modern-day amphibians, such as frogs and salamanders, carry on this type of reproduction. Only in the adult stage does the animal develop stout limbs that are capable of supporting it on land.

The best known of these early amphibians are the **labyrinthodonts** (Latin, meaning "labyrinthine [very complex] tooth"), animals superficially similar to crocodiles but much more primitive. The limbs of the labyrinthodonts show the greatest departure from the structure of their fish ancestors. The *proximal* elements (bones nearer the body) of both front and back limbs are single (the humerus and femur, respectively), and the distal elements (bones farther from the body) are paired (the radius and ulna, and tibia and fibula, respectively; see Figure 5–8 and Appendix 1). There are small block-shaped bones making up the hand and foot skeletons, and five digits on each. We share this primitive skeletal arrangement and associated musculature with the labyrinthodonts and with all other land vertebrates.

What fossil evidence do we have of these early tetrapods? In 1992 on Valentia Island off the isolated southwest coast of Ireland, fossilized footprints of such an animal were discovered. Until that time our knowledge of Devonian tetrapods was scant: Only one nearly complete early species, *Ichthyostega*, had ever been found; it was discovered in Greenland in 1929. The Valentia footprints as yet have no fossil remains associated with them; however, measurements of the distance between prints suggest that the animal was more than 1 meter (3 feet) long. Curiously, if this was a land animal, the fossil trail shows no indication of a tail being dragged behind. The conclusion is that the animal was not walking on land but in shallow water, its tail floating behind.

Evidence that limbs evolved while tetrapods were still aquatic has also come from other fossils found in Greenland in 1987. Among these fossils, now called *Acanthostega* (about 360 million years old), is one of the most complete tetrapod specimens known (Figure 5–9, p. 114). Dr. Jenny Clark at the Cambridge University Museum of Zoology reconstructed the fossil she calls Boris, which gives us the first good look at these animals. According to Clark, *Acanthostega* also did not walk on land, because its wrists and ankles were too weak to support the weight of its body, and its ribs were too small for the attachment of muscles needed to hold the body up above the ground. Like other labyrinthodonts, it also possessed lungs as well as gills (Westenberg, 1999:122).

Only one Devonian fossil, *Hynerpeton*, discovered in 1993 at a site called Red Hill in Pennsylvania, shows any signs of living on land (see Figure 5–7). From the fossil remains of its shoulder, the muscles that would have attached from there to the limbs are robust enough to support its body weight on land. At 365 million years old, *Hynerpeton* is the third-oldest tetrapod thus far known.

As the fossil record improves it shows that the transition between fish and land vertebrates took place within a series of radiations that began in aquatic environments

Amphibia: vertebrate class that includes frogs, salamanders, and extinct species living much of their lives on land but whose reproduction remains tied to water.

labyrinthodonts: extinct, predatory amphibians of the Carboniferous period, some of whom were ancestral to the first reptiles.

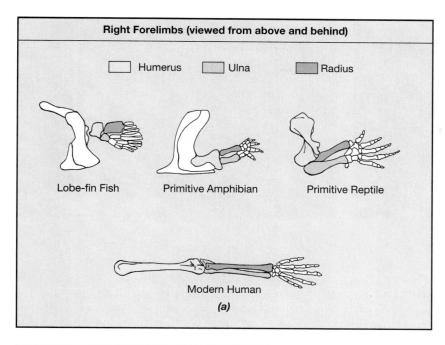

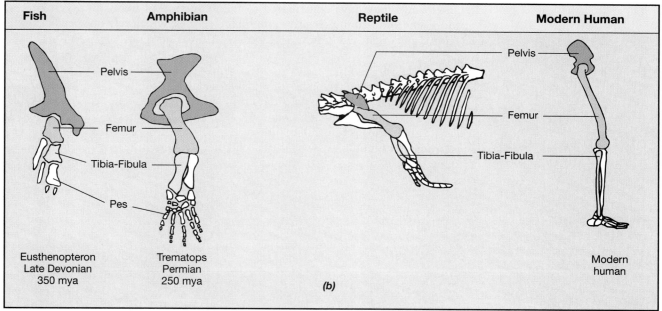

FIGURE 5-8 Homologous structures in limbs of fish, amphibians, reptiles, and humans.
(*a*) Comparison of forelimb bones to show homologues from lobe-fin fish to humans.
(*b*) Comparison of hindlimb bones to show homologues from early fish to modern humans.

and ended in fully terrestrial ones. Anatomical changes in this group of vertebrates are the result of a progressive adaptation to increasingly shallower water. The increase in the number of different species of large amphibians was brought to a dramatic close by the end of the Permian period (290 million to 245 million years ago). This final period of the Paleozoic brought with it the worst of the mass extinctions ever recorded; fully 95 percent of all species that lived both on land and in the water were wiped out.

During the Permian, earth's landmasses formed a single supercontinent called Pangaea, which was surrounded by an ocean that covered the rest of the planet

FIGURE 5–9 *Acanthostega* (top), a tetrapod originally found in Greenland in 1987, as reconstructed by Dr. Jenny Clark (right, in blue) of Cambridge University and her assistant, Sarah Finney.

(Figure 5–10). This configuration of land and water, researchers believe, created vast pockets of deep stagnant water whose oxygen content became increasingly diminished and was replaced by carbon dioxide. This massive buildup of carbon dioxide poisoned most of the passive breathing species, such as corals, causing their extinction. Although carbon dioxide poisoning decimated life in the oceans, rapid climatic swings may have contributed to the extinction of many land vertebrates. The more environmentally sensitive amphibian species, which rely on specific conditions both on land and in the water for their survival and reproduction, suffered the worst.

None of the fossils of these vertebrates have been found from the succeeding 20 million years, during which time all of the main groups of later land forms appeared. Permian extinctions, no doubt, opened up many niches that other, more adaptable life forms would later come to occupy. By the Triassic period, only small species related to frogs and salamanders survived. Coincident with the disappearance of the early amphibians was the ascendancy of the reptiles, a group much better adapted to full terrestrial life (Figure 5–11).

FIGURE 5–10 Pangaea, the supercontinent that formed 225 million years ago, during the Permian period. About 150 million years ago, Pangaea began to split into two continents, Laurasia and Gondwanaland. The outlines of most of the present-day continents can be seen in these two giant landmasses.

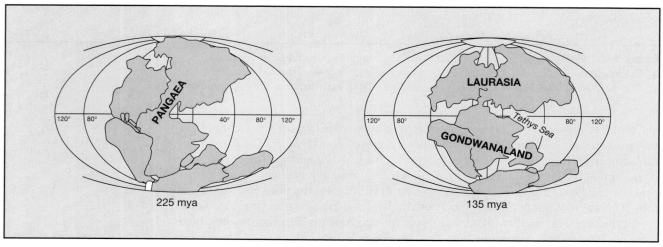

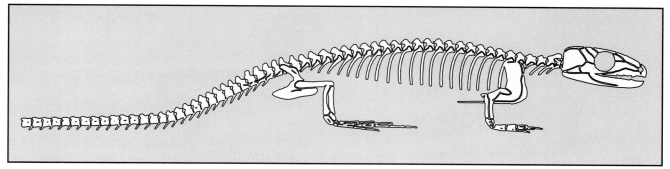

FIGURE 5-11 Skeleton of the earliest known reptile, *Hylonomus,* which lived approximately 300 million years ago in Nova Scotia. *Hylonomus* was a small, slender, and agile creature.

Reptiles Conquer the Land

As we have seen, the major problem that limited the spread of amphibians was their manner of reproduction. Amphibian eggs must be laid in water, and the larvae that result are tied to their aqueous environment. As greater numbers of living species diversified and grew in number, more and more species preyed on defenseless eggs and larvae.

These problems were solved for reptiles with the evolution of the **amniote egg**, which could be laid and hatched on land. This adaptation required internal fertilization and the development of behaviors that encouraged mating of this kind. Reptile offspring had a much higher chance of survival than amphibian offspring, because they were better protected from predators and were, therefore, favored by natural selection. Although the earliest reptiles still lived close to water and preyed on water-living species, the land-laid egg led to the adaptive radiation of land vertebrates.

The amniote egg takes its name from an inside membrane, the *amnion,* which surrounds and protects the developing embryo (Figure 5–12). In amphibians, the developing embryo receives oxygen and food, and releases wastes, through the egg

amniote egg: an egg characteristic of the reptiles that could be laid and developed out of water.

 **FRONTIERS**

How Did Limbs Evolve? Alternative Views

There are alternative viewpoints that contend that the evolution of limbs did not arise as a response of ancient freshwater fish to episodic drought conditions. Hans Bjerring of the Swedish Museum of Natural History believes that *Ichthyostega,* along with the other Devonian tetrapods, evolved in water-plant clogged swamps in which swimming would have been exceedingly difficult. Having limbs rather than fins would have made it easier to survive in these conditions (Westenberg, 1999). Grasping vegetation to hold your position in streams, feeling your way through murky waters, digging in the mud for prey, and crawling into vegetation masses to avoid predators are all good reasons for limbs to have evolved to cope with the stresses of an aquatic environment. Contrary to the earlier views, Bjerring doubts that *Ichthyostega* ever walked on dry land. The footprints found in Valentia Island, Ireland, add support to his views (Westenberg, 1999:119).

If limbs evolved as an adaptation for aquatic living, how is the evolution of lungs part of this picture? One explanation suggests that lungs were used by these swamp dwellers for breathing air when plant decay used up water's dissolved oxygen. And if periodic drought was not the whole explanation for the first forays onto dry land, what other situations might have promoted terrestrial locomotion? One popular explanation suggests that early tetrapods invaded land in order to escape aquatic predators and, at the same time, avoid competition with other life forms for space, food, and breeding sites in these humid swampy habitats.

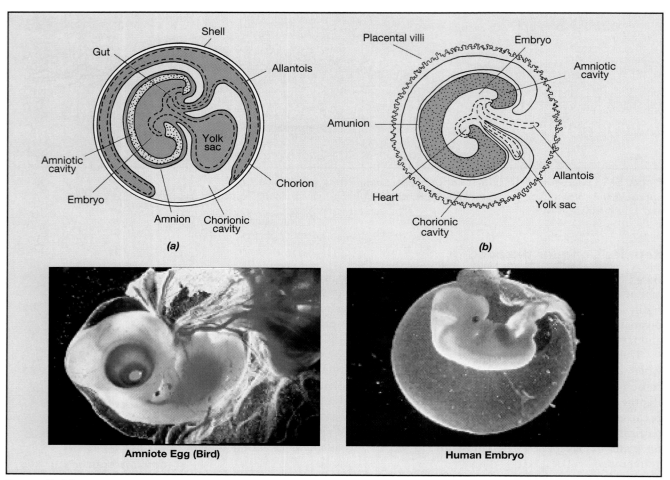

FIGURE 5–12 (*a*) Top: Amniotic egg structure, inherited from reptiles by both birds and mammals; bottom: photo of bird embryo. (*b*) Top: Human embryo, with parts homologous to the amniote egg labeled; bottom: photo of human embryo.

wall, in direct connection with the surrounding water. The water also protects the embryo from mechanical injury. Because reptilian eggs are laid outside water, four additional structures have evolved to carry out these functions: (1) the *shell* provides the interface between the dry air and the wet ancestral amphibian environment, as well as protecting the egg from breakage; (2) the *chorion*, a membrane just inside the shell, takes in oxygen and gives off carbon dioxide through the shell; (3) the *allantois* forms a sac into which body wastes are deposited; and (4) the *yolk sac* provides nourishment to the embryo.

Adaptive Radiation of Reptiles

From the earliest reptiles evolved the wide diversity of more advanced reptiles that characterized the Mesozoic Era (245 million to 265 million years ago), referred to as the "Age of Reptiles": sharklike ichthyosaurs, lizards and snakes, marine plesiosaurs, mammal-like reptiles, dinosaurs, and eventually birds (Figure 5–13). As the giant Pangaean landmass began to break apart about 150 million years ago (refer back to Figure 5–10), the largest land vertebrates ever to roam the planet surface emerged. Among the immense herbivores that walked quadrupedally, one individual found in

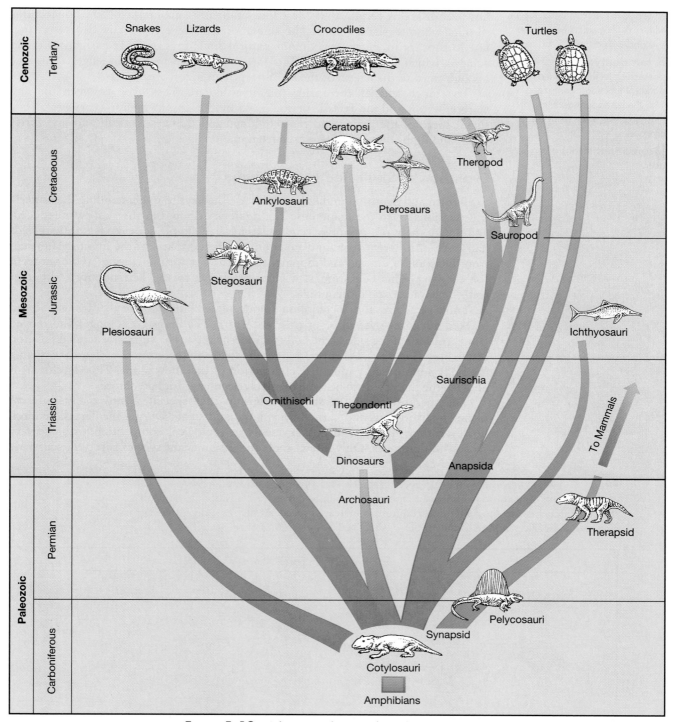

FIGURE 5–13 Adaptive radiation of reptiles during the Paleozoic and Cenozoic.

western Colorado called *Supersaurus* is probably the longest. Recently reconstructed by Brian Curtice of the State University of New York at Stony Brook, this fossil had an overall length of 134 feet.

Among the bipedal carnivores, a number of similar fossils found in North America, South America, and Africa are record holders. Finding three closely related dinosaurs living on three different continents is surprising to paleontologists;

therapsid: mammal-like reptile with a skull opening behind the eye and with differentiated teeth.

heterodonty: the condition of possessing teeth differentiated for different functions; contrasted with the homodont dentition of many reptiles, such as living crocodiles.

locomotion: means of moving about.

however, it seems certain that Mesozoic landmasses maintained some connections through various island chains. The similar size of these reptiles is also surprising, but it appears to be the maximum natural limit in size these carnivores could achieve, which was only about 40 to 45 feet (13 to 15 meters) in length. This was about a third of the length of the largest reptilian herbivores.

The much smaller **therapsids** (mammal-like reptiles) lived between the late Carboniferous and the Triassic periods (245 million to 215 million years ago). They signal some of the major and most fundamental changes in skull and jaw form, teeth, and limbs that separate reptile from mammal.

Evolution of Skull, Teeth, and Limbs

Skull form and dentition in the therapsids are the keys to understanding their ancestral relationship to the mammals. The number of bones in the skull was reduced, and unlike the more primitive reptiles, which had simple conelike teeth, therapsids had teeth of different form and function in different parts of the mouth. They had front incisors for cutting and nipping, single canines for puncturing, and back teeth for chewing. This condition is a clear precursor to the **heterodonty** ("different teeth") characteristic of mammals.

Limb structure and **locomotion** (mode of walking) in the therapsids showed marked advances over those of their ancestors. The limbs grew longer and moved from positions at the side of the body to underneath it. The vertically aligned skeleton of the limb (Figure 5–14) supported the body above the ground, rather than having the body supported by muscular contraction of the limbs alone. This development allowed the therapsids to become relatively fleet terrestrial predators.

The therapsids were a successful group that speciated into many different niches—herbivorous and carnivorous, large and small. During the Triassic period, however, they largely died out, probably in ecological competition with the very successful dinosaurs. Only a few small and insignificant species survived, scurrying

FIGURE 5–14 Compared with quadrupedal reptiles, early mammals showed more efficient adaptations for locomotion. In mammals, the limbs moved to a position underneath the body and closer to the center line, resulting in increased speed. At the same time, the side-to-side bending motion of the reptile was reduced.

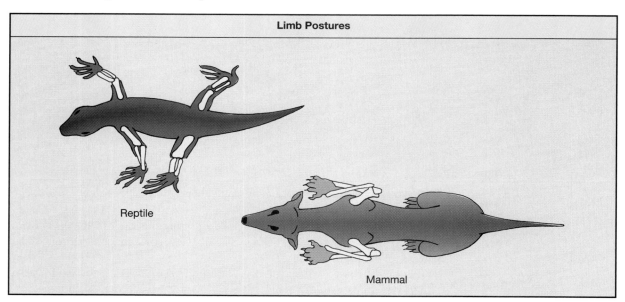

about in the shadows of their ponderous contemporaries. These evolved into the first mammals.

Late Cretaceous Extinctions

The dinosaurs of the Mesozoic were remarkably successful animals that survived for more than 150 million years. Over a relatively short period of time, however, at the end of the Cretaceous period, all of the large dinosaurs, along with many other animal species, became extinct. It is difficult to explain such a massive extinction. Assuming that the dinosaurs were ectothermic (cold-blooded) like modern reptiles, their large size certainly would have put them at a distinct disadvantage to cope with the variable climate that ushered in the succeeding Age of Mammals. They would have found it difficult to lose heat in the hot summers or retain it during the cold winters. In contrast, endothermic (warm-blooded) mammals would have encountered little difficulty in adapting to the fluctuating temperatures of the more seasonal Cenozoic period. This reasoning, however, was jolted by the discovery of a fossilized heart found inside the ribcage of a nearly complete skeleton of a small, plant-eating dinosaur called *Thescelosaurus*. The discovery, made in 1993 in South Dakota's Hell's Creek Formation, was unique in several respects. First, it was the only example of a dinosaur heart ever found. Second, the heart had four chambers, like those of birds and mammals, rather than three chambers, like most reptiles. This suggests that this dinosaur had an exceptionally high metabolic rate. This find, however, is not without its detractors. CT scans of the fossil reveal some, but not all, of the expected blood vessels, such as the carotid arteries, and the missing pieces leave the heart's anatomy and physiology open to debate. Meanwhile, the team of researchers studying the heart plan are using CT scans to address the questions. The dinosaur heart may be viewed at www.dinoheart.org (Fisher et al., 2000).

Overall, about 50 percent of all genera that lived before the end of the Cretaceous period became extinct, and marine organisms fared worse than did the terrestrial species, with the exception of the dinosaurs. But what caused this climatic catastrophe? The reasons range from the geologic (intensive volcanic activity), to the biologic (epidemics of new diseases), to the extraterrestrial (dust clouds caused by a colliding asteroid). Whatever the ultimate cause, those terrestrial species that did survive must have possessed adaptations that gave them some advantage over the others. Small size and possibly endothermy may well have proven beneficial to some species. That, with a bit of luck, enabled the explosive Cenozoic radiation of the mammals.

MAMMALS EVOLVE AND RADIATE

The evolution of Mesozoic mammals is obscure, and researchers are not certain when the living branches split from their common ancestors. Part of the problem lies in the fact that most fossils of early mammals older than 65 million years are represented by little more than isolated teeth and fragmented bones. This lack of more complete fossils was overcome, however, in 1998 when Ji Qiang, a paleontologist from the National Geological Museum of China, discovered a fully articulated fossil of an early mammal that he named *Jeholodens jenkinsi* (Zimmer, 1999). Discovered in deposits of the Liaoning Formation located about 250 miles northeast of Beijing, this fossil represents the oldest, most complete early mammal thus far known, and it came with a number of surprises. The reconstructed animal, belonging to a group called the *triconodonts,* was most surprising in its postcranial

The Interaction of Climate, Environment, and Evolution

LLOYD H. BURCKLE

Many new areas of research have shown that there is a general correspondence between times of major climate change and episodes of evolutionary change. Why should this be so? One idea is that during periods of worldwide cooler temperatures ("global cooling"), the animal and plant species in the far north and far south, those most affected by colder temperatures, suffered some extinction and tended to move toward the equator. Ecological pressure would then have been placed on the species already resident near the equator as the immigrant species competed for food and space. A great deal of extinction of the resident low-latitude species would have resulted. When conditions became warmer, species were free to repopulate the higher latitudes again, and evolution acted to increase the diversity of species. In this scenario most of the newly evolved species in the world would have derived ultimately from higher-latitude populations.

Even if this scenario is accurate, and it is not by any means the only explanation for evolutionary change, many other factors may complicate the story. For example, there have been periods, unlike the present, during which climatic cooling was not the same at both the North Pole and the South Pole. If, because of continental drift, a continent was centered at one pole, and the open ocean was centered at the other, the pole without the insulating effect of water would suffer greater temperature change, and hypothetically would witness the greater effect on its animal and plant communities. Further changes can occur on land as ice builds up during periods of cold. These episodes are known as *glaciations*. The massive buildup of ice on land takes up so much of the earth's water that sea level is lowered worldwide. Islands can become connected with mainland areas, and

previously open land connections can become blocked by ice formation. These changes in land routes can have important effects on the dispersal of species and their subsequent evolution.

What causes the changes in the earth's climate that we see? Major changes are dictated by astronomical cycles related to the earth's relationship to the sun. These cycles lead to periodic and predictable changes in global climate. The severity and mosaic pattern of that climate change, however, is dictated by other factors as well. Surface and near-surface earth movements, known as *tectonism*, are one of the most important factors. Tectonic effects include mountain building, continental drift, and long-term vertical uplift or subsidence. Only recently have geologists and climatologists come to appreciate the role that tectonism plays in climate and climate change (and, by extension, its effect on evolution).

Another important factor affecting climate is *weathering*, or the physical and chemical wearing away of the rock of the earth's surface. Increased rates of weathering, caused by higher continental elevations (in turn related, of course, to tectonic activity), cause greater amounts of calcium carbonate from chemical weathering of rocks to be deposited into the world's oceans. This, in turn, reduces the amount of carbon dioxide in the atmosphere, and in a reverse greenhouse effect, reduces global temperature. The relationship among mountain and plateau uplift, increased chemical weathering, and global climate cooling seems to hold both for the recent periods of earth history during the Tertiary period and for much of geological history.

The Tertiary period is particularly important for primate and hominid evolution and provides a good illustration of the interaction of tectonic change, regional climate, and evolution. Within the past 50 million years, Antarctica separated from South America and Australia, while the north polar regions became landlocked. India collided with Asia some 40 million to 50 million

years ago, and this initiated the rise of the Himalayas. In addition to the formation of this large mountain barrier, the uplift of the Tibetan plateau began. The American West also witnessed uplift during this time, the most significant of which became the Colorado plateau. Finally, regions such as eastern and southern Africa underwent broad vertical uplift, which caused fracturing and rifting at the earth's surface.

The climatic effects of these tectonic changes included the thermal isolation of the south polar region and the initiation of major glaciation in Antarctica about 54 million years ago. This ice sheet increased 34 million years ago, leading to a global drop in sea level. The rise of the Himalayas not only caused increased weathering and reduction of atmospheric carbon dioxide, thus reducing global temperature, but also their height redirected wind patterns in the entire Indian Ocean area, creating a seasonal, or "monsoonal," rain pattern in Africa and southern Asia. Uplift of the Colorado and Tibetan plateaus, aside from influencing local climate, diverted high-level jet stream and low-level winds to the north, causing further cooling, particularly in the northern hemisphere. Two more recent global cooling events are recorded at 14 million years ago, when the Antarctic ice sheet greatly enlarged, and at 7 million years ago, when the Greenland ice sheet was initiated. Many interrelated changes in environment accompanied these broad changes in climate. The subtropical and temperate belts, for example, had been of broad extent some 50 million years ago, but they have moved progressively closer to the equator through the Tertiary and have created a series of new climatic zones in their wake. The interplay among climate, tectonics, and evolution is an active field of research, and we can expect to see much progress as research proceeds.

Lloyd H. Burckle is senior research scientist at Lamont Doherty Earth Observatory, Columbia University, New York.

anatomy (Figure 5–15). Rat-sized, it walked on what resembled mammalian front limbs with the elbows pointing backward and splayed reptilian hind limbs with the knees pointing to the sides. If *Jeholodens* is in fact closely related to the common ancestral group that gave rise to all mammals, then the evolution of the mammalian limb presents us with a problem. If the flexible forelimb is a characteristic of common ancestry, then it must have been secondarily lost in the *monotremes* (egg-laying mammals), whose limb structure is characterized by a more reptilian stance, and who diverged from the stem mammalian lineage earliest in the evolution of this group. The later diverging *therians* (the placental mammals) and the *marsupials* (such as the kangaroos) retained the flexible forelimb and then evolved flexible hindlimbs to match (Zimmer, 1999).

FIGURE 5-15 A reconstruction of *Jeholodens jenkinsi*, which lived 120 million years ago. *Jeholodens* is believed to be the ancestor of all modern mammals.

Major Adaptations of Mammals

We live today in a world replete with many varieties of animals of the class Mammalia. Many characteristics distinguish mammals from their reptilian antecedents. Among these are a four-chambered heart (however, note the possible exception to this mentioned earlier in this chapter); adaptations to homeothermy; live birth; mammary glands, and, thus, the ability to lactate; skeletal changes in the skull and head region that mark the beginning of an enlarged and more complicated brain; teeth that are replaced only once, and a diaphragm. Such is the diversity of advanced mammals that it is at first difficult to believe that they are all descended from common ancestral populations that radiated only at the beginning of the Cenozoic era, the "Age of Mammals," some 70 million years ago (Figure 5–16).

Since their origin, mammals have diversified into a number of habitats. Changes in the limbs have been of primary importance in the mammalian adaptive pattern, and in the different groups of mammals the limb evolutions formed the basis for adaptations to different ways of life. The process of moving the front and hindlimbs under the body, begun in the therapsids, was completed. The toe joints were reduced to three in all digits except the first (the thumb, or *pollex*, and the big toe, or *hallux*), which have two joints—the same pattern that we possess.

The most primitive living order of placental mammals are the *insectivores,* composed of small, usually forest-dwelling animals with high metabolisms, such as tree shrews (Figure 5–17, p. 123). They are probably very similar to the ancestors of all placental mammals in the Cretaceous period. Using modern shrews as an analog, our Mesozoic ancestors were likely small, voracious, nocturnal animals. Our earliest primate ancestors constituted one of the first stems off this basic mammalian trunk.

The insectivores, primates, and rodents (rats, squirrels, and their kin) have remained structurally primitive, or similar to the early common ancestors. Other placental mammals have radiated into a large number of ecological niches, that is, particular morphological and behavioral specializations for specific habitats (refer back to Figure 5–16). The first of these radiations came about in the Paleocene epoch, beginning about 70 million years ago. In simplified terms, we can categorize the Cenozoic radiation of mammals into five major adaptive zones: aerial, aquatic, fossorial (burrowing), arboreal, and cursorial (running).

Bats and some other small gliding mammals (the *dermopterans*), such as flying squirrels and flying "lemurs," constitute the only members of the aerial radiation. Biochemical studies, and more recently fossil discoveries, indicate that these aerialists (Figure 5–18, p. 123) may be closely related to the primate stem (see Chapter 6). Mammals have also adapted to marine niches. This group includes the whales and porpoises, along with the sea cows and carnivorous seals and otters. Fossorial mammals are burrowers, such as moles and aardvarks. The arboreal mammals are evolutionarily the most conservative of the entire class, and our own order,

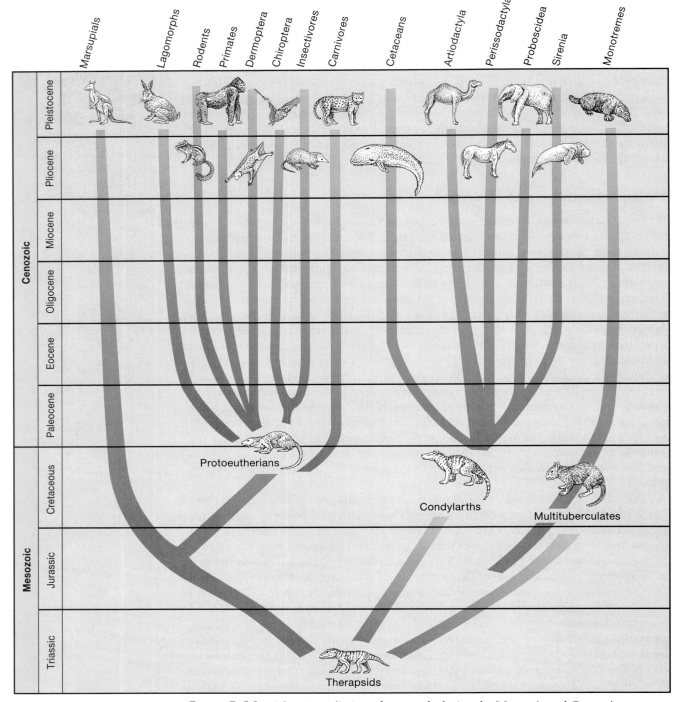

FIGURE 5-16 Adaptive radiation of mammals during the Mesozoic and Cenozoic eras.

primates, is the most arboreal of the mammals. Cursorial, or running, mammals are by far the largest ray of the adaptive radiation of Cenozoic mammals. Foremost among the cursorial mammals are the hoofed mammals: the odd-toed perissodactyls (horses and rhinoceroses), even-toed artiodactyls (pigs, antelopes, deer, hippopotamuses, and giraffes), and the carnivores.

The first mammals are identified by their teeth, which, unlike those of the earlier reptiles, possessed a *heterodontic* pattern (Figure 5–19). The molars have a triangular outline with three well-defined *cusps*. The ridges between the cusps on upper and lower molars slice past each other as the mouth is closed, affording an effective mechanism for cutting up and chewing food. From this basic design all other mammalian chewing teeth have evolved.

New Reproductive Strategies

The earliest mammals may have been egg-laying, like their reptilian ancestors. In fact, the two most primitive living mammals, the platypus and the spiny anteater, members of the monotreme group that live in Australia, bear their young in this way. The general history of mammalian reproduction is one of greater protection of progeny, both before and after birth, and in the Mesozoic era a new type of reproduction evolved in which young were born alive. Mammal mothers retained the reptile-type egg, but internally, in special structures in their bodies where the embryo developed. The production of milk, a unique mammalian adaptation, may have first evolved as an antibacterial fluid designed to protect the eggs and, secondarily shifted in function for nutrition of postnatal offspring. This interpretation suggests that *lactation* evolved before *viviparition*, or live births. The result was that the egg was better protected, and thus, mammalian offspring survived at higher rates. Because the rate of predation on newborn and immature mammals was still high, selection favored offspring that were protected by an adult until they were capable of making their own way. Thus successive species have cared for their young for longer and longer periods, culminating, as we will see, in the primates.

During the Cretaceous period the **marsupials** (Latin, meaning "pouch" [*marsupium*]) and the **placentals** (referring to the membranous structure in the uterus, the *placenta,* which provides prenatal nourishment to the developing embryo and fetus), the two dominant forms of mammals, appeared. Marsupials were more common during the Cretaceous (145 million to 65 million years ago), when the dinosaurs still reigned. The marsupials are pouched mammals, two living examples of which are the opossum and the kangaroo. They bear their young in a very immature

FIGURE 5-17 A common insectivore, the southeast Asian tree shrew.

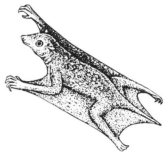

FIGURE 5-18 Flying lemur, *Cynocephalus volans,* whose order, Demoptera, is closely related to those of the insectivores and primates.

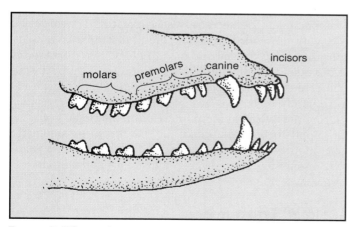

FIGURE 5-19 Early mammal heterodont tooth patterns. This generalized reconstruction includes three molars, used for crushing and chewing; as many as four premolars, which function the same as molars; one canine tooth, used for piercing; and up to three incisors, used for nipping. Numbers refer to the number of teeth on either side of the upper or lower jaw.

marsupials: pouched mammals.

placentals: evolved mammals with very efficient reproductive systems, which include the placenta, a structure that provides the developing embryo with well-oxygenated blood and food, and that takes away carbon dioxide and waste.

state of development after a brief period of gestation. The baby then climbs tenuously along the mother's abdomen into the pouch and clasps onto a teat (the nipple end of the *mamma,* or mammary gland, from which the name of the class derives), where it nurses until fully developed.

Although the marsupials' reproductive adaptation did little more than internalize the reptilian egg while the young were still nurtured externally, the more advanced placental mammals internalized both processes and improved the method of nurturance of the embryo. The *chorion,* a membrane that surrounds the embryo, became fused with the wall of the mother's uterus, forming the placenta, richly supplied with blood vessels (refer back to Figure 5-12). The placenta attaches to the embryo via the *umbilical cord,* carrying oxygen and nutrients to the embryo and carrying wastes away. That the placental form of gestation proved ultimately more successful is evidenced by the placental species having generally replaced marsupials when they have come face-to-face in ecological competition.

Endothermy

The early mammals physiologically were probably capable of maintaining their internal body temperature at a more constant level than their reptilian ancestors had been able to do. This ability, termed **endothermy** (Latin, meaning ("internal heat")), or, more commonly "warm-blooded," allowed mammals to be active during relatively cool periods, such as at night. Similar-size (small) reptiles today are quiescent when they are cold and must raise their body temperature behaviorally through activities such as sunning themselves. Endotherms use muscular contraction (in movements and shivering), constriction and dilation of surface blood vessels, sweating, panting, and insulation by hair and fat to maintain body temperature.

Warm-bloodedness allowed a greater range of activities, particularly in hunting and escape from predators, and especially at night and in cooler seasons of the year in temperate regions. At least one other nonmammalian group independently evolved endothermy—the birds.

As part of their more active physiology, mammals evolved a heart and circulatory system that kept oxygenated and deoxygenated bloodstreams separated and created higher blood pressure. Because more oxygen and more blood could be delivered to the tissues per unit of time, a higher **metabolic rate** (oxygen consumption and energy production) was possible. The ancestral fish circulation system was a simple pumping mechanism, with the *ventricle* pushing blood through two systems of capillaries: first to the gills to pick up oxygen and then to the body to nourish the tissues and pick up carbon dioxide waste. In amphibians, with the advent of the air-breathing lung, a three-chambered heart evolved (Figure 5-20*a*). The right and left *atria* received blood from the body (deoxygenated blood) and lungs (oxygenated blood), respectively. Blood from the two atria then emptied into the single ventricle, which in turn pumped the blood to both the body and the lungs. In mammals, as well as in some advanced reptiles and birds, the four-chambered heart evolved (Figure 5-20*b* and *c*), in which one side of the heart pumps oxygenated blood and the other side pumps deoxygenated blood.

Enlarged Brain and Related Structures

endothermy: the maintenance of constant body temperature; "warm-blooded."

metabolic rate: the rate at which energy is expended in all the chemical reactions in an animal's cells and tissues.

The earliest mammals had as one of their major adaptations a significantly larger brain for their body size compared with that of the reptiles. The enlargement was particularly observable in a part of the brain originally concerned with the sense of smell, the cerebrum. The *cerebrum* assumed new and expanded functions in the mammals. Sensory information—visual, auditory, taste, and smell—was recorded and remembered in the outside part of the brain, the *cerebral cortex*. This increased memory and ability to receive and act on environmental information with effective

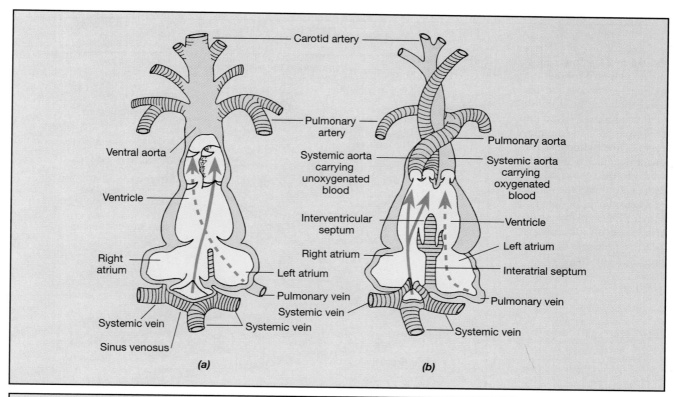

Carotid artery

(a)
- Pulmonary artery
- Ventral aorta
- Ventricle
- Right atrium
- Left atrium
- Pulmonary vein
- Systemic vein
- Systemic vein
- Sinus venosus

(b)
- Pulmonary aorta
- Systemic aorta carrying unoxygenated blood
- Systemic aorta carrying oxygenated blood
- Interventricular septum
- Ventricle
- Right atrium
- Left atrium
- Interatrial septum
- Pulmonary vein
- Systemic vein
- Systemic vein

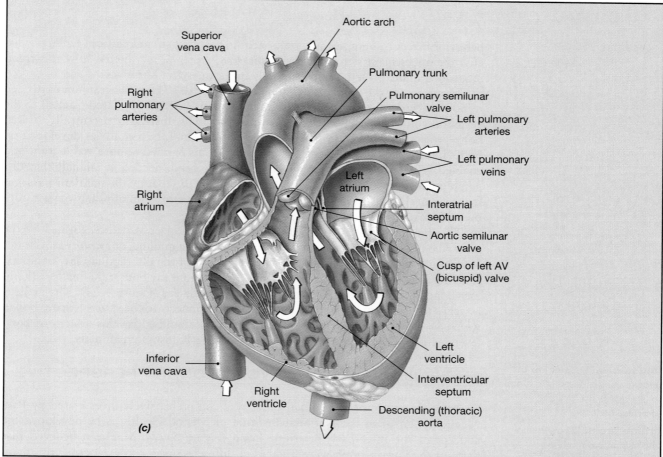

- Superior vena cava
- Aortic arch
- Right pulmonary arteries
- Pulmonary trunk
- Pulmonary semilunar valve
- Left pulmonary arteries
- Left atrium
- Left pulmonary veins
- Right atrium
- Interatrial septum
- Aortic semilunar valve
- Cusp of left AV (bicuspid) valve
- Inferior vena cava
- Left ventricle
- Interventricular septum
- Right ventricle
- Descending (thoracic) aorta

(c)

FIGURE 5–20 Comparison of hearts of (*a*) amphibian, (*b*) reptile, and (*c*) human. Mammals have four-chambered hearts in which oxygenated blood flows on one side and deoxygenated blood on the other.

FIGURE 5-21 Stages in the development of the mammalian middle ear. The hyomandibular bone in fish (shown in blue) evolved into the stapes bone in amphibians, reptiles, and mammals. The quadrate and articular bones, which formed the reptilian jaw, evolved into the malleus and incus bones of the middle ear, and a new mammalian jaw joint evolved because of selective pressures that favored improved chewing ability.

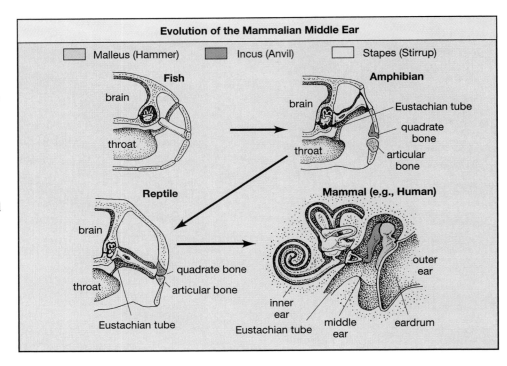

behavior became an important component in mammalian adaptation. Later, we discuss the ancestral structure of the brain. In Chapter 6, we discuss how this trend intensified in the primates and especially in the apes and ourselves.

The shape of the skull also changed in mammals. The neurocranium expanded to hold the larger brain. A new design, in which the head articulated (joined) to the vertebral column, became perfected in the mammals. Instead of a centrally located bony projection, the *condyle,* on the back of the skull, two condyles developed on both sides of the opening for the spinal cord. This formed a more stable joint and enabled faster, more accurate movements of the head, needed in animals that dispatch prey with their teeth. A *hard palate* evolved to separate the nasal air passages from the oral food passages, thus allowing mammals to maintain their oxygen supply while eating.

The mammalian jaw, or **mandible,** became a stronger structure, formed by the same two bones as in the reptiles but now fused at the midline, or *symphysis.* Greater force could be exerted in biting and chewing. Two of the old reptilian jaw bones assumed a new function in the mammals. They became ear bones: the *malleus* (hammer bone) and the *incus* (anvil bone) of our middle ear (Figure 5–21). The malleus attaches the eardrum to the incus, and the incus connects to the *stapes* (stirrup bone), which first evolved in the amphibians. Sound is amplified by this system of bony levers, which constitutes a finely tuned hearing mechanism in mammals.

mandible: the lower jaw of mammals, composed of a fusion of the reptile dentary and articular bones.

triune brain: the division of the human brain by Paul MacLean into three broad divisions based on phylogenetic and functional patterns.

THE HUMAN BRAIN IN EVOLUTIONARY PERSPECTIVE

The mosaic nature of the human brain was comprehensively investigated by Paul MacLean (1990) of the National Institute of Mental Health as he developed the concept of the three-part, or **triune brain** (Figure 5–22). MacLean believed that parts of the human brain were legacies of different stages of development in mammalian brain evolution. The three-part brain is built on the most ancient "neural chassis"—the spinal cord and the mid- and hindbrains that are inherited from our

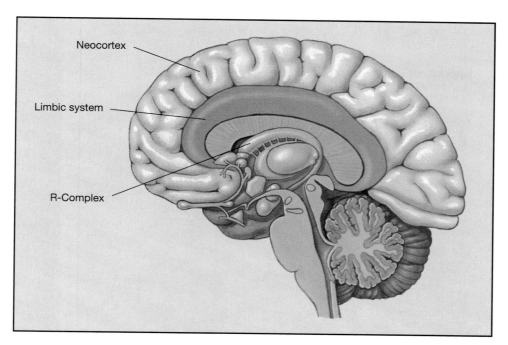

Figure 5-22 The three parts of the triune brain, R-Complex, limbic system, and neocortex, as they appear in cross-section in the human brain.

early fish and amphibian ancestors. These most ancient parts of our brains allow us to breathe, allow our hearts to beat, and provide our instincts for survival and reproduction. MacLean called this first part of the triune brain the **R-Complex,** because he believed that it evolved during the period of the early Mesozoic reptiles.

The second part of the brain is the **limbic system** (Figure 5–23), a term introduced in 1952, though components of the system were recognized as early as 1878 by French neuroanatomist Paul Broca. This is the part of the mammalian brain that provides the emotional basis of behavior. MacLean believed that the limbic system appeared early in the evolutionary history of mammals. Current opinion holds that the limbic system may be far older than the early mammals, because evidence indicates that it evolved before the advent of any amniote vertebrates (Butler and Hodos, 1996).

The third part of the triune brain, the **neocortex,** allows mammals, including primates, to reason.

The R-Complex

The reptiles of 250 million years ago possessed several evolutionary advances in brain function over their amphibian forerunners. These reptilian structures are located in the base of the forebrain of all reptiles, birds, and mammals and include several structures, collectively called the **basal ganglia.** A *ganglion* (Greek, meaning "knot" or "swelling") is a concentration of nerve cell connections. The basal ganglia contribute to both movement and cognitive functions. The R-Complex is rich in chemical messengers, called *neurotransmitters,* including *dopamine,* which is responsible for controlling higher cognitive functions (decision making) and motor pathways (voluntary muscle movement); *serotonin,* which regulates emotional behavior; and *endorphins,* which function much like opiates in pain reduction.

What parts of our thoughts and actions can be traced to this ancient but still functioning part of our brain? What does the R-Complex do? MacLean (1990) carried out a series of experiments designed to establish the role of the R-Complex. His research suggests that it controls primarily ritualistic, stereotypical behavior,

R-Complex: the most primitive part of the triune brain model of Paul MacLean; the site that controls certain ritualistic, stereotypical, and social communication behaviors.

limbic system: an adaptation of the primarily olfactory part of the forebrain, important in sexual and maternal behavior.

neocortex: the evolutionary "new" part of the cerebral cortex, characteristic of mammals.

basal ganglia: structures in the forebrain of vertebrates that form part of the R-Complex.

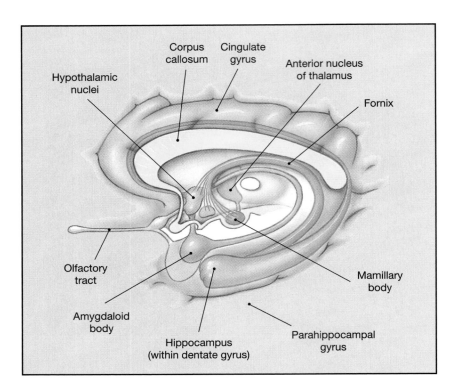

FIGURE 5-23 Three-dimensional view of the human limbic system.

movement, and communication. More specifically, the R-Complex functions in the recognition of individuals, in behavior control and interpretation of the behavior of other animals, in the mediation of aggression, and in the maintenance of social hierarchies and territory (Figure 5–24). MacLean's experiments showed, however, that destruction or disease to parts of the R-Complex did not result in actual motor deficits, nor did direct electrical stimulation of this complex result in movement. Apparently, the R-Complex only indirectly aids movement; rather, it is more involved in planning and organizing movement. Other research (Hoover and Strick, 1993) suggests that the R-Complex receives information about appropriate motor action and then sends it on to another forebrain structure that directly selects and then controls specific muscle movement. MacLean's experiments on lizards and monkeys demonstrated the R-Complex's basic role in displays used in social communication.

In humans and other mammals R-Complex behavior is modified by more evolved parts of the brain, such as the neocortex (discussed shortly). In the higher vertebrates, connecting tracts between R-Complex structures and other parts of the brain permit emotional as well as learned input to affect R-Complex output, producing variable and highly complex behavioral responses to different situations and circumstances.

The Limbic System

Structural elements of the limbic system (Latin, meaning "bordering, peripheral") are located in an area called the forebrain that surrounds the brainstem and R-Complex (refer back to Figures 5–22 and 5–23). The limbic system consists of three main components: the *medial pallium,* which contains the *hippocampal formation* (Greek, meaning "mythological sea monster") and *fornix;* the *septal nuclei* and the *amygdala* (Greek, meaning "almond"); and the *thalamus* and *hypothalamus.* Our current understanding of the evolution of the limbic system suggests that many of these structures appeared early in the history of vertebrates. The medial pallial, septal, and amygdala components, for example, may be found in all jawed vertebrates, and multiple subdivisions of the amygdala are found in birds and reptiles as well as in mammals.

FIGURE 5-24 Agonistic (hostile) displays in the komodo dragon and mountain gorilla; a function of the ancient R-Complex?

In the lower vertebrates, limbic structures function to relay sensory information. In the higher vertebrates, the medial pallium becomes progressively more concerned in the analysis of complex information integrated from many sensory sources. In mammals, the medial pallium further expands in size and differentiates into specialized areas that play major roles in learning and memory and provide the basis for motivation and emotion that may be necessary for appropriate responses to external stimuli. In humans, interconnections within the system are the most numerous of all the mammals.

In mammals, generally, the limbic system functions in the production of motivated and emotional behaviors, such as eating, drinking, sex, anxiety, and aggression. Understanding the functions of the various components of the system has come about primarily through studies of behavioral deficiencies caused by lesions (damage) to specific parts and by experimentation involving the stimulation of various structures through implanted electrodes. Information gathered in these ways suggest that the hippocampal formation is essential for short-term memory; thus, it is considered the gateway for the storage of long-term memory of new events. If the hippocampus is in some way damaged, old memories stored prior to damage are preserved but new information is not. Apparently the role of the hippocampus in memory is to relate different elements of experience, a role that is suggested by the fact that it receives information from many brain regions.

The fornix functions to interconnect the hippocampal formation with the septal nuclei and parts of the brainstem. Damage caused in the septal nuclei will result in the immediate increase in rage and hyperemotionality, after which behaviors usually return to normal over time. Increase in aggressiveness, however, may secondarily result from an increase in defensiveness, the primary motivator.

The amygdala is an important point of interface for multiple systems, and it receives the direct sensory input of smell from the olfactory bulb. Because of this, the amygdala is critical in the relay of chemosensory information to the hypothalamus, especially as it involves sexual behavior. Electrical stimulation of the *rostral* (anterior) part of the amygdala evokes flight and fear responses, whereas stimulation of the *caudal* (posterior) part brings out defensive and/or aggressive behaviors in cats and monkeys.

In a general sense, the amygdala appears to be essential for the maintenance of normal social behavior. High-ranking monkeys, for example, drop to the bottom of the social hierarchy following damage to the amygdala. Damage may also result in the disruption of some learning tasks and in the failure to acquire certain emotional responses.

The third area of the limbic system includes the dorsal part of the *thalamus* (Greek, meaning "chamber") and the *hypothalamus*. This area is important in co-operative social behavior and some aspects of sexuality. This region is larger in primates than it is in most other mammals. The hypothalamus is involved in the activities of the autonomic nervous system and the endocrine system by controlling the endocrine system's production of hormones through the *pituitary* (Latin, meaning "mucous secreting"), to which it is directly connected. The hypothalamus is able to control and regulate behavior patterns that depend on the levels of hormones in the blood, such as sexual and maternal behavior. It also plays a role in feeding and drinking, aggression, temperature regulation, and territoriality.

Much of the influence that the limbic system exerts on behavior derives from chemical messengers called *hormones*. Hormones are produced in glands, such as the pituitary, carried by the blood to their target organs, and generally have long-term effects. In contrast, another source of limbic influence, also found in the R-Complex, are neurotransmitters and neuromodulators. These chemicals are released directly adjacent to a target cell and produce shorter but more immediate responses than hormones. Although there are relatively few neurotransmitters, such as serotonin and dopamine, there are more than 30 different neuromodulators, of which insulin is one example.

Neurotransmitters function to excite or inhibit the synapses of nerve cells, depending on the type of receptor that is present. Neuromodulators function somewhat differently, in that they influence the duration or intensity of the neurotransmitter's actions by affecting, for example, the reuptake of transmitters and the rate of transmitter release. As a result, these chemical substances facilitate the possibility of many subtle and sophisticated modifications of the transfer of information between neurons and, thus, of behavior. The effects of hormones on behavior overlap with the effects of the neurotransmitters and neuromodulators.

The Neocortex

The third part of the triune brain is the neocortex (Latin, meaning "new covering"). Human behavior is a function of an expanded mammalian part of the neocortex—the cerebral cortex (Figure 5–25).

The link between the cerebral cortex and voluntary movement was discovered by a British neurologist, John Hughlings Jackson, who in the 1860s researched the behavior of individuals suffering from seizure disorders. He discovered that seizures always started with uncontrolled movements of one part of the body. By recording where in the brain an injury occurred, and what part of the body was subsequently affected in an epileptic seizure, Jackson was able to map out the whole body along a strip of brain tissue.

Jackson had discovered the **motor cortex,** a loop of brain in the front part of the cortex, also termed the *precentral gyrus* (see Appendix 1). One writer described the motor cortex as "the keyboard of an instrument whose strings are the muscles, which finally play the melody of movement" (Blakemore, 1977:79). There are larger "keyboard" areas for certain parts of the body, where more finely tuned muscular control is required, such as for the thumbs and lips in humans.

A similar area, the **sensory cortex,** is directly behind the central sulcus, and thus it was named the *postcentral gyrus*. Sensations from the skin of touch, heat, cold, and pain are perceived in the brain in a clearly organized pattern. As in the motor

motor cortex: the part of the cerebral cortex located in the precentral gyrus that controls voluntary movements of the body.

sensory cortex: the part of the cerebral cortex located in the postcentral gyrus that senses touch, temperature, and pain on all parts of the body.

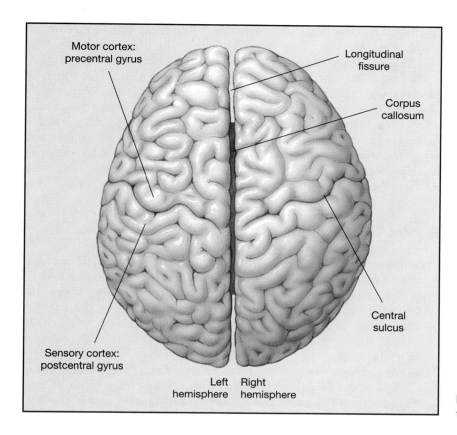

FIGURE 5–25 Dorsal view of the human cerebral cortex.

cortex, the proportion of cortical area allotted for sensations correlates with the importance of particular sensations in an animal's adaptation. Human brains have a very large sensory area for the hands, as do most primates. In contrast, dogs have larger sensory areas for perceiving touch on the nose.

Understanding the structure and function of the human brain is one of the most challenging frontiers for modern science. The model of the triune brain is one way to understand some very complex structures in an evolutionary framework. The model will certainly need to be modified as new discoveries are made.

UNDERSTANDING HUMAN MORPHOLOGY

The vertebrates, and particularly the mammals, provide an essential background for understanding human evolution. The human body is a mosaic of many anatomical structures and physiological mechanisms derived from ancestors at many stages in a long evolutionary development. At each stage those traits were important parts of the species' adaptation to its environment. Clearly, there was no *orthogenetic,* or predetermined, trend toward the human condition. The story of our early preprimate evolution, with all its twists and turns, is a much more complicated and, indeed, exciting one than a simple plodding progression toward ourselves.

Many of the main *adaptive grades* (roughly, stages in evolutionary development) in our vertebrate heritage have been recognized for some time, having been discovered by several generations of comparative anatomists, embryologists, and paleontologists. These nonprimate data continue to provide important contributions to our understanding of human evolution. Vertebrate paleontology is also providing important information on the context of human evolution: the environmental conditions, regional connections, and ages of fossil faunas that tell us about the world of our ancestors.

The human body is not a well-designed machine unique unto itself. Each part has a long history of evolutionary change behind it. It is, therefore, important in human anatomy, and its practical applications in medicine, to appreciate the evolution and development of structures as well as their present functional configurations. Comparative anatomical, paleontological, embryological, and biochemical data provide compelling evidence of human beings' connections with and evolutionary differentiation within the animal world. Regardless of how dramatic the later developments of human evolution may seem to be, their bases lie in the adaptations inherited from our chordate and vertebrate ancestors.

◀ SUMMARY

1. **What structural and paleontological clues do biological anthropologists use to reconstruct human and nonhuman primate evolution?**

   We can trace the ancestry of people through the vertebrates (animals with backbones) by using information derived from studies in comparative anatomy, embryology, and paleontology. Contrary to an anthropocentric view of life, people and their immediate ancestors were, until quite recently, minor components of life on earth.

2. **What characteristics distinguish all chordates, including humans?**

   Chordates can be distinguished from members of other phyla by the presence of paired series of clefts or gills present in all embryos and in the adults of some vertebrate groups; an internal skeleton, the structure of which is bilaterally symmetrical, including the embryologic presence of a flexible rod, or notochord; a tail that may be quite prominent in all embryos, although not in all adults, such as people; and a single hollow nerve cord that runs dorsally above the notochord. These characters are unusual if they are compared to those of other phyla. A direct fossil connection from the chordates to other phyla remains elusive.

3. **What adaptations occurred in the evolution of bony fishes?**

   Early fish evolved internal skeletons of cartilage and bone, which allowed for an increase in body size. The development of biting jaws among the placoderm fish was a milestone in the evolution of a predatory way of life.

4. **What major adaptations led to the evolution of amphibians, reptiles, and therapsids?**

   Land vertebrates evolved from lobe-finned fish some 360 million years ago. These animals possessed air bladders and were capable of occasional, opportunistic terrestrial locomotion on limbs that had earlier evolved on aquatic animals. By developing the drought-resistant amniote egg, early reptiles who followed next, about 245 million years ago, evolved as animals free from life in the water. Mammal-like reptiles, the therapsids, evolved many features of the skulls, jaws, teeth, and limbs characteristic of the later mammals.

5. **What major adaptations occurred in the early evolution of mammals, and what was their significance?**

   Early mammals differentiated from the reptiles in adaptations that provided for (a) a constant internal body temperature (endothermy), (b) birth of live young, (c) nourishment of the young by lactation, and (d) a considerably larger brain that expanded on more ancient neural structures, such as the limbic system, and developed new ones, such as the neocortex.

6. **What were the major steps in the evolution of the human brain?**

   The evolved mammalian brain expanded the way in which these animals perceived the world around them and their ability to respond to it. Emotion and rational thought hallmarked the mammalian behavioral response to conditions in the environment and formed the basis on which a strong mother–infant bond and sociality among members of a species could be achieved.

7. **What does it mean to say that no predetermined trends led inevitably toward the present human condition?**

The morphology of modern humans is the result of many individual changes affecting the structure of every body part and system. The human lineage evolved over vast periods of time in response to specific environmental changes and pressures, not as a result of an overall plan.

◀ CRITICAL THINKING QUESTIONS

1. A scientist's understanding of the evolution of life on earth usually starts with a conjecture, which is later either abandoned or modified as pertinent new fossil evidence is discovered. Discuss examples of how early ideas of vertebrate evolution have changed as a result of new fossil finds.

2. Homology, homoplasy, and analogy are useful terms in describing anatomical structures in terms of their evolutionary history. Give examples of structures that could be considered homologous, homoplastic, or analogous and discuss the reasons you consider them to be so.

3. What are the advantages of endothermy? If Mesozoic reptiles were endothermic, might their descendants still be alive today?

4. When individuals find themselves in frightening circumstances, what parts of the brain react? In what specific ways?

5. Adaptive radiations are a feature of the expansion of living forms. These radiations are opportunistic, however, because they are usually time- and place-specific. Niches must be available for species to spread into, and individuals must be preadapted to be successful in their new niches. Provide examples of an adaptive radiation in a group of vertebrates, and explain the preadaptations that made the radiation a successful one.

◀ INTERNET EXERCISES

Critical Thinking

Sea Cows and Sea Squirts. All vertebrates are chordates, but not all chordates are vertebrates. Why? Answer the following questions:

1. What characteristics do all chordates share?
2. What subgroups are included within the phylum Chordata?
3. Why are classifications, such as Chordata or Mollusca, important?

Writing Assignment

The Tetrapods. For this assignment, find out more about living and extinct tetrapods and answer the following questions:

1. What living animals are considered tetrapods? How is the group defined?
2. When did the first tetrapods evolve? Under what ecological conditions?

See Companion Web site for Internet links.

Continental Drift: Where Were They When . . . ?

Why study continental drift in a book about biological anthropology? Continental drift played an important role in the evolution of complex life. As we saw in the chapter, during the Permian, earth's land masses formed a single supercontinent, called Pangaea, surrounded by an ocean that covered the rest of the planet. It is thought that this process created vast pockets of deep stagnant water whose oxygen content became increasingly replaced by carbon dioxide. This buildup of carbon dioxide poisoned many ocean species, causing their extinction, at the same time that rapid climatic swings may have contributed to the extinction of many land vertebrates. The environmentally sensitive amphibians suffered the most, and their extinction opened up many niches that other, more adaptable life forms, such as reptiles, would occupy.

This MediaLab allows you to witness the breakup of Pangaea and the formation of the present continents over time. Thinking about these events in terms of the evolution of specific groups of animals will shed new light on the topic.

WEB ACTIVITY

Study the animation and note the order in which the continents broke apart. Also note carefully which continents were in tropical and which in temperate zones at various times.

Activity

1. Where was Antarctica when Pangaea began to break up? Where were Africa and Australia? What types of fossils would you expect paleontologists to find from that time period on those continents?

2. When did Africa and South America separate? What effect did their relatively late separation have on the evolution of Old World and New World monkeys? (You might want to skip ahead to Chapters 6 and 7 for more information on this topic.)

3. Scientists speculate that before Pangaea formed, other continents existed. What evidence would you expect paleontologists to have for the existence of earlier continents?

The MediaLab can be found in Chapter 5 on your Companion Web site http://www.prenhall.com/boaz

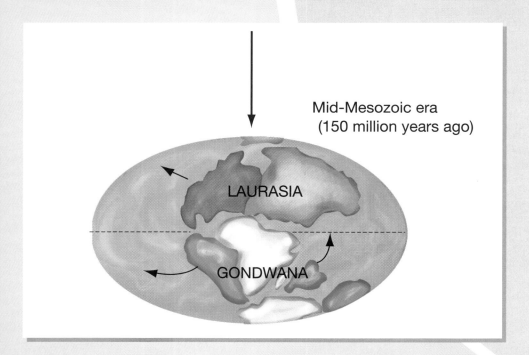

Mid-Mesozoic era
(150 million years ago)

LAURASIA

GONDWANA

PRIMATE EVOLUTION

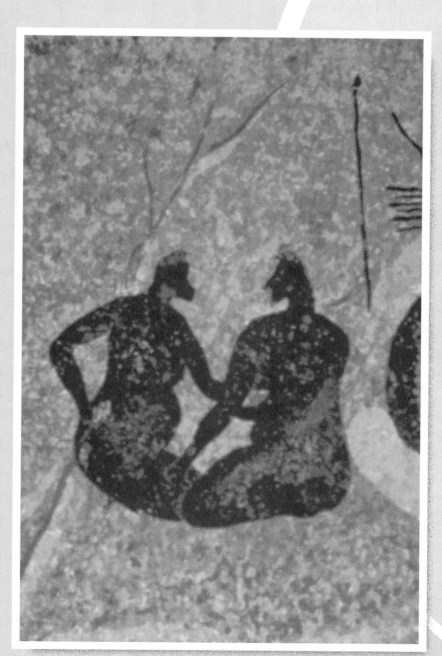

With the evolution of flowering plants, including trees, in the latter part of the Mesozoic era, forests became complex environments. There were more niches available for exploitation. One group of mammals, the primates, radiated to fill the new tree-living niches. These were small creatures that climbed in the trees by grasping. In this chapter, we answer the question, "What is a primate?," and survey the earliest forms.

WHAT IS A PRIMATE?

The term **primate** was coined by Linnaeus in 1758 to name the order of mammals that includes monkeys, apes, and humans. "Primate" comes from the Latin *primas,* meaning "of the first rank." Linnaeus considered the order that contained humans to be first among the animals. Today, nonhuman primate species are numerous throughout the Old and New Worlds, from Africa and Asia to South and Central America (Figure 6–1), and most of these are tree living, or *arboreal.*

Primates are subdivided into two major groups (Figure 6–2, p. 138). The **prosimians** (Latin, meaning "before monkeys") are the most primitive of living primates; that is, they retain many characteristics of their earliest ancestors. Most species of prosimians, such as the lorises, galagos, and tarsiers, are small, solitary foragers that are active only at night. **Anthropoids** (Greek, for "humanlike"), often called the "higher primates," include the monkeys, apes, and humans. They share derived characteristics that distinguish them from their earliest primate ancestors. As a group, anthropoids are generally larger in body size than prosimians, and they are organized into social groups. Almost all anthropoids are active during the day. We describe the living groups of prosimians and monkeys in Chapter 7.

The anatomist Sir Wilfrid Le Gros Clark (1964) set out a number of trends that typify most, if not all, primates.

1. Primates tend to have *well-developed visual senses,* which includes good depth perception. This characteristic includes overlapping fields of vision for each eye (binocular vision), which, when integrated in the brain, yields a perception of three dimensions, **stereoscopic vision.** Primates have eyes that are directed forward, medially positioned in the front of their face, a condition known as *orbital frontality.* Prosimian eyes are more side-directed, or laterally positioned, than are the eyes of the anthropoids. In all modern primates, as a consequence of forward facing eyes, the lateral wall of the orbit is constructed through contact between part of the

primate: the order of mammals that includes living and extinct monkeys, apes, and humans, as well as more primitive taxa.

prosimians: primates typified by small body size and frequently nocturnal adaptations in the living forms.

anthropoids: "higher" primates, including monkeys, apes, and humans.

stereoscopic vision: the ability to perceive depth by virtue of the fact that the fields of vision of each eye partially overlap, thus giving the brain information sufficient to reconstruct an accurate impression of depth or distance.

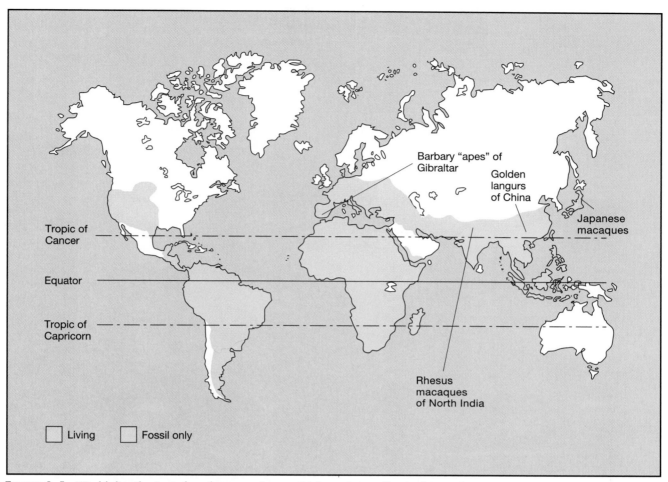

FIGURE 6-1 World distribution of nonhuman primates. Living primates live in the tropics or subtropics, with the exception of some species of Old World monkeys, such as the Japanese macaque, which have adapted to a temperate climate. Fossil primates are found in areas of the world that were formerly in the tropics.

frontal bone, which extends downward, and part of the cheekbone (or malar), which extends upward, to form the postorbital bar (see Figure 6–2).

2. Primates have *color vision*. The ability to discriminate a wide range of the color spectrum is another characteristic of all primates except the nocturnal prosimians. Color vision in primates may have arisen by selection for a fruit-eating diet, which required the ability to determine the ripeness and edibility of particular food.

3. Primates in general have *larger brains for their body sizes* than do other mammals. This is particularly true for anthropoids, and it is especially true of the apes and humans. The trend toward increased brain size, which relates in a general way to increased intelligence, may result from a predatory lifestyle that requires primates to outsmart and capture prey (Cartmill, 1982). It may have been further developed in higher primates because of their complex social adaptations to life in well-integrated groups (see Chapter 8). Human ancestors probably underwent extensive brain development because of their increasing reliance on a peculiar social adaptation of learned behavior, known as *culture* (see Chapter 12).

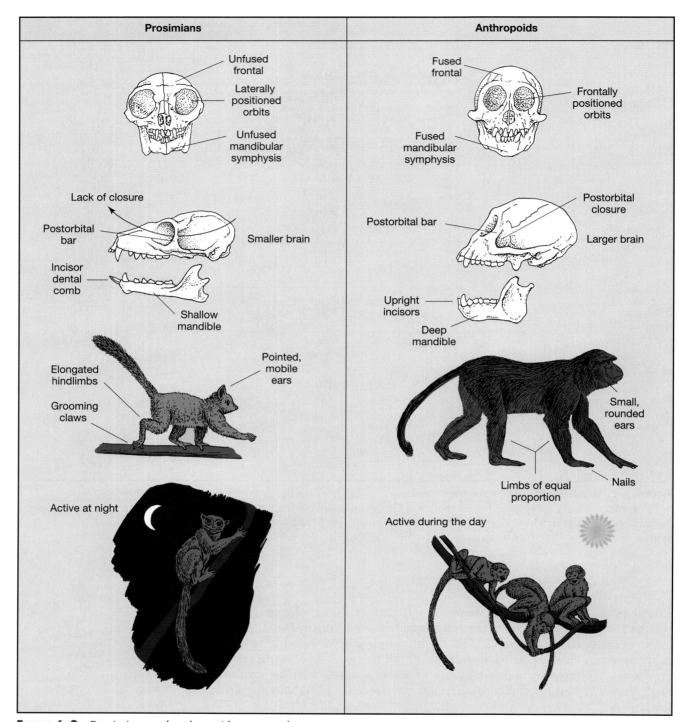

FIGURE 6–2   Prosimians and anthropoids compared.

4. Primates have *increased parental investment in offspring.* Primates give birth to fewer offspring than do many other mammals. There is a greater degree of parental investment in caring for offspring throughout the relatively long period of infant dependency after birth, and, as a consequence, lower infant mortality. Aspects of primate anatomy and physiology reflect this reproductive strategy. Because most primates usually give birth to only a single offspring at a time, females have only two nipples for suckling infants, whereas many other mammals, which give birth to litters, have a series of nipples.

5. The *period of development is longer in anthropoids than it is in prosimians.* This includes the time required for development of the fetus (gestation), as well as the other stages of the lifespan, including infancy (birth to the eruption of the first permanent teeth), the juvenile period (prepubertal), and adulthood. All of these periods increase in length from prosimians to anthropoids. Humans have the longest spans of all of these stages.

6. Primates show a *diversity of modes of locomotion.* Figure 6–3 classifies the various types of locomotion in living primates (Napier and Napier, 1967). The earliest primates probably were arboreal quadrupeds (Figure 6–3a), somewhat similar to but less specialized than modern prosimian vertical clinging and leaping forms (see Figure 6–8). **Vertical clinging and leaping** is a type of locomotion typified by grasping a vertical tree trunk with the hands and feet encircling the trunk, and then jumping to another such perch (Figure 6–3b). Prosimians thus possess hands and feet capable of grasping. Some of the traits associated with these adaptations for locomotion are an opposable thumb and a big toe that can be flexed, or "opposed," against the other digits; flat nails, instead of claws, to support sensitive finger and toe tips; fingerprint ridge patterns to increase friction in grip; and relatively short fore- and hindlimbs of nearly equal length. The last of these is a generalized mammal trait (Figure 6–2).

Body size increased in a number of descendant primate groups, and new locomotor adaptations appeared: Fore- and hindlimb lengths increased in ground-running primates, which increased stride length and speed (Figure 6–3c). In the tree-living apes ("arm swingers," or *brachiators*), forelimbs increased in length, which increased both speed and reach (Figure 6–3d). In the ground-dwelling African apes (gorillas and chimpanzees), longer forelimbs facilitated a unique form of locomotion called *knuckle walking* (Figure 6–3e). Finally, length of the lower limbs increased in the human lineage, which allowed for greater stride length and a new form of terrestrial locomotion, *bipedal walking* (Figure 6–3f).

7. Primates have low-crowned (*bunodont*) molar and premolar *teeth adapted to grinding and crushing food,* as opposed to slicing, cutting, and piercing food (Figure 6–2). Primates have been described as an "order of omnivores" (Harding and Teleki, 1981). Animal protein in the form of insects and small vertebrates probably made up a large part of early primates' diets, along with fruit and other types of vegetation. Later, and generally larger, primates followed one of several components of this basic dietary adaptation.

Primates' tooth patterns, or *dentition,* clearly correlate to diets. In general, primate molars are flat, rounded structures, which indicates their function in crushing and chewing food. The Old World monkeys have shearing crests on their molars (*bilophodonty*), which allows them to cut through tough plant food.

8. *Primates are generally tropical animals.* However, some macaque monkeys, such as Japanese macaques, have been able to extend their range into cold regions. Their adaptations to the cold include heavy fur and short, stubby tails. Later members of the genus *Homo* and modern people extended their range by means of certain physiological adaptations (which is discussed in Chapter 15) and by culture.

9. Most primates are *active in the daytime,* which is related to their highly developed vision. Food is located, predators are avoided, and movement is effected by means of visual referents. Most primates spend the night in secure locations in the trees or on cliff ledges that are difficult to access.

Classification of Primates

One popular way to classify the living members of the order primates is to separate them into two suborders: the prosimians and the anthropoids (see Figure 6–2 and

vertical clinging and leaping: the method of locomotion characteristic of many living prosimians, and inferred to have been a method of locomotion in some early primates.

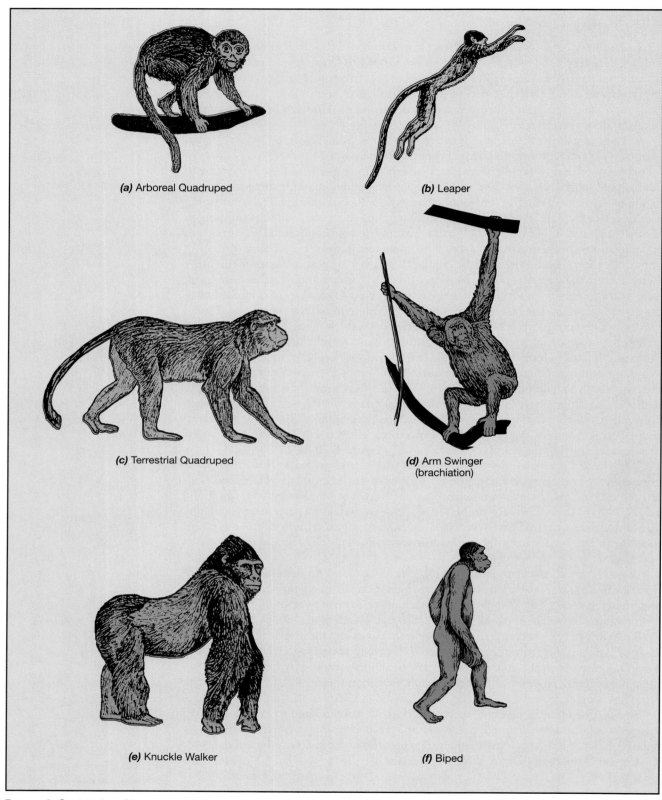

(a) Arboreal Quadruped

(b) Leaper

(c) Terrestrial Quadruped

(d) Arm Swinger
(brachiation)

(e) Knuckle Walker

(f) Biped

FIGURE 6–3 Modes of locomotion in primates.

✳ FRONTIERS

The Ancestral Primate Niche and the Origin of Primate Adaptations

Primates are distinguished from other mammals, including the *plesiadapiforms,* by many anatomical adaptations. Although we are still unclear about which of the early mammal groups gave rise to the primates, many researchers now agree about why primates adapted as they did. For most of the twentieth century, the idea of tree-living (arboreality) was used to explain primate origins and unique characteristics. In the past few decades a number of other proposals have considered primates' eating habits and their foraging practices, rather than their movement within their habitats.

Fred Szalay (1972) opened the debate when he proposed that a shift to a herbivorous diet, accompanied by a leaping kind of locomotion, promoted the shift to a dentition characterized by rounded molar cusps and a more agile postcranial skeleton. Matt Cartmill (1992) thought that the stereoscopic (binocular) vision of primates (and of carnivores as well, as he pointed out) demanded a different explanation. He believed that this visual adaptation was the result of foraging activities, which involved the capture of moving prey (as opposed to stationary vegetation). He argued that just as carnivores rely on stereoscopic vision to detect their prey, so did the early primates. The grasping hands (found only in primates) might simply represent an evolutionary improvement in the catching ability.

Robert Sussman (1991) is credited with the idea that the earliest primates developed strategies that exploited fruit, flowers, and nectar while feeding on small branches. Feeding on small or terminal branches requires dexterity and a nimble body construction. Sussman also pointed out that the mammals that show the greatest resemblance to primates in their visual adaptation are the fruit-eating bats.

R. H. Crompton (1995) proposed that the earliest primates may have been nocturnal and that the leaping behavior of many nocturnal animals, which requires the precise estimation of distance for a jump to be successful high in the trees, was the selective force in the evolution of stereoscopic vision.

Finally, D. Tod Rasmussen (1990), looking at an entirely different group of mammals, the marsupials, discovered one genus, *Caluromys,* that possessed characteristics strikingly similar to those of primates and was also more arboreal than any other related marsupial group. However, because *Caluromys* foraged for both fruits and insects on terminal branches, Rasmussen was unable to clarify which of the competing hypotheses stated previously was most reasonable. He speculated that stereoscopic vision evolved for predation purposes in mammals that were already adapted for foraging for plant food on terminal branches. This lends support to all of the hypotheses, but specifies an order in which the different adaptations appeared. According to John Fleagle,

> The key to reconstructing the history of any seemingly integrated suite of evolutionary adaptations lies in having a record of the sequence in which the features were acquired. Did the primate visual adaptations precede or follow the grasping abilities and the reduced molar cusps? Until we have a better fossil record of the intermediate forms preceding the first appearance of "real primates" at the beginning of the Eocene, the details of primate origins will remain shrouded in the mists of time. (1999:347)

Appendix 1). The prosimians are further divided into three superfamilies: the lemurs, the lorises, and the tarsiers. These superfamilies include eight families, most of which live in nocturnal habitats in the forests of Africa and Asia.

The anthropoids also have three superfamilies, including the New World monkeys (Ceboidea), the Old World monkeys (Cercopithecoidea), and the group that incorporates the apes and humans (Hominoidea). These three anthropoid superfamilies include six families. We survey the physical features of the living primates in Chapter 7 and aspects of their social organization in Chapter 8.

In addition, within the primates, there is generally considered to be a third suborder of extinct primatelike mammals, the plesiadapiforms, which we discuss shortly. The plesiadapiforms were a widespread and very successful group of mammals that were common throughout the Paleocene and Eocene landscapes of North America and Europe. Recently, new fossil discoveries of the plesiadapiforms have also been reported in Asia (Beard and Wang, 1995).

THE FIRST PRIMATE RADIATION: PRIMATELIKE MAMMALS OF THE PALEOCENE

The extinction of the dinosaurs left many ecological niches vacant that subsequently were occupied by the birds and mammals. In addition, significant changes in the earth's environment that occurred at the boundary of the Mesozoic and Cenozoic eras contributed to the formation of new niches. Flowering plants, characterized by a covered seed coat, first appeared in the late Mesozoic, and as these plants diversified, they formed forests of great complexity, opening up new niches for animal life.

During the Paleocene, numerous kinds of mammals appeared, and although none of them even remotely approached the size of the dinosaurs (most were no larger than medium-size dogs), they were very successful, as their numbers attest. Among the most successful of the early mammals were the **plesiadapiforms.** More than 75 species in 35 genera are now known (Fleagle, 1999:332). The name of this group, plesiadapis, comes from the Greek word *plesi,* meaning "like," and *Adapis,* the first fossil primate to be named (by Cuvier in 1821; Figure 6–4.) Cuvier originally thought that his new fossil was an ancestor of the ungulates (hoofed mammals, such as cattle), so he named the fossil after the ancient Egyptian bull god Apis, prefixing this name with the Greek word *ad,* meaning "toward" Apis.

The status of the plesiadapiforms as true primates has been questioned by a number of researchers for many years (Martin, 1968). The teeth of the plesiadapiforms show similarities to those of primates, but the cranial and postcranial skeletal fossil material is ambiguous. At present the general consensus is to establish a separate order for the plesiadapiforms, noting some of the similarities that they share with the primates. This group is discussed here because they are one of the best represented groups of early mammals. More important, they were the most primatelike of any mammal that lived during the time in which early primates diverged.

Most of the fossil remains of the plesiadapiforms consist of fragmentary jaws and teeth. Several features of the dentition are similar to those seen in later

plesiadapiforms: archaic primates of the Paleocene and early Eocene epochs.

FIGURE 6–4 (*a*) Reconstruction of *Plesiadapis.* (*b*) Relative abundance of plesiadapiforms in relation to other Paleocene mammals. (*c*) Skull of *Plesiadapis,* showing low-cusped molars; rodentlike incisors; low, flat skull; and long snout.

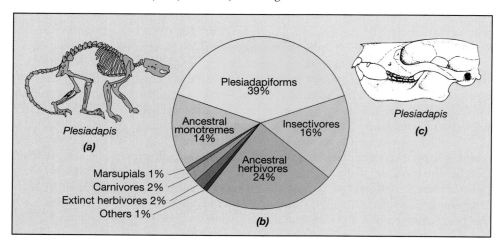

prosimians, including molar teeth with relatively low cusps. Because the complete number of teeth in the upper and lower jaws is known, we can describe the different number and kinds of teeth by using a dental formula. A *dental formula* indicates the number of teeth of each type present in one side of the upper or lower jaw. The primitive plesiadapiform dental formula, for example, is 3.1.3.3. This means that each side of the upper and lower jaw contains three incisors, one canine, three premolars (or bicuspids), and three molars.

Because all of the members of this group possess three or fewer premolars, the plesiadapiforms are not considered to be ancestral to the earliest prosimians. Many of the known early prosimians possess four premolars. In addition, the plesiadapiforms had extremely large and *procumbent* (slanting forward, like a rodent's) upper and lower central incisors, features that are also uncommon among the prosimians. The plesiadapiforms do show, however, a great diversity of dental forms, and this in turn indicates a wide range of dietary adaptations.

Cranially, the plesiadapiforms have a low flat skull, a long snout, and no bony rings surrounding the orbits of the eyes. Because these features are so different from those of any living primate, it is useless to speculate about whether the plesiadapiforms were nocturnal or diurnal in habit.

Fossil remains of the limb and trunk skeleton are rare, with one exception. The one genus that is represented by a substantial number of postcranial fossils is *Plesiadapis* (see Figure 6–4). These fossils show an animal that possessed short, heavily constructed limbs; hands with nonopposable thumbs; and claws at the ends of all of the digits, all features that are more primitive than those generally seen in primates. Judging from the differences in size of some of these limb bone fossils, the overall body size of different species ranged from that of a large New World monkey, such as the howler monkey (about 10 kg, or 4 lb), to those smaller than any living primate.

The genus *Purgatorius,* a tiny fossil mammal found in deposits of the earliest Paleocene in Montana, is probably the oldest representative of this group. Of all of the plesiadapiforms, *Purgatorius* is generalized enough in its dental formula, 3.1.4.3, and in its dentition to be ancestral to the later plesiadapiforms as well as to the primates. Although we know of intermediate fossils that link *Purgatorius* to the plesiadapiforms, a conclusive link with the primates awaits the appropriate fossil discoveries.

THE SECOND PRIMATE RADIATION: PROSIMIANS

The end of the Paleocene epoch marked a period of global warming that caused greater rainfall and higher temperatures over much of the earth (Figure 6–5; Appendix 2). Evergreen, tropical forests extended over much of Africa, North America, and Eurasia at this time. The increased size of tropical forests and warmer temperatures facilitated the spread and adaptive radiation of primates into new areas.

The initial radiation of early primates during the Eocene epoch, beginning some 54 million years ago, came after the extinction of most of the plesiadapiforms. This radiation marks the first appearance of primates that show many similarities to the living prosimians. Prosimians possess such distinguishing characteristics as postorbital bars, which complete the lateral or outside rings of bone around the eye sockets; shorter snouts and larger, more rounded braincases than the plesiadapiforms; thumbs and great toes that diverge from the other four digits, allowing opposability and grasping; and nails at the ends of most of the digits instead of claws (Figure 6–6; see also Figure 6–2).

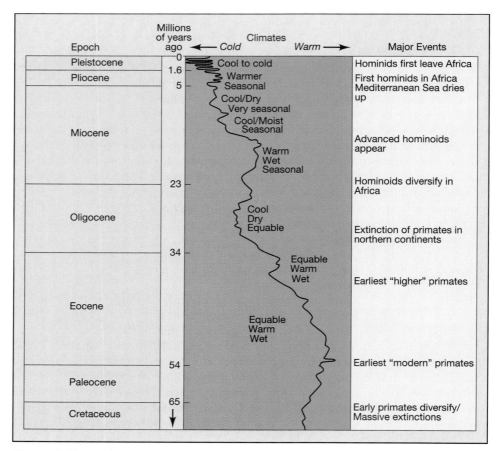

FIGURE 6–5   Geological time and environmental history of the Cenozoic era, in which the primates evolved.

Two superfamilies of early primates are recognized, consisting of multiple genera and species. The first of these two groups are the lemurlike **adapoids.** In their tooth pattern, the adapoids are in many respects the most primitive of these early primates. The dental formula is 2.1.4.3, and both the upper and lower canines are larger than the upright positioned incisors. In some species the canine teeth are sexually dimorphic (in other words, the male's canine teeth are much larger than the female's).

The second group, the tarsierlike **omomyoids,** initially shared the dental formula of the adapoids, but later the number of antemolar teeth were reduced. Many members of this group possessed large procumbent incisors and small canine teeth, unlike those of the adapoids.

The adapoid primates have traditionally been called Eocene lemurs and do show derived features that point to a possible ancestry of modern lemurs (Figure 6–7). Several features found in the omomyoids, such as the structure of the orbit, the leg where the tibia and fibula are commonly fused, and the elongated calcaneus (heel-bone) of the foot, link these primates to modern tarsiers.

Although we have not yet found any fossil remains that would qualify as representing the direct ancestors of the early prosimians, several genera from Africa and Asia may be close to the original stock. The first one, *Altanius,* a tiny primate [about 10 g (.3 oz)] known from many specimens from the early Eocene of

adapoids: lemurlike fossil prosimians of the Eocene age.

omomyoids: tarsierlike prosimians, among the earliest haplorhines of the Eocene age.

Mongolia, is considered by Gingerich et al. (1991) to be a basal primate ancestral to both adapoids and omomyoids. *Altiatlasius,* a larger African primate [50 to 100 g (1.5 to 3 oz)] from the Paleocene of Morocco, known from only 10 isolated teeth, is dentally related to modern prosimians, but the lack of other fossil remains makes a specific relationship unclear (Sige et al., 1990).

Climatic cooling at the end of the early Eocene, coupled with mountain formation in western North America and Europe, made for diversifying environments over the ranges of prosimians. In both Europe and North America, where the best fossil record of these forms exist, the adapoids and the omomyoids were a diverse group of primates that occupied a wide range of habitats. The adapoids, however, seemed to have occupied adaptive niches more similar to those of the living anthropoids. Species of the adapoid group were generally larger in size (from about 1,000 to 7,000 g) and were diurnal. Based on their dentition patterns, they ate fruit (frugivores) and leaves (folivores). In North America they were represented by only five or six genera.

The omomyoids were, at least in the beginning, more comparable in adaptation to the modern galago, an African prosimian, in that they were small in size [less than 500 g (15 oz)] and appear to have been nocturnal (illustrations of many living prosimians appear in Chapter 7). Later, during the Oligocene, omomyoids developed larger body size and adapted to a folivorous diet. In North America, unlike in Europe, the omomyoids were taxonomically diverse (about 19 genera). Although the postcranial fossil materials for most of these early primates are poorly known, the remains of elongated hindlimbs generally indicate a leaping ability for both the omomyoids and adapoids.

Though the prosimians have left a trail of their evolutionary history with scattered fossils through the Eocene and into the Pleistocene, prosimian dominance was well on the wane by the beginning of the Oligocene, some 37 million years ago. They disappeared from the fossil record in North America during this period.

The living prosimians are relics of what was once a widely distributed and ecologically diverse group. Today, in the mainland areas of Southeast Asia and tropical Africa, the prosimians have been displaced from the daytime world by the anthropoids because of competition for natural resources. With the exception of the isolated case of Madagascar, a large island off the southeast coast of Africa, now only nocturnal prosimian species survive.

In Africa and Southeast Asia, prosimians range into tropical woodlands, deciduous forests, and rain forests. In addition, the largely diurnal lemuroid groups live in the dry, spiny forests and the rain forests of Madagascar (see Figure 6–7). Three species of bush babies ("galagos") are found in habitats throughout the forests of central to southern Africa. Two additional prosimians in the lorisid family, the potto (*Perodicticus*) and the angwantibo (*Arctocebus*), live together with the galago in much of their forested range. In Asia the nocturnal prosimians include the slender loris (*Loris*) and the slow loris (*Nycticebus*), as well as the leaping form, the tarsier.

Napier and Walker (1967) described prosimian locomotion as primarily a form of vertical clinging and leaping (Figure 6–8). Extremes in locomotor speed exist among the prosimians. The tarsier and galago move by rapid jumping and clinging to branches, whereas the potto and slow loris move, as the latter's name implies, at a casual, cautious pace along the branches. The limb skeleton of each reflects their locomotor capabilities. The tarsier, perhaps the most dramatic jumper, has extremely elongated hindlimbs. The lower portion of the hindlimb has a largely fused tibia and fibula. This adaptation increases the stability of the lower limb and at the same time adds greater strength to withstand the compressive shock in

FIGURE 6–6 Reconstruction of the Eocene adapoid *Notharctus,* from North America.

FIGURE 6–7 Ring-tailed lemur in native habitat in Madagascar.

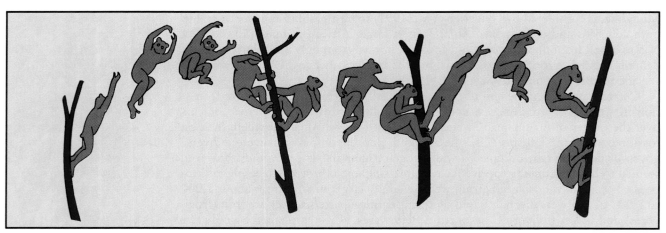

FIGURE 6-8   Vertical clinging and leaping among prosimians.

landing after long jumps. Two of the tarsier's tarsal (foot) bones, the calcaneus (heel bone) and talus (ankle bone), are also elongated (see Figure 7–10). This elongation of the tarsal bones provides greater leverage in jumping and gives the tarsier its name.

THE THIRD PRIMATE RADIATION: ANTHROPOIDS

The latter half of the Eocene epoch and the beginning of the Oligocene epoch (34 million to 23 million years ago) was a period of global cooling and of increasingly open, less forested habitats (refer back to Figure 6–5). These significant changes in the environments of the world were the result primarily of the shifting positions of the continents. Most importantly, South America and Australia separated from Antarctica, making possible the first deep water currents around Antarctica and allowing colder water to circulate toward the equator. Changes in these ocean currents resulted in a great decrease in global temperatures.

Faunas worldwide changed as well. For one thing, more terrestrial browsing (herbivorous) species appeared. For another, the higher primates, the anthropoids, made their debut suddenly, without any clear antecedents, in regions of the world, such as Africa and possibly Asia, that remained mostly warm and tropical. One of the earliest possible anthropoids thus far discovered is a new fossil from the middle Eocene of southern China called *Eosimias*. This fossil has been classified as an anthropoid on the basis of its dental features, which include small spatulate (flat) incisors and enlarged canines positioned on a deep mandible (Figure 6–10, p. 148).

Two other possible early anthropoid genera are also Eocene in age and come from deposits in Burma (now Myanmar). As with *Eosimias*, the anthropoid affinities of *Amphipithecus* and *Pondaungia* are based on features of the dentition and jaws. A third possible early ancestral group is represented by a fossil genus named *Siamopithecus*. This fossil, discovered in late Eocene sediments in Thailand, shares the dental characteristics of the previous three candidates (Chaimanee et al., 1997). Presently, however, not enough of these fragmentary fossils are available for us to make conclusive diagnoses of their affinities (Ciochon and Holroyd, 1994). It is possible that some of these fossils are not anthropoids at all.

The Prosimian Origin of the Anthropoids

It is certain that the earliest anthropoids had nonanthropoid ancestors. But who were these ancestors? We can condense most of the hypotheses about these ancestors into four possible cases, each of which has strengths and weaknesses (Figure 6–9). The question is difficult to resolve, given our current state of knowledge, for two reasons. On the one hand, many of the early anthropoids retain primitive features, such as simple premolars and unfused mandibular symphyses (chin). On the other hand, many Eocene prosimians have features that are anthropoidlike, including fused symphyses and sexual dimorphism of the canine teeth. It is also certain that most of the hypotheses regarding anthropoid origins are incorrect in their fine detail. The question will only be resolved with the discovery of new fossils that will fill in the gaps and tell us about the intermediate morphologies that link one group to its descendants. In the meantime, the four current theories are as follows:

Tarsier Origin (Figure 6–9a)

Postorbital closure and middle ear morphology are the main features that distinguish the anthropoids from the prosimians. Only the living tarsiers share these characters with anthropoids. Dental evidence from the fossil *Eosimias*, a genus more fully described later in the chapter, supports the theory of a tarsier origin for anthropoids (Kay, Ross, and Williams, 1997). However, the absence of the anthropoid middle ear features in *Eosimias* suggests that this feature may have evolved in parallel in tarsiers and anthropoids (see Figure 6–11).

Omomyoid Origin (Figure 6–9b)

Many researchers view the omomyoids as good candidates for the ancestors of both tarsiers and anthropoids. This hypothesis is in agreement with recent molecular studies that link the tarsiers to the anthropoids (Rosenberger and Dagosto, 1992). However, the anthropoid features of the middle ear and postorbital closure are not seen in any known omomyoid. We have, however, only a few skulls that are complete enough to show whether these anthropoid characters are present in the omomyoids, so the question may be considered open.

Adapoid Origins (Figure 6–9c)

Arguments in favor of adapoid origins are largely based on the similarities in the anterior dentition (small canines and large canines) and frequently fused mandibular symphyses that the adapoids share with anthropoids. In this point of view the omomyoids are too specialized a group in many features and their postcanine dentition suggests that they are more closely aligned with the later oligopithecids than with the anthropoids. There is no evidence at present, however, to suggest that the adapoids possessed those anthropoid features of the middle ear or orbit of the eye.

Ancient or Other Origin (Figure 6–9d)

Hypotheses that promote a separate, ancient position derive from our present inability to identify an ancestral group from any of the known prosimian groups. Therefore, researchers argue that the origin of the anthropoids must be ancient, derived from some yet undiscovered Paleocene prosimian that may have lived on continents that, as yet, have not been well explored for their fossil content, such as Africa or Asia (Beard and MacPhee, 1994). However, according to Fleagle,

> arguing for a nonadapoid, nonomomyoid, nontarsier origin for anthropoids is little more than a claim for ignorance regarding the origin of the group . . . and suggests that we might expect identification of their correct phylogenetic relationships to be more difficult to reconstruct, because each (group) would have had even more time to develop parallelisms. (1999:421)

FIGURE 6–9

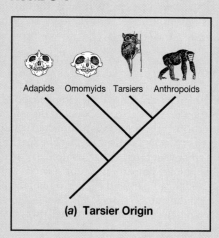

(a) Tarsier Origin

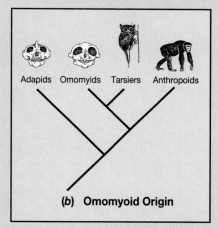

(b) Omomyoid Origin

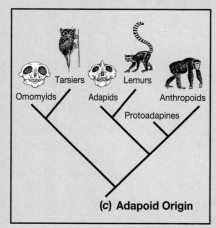

(c) Adapoid Origin

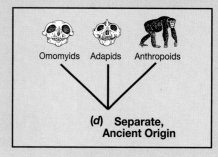

(d) Separate, Ancient Origin

FIGURE 6–10 Recent discoveries of ankle and foot bones of the 45-million-year-old *Eosimias* (shown here in a reconstruction) establishes this primate as an extremely primitive member of the anthropoid lineage and the smallest primate ever found. Specimens of *Eosimias* range in size from about 12 g (.5 oz) to about 100 g (4 oz). These differences may represent distinct species or sexual dimorphism. The discovery of *Eosimias* supports the view that anthropoids originated in Asia and then migrated into Africa.

Certainly, one diagnostic feature that separates the Old World anthropoids and tarsiers from other modern prosimians is the bony anatomy of the middle ear (Figure 6–11). This region of the skull is important in general in determining relationships among different primates. In particular, in tarsiers and Old World primates, including humans, the bony ring that surrounds the eardrum expands outward to form a tubular opening. This advanced feature has not been found in any of the known fossil Eocene primates, such as *Eosimias,* and this casts some doubt on the claims of anthropoid affinities for any of these groups.

Discoveries at the Fayum Depression

From the beginning of the twentieth century, most of our knowledge of anthropoid evolution has come from fossils recovered in a region of Egypt called the Fayum Depression (Figure 6–12 and Figure 6–13, p. 150). Surrounding this basin is a series of sedimentary deposits, the Jebel Qatrani Formation, that likely date, at the bottom of the series, from the latest Eocene and, at the top, from the earliest Oligocene. Our knowledge of the paleoenvironment suggests that these times were warm, wet, and seasonal, in marked contrast to the desert conditions found there today.

The fossil plants preserved in Fayum deposits provide an important glimpse at the world of the early anthropoids. The fossil wood preserves the remains of mangrove trees, which characteristically live in low-lying swamps near the sea, and large broad-leaved trees and climbing, vinelike plants that live abundantly in dense rain forests (Bown et al., 1982).

The Eocene–Oligocene primates that lived in the Fayum shared it with many large and small mammals, but the diverse primate fauna included at least five groups of prosimians and three well-known groups of anthropoids. Of the anthropoid

FIGURE 6–11 The structure of the tympanic bone, or ring, that surrounds the eardrum, and its position in relation to the bones of the middle ear, vary among the modern primates. (*a*) Cross-section of the primitive mammalian condition, in which the ring is exposed and the middle ear cavity lacks a bony floor. (*b*) The structure found in lemurs, in which the ring is enclosed in a bony auditory bulla, a bulblike protrusion of bone below the level of the base of the skull. (*c*) The structure found in lorises and New World monkeys, in which the ring is at the surface and forms part of the outer wall of the bulla. (*d*) Structure found in Old World primates, including tarsiers, apes, and humans, in which the ring extends outward to form a tubular opening, the external auditory meatus.

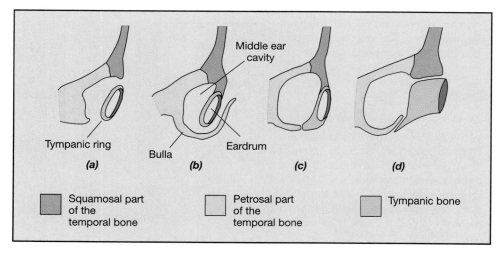

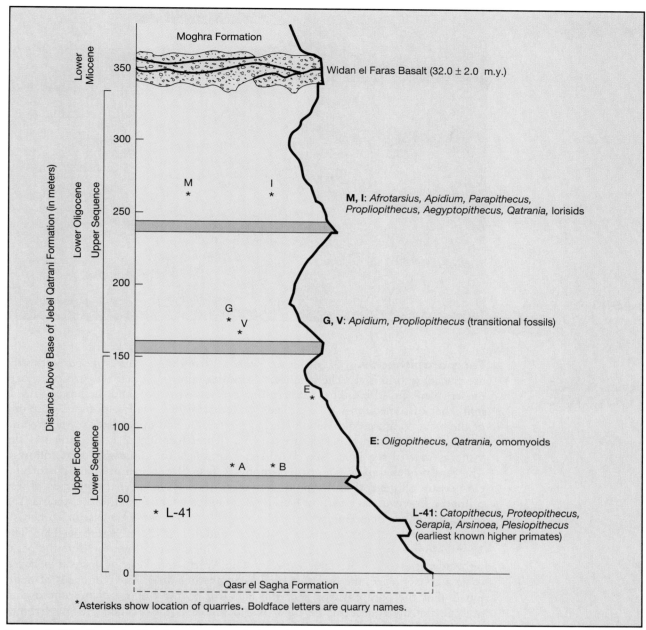

FIGURE 6-12 Geological levels and primate finds in the Fayum, Egypt. Levels E and L contain the earliest known fossil primates of this time range.

groups we can distinguish three families: the **parapithecids**, the **propliopithecids**, and the **oligopithecids** (Figure 6–14). As Figure 6–12 shows, fossil primates have been recovered primarily from three levels in the formation. The most recent primates come from the uppermost levels (quarries M, I), where they are the most common of all of the fossil mammals. In contrast, the middle levels (quarries G, V) have yielded only a few primates, but these are important transitional fossils. At the lowest levels (quarries E, L-41), many incompletely described discoveries of the earliest higher primates (Simons and Rasmussen, 1994) have changed our views of the origin of this group.

parapithecids: Oligocene anthropoids, the most primitive of the known species from Fayum, Egypt.

propliopithecids: the largest anthropoid (catarrhine) primates from the Oligocene of Egypt, sometimes considered the earliest hominoids.

oligopithecids: Oligocene anthropoids whose affinities to later hominoid primates remains obscure.

Figure 6–13 The Fayum site, Egypt.

The parapithecids. Of all higher primates from the Fayum, the parapithecids are the most primitive. The smallest (*Qatrania*) approximated the size of a marmoset (New World monkey, about 500 g, or just over 1 lb), and the largest (*Apidium*) that of a medium-size dog. The parapithecids, especially *Apidium*, were one of the most common mammals found in the middle and upper beds of the Fayum. In dentition the parapithecids possessed a dental formula, 2.1.3.3, which is the same as that of the later New World monkeys (see the discussion that follows). The fusion of the mandible at the symphysis, fused frontal suture, and postorbital closure are all general anthropoid characteristics seen in the parapithecids. These primates, however, lack certain features seen in later Old World forms, such as the reduced number of premolars to two instead of three, the broad ischial tuberosities, and the tubular tympanic of the middle ear (see Figure 6–11). The bilophodont pattern seen on the molar teeth, which would seem to relate the parapithecids directly to the later evolving Old World monkeys, is instead believed to be a convergence, the result of similar frugiverous diets. The consensus of opinion is that the parapithecids probably lie close to the origin of anthropoids but precede the divergence of the New World monkeys, also called the **platyrrhines** (see Figure 6–14).

The propliopithecids. The propliopithecids are the best-known higher primates that are larger than the largest parapithecid. They possessed the same dental formula, 2.1.2.3, as modern Old World higher primates (catarrhines). Their molars are apelike, in that they show broad basins (called *talonids*) surrounded by five rounded cusps and lack the bilophodont pattern of the Old World monkeys. The canine teeth of many species are large and sexually dimorphic. Of the many species of propliopithecids, *Aegyptopithecus* is one of the largest (6 to 8 kg, or 13 to 18 lb) and best known of all of the fossil anthropoids (Figure 6–15). It has relatively small orbits of the eyes, suggesting that it was actively diurnal, an adaptation that appears to be common among many of these anthropoids.

Aegyptopithecus possessed anthropoid characteristics in the eye orbits, which are completely walled off posteriorly from the skull, a result of increased conver-

platyrrhines: New World monkeys.

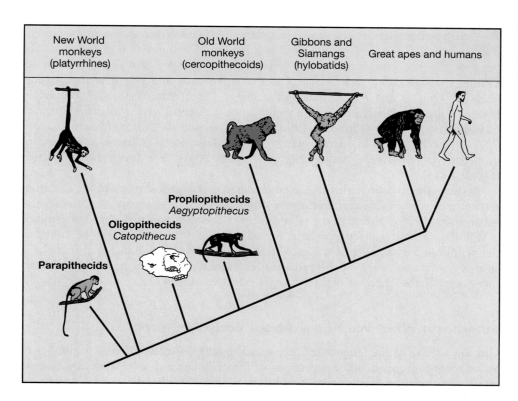

New World monkeys (platyrrhines) | Old World monkeys (cercopithecoids) | Gibbons and Siamangs (hylobatids) | Great apes and humans

Propliopithecids
Aegyptopithecus

Oligopithecids
Catopithecus

Parapithecids

FIGURE 6–14 Evolutionary relationships among early anthropoids. Extinct groups are shown in boldface type.

gence (frontal positioning) of the orbits. It also had a large brain with relatively large parietal regions for primates of these times. It possessed some primitive features, however. In the ear region, the tympanic is a bony ring fused to the lateral surface of the auditory bulla with no bony tube (see Figure 6–11), and the limb bones show greater similarities to New World monkeys and the prosimians. Researchers believe that the propliopithecids are a primitive group that preceded the subsequent divergence and evolutionary radiation of the Old World monkeys and apes (Fleagle 1999:413).

FIGURE 6–15 Reconstruction (left) and skull and lower jaw (right) of *Aegyptopithecus zeuxis,* a member of the propliopithecine group of early anthropoids.

The oligopithecids. The most enigmatic of the Fayum anthropoids are the oligopithecids. They possess most of the anthropoid features that characterize the propliopithecids, but dentally they possess many unique features, such as small canines that are compressed in size from front to back and primitive molar morphology. One of the earliest oligopithecids is *Oligopithecus savagei,* named in honor of the late Donald Savage, a well-known paleontologist from the University of California, Berkeley (Simons, 1990). Closely related to *Oligopithecus* is *Catopithecus* (see Figure 6–14), from quarry L-41, whose fossil remains, consisting of numerous jaws, several skulls, and some limb bones, are much better known (Figure 6–16).

Because the fossil remains of *Catopithecus* represent most parts of the skeleton, researchers can be fairly certain that the oligopithecids are anthropoids (Simons and Rasmussen, 1996). Although the relationship of this group to the other anthropoids is still obscure and subject to debate, the oligopithecids are believed to be linked to the propliopithecids. Even if we know little more than this, the oligopithecids have shown us that the base of the radiation of higher primates is much bushier and more complicated than we earlier thought (Fleagle, 1999:417).

Summary: What We Know About Early Anthropoids

Our knowledge of the Oligocene anthropoid fossil record has clarified a number of issues regarding the earliest adaptations of the early anthropoids. With new discoveries of anthropoid fossils from North Africa and Asia, however, the diversity of these species makes it difficult to describe a single basic anthropoid adaptation. The fossil record shows us that the early anthropoids were diverse and successful primates consisting of a large number of species, mostly very small. Based on their small size and the morphologies of their dentition, we think that these species were probably insectivorous in diet. There is no evidence that any of them were folivores like the modern colobine monkeys, which we discuss in Chapter 7. The fossil limb bones suggest that they generally moved by arboreal quadrupedalism and leaping, and resembled in their primitive morphologies the New World monkeys, which are discussed in the next section. At this point there is no evidence for locomotion by either terrestrial quadrupedalism or arboreal suspension, such as we describe for the modern apes in the next chapter.

ORIGINS AND EVOLUTION OF THE MONKEYS

The anthropoid primates of the early Oligocene were directly ancestral to the early groups of monkeys and apes, both of which appeared more or less simultaneously in the fossil record in deposits primarily in Africa about 25 million years ago (late Oligocene). Monkeys were also, for the first time, found in South America during this period.

During the final phases of the Oligocene world, temperatures began to climb once again, reaching another peak during the succeeding Miocene epoch (see Figure 6–5). About 15 million years ago, the average temperature, 20 degrees centigrade, was about 10 degrees higher than during the earlier Oligocene low. Although forests increased in size in some areas, seasonal variations in temperature became the pattern, and in many parts of Africa more arid climates resulted in ecosystems like the broad savannas we see today.

The early Miocene deposits exposed along the East African rift system have given us the fossils of the earliest monkeys and apes. The fossil record shows relatively few kinds of monkeys and a great diversity and abundance of primitive apes.

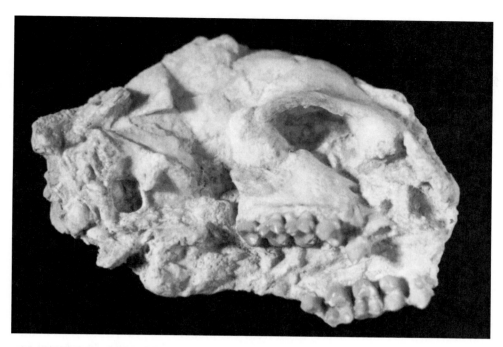

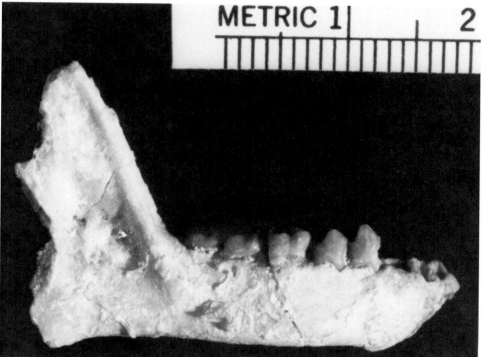

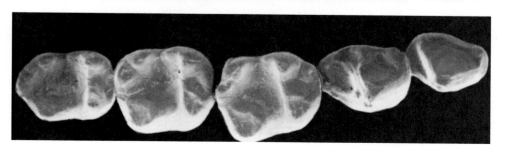

FIGURE 6-16 *Catopithecus brownii,* from Fayum quarry L-41, the first undisputed anthropoid: (*a*) skull and mandible; (*b*) lower teeth, viewed from the side; and (*c*) lower teeth, seen from the top.

We explore this fossil record, along with that from South America, in an attempt to understand the origins and diversity of these groups.

New World Monkeys

The French naturalist Buffon (1767) was the first to recognize the primates of the New World and to differentiate them from the better-known monkeys and apes of the Old World. He based his early, simple classification primarily on external morphological features, the three most visible characteristics of which are an absence of cheek pouches and ischial callosities (areas of hardened skin on the buttocks), both of which are found only on the Old World monkeys, and more widely spaced nostrils (Figure 6–17). Later, in the nineteenth century, came the discovery of the smallest members of this group, the marmosets and the tamarins, whose tails lack the prehensile (grasping) ability common to a number of other New World primates.

New World monkeys belong to the family **Cebidae** and are divided into six subfamilies. Again, we discuss these and the other modern primate species in Chapter 7.

The fossil record of the New World monkeys (the platyrrhines, Greek meaning "flat-nosed") is not extensive (Figure 6–18). The earliest known forms, discovered at the late Oligocene locality of Salla, Bolivia, consist of only two genera, *Branisella* and *Szalatavus*. A more diverse fossil record of monkeys appears in early to middle Miocene deposits in the southern regions of Argentina and Chile. The dental formula of these early monkeys and most other New World species, with the exception of the marmosets and tamarins (of the subfamily **Callitrichinae**), is 2.1.3.3. The low, rounded cusps of the molars and premolars are characteristic of the diets of frugivorous animals.

Cebidae: family of New World monkeys.

Callitrichinae: subfamily of marmosets and tamarins.

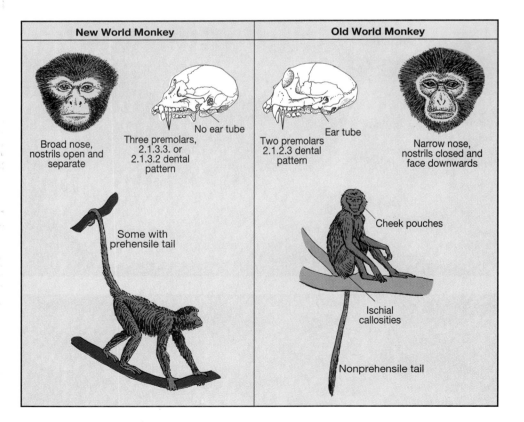

New World Monkey	Old World Monkey
Broad nose, nostrils open and separate	Narrow nose, nostrils closed and face downwards
Three premolars, 2.1.3.3. or 2.1.3.2 dental pattern	Two premolars 2.1.2.3 dental pattern
No ear tube	Ear tube
Some with prehensile tail	Cheek pouches
	Ischial callosities
	Nonprehensile tail

FIGURE 6–17 Major differences between New World and Old World monkeys.

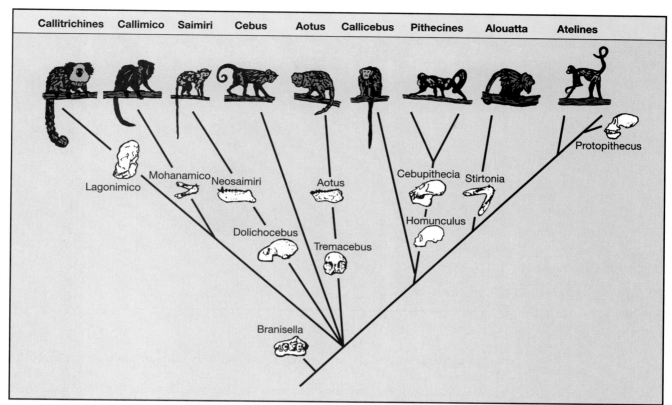

FIGURE 6-18 Evolutionary relationships among New World monkeys. Many early forms show close similarities to their modern descendants.

The most striking feature of New World monkey fossils is their similarity to the living species, and it seems apparent that many lineages of living New World monkeys have been separate from one another since the middle Miocene. For example, the Argentinean fossil *Tremacebus* in its dental and cranial features shows great similarity to living forms of *Aotus,* the owl or night monkey (Rosenberger, 1984).

One of the most intriguing questions about the New World monkeys is, "How did they get to South America in the first place?" South America until about 3 million years ago was an island continent separated from Africa by the south Atlantic Ocean and from North America by the Caribbean Sea. If primates came across these bodies of water from either continent, they would have had to accomplish this feat by rafting (Figure 6–19). The only possible alternative explanation is that the New World monkeys evolved from earlier prosimian primates who were already in South America. There is no fossil record, however, of any earlier primate native to South America.

This fact leaves us with the only other option for New World monkey origin—colonization. But from where? During the Oligocene ocean levels were considerably lower than they are today. As a consequence, many islands would have been exposed in the South Atlantic, and the ocean currents would have been favorable for primates to cross from Africa to South America. Other facts, as well, support the hypothesis of an African homeland for the New World monkeys. Most important, the primate fossil record from South America consists only of anthropoid (monkey) forms, and the only regions that have yielded early anthropoids are in the Old World. We have already seen that while prosimian primates abounded in

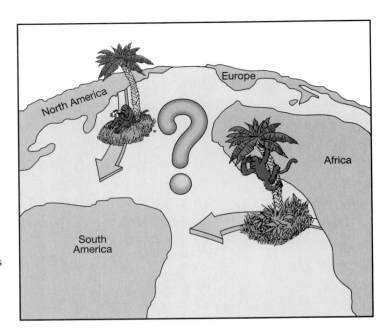

FIGURE 6–19 Possible routes of dispersal of the ancestors of New World monkeys from either Africa or North America.

North America during this period, there are no records of anthropoids in North America.

There are many similarities between the anthropoids of the Fayum and the fossil monkeys of South America. The parapithecid primates are especially interesting in this regard, because they clearly evolved before the New World and Old World anthropoids diverged, and they possess a dental formula, 2.1.3.3, the same as that of most New World anthropoids. Finally, like primates, rodents apparently also colonized South America during the Oligocene, and these rodents are most closely related to African forms, such as the porcupine (Hoffstetter and Lavocat, 1970).

Some researchers (Simons, 1976) believe that long-distance rafting is a highly unlikely way for animals, such as anthropoids, which do not hibernate, to move from one continent to another. Food requirements would making successful travel over a long period of time highly problematic. We know, however, that large rafts of vegetation, some large enough to support standing midsize trees, occasionally break off from banks of tropical rivers and drift out to sea. Such rafts, emanating from, perhaps, the Congo or Niger rivers of west Africa, may have launched some primates on new evolutionary journeys to the shores of South America. Given our current knowledge of the fossil record of primates around the world, rafting (probably from Africa) is the only plausible explanation we have of how primates came to inhabit South America.

Old World Monkeys

catarrhines: primates of the Old World, including monkeys, apes, and humans.

cercopithecines: subfamily of Old World monkeys with generally omnivorous or graminivorous diets.

colobines: subfamily of Old World monkeys, leaf-eating and mostly arboreal.

Modern monkeys of the Old World are members of the **catarrhine** group and belong to one family, the cercopithecids, that is divided into two subfamilies, the **cercopithecines,** consisting of baboons and macaques, and the **colobines,** or leaf-eating monkeys. Living colobines are clearly distinguished from cercopithecines by dental, cranial, and soft-tissue features. Cercopithecines possess specific distinguishing characteristics, such as molar teeth with high crowns and low cusps, and skulls that are longer in snout length and narrower in interorbital width. All cercopithecines have cheek pouches in which they store undigested food. Colobines have molar teeth with cusps that are higher than those of the cercopithecines and stomachs, like those of cows, that allow them to digest mature vegetable matter, such as leaves. We discuss all these features in great depth in Chapter 7. These two subfamilies can be distinguished in the fossil record by the late Miocene (5 million to 7 million years ago) in Africa, Asia, and Europe.

The earliest fossil monkeys, however, cannot be assigned easily to either subfamily of modern Old World monkey. They belong instead to a group called the **victoriapithecids,** which apparently predated the split of the cercopithecines from the colobines. Fossils of these early monkeys have been discovered in several sites in both northern and eastern Africa but are quite rare when compared to the number of early ape fossils that have been found in the same regions. These fossil monkeys, however, do provide us with good evidence, especially in their dentition, of the intermediate stages in the evolution of the Old World monkeys of the Oligocene to the modern species.

There are two known genera of victoriapithecids: *Prohylobates,* found in Miocene sites in Egypt and Libya, and *Victoriapithecus,* from the middle Miocene site of Maboko Island, Lake Victoria, Kenya, a site also known for its fossils of primitive apes. These monkeys are small to medium in size (4 to 22 kg; 2 to 10 lb) and are distinguished from early apes by the presence of bilophodont lower molars. They possessed canines that were sexually dimorphic, but they had relatively small brains as compared to modern species, and their overall facial morphology was similar to that of *Aegyptopithecus.* The fossil limb bones of the victoriapithecids are those of a quadruped adept at locomotion on the ground or in the trees.

Very few fossil monkeys from the middle Miocene to the late Miocene are known. By 5 million years ago and continuing on through the Pleistocene, however, fossil monkeys become increasingly more abundant and diverse. One notable feature of these fossil cercopithecids is their larger body size compared to that of modern species. For example, one fossil species of gelada baboon (*Theropithecus oswaldi*) weighed about 96 kg (44 lb), as compared to the modern gelada males, which weigh about 19 kg (9 lb). Most of these larger primates, along with many other large mammals, became extinct for unknown reasons during the middle Pleistocene.

The increase in monkey diversity corresponds to a decrease in diversity of the Miocene apes. It may be that the change over time of the relative abundance of the monkeys and apes is an ecological replacement of apes by the more competitive monkeys. Evidence suggests that climatic change also played a role, however, and that the decrease in the number of apes is not simply the result of the monkeys outcompeting the apes for resources (Kelley, 1998).

The earliest fossil cercopithecines appear in the fossil record during the late Miocene. Representatives of the genus *Macaca* (macaques), the most widespread of this group, ranged from Europe and North Africa to Asia. In contrast with the fossil cercopithecines, which are often described as being similar morphologically to the living species, many of the fossil colobines are quite different in appearance, ranged over a wider geographical area, and occupied more diverse ecological niches than did their successors.

The oldest fossil colobine from the late Miocene is *Mesopithecus,* which is found in Europe and western Asia (Figure 6–20). *Mesopithecus* (about 7 kg; 3 lb) and its close relative *Dolichopithecus,* a larger form (about 13 to 18 kg, or 6 to 8 lb), both possess postcranial features that suggest terrestrial quadrupedalism as a mode of locomotion. Reconstructions show these primates living in woodland savannas and forests, environments that would have lent themselves well to terrestrial quadrupeds.

Questions about the origins of the living species of monkeys, although not completely resolved, do not present the same degree of difficulty as those about the

victoriapithecids: earliest fossil Old World monkeys of the Miocene, ancestral to later cercopithecines and colobines.

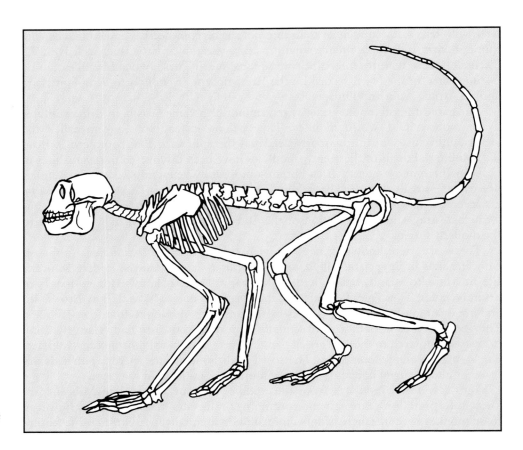

FIGURE 6–20 Skeleton of *Mesopithecus,* a late Miocene fossil colobine.

origin of modern apes. The great diversity and abundance of the fossil apes of the Miocene have not clarified our understanding of the lineages that produced modern apes. The almost complete lack of any ape fossil record from the late Miocene through the Pleistocene complicates the issue further. We turn our attention to these apes and their adaptive radiation at the beginning of the Miocene in Chapter 9.

◖ **SUMMARY**

1. **What is a primate?**
   Primates are animals that developed a number of unique morphological features, including stereoscopic vision and, in many species, color vision as a way of catching prey as well as locomoting rapidly in the trees. The earliest primates were distinguished from other kinds of closely related mammals, such as the bats, insectivores and "flying lemurs," by their dentition, which, in terms of function, was best suited to a vegetarian diet. Later-developed characteristics, such as the grasping hands and feet and an enlarged brain, allowed primates to become adept in arboreal locomotion.

2. **When did the first primatelike animals appear, and what were their characteristics?**
   Primates as a distinct order of mammals originated during the early Paleocene as tropical animals that evolved hands and feet for grasping and for locomotion in the trees. The ancestry of the primates is perhaps most closely related to that of the insectivores who today are represented by one common form: the tree shrew of Southeast Asia. An omnivorous diet, as reflected in bunodont cusp tooth

structures, distinguished the earliest or archaic primates, including the plesi-adapiforms from other mammals.

3. **What are the characteristics of the prosimians, and when did they evolve?**

The evolution of the archaic primates was followed by a series of three adaptive radiations that characterized the evolution of the early prosimian-like primates through the evolution of the higher primates or anthropoids. The first radiation, which occurred during the Paleocene and Eocene is marked by the diversification of the plesiadapiforms. The second radiation, which began at the end of the Paleocene, produced the arboreal prosimians, the ancestors of the living lemurs, lorises, and tarsiers. The relationship between the plesiadapiforms and these archaic prosimians remains unclear.

4. **What adaptations distinguish the anthropoids?**

The third radiation occurred in the Eocene, when the anthropoid primates appeared and apparently spread out of Africa. Compared with the prosimians, they have frontally positioned orbits, a fused mandibular symphysis (jaw), larger brains, upright incisors, and limbs of equal proportions. They are also active during the day rather than at night.

5. **What are the two major groups of monkeys, and what are their evolutionary relationships?**

In South America the platyrrhines diversified into the highly variable modern New World monkeys, which possess both unique characteristics, such as the prehensile tail, and parallel characteristics, such as larger brains, with the monkeys that evolved at the same time in the Old World. In the Old World, two groups of monkeys diversified: the more generalized cercopithecines, a group to which the baboons and macaques, among others, belong, and the more specialized colobines. The colobines evolved specialized adaptations in the stomach and gut that allowed them to digest mature leaves, something the cercopithecines could not do. Both groups of Old World monkeys are found throughout many different ecosystems in Africa and Asia. The separation and subsequent diversification of the Old World and New World monkeys probably began in the early Oligocene some 30 million years ago.

◀ CRITICAL THINKING QUESTIONS

1. Prosimians and plesiadapiform primates existed side by side for much of the Eocene. We have not as yet identified any fossil species that might link these two groups. Under the circumstances, what possible explanations for the origins of the prosimians can be derived from the available data?

2. There are a number of competing hypotheses regarding the reason for the appearance of early primate traits, such as grasping feet and hands, and stereoscopic and color vision. Develop a time sequence of events and causes relating what we know about ecology, anatomy, and the behavior of these animals, and reconstruct the "best fit" evolutionary scenario that accounts for this knowledge.

3. The origin of anthropoid primates from some prosimian stock is problematic. Discuss the various competing hypotheses in light of the known fossil record, and compare each idea from a pro and con point of view.

4. The earliest fossil remains of primates in South America are Oligocene in age and more similar to monkeys than prosimians. If rafting is used to explain the colonization of South American primates from Africa, why are there no

prosimians in South America if both anthropoids and prosimians were equally common in Africa at the time?

5. The evolutionary split of the Old World monkeys into the cercopithecine and colobine subgroups was marked by dietary adaptations that were reflected in the dentition of each group. As monkeys of both subgroups are often found together in the same forests, what is the real significance of these dietary adaptations regarding competition between species and habitat exploitation?

◀ **INTERNET EXERCISES**

Critical Thinking

Teeth? Middle Ear Bones? Throughout this chapter and the previous one (and the next chapters as well), we have emphasized the distinguishing features of such minute features as teeth and middle ear bones. Why are these features so important to biological anthropologists? Find an answer by considering the following questions:

1. Why do biological anthropologists concentrate on particular features in speculating on evolutionary relationships?
2. What can physical features tell scientists about an animal's life and the environment in which it lived?

Writing Assignment

Early Primates. Choose one topic discussed in this chapter and write a brief paper about it. Some possibilities include origin of New World monkeys, ecological niches of early primates, evolutionary origins of anthropoids, evolution of the mammalian jaw and earbones, primate vision, or a topic of your own choosing. The following Web sites will get you started in your research.

See Companion Web site for Internet links.

The Primate Family Tree

Chapter 6 surveys the evolution of the earliest primates, the prosimians and first monkeys. The living prosimians retain many characteristics of their earliest ancestors. Most are small, solitary foragers that are active only at night. Monkeys, apes, and humans, who evolved later, are classified as anthropoids. They share derived characteristics that distinguish them from their earliest primate ancestors. As a group, anthropoids generally have larger body size than prosimians, and they are organized into social groups. Almost all anthropoids are active during the day.

The Web Activity provides an overview of primate evolution. The timeline shows how all groups of primates, from lorises to humans, fit into the evolutionary timeline.

WEB ACTIVITY

The story of primates begins at the time of the evolution of flowering plants, including trees, in the latter part of the

Mesozoic era. At that time, forests became complex environments, with more niches available for exploitation. By 50 million years ago, the early primates had radiated to fill the new tree-living niches. These small creatures climbed in the trees by grasping. Gradually, other groups of primates, the Old World and New World monkeys, the apes, and hominids, evolved.

Activity

1. View the animation. When did the two groups of monkeys radiate? When did apes radiate?
2. Redraw the evolutionary tree to include the plesiadapiforms. Where do they "fit"?
3. Which part of the chart shows the adapoids and omomyoids? Include these groups and their characteristics in the chart you drew for question 2 above.

The MediaLab can be found in Chapter 6 on your Companion Web site http:www.prenhall.com/boaz

PRIMATES OF THE NEW AND OLD WORLDS

In Chapter 6 we followed the evolutionary history of the primates from their appearance during the Eocene epoch, some 50 million years ago, to their divergence as anthropoids, beginning in the late Eocene to early Oligocene epochs. Although many of the connecting links between this diverse group of animals are missing from the fossil record, with the discovery of new fossils a clearer picture of primate relationships is gradually emerging. In this chapter we survey the living members of the primate order and examine their morphology and physical adaptations.

There is a wide range of variation in much of primates' life histories. Table 7–1 lists a few of these differences. Both anatomy and behavior play important roles in determining how each of these differences is expressed. In Chapter 8 we turn our attention to the social organization and behavior of these groups.

THE PRIMATE ORDER

The primate order has traditionally been divided into two major groups, or suborders (see Appendix 3). The prosimians (meaning "before apes") include the lemurs, lorises, and tarsiers; the anthropoids consist of the monkeys, apes, and humans. The

TABLE 7–1	Life History Differences Among Nonhuman Primate Species
Gestation length	60–250 days
Litter size	1–3 (rare) infants
Nursing (lactation)	2 months–5 years
Age at weaning	50 days–1,500 days
Age at sexual maturity	<1 year–9 years
Life span	10 years–50+ years

The lower ranges of these categories, with the exception of litter size, characterize the prosimians, whereas the upper ranges characterize the great apes.

SOURCE: Data from Fleagle, 1999.

living prosimians are relics of what was once a widely distributed and ecologically diverse group. Today, in Asia and Africa the prosimians have been displaced from the daytime world by the anthropoids, as a result of competition for natural resources. Only on the large island of Madagascar, located off the east coast of Africa, do any prosimians still live as day-active species, most likely because there are no anthropoids, besides humans, to compete with them.

In Africa the nocturnal prosimians consist of three species of galagids (the bush babies) and two additional species of the lorisid family, the potto (*Perodicticus*) and the angwantibo (*Arctocebus*). All of these species may be found overlapping in habitats throughout the forests of central to southern Africa.

In Southeast Asia and India the nocturnal lorisid prosimians include the slender loris (*Loris*) and the slow loris (*Nycticebus*). Southeast Asia is also the home of the single member of the tarsiid family, the *Tarsius*. Phylogenetically speaking, however, the tarsiers may be more closely related to the anthropoids than to the prosimians. Because tarsiers share some derived anatomical features with members of the anthropoids, in some taxonomic schemes, anthropoids and tarsiers are grouped together, rather than being separated in another suborder, the **haplorhines** (Greek, meaning "single nose"). The remainder of the prosimians are, in turn, grouped as **strepsirhines** (Greek, meaning "twisted nose").

Dividing the primates into haplorhines and strepsirhines has the benefit of expressing the phyletic, or evolutionary, relationships among the living primates: that is, ancestral tarsierlike primates were basal stock for both tarsiers and anthropoids (Yoder, 1997). The taxonomy that divides primates into prosimians and anthropoids "expresses the fact that the prosimians are primitive primates that lack anthropoid features" (Fleagle, 1999:82). The difference between these two schemes of dividing the primate order taxonomically may be expressed in the following manner: Prosimian − Tarsier = Strepsirhine, and Anthropoid + Tarsier = Haplorhine. In other words, all prosimians *except* tarsiers are strepsirhines, and haplorhines include anthropoids (monkeys and apes) and tarsiers.

THE STREPSIRHINES: PRIMATES OF AFRICA AND ASIA

Living strepsirhines are grouped together because they, on the whole, have retained more primitive characteristics than other prosimians. In many morphological features of the teeth, skull, and limbs they are quite similar to their 60-million-year-old Eocene ancestors, such as the adapoids described in Chapter 6. Unlike the adapoids, however, strepsirhines do share a number of specialized features that make them unique among the primates (Figure 7–1). The first specialization is the dental comb, which is made up of the procumbent lower incisors and the corresponding small upper incisors. Together these teeth function in social grooming. The grooming claw on the second digit of the foot is another unique anatomical feature, along with the outwardly (lateral) flaring heel bone, or talus.

The strepsirhine skull shows many primitive features. The orbit of the eye is surrounded on the outside by a postorbital bar, and the back of the socket is not enclosed as it is in the anthropoids (refer back to Figure 6–2). In the ear, the lemurs possess a tympanic ring surrounding the eardrum that is enclosed within a primitive auditory *bulla* (the bony housing at the base of the skull for the middle ear; see Figure 6–11). In the lorises, as well as in the New World monkeys, the tympanic ring expands and actually contributes to the formation of the bulla. As we saw in Chapter 6, the structure of the ear canal is important in determining evolutionary relationships among primates.

The elongated strepsirhine skull houses a relatively small brain whose olfactory lobes are slightly larger than the optic lobes. Strepsirhines also possess moist noses,

haplorhines: taxonomic grouping that includes the living tarsiers and their direct ancestors.

strepsirhines: taxonomic grouping of lemurlike prosimians, both living and extinct.

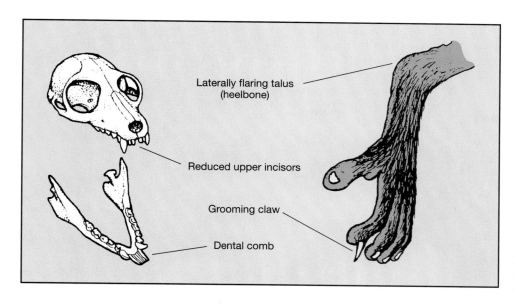

Laterally flaring talus
(heelbone)

Reduced upper incisors

Grooming claw

Dental comb

FIGURE 7–1 Specialized features of strepsirhines. This group includes the lorises and galagos.

a trait common to many other groups of mammals. The primitive dental formula is 2.1.3.3, although different families show a reduction in numbers of different teeth. For example, the indri, which lives on the island of Madagascar, has only two premolars, and the aye-aye, showing the most extreme dental specialization of any living primate, has a greatly reduced dental formula of 1.0.1.3 (Figure 7–2). Its incisor teeth are also unique in that they are large and grow continuously, like those of rodents.

Postcranially, many strepsirhines are specialized as leapers, and they leap from a position that has been described as **vertical clinging** (Napier and Walker, 1967; refer back to Figure 6–8). To maximize the effectiveness of leaping, the hindlimb is considerably elongated, to the point where in the sifaka (*Propithecus*) of Madagascar, locomotion on the ground takes the form of bipedal hopping. The hindlimbs are so much longer than the forelimbs that terrestrial quadrupedal locomotion is impossible.

Many strepsirhines have claws at the ends of some of their digits instead of nails. Many of these claws serve special uses, such as the grooming claw of the second digit of the foot, or the clawed third digit of the hand of the aye-aye. The aye-aye uses this claw and its elongated finger to probe for various kinds of food (see Figure 7–2).

FIGURE 7–2 The aye-aye, a solitary nocturnal strepsirhine of Madagascar.

Strepsirhines of Madagascar

Most strepsirhines live in forested environments, although on Madagascar they fill many different ecological niches (Figure 7–3). The sifaka, for example, lives quite successfully in the dry, spiny forest of the southern part of the island. The mongoose lemur is perhaps the most versatile of the Madagascar primates in terms of habitat usage. Although they live in the forested areas in the northern region of the island and are almost exclusively arboreal, field observations have shown that during the dry season these animals forage nocturnally, whereas in the cold, wet season, they are active during the day.

Despite their current diversity, the living Madagascar primates represent only a fraction of the number of different primates that inhabited the island as recently as 1,000 years ago. Many of these island primates (and other plants and animals) have become extinct, some as a direct consequence of human activities. The fossil record shows that most of the extinct species were large and probably diurnal. In size they

vertical clinging: a type of posture and locomotion characteristic of many strepsirhines in which these primates, clinging to vertical supports, move by leaping between the supports.

FIGURE 7–3 Most strepsirhines live in forested environments, although they inhabit various environmental niches. This drawing shows three lemurid species from different parts of Madagascar: the canopy-dwelling brown lemurs (*Eulemur fulvus*); ruffed lemurs (*Varecia variegata*), which inhabit understory trees; and the ground-dwelling, ring-tailed lemur (*Lemur catta*).

may have ranged from the small mouse lemur (30 g; 1 oz) to *Archaeoindris*, a prosimian that was almost as large as a gorilla. Some were apparently terrestrial foragers, whereas others may have used an apelike kind of suspension to feed (see Figure 7–25). Both kinds of activities are rare among the living Madagascar primates. As John Fleagle (1999:109) observed, "The Malagasy lemurs were a natural experiment in evolution. Isolated from competitors lemurs evolved a diverse array of species with dietary and locomotor adaptations for exploiting a wide range of ecological conditions."

Perodicticus potto

Galagoides demidovii

Euoticus elegantulus

Galagoides alleni

Arctocebus calabarensis

FIGURE 7–4 Five species of lorises that inhabit different niches of the same forested habitat in Gabon, in central Africa.

Strepsirhines of Africa and Asia

In contrast to the large number of Madagascar primates, there are only a limited number of African and Asian strepsirhines, the lorises and galagos. All of these animals are small and exclusively nocturnal in habit (Figure 7–4). They likely overlap in their home ranges with the larger diurnal monkeys and apes. Also unlike the Madagascar primates, the lorises and galagos show little variation in social organization, all appearing to be solitary foragers that vary in their disposition to sleep alone or in small groups.

Several cranial features differentiate the mainland strepsirhines from their Madagascar Island cousins. For example, in the ear region the tympanic ring is

FIGURE 7-5 Two Asian lorises. Left, a slow loris (*Nycticebus coucang*) from Southeast Asia. Right, a slender loris (*Loris tardigradus*) from India and Sri Lanka. Compared with the galagos, they have smaller ears and shortened hindlimbs.

fused to the lateral wall rather than being suspended within the bulla as is seen in most of the Madagascar species (see Figure 6–11). Although the overall cranial morphology of galagos and lorises is similar, these two families differ considerably in their postcranial anatomy, which reflects their locomotor abilities: galagos are leapers, whereas lorises are slow climbers.

Although there is debate among taxonomists as to the exact division of this group, most researchers agree that the galagos consist of at least three or four genera and as many as 10 species, all found in African forested habitats. Galago leaping anatomy is most strikingly shown in the relatively long lower limbs compared to the forelimbs, the elongated ankle bones (the calcaneus and the navicular), and the long tail, which is used for balance.

The lorises are found in both Africa and Asia. In Africa, as we mentioned earlier, there are two groups: the potto, which is geographically distributed from Liberia in the west to Kenya in the east; and the angwantibo, a smaller and more slender version of the potto found in more restricted localities in west central Africa.

In Asia the slender loris is found on the island of Sri Lanka and in mainland south India (Figure 7–5). The slow loris, which is found in many parts of Southeast Asia, is the stockier of the two Asian lorises. Virtually nothing is known about the social behavior of these animals.

The lorises are characteristically slow and move stealthily. They have smaller ears than do the galagos, and their hindlimbs and forelimbs are more equal in length. They also lack the long tails of the galagos. Lorises have been described as *olfactory foragers,* animals that rely heavily on their sense of smell, and are often seen moving on large branches with their noses pointed downward. Compared with the galagos, the lorises seem to show less dependence on locating their prey by hearing. This probably accounts for the lorises' smaller ears.

The living strepsirhines form a diverse group of primates that show a number of unique specializations in anatomy and habitat usage. Most of the members of this group are distantly related to one another, but the exact relationships between many of the families are yet to be completely worked out. Figure 7–6 represents a reasonable phylogenetic reconstruction of the strepsirhines based on comparative anatomy and molecular studies of the group.

FIGURE 7-6 Evolutionary relationships among strep- sirhines, including forms known only as fossils. Asian and African species are shown on the left, Madagascar species are shown on the right.

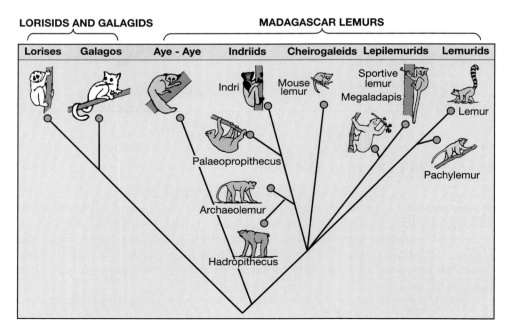

LORISIDS AND GALAGIDS | MADAGASCAR LEMURS

Lorises   Galagos   Aye - Aye   Indriids   Cheirogaleids   Lepilemurids   Lemurids

Indri   Mouse lemur   Sportive lemur   Megaladapis   Lemur

Palaeopropithecus

Pachylemur

Archaeolemur

Hadropithecus

THE HAPLORHINES: TARSIERS

The Tarsiers of Southeast Asia

The five species of tarsiers are spread out geographically over the islands of the Philippines, Borneo, Sumatra, and Java (Figure 7–7). These primates are different enough from the strepsirhines to be placed in a different lineage, one that includes monkeys, apes, and people, the haplorhines, although their evolutionary history is still debated, as we saw in Chapter 6. These small and unusual primates show a mixture of prosimian and anthropoid features (refer back to Figure 6–2). Separating them into their own grouping is supported by cranial and postcranial morphology and by DNA analyses.

Tarsiers show the largest eye sockets in proportion to facial size of any living primate (Figure 7–8). Their enormous eyes are in fact larger than their brains. A lateral bar and partially enclosed posterior wall make up the eye socket, a condition similar to the anthropoids. Likewise, in the ear region the tympanic ring is outside of the auditory bulla and extends laterally to form a bony tube called the external auditory meatus, the passage of the outer ear (refer back to Figure 6–11). In the

FIGURE 7–7 Tarsiers, a haplorhine species native to Southeast Asia.

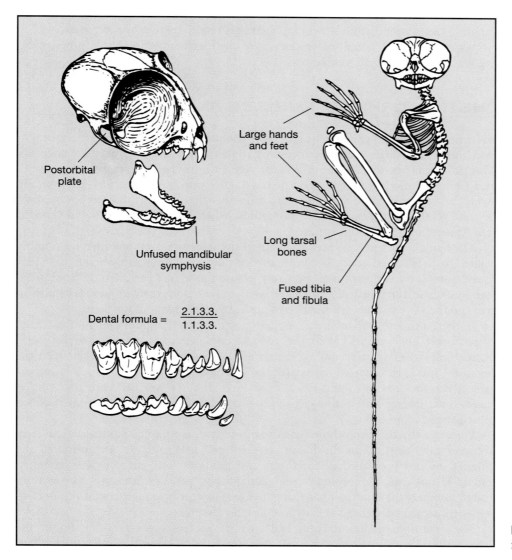

Postorbital plate

Large hands and feet

Unfused mandibular symphysis

Long tarsal bones

Fused tibia and fibula

Dental formula = $\dfrac{2.1.3.3.}{1.1.3.3.}$

FIGURE 7–8 Distinctive features of tarsiers.

tarsiers, as in the anthropoids, the major blood supply to the brain passes through the promontory branch of the internal carotid artery.

Tarsiers possess anthropoid-like dentition in that their incisors are broad and upright and they lack the dental combs that are common in the strepsirhines. The canine teeth are projecting. As a group, however, they show a unique dental formula with only one incisor on either side of the lower jaw.

Tarsiers, which are perhaps the most dramatic jumpers among all the primates, have extremely elongated hindlimbs. As we saw in Chapter 6, the fossil tarsiers (the omomyoids) as well as the living species have largely fused tibias and fibulas in the lower hindlimbs. This adaptation increases the stability and strength of the lower limb, allowing the limb to withstand compressive shock in landing after long jumps. Two of the tarsier's tarsal (foot) bones, the heel bone (calcaneus) and ankle bone (talus), are also elongated. This elongation provides greater leverage in jumping (and incidentally gives the tarsier its name). The hands and feet are large, and the terminal digital pads resemble suction cups. Both these features allow the tarsier to grasp branches securely while clinging. The second and third digits of the foot have claws, which apparently function in self-grooming.

We have little information about the behavior of tarsiers besides the fact that they, like many of the strepsirhines, are nocturnal foragers. It appears, however, that they can form different patterns of social organization, from single foragers whose ranges overlap to individuals who are members of polygynous social groups.

We now turn our attention to the rest of the members of the haplorhines, starting with the New World monkeys.

THE HAPLORHINES: MONKEYS AND APES

Morphologically and genetically, the living monkeys and apes represent a group of primates with a single common ancestry from an as yet unknown primate ancestor. This group may be divided into the New World Monkeys, or *platyrrhines,* of South and Central America; and the Old World higher primates of Africa, Europe, and Asia, the *catarrhines.* The catarrhines are further divided into the *cercopithecoids,* or Old World monkeys, and the **hominoids,** which include the apes and humans (see Appendix 3).

The haplorhine primates possess distinguishing features of the skull, most notably related to an enlarged brain. The brain-to-body ratio is considerably higher than that found among the strepsirhines. They rely less on the sense of smell and communication by chemical signals and more on vision. Consequently, their snouts are smaller in size and their eye sockets are positioned medially, in the front of the face.

In these primates the frontal, zygomatic, and sphenoid bones expand the lateral or postorbital bars of the eye sockets to form completely encapsulated sockets with postorbital closure (refer back to Figure 6–2). This separates the socket from the temporal fossa, through which passes the large temporal muscle, which is important in the movement of the lower jaw. In the ear region the tympanic ring is fused to the lateral wall and may or may not expand to form an external auditory meatus (see Figure 6–11).

Postcranially the haplorhines as a whole show few unique characteristics. They are generally larger than the living strepsirhines, and with the exception of the langurs, most cercopithecoid forelimbs and hindlimbs are more or less equal in length. In the apes, the forelimb is elongated for suspensory (hanging) locomotion, and in humans, the hindlimb has elongated for efficient bipedal locomotion. Both of these features are discussed shortly and in later chapters.

The dentition of the monkeys and apes shows few specializations, unlike the unique traits seen in the strepsirhines (for example, the dental comb). In the haplorhines the front teeth (the incisors) are upright and broad, and the canines are

hominoids: taxonomic superfamily to which the apes and people and their immediate ancestors belong.

projecting and usually display some pattern of sexual dimorphism. Cusp patterns on the premolar and molar teeth reflect dietary adaptations made by the various members of the group. In the dental formula the catarrhines have two premolars, whereas the New World monkeys have three. All haplorhines have three molars, except the New World marmosets and tamarins, which have only two. Unlike the strepsirhines, all haplorhines have lower jaws that are fused at the symphysis (chin).

THE NEW WORLD MONKEYS

The modern species of New World monkeys (the *platyrrhines,* a name derived from the broad, flat shape of their noses) are all arboreal and, with one exception, the night or owl monkeys (*Aotus*), are active during the day (refer back to Figure 6–17 for distinctive features of New World monkeys). Geographically, they range as far north as the Yucatan in Mexico and as far south as the southernmost expansion of the tropical rain forests of South America. Most species live within the reaches of the Amazon rain forest basin. Although great expanses of open, savannalike habitats do exist in South America, a striking feature of New World monkeys is that none of them ever adapted primarily to life on the ground, as did the baboons of Africa. On occasion some species do forage terrestrially, but none of them spend much time doing so.

Morphologically the platyrrhines are a widely divergent group of monkeys. The divergences that are seen in the New World monkeys clearly demonstrate the fact that evolution can produce almost infinite variations in response to differences in habitats and ecological niches. As we will see, the New World monkeys inhabit all levels of the tropical rain forests and consume a wide variety of foods (Figure 7–9).

Various groups exhibit specializations, both cranial and postcranial, that are not seen in the monkeys of the Old World. The New World monkeys evolved in South America in the absence of any competing prosimian or ape group, a fact that might account for adaptations that are prosimian- or apelike. For example, the spider monkey (*Ateles*) developed tail-assisted suspensory movement and great mobility in the upper limbs (Figure 7–10). These adaptations parallel in some respects the arm-swinging (or brachiating) form of locomotion observed in the apes (see Figure 7–25). In the marmosets and tamarins (a group referred to as *callitrichines*), all of the digits of the hands and feet are clawed. Although the exact anatomical makeup of these claws differs from that of true claws of other mammals, in the marmoset group these claws function in much the same way as the claws of rodents: They allow these very small primates to vertically ascend and descend large trees and to engage in clinging and leaping locomotion.

There are six subfamilies of New World monkeys, representing evolutionary lineages that are quite old compared to the lineages of Old World monkeys. Many subfamilies of New World monkeys probably split from common ancestors as far back as the late Oligocene (about 30 million years ago). Within these subfamilies 16 genera are recognized, all of which exhibit substantial diversity in terms of both ecological adaptation and social organization. Presently there are arguments over how many platyrrhine subfamilies should be recognized. Molecular studies consistently show that three of these subfamilies, the pithecines, atelines, and callitrichines, are distinct groups, but beyond that there is little agreement. Figure 7–11, p. 173, is a working approximation of the evolutionary groupings among the members of this group. The origin of many of the adaptations of the New World monkeys are the subject of current investigations.

New World monkey limb proportions overall are similar to those of the Old World monkeys: the forelimbs are equal to or slightly shorter than the hindlimbs. Unlike the Old World species, however, the New World monkeys lack a true **opposable thumb.** True opposable thumbs, found only among catarrhine (Old World)

opposable thumb: a central primate characteristic that contributes to the prehensility of the hands and feet and the mode of locomotion, climbing by grasping.

FIGURE 7-9 Seven species of New World monkeys that inhabit the Suriname rain forest, filling different ecological niches of the same habitat. In the canopy are the (*a*) bearded saki (*Chiropotes satanus*) and (*b*) black spider monkey (*Ateles paniscus*). Below them are (*c*) tufted capuchins (*Cebus apella*) and (*d*) red howling monkeys (*Alouatta seniculus*). On the lowest levels are (*e*) squirrel monkeys (*Saimiri sciureus*), (*f*) golden-handed tamarins (*Saguinus midas*), and (*g*) white-faced sakis (*Pithecia pithecia*).

FIGURE 7-10 The spider monkey, a New World monkey that uses its prehensile (grasping) tail for locomotion.

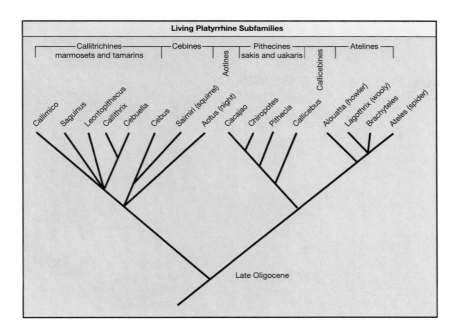

FIGURE 7-11 Evolutionary relationships among the New World monkeys. The platyrrhines are grouped into six subfamilies based on recent molecular studies.

species, are characterized by a saddle-shaped joint at the base of the thumb. This allows the thumb to be rotated into opposition to the other digits in a way that allows the friction surfaces of each to touch (try it yourself). The rotational ability of New World monkeys is more limited, and thus their thumbs are considered to be *pseudo-opposable*.

Quadrupedalism and leaping seem to represent the earliest arboreal locomotor adaptation in the evolution of this group (Gebo, 1989a). The fossil remains of early New World monkeys show a widened foot, a lengthened great toe for purposes of grasping, and an increased mobility of the limb joints, at least in some species. Only 5 genera out of the 16 have long prehensile tails that, at the distal end, underneath, have a friction surface with ridges similar to fingerprints. This friction surface allows these primates to wrap their tails around branches and hang by the tail exclusively while they feed (Figure 7–12). Four of the five genera of monkeys that possess prehensile tails are members of the ateline subfamily, to which the spider (*Ateles*), howler (*Alouatta*), and woolly monkeys (*Lagothrix*) belong. The fifth genus of prehensile-tailed monkey is the familiar capuchin (*Cebus*) monkey. Curiously, the capuchins, which share the prehensile tail adaptation with members of the atelines, are not phylogenetically very closely related to them (see Figure 7–11).

The following brief narrative describes the six subfamilies of New World monkeys and some of their most distinguishing adaptations.

- *The callitrichines.* This subfamily includes the marmosets and the tamarins, which are some of the smallest (100 to 750 g; 4 oz to less than 2 lb) and most colorful of all of the New World monkeys. They are also one of the most taxonomically diverse groups, with somewhere around 30 species. The largest of the callitrichines is the lion tamarin, which weighs more than 600 g (1.5 lb), and the smallest (the smallest of all anthropoids, in fact) is the pygmy marmoset (*Cebuella*) at about 100 g (4 oz). The tamarins (*Saguinus*) are the most widespread and diverse (10 to 12 species) members of the group.

Marmosets and tamarins show little sexual dimorphism in body size, but they do boast a unique dental formula, 2.1.3.2., showing loss of the third molar tooth (Figure 7–13). All of the digits of the hands and feet have claws instead of nails, which allows these animals in their many ecological niches to cling to the trunks and branches of large vegetation while they feed on tree gums and saps. As in some other New World primates, males play a major role in infant care

FIGURE 7-12 The muriqui, or woolly spider monkey, from southeastern Brazil demonstrating the use of the prehensile tail that allows it to hang from its tail while feeding.

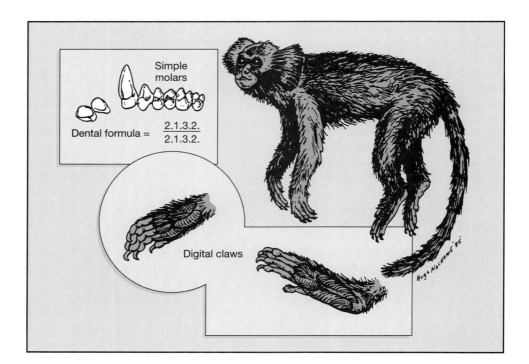

FIGURE 7-13 Unique features of the callitrichines, the group that includes marmosets and tamarins.

and transportation. This is made more complicated for these fathers by the fact that the mothers most often give birth to twins (Figure 7–14).

- *The cebines.* Capuchin monkeys and squirrel monkeys, the most omnivorous of all New World monkeys, make up the subfamily Cebinae. Although the capuchins are perhaps the best known of all the New World monkeys because of their widespread use by the media for various advertising or entertaining purposes (for example, the well-known "organ-grinder" monkeys), the squirrel monkeys are the most morphologically distinctive. Squirrel monkeys (*Saimiri*) show a distinctive cranial anatomy. The occipital bone is unusually long, and the foramen magnum lies directly under the skull base, almost in the position commonly seen in bipedal humans. This is unlike the condition found in most quadrupedal monkeys, where the occipital region is short and the foramen magnum opens to the back of the skull rather than below it.

   The cheek teeth have sharp cusps that reflect the insectivorous part of their general diet. Like the tarsier, but not to the same extent, the tibia and fibula are fused distally (refer back to Figure 7–8). This adaptation, although it restricts movement at the ankle joint, also provides greater stability in the absorption of compressive shock from landing after long leaps.

- *The aotines.* The "owl" or "night" monkeys are a group of eight or more species of the subfamily aotinae. These are the only nocturnal higher primates, and as with other nocturnal primates, the orbits of the eyes are large; in fact, the owl monkey has the largest orbits of any anthropoid. These primates, which are widely dispersed throughout South America, are also the only anthropoids that lack color vision. Postcranially the aotines show one unique feature: a compressed clawlike grooming nail on the second digit of each foot.

- *The pithecines:* Three genera of monkeys belong to the pithecines, including *Pithecia*, the most remarkable leaper of all the New World monkeys. The most curious-looking pithecine is the bald-headed *uakari* (the *Cacajao*), which often uses a specialized hindlimb suspension while feeding (Figure 7–15). Dental specializations within this subfamily include large procumbent incisors and large canines that are used to get at fruits and seeds encased in tough outer coats.

FIGURE 7-14 A pygmy marmoset.

- *The callicebines.* The callicebines include the "titi" monkeys, an ancient lineage whose skeletal anatomy is considered the closest to that of the earliest ancestral group. These are relatively small primates (about 0.9 to 1.3 kg; approximately 2 lb), and, as with many New World monkeys, the young are carried by the males in the group from about one week after their births. These newborns are usually returned to their mothers only for nursing.
- *The atelines.* Four genera make up the ateline subfamily. Members of this group are the largest of all the platyrrhines, weighing up to 10 kg (22 lb). All have a long prehensile tail. Many aspects of their postcranial skeletons are similar to those of the living apes, including the kind of suspensory locomotion these monkeys use in feeding (see Figure 7–12). In the howler monkeys (*Alouatta*), the mandible is large and quite deep. The hyoid bone in the throat is expanded to form a large resonating chamber, allowing these monkeys to produce one of the loudest and longest-ranging calls of any primate (Figure 7–16).

In this section we have hinted at the great variety of New World monkeys, which corresponds to the variety of niches they fill. In the next chapter we discuss their behavior in more detail. We turn now to a discussion of the Old World monkeys.

FIGURE 7–15   The cacajao uses a unique hindlimb suspension while feeding.

THE OLD WORLD MONKEYS

Instead of the one very diverse radiation that characterizes primate evolution in the New World, in the Old World there are two distinct radiations of primates, the Old World monkeys (Cercopithecoidea) and the apes (Hominoidea) (Disotell, 1996). These two superfamilies are grouped into a single larger group (an infraorder), called the catarrhines, or Old World higher primates, which share certain distinctive features as described shortly. Although similar adaptations occurred in both the New World and Old World monkeys, the tempo and mode of evolutionary change were different.

The living monkeys of the Old World resemble each other much more closely than do the more diverse monkeys in the New World. This reflects, in part, a more recent common ancestry of the different groups of the Old World monkeys than the more distant common ancestry of the New World forms. It also suggests that

FIGURE 7–16   The howler monkey is a member of the ateline subfamily. Howler monkeys produce the loudest cry of any primate.

ischial callosity: the callused pads that cover the ischial tuberosity in all Old World monkeys and gibbons. This pad is used primarily for sitting for long periods usually while the animal sleeps.

loph: a crest of enamel on the occlusal surface of the dentition.

bilophodont: two-lophed tooth. Characteristic occlusal surface pattern of Old World monkeys where the mesial two cusps and the distal two cusps, respectively, are each connected by a loph.

sectorial: literally "cutting," first lower premolar of apes and some monkeys, a unicuspid tooth whose forward edge shears against the back edge of the occluding upper canine, honing it to sharpness.

adaptations found among some species of both the catarrhines and platyrrhines, such as suspensory locomotion, appeared at different times in these groups and, no doubt, for different specific reasons. Thus, despite the fact that broad similarities between the two groups exist, they have quite different evolutionary histories.

The catarrhines share many anatomical specializations that distinguish them from their more primitive New World cousins (refer back to Figure 6–17). The name *catarrhine* reflects one of these basic differences: The nostrils are narrow and face downward in the Old World primates. The catarrhine dental formula is 2.1.2.3., showing a reduction of one premolar on each side of both jaws. In the ear region, the tympanic bone extends out to the side of the cranium to form the tubular external auditory meatus (see Figure 6–11). With the exception of the great apes and humans, all catarrhines have expanded ischial tuberosities of the pelvis. These bony projections are covered with thick calluses (the **ischial callosities**), which these animals use as sitting pads (Figure 7–17).

Today the living Old World monkeys (the cercopithecines) are taxonomically more diverse, geographically more widespread, and numerically more abundant than the hominoids, with the exception, of course, of people. Part of the monkeys' success story is the result of the more generalized adaptations that they have made and retained, which have allowed them to diversify to such a degree. To a large extent the more specialized hominoid (ape) adaptations became tied to ecosystems that are more perishable and fragile. Consequently, the hominoids' success is more limited than that of their monkey cousins.

The cercopithecoid monkeys are found throughout Africa and Asia in a wider range of latitudes, climates, and habitats than any other nonhuman primate. Within this group there are two subfamilies: the *cercopithecines,* or cheek-pouched monkeys, which are predominantly fruit eaters; and, the *colobines,* or leaf-eating monkeys (Figure 7–18). Both groups display a specialized cusp pattern on the molar teeth, which usually have four cusps. This cusp pattern reflects their basic dietary adaptations as vegetarians: on the molar teeth, the two forward cusps and the two back cusps are connected by a ridge of enamel called a **loph**. This two-lophed tooth pattern is referred to as **bilophodont** (see Figure 7–18).

In addition to the unique molar cusp pattern, most cercopithecoids have sexually dimorphic canine teeth and first lower premolars that are described as **sectorial.**

FIGURE 7–17 A savanna baboon, an example of an Old World monkey, sitting on its ischial callosities.

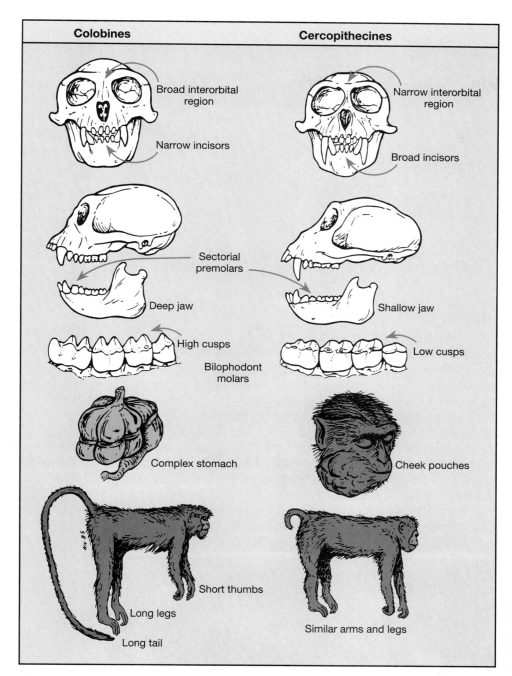

Colobines | **Cercopithecines**

Broad interorbital region

Narrow incisors

Narrow interorbital region

Broad incisors

Sectorial premolars

Deep jaw

Shallow jaw

High cusps

Low cusps

Bilophodont molars

Complex stomach

Cheek pouches

Short thumbs

Long legs

Long tail

Similar arms and legs

FIGURE 7-18 Distinguishing characteristics of cercopithecines and colobines, the two subfamilies of Old World monkeys.

The front (anterior) edge of these sectorial premolars hones against the back edges of the upper canine teeth, keeping these teeth razor sharp, primarily for matters of social display and occasional overt aggression. The large size of these teeth also results in relatively elongated and protruding jaws. The extent of this adaptation is observed best among the baboons (Figure 7–19).

With the exception of their remarkable variety in coat coloration and hair patterns, the cercopithecoids have few divergent specializations compared with the prosimians, the New World monkeys, or the hominoids. Size differences, also, are not as great as those found in the other primate groups: the smallest cercopithecoid, the talapoin, weighs about 1.2 kg (3 lb), and one of the largest, the mandrill, about 30 kg (66 lb). In most species, however, males are significantly larger than females. Certain Old World monkeys exhibit unique sexual differences in such features as the

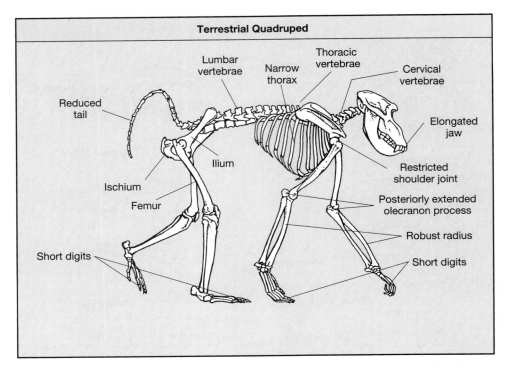

Terrestrial Quadruped

Reduced tail

Lumbar vertebrae

Narrow thorax

Thoracic vertebrae

Cervical vertebrae

Elongated jaw

Ilium

Ischium

Femur

Restricted shoulder joint

Posteriorly extended olecranon process

Robust radius

Short digits

Short digits

FIGURE 7–19 Typical structural traits of Old World monkeys as seen in the baboon (genus *Papio*). The baboon exhibits an extreme example of jaw elongation (prognathism), however, especially in males, as a result of large canine teeth.

shape of the ischial callosities, on which both males and females sit or sleep during the night, the size of the cheek pads, and the size of the nose (Figure 7–20).

The Old World monkeys show few locomotor specializations, with the exception of the relative elongation of the hindlimb as seen in the colobines, the best-adapted leapers in this group. Limb proportions, as measured by the intermembral index (the length of the forelimb divided by the length of the hindlimb, multiplied by 100), differ far less in the Old World monkeys than in other primate groups. The Asiatic gibbons, the most active of the arm-swingers, or brachiators, show the longest relative arm lengths.

The longest relative leg lengths belong to humans and to the leaping Asiatic tarsiers. In the Old World monkeys, leaping is generally less developed than in the

FIGURE 7–20 Sexual dimorphism in Old World monkeys. Shown are male, female, and juvenile proboscis monkeys (*Nasalis*). Note the male's significantly larger body size and nose.

prosimians. Monkey leaps have a downward direction, a spread-eagle midair posture, and a crashlike mode of landing. Old World monkeys do not possess prehensile tails, although they may use their tails for balancing, for assisting in vertical climbing, and even for social display. Tail length varies considerably among species in the Old World monkeys from short stublike tails seen in the Japanese macaques to tails that are as long as the body in monkeys such as the colobines.

The cercopithecine subfamily. The cercopithecine monkeys are predominantly an African group, with the important exception of the macaques of Asia (some macaques also remain in northwest Africa and in Europe on Gibraltar). In fact the genus *Macaca* is the widest geographically ranging genus of living nonhuman primates and consists of as many as 19 species. One important factor may account for the success of the macaques. They are unusual in their ability to cope with a wide range of habitats and to coexist closely with humans in a range of modified environments. The rhesus macaques of India, for example, live side by side with people in crowded cities.

The savanna-dwelling African baboons (*Papio*) are one of the largest of the cercopithecines and are the best studied in the wild. Baboons are the most sexually dimorphic of the Old World monkeys; the males are about twice the size of the females. Baboons are found throughout the forest and savanna regions of sub-Saharan Africa and in the deserts of the southern Saudi Arabian peninsula. The different groups of baboons live as geographically distinct, or **allopatric**, populations that variously interbreed at their boundaries. Although at least five different baboon species have been named, because of extensive interbreeding between them it may be more appropriate to consider the African savanna baboon as a single species, *Papio hamadryas* (Fleagle, 1999:195). Savanna baboons have figured prominently in models developed to explain aspects of early human evolution, because it was believed that early humans shared the open savanna regions of Africa with the baboons and thus were similarly adapted (Washburn and DeVore, 1961; Strum, 1987).

There are at least two other kinds of baboons, the highly colorful, forest-living drills and mandrills, and the highland montane grassland baboons, the geladas. The geladas are distinctive-looking animals that can retract their upper lips completely over their upper jaws to produce a startlingly aggressive facial gesture. Because of their external appearance and cranial morphology, geladas are commonly placed in their own genus, *Theropithecus* (Figure 7–21).

allopatric: two species or populations that live in distinct geographical ranges that do not overlap. Contact at the boundaries of two populations may result in the formation of hybrid groups.

FIGURE 7–21 Gelada baboons can completely retract their upper lips, allowing males to produce dramatic facial displays.

FIGURE 7-22 A red guenon, *Ceropithecus*, and patas monkey, *Erythrocebus*, two examples of cercapithecine monkeys from Africa.

FIGURE 7-23 A black and white *Colobus* monkey from Africa. Old World monkeys do not possess prehensile tails, although some species, such as colobines, have extremely long tails. Leaping is an important locomotor specialization in colobine monkeys, which have the longest relative hindlimb length of Old World anthropoids.

sympatric: two species or populations whose geographical home ranges overlap.

The forest-living guenon (*Cercopithecus*) monkeys of Africa are the most diverse of the entire subfamily, with about 19 named species. The smallest members of this group, in fact the smallest of all the Old World monkeys, are the talapoins (*Miopithecus*). Although the guenons are generally fairly uniform in body size (averaging about 4 to 5 kg, or 9 to 11 lb) and proportion, their appearance is remarkably colorful, making each species quite distinctive. Close relatives to the guenons, the vervet and patas monkeys, differ from them in that they are mostly terrestrial, living in the open savanna grasslands along with the baboons (Figure 7–22). Although these monkeys generally act peacefully toward one another, baboons have been known to hunt and kill young vervets for food.

The colobine subfamily. The colobines are the specialized leaf-eating monkeys of the Old World group. Colobus monkeys of several species are found in the forests of Africa, and the langur monkeys have reached the greatest diversity and abundance in Asia of all the members of this subfamily. Langur monkeys are so common that in any given area one can find two to three different species living **sympatrically.** Of all the langurs, the sacred or Hanuman langur of India and Sri Lanka is the most ecologically diverse. These primates figure as heroes in Hindu religious texts for rescuing an Indian queen from her kidnappers, and as a reward for this deed, they are considered sacred. Because of their preferred status, today the Hanuman langur exists in various habitats in India from the deserts of Rajasthan in the west, to tropical rain forests and the high Himalayan mountains in the north.

The colobines are the most acrobatic of the Old World monkeys. Some colobines, such as the banded leaf monkeys of western Malaysia, are extraordinary leapers and occasionally use forelimb suspension in feeding. These and other colobines have elongated hindlimbs that enable them to leap quite long distances in the trees (Figure 7–23). As part of their locomotor specializations of leaping and arboreal suspension, colobines are capable of greater forelimb abduction (lifting the arm upward), including shoulder rotation with the elbow joint fully extended, than other Old World monkeys. This larger range of forelimb movement allows them to sit on branches and, from overhead, pull down small twigs containing food (Tuttle, 1975). They also use their forelimbs and hands to grasp overhanging limbs in order to steady themselves while negotiating their way through the branches of the forest canopy (Morbeck, 1979).

The remaining colobines can be grouped in a category we might call the "odd-nosed" monkeys. The best known of this group is the proboscis monkey of Borneo (refer back to Figure 7–20). The sexually dimorphic nose of the male is about two times the size of the nose of the females. Although the function of the large male nose is not completely understood, it may be the result of sexual selection, much like the colorful tail feathers of the male peacock. The golden monkey (*Rhinopithecus*) is another odd-nosed primate and is also the largest of all the colobines, with males weighing about 30 kg (66 lb). Perhaps not surprisingly, because of their large size, these monkeys, which are found throughout Vietnam and southern China, are also the most terrestrial of the colobines.

Unlike the situation we have seen for other primate groups, phyletic relationships among Old World monkeys are fairly well understood and agreed on by researchers. There are only a few minor taxonomic issues that remain unresolved at present (Figure 7–24). The Old World monkeys are generally successful species that have populated many diverse ecosystems of Africa and Asia, including some of those presently occupied by people. The relative success of the Old World monkeys is in stark contrast to the poor state in which we find the living apes. As we will see, the ancestral apes were diverse and plentiful early in their evolutionary history compared to the contemporary monkeys, which were seldom found in the fossil record. This situation changed dramatically as the Miocene period drew to a close, with the

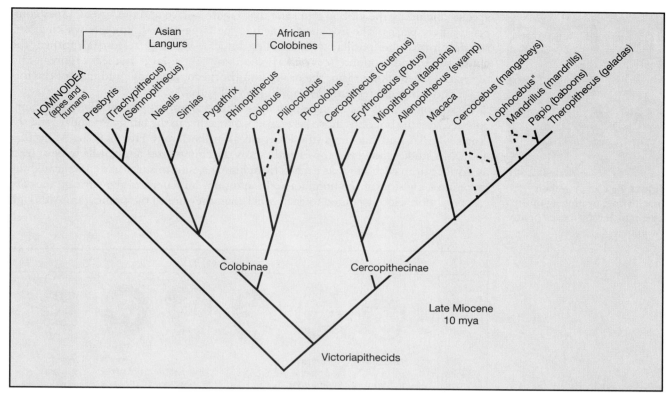

FIGURE 7–24 Evolutionary relationships among Old World monkeys, based on morphological features.

monkeys pulling ahead in the evolutionary race of competition. In terms of number of species and diversity, the shift in predominance from apes to monkeys is one of the most intriguing mysteries of primate evolution. However, knowing what you now know about the living monkeys, you will be better able to understand the fate of the apes.

THE LIVING HOMINOIDS MINUS HUMANS: THE APES

By the middle Miocene, about 15 million years ago, apes had expanded from Africa into Europe and Asia (see Chapter 9). During this period, forests and dense woodlands connected Africa and Asia, so as hominoids expanded their ranges they came into contact with an increasing diversity of environments. By 10 to 14 million years ago, there were fewer species of apes, but they were found throughout Africa and Eurasia. During the late Miocene, the radiation of apes began to draw to a close: By about 5 million years ago, most species had become extinct, with only a few forms surviving to the present day. What remained were the ancestors of the living gibbons, siamangs, and orangutans, and the common ancestor of humans, chimpanzees, bonobos, and gorillas. As the apes were declining, monkeys were successfully increasing in number of species and in geographical range—as we have seen, a likely result of broad ecological competition between the two groups.

The hypothesis of monkey–ape competition in the late Miocene may explain why today we have five separate hominoid adaptations, all quite different from one another and from their more monkeylike early ancestors. Today, among the hominoids there are two major groupings: the "lesser" apes, the small-bodied suspensory

FIGURE 7–25 A gibbon brachiating, or moving under tree branches by means of arm swinging.

species, including the gibbon and siamang (Figure 7–25); and the "great" apes comprising five species. The five species include the large-bodied, knuckle-walking, terrestrial form, the gorilla; two smaller knuckle-walking terrestrial forms, the chimpanzee and bonobo (or pygmy chimpanzee); a large-bodied arboreal and terrestrial fist-walking form, the orangutan (Bornean, meaning "old man of the forest"); and a bipedal terrestrial form, humans (Figure 7–26).

Traditionally, all the living great apes, the orangutans, the gorillas, the chimpanzees, and the bonobos, have been grouped together in the family Pongidae, and the Asian gibbons and siamangs (the lesser apes) in the family Hylobatidae. Molecular and DNA studies, however, consistently show the chimpanzee and gorilla to be at least as distinct from each other as each is from humans, and this fact has complicated the taxonomic division of the hominoids. In addition, humans and the African apes are certainly more closely related to each other than they are to the orangutan. Although

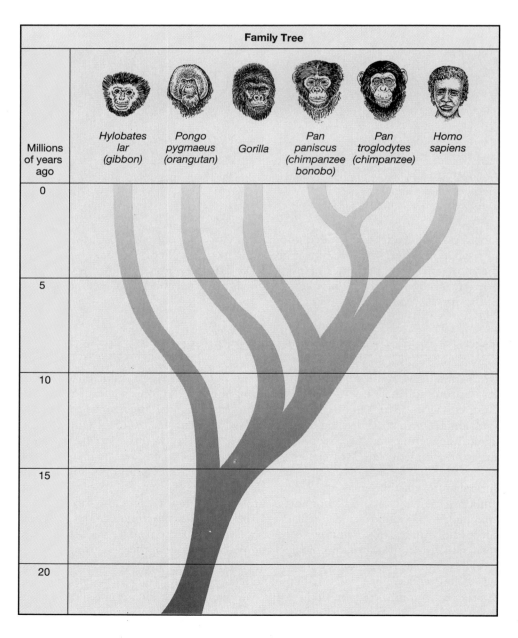

FIGURE 7–26 Evolutionary relationships among living apes, based on fossil and molecular evidence.

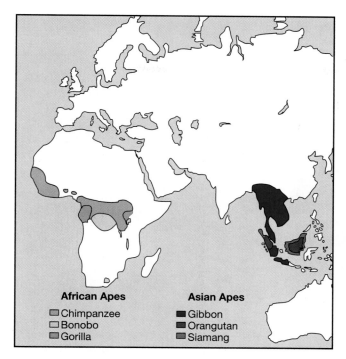

FIGURE 7-27 Distribution of the living apes. The African apes are found throughout west and central Africa. The Asian apes are found in Southeast Asia. The orangutans are restricted to forest habitats on the islands of Borneo and Sumatra. The larger of the "lesser" apes, the siamangs, are less common than gibbons and are found only along the west coast of Sumatra and the southwestern coast of Malaysia.

we are aware of these phyletic relationships among the hominoids, we will continue to use in this chapter (following Fleagle, 1999) the more traditional taxonomy.

Apes today are found in tropical rain forests and forest woodlands from sea level to heights of 12,000 feet (4,000 meters), the altitude at which the few remaining mountain gorillas make their home in the Virunga Volcanoes of Congo (formerly Zaire), Uganda, and Rwanda (Figure 7–27). The apes have fared poorly at the hands of fate and of humans. Few in number and pushed to the limits of their environmental resources, the living apes face a dismal future today in the wild. On a sliding scale of evolutionary success in the primates, apes rate near the bottom, barely holding their own. Their seriously threatened condition makes it important not only that we study them in the wild while there is still time but also that conservation efforts go hand in hand with the scientific study of the species.

What Is an Ape?

The "great" apes are larger than monkeys, and as adults they exhibit marked sexual dimorphism. In terms of cranial anatomy the apes are all largely similar at birth (Schultz, 1924; Biegert, 1963). Changes in infant cranial structure are mostly determined by brain size and housing for the special senses (sight, hearing, taste, and smell). As the teeth erupt, however, the mechanical requirements of the developing teeth and jaws begin to show their effect on the cranial anatomy; the face becomes more **prognathic** (forward thrusting), a trend that continues until adulthood. With the eruption of the permanent canine teeth (which are substantially larger in males than in females), the patterns of growth of the different skull regions begin to change dramatically, giving rise to the adult pattern of sexual dimorphism (Schultz, 1969). The cranial anatomy of the gorilla, for example, is dominated by the large upper and lower canines, the large prognathic jaws that give support to them, and the massive **muscles of mastication** that attach to the jaws (Figure 7–28). The skull itself is covered by the temporalis muscles and, in the cheek region, by the masseter muscles. As gorillas mature, the left and right temporalis muscles meet at the top of the skull and attach to it, producing a bony **sagittal crest**, the largest of its size in any primate.

prognathic: forward jutting, as in the jaws of many primates, primarily as a result of large canine teeth.

muscles of mastication: muscles of the jaw, primarily the temporalis and masseter, that provide the power in chewing.

sagittal crest: crest of bone that develops as some large primates, as well as other mammals, age. The result of an ever-enlarging temporalis muscle that covers the walls of small braincases.

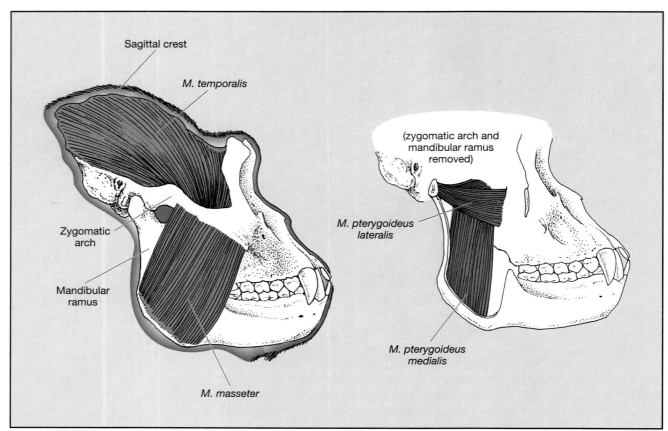

FIGURE 7–28   Muscles of mastication and associated cranial structures of the gorilla. Note the large canine teeth and the sagittal crest.

bunodont: the surface or occlusal anatomy of the cheek teeth where the cusps are rounded in shape and low in height.

Y-5 pattern: cusp pattern on hominoid cheek teeth. Lower molars have an expanded talonid basin surrounded by five rounded cusps.

brachiation: arboreal locomotion in the apes where progression below branches is accomplished by using elongated forelimbs only; "arm-swinging."

Like the Old World monkeys, all of the apes have the tubular tympanic bone in the ear region (refer back to Figure 6–11) and a dental formula of 2.1.2.3. Apes lack, however, the specialized bilophodont cusp pattern and instead show molar teeth with more primitive, rounded, **bunodont** cusps arranged in a **Y-5 pattern** (Figure 7–29). The first lower premolars are typically shaped like shearing blades (referred to as *sectorial*), but the adjacent canine teeth vary considerably from those of monkeys, both in shape and degree of sexual dimorphism.

Apes differ from monkeys in a number of other significant traits (see Figure 7–29). All apes are capable of a wide range of arm movements, giving them their unique ability to raise their arms above their heads (full abduction of the forelimb), as we do when we do chin-ups or hold onto a strap while standing on a bus. Apes raise their arms when they hang from tree limbs or climb in trees (see Figure 7–25). When they move in trees by suspension, this type of locomotion is called arm swinging, or **brachiation** (from Latin for "arm"). In addition, as part of this brachiating adaptation, all apes and humans lack tails.

The direct ancestors of modern apes developed the ability to suspend themselves by their arms from tree branches and even to swing from branch to branch as a unique form of locomotion. Washburn (1963) stressed the importance of apes' ability to hang with one hand, grasping a branch while feeding with the other hand. He realized that apes' locomotion was in reality an arboreal feeding adaptation: Its adaptive advantage is in obtaining food in trees (primarily fruit) from the ends and the tips of branches. Knowledge of tropical forest ecology shows that the best and sometimes the only digestible foods in a tree are at the edges. These include fruits,

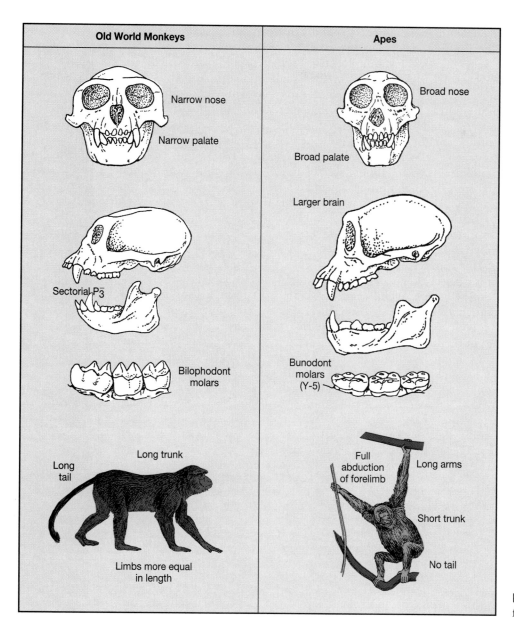

FIGURE 7-29 Apes differ from Old World monkeys.

nuts, flowers, and, perhaps on a more regular basis, new leaves—those whose internal chemistry has not yet built up the defense systems that make the most mature leaves indigestible to the average vegetarian.

Brachiation reaches its greatest efficiency in the small-bodied Asian apes: the gibbons and siamangs (see Figure 7–25). In fact, Napier and Napier (1967) describe these forms as the true brachiators, as opposed to the great apes, which they describe as modified brachiators. Movement through the trees in these small apes is rapid because of the greater elongation of the forelimbs and fingers of the hands, with the exception of the shortened thumb, which apparently functions to increase the breadth of the grasping hand in vertical climbing, an important additional gibbon locomotor component. On the ground and in the trees, gibbons and siamangs are also unique in that both occasionally adopt bipedal posture in locomotion (Figure 7–30).

The great apes move much more carefully (and slowly) because of their larger size. They usually support their weight with their hindlimbs while in the trees. On

FIGURE 7-30 Bipedal locomotion by a gibbon on the ground. Apes also employ bipedal locomotion on tree branches.

FIGURE 7-31 An adult orangutan moving through tree branches. Because of their large size, great apes move more cautiously than lesser apes while brachiating.

knuckle walking: a unique form of quadrupedal locomotion observed only in the African apes. Specialized anatomical adaptations in the wrist and hand allow the upper body weight to be supported on the dorsal surface of the middle phalanges while the rest of the weight is supported by the plantar surfaces of the feet.

the ground, these animals generally move quadrupedally and, on occasion, bipedally. The orangutan (*Pongo pygmaeus*) often travels arboreally, but generally climbs rather than swings along branches (Figure 7–31). The brachiating anatomy we described for gibbons and siamangs is much the same for the orangutans, except that orangutans' size is a limiting factor to rapid arboreal locomotion. Infant and juvenile orangutans are much more mobile than adults, both in the trees and on the ground.

When moving on the ground, apes rarely run with their hands palmigrade (flat on the ground), but either knuckle walk, as with chimpanzees, bonobos, and gorillas (Figure 7–32); fist walk, as with orangutans (Figure 7–33); or walk on two hindlimbs, as with gibbons (see Figure 7–30) and humans. Although the orangutan's quadrupedal locomotion is usually accomplished with the fists in a clenched position, they have been observed occasionally to use a palm-down stance like monkeys.

British paleontologist Richard Owen (1859) first recognized **knuckle walking** as a form of ape locomotion, but the distinctive anatomy of knuckle walking seen only in the hands of African apes was recognized somewhat later (Keith, 1899). On anatomical grounds it was argued that the African apes were phylogenetically more closely related to each other than either was to the orangutan (Andrews, 1987). In the skeletal elements of the wrists of African apes (as well as in that of humans), the primitive os centrale (Latin, meaning "central bone") fuses with the scaphoid (Greek, meaning "shiplike," in reference to its shape) (see Chapter 9). Additionally, the unique shape of the heads (distal end) of the metacarpals is especially related to knuckle walking (Tuttle, 1967). Because the African apes and humans share some of these skeletal characteristics, might this indicate that the common ancestor of all three living species was a knuckle walker as well? Both Washburn (Washburn and Moore, 1980) and Begun (see Frontiers box: Miocene Apes and Early Hominoids in Chapter 9) stress the possibility of a knuckle-walking stage in human ancestry. Washburn and Moore discussed the potential advantages of this form of locomotion:

> This method of walking was the key to eventual upright walking, and to human evolution. By knuckle walking, an ape on the ground could move [quickly] from one isolated group of trees to another. If danger threatened, it still could climb to safety; the knuckle gait did not interfere with the structures that enabled it to climb or move around in the trees. Knuckle walking got the new ground dwellers around the possible fatal dangers of being slow, inefficient bipedalists, as most monkeys are. [Additionally,] an ape whose hands were not totally involved in locomotion was freer to use them in other ways, a great advantage. (1980:64)

Although this viewpoint has been criticized on anatomical grounds (Tuttle, 1975) and as yet no fossil evidence has emerged to demonstrate conclusively early hominid knuckle walking, the question is intriguing and still remains open.

The Lesser Apes: The Gibbons and Siamangs

Of all of the living apes, the gibbons (*Hylobates*) are the most successful in terms of species diversity and geographic distribution. Gibbons are also the most numerous of all the apes. Gibbons are the smallest of the apes, ranging in size from 5 to 11 kg (11 to 24 lb), with no sexual dimorphism. They are the most primitive of the living apes anatomically, retaining many monkeylike traits, such as the ischial callosities. Gibbons are found throughout Southeast Asia and the islands of Borneo, Sumatra, and Java. Biologists have recognized four major groups, consisting of up to nine different species, including the siamang (*Hylobates syndactylus*). Of all of the gibbon species, only two are sympatric, the siamang and the white-handed gibbon, *H. lar.* Both are found together in the forests of western Malaysia and Sumatra. The remaining gibbon populations are allopatric and have distinct vocalizations that distinguish them.

Considering the broad geographical distribution of the gibbons, the various species' behaviors and habitats are quite similar. Gibbons share a preference for primary, lowland rain forests and prefer diets consisting of ripe fruit, new leaves, and some species of invertebrates. Only the siamangs are found in high, mountainous regions. Families of siamangs, whose diet includes a higher proportion of leaves than does that of other gibbons, usually forage as a unit. In contrast, members of gibbon families often forage individually over large home ranges. Because the gibbons prefer to eat fruit rather than leaves, the widely scattered fruits are more efficiently foraged by individuals.

Gibbons move and feed in the middle to upper canopy of forests and are almost never found on the ground. In those rare instances when they do move terrestrially or above branches in the trees, they do so using a type of shambling bipedalism rather than some form of quadrupedal knuckle walking as seen in the great apes. Gibbons have the longest forelimbs relative to body size of any primate. As a consequence, on the whole gibbons are the most suspensory of all primates, moving arboreally almost exclusively by two-armed rapid brachiation.

The Great Apes of Africa and Asia

There are four living species of great apes. Of the four, only the orangutan lives in Asia, in very restricted habitats on the islands of Borneo and Sumatra (Figure 7–34). The gorillas, chimpanzees, and bonobos all live in the rain forests and woodlands of central Africa from the west coast to regions along the western rift of East Africa (see Figure 7–27). The great apes share with the gibbons and siamangs the brachiating anatomy of the upper torso, a shorter lumbar section of the vertebral column, shorter lower hindlimbs, and absence of a tail. The upper torso is characterized by a broad chest and long clavicle, longer arms than legs, and greater mobility at the wrist, elbow, and shoulder joints that allows for the full abduction of the forelimb in suspensory climbing and hanging.

Although the great apes differ from the gibbons in relative size, more specific differences also exist. The most important of these is the larger canine teeth, which in turn contribute to the massiveness of the face and prognathism of the upper and lower jaws (see Figure 7–28). These skeletal and dental features are accompanied by larger muscles of mastication, such as the temporalis, a muscle that originates on the sides of the skull, and the masseter, a muscle that originates along the zygomatic arch, a bridge of bone connecting the cheekbone (malar) with the temporal bone of the skull.

FIGURE 7–32 Knuckle walking in a gorilla.

FIGURE 7–33 Fist walking in an orangutan.

FIGURE 7–34 Male and female orangutans.

The orangutan. Orangutans, *Pongo pygmaeus*, are the largest living arboreal mammals, and they are highly sexually dimorphic, with males weighing as much as 83 kg (183 lb). Females weigh about half as much as the males, averaging 37 kg (81 lb). The extreme difference in body form between adult male and female orangs is comparable to that seen in gorillas and baboons (see Figure 7–34). Orangutans inhabit forested regions on the Southeast Asian islands of Borneo and Sumatra. Populations living on these islands are recognized as two separate subspecies, *pygmaeus*, on Borneo and *abelii*, on Sumatra, and may have shared a common ancestor a little more than 1 million years ago (Delgado and Van Schaik, 2000:205).

At full maturity, one striking characteristic of the male is the large cheek pads of subcutaneous (Latin, meaning "under the skin") tissue located between the eyes and the ears. The exact function of the cheek pads is unknown, but it appears to be related in some fashion to full maturity and high-dominance rank. The appearance and development of these pads may be slowed down in younger males if older and more dominant adult males are present in the local area. Adult males also possess large **laryngeal sacs** that are inflatable, producing their characteristic "long call," the function of which is probably to keep groups spaced apart. Orangs also have a unique set of **sternal glands** on their chest that may function in territorial scent marking.

In postcranial structure orangutans have long forelimbs with hooklike hands and long curved phalanges. The length of the forelimb relative to hindlimb length approaches that seen in gibbons. Orangutans have a very mobile hip joint and a more fully opposable big toe than is found in the African apes. These adaptations allow the large-bodied orangutans to move through the forest by quadrumanous (four-handed) scrambling.

The gorilla. The gorilla is found in different regions of central and west central Africa as three subspecies: the western lowland gorilla (*Gorilla gorilla gorilla*), the eastern lowland gorilla (*G. g. graueri*), and the mountain gorilla (*G. g. beringei*; Figure 7–35).

The gorillas are the largest of all the wild species of primates and show extreme sexual dimorphism; the males weigh more than 180 kg (400 lb) in the wild and up to 300 kg (660 lb) in captivity, and the females weigh 70 to 115 kg (154 to 253 lb). Gorillas have elongated faces because of their large canine teeth and well-developed

laryngeal sacs: the larynx or "voice box" is expanded, creating a resonating chamber used in the production of loud vocalizations. Characteristic of howler monkeys of South America, and the siamangs and orangutans of Southeast Asia.

sternal glands: scent-producing glands of the chest common in many prosimians and the anthropoids such as the orangutan. The scent is used in territorial display and marking.

bimaturism: phenomenon of physically distinct morphs of adult males, males that have developed the full set of secondary sex characteristics and those that have not.

Orangutan Genders

Researchers have recognized sexually mature male orangutans with two physically distinct forms (or *morphs*), differing both in body structure and in behavior. Fully adult male orangutans show striking secondary sex characteristics, such as the wide cheek pads, well-developed laryngeal sac, and long dense capelike hair (see Figure 7–34). Subadult males, who are generally over the age of 10 years, lack the large size of the fully adult male and the secondary sex characteristics, including the large flanged cheek pads. These younger males normally attain only the size of large adult females, about 35 to 55 kg (77 to 110 lb). The subadult males may maintain this relatively small size for as long as 10 to 20 years after they mature. These physically distinct morphs of the adult males represent a phenomenon called **bimaturism.**

Subadult males ultimately develop the full set of secondary sex characteristics and large body size of adult males, but until they do, their reproductive efforts are almost entirely restricted to forced copulations with neighboring females, who try to avoid subadults if they can. The two male forms probably represent long and highly variable developmental phases in the male orang-

utan life history rather than alternative pathways of growth or arrested development. However, we cannot really understand bimaturism until we obtain detailed knowledge of orangutan maturation and growth curve data in the wild. Social contact between males in the wild is limited and often aggressive. Auditory signaling by fully adult males may affect younger males, acting to suppress for awhile their full development (Delgado and Van Schaik, 2000). Certainly, one effect of bimaturism is that it helps to limit the number of fully adult males that are competing for females at any given time.

FIGURE 7-35   Male and female mountain gorillas in the Virunga Mountains, Rwanda.

browridges over the eyes. In the adult males both sagittal crests and nuchal crests (found along the back of the skull) are prominent.

The gorilla shares with the other apes the brachiating anatomy of the upper torso, but because of its large size, arm swinging and suspensory hanging from all but the largest branches are uncommon, except in young animals. Adult mountain gorillas spend most of their time on the ground. Lowland gorillas are much more arboreal, and unlike their mountain cousins often build their sleeping nests in trees instead of on the ground. Like chimpanzees, gorillas move quadrupedally on the ground by knuckle walking, supporting the weight of their forelimb on the dorsal surface of the third and fourth fingers of the flexed hands (see Figure 7-32).

Gorillas are the most herbivorous of all of the apes. They eat mainly leaves and the *pith* (tender centers of woody stalks) of certain plants. Although they do consume fruit on occasion, gorillas have not been observed hunting or eating meat. Gorillas also do not appear to use tools in the wild.

The chimpanzee.   The first descriptive anatomy of the common chimpanzee, *Pan troglodytes,* was credited to the Dutch anatomist Nicolaas Tulp, who dispelled most of the early half-man/half-beast myths surrounding the chimpanzee in a paper he published in 1641. The species name *troglodytes* (Latin, meaning "cave-living") reflected early thinking on the behavior of the chimpanzee based on travelers' tales brought back to Europe. We now know, of course, that chimpanzees do not live in caves. In 1699 the English anatomist Edward Tyson was given the opportunity to dissect a chimpanzee and thus demonstrated the correct anatomical relationships to humans. Darwin was aware of Tyson's work, and on that basis he believed that the African apes were more closely related to humans than were the Asian apes, but it was not until the early twentieth century that the extent of chimpanzee diversity was discovered. The taxonomy of the chimpanzee offered by Schwarz in 1934 reflected the range of that diversity and established three subspecies: *troglodytes, verus,* and *schweinfurthi.*

Chimpanzees are found throughout central Africa and in isolated areas along the west coast (see Figure 7-27). Overall they occupy more diverse habitats than do the gorillas, ranging from tropical rain forests to the more open and drier forest woodlands. Chimpanzees have been studied in different ecological habitats in their range, and the literature is voluminous, with published data from more than 35 wild populations across sub-Saharan Africa from Senegal to Uganda and south to Tanzania.

FIGURE 7-36 Male and female chimpanzees; a juvenile is on the left.

The chimpanzees are anatomically similar to the gorillas in form but are less massive. The average weight of a male chimpanzee is about 40 kg (88 lb), and that of the female is less than 30 kg (66 lb). Sexual dimorphism between male and female chimpanzees is less marked than in the gorilla (Figure 7–36). In terms of overall body size differences, chimpanzees show less prognathic jaws, less massive cheek and temporal muscles than gorillas, and, consequently, in males, a commonly absent sagittal cresting on the top of the skull.

In postcranial anatomy, the limb proportions are much the same as the gorilla's. The morphology of the limbs, however, is much less robust, and the digits of the hands and feet are more slender and curved. These differences bear witness to the fact that even adult chimpanzees are overall much more active arborealists than gorillas. The diet of chimpanzees is opportunistic; fruit (60 percent of the total diet) and leaves (20 percent) constitute the majority of food types, although chimpanzees are known to eat insects (especially termites) and small game, including other primates (baboons and colobus monkeys). Movement from food source to food source on the ground is generally accomplished by quadrupedal knuckle walking, whereas arboreal locomotion may be either quadrupedal or by suspension and arm swinging (Figure 7–37).

The bonobo (pygmy chimpanzee). There is only one species of bonobo, *Pan paniscus* (Figure 7–38), which is limited in its distribution to the more heavily forested regions of central Congo (formerly Zaire). Pygmy chimpanzee anatomy, possibly because of the animal's small size, is at first glance more similar to human anatomy than to that of the common chimpanzee. *Pan paniscus* is not in fact much smaller than *Pan troglodytes,* and when skeletal size differences between the two are compensated for, very few traits are significantly different (McHenry, 1984).

Recent research calls into question whether the bonobo is a distinct species from the common chimpanzee. Molecular studies show that the last common ancestor of both chimpanzees lived only 1.5 million years ago (Ruvulo, 1997), and hybrids have been produced from captive chimpanzees housed in primate research centers.

The bonobos, like other African apes, are sexually dimorphic in body size; females weigh only about 75 percent of what males weigh. In their cranial anatomy, bonobo skulls are less robustly constructed than those of common chimpanzees, with smaller brow ridges, and less prognathism in their jaws. Overall bonobos appear more *pedomorphic* (childlike) in body form, possessing more slender limbs and longer hands and feet than common chimpanzees.

FIGURE 7-37 A chimpanzee foraging and feeding.

Like gorillas and common chimpanzees, bonobos usually knuckle walk as they locomote on the ground or above branches in the trees. However, they do move bipedally, most often when they are carrying food (Figure 7–39). In other forms of arboreal locomotion, the bonobos are more agile than the common chimpanzees at both arm swinging and climbing, again no doubt because of their lighter body build. In fact, the bonobos use suspension as a form of arboreal locomotion more than any other African ape (Doran and Hunt, 1994).

Like that of the common chimpanzee, the diet of the bonobo is varied. They eat leaves, pith, and fruit along with occasional small mammals, snakes, and invertebrates. Unlike common chimpanzees, bonobos in the wild show little interest in making or using tools. This, as we see later, is in sharp contrast to the tool-making abilities they display in captivity.

This chapter has surveyed the enormous ecological, geographic, and morphological diversity of the living primates. In Chapter 8, we examine the corresponding behavioral diversity of this fascinating order of animals.

FIGURE 7–38 Male and female bonobos.

◀ SUMMARY

1. **Where are most living strepsirhines found? What are their evolutionary relationships with other primate groups?**

Living strepsirhines, though fewer in number today than in past times, are found in great diversity on the island of Madagascar, and in more limited nocturnal niches in the forests of Africa and Asia. The living strepsirhines are only remotely related to the monkeys and apes, having diverged from a common ancestor during the Eocene some 40 or so million years ago.

2. **What are the basic groups of New World monkeys and the evolutionary relationships among them? What is the primary form of locomotion among New World monkeys?**

The most diverse group of the monkeys are the platyrrhines, or New World monkeys. Six subfamilies of New World monkeys are recognized, and each has anatomical as well as behavioral specializations not found in any of the other anthropoids. New World monkeys are all diurnal species except for one, the nocturnal owl or night monkey. All species live exclusively in arboreal niches, seldom venturing to the ground except on rare occasions to feed. There are no fully terrestrial species of New World monkeys as are found among Old World species, such as the baboon.

3. **What are the basic groupings of Old World monkeys and the evolutionary relationships among them?**

The primates of the Old World, the catarrhines, are divided into the Old World monkeys, the cercopithecoids, and the hominoids, which includes the apes and humans. The Old World monkeys consist of two basic kinds, the cercopithecines, which are omnivorous, and the leaf-eating specialists, the colobines. Both kinds of Old World monkey are found in arboreal as well as, for some, terrestrial habitats. The colobines, however, tend to be more arboreal than the cercopithecines, such as the macaques and the baboons who use a wider range of habitats.

4. **What are the groups of living apes, and where do they live? What ecological pressures do these species face in the wild?**

The living apes are much fewer in number and more restricted both geographically and in habitat use than the monkeys. Most apes are forest-living species. Chimpanzees live in west and central Africa, and the gibbons and siamangs live in Southeast Asia on the mainland and neighboring islands. Orangutans are now limited exclusively to forest reserves on the islands of Borneo and Sumatra. All species of apes have developed greater forelimb mobility and elongation that

FIGURE 7–39 A bonobo walking bipedally.

allows them, depending on their size, to variously display a unique form of arboreal locomotion, brachiation. The great apes also spend a great deal of time on the ground, and gorillas and chimpanzees have developed anatomical specializations in the hands that enable them to knuckle walk. The living apes are few in number primarily because of adverse competition with monkeys over millions of years and, more recently, with people. Ape conservation programs are critical to ensure the continuing existence of these species in the wild.

◖ CRITICAL THINKING QUESTIONS

1. How might differences in life history strategies, as shown in Table 7–1, play a role in the relative abundance and distribution of the varied primate groups?
2. Discuss the pros and cons of taxonomically dividing the primates into prosimians and anthropoids rather than haplorhines and strepsirhines.
3. Account for the fact that the New World monkeys are the most diverse of any other single primate group. How does the evolutionary concept of parallelism play a role in this diversity?
4. What aspects of cercopithecoid anatomy have made these monkeys the most successful primate of the Old World with the exception of humans?
5. If all of the hominoids share in common a "brachiating" anatomy of the forelimb, would you expect the common ancestor of this group also to have been a brachiator? Why or why not?
6. How does knuckle walking as a locomotor adaptation figure in the common ancestry of chimpanzees, gorillas, and people, considering that chimpanzees may be more closely related to humans than they are to gorillas?

◖ INTERNET EXERCISES

Critical Thinking

Baboons. Most researchers classify baboons into five separate species. For this activity, research the genus *Papio* and answer the following questions. Display your findings in a table or chart.

1. What are the scientific and common names of the five species, and what is the range of each? How do the species compare in terms of size, weight, appearance, and sexual dimorphism?
2. What are the different species' diets and ecological adaptations? How do they differ from those of other groups of Old World monkeys? What adaptations define a baboon?
3. Which baboon species is most similar to the ancestor species of the others? How do you think that speciation occurred?

Writing Assignment

Endangered Apes. The four living species of great apes are among the most endangered mammals on the planet. For this activity, investigate the current status of one of the great ape species and the risks to its long-term survival. Write a research paper in which you explore the reasons for the species' endangered status. Be sure to discuss the species' ecological needs as well as its relationships with its human neighbors.

See Companion Web site for Internet links.

Characteristics of Primates

Compared with other mammals, primates have several distinguishing features of the skull, most notably related to an enlarged brain. The brain-to-body ratio is considerably higher than that found among other mammal groups, and the ratio increases as we move through the primate evolutionary tree from prosimians, to monkeys, and to apes. Compared to other mammals, primates rely less on the sense of smell and communication by chemical signals and more on vision. Consequently, their snout is reduced in size and their eyes are positioned in the front of the face. In addition, adaptations of the arm, hip joint, foot, and hand allowed the primates to live and travel freely in the forest canopy.

The Web Activity allows you to view a montage of the many forms of living primates to observe the way they move, feed, and use their senses. You will also see how the primate grasping thumb functions in humans, monkeys, and apes.

WEB ACTIVITY

The video montage focuses on primates' facial features, brains, and opposable thumbs. Although primates are a diverse group of animals, the video makes clear the underlying unity of the order.

Activity

1. View the video. What is the significance of the primates' flat faces and short snouts?
2. How does the position of primates' eyes affect their ability to locomote and find food high up in the forest canopy?
3. What advantage did the grasping thumb give to the earliest monkeys? To the earliest hominids?

The MediaLab can be found in Chapter 7 on your Companion Web site http://www.prenhall.com/boaz

PRIMATES: PATTERNS IN SOCIAL BEHAVIOR

After reading this chapter, you should be able to discuss the following questions:

1. What benefits do primates derive from group living?
2. What methods are used to study primates' social relationships? What models are most useful for understanding the functions of primate social groups?
3. In what kinds of social groups do strepsirhines live?
4. What are the goals of female reproductive strategies, and what types of strategies do individuals and groups use to achieve these goals?
5. What are some typical male reproductive strategies?
6. Explain optimal foraging theory. What behaviors does the theory explain?
7. What are some common behaviors that promote social solidarity among primate groups? How is aggression channeled within groups?
8. What are the functions of communication and play in primate social groups? Why are they important?

Chapter 6 examined primate evolution by looking at the fossil record, and Chapter 7 surveyed the morphological adaptations of modern primates. This chapter explores aspects of the **social behavior** of prosimians, monkeys, and apes. In the previous chapter, we divided the primates into the strepsirhines and the haplorhines because this grouping is appropriate from an anatomical and phylogenetic point of view. As we turn to a study of the nonhuman primates, we use the terms *prosimian* and *anthropoid* because the grouping *prosimian* (which includes the nocturnal tarsier) better describes the similarities in behavior that tarsiers share with the other lemurs and lorises. Such studies of modern nonhuman primates, both in the wild and under laboratory situations, are instructive in two broad areas, both of which we consider throughout this chapter.

First, in a general sense, *behavior is ecologically constrained,* or determined by environment: Behavior is usually ecologically adaptive, so that variations in behavior patterns can be explained by how different species exploit their natural resources. For example, the single-male harem social units of hamadryas baboons are an adaptive pattern for a species that forages in a desert environment. Survival or life history strategies of a species must be successful in the species' environment if an animal is to eat, mate, and avoid predators.

Second, the study of *behavior sheds light on evolutionary problems.* Behaviors that are universal among modern primates provide us with some clues as to the kinds of behaviors that our ancestors may have practiced. With such clues, we can develop behavioral models of how our early ancestors acted. For example, the social behavior of modern prosimians provides us with information on those basic primate behavioral adaptations from which the more complex behaviors of the higher primates have evolved.

ADVANTAGES OF GROUP LIVING

One of the most important primate characteristics is *sociability*. In primates, social behavior is organized around the continuous interactions of a group of animals. Some members of the group may continue to interact with certain other members

social behavior: actions and interactions of animals within groups.

FIGURE 8-1 Chimpanzee (*Pan troglodytes*) extended family and others relax. Group cohesion depends on each member's cooperation. Deviant or antisocial behavior is constrained.

observational learning: learning by seeing and hearing.

reproductive fitness: relative reproductive success of certain individuals over others as measured by survival of offspring into adulthood in a particular environment; the ability of one genotype to produce more offspring relative to this ability in other genotypes in the same environment.

throughout their entire life spans. Long-term interactions, such as those between a mother and her offspring, support group cohesiveness and make social living possible. Because group living demands complicated social interactions, each animal must spend a substantial amount of time learning about other animals and the roles they play in the group. The individual's ability to recognize other individuals and act according to what is known about them based on past experience forms the basis for group interaction. Primate group living on a year-to-year basis also demands a great measure of social control over each individual's actions, because individual deviant behavior, for the most part, must be constrained if the group is to survive as a unit (Figure 8–1).

All social animals must balance the advantages and disadvantages of group living. Perhaps the first advantage is that social living *sets the stage for* **observational learning** by individuals and thus reduces the necessity for experimentation by any single animal. Infants learn how to behave in the group by observing their elders, and knowledge of group traditions and the adaptive solutions to recurring problems allows an animal to survive within its ecological setting. The advantage of sociability is that such information is transmitted easily among animals living in a group. Through the socialization process, the group makes available to its members more knowledge than a single individual could acquire in its own lifetime.

A second advantage of social behavior is biological: *It increases the possibility of resistance to disease and parasites.* The development over time of such resistance is less likely among solitary animals than among social animals.

A third advantage is that social behavior *increases the overall* **reproductive fitness** *of group members.* Generally, group living is organized in a dominance hierarchy in which all members are ranked according to various criteria. This hierarchical structure may result in reduced reproductive fitness of subordinate group members relative to fitness of high-ranking individuals. But even a subordinate group-living individual probably has a relatively higher fitness, because of the availability of mates, than do individuals living a solitary existence (Figure 8–2).

FIGURE 8–2 (*top*) Savanna baboons on the move and foraging. (*bottom*) A baboon troop (*Papio anubis*) at rest in Nairobi National Park.

Finally, social groups *are more efficient in finding food resources,* because foraging becomes more effective with larger numbers of individuals looking for food. For females, an additional benefit of social groups is the reduced chance of infanticide by nonmember males, because resident males often protect group females and their young from attack. These benefits must be weighed against the costs of social group living, as shown in Table 8–1.

We turn now to a brief history of the study of primates in the wild.

FIELD STUDIES AND BEHAVIORAL MODELING

Field Studies

Arguably, the first successful study of a primate species done in the wild was C. R. Carpenter's work on the howler monkeys of Barro Colorado Island, Panama, in 1934. Since then, **field studies, semi–free-ranging studies,** and **laboratory studies** on

field studies: in primatology, studies of species in their natural habitat, uninfluenced or influenced to a minor degree by interactions with humans.

semi–free-ranging studies: in primatology, the study of primate groups that are in some way affected by or are dependent on humans, yet live more or less "normal" social lives.

laboratory studies: in primatology, controlled studies of captive primates.

TABLE 8-1	Risks and Benefits of Group Living
Risk	**Benefit**
Reduced fecundity (reproductive output) of individuals, because of the stress of group living	Increased reproductive fitness because of an increased number of available mates
Increased competition for food, increasing with group size	Higher likelihood of finding food, because of an increased number of foragers
Increased possibility of killing of infants whose mothers shift their group membership or resident males leave the group	Decreased possibility of infanticide for infants whose mothers remain in the group
Increased spread of disease and parasites	Acquired resistance to disease and parasites

primates of both the Old and the New Worlds have expanded dramatically. Interest in general social behavior of a wide variety of primate species was followed by more specific studies on communication, mother–infant behavior, matrilineal kinship, and dominance, as well as the relationships between behavior and ecology. Long-term studies (more than one year in length) have been undertaken on genealogical relationships and life histories of animals of such species as the common chimpanzee (Goodall, 1986), the gorilla (Fossey, 1983), the savanna baboon (Strum, 1987), the orangutan (Galdikas, 1979), and the Japanese macaque (beginning with Itani, 1954).

In the late 1950s, K. R. L. Hall studied the chacma baboons of South Africa; Sherwood Washburn and Irven DeVore (1961) studied the yellow and olive baboons of the Serengeti Plain in Kenya (Figure 8–3); Hans Kummer and Fred Kurt (1963) studied the desert baboons (*Papio hamadryas*) of Ethiopia; and Phyllis Jay Dolhinow (1965) studied the langurs of North India. During the 1970s, studies on almost every genus and most species followed, all of which have increased our awareness and concern for those conservation measures that might help stem the alarming trend of habitat destruction, which threatens the survival of many species throughout the world (Southwick and Smith, 1986).

FIGURE 8-3 Irven DeVore studying baboons in Nairobi National Park.

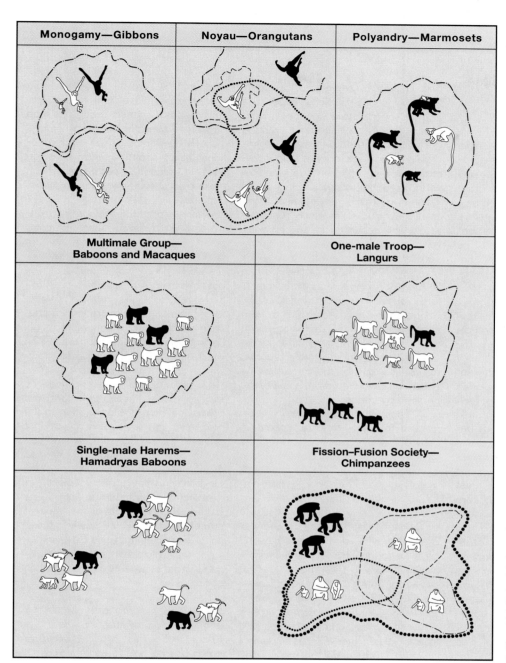

Monogamy—Gibbons	Noyau—Orangutans	Polyandry—Marmosets

Multimale Group—Baboons and Macaques	One-male Troop—Langurs

Single-male Harems—Hamadryas Baboons	Fission–Fusion Society—Chimpanzees

FIGURE 8–4 Common types of primate social organization. Social groupings vary from monogamous partnerships, as observed in gibbons, to opportunistic mating in multimale groups, as seen in baboons and macaques. Single-male units vary from the noyau pattern of orangutans to one-male troops, as observed in South Indian langurs, to single-male harems, which are the small foraging units within the larger troops of hamadryas baboons. The most fluid social grouping is the fission–fusion society of chimpanzees.

Models of Behavior

As information from numerous field studies has accumulated, models of behavior have been developed to explain various patterns of primate social organization (Figure 8–4). Each primate species follows a general pattern of social behavior that is determined by its evolutionary history and ecological constraints. Primates are complex and intelligent animals, and many variations in social behavior patterns have been observed. These variations have been integrated with the ecological and demographic data collected by field-workers.

Some of the early attempts to synthesize primate behavioral data borrowed theories from ethological studies of other animals, mainly birds and the social insects. One of

FRONTIERS

Insights from Field Primatology

LINDA D. WOLFE

Field primatology encompasses social behavior, sexual behavior, demography, activity budgets, foraging and ranging strategies, and the environmental factors that impinge on the lives of the primates. In order for researchers to view the full range of adaptations and social behaviors, species must be studied in their natural habitats. Because primates are long-lived, long-term field studies produce the most valuable insights into behavior.

Much of what we know about behavior comes under the rubric of primate ecology and primate socioecology. *Primate ecology* involves a field study of ecological adaptations of a particular group of free-ranging primates. During the field study, a primatologist collects and analyzes data on foraging and ranging patterns, specific foods ingested, activity budgets (how the group spends its time during the day), relationships with other species, and the group composition (the individual primates making up the group). Primates consume fruit, leaves, seeds, flowers, gum, insects, and in some cases, meat. There is also evidence that chimpanzees deliberately eat plants for their medicinal effects (Jisaka et al., 1992). With the exception of the colobines, whose digestive systems allow them to do so, most primates learn to avoid eating plants with high levels of toxins.

Almost since the inception of field primatology in the 1930s there has been interest in *primate socioecology,* the study of the relationship between primate social systems and the environment through comparative studies (Richard, 1985a). The literature on primate socioecology includes both large-scale studies, which use multiple variables from field studies to link social systems and the environment, and small-scale studies, in which the adaptations of members of one species living in different environments are compared. An example of the latter is Mitani's (1992) study of the western lowland gorilla in the northern tropical forest of the People's Republic of the Congo. Mitani has shown that gorillas in these forests have a fission–fusion type of social system rather than the single-male grouping usually reported for gorillas, possibly as a result of the patchy distribution of fruit, some of the gorillas' favorite food.

A number of researchers have attempted to demonstrate a relationship between primate social systems and the environment (Crook and Gartlan, 1966; Eisenberg et al., 1972; Clutton-Brock and Harvey, 1977; and Wrangham, 1980). None of these attempts has proved entirely satisfactory, because evolutionary history or random changes in the behavior of a species may be more important than current environmental factors in determining present-day social systems. Further complicating the issue is Rowell's (1993) suggestion that nonhuman primates do not perceive a social system and that analyzing their social behavior with this theoretical construct is, therefore, not productive.

Dunbar (1992) has suggested that brain size (neocortical volume) more accurately predicts primate group size than does environmental variables. Finally, there is considerable individual variation in behavior and in behavioral traditions in different troops, which can make cross-species comparative studies difficult.

There is a debate among field primatologists as to whether primates other than humans have culture (McGrew, 1992). It is evident that there are behavioral traditions, such as potato-washing (Kawamura, 1959) and branch-shaking displays (Wolfe, 1981) among Japanese macaques, and tool-use and grooming postures among chimpanzees (McGrew, 1992), which may vary from group to group within the same species. If culture is behaviorally based and defined as learned, shared behaviors that are passed on from one generation to the next, then we would have to say that primates have culture. If, however, culture is based on symbols and defined as the rules in the mind used to generate behavior, then it would seem evident that other primates do not possess culture. The resolution of the issue of primate culture will ultimately depend on greater communication between cultural anthropologists and primatologists, and a consensus on the definition of culture.

Linda D. Wolfe is professor and chair of anthropology at East Carolina University. She has conducted extensive primatological field research in Asia.

ethology's pioneers was Konrad Lorenz (1964; see Chapter 2). He focused on stereotypic (species-specific) aspects of behavior that clearly reflected evolutionary patterns. The complex social behavior of mammals, and of primates in particular, remained mostly outside this field of study. The primary reason was that species-specific behaviors, which are primarily genetically programmed, were considered to be relatively minor components of the total behavior patterns of mammals. In addition, ethologists believed that behavioral variation within a species, which is common among mammals, had little evolutionary or adaptive importance. For all of these reasons, ethology has limited use for explaining the complex social behaviors of primates.

During the mid-1960s, new theoretical perspectives emerged through the efforts of William Hamilton (1963), George Williams (1966), and J. Maynard

Smith (1966). From these perspectives evolved the concept of inclusive fitness. **Inclusive fitness** is the sum of an individual's reproductive success *and* that of its relatives, in proportion to their percentage of shared genes. It involves the success of individual strategies of game playing and optimality. *Game playing* refers to the development of specific behavior patterns that maximize an individual's reproductive success, and *optimality* refers to alternative behaviors available to an individual. Along with this body of work, Dawkins (1989) developed the model of the "selfish gene," which argued that the basic unit of selection was the gene, not the individual. These concepts replaced the earlier ethological views with notions that animal behavior is flexibly opportunistic rather than stereotypic. Behavior is thus designed to maximize reproductive fitness through various strategies of self-interest.

These ideas were incorporated in a new field of animal behavior called **sociobiology** (Wilson, 1975). Sociobiology turned its attention to the behavioral adaptations that are most important to an animal's reproductive strategies. It argued that the evolution of sociability must be explained at the level of reproductive costs and benefits to the individual (Alexander, 1974). As a consequence, behavioral variation, especially between the sexes, became the focus of research, and behavioral decisions were viewed in terms of how they were influenced by social and ecological variables. Within the scope of reproductive strategies (strategies used to increase reproductive success), an animal's primary interest involved *sex-ratio manipulation* (how to alter the number of male or female offspring produced in relation to environmental demand), *parental investment* (how much time and energy to spend on any given offspring), and *parent–offspring conflict*.

The second field of interest to arise from the ethological perspective is behavioral ecology, or **socioecology,** which examines ways in which environmental variables, such as the availability of food or the threat of predators, can determine or constrain behavior. Whereas sociobiology measures *genotypic* success, based on gene propagation or spread, socioecology measures *phenotypic* success, that is, how successful animals are at food acquisition, resource defense, and mating (Terbough and Jansen, 1986; Wrangham, 1987a; Isbell, 1991).

Causes of Behavior

The question of why individuals perform specific behaviors in given situations requires answers at different levels of understanding. Evolutionary biologists have separated the causes of individual behavior into two main types, proximate and ultimate. *Proximate causes* are directly linked with physiological, neural, or hormonal factors. For example, the expression of aggression may be directly related to stimulation in the part of the brain that causes rage. In primates, however, aggressive behavior is usually modified by further proximate causes, such as social group size and individual dominance rank. *Ultimate causes* refer to evolutionary origins. For example, natural selection may be the ultimate cause of aggressive behaviors, favoring them as part of the overall defense and reproductive strategies of males and females.

In an attempt to reconcile the notion of behavioral flexibility with that of biological determinism in primate behavior, biological anthropologists develop models in which social and environmental factors play key roles in determining behavior, within a context of genetic and physiological influences. All of the elements of genetics, ecology, sociability, and learning are used in explaining behavior (Figure 8–5). We now consider specific aspects of behavior among primate groups, beginning with the prosimians and focusing on behaviors that have formed the cornerstones of sociobiology: male and female reproductive strategies.

inclusive fitness: the sum of an individual's reproductive success and that of its relatives, in proportion to their percentage of shared genes.

sociobiology: evolutionary study of social behavior emphasizing relative reproductive success of individuals, including their inclusive fitness within a population.

socioecology: evolutionary study of social behavior emphasizing the adaptation of species to their environment and ecological conditions.

FIGURE 8–5 A bonobo (*Pan paniscus*) mother and her infant. Play? Distraction? Transmission of cultural information? In order to explain a specific primate behavior, a biological anthropologist would consider many different factors.

BEHAVIOR AND SOCIAL ORGANIZATION OF PROSIMIANS

We do not know how the earliest prosimians behaved or how their social groups were structured. The only clues that we have, as we saw in Chapter 6, are from fossil prosimians, whose small, medially positioned eye sockets suggest a diurnal, or day-active, lifestyle. Additionally, fossils that display sexually dimorphic canine teeth could be evidence of a promiscuous mating system among individuals who belonged to a multifemale, multimale social group.

Today, we know a good deal about the behaviors of living diurnal and nocturnal prosimians from field and laboratory studies, and as a result, we can speculate cautiously on what early prosimian behavior might have been like. In our attempt to create behavioral models of early prosimian life, however, we must remember that these primates coped with a substantially different environment from that of today and lived in places of the world where prosimians are no longer found in the wild.

Nocturnal Prosimians

We described in Chapter 7 the five lemur families of Madagascar and three lorisid families from mainland Africa and Asia. All of the mainland African and Asian species, as well as the dwarf lemur and aye-aye of Madagascar, are nocturnal.

Charles-Dominique (1977) noted that "all lemurs are social, even those which are not particularly gregarious." Although the males and females of these nocturnal species generally avoid contact with one another, except during the breeding season, their successful reproduction depends on the continuing knowledge of each other's whereabouts. This knowledge is imparted by urine or fecal marking, commonly practiced by most prosimians throughout their individual **home range**—the area that a group of animals occupies all through the year. Other prosimians possess glands on the neck and chest from which the males deposit scent on branches as well as on nearby females.

Pair-bonding is reinforced by tactile signals, such as grooming and side-by-side contact, both of which increase in frequency as the annual breeding season approaches. Even during solitary foraging, the nocturnal prosimians maintain a network of social interactions through scent markings, vocal calling, and, at times, direct contact.

The adult female of each species generally occupies a distinct home range. During the day, female lorises often sleep alone or with immature offspring (Figure 8–6). Galagos forage alone at night in overlapping home ranges, but females

FIGURE 8–6 Slender loris (*Loris tardigradus*) female, with a clinging infant, during solitary nocturnal foraging.

home range: the area that a group or population inhabits and ranges over, the boundaries of which, unlike a territory, are not defended.

often sleep in groups of two or three with their young. Males of all of these species usually forage and sleep by themselves. The home ranges of one or more of the females overlap with that of a single male. The male keeps constant vigil throughout his range, periodically visiting females and mating with those who are in **estrus** (see following discussion). Young males, in order to find a spot devoid of another "central" male, may travel substantial distances from their natal home ranges to establish themselves in another social group. Females, however, usually remain near the area of their birth throughout their lives.

estrus: the period within the female reproductive cycle that usually corresponds to ovulation and where the female may engage in sexual activity.

Diurnal Prosimians

The diurnal prosimians, the lemurs, are found only on the island of Madagascar, where they have avoided ecological competition with the higher primates. The lemurs of Madagascar were first studied by Jean-Jacques Petter, beginning in 1956. Later Alison Jolly (1966) began work at her team's study site at Berenty, southern Madagascar, where research has been ongoing since 1963. In 1987, Robert Sussman and his team began long-term observations of ring-tailed lemurs at the study area of Beza Mahafaly, also located in southern Madagascar. These studies have brought to light the unique adaptations and behavior of these primates. The lemurs are gregarious in their social behavior, forming year-round social groups of females, males, and young. The best-studied species have been the ring-tailed lemur (*Lemur catta;* Figure 8–7) and the sifaka (*Propithecus*).

The ring-tailed lemurs form social groups numbering between 5 and 22 animals of all ages and sexes. The core of the group consists of females and their young, with several adult males spatially peripheral to the core. Adult males often move between groups and sometimes form temporary all-male groups. Lemur home ranges may be exclusively used by a single group, or they may overlap between groups, which mutually avoid one another by adjusting their foraging patterns and times.

Dominance rank interactions are displayed by both the adult males and females of the troop; however, in many lemur species females exhibit dominance over males. This is usually expressed in terms of feeding priorities: When the troop finds a food source, females feed first. The most recent research suggests that female dominance over males allows them priority access to food, which is especially important during the dry seasons when resources are scarce. Sauther, Sussman, and Gould (1999) suggest that among females, high rank is related to greater reproductive success and to improved infant survival.

Aggressive behavior among males is common, but only during the mating season do these aggressive interactions result in physical injury. During the breeding season the male dominance hierarchy breaks down, and the males interact in a free-for-all for sexual access to the females in estrus.

The sifaka social group consists of adult males and females, but group size tends to be small, ranging between 2 and 12 animals. Sifakas, which occupy the drier, spiny forests of southern Madagascar, establish and defend their home ranges, called *territories.* Territorial behavior includes ritualized aggression toward other groups, although this aggression seldom results in actual physical violence. In other areas of Madagascar, however, sifakas show no defensive behavior when their home ranges overlap. As with the lemurs, male social dominance hierarchies disappear during the annual breeding season.

The indri exhibits a particularly interesting social organization that is similar to the organization of the marmosets (small monkeys of South America). The indri live in monogamous family groups that, in addition to the adult male and adult female, may also include older siblings of the monogamous pair and, occasionally, unrelated younger males (Richard, 1985a:296). How these additional individuals function in the indri group is as yet unknown. It may be, however, that these hangers-on are put to work baby-sitting newborns of the troop.

FIGURE 8–7 Ring-tailed lemurs (*Lemur catta*), a diurnal, or day-active, species native to Madagascar. (*top*) A female and a juvenile on a branch. (*bottom*) Interspecies encounter between a troop of ring-tails and a single *Lemur macaca.*

Although the prosimians are anatomically more primitive than the monkeys and apes, they do display many behavioral patterns that parallel those observed in their more advanced cousins, the anthropoids. We turn now to patterns of monkey and ape behavior. We organize our discussion into a number of themes, beginning with reproductive strategies of females and males.

FEMALE REPRODUCTIVE STRATEGIES

Primate social structure and organization are, in part, the result of the interplay between male and female reproductive interests, which unfold under unique ecological and demographic circumstances. Female behavior and female social organization relate to habitat characteristics. That is, where do females find food and safety, as well as a selection of mates? In contrast, male behavior mostly revolves around the ability to find mates. Thus, male social organization is primarily correlated with the distribution of females and only secondarily correlated to the demands of the environment.

British anatomist Sir Solly Zuckerman, who wrote one of the first books on primate social behavior, *The Social Life of Monkeys and Apes* (1932), was convinced, on the basis of his studies of captive primates, that the primary reason for their year-round social bonds was sexual attraction. He was wrong, however, because most subsequent studies have shown, for primates living in the wild, sexual behavior for any given adult on a yearly basis is usually quite limited. Certainly, one limiting factor of sexual behavior is the fact that for many primate species the breeding patterns are seasonal.

That part of the female reproductive cycle when the egg is released from the ovary and the female is hormonally receptive to sexual advances is termed *estrus*. A common example of estrus is the domestic dog or cat in "heat." During this period, females are most willing to mate, and in most mammalian species it is the only time in their reproductive cycles that they actually do mate. Biologically speaking, estrus is that part of the mammalian reproductive cycle when females ovulate, the most likely time for them to conceive (Figure 8–8).

Just before **ovulation**, females undergo many hormonal changes, such as increases in their levels of estrogen and testosterone, which may lead to specific external physical and behavioral changes. External changes resulting from estrus may include any of the following:

1. *Visual signals:* Some primate species have a specialized **perineal** skin that reacts to ovarian steroids by swelling and reddening (Figure 8–9). This signals that the female is receptive to males.

ovulation: release of a mature egg cell from the female's ovary, after which it can be fertilized by a male sperm cell.

perineal: relating to the area between the anus and the external genitalia, the perineum.

FIGURE 8–8 The mammalian reproductive cycle from conception through weaning. Female sexual cycling, which culminates in ovulation (estrus), continues until the female becomes pregnant, at which time cycling may cease until after her infant has been weaned. In many primate species, periods of estrus are seasonal. The duration of gestation (the period of infant development inside the uterus) and lactation varies among different species.

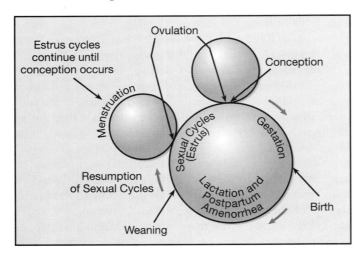

FIGURE 8-9 Swollen perineal region of female baboon during estrus.

2. *Olfactory signals:* **Pheromones** (Greek, meaning "carriers"), hormones that carry scent messages, as well as a scent in urine, are produced.
3. *Behavioral signals:* Females that are in estrus approach males.

All of these signals have the effect of signaling receptivity and willingness to mate to the males.

This sort of reproductive signaling was remarked on in 1872 by Charles Darwin, who concluded that the swelling of the perineum functioned to attract males. Among species whose females do exhibit perineal swelling, including baboons, many other Old World monkeys, and the common chimpanzee, copulations become much more frequent as the size of the perineal area increases. During the period of maximum swelling, as male arousal becomes more intense, ejaculations are also more frequent. It appears now, however, that the visual cue of the swollen perineum by itself, independent of olfactory/pheromonal cues, is the arousing stimulus that affects male sexual behavior.

Some primates are sexually receptive throughout their reproductive cycles (Loy, 1987). The prosimians, however, are more similar in their reproductive behavior to other mammals: Their reproductive activity is exclusively tied to ovulation and is rarely observed during other phases of the cycle. Although some species of the higher primates do breed seasonally and may also restrict their entire sexual activity to this one period during the year, there are numerous exceptions to this rule. Some species have breeding seasons but continue sexual activity throughout the year. The crab-eating macaque (*Macaca fascicularis*) of Southeast Asia, for example, breeds year round and copulates throughout the female's reproductive cycle and during her pregnancy. Among the apes, the bonobos maintain intense sexual activity throughout the year.

In primates there is not necessarily a simple cause-and-effect relationship between hormones and sexual behavior. Gordon and colleagues (1979) showed that, in laboratory situations, when male rhesus macaques were removed from their normal mixed-sex groups and isolated, they failed to show any sexual activity at all, even during a mating season when they would normally associate with receptive females. These studies show that primates differ from other mammalian species: In primates, hormonal influences on both sexes act on the brain's motivational systems rather than directly on the specific motor activity of a species' sexual behavior patterns. Consequently, sexual behaviors in the higher primates are affected by context and by other external factors.

pheromones: hormones that produce their effect by the sense of smell.

The estrus cycle among nonhuman primates is similar to that of human females but with a number of important differences. The first difference is that human females show very little obvious indication of ovulation. In humans, ovulation may be detected by a slight rise in body temperature, as measured by thermometer; by testing for a change in levels of hormones; and by, perhaps, subtle changes or shifts in some behavioral patterns. In contrast, the end of the reproductive cycle, or **menstruation,** which occurs if the female fails to become pregnant, is made quite obvious by the discharge of blood and tissue of the built-up uterine lining. It is important to point out, however, that for most of human evolution, and for most women in the world today, menstruation is a rare occurrence, because of repetitive pregnancies and subsequent long periods of **lactation** or breast feeding.

The second important difference lies in the area of sexual activity, which for humans, as well as for a few of the monkeys and apes, may be ongoing and continual throughout the entire reproductive cycle, including pregnancy and lactation. *Lactational amenorrhea* (the cessation of estrus cycling while the female is lactating) may occur, but it depends on the frequency of nursing and the mother's nutritional status. The relationship between lactation, lactational amenorrhea, and weaning is complex. In the nonhuman primates, suckling/lactation may continue for months following the return of estrus cycling. In humans, lactation may continue for years following the return of menses/ovulation. It is possible in well-nourished primates for a mother to lactate through a subsequent pregnancy and then to nurse offspring of two different ages. This is well known in the United States, where it is called *tandem nursing*. It has been reported that some women have even nursed three children of different ages. Tandem nursing was also observed by Jane Goodall (1986) in chimpanzees (Fifi) and in captive gibbons.

Seasonality and Behavior

Given the large differences in primate **life history strategies** and the complexity of ecological relationships, biological anthropologists have not been able to clearly tie environmental variables to the timing of reproductive events among all primate species. Nevertheless, it is obvious that some breeding seasons are environmentally related. Because seasonal reproduction is part of the reproductive strategies of some species, natural selection may favor individuals who time their births to coincide with optimal environmental conditions, guaranteeing a better chance for survival of both offspring and mother. For example, among yellow baboons, infants who are born later in the season than other newborns are at some disadvantage. Mortality rates for these latecomers increases about 30 percent during their first two years of life over those born earlier in the season.

Where yearly variation in temperature is small and the **predation rate** on both parent and young is low, seasonal availability of food is generally the most important variable to explain the timing of births. For *Cercopithecus* monkeys, food apparently is the primary determinant of when a female should give birth, and rainfall, through its effect on the food supply, plays a major indirect role. In regard to food, however, it is not so much what the mother eats as what is available to newly weaned young. Their diet at this critical time may be the most important causative factor in birth seasonality.

Female Sexual Strategies

Females are not passive objects of males' reproductive strategies (Hrdy, Janson, and Van Schaik, 1995). In order to avoid male infanticide, females, even when pregnant, will often engage in sex with numerous males. Hrdy theorized that females use **promiscuity** to confuse paternity, and she believes that mating with many males increases the number of males who might befriend a female.

menstruation: monthly, cyclic shedding of the lining of the uterus by nonpregnant female primates, particularly noticeable in humans.

lactation: in mammals the period following birth of offspring, during which time the offspring receive breast milk from the mother.

life history strategies: behavioral decisions that each animal in a species must make to acquire food, avoid predators, and find mates. These decisions may increase inclusive fitness and, thus, vary the reproductive success of different individuals.

predation rate: frequency of killing and eating of individuals of a prey species by predator species living in the same environment.

promiscuity: sexual relations with a number of partners.

In some species, however, females can reduce the risk of aggression by forming long-term breeding relationships with one male. Van Schaik and Dunbar (1990) believe that **monogamous** relationships are best explained by the protection the male provides against **infanticide** by other males. They cite studies on the incidence of infanticide in gorillas (Watts, 1989), showing that in 8 out of the 11 observed cases of male infanticide, a mother and her infant were attacked when they were unaccompanied by a mature male. One explanation is that females live in social groups to reduce the possibility of infanticide.

The **dominance rank** of the mothers has shown to be an important variable in infant production, infant survival, and offspring maturation rates. The subtle social hierarchies to which females belong exert a strong influence on the reproductive success of every female in the group. Infants born to females of high rank are much more likely to survive than are those born to subordinate females. In fact the survival of weaned offspring of dominant females is almost twice that of mothers who hold subordinate ranks. In addition, daughters of dominant females reach sexual maturity substantially earlier than daughters of lower-ranking mothers. Earlier maturity offers an enormous evolutionary advantage, because it offers the potential to produce more offspring (Pusey et al., 1997; Wrangham, 1997). One recent study showed that the rate of production of weaned offspring by dominant females is almost twice that of subordinate females.

Dominant females can affect the reproductive success of their low-ranking competitors by harassing them during copulation. Among langur monkeys, for example, rank plays some role in the frequency of harassment: Females disrupted only 50 percent of the copulations that involved the top three females in a troop. In contrast, females disrupted almost 96 percent of copulations involving the three lowest ranking females. Dunbar (1986) demonstrated with gelada baboons that social stress caused by dominant females harassing subordinate females limited the subordinates' reproductive success, probably by suppressing ovulation. Pusey and colleagues (1997:828) proposed that high rank may influence reproductive success by allowing these females to "establish and maintain access to good foraging areas rather than by sparing them stress from aggression." In spider monkeys, for example, dominance rank must play some role in the timing and sex determination of a newborn. Low-ranking females have much longer birth intervals than do high-ranking ones, about 36 months as compared with 29 months, and they almost exclusively give birth to daughters, whereas high-ranking females produce mostly sons. By chance alone, the ratio of males to females at birth should be about 50:50. The skewed birth ratio, about three females to one male, which is correlated heavily with maternal rank, presupposes some postconception mechanism that results in differential male mortality in utero.

After the birth of the infant, aggressive harassment by adult high-ranking females further reduces the chance of survival of young males. Attacks resulting in injury occur about 1.7 times more often to young males than to young females (Chapman et al., 1989). One explanation is that under the conditions of intense resource competition, it may be advantageous for adult females to reduce the production and survival of male offspring of other females in order to decrease competition later for their sons. The consequences of these behaviors give an additional advantage to sons of higher-ranking females.

Birth and the Mother–Infant Bond

All mammalian mothers nurse, protect, and care for their young during lactation and beyond. However, the duration and intensity of the mother–infant relationship varies considerably. Among mammals, with the exception perhaps of elephants, the primate (including human) mother–infant bond seems to be the most intense and longest lasting.

monogamous: referring to one male–one female pair bonding.

infanticide: killing of infants.

dominance rank: the relative hierarchical position of an individual in a social group.

Primates are usually born during the night or in the early morning hours, before the group begins to forage in search of food. Births at night have the advantage of allowing some time for the recovery of both mother and newborn before the group's social life resumes its daily pace. Within hours after birth, the new mother and her infant must be able to move away from the sleeping area with the group in search of food, and the infant must be able to cling to its mother's hair (see Figure 8–6). An adult male may linger behind the group to assist the new mother or to thwart aggression, but this often depends on the mother's earlier friendships or her kin relationships. The group as a whole rarely modifies its behavior to suit a new mother.

During the first few months of an infant's life, it remains in close proximity to its mother. While traveling, the mother transports the infant under her belly in a **ventro-ventral position.** Infant monkeys attract attention in the social group, and in the first few weeks after birth, mothers receive frequent social contacts from other members of the group (Figure 8–10). Some mothers appear to be very responsive to other individuals' curiosity about their newborn; others are quite restrictive and intolerant of other animals' presence.

Nonlactating females or those who have not yet given birth may "kidnap" an infant for a period of time if they can. This "aunt" behavior of caring for and holding the infant, however, may, for a short time, help the real mother. It is certainly a way by which young females learn about infant care before they have offspring of their own. In contrast to earlier views, we now know that much of the increased interaction that occurs between new mothers and other group members is antagonistic rather than friendly. New mothers often direct aggression toward juveniles and experience more aggression from adult males than they do when they are not pregnant or lactating.

If a mother dies, other females in many species may adopt the orphaned infant. Adoption has been observed in both New and Old World monkeys and apes. Parental care by other females of older infants may afford them some protection against the aggressive behavior of other animals. When an infant who is still dependent on its mother's milk is orphaned, however, the adopter must be a lactating female. Often an adopter is kin. Lynn Fairbanks (1988) demonstrated that grandmothers form affiliative relationships with their grandinfants, though the intensity of this relationship

ventro-ventral position: two individuals facing each other with bodies in contact.

FIGURE 8–10 An infant stump-tailed macaque in its mother's lap surrounded by other adults. Adults often display intense interest in infants, and infant primates often have facial features or coat colors that attract attention because they are so different from those of adults. This infant is snow-white, in striking contrast to the dark-haired adults around it.

varies considerably with the dominance rank of the grandmother. High-ranking grandmothers associated with their grandinfants more often, assisted them by providing social support and protection, and groomed them more frequently than did lower-ranking grandmothers. According to Fairbanks, grandmothers contribute to the reproductive success of their daughters by helping them protect the offspring.

Psychologist Harry Harlow demonstrated in his early experiments on bond formation and "love" in monkeys that an infant's clinging plays a vital role in its development (Figure 8–11). In fact, if the infant becomes agitated or frightened, body-to-body contact is more important to it than nursing. The mother is a safe, secure home base from which the infant launches an exploration of its environment, observing its mother's varying reactions to specific individuals and later to specific situations while clinging to her.

The social development of a young primate passes through a series of discrete phases. Each successive phase is linked by transitional steps in which relationships may change considerably. The sex of the infant seems to be a crucial variable during these transitions. In most species, sex differences during the infant (from birth to the eruption of the first permanent teeth) and juvenile (from the eruption of first permanent teeth to the eruption of the last permanent teeth) periods show a mixture of behavioral patterns that resemble those of the adults together with those that are specific to the particular demands of the early stage. For example, juveniles may regularly incorporate in their vocalization a mixture of signals, some typically infantile as well as some common to adults.

During the transitional phase from infant to juvenile, young males transfer much of their affiliative behavior away from their mother toward others, usually adult males. Loy (1992) notes this especially in his studies of patas monkeys. The juvenile's successes in achieving a friendly bond with the adults will be limited primarily by the youngster's own rank relative to that of its older friends, the interest or behavioral reciprocity its friends have in the juvenile, and any kin relationship the young male might have to a "friend" (Smuts, 1987). If a young male forms bonds with high-ranking males, his chance of being forced out of the group later is diminished. Female yearlings, however, usually maintain their close associations with their mothers, their kin, and friends.

FIGURE 8–11 Harlow's experiments with mother–infant interaction. The infant is clinging to a cloth "mother" for comfort. Harlow found that infants prefer clinging for comfort to food: They cling to a soft mother substitute that does not provide food, rather than a hard wire "mother" that does.

MALE STRATEGIES AND BEHAVIORS

Whereas females in many nonhuman primate species are known to exhibit seasonal reproductive behavior, seasonal changes in male *testosterone* (an androgen) levels are less well understood. It is apparent, however, that in many nonhuman primate species they also vary. The influence, for example, of female receptivity on male cyclicity has been documented for squirrel monkeys (DuMond and Hutchinson, 1967). During the mating season, plasma testosterone levels in adult males are considerably higher than at other times of the year, accounting for distinct birth peaks. In contrast to those species that show a restricted breeding season, others, such as the stump-tailed macaque of Southeast Asia, breed all year long, and testosterone levels do not show a seasonal pattern.

Carpenter (1942) studied rhesus monkeys colonized on Cayo Santiago Island near Puerto Rico. On the basis of his observations he hypothesized that the number of females with which any male mated was directly proportional to the individual male's dominance rank. Since that time it has been shown that male rank and copulatory frequency are not significantly interrelated. Copulation frequency of low-ranking males is usually underestimated, because, as part of these individuals' reproductive strategies, they often conceal themselves from the view of others, knowing that dominant males will usually disrupt their copulation attempts if they can see them.

On Cayo Santiago fully one-third of all rhesus males born into a group migrate by the time of puberty. In fact the average stay of any one male in a group is only 17 months. Males choose to lose the dominance status they have achieved in one group in order to improve their reproductive success by migrating to another group. Apparently, many females often choose to mate with strangers rather than males, even high-ranking ones, from their own group. In fact, familiarity is often a disadvantage in regard to mate choice. Choosing a stranger as a mate may help primates avoid mating with close kin; indeed, field studies have shown that matings between close matrilineal kin (especially between sons and their mothers) are extremely rare. Certainly, one important consequence of avoidance of some kinds of close-kin breeding is that it significantly reduces the problem of inbreeding. Genetic heterogeneity within groups is thus maintained.

In many species of nonhuman primates, attempts at copulation by young males rise sharply 6 to 12 months prior to the descent of their testes, which occurs as they reach sexual maturity. Up to this point and a few months beyond, young males attempt mating with willing females openly in view of other group members without interruption from other adults. Starting about a year following testicular descent, however, this sexual freedom for the most part ends, because of increasing intolerance of these males by fully adult males, as well as by females. It is this growing intolerance of the presence of the young adult males that ultimately forces them to the periphery of the group and then forces them to migrate into nearby all-male or other mixed sex groups.

Although paternity will always be to some extent uncertain in **multimale groups,** males that have mated and then remain in the group during the birth of infants are usually assumed to be the fathers by primatologists who study them. These males also associate with newborns far more than do more transient males. From the point of view of the infant, "paternal" protection often prevents harassment and aggression by other males or females. From the protector's point of view, protective behavior may serve to develop or further social relations with the infant's mother. Such nonkin alliances or "friendships" are often maintained for long periods of time (Smuts, 1987).

Interactions between adult males and infants may benefit the adult male as well as the mother and infant. Sometimes males "kidnap" infants temporarily and use the infants as buffers or "shields" in **agonistic** encounters with other males. In baboons a very common three-way interaction has an adult male holding or carrying an infant while accompanied by another adult male (Figure 8–12). In this way, potential aggression between males is often thwarted.

multimale groups: in reference to primate social organization, groups of primates where a number of males of various dominance rank live together in the same group.

agonistic: behavior that appears in aggressive encounters.

FIGURE 8–12 Use of an infant as a shield in a potentially agonistic encounter between adult male baboons.

Paternity is most easily determined in species that are (at least serially) monogamous, and in which males make regular contributions to the care of offspring. In the New World monkeys—among the marmosets, tamarins, titis, and owl monkeys—males usually do most of the infant carrying and return infants to their mothers only for nursing. Fathers, with the help of juveniles and in some cases even unrelated subdominant males, carry infants on their backs, share food after the infants are weaned, and play with infants, as well as protect them from predators and other dangers (Figure 8–13). Fathers, however, will avoid "baby-sitting" if they can, and will relieve themselves of the chore if they have available helpers (McGrew, 1988). Among marmosets and tamarins, one primary function of paternal care is to aid the mother in carrying multiple offspring, as twinning (producing twins) is the norm rather than the exception for this group. Among the Old World monkeys, males do not habitually carry infants. In single-male, multifemale **harem species,** such as the hamadryas and gelada baboons, males may adopt prepubescent females, carry them about, and protect them much as their mothers would, and, ultimately, when they become adults, incorporate them into the "harem."

Under certain circumstances, adult males kill infants. The most common instance of infanticide occurs when an unfamiliar male migrates into a troop and usurps the position of the resident dominant male. When the new male has established his position of dominance in the group, he may systematically kill infants belonging to the group's resident females. Sarah Hrdy's (1977) study of langurs in India revealed that on the average, every 27 months, a female's infant was killed in this manner. One apparent result of this behavior is that females begin to ovulate soon after the death of their offspring and become sexually receptive. Langur infanticide is explained as part of a male's reproductive strategy: It brings females into estrus and thus ensures his paternity for the next round of infant births.

Other examples of infanticide have been observed among baboons, red colobus monkeys, silver leaf monkeys, and the New World red howler monkeys. This is also not uncommon behavior among other species of mammals, such as lions. In these cases infanticidal males were **natal residents** of the troop. Apparently, the trigger for this sort of behavior was the male's rise to higher dominance status.

PRIMATE FORAGING AND FEEDING

A group's **foraging strategies** must be modified to accommodate the number of animals in a social group that feed on relatively concentrated food sources (or patches). Having to compete among themselves for food may give rise to higher frequencies of dominance interactions, and the resultant increase in social friction may be considered as one cost of social group living. Alexander (1974) proposed that predator pressure was the primary determining factor for sociality. He believed that intragroup competition in foraging was a cost of group living. When too many animals feed in the same area at the same time, they tend to reduce foraging efficiency by depleting available resources. To solve these problems, there must be some optimal group size for which foraging efficiency is maximized. Optimal group size, however, may vary from group to group, species to species, and year to year (Figure 8–14).

When food sources are scarce and the geographical location of these patches and their annual productivity is unpredictable, a large number of foragers may be advantageous, because it increases the group's chance of finding food quickly (Ward and Zahavi, 1973; Clutton-Brock and Harvey, 1977; Rodman, 1988; Isbell, 1991). As an example, when a few chimpanzees locate a particularly coveted food, they hoot loudly as a signal for others to join them. Sharing information on preferred food sources is clearly of benefit to group members.

FIGURE 8–13   New World adult male monkey (*Callimico* species) carries single infant on his back.

harem species: in primatology, species characterized by social groupings of one dominant male and a number of females and their young.

natal residents: residents of a group that were born in the group.

foraging strategies: behavior patterns that result in the discovery and procurement of food.

FIGURE 8-14 A foraging unit, in this case a gelada baboon harem, at rest. Group members spend much of their time grooming one another.

These ideas have been formally organized into what has become known as the **optimal foraging theory.** The theory states that optimal behavior will develop when returns and benefits are maximized in relation to costs and risks, within the context of resource availability and socioecological factors. As Robinson (1986) has shown from his field studies of the wedge-capped capuchin, a New World monkey, foraging groups possess considerable knowledge of the resources in their home ranges, and they use this knowledge effectively to find seasonal fruit. The capuchin's large home range ensures that some fruiting species are available throughout most of the year and, because the home ranges overlap extensively, intergroup competition makes social living and large group size the practical solution to their feeding problems (Wrangham, 1980, 1983; Rodman, 1988).

DEFENSIVE BEHAVIOR, AGGRESSION, AND DOMINANCE PATTERNS

Whereas a solitary animal must depend solely on its own ability to detect a predator, group living in primates almost always ensures early detection of a predator by many animals (Hamilton, 1971). The subsequent emission of a warning signal reduces each member's chance of being attacked. A number of species have elaborated on this defense strategy and, in addition to warnings, have developed some form of *cooperative defense* against the predator. The African savanna baboon may use cooperative, adult, male threat behavior to ward off predators (DeVore and Washburn, 1963). Young adult males typically stay on the group's periphery and are usually the first animals to confront a predator. In a similar fashion the juveniles and females often form the center of the group (Figure 8–15). Dominant adult males may act cohesively to threaten predators and thus protect the females and young if safe retreats are not close at hand. But in many cases if refuge is nearby, then it's every animal for itself in the mad dash to safety.

The potential effect of predation on the survival of solitary males may help explain why multimale associations persist in seasonally breeding species. Van Schaik (1983) believed that predation avoidance offered the only universal selective advantage of group living. He believes that predation is what sets the lower limit for group size, whereas intragroup feeding competition is what sets the upper limit. Broad generalizations about the relative influence of predation pressure on primate social organization, however, may be difficult to prove.

optimal foraging theory: a predictive theory based on food-getting behavior selected to balance a group's needs to find food against the costs of getting it.

FIGURE 8–15   Positioning of baboon troop members during foraging. Adult males tend to lead and follow the main group. Compare with Figure 8–2, p. 197. Which individuals in Figure 8–2 are the adult males?

Aggression and Dominance Interactions

Primatologists have looked at the ways nonhuman primates maintain group cohesion in spite of occasional aggressive acts by members within the group itself (Figure 8–16). Most often primates resolve their conflicts through a series of *reconciliation behaviors*. These behaviors usually follow some aggressive act. By seeking out one's former opponent in an attempt to reconcile the damage that was done, the relationship is repaired and peace is restored. Kinship plays an important role: Two opponents are much more likely to reconcile if they are matrilineal kin than if they are unrelated. For most primates, kinship functions as a major feature of intra-group behavior and is useful in explaining many patterns of grooming, dominance, and aggression. Some species of primates have specific gestures and social displays to accomplish a reconciliation, such as lip smacking (Figure 8–17) and presenting their hindquarters to an adversary, commonly observed in baboons and macaques. Other species, such as patas monkeys and some species of *Cercopithecus*, use adjustments in proximity to one another to accomplish the same end.

Some nonhuman primates exhibit behaviors aimed at preventing aggression in the first place. Keeping adult males at the periphery of the group is an extremely

FIGURE 8–16 Aggressive interaction between two subadult male gorillas. Primates may resolve their hostilities by carrying out a series of reconcilation behaviors, which may include facial gestures, grooming, or food-sharing.

FIGURE 8–17 Lip-smacking is a facial gesture of appeasement and reconciliation in chimpanzees.

good way to do this: It separates the males from one another. But when males cannot avoid interacting, they may exhibit behaviors to help maintain a peaceful coexistence (Dohlinow and Taff, 1993). Male–male mounting behaviors, for example, may function in this manner. Because a significant number of these mounts are made by subordinate individuals over more dominant animals, this behavior cannot be explained in terms of an expression of higher-dominance rank. Mountings of this type frequently occur before friendly relations are established between two individuals, in which case they may function cohesively by promoting nonaggressive social contact.

Grooming behavior also prevents aggression and at the same time helps maintain group solidarity (see Figure 8–14). In fact, grooming is a good example of a behavior pattern that serves a multitude of social functions. From a hygienic point of view, grooming is necessary for the maintenance of good health, because ticks, lice, and other parasites infest many species, and grooming generally concentrates on those regions of the body that are difficult to get at by oneself. Also, grooming may be traded for sexual access, for proximity to a mother with a new infant, or for forming an alliance with another animal for assistance in future aggression against a third party. Mothers spend a good deal of time grooming their infants, although as their offspring mature, mother monkeys tend to groom them less, and they groom sons less than daughters.

Patterns of dominance, based on the rank of the adult males and females, organize most of the social interactions in the nonhuman primate group. Dominance rank is established and maintained by aggressive interactions, yet aggressive behavior is usually not disruptive of social order. In fact, because aggression most often takes the form of a threat rather than actual fighting, it functions positively to maintain social integration and group cohesion. Although the biological elements of aggression are similar in most nonhuman primates, the pattern and degree of the development of aggressive behavior differs between species and within species in different habitats.

The expression of dominance occurs in many ways. One individual may displace another in a favored resting place, or an individual, usually a high-ranking individual (a male or a female), may purposefully break up disputes to restore peace within the group (Figure 8–18). Interference behavior of this sort may be a defense of self-interest, because an interfering animal might be supporting kin, a friend, or a potential sex partner. Finally, interference interactions may have the continuing function of improving (or at least monitoring) one's dominance position.

Female dominance rank relationships are generally stable and continue over long periods, because females usually do not emigrate from their natal troops, as males often do. Until puberty, both males and females, even fostered infants, assume the rank of their real or foster mothers. If a mother dies while her daughter is

grooming behavior: slow systematic picking through the hair of another individual to remove foreign matter; important in primate social interactions.

FIGURE 8–18 The dominant male in this group of chimpanzees (center, facing camera) breaks up a fight between two females (right and left). The two females began to fight over the pile of food in the center of the picture, and the dominant male immediately rushed in.

still a juvenile, however, the daughter's rank may be diminished. Apparently, the most important factor in determining a daughter's rank is the memory others have of those dominance relations that existed while her mother was still alive. Some females, however, from an early age can significantly elevate their rank through their associations with older males and females (Small, 1989).

In most nonhuman primate species, males leave their natal group at about the age of puberty (Pusey and Parker, 1987). Field data indicate that the percentage of males that actually move from group to group range from a low of 30 percent to a high that includes almost every male in the group. Because males migrate frequently, both at puberty and later in life, male dominance hierarchies tend to be unstable over time. Many different males may, at one time or another, reach the highest position in the group's dominance hierarchy, but sooner or later each of them will be replaced by a younger individual. Factors other than current dominance rank affect the behavior and social interactions of adult males, including their age, physical strength, residence time, and previous mating successes.

COMMUNICATION AND LEARNING

Communication

Considering that nonhuman primates have no spoken language in the human sense, they communicate a great deal. To live together peacefully year after year, animals must communicate their needs and emotions by means of various signals. **Communication** usually results in cooperative action of a give-and-take nature. Communication is necessary to all primates, even the less gregarious ones, for purposes of reproduction at least. For highly social primates, precise communication of emotional states and information about the environment is critical to social life. As a result, primates have developed elaborate communication systems that incorporate both specific anatomical structures and specific types of signals that vary depending on the environmental situation. For instance, monkeys that live high in the forest canopy often rely on discrete vocalizations, because individual animals cannot usually see each other in the dense foliage. By contrast, savanna baboons, which are almost always in sight of one another (see Figure 8–2), usually rely on visual or postural cues to communicate their intent.

Most primate species communicate using a number of different signals or modes. For example, vocalizations, facial gestures, postures, and touch may all be incorporated in a single message, often simultaneously. One evolutionary trend in primate communication has been to reduce the emphasis on signals based on olfaction (sense of smell) and to increase those based on vision. This change is understandable, considering the importance of vision to arboreal locomotion in all primate species. The Old World monkeys and apes rely on visual means of communication and use a more extensive array of facial gesturing and expression than do their New World and prosimian cousins. The increased use of visual signaling in all Old World higher-primate species, including humans, is, in part, related to a more elaborate and complex facial musculature (Figure 8–19).

Many primates relay subtle changes in their emotional state during an interaction. For instance, most expressions of dominance involve signals that are variable in intensity. We once believed that primates communicated only about their emotional state and that they could relay little information about objects or events around them. The recording of individual vocalizations and their subsequent playback to the animals have revealed a much greater complexity in the kinds of information relayed. Apes as well as monkeys produce variable vocal signals that can give information about the sender's sex, the kinship group to which the sender belongs, and the sender's social status. For example, wild forest mangabeys respond

FIGURE 8–19 Bonobo facial expression. The facial and hand position are remarkably human, as is the ability to communicate complex emotional states by means of expression and gesture.

communication: transmission of information by sensory means.

Theory of Mind in Nonhuman Primates

Until recently, researchers were puzzled by the lack of vocal response of nonhuman primate mothers to calls from their separated infants. It is clear from earlier work that the mothers can recognize the calls of their own infants and discriminate among calls that other infants, not their own, might make. But the mothers seldom respond vocally to their infants, even though it seems obvious that hearing a response from one's mother would certainly be reassuring to a frightened, lost infant. Perhaps a mother's reply to the calls of a lost infant might bring attention to it and, therefore, put the infant at greater risk from predators. Observations made over a 14-month-long field study of baboons in Botswana by Drew and Karen Rendall (Rendall, Cheney, and Seyfarth, 2000) have provided us with another explanation.

These researchers believed that baboons did not have a "theory of mind" to understand how their own vocalizations affect others' behaviors.

According to these researchers, baboons lack the ability to recognize that other baboons have knowledge, thoughts, and feelings apart from their own. This is the reason that baboon mothers do not vocalize to call back to their separated infants: They do not understand that their vocalizations could be important for the well-being of their infants. They cannot comprehend another animal's thoughts.

Many primatologists believe that the only difference between human and nonhuman animal communication is syntax: We have it and the nonhuman primates don't. This new research points to a more fundamental difference in psychological mechanisms that underlies communication in human and nonhuman primates. Humans, except for autistic humans, have a *theory of mind*—the ability to think about what another animal is thinking.

There are three levels at which animals can respond to another animal's presence or communication: (1) purely automatically, without any thought involved; (2) with thought about what the other animal is doing; and (3) with thought about what the other animal is thinking. It is the third level that requires a theory of mind. Even without a theory of mind, baboons can extract information from another baboon's vocalizations, but they still are unlikely to vocalize themselves with the intention of influencing others' behavior. Among the apes, chimpanzees represent a higher level of cognitive ability in that they apparently realize that the sounds they make will alert other chimpanzees to a newly discovered source of food. They understand the effect their communication will have on others.

This research adds a new perspective to what we know about the theory of mind in human children. The consensus is that development of a theory of mind—an understanding that other individuals have minds that allow them to think, remember, infer, and even deceive—is one of the milestones of early childhood that becomes evident some time around the age of four in human infants. Whether other primates develop a fully realized theory of mind is the subject of ongoing study and debate.

---

selectively to the long-distance calls of adult males from outside their group. Presumably group members' responses to these vocalizations are based on their past experience with the individuals making the calls. For some species, signals are discrete to avoid ambiguity. For example, vervet monkeys use distinct vocal calls to distinguish between snake and bird predators.

Within the vocal repertoire of many species, calls may be age- and sex-specific. The colobine genus *Presbytis* uses between 18 and 21 discrete vocalizations, of which four calls are used exclusively by adult males and one by adult females. In *Presbytis*, alarm calls of adult females and juveniles of both sexes differ in structure from the harsh bark of adult males. Marler (1973), however, found certain structural similarities in the alarm calls of many species living in the same habitat that were endangered by the same predators, indicating how minimizing the difference in specific vocalizations that function solely as alarm signals could mutually benefit different species.

Expanding these notions in terms of the origin of human language, Seyfarth, Cheney, and Marler (1980) have suggested that the simplest sort of "representational" signaling, such as the alarm calls of vervet monkeys that distinguish specific predators, provides a considerable adaptive advantage to individuals who use it. Success in alarm call signaling might support the further development of this ability into many other social situations. Studies of the titi monkeys of South America have further blurred the distinction between the communications of nonhuman primates and human language: These primates have been known to repeat calls to form what might be considered phrases and to combine them in sequence, mimicking the elementary rules of syntax (Mueller, 1995).

Learning as Adaptation to Sociability

Primates have the ability to **learn** a great number of things, and they require more developmental time for learning than any other order of mammals. It is not surprising that the two most important ingredients for learning in the nonhuman primates, one's mother and interactive play, form a substantial part of an individual's lifetime experience. Situational responses are easily learned within the context of the group and the affectional bonds and stability that the group affords.

The ability to learn can be explained in part by the expansion of that part of the brain known as the neocortex (Chapter 5). Primates have a large brain-to-body weight ratio. But bigger brains are only part of the answer. We have to be motivated to learn, and effective learning requires strong motivation. Psychiatrist David Hamburg (1963) has described the primate learning process as an emotionally pleasurable experience. Natural selection has endowed that part of the brain that moderates pleasurable responses, the limbic system, with the ability to motivate individuals to do what they have to do in order to survive and reproduce successfully. This system makes it pleasurable to form social bonds and thus makes it easy to learn them.

However, primates live in complex hierarchical societies where social context and rank affect daily lives. Therefore, for any given animal, what is learned, as opposed to what is acted out, often depends on context and rank. These elements are not usually part of the experimental design in laboratory studies of learning, from which most of our knowledge on this subject emerges—generally speaking, only single animals are used in tests.

Recent laboratory studies (e.g., Drea and Wallen, 1999) have altered this approach, with surprising results. In these experiments two groups of rhesus monkeys were tested. One group consisted of high-ranking individuals, the other, of individuals of low rank. Performance of high-ranking individuals, who excelled in all tests, remained constant regardless of whether low-ranking animals were present. Members of the low-ranking group, on the contrary, excelled only when the high-ranking individuals were not present. The researchers concluded that the low-ranking animals had learned the appropriate skills but would only express their knowledge when no high-ranking individual was present. This research provides the experimental evidence that performance in any given situation may be socially modulated and rank-related, and that subordinate animals may "play dumb" in hierarchical social groups. It also points out the fact that social factors must be given greater consideration when assessing learning, not only for the nonhuman primates but also, potentially, for humans as well.

A young nonhuman primate's learning is **imitative**, usually of its mother's actions or reactions to individuals or objects. Typically these concern what foods to eat and where to find them, where to sleep and where to find water, and which animals can be approached and which should be avoided. The major part of a young primate's education, however, is not the simple facts about its physical environment but learning to live successfully with other members of its group. Depending on the species, the infant gradually decreases its independence on its mother over time and is finally weaned. As weaning progresses, the mother may refuse to carry her infant or to allow it to suckle (Figure 8–20). Nevertheless, through this transitional stage, the infant continues to be influenced by its mother, most importantly by her personality and social rank. As infants become older, they leave their mothers for longer

learn: to remember information or an experience and retain for use in future behavior.

imitative: relating to information gained through observing other individuals and not through one's own experience.

FIGURE 8-20 A juvenile chimpanzee (left) has been weaned, but continues to "nurse" at its mother's armpit. Such compromises, which are common among chimpanzees, help promote enduring relationships between mothers and their young.

periods of time, widening their explorations and increasing their social relationships, usually through play with their age-mates, but frequently through interactions with older adults.

An important component of learning in the young primate is **play** (Figure 8–21). Play is not a frivolous activity, but a behavior pattern that promotes skill acquisition and problem solving throughout life. Play provides the secure, largely carefree environment and the emotional motivation needed to sustain an individual's attention to a specific object or activity. Play is pleasurable, and, because it involves a seemingly endless series of imitations, repetitions, and experimental variations that usually occurs in the proximity of adult animals who are vigilant to danger, young animals are seldom badly injured during play.

Initially, as young primates leave their mother for short periods of time, their play is solitary and consists primarily of locomotor explorations, which ultimately become explorations of the environment. Because primates are extremely curious animals, over time their play helps them explore and become familiar with the entire area over which their group wanders. For exploratory play to remain interesting, however, it must constantly change. But there are only so many trees to climb and so many ways to climb them, and considering how much time a young primate spends in play, the environment's novelty soon disappears.

Social play then becomes the logical continuation of the process. Peers are perfect play subjects. They are familiar and secure; they are mobile and not always predictable. Hence, peers are endlessly interesting. It is certainly more "fun" to play with

play: behavior that is not directed toward any clearly defined end result, such as food getting, and which is frequently characteristic of young mammals.

FIGURE 8-21 Young bonnet macaques at play. Play allows young primates to practice motor skills and provides an opportunity for social learning.

one another than with a twig. Although observers readily see the importance of social play for learning the basic social skills needed in adult life, this probably is not the reason young primates themselves are motivated to play. The most likely reason critical information and behavior skills necessary for an individual's survival are learned during play is because it is emotionally pleasurable. Under these circumstances, new information is easily and rapidly assimilated into an individual's body of knowledge.

In order to play socially, the young primate must be social; that means it must make adjustments in its own behavior so that it can get along with others (Figure 8–22). Play allows the young animal to learn from its experiences which behaviors are acceptable and which are not (Figure 8–23). This knowledge is important later to adult membership in the group. In this sense, social play serves as a model of later adult social interactions. For example, the social skills required in juvenile play fighting are the same as those required in adult real fighting. An individual must be able to rapidly and correctly appraise a situation and through effective communication use this information to its advantage. This development of effective communication is the basis of all adult interaction. Fortunately, play has an advantage: While using all these social skills, it allows the players to make mistakes, misinterpret intent, and communicate ineffectively without suffering serious punishment. In contrast, generally speaking, adults making these kinds of errors must pay for them.

There is danger in play, however, because it makes young animals inattentive to external events and may attract predators. Hausfater (1976) observed play groups of African vervet monkeys that typically occurred at some distance from the adults. Juveniles of this species were often stalked and killed by adult baboons. The adults of other species may exhibit more vigilant behavior while their young are engaged in play. Squirrel monkey mothers, for example, respond quickly to the alarm calls of their close associates, the capuchins. Although loud vigorous play may provoke the curiosity of a predator, it also seems to alert the adults that play is going on, and, perhaps because of this, juvenile vocalizations stimulate greater vigilance in predator detection by the adults.

The study of the behavior of the living nonhuman primates has provided us with many insights into what makes us human. We have discovered many of the variables that make us the kind of social animal we are from observing the behavior of

FIGURE 8–22 An adolescent bonobo plays with an infant. In order for the play to be mutually satisfying, the older and larger individual must learn to adjust his behavior and restrain himself. Such adjustment requires complex social learning.

FIGURE 8-23 Young chimpanzees test social relationships with members of their communities by teasing their elders. Young chimps of higher rank are bolder in these interactions. Even then, the young quickly learn the reactions different adults may display toward them.

our closest living relatives, both in the wild and in the laboratory. Although the human fossil record, the subject of Chapters 10 through 12, tells us something about the evolution of our distinctive anatomy, this record is limited in what it can tell us about how our ancestors lived and acted. Our knowledge of nonhuman primate behavior, especially that of the great apes, offers clues to an understanding of this part of our past. We have seen that the nonhuman primates display many sophisticated behavioral strategies in the realms of finding mates and food and avoiding predators. New behavioral research in these areas will allow us to refine earlier hypotheses and formulate new ones in our search for the explanation of human origins and the emergence of modern *Homo sapiens*.

◖ SUMMARY

1. **What benefits do primates derive from group living?**
   One of the most important behavioral characteristics of primates is that they live in year-round social groups. Social living provides a number of significant advantages to members of the group. In mixed-sex troops, as observed in the baboons, there is a greater opportunity to find mates. Because there are more animals who are alert to danger, the chance for any individual to avoid predators is increased. Protection by the adults who will defend them against predation increases the chances of infants surviving into adulthood. In addition, orphaned infants may be adopted by other females in the troop. All of these benefits increase the overall reproductive success of individuals in the group.

2. **What methods are used to study primates' social relationships? What models are most useful for understanding the functions of primate social groups?**
   From studies of primates in the wild, we have come to understand many of the reasons for variability in their social organization. We have also observed diverse behaviors. Whereas earlier field studies focused on the daily activities of members of a single group, recent studies have concentrated on the ecological variables affecting primate societies and the life history or survival strategies that animals have developed in response to the surrounding environment. Primatologists have borrowed from studies of other animal species in their attempt to synthesize primate behavioral data. The ethological perspective focused on the phylogenetic as-

pects of behavior, those which are more controlled directly by the genetics of the species. Sociobiological analysis looked at an individual's reproductive strategies, and socioecology looked at ways in which animals were successful in finding food and in defending themselves and their resources from attack by other animals.

3. In what kinds of social groups do prosimians live?

Nocturnal prosimians, with the exception of mothers and their infants, generally live alone as adults and come together only for breeding. Each animal adopts a distinctive home range, which it delineates by chemical marking with scent from body glands. Diurnal prosimians are more gregarious and live in social groups of up to 20 or more animals of all ages and both sexes.

4. What are the goals of female reproductive strategies, and what types of strategies do individuals and groups use to achieve these goals?

Female reproductive strategies relate primarily to habitat, such as the availability of food, safety, and a selection of mates. Females use a variety of strategies to optimize reproductive success, such as promiscuity (to confuse paternity) and long-term breeding relationships with a single male. A female's dominance rank has an important relationship to her reproductive success. The mother–infant bond is intense and long lasting.

5. What are some typical male reproductive strategies?

Androgen levels in species with a distinct breeding season fluctuate in reponse to female receptivity to mating. Before sexual maturity, young males attempt mating freely, but after reaching maturity their attempts are thwarted by dominant males. As a result, many males leave the natal group and live in all-male groups or migrate to a different mixed-sex group. In species that are at least serially monogamous, fathers do most of the infant carrying, usually in harem-type social groups. When a new dominant male establishes his position in a group, he may try to kill the infants in the group unless their mothers successfully thwart the male's efforts. If infants are killed, their mothers soon afterward usually go into estrus and become once again sexually receptive.

6. Explain optimal foraging theory. What behaviors does the theory explain?

Optimal foraging theory attempts to explain how animals find food using strategies that maximize return against the costs of the foraging activities. The theory states that optimal behavior will develop when returns and benefits are maximized in relation to costs and risks within the context of resource availability. It helps explain different foraging strategies as these relate to the number of animals that forage together as a group.

7. What are some common behaviors that promote social solidarity among primate groups? How is aggression channeled within groups?

To maintain social cohesion in spite of occasional aggression, primates use a variety of reconciliation behaviors. They also use strategies that avoid aggression in the first place, such as keeping adult males separate from one another. Grooming behavior is also important in maintaining group solidarity. Finally, expressions of dominance, such as interference with another animal's activities, maintain social integration within the group.

8. What are the functions of communication and play in primate social groups? Why are they important?

Communication, in addition to warning of danger, to alerting others to food sources, and to accompanying behaviors related to breeding activities, is critical as a means by which group solidarity is maintained. Play, an important component of learning in young primates, aids in the acquisition of skills necessary for adult life, including social skills.

◀ CRITICAL THINKING QUESTIONS

1. What is meant by the statement that female social organization and use of space depends primarily on the distribution of food, whereas male strategies depend on access to females?
2. What factors determine the contact a mother will allow for her infant with other group females? What factors determine whether an infant will survive its infancy?
3. What is the nature of primate social groups? What factors make a social group adaptive for primate individuals of different ages and sex?
4. Individual primates interact on a daily basis with others, within and sometimes outside of their social groups. As we come to know individuals through close observation, we become familiar with the way they act. Yet individual behavior is never completely predictable. Why?
5. Primates communicate among themselves and often with members of other species using different modes. What determines which modes will be used in a particular social setting, and why are some modes more appropriate than others for any given situation?

◀ INTERNET EXERCISES

Critical Thinking

Sexual Selection and Reproductive Strategies. In Chapter 2, you read about Darwin's original theory of sexual selection and its modern permutations; in this chapter, you read about male and female reproductive strategies in primates. This exercise asks you to link the two topics. Consider the following questions:

1. What is the underlying purpose of the different reproductive strategies used by male and female primates and other animals? (Can researchers determine the "purpose" of an animal's actions?)
2. Consider the connection between the theory of sexual selection and specific reproductive strategies you read about in this chapter or elsewhere. Do the strategies represent evidence in support of the theory?
3. Why are male and female strategies so different?

Writing Assignment

Primate Communication. For this activity, write a paper about some aspect of communication in primates (avoid the "ape language" controversy, which we address in Chapter 13). Choose a particular primate species and find out as much as you can about the way it communicates. Use video, Web, audio, and print sources. Try to answer the following questions:

1. What is the difference between communication and language?
2. What types of vocalizations does the primate you have selected produce? In addition, what types of gestures and facial expressions are used for communication?
3. Do males and females produce different calls? Juveniles and adults? What is the purpose of the different types of calls?

See Companion Web site for Internet links.

MEDIALAB

Do Nonhuman Primates Have Culture?

The chapter describes the techniques of field primatology and surveys the important discoveries that have been made since the field originated in the 1930s. Because primates are long-lived animals that exhibit complex behavior patterns, long-term field studies produce the most valuable insights into behavior. Dr. Jane Goodall, world famous for her research among the chimpanzees of Gombe, is an eminent scientist in this field.

Chapter 8 discusses the question of whether nonhuman primates have culture and finds the answer as yet undetermined. In the video on your Companion Web site, Dr. Goodall states her firm opinion that chimps, at least, have culture and that chimpanzee culture differs among the various populations that have been studied.

WEB ACTIVITY

The resolution of the issue of primate culture will ultimately rest on the definition of culture. If culture is behaviorally based and defined as learned, shared behaviors that are passed on from one generation to the next, then primates have culture. If, on the other hand, culture is based on symbols and defined as the rules in the mind used to generate behavior, then nonhuman primates do not possess culture.

Activity

1. View the video. What behaviors does Dr. Goodall describe?
2. What definition of culture can you derive from Dr. Goodall's assertions about chimpanzees?
3. What is the significance of the fact that some groups of chimpanzees use sticks to fish for termites, whereas others use rocks to crack nuts? What is the relationship between tool use and culture?

The MediaLab can be found in Chapter 8 on your Companion Web site http://www.prenhall.com/boaz

INTRODUCTION TO THE HOMINOIDS

OUTLINE

After reading this chapter, you should be able to discuss the following questions:

1. What characteristics distinguish the proconsulids from other hominoids? What were the key characteristics of nonproconsulid African hominoids?
2. What is the significance of the discovery of several distinct groupings of Miocene hominoids in Eurasia?
3. What are the evolutionary relationships among the extinct and living hominoids?

Hominoids (Latin, meaning "like humans") are members of the zoological superfamily Hominoidea, which includes the many lineages of fossil and recent species of apes and humans. As we saw in Chapter 7, the first apes appear in the fossil record during the Miocene epoch, some 20 million years ago. Our survey of the living primates showed the diversity of this order and the variety of habitats to which they are adapted. Now we turn to the evolution of the hominoid line.

ANATOMY OF A CLIMBING HERITAGE

Hominoids first appeared in Africa in dense, lowland, forested environments. As we saw in Chapter 7, all living nonhuman hominoids share similar anatomy of the forelimb, shoulder, and upper back, traits that reflect their **suspensory** posture and arm-swinging locomotor, or *brachiating,* heritage. Members of the human lineage also share these anatomical structures—similarities that were recognized early on by Tyson (1699). The evolutionary origins of this body structure are far from clear, because the fossil record that might throw some light on this issue is nearly nonexistent. The scarcity of fossils may be because these hominoid species lived in dense tropical forests, whose acidic forest floors and abundant bacteria tend to chemically degrade their skeletal remains. But equally important is the fact that modern forests still cover most of the forest areas of the past, making paleontological investigations of these important areas difficult. Where adequate sediments have buried the fossil levels, even forest-living animals of the past, including fossil apes, have been discovered.

By the Pliocene (about 4 million years ago), an early form of the hominid *Australopithecus* (see Chapter 10) showed all of the anatomical characteristics of a climbing heritage, although it was clearly also adapted to a bipedal mode of terrestrial locomotion. The ancestors of modern apes must surely have shared the anatomical characteristics of brachiation with *Australopithecus,* but we have, as yet, no fossils to show it.

In the hominoids, the anatomical adaptations made for brachiation (Figure 9–1) have been well described by such prominent anatomists as Sir Arthur Keith (1896) and Adolf Schultz (1936). These include changes that increased rotational movement at the wrist joint, permitting a 180-degree *pronation* (turning the palm of the hand up or down); at the elbow joint, allowing for 180-degree *extension* (unbending the elbow); and at the shoulder joint, permitting full *abduction* of the forelimb (lifting the arm away from the body and over the head; see Appendix 1). The sternum and thorax (chest region) broadened, and the scapula became

hominoids: modern apes, modern humans, and their immediate ancestors.

suspensory: positional behavior; ability of hominoids to hang (from branches) using one or both fully extended forelimbs.

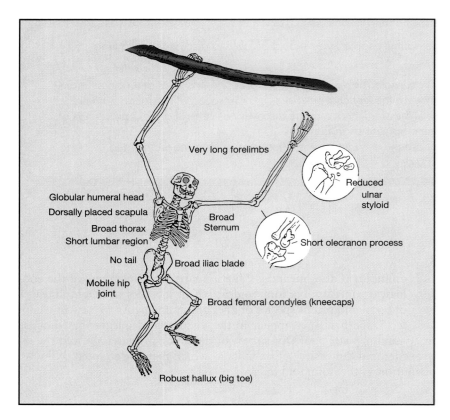

FIGURE 9–1 Anatomy of climbing and brachiating: Compared with anthropoids, hominoids have increased rotation of the wrist (reduced ulnar styloid); increased extension of the elbow (reduced olecranon process); full abduction of the forelimbs at the shoulder joints; broadening of the chest cavity (thorax); elongation of the shoulder blade (scapula); and change in the shape of the shoulder joint.

Labels in figure: Very long forelimbs; Globular humeral head; Dorsally placed scapula; Broad thorax; Short lumbar region; No tail; Mobile hip joint; Broad Sternum; Reduced ulnar styloid; Short olecranon process; Broad iliac blade; Broad femoral condyles (kneecaps); Robust hallux (big toe)

positioned more on the back of the ribcage, rather than down on its side as in the monkeys. Effectively, these changes allowed hominoids to raise their forelimbs over their heads while at the same time maintaining a vertical posture.

In the lower torso, the *lumbar* (lowermost) section of the vertebral column shortened, becoming more rigid (less able to flex and rotate), and the tail was lost, all features that improved an individual's ability to brachiate. The ape's elongated forelimbs allow for a longer reach as the animal swings from branch to branch (see Figure 9–13). The reduced length of the hindlimb; increased rigidity of the hindlimb, caused by morphological changes in the lumbar vertebrae; and the loss of the tail function, all helped eliminate any lower body movement that might interfere with, and thus compromise, the efficiency of the pendulum-like swing of the body.

Changes in the hand also occurred, leading to the development of a curved, hook-like arrangement of the *metacarpals* and *phalanges* (hands and fingers). This solved the potential problem of hand fatigue for an animal hanging for a considerable period of time in one spot. Of all of the suspensory adaptations that humans share with the apes, only the hook-shaped hand was not retained. The human hand developed in a direction that allowed for finer motor coordination and precise gripping ability.

As we saw in Chapter 7, the African apes form a group of quadrupeds that, while on the ground, support the weight of the upper body on the knuckles of the hands rather than on the fingers or palms. This allows them to locomote quadrupedally quite rapidly and at the same time retain the long, curved fingers that are important in arboreal suspension. This unique form of locomotion was first recognized by Sir Richard Owen in 1859, who coined the termed "knuckle walking" and included the Asian orangutan in the group. Subsequent work on the anatomy of the hand and wrist have excluded the orangutans as true knuckle walkers (Tuttle, 1975). The true knuckle-walking apes, the gorillas and chimpanzees, share certain anatomical specializations in the hand and wrist that function to limit the degree of wrist extension, which in turn increases wrist stability (Figure 9–2). Limited wrist extension is reflected in a number of unique anatomical features.

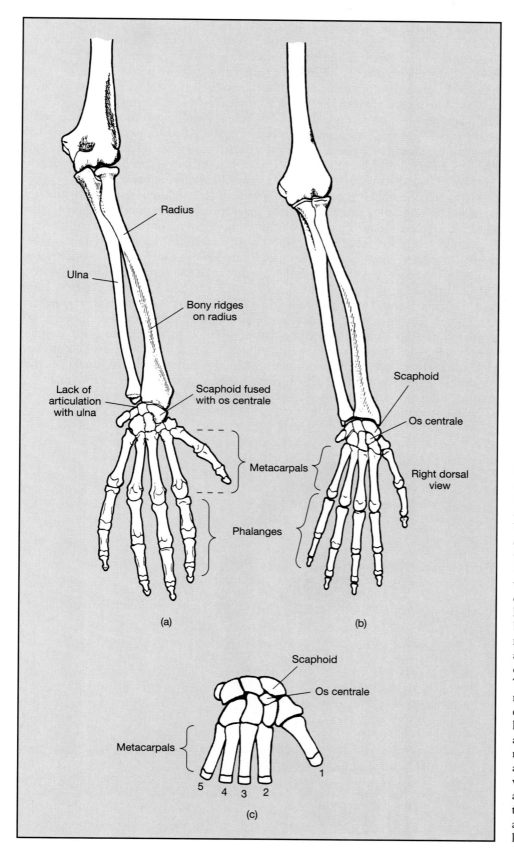

(a)

(b)

(c)

FIGURE 9-2 Comparison of wrist structure in (a) chimpanzee, (b) dryopithecid, and (c) macaque (Old World monkey). The chimpanzee's wrist shows three major adaptations: (1) The *os centrale* is fused with the scaphoid in the chimpanzee (and in modern humans) but is an independent bone in the dryopithecid and macaque. (2) Chimpanzees also have bony ridges on the dorsal side of the radius. These provide a locking mechanism that prevents extension of the wrists during knuckle walking. This ridge is absent in dryopithecids and monkeys. Both these adaptations allow for knuckle walking. (3) The ulna does not articulate with the bones of the wrist. This adaptation allows for suspensory locomotion.

Other skeletal specializations that stabilize the wrist and allow it to support the animal's weight can be found in the fusion of the *os centrale* to the scaphoid bone. This condition is present in the wrists of gorillas, chimpanzees, and humans but not in known fossils of Miocene hominoids, such as the dryopithecines. At the proximal ends of the phalanges (fingers), where they contact the metacarpals, a bony ridge is present that also stabilizes the hand as it bears weight in this flexed position. Although we have no fossil evidence for knuckle walking in the Miocene hominoids, it is likely that the common ancestor of the African apes and humans will show these features. Recent discoveries of wrist traits that researchers believe are leftovers from a knuckle walking ancestor of the earliest australopithecine support this view. These discoveries are reviewed more closely in Chapter 10.

Given the brachiating adaptations found in all modern hominoids and the knuckle walking adaptations limited to the African apes, studies of the Miocene fossil record reveal that the early evolution of hominoids consisted of small changes in a number of different areas of the body (a pattern of evolutionary change that biological anthropologists refer to as *mosaic evolution*). The fossils reveal that morphological changes associated with the emergence of the earliest apes were concentrated in the face; the distinctive characteristics of the locomotor skeleton came later. Derived features of the hominoid face include a flat interorbital region (the nasal bones lie relatively flat across the top of the nose, unlike the condition seen in monkeys) and a wide anterior palate that contributes to the makeup of the upper jaw (Figure 9–3). These features, among others, characterize the faces of all modern hominoids as well as members of the proconsulid family, a group of fossil apes that we discuss next. Although the fossil record leaves us with many examples of the unique hominoid face, the selection pressures that led to their appearance are not yet well understood (Rae, 1999).

FIGURE 9–3 Derived features of *Dryopithecus* facial anatomy shared by later hominoids.

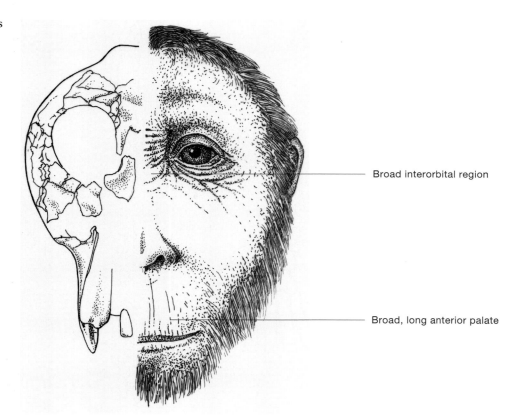

Broad interorbital region

Broad, long anterior palate

THE EARLIEST HOMINOIDS

The Miocene epoch, extending in time from 23 million to 5 million years ago, was a time of a large-scale adaptive radiation of apes. It is important to stress, however, that although there were many different kinds of hominoids living during this epoch, with very few exceptions, paleontologists have established no links between these fossils and the living apes. Taxonomic changes also contribute to the confusion in this picture, because the same fossil has often been described using different taxonomic names. We attempt to describe only a few of the many Miocene hominoid fossils in this chapter, particularly those that shed some light on the origin of the adaptations seen in the living species. Despite the fact that the discovery of some Miocene apes, such as *Dryopithecus,* were made more than 150 years ago, their study remains a perplexing one.

The Proconsulids

In the early Miocene, dating from approximately 23 million to 18 million years ago, the earliest family of fossil apes, known as the **proconsulids,** appeared. At least 15 species belonging to 10 genera of these hominoids have been recognized (Figure 9–4). Of these only two genera, *Dionysopithecus* and *Platydontopithecus,* have been found outside of Africa. The proconsulids range in size from the diminutive, cat-size *Micropithecus* (3.5 kg; 7 lb) to the large *Afropithecus,* the size of a female

proconsulids: family of early Miocene hominoids known mostly from sites in eastern Africa.

FIGURE 9–4   Fossil hominoid sites for the Miocene epoch. African sites date from the early Miocene (23 million to 18 million years ago). Sites in Europe and Asia date from the middle to late Miocene (15 million to 9 million years ago). Sites in Europe and Asia have yielded fossils of hominoids that are the descendants of those who earlier migrated out of Africa.

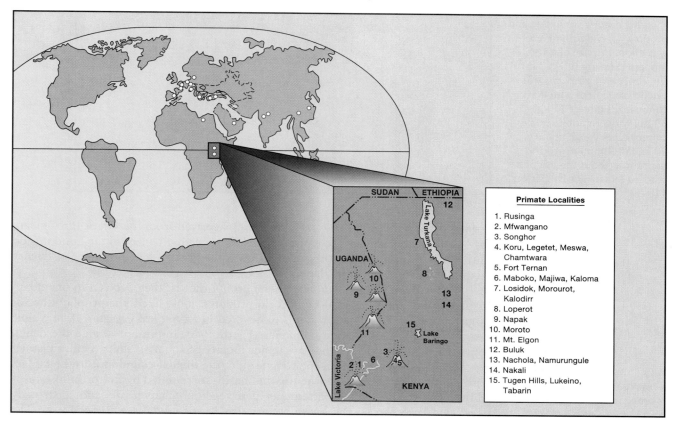

Primate Localities

1. Rusinga
2. Mfwangano
3. Songhor
4. Koru, Legetet, Meswa, Chamtwara
5. Fort Ternan
6. Maboko, Majiwa, Kaloma
7. Losidok, Morourot, Kalodirr
8. Loperot
9. Napak
10. Moroto
11. Mt. Elgon
12. Buluk
13. Nachola, Namurungule
14. Nakali
15. Tugen Hills, Lukeino, Tabarin

(a) Dendropithecus macinnesi

(b) Proconsul africanus

(c) Proconsul major

FIGURE 9–5 Reconstruction of three proconsulid species, showing differences in size and posture. (*a*) *Dendropithecus* was about the size of a modern siamang (9 kg; 2 lb). (*b*) *Proconsul africanus* was a smaller version of a modern chimpanzee (about 15 kg; 33 lb). Modern adult female chimpanzees weigh about 40 kg (88 lb). (*c*) *Proconsul major* was about the size of a modern female gorilla (50 kg; 110 lb).

cingulum: a "belt" (from Latin), referring to a raised ridge of enamel encircling a tooth crown.

gorilla (50 kg; 120 lb). The name *Proconsul* is derived from the Greek (*pro-* meaning "before" and Consul, the name of a well-known chimpanzee in the London Zoo in the 1940s). Members of this family show a diversity of locomotor types, dietary adaptations, and body sizes (Figure 9–5).

The proconsulids are a *monophyletic* group; that is, they evolved in one adaptive radiation from ancestral Old World primates, most likely the propliopithecids (a group of Old World anthropoids discovered in Egypt; see Chapter 6), at a time near the Oligocene–Miocene boundary (Figure 9–6). Important among the dental traits that heralded this change are upper molars of squarish shape with a distinctive belt of raised enamel on the tongue side (the lingual **cingulum**); lower molars with a broad posterior basin (the trigonid basin) surrounded by five prismlike cusps (forming a so-called Y-5 pattern, as described in Chapter 7); and a strongly developed last cusp on the lower molars (the *hypoconulid*; see Appendix 1). The

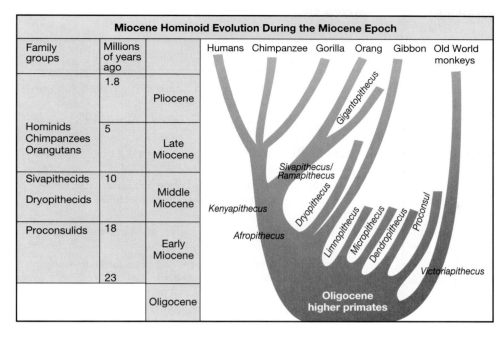

Miocene Hominoid Evolution During the Miocene Epoch		
Family groups	Millions of years ago	
Hominids Chimpanzees Orangutans	1.8	Pliocene
	5	Late Miocene
Sivapithecids Dryopithecids	10	Middle Miocene
Proconsulids	18	Early Miocene
	23	
		Oligocene

FIGURE 9–6 Evolutionary relationships among the hominoids, shown in relation to the geologic periods in which the species evolved.

teeth of the proconsulids show that they had a range of dietary patterns. Some were primarily fruit eating, indicated by low, rounded molar cusps, whereas some were leaf eating, indicated by a greater development of shearing crests and cusps on the molar teeth than seen in earlier primate fossils.

The proconsulids also share many primitive catarrhine cranial traits (traits typical of all Old World primates). These include a tubular ectotympanic bone in the middle ear region (refer back to Figure 6–11). The relative size of the brain, compared with overall body size, also seems to be similar in the proconsulids and in the living Old World monkeys.

Postcranial remains (those other bones of the body besides the skull) that are clearly hominoid are mostly unknown before 18 million years ago (Pilbeam, 1996). Even at that date, postcranial fossils attributable to the proconsulids show very few similarities to modern hominoids. Proconsulid vertebral columns probably had six lumbar vertebrae, and at least the last thoracic vertebrae had lumbarlike articulations. The thorax appeared to be narrow and deep, features most similar to quadrupedal monkeys (Figure 9–7). However, there appears to be a range of adaptations within this general pattern. For example, there were suspensory species such as *Dendropithecus macinnesi* (similar to the modern spider monkey), gibbonlike species of *Limnopithecus* and *Simiolus,* and a terrestrial quadruped, *Proconsul nyanzae.* Based on studies of differences in size of canine teeth, the proconsulids show considerable sexual dimorphism in body size (Kelley, 1987).

Other African Hominoids

In addition to the proconsulids in Africa, other fossils have been discovered whose taxonomic status remains unclear (Table 9–1). Within this group are animals that possess a wide range of features, ranging from primitive, to considerably more advanced, to those found in the modern apes.

Discovered early in the 1960s, one of the most interesting of these fossils, which included facial, dental, and postcranial remains, was recovered from Moroto, a site in Uganda. The fact that these fossils differed from known proconsulids and modern monkeys suggested to paleontologists that they had recovered a new hominoid species, for which they proposed the name *Morotopithecus bishopi,* after the late

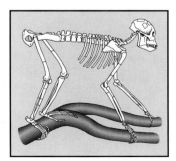

FIGURE 9–7 Skeletal reconstruction of *Proconsul.*

TABLE 9–1	Nonproconsulid Miocene African Apes

Genus

Afropithecus (early to middle Miocene) also found in Saudi Arabia. Two species: *turkanensis, leakeyi*

Morotopithecus (early Miocene) modern anatomical features adapted for brachiation seen in the lower lumbar vertebrae and shoulder joint. One species: *bishopi*

Turkanapithecus (early Miocene) reduced size of the olecranon process at the elbow suggests suspensory posture. One species: *kalakolensis.*

Kenyapithecus (middle to late Miocene) Some characteristics of the limb bones show adaptations for terrestrial locomotion. Two species: *wickeri* and *africanus* (*africanus* has now been included in the genus *Equatorius*)

Otavipithecus (late Miocene) first fossil ape found south of equatorial Africa. Neck vertebrae indicate a more upright posture. One species: *namibiensis*

Samburupithecus (late Miocene) Possessed molar teeth that are long mesiodistally, thus differing from all other Miocene apes and resembling the modern ape condition. One species: *kiptalami*

geologist W. W. Bishop, who did the original work at the Moroto locality (Figure 9–8). The surprisingly modern anatomy of the lumbar vertebrae, resembling features found only in living hominoids, contrasted with the more primitive features of the skull and teeth. The vertebrae indicated a lower back region that was shorter and stiffer than that of other proconsulids and more compatible with the brachiating form of locomotion and arm-hanging posture of the modern apes.

New postcranial fossils recovered in 1994 and 1995 consisted of part of a shoulder blade and the socket of the shoulder joint. The socket was cup-shaped, like that of chimpanzees and orangutans, suggesting a wide range of forelimb mobility and abduction. The fossil evidence suggests that *Morotopithecus* was the first Miocene ape to be able to hang and swing from branches (see Figure 9–8). Other early apes traversed along the branches on all fours. This fossil primate was large, weighing somewhere between 40 and 50 kg (90 to 110 lb). *Morotopithecus* is surprisingly modern in aspects of its anatomy, considering how old it is. It has been dated to an early Miocene age of more than 20 million years ago (Gebo et al., 1997). We can compare *Morotopithecus* to another member of this group, the later middle Miocene species *Kenyapithecus wickeri,* which had a more primitive quadrupedal monkeylike postcranial anatomy.

During the early 1990s the remains of yet another new species of fossil hominoid were recovered from a cave in Namibia by a team led by Glenn Conroy of the Washington University Medical School. The new species, named *Otavipithecus namibiensis* by its discoverers, is so far the first Miocene hominoid found south of equatorial East Africa, significantly expanding the known hominoid range (Figure 9–9). The first published descriptions of this fossil consist of a single, partial mandible (jawbone). It shares dental features, such as relatively thin enamel, with the middle Miocene European hominoid known as *Dryopithecus.* A recently discovered first cervical vertebra (the atlas) from *Otavipithecus* is morphologically intermediate between those belonging to modern Old World monkeys and hominoids, and this may be another instance of hominoids becoming more upright in posture.

In contrast to *Morotopithecus, Otavipithecus* is relatively recent. It is dated by faunal remains to about 13 million years ago (later middle Miocene). *Otavipithecus,* whose size is somewhat smaller than that of a pygmy chimpanzee, at present is best interpreted simply as another type of Miocene large-bodied hominoid whose ancestral relationships to modern hominoids is still unclear (Conroy, Pickford et al., 1992a, 1992b; Conroy, Senut et al., 1996).

FIGURE 9–8 Reconstruction of *Morotopithecus,* a hominoid that lived approximately 20 million years ago in Africa.

 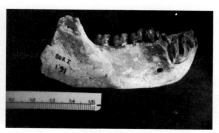

FIGURE 9–9 Two views of the lower jaw of *Otavipithecus namibiensis,* a 13-million-year-old hominoid species discovered in Namibia in the 1990s.

Appearance of Hominoids with Thick Molar Enamel

During the middle Miocene in Africa, hominoids appeared that for the first time possessed molar teeth with thick enamel, a trait that was probably a common ancestral one to all later hominoid groups, but one that survived only in the hominids from *Australopithecus* onward (Figure 9–10). This most likely represented an adaptation for the biting and crushing of hard foods. *Kenyapithecus,* yet another of these taxonomically uncertain genera, which inhabited dry forests, open savannas, and woodlands in Africa, is typical of this type of hominoid. Fossil remains of this species, known primarily from the teeth and jaw fragments, have been discovered at the Kenyan sites of Maboko (about 15 million years ago), Fort Ternan (13 million to 14 million years ago), and Samburu Hills (9 million years ago). (See Figure 9–4.) The pattern of thick enamel on the molar teeth is also a dental feature of the hominids, or members of the human lineage, all of whom were also adapted to open savannas and woodlands.

FIGURE 9–10 Cladogram showing the evolution of thickness of tooth enamel in fossil and living hominoids. The common ancestor of the modern great apes and humans possessed molar teeth with thick enamel. Fossil apes, such as *Sivapithecus,* show these characteristics. Modern African apes and *Ardipithecus,* a later hominoid, lost this type of enamel in favor of one that is thin. Thin enamel is, therefore, a derived characteristic for modern apes. An alternative viewpoint (Shellis et al., 1998) suggests that the last common ancestor of the great apes and humans had average enamel thickness. In this case, the thick enamel of humans and the thin enamel of African apes would both be derived traits from the common ancestor.

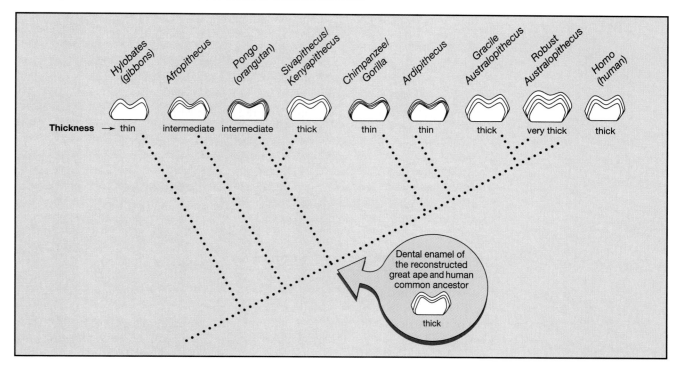

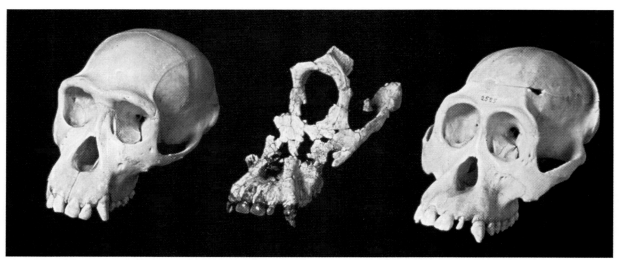

FIGURE 9–11   Face of *Sivapithecus* (GSP 15000, center), compared with orangutan (left) and chimpanzee (right). The facial anatomy of *Sivapithecus* most resembles that of the orangutan, a modern Asian ape, suggesting that it may be ancestral to the organutan. Molecular studies indicating a date of 10 million to 12 million years ago for orangutan divergence is in agreement with this fossil data.

From the 1960s to the early 1980s, the middle-Miocene fossils of *Kenyapithecus wickeri,* along with fossils discovered in India and Pakistan called *Ramapithecus,* were considered by many researchers to be direct human ancestors. These fossils were used by paleontologists to support the Early Divergence Hypothesis, an idea that is described later in this chapter. In the early 1930s, paleontologist G. E. Lewis suggested that *Ramapithecus* showed some hominid features in its dentition. Some characteristics that these fossil apes share with humans are thick molar enamel, a more *orthognathous* or "straight-faced" profile, and somewhat reduced canine tooth size compared with that of most other apes. The most likely case, however, based on the resemblances of known cranial and dental features, is that *Ramapithecus* belong to a group of Asian fossil hominoids that we now call *Sivapithecus* (Conroy, 1990), a genus that is described later in this chapter. Sivapithecine dental and facial characteristics link this genus as a possible common ancestor of the modern Asian great apes, the orangutans, even though analysis of the postcranial remains shows no features of the knuckle-walking terrestrial locomotor adaptations of the modern African apes (Benefit and McCrossin, 1993; Figure 9–11).

The fossil record of African apes after the middle Miocene is a blank, except for a possible gorillalike fossil canine tooth reported by Pickford and colleagues (1988) from the Pliocene deposits of the Western Rift Valley of Uganda. Interestingly, there are no fossil apes in the Pliocene hominid sites of eastern or southern Africa, implying that these areas were either isolated from the forests of Central and West Africa by corridors of open vegetation, or were too arid and unforested to serve as appropriate ape habitats. Future paleontological work in Central and West Africa may improve our understanding of the history of modern ape habitats and their fossil record.

APE EVOLUTION IN EURASIA

A newly described partial skeleton of a fossil ape recovered from deposits located in the Tugin Hills, in the Lake Baringo area of Kenya, now sheds light on the relationship of the African Miocene apes and hominoids found in later Miocene deposits in Europe and Asia. Recently described fossils of a new genus, *Equatorius africanus,* were discovered from several localities and have been dated to about 15 million years ago, when the African rain forests were being replaced by drier, more open woodlands. This is the earliest known hominoid to possess some adaptations that allowed it to occasionally come down to the ground. Fossils originally discovered by Louis Leakey in 1965 from sites on Moboko Island, Lake Victoria, and dated to about 15.5 million years ago, which he called *Kenyapithecus africanus,* have now also been included as members of *Equatorius.* Because of characteristics *Equatorius* shares with some European Miocene hominids, it may provide important clues to the identity of the early African apes that eventually, during the middle Miocene, migrated out of Africa (S. Ward et al., 1999).

Eurasian hominoids, having migrated from Africa, appear in the fossil record for the first time beginning in the middle Miocene, about 17 million years ago. The Eurasian fossil apes are more distinct from one another than are the earlier proconsulids. There are five major groups of Eurasian Miocene fossil apes:

1. The oldest and most primitive apes, the **pliopithecids**
2. The enigmatic late Miocene primate represented by a single genus and species, *Oreopithecus bambolii*
3. Species of the genus *Gigantopithecus,* the largest primate that ever lived. A smaller species, *G. giganteus,* about the size of living gorillas (125 kg; 275 lb), was found in deposits of the latest Miocene in India and Pakistan. Remains of its larger descendant, *G. blacki,* whose estimated weight approached some 300 kg (650 lb), have been found in middle Pleistocene caves in southern China and other areas of Southeast Asia.
4. Different genera and species of groups called the **sivapithecids**, named by Pilgrim (1915) for the Hindu god Siva
5. The **dryopithecids**, named by Lartet (1856) (from Greek, *dryo-* meaning "oak")

Many of these fossils are known only from jaw and tooth remains. As a consequence, separation of individual fossils into different groups is commonly based on differences in enamel thickness (thin versus thick; see Figure 9–10), shape of the mandible, and structure of the lower face. Even applying these criteria, different classifications relating specific fossils to one another are possible.

The majority of Miocene apes probably belong to a separate radiation from the one that led to the living hominoids. Currently, only *Oreopithecus, Morotopithecus* (see Figure 9–8), and, possibly, *Dryopithecus* show any significant postcranial resemblances to living hominoids. According to Pilbeam, there are essentially no Miocene fossil hominoids that are "directly relevant to the extant apes and especially to the chimp–gorilla–human clade. Hence, there is no fossil record directly relevant to the question of hominid origins, except for Pliocene hominids, the earliest of which date back to about 4.5 million years ago" (Pilbeam, 1996:157).

The dryopithecids apparently lived in densely forested environments, commonly in Europe and possibly in China, during the middle and late Miocene, at the end of which time they became extinct. Their remains, the first hominoid fossils ever to be discovered, were found in 1856 at a site in the Paris Basin of France. Subsequently, as more fossils were discovered, the genus and subfamily names were applied to a wide range of Miocene hominoids (Simons and Pilbeam, 1965).

Although fossil remains of the dryopithecids' jaws and teeth are well known, the cranial remains that do exist have not, as yet, been described fully. The few pieces that represent the postcranial skeleton, including an ulna with a reduced olecranon process (elbow), suggest that some of these species were suspensory (Morbeck, 1983; see Figure 9–1). Recent evidence from Hungary suggests that the dryopithecids had facial anatomy similar to that of the modern African apes (Begun, 1992). In summary, the middle to late Miocene European hominoids most likely represent a separate radiation of apes that became progressively cut off from the forests of Africa and Asia as the Miocene epoch drew to a close.

pliopithecid: medium-size, folivorous hominoids known from the middle-late Miocene of Eurasia.

sivapithecid: family of middle to late Miocene hominoids found mostly in Asia. Species of this group may be ancestral to the modern orangutan.

dryopithecid: family of middle Miocene hominoids found mostly in Europe.

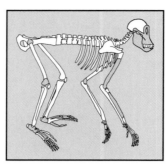

FIGURE 9–12 Schematic representation of *Sivapithecus*. Known parts are shown in orange. Compare with *Proconsul* (see Figure 9–7).

The Sivapithecids

The widespread sivapithecids were originally discovered in India in sediments of the Siwalik Hills, an area that follows the base of the Himalayas from western Pakistan to northeast India (see Figure 9–4). Since the 1970s, Elwyn Simons, David Pilbeam, and colleagues from the Geological Survey of Pakistan have uncovered hundreds of new fossils representing more than 100 individuals. Of these, however, only a very few postcranial remains have been found in direct association with the fossil teeth (Figure 9–12).

Sivapithecids are best known from the later Miocene in Asia, with some species spreading into eastern Europe. This family of fossil apes was composed of a geographically wide-ranging group of probably three species from Eurasia, the largest of which approached the size of a male orangutan (Fleagle, 1999:475). Dentally, *Sivapithecus* shows a relatively small amount of canine sexual dimorphism compared with modern anthropoids, thick, fast-developing molar enamel (see Figure 9–10), an absence of a cingulum, and relatively low flat molar cusps that allowed the teeth to wear flat. These dental features resemble those of modern monkeys whose diet consists mainly of hard objects, such as nuts, seeds, and fruit with pits. A reconstruction of the paleoenvironment of the sivapithecids shows a mixed woodland and dry forest habitat.

Other European Hominoids

Europe was also home to two other descendants of early Miocene proconsulids. The first group, the pliopithecids (Greek, meaning "lesser ape"), were small-bodied, forest-living, climbing and suspensory hominoids frequently found associated with *Dryopithecus*. Members of the family Pliopithecidae are the earliest hominoids to appear in Eurasia, at about 16 million years ago. The best-known species was *Pliopithecus vindobonensis*. Although they were gibbonlike in their postcranial adaptations and size, details of their teeth and cranial anatomy are too primitive to indicate a close relationship with modern gibbons. The canine teeth show a high degree of sexual dimorphism, and the well-developed shearing crests of the cusps of the premolar and molar teeth indicate that *Pliopithecus* ate foliage.

The second group, the Oreopithecidae, is enigmatic in that fossil remains of this form have been very difficult to place phylogenetically. There is irony in this, because these fossils are the best-known skeletal remains of all the Miocene hominoids. *Oreopithecus* (Greek, meaning "forest ape") was first discovered at an 8-million-year-old site at Mount Bamboli in Italy. Paleoecological studies show that members of this group lived in swamp forests, even though aspects of their postcranial anatomy suggest the possibility of some terrestrial locomotion (Figure 9–13). *Oreopithecus* is unique in its postcranial anatomy in other ways. Recent functional analyses of the hand bones of *Oreopithecus* show structural modifications that are, in several respects, quite hominidlike. Improved grasping capabilities and a finer

FIGURE 9–13 Skeleton of *Oreopithecus* and a reconstruction of its appearance. In size, *Oreopithecus*, a late Miocene proconsulid from Europe, was most similar to a female orangutan.

precision grip, suggested by hand length, relative thumb length, and an extensive area for the insertion of the tendon of the long thumb flexor, approach the condition seen in modern humans. These features are not present in any other fossil or living ape (Moya-Sola et al., 1999).

Oreopithecus possessed a broad thorax, short lumbar region of the vertebral column, long forelimbs, and short hindlimbs. In comparison with the rest of the Miocene hominoids, *Oreopithecus* shows the clearest early adaptations for forelimb suspensory locomotion. In its locomotor adaptations it is most similar to the modern orangutan. Its very different cusp pattern on the molar teeth, however, shows that it had no close phylogenetic connection with any modern hominoids. Harrison (1986) showed possible ties to earlier African proconsulids, suggesting that the origins of the oreopithecines may perhaps be traced back to East Africa in the early Miocene.

EVOLUTIONARY RELATIONSHIPS AMONG HOMINOIDS

The question of when our earliest hominid ancestors diverged from the ancestors of our closest living relatives, the African apes, has been one of the most controversial in biological anthropology. Our understanding of the evolutionary relationships of the Miocene hominoids has undergone a revolution in recent years. At one time most researchers of human evolution, such as Elywn Simons and David Pilbeam (1965), believed that there was a straightforward connection between Miocene forms and living species. *Proconsul africanus* was hypothesized to be ancestral to the chimpanzee; *Proconsul major,* to the gorilla; possibly *Sivapithecus indicus,* to the orangutan; and *Ramapithecus,* to hominids. Greenfield (1980) termed this hypothesis the **Early Divergence Hypothesis,** which stated that the branching of the lineages leading to the modern apes occurred prior to the early Miocene (Figure 9–14).

Developments in two areas of biological anthropology, however, changed this general opinion. First, biomolecular studies and the development of the concept of the molecular clock showed that humans shared a recent common ancestor with African apes, diverging from one another only some 4 million to 6 million years ago

Early Divergence Hypothesis: hypothesis that postulates an ancient evolutionary split (more than 15 million years ago) of African apes and humans from a common ancestor.

FIGURE 9–14 The Early Divergence Hypothesis (left), compared to the Late Divergence Hypothesis (right). Almost all biological anthropologists now agree that the Late Divergence Hypothesis better reflects the actual evolutionary relationships and dates of divergences of humans and great apes. According to this view, the human lineage diverged from that of the chimpanzee, our closest living relatives, about 5 million years ago.

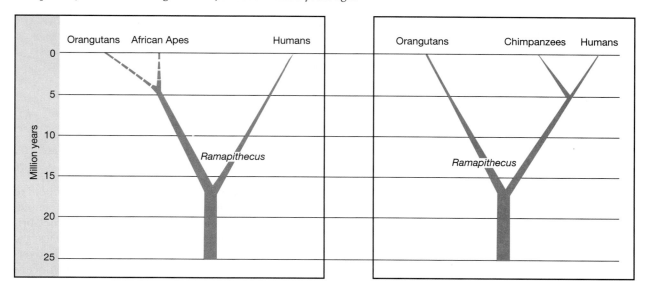

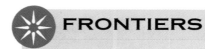

Miocene Apes and Modern Hominoids

DAVID R. BEGUN

The results of the past 20 years of research in Miocene hominoids have produced some dramatic changes in interpretations of hominoid evolution. Hominoid evolution is much more complicated than was once thought; at least 25 different genera are now known, dating from about 20 million to 6 million years ago. Living hominoids are but a mere shadow of the former diversity of this group.

The earliest well-documented Miocene hominoid is *Proconsul*, who dwelled in Kenya up to about 20 million years ago. Many fossil hominoids are known from these sites. Most are probably related to *Proconsul*, but some, like *Dendropithecus*, may represent a different kind of hominoid, or may not be a hominoid at all. The common ancestor of modern hominoids must have been very similar to *Proconsul*.

The middle Miocene lasted from about 16.5 million to about 11.5 million years ago. The Kenyan site of Maboko, dating to about 15 million years ago, preserves a new type of hominoid with thick molar enamel, known as *Griphopithecus* (or *Equatorius*). A bit later in time the more modern-looking *Kenyapithecus* appears at the nearby site of Fort Ternan, Kenya. *Kenyapithecus* and *Griphopithecus* are more advanced than early Miocene hominoids in molar morphology but retain many primitive features also found in *Proconsul*. Certain characteristics of the shoulder joint in *Griphopithecus*, combined with its thickly enameled molars, however,

suggests a greater dependence on terrestrial sources of food, which tend to contain more grit and, therefore, tend to wear teeth more rapidly. More will be known about the cranial and postcranial anatomy of these early more modern-looking forms when closely related taxon from Nachola, Kenya, known as *Nacholapithecus*, are described. Dentally and postcranially similar hominoids are also known from the middle Miocene in Europe and Turkey. These forms, called *Griphopithecus*, may, together with *Kenyapithecus*, be the earliest members of the lineage that includes the living great apes and humans. *Kenyapithecus* has more modern-looking molars that lack a ridge common to earlier forms (a cingulum) and also has a more modern-looking maxilla.

By the end of the middle Miocene and into the late Miocene, modern great ape anatomy becomes evident. Two forms appear at nearly the same time—*Sivapithecus* in South Asia (India and Pakistan) and *Dryopithecus* in Europe. The discovery of a remarkably complete face of *Sivapithecus* (see Figure 9–11) has now convinced most paleoanthropologists that *Sivapithecus* was not a "dryopithecine" but an early member of the orangutan lineage.

The interpretation of *Dryopithecus* has also changed considerably because of new discoveries. Four partial crania and large numbers of jaws, teeth, and limb bones from various sites in Europe show that *Dryopithecus* has characteristics only found in African apes and humans, and one other Miocene hominoid, *Ouranopithecus*, from the late Miocene of Greece. The new interpretation that links *Dryopithecus* and *Ouranopithecus* from Europe, rather than Asian *Sivapithecus*, more closely to

African apes and humans, is almost exactly the opposite of the interpretation of these genera 25 years ago.

A major conclusion from recent research in Miocene hominoids concerns our understanding of the relations among living hominoids and the place humans occupy among them. Some paleoanthropologists who focus on morphology believe that chimps and gorillas are closer to each other than either is to humans, citing such specializations as knuckle walking and thinly enamelled teeth. But the significance of these characteristics is not so clear-cut. Enamel thickness is a poor indicator of evolutionary relationships, because it changes so often in response to dietary requirements. Knuckle walking, which is unique among living forms of African apes, is commonly considered to be a recent specialization of the African apes. A more likely view is that knuckle walking characterized our ancestors, too. After all, humans do share unusual features of the hand and wrist only with African apes, such as fewer wrist bones, more stability of the joints of the wrist, and shorter hand and finger bones. One real possibility is that humans retain these characteristics because we evolved from a knuckle walker that needed them to ensure wrist and hand stability while walking on the knuckles. When humans shifted to two feet, we may have lost many features still found in knuckle walkers, whereas other characteristics suitable to the tasks important to early bipeds, such as enhanced manipulation, were retained.

David R. Begun is professor of anthropology at the University of Toronto. He studies hominoid morphology and evolution, and excavates in Europe and Turkey.

(Sarich and Wilson, 1967). Therefore, *Ramapithecus*, dating from 13 million to 8 million years ago, could not be a direct hominid ancestor: According to the molecular clock, which measures differences in protein structure between different primate species and calibrates the dates of divergences between the modern species, the hominid–ape split did not occur until millions of years later. And second, discoveries of more complete remains, as well as of many new fossil apes from the Miocene of Africa and Eurasia, also began to cast doubt on this simple, straightforward interpretation. As we have seen, a relatively complete fossil facial skeleton of *Sivapithecus* (see Figure 9–12) discovered in Pakistan showed that this genus shared many facial characteristics with the orangutan. This realization removed the best candidate for a Miocene ape uniquely ancestral to the hominid lineage and argued strongly against the Early Divergence Hypothesis (Pilbeam et al., 1980).

The Early Divergence Hypothesis has been replaced by the **Late Divergence Hypothesis,** a term also coined by Greenfield (1980). Both fossil evidence and molecular evidence played important roles in the acceptance of this hypothesis. For some years it has been known how close the genetic relationships are between apes and humans (Goodman, 1961, 1962, 1973; Hafleigh and Williams, 1966). Data that have supported this position have now been amassed from DNA studies, **globin** sequences, **fibrinopeptide** sequences, and immunology (Table 9–2).

The molecular data argue for a single grouping of hominoids, with a separation from the Old World monkeys some 20 million years ago, and, subsequently, for four major changes that led to the evolution of the hominoids (refer back to Figure 9–6). First is the separation of the gibbon and its relatives from the line leading to the great apes and hominids. This lineage split from the common great ape-hominid line between 12 million and 15 million years ago. Fossil apes such as *Micropithecus* from the middle Miocene of Kenya and *Dionysopithecus* from the early Miocene of China, nearly identical primates in features of their dentition, are possible candidates for the earliest gibbon ancestor (Fleagle 1999:463).

Second is the subsequent divergence of the orangutan from the lineage leading to the African apes and hominids. There is now overwhelming evidence in favor of a common lineage leading to the African apes and humans, with orangutans as a sister group. The orangutan divergence occurred, according to molecular estimates,

Late Divergence Hypothesis: a hypothesis that postulates a recent evolutionary split (5 million to less than 15 million years ago) of the African apes and humans from a common ancestor.

globin: a protein of hemoglobin that is found inside red blood cells.

fibrinopeptide: blood protein related to blood clotting.

TABLE 9–2	Differences in Amino Acid Sequences of Human and Chimpanzee Polypeptides
Protein	**Amino Acid Differences**
Fibrinopeptides A and B	0
Cytochrome C	0
Lysozyme 1	0[1]
Hemoglobin (alpha)	0
Hemoglobin (beta)	0
Hemoglobin (A gamma)	0
Hemoglobin (G gamma)	0
Hemoglobin (delta)	1
Myoglobin	1
Carbonic anhydrase 1	3[1]
Serum albumin	6[1]
Transferrin 1	8[1]
Total	19

[1]Comparison of the amino acid composition of a number of polypeptide molecules from humans and chimpanzees. The first seven molecules are identical in their amino acid composition in both species. The protein transferrin shows the greatest number of amino acid differences (8) between the two species. Compare these small differences with the 12 differences found to exist between humans and Old World monkeys and the 43 differences between humans and horses for alpha hemoglobin, which exhibits no difference in the human–chimpanzee comparison.

SOURCE: Adapted from M.-C. King and A. C. Wilson (1975). Evolution at two levels in humans and chimpanzees. *Science* **188**:107–16. Copyright ©1975 American Association for the Advancement of Science.

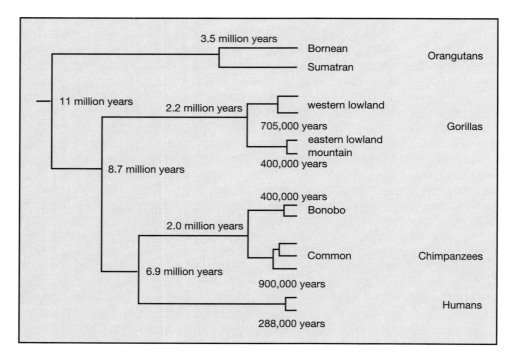

FIGURE 9–15 Evolutionary tree of hominoids, based on mitochondrial gene data. Humans have the least variation within species and, therefore, have the most recent common ancestor of all hominoid species. Orangutan subspecies, which diverged about 3.5 million years ago, are more different from each other than are the two species of chimpanzees, which diverged only 2 million years ago.

bonobo: *Pan paniscus*, a species (?) of chimpanzee distinct in some morphological ways, but not reproductively isolated, from the common chimpanzee, *Pan troglodytes,* and living in a different, nonoverlapping range—the Central Congo (formerly Zaire) forest basin; also termed the "pygmy chimpanzee."

DNA hybridization: method of assessing genetic relationships by splitting and "reannealing" strands of DNA from different species.

between 10 million and 12 million years ago. This corresponds with the known range of *Sivapithecus* and *Ramapithecus* in the fossil record (Andrews and Cronin, 1982).

Third is the split of the gorilla from hominids and chimpanzees. Earlier data were unable to separate the time of divergence of the gorilla and the chimpanzee lineages (e.g., Sarich and Wilson, 1967). More recently, however, Horai and colleagues (1995) have sequenced the entire mitochondrial genome in these hominoids, and their data show a clear chimp–hominid grouping with a long time of separation after the divergence of gorillas. Other work on DNA has also suggested that humans and chimpanzees share a common lineage to the exclusion of the gorilla, which diverged about 8 million years ago (Sibley et al., 1990). According to Pilbeam, "in the case of the hominoids it is difficult to explain the genetic patterns reported here as supporting anything other than a chimp–human clade, given what is known of molecular biology and molecular evolutionary process" (1996:159). At this point, however, fossil evidence that would confirm the evolutionary histories of the modern chimp and gorilla lineages is virtually nonexistent. The three living subspecies of the gorilla may have separated into western and eastern populations as recently as 1 million years ago.

The fourth change is the split of the hominid and chimpanzee lineages. According to the molecular data, this occurred between 5 million and 8 million years ago (Cronin, 1983). Molecular work further reveals genetic differentiation within the modern chimpanzee (*Pan*) species: the **bonobo** (*Pan paniscus*) and the common chimp (*Pan troglodytes*), which shared a common ancestor about 1.5 million years ago (Figure 9–15).

DNA hybridization data are now available on several primate species (Sibley et al., 1990). This technique compares the temperature (measured in degrees centigrade) required to break apart the two strands of the DNA molecule of any species (called the *dissociation temperature,* or *Tm*) with the reduced temperature it takes to break apart a "hybrid" DNA: DNA whose two strands come from two separate species. This technique assumes that the hybrid DNA of species more distantly related will dissociate at a temperature lower than the hybrid DNA of species that are more closely related. This assumption is based on the fact that more distantly related species will have fewer nucleic acid sequences in common, and, thus, the strands of the hybrid DNA will bond together less completely. Chimpanzee–human hybrid DNA dissociates at a temperature somewhere between 0.7° and 1.5° C (1.3° F to 2.7° F) lower than the dissociation temperature of either human or chimpanzee DNA by itself.

DNA hybridization results have proven to be extremely useful in primate phylogenetic analysis. For example, hybrid human–capuchin monkey DNA (a New World monkey) dissociates at a temperature about 10.5° C lower than the pure DNA of either species. If we assume that the New World and Old World monkeys diverged about 35 million years ago, then the human–chimpanzee difference of 1.5° C translates to about a 5-million-year divergence time. Similarly, a difference of 6.3° C between human and green monkey DNA (an African Old World monkey) translates to a time of separation of 21 million years, and the human–gibbon difference of 3.5° C translates to a divergence estimate of 11.7 million years. All are in excellent agreement with the time of divergence calculated using the amino acid sequence data (Table 9–2).

An integrated biomolecular and paleontological perspective argues increasingly for an entirely African origin for the common ancestral hominid–chimpanzee-gorilla and hominid–chimpanzee lineages. These lineages, which diverged at about 9 million to 11 million years ago and 5 million to 8 million years ago, respectively, arose close to the dates of significant late middle Miocene global cooling (11 million to 14 million years ago); the formation of the Western Rift Valley in Central Africa (about 8 million years ago); and the "Messinian Event," the drying up of the Mediterranean Sea, between about 6.2 million and 5 million years ago (Boaz, 1997). These events and the significant climatic effects that resulted may have contributed to the evolutionary origins of these various hominoid lineages.

◄ SUMMARY

1. **What characteristics distinguish the proconsulids from other hominoids? What were the key characteristics of nonproconsulid African hominoids?**
   The earliest members of the hominoid group, the proconsulids, appeared in Africa during the early Miocene, more than 20 million years ago. The proconsulids differed from fossil monkeys at the time in molar cusp morphology (the hominoids shared a Y-5 pattern that is different from the derived bilophodont molar pattern seen in the Old World monkeys); in locomotor abilities (the hominoids were more dexterous climbers); and, in some later forms, in unique patterns of locomotion (such as brachiation and knuckle walking). Other Miocene African hominoids, such as *Morotopithecus*, showed more advanced adaptations for brachiation than did the proconsulids.

2. **What is the significance of the discovery of several distinct groupings of Miocene hominoids in Eurasia?**
   Hominoids spread throughout the Old World by 15 million years ago. In Europe they appeared as the dryopithecids and in Asia as the sivapithecids, in addition to a number of smaller species that were possibly ancestral to the modern gibbons. By 5 million years ago most of these early species had become extinct, possibly because of unsuccessful competition and ecological replacement with a growing number of monkeys. It is, of course, equally likely that the reduction in the number of ape species during the late Miocene and early Pliocene reflects climatic changes during this period.

3. **What are the evolutionary relationships among the extinct and living hominoids?**
   Molecular studies of the living apes have changed our ideas about their phylogenetic relationships with earlier Miocene species. We once considered middle Miocene species such as *Ramapithecus* and *Kenyapithecus* to be contenders for

direct human (hominid) ancestry. *Ramapithecus,* now taxonomically included with *Sivapithecus,* is believed to be related, if not ancestral to, the orangutan, rather than the human. The Early Divergence Hypothesis predicted independent lineages for the modern apes and humans extending back more than 15 million years. Molecular studies involving techniques such as immunology and protein sequencing and DNA hybridization, as well as a more complete fossil record, now support a Late Divergence Hypothesis and a more recent date of about 5 million to 6 million years for a point of common ancestry of the chimpanzees and humans, with an earlier split of this group from gorillas.

CRITICAL THINKING QUESTIONS

1. Brachiation is reflected in a number of specific anatomical features found in all living hominoids. Although we have no fossil record of the direct ancestors of the modern apes, what would you predict this ancestor to have looked like, based on what we know about the anatomy of the modern apes?
2. The spread of the early African proconsulids into Europe and Asia was underway by the middle Miocene. What environmental conditions might have encouraged this dispersal at this time? What subsequent change might have forced their retreat from these areas by the end of the Miocene?
3. From a morphological point of view, describe the evolution of the Miocene hominoids and the adaptive niche that they occupied.
4. If the molecular and DNA evidence show that the chimpanzee and human are more closely related to each other than either is to the gorilla, how do you account for the presence of knuckle-walking adaptations in these apes and, except for the retention of a few features, their absence in modern humans?

INTERNET EXERCISES

Critical Thinking

Miocene Apes. The Miocene was a period of complex radiation of apes. Many different groups of apes evolved, first in Africa and later in Europe and Asia, and most of them have no modern descendants. This period is a controversial one for those who study human origins, because so many gaps in the fossil record exist. For this exercise, consider what is known about ape evolution during the Miocene in relation to the following questions:

1. What major gaps in knowledge exist? In other words, what important questions remain unanswered?
2. What is known about evolutionary relationships among various genera of Miocene apes, and what remains to be learned?
3. What is known about the relationship between Miocene apes and early hominids? What research is available?

Writing Assignment

Finding Links. Speculate on what kind of fossil evidence would be required to link Miocene forms with modern apes. Discuss what a common ancestor of the great apes would have to look like (or what we would expect it to look like, given what we know from modern comparative anatomy of the apes and the molecular data). What anatomical features would such an ancestor show? What evidence would be needed to demonstrate that a fossil species was the common ancestor? Discuss your ideas in a research paper.

See Companion Web site for Internet links.

MEDIALAB

What Can We Learn About the Past?

This chapter covers the Miocene epoch, a time of a large-scale radiation of apes. This is a confusing period for those who study human origins, because of the large number of hominoid species, the paucity of links between these species and the living apes, and much disagreement over taxonomy and nomenclature. Many of these hominoids lived in dense tropical forests, whose acidic forest floors and abundant bacteria tend to chemically degrade their skeletal remains. Equally important, modern forests still cover most of the forest areas of the past, making investigations of these important areas difficult.

So why attempt to put together a fossil record of this difficult period? In this Web Activity, you will hear working paleoarchaeologists discuss some of the reasons for studying the past.

WEB ACTIVITY

Hominoids first appeared in dense lowland forests of Africa about 20 million years ago. Throughout the Miocene, many genera and species evolved. Subsequently,

four major changes led to the evolution of the hominids: separation of the gibbon and its relatives from the line leading to the great apes and hominids (about 12 million to 15 million years ago); divergence of the orangutan from the lineage leading to the African apes and hominids (10 million to 12 million years ago); the split of the gorilla from hominids and chimpanzees (about 8 million years ago); and, finally, the split of the hominid and chimpanzee lineages (between 5 million and 8 million years ago). Work on the identification and taxonomy of early hominoids is key to confirming and refining these dates.

Activity

1. View the video. Based on the interview, what are biological anthropologists ultimately trying to discover?
2. Which adaptations led to the evolution of the hominoids and the modern apes?
3. Based on the chapter and the video, can you think of reasons why it is more difficult to find hominoid remains than human remains?

The MediaLab can be found in Chapter 9 on your Companion Web site http://www.prenhall.com/boaz

10

THE AUSTRALOPITHECINES

After reading this chapter, you should be able to discuss the following questions:

1. What characteristics define the hominid family?
2. What are the most important sites at which australopithecine remains have been found? What are current beliefs about the evolution and definition of the subfamily?
3. Summarize what is known of the structural and ecological characteristics of the robust australopithecines. What is currently believed about their evolutionary relationships with early *Homo* species?
4. What selective advantages did bipedalism provide to early hominids? What is the relationship between bipedalism and environmental change?

The origins of the hominid family, the family to which humans belong, is one of the most active areas of investigation in human evolution. As paleoanthropologists have discovered successively older and more primitive fossil remains of hominids, the definition of the family Hominidae and its distinction from apes has been continually reassessed. Past definitions have been based primarily on characteristics of *Homo sapiens*, our own species, which is the best-known member of the family. The fossil record now presents several species of hominids that, in varying degrees, are unlike modern humans. Where to draw the line between human and ape has had to be spelled out in ever greater detail. This chapter covers the **australopithecines**, the earliest group of hominids that share important traits with *Homo sapiens*.

WHAT IS A HOMINID?

The ancient Greeks defined people in the natural world as "featherless bipeds." The term *biped* separated people from all four-footed animals, and *featherless* removed people from the largest category of bipedal animals, the birds. But such living animals as the kangaroo, gerbil, and gibbon, and fossil animals, such as the *Tyrannosaurus*, also fall in this category.

The British anatomist Sir Wilfrid E. LeGros Clark (1964) provided what has been the most widely accepted definition of Hominidae (Table 10–1). Hominidae, or hominids, are relatively large-brained bipedal members of the primate order. Compared with apes, their facial anatomy has two distinct features: They have *orthognathous* ("straight-jawed") facial skeletons that protrude less, and their canine teeth are reduced in size relative to their other teeth. However, as more primitive hominid fossils have become known, some of these distinctions have become less absolute. The earliest known hominids show characteristics only slightly more advanced than those of apes. Nevertheless, these early hominids were well-adapted bipeds, notwithstanding significant climbing abilities, and bipedalism still serves as the most useful distinguishing characteristic of the family.

Hominidae: the zoological family in which humans and their more recent fossil antecedents are classified; bipedal hominoids with increased brain-to-body-size ratio.

Australopithecines: small-brained, bipedal members of an early genus of the family Hominidae; flourished from the early Pliocene (about 4 million years ago) to early Pleistocene (1 million years ago) and was replaced by members of the genus *Homo*.

TABLE 10–1	**Characteristics Defining the Family Hominidae**

Skeletal adaptations to erect bipedalism, especially proportionate lengthening of lower extremity and changes in proportions and structural details of the pelvis, femur, and foot

A well-developed thumb

Loss of opposability of the big toe

Increasing flexion of base of the skull, with increasing cranial height

Forward positioning of occipital condyles (the bony prominences surrounding the foramen magnum)

Restricted area on occipital bone for attachment of posterior neck muscles

A strongly developed pyramid-shaped mastoid process of the temporal bone

Reduced forward projection of the lower bony face

Canine teeth spatulate in form, showing little or no interlocking, and lacking sexual dimorphism

No gaps in the tooth row related to the canine teeth

First, lower premolars bicuspid and nonshearing

Tooth wear largely even and horizontal on the crowns

Dental arcade evenly rounded

In later stages of evolution, reduction in size of the molar teeth

Accelerated replacement of deciduous teeth in relation to the eruption of the permanent molars

"Molarization" of the first deciduous molar

In later stages of evolution, marked and rapid expansion of cranial capacity, associated with reduction in the size of the jaws and in the attachment areas for the muscles of mastication, and with presence of a chin

SOURCE: Modified from LeGros Clark (1964).

The Earliest Hominids

Despite intensive searching for more than 100 years, no fossils that document the common ancestor of the ape–human grouping have been discovered. The hominoid fossils of the late Miocene are fragmentary and predate the earliest known definitive hominids. The sites from which these fossils come are in Africa and date between 5 million and 11 million years ago.

An isolated upper molar tooth from Ngorora, Kenya, is the earliest possible fossil evidence for hominids in Africa. It is dated to about 11 million years ago. The specimen is similar to that of a modern chimpanzee, except that it is larger and likely had a thick, enamel capping on the crown of the tooth. Both of these characteristics differentiate the tooth from that of modern African apes, and, in this respect, the tooth resembles the teeth of modern humans. Because thick enamel is a primitive characteristic for the great-ape–hominid ancestor, however, as we saw in Chapter 9, it does not give the Ngorora fossil definitive hominid status. Without associated postcranial bones it is impossible to determine the body size of the Ngorora hominoid and thus to decide whether its molar teeth were relatively enlarged, as in hominids. It may represent the earliest hominid, or, more likely, it may be one of several still poorly known late Miocene East African species of apes. A second hominoid specimen found at Ngorora is a premolar that Hill and Ward (1988) have suggested represents the last surviving *Proconsul* (see Chapter 9).

Another isolated molar tooth, also from Kenya, comes from the site of Lukeino, dated to about 6 million years ago. In overall appearance it is also chimpanzee-like,

New Faces in the Human Tree

The discovery of one new fossil hominid genus and species is noteworthy for any year. The fact that two new hominids were described in 2001 makes it exceptional. The first new millennium fossil described by Martin Pickford and Brigette Senut (2001) was unearthed from a site in the Tugen Hills area near Lake Baringo, Kenya. Earlier dating of these deposits by Andrew Hill and colleagues from Yale University, who had explored this region over the past 20 years, suggests that the fossils are at least 6 million years old. The fossils, named *Orrorin* (meaning "original man" in the local dialect) *tugenensis*, consist of twelve fragments of femora and dentition of at least five chimpanzee-size individuals. The discoverers maintain that the head (proximal end) of the femora, which is large and humanlike in relation to the size of the neck, is a good indicator that *Orrorin* was a biped. These researchers also point out that the reduced size of the canine teeth and large molars make this fossil an excellent candidate for the earliest hominid. Critics of this interpretation believe that *Orrorin* is more likely to be an early species of chimpanzee, it in itself being a significant discovery as

the African ape fossil record is nearly nonexistent.

A team led by Meave Leakey (Leakey et al., 2001) of the National Museums of Kenya announced yet another new genus and species, *Kenyanthropus platyops* (Figure 10–1). These fossils were recovered from a site, Lomekwi, located on the western side of Lake Turkana and consist of more than 30 skull and dental fragments reliably dated to between 3.2 million and 3.5 million years ago. Paleontological work at the site suggests a similar environment, grassland and wooded habitats, not unlike Laetoli and Hadar where the fossil remains of the better known contemporary *A. afarensis* have been found.

The most important fossil specimen so far recovered is a nearly complete cranium, KNM-WT 40000 found in August 1999. Fossils of *Kenyanthropus* show a mosaic of features, some of which it shares with *A. afarensis*, such as thick-enameled cheek teeth, and some features that are derived, such as the existence of a flat plane beneath the nose bone and a tall vertically oriented cheek region. The overall size of the cranium falls within the gracile australopithecine range. Based on the description of the fossil evidence by

Leakey and colleagues (2001), the new specimen does not fit well in the diagnosis of any existing genus of Pliocene hominid. As Daniel Lieberman (2001:420) sums it up, "I suspect the chief role of *K. platyops* in the next few years will be to act as a sort of party spoiler, highlighting the confusion that confronts research into evolutionary relationships among hominins."

FIGURE 10–1   Proposed new genus and species, *Kenyanthropus platyops* found in deposits in the West Turkana region of Kenya. *K. platyops* dated to about 3.5 million years ago is a contemporary of the better known *A. afarensis* that has been found at many sites in East Africa.

but for the same reasons as with the Ngorora specimen, its affinities are difficult to determine with certainty.

One of the earliest fossils generally accepted as representing hominid remains is the Lothagam mandible (Figure 10–2), which is about 5.5 million years old. This specimen consists of a right portion of a jaw, with the first molar and the root of the last premolar preserved. The thickness of the mandible and the squared shape of the molar, as well as a number of structural details, show that this specimen was similar to those of later hominids and significantly different from those of apes. A second jaw discovered at Tabarin, Kenya, and dating to about 5 million years ago, confirms that hominids were present in East Africa by the end of the Miocene epoch.

The earliest fossil evidence for hominids, whose primary definition is based on a postcranial locomotor adaptation, bipedalism, thus ironically consists solely of dental and mandibular remains. There is no clear indication of whether the Lothagam and Tabarin hominids were in fact bipeds, because relevant portions of the postcranial skeletons, especially lower limb bones, are lacking.

The earliest possible, but quite fragmentary, postcranial fossil evidence indicative of bipedal adaptation may be that of *Aridpithecus ramidus* from Ethiopia or

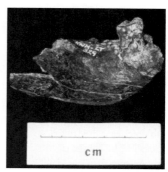

FIGURE 10–2   The Lothagam mandible, from Baringo Basin, Kenya, dated to 5.5 million years ago. The earliest possible hominid fossil known, it shows that hominids were in East Africa by this time.

Orrorin tugenensis from Kenya, discussed later in this chapter. A femur fragment from the Middle Awash area, Ethiopia, dated at less than 4 million years ago, is clearly hominid in its long, straight neck and small greater trochanter (the laterally projecting bony prominence at the base of the femoral neck). The straightness of the head, neck, and shaft indicates that weight was transferred in a more or less vertical manner, as expected in a biped.

What Did the Earliest Hominids Look Like?

When paleoanthropological research succeeds in uncovering remains of hominids more primitive than are currently known, what sort of creature will they reveal? Equally intriguing is the question of what the common African ape–hominid ancestor was like.

If hominids share a common ancestor with chimps and gorillas, which of the three is the least changed from the common ancestor, and which is the most derived? Comparing only the living species (humans, chimpanzees, and gorillas), the answer to this question has seemed to be that humans are the most derived and that chimps and gorillas are the most primitive, because they are more similar to each other than to humans. The deduction follows, therefore, that our common ancestor would have been a knuckle walking, apelike form (Washburn and Moore, 1980). Zihlman and colleagues (1978) suggested that the common ancestor would have been very similar to a small chimp, specifically the pygmy chimpanzee or bonobo, *Pan paniscus.*

With the extension of the hominid fossil record back to more than 4 million years ago and with greatly expanded morphological and molecular studies, this situation has now changed. As we saw in Chapter 9, humans and chimps share a more recent common ancestor than either share with gorillas (Sibley et al., 1990). This implies that many of the traits common to chimps and gorillas, including possibly knuckle walking, are derived traits that developed in parallel, and not primitive at all. The fossil record of hominids now shows that the earliest known representatives of the lineage were bipedal and small bodied, about the size of a baboon. Using extensive anatomical studies as a basis in support of this hypothesis, Tuttle (1975) has suggested that the common ancestor would have been more gibbonlike than chimplike, in keeping with his findings that there are no anatomical remnants of a knuckle-walking heritage in the modern human hand and forelimb.

Some fossil evidence exists, however, that supports the suggestion of a knuckle-walking ancestry for the hominids. Brian Richmond and David Strait (2000) of George Washington University pointed out what they believe to be ancestral knuckle-walking characteristics in two early species of australopithecines, **A. afarensis** and **A. anamensis.** But these conclusions are contested by other observations from a new early australopithecine discovery at South Turkwel in Kenya by Carole Ward and colleagues (1999), who state "[t]here are no indicators of adaptations to knuckle-walking or suspensory locomotion in the hand, and the pedal phalanx suggests that this hominid was habitually bipedal." Thus, further research is needed to resolve the question of locomotion in the earliest hominids.

Why Are Hominid Fossils Rare?

It has been said that paleoanthropology is a unique scientific discipline, because its practitioners probably outnumber the scientific specimens available for study. Several reasons account for the rarity of hominids and their relatives in the fossil record. Some of these reasons are *taphonomic* (Greek, *taphos,* meaning "burial," and *-nomy,* meaning "law"). That is, the scarcity of hominid fossils relates to the conditions under which bones were deposited in a fossil site. In addition, some reasons are *paleoecological;* that is, they relate to aspects of the species adaptations,

Australopithecus afarensis: gracile species of *Australopithecus* found at sites in East Africa and dated from 4 million to 2.5 million years ago; most famous representatives of this taxon are "Lucy" from Hadar, Ethiopia, and the Laetoli footprints in Tanzania.

Australopithecus anamensis: new species of *Australopithecus* discovered at two sites around Lake Turkana, described in 1995 by Meave Leakey and Alan Walker, and dated to 4.0 million years ago.

which affect whether their fossils were preserved. **Taphonomy** is the paleontological study of how bones become buried and preserved as fossils. Perhaps the most important taphonomic factor accounting for the rarity of hominid fossils is that hominids, especially early in the record, were small animals. All the various destructive forces of erosion, weathering, and scavenging by other animals, therefore, affected the hominid bones much more than they did the bones of larger animals, such as horses or giraffes.

Paleoecological aspects of this problem relate to the probability that hominids were not common animals in the environment. They were relatively rare animals that had large home ranges (Boaz, 1979a). Thus, they were unlike prey species, such as antelopes, that were common in the environment and thus contributed their bones to the fossil record in proportion to their population numbers. At Omo, Ethiopia, early hominid fossils, usually single teeth, make up only approximately 1 percent of the mammalian fossil record recovered in excavations and fossil surveys of surface exposures (Boaz, 1985).

Finally, there is the problem of **collector bias.** Paleontologists in the past have not always been interested in or aware of the smaller animals at their sites. Fossils of elephants, hippos, rhinos, antelopes, giraffes, and even pigs are larger, more impressive, and easier to spot in the field. Today a number of paleoanthropologists focus on the smaller elements of fossil faunas, which are termed **microfauna.** These smaller fossils are particularly important in recovering information about ancient environmental conditions, because they are usually more sensitive to changing conditions than the larger animals.

THE AUSTRALOPITHECINES

The term *australopithecine* refers to the subfamily of hominids, the Australopithecinae. It is used as an inclusive term for species of hominids that are more primitive than members of the genus *Homo*. Members of the genus *Homo* are referred to as hominines, from the subfamily term, Homininae (see the discussion of taxonomy in Chapter 1). Australopithecines are characterized as a group, and set apart from *Homo,* by their small cranial capacity, protruding facial profile, somewhat larger overall dentition, and different hip and lower limb structure. In contrast to great apes, the australopithecines were bipedal, possessed smaller and functionally different canine and premolar teeth, and showed many anatomical details of the skull and face that ally them with more advanced hominids.

The number of species attributable to the genus *Australopithecus* continues to grow with the discovery of new fossil remains (Table 10–2). This is a common phenomenon in paleoanthropology, because different discoverers of fossils vie to establish the importance of their finds. Whether the taxonomic names that have been given to different fossils represent legitimate species has been and remains a matter of considerable debate. A conservative stance on this issue would argue against the establishment of new species without exhaustive comparison with other known fossils, while, at the same time, giving attention to established ranges of variation in modern primate populations (Henneberg and Thackery, 1995).

There are no certain occurrences of australopithecines outside Africa. Dutch paleontologist G. H. R. von Koenigswald reported some single teeth from mainland China that he purchased in drug stores in Hong Kong during the 1930s and considered to be australopithecines. These specimens, however, are undated and are poor evidence for confirming the presence of *Australopithecus* in China. Three mandibles collected in Java were considered by J. T. Robinson, an expert on the South African australopithecines, to be robust australopithecines. But most other anthropologists consider these specimens to be large individuals of early *Homo.*

taphonomy: the paleontological study of burial processes leading to the formation and preservation of fossils.

collector bias: the selection choices that an individual makes in assembling a collection of specimens.

microfauna: the smallest members of a fauna, commonly small mammals, such as rodents, insectivores, and prosimian primates.

TABLE 10-2	Major Fossil Australopithecines			
Species	**Locality**	**Specimen Number**	**Body Part**	**Geological Age**
Orrorin tungenensis	Tugen Hills, Kenya	"Millennium Man"	Various skeletal elements	about 6 million years
Ardipithecus ramidus	Middle Awash, Ethiopia	ARA (Aramis Location) VP-6/500 "Ardi Ram"	Dentition, partial skeleton	4.3–4.4 million years
Australopithecus anamensis	Kanapoi Allia Bay, Kenya	KNM ER 20419	Various cranial, postcranial, and dental specimens	3.9–4.2 million years
Kenyanthropus platyops	West Lake Turkana, Kenya			3.2–3.5 million years
Australopithecus afarensis	Laetoli, Tanzania Hadar, Ethiopia	LH (Laetoli Hominid) 4 AL (Afar Locality) 288-1 ("Lucy")	Mandible with teeth Partial skeleton	3.6–3.8 million years 3.2–3.4 million years
		AL 333 ("The First Family")	Various cranial, postcranial, and dental specimens of some 14 individuals	
		AL 442-2	Complete skull	
	Bahr el-Ghazal, Chad	KT (Koro-Toro) 2	Mandible with teeth	3–3.5 million years
Australopithecus africanus	Taung, South Africa	Taung 1 ("The Taung Child")	Complete skull and mandible with teeth	about 2.5 million years
		Stw 505, Stw 593	Skull	3–3.6 million years
	Sterkfontein, South Africa	STS (Sterkfontein Type Site) 5 ("Mrs. Ples")	Skull lacking teeth	3–3.6 million years
Australopithecus garhi	Middle Awash, Ethiopia	Bouri	Partial skull and postcrania	2.5 million years
Australopithecus aethiopicus (also considered *A. boisei*)	Omo, Ethiopia	Omo 18-67-18	Mandible with tooth roots	2.8 million years
	West Turkana, Kenya	KNM WT (Kenya National Museum, West Turkana) 17000 ("The Black Skull")	Skull lacking teeth	2.5 million years
Australopithecus (or *Paranthropus*) *boisei*	Olduvai Gorge, Tanzania	OH (Olduvai Hominid) 5 ("Nutcracker Man" or "Dear Boy")	Complete skull with teeth	1.8 million years
	East Turkana, Kenya	KNM ER (Kenya National Museum, East Rudolf) 406	Skull lacking teeth	1.9 million years
Australopithecus (or *Paranthropus*) *robustus*	Swartkrans, South Africa Drimolen, South Africa	SK 47	Skull with partial dentition	about 2 million years

In the remainder of this section we survey the major australopithecine fossils and describe how the subfamily came to be defined (Figure 10–3).

Australopithecus africanus

Controversy surrounded the original australopithecine find, a skull of a juvenile hominid from a cave site quarried for lime in northern South Africa known as

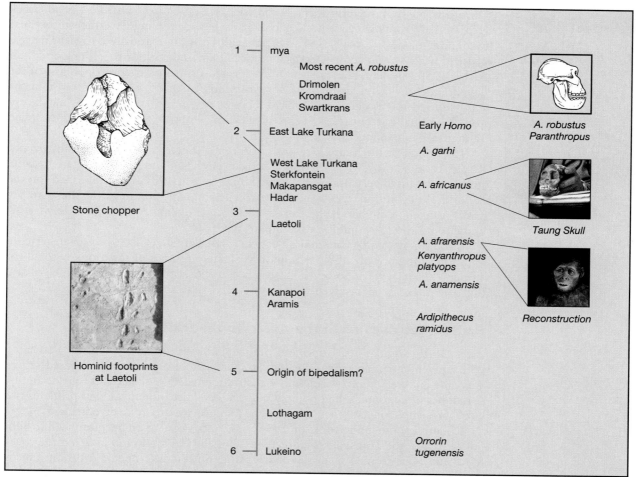

FIGURE 10–3 Timeline: hominid sites and fossils of the australopithecines.

Taung, meaning "place of the lion" in the Tswana language. Nevertheless, the discovery is a singularly important event in the history of human evolutionary studies, because it brought to light a totally unknown, though not unexpected, primeval state of human existence.

The specimen was blasted out of a lime deposit by a quarryman with the Northern Lime Company. He immediately recognized that it was not that of a baboon, the skulls of which he had come across in the same manner. He speculated that it belonged to a fossil bushman, possibly an ancestor of the San people who still inhabit the region. The specimen, still imbedded in a large chunk of rock, made its way to Johannesburg and to Raymond Dart, an assistant professor in the anatomy department of the University of the Witwatersrand Medical School (Figure 10–4). Dart broke away from the final preparations of hosting his daughter's wedding to receive and examine the shipment of rock-imbedded bones arriving from Taung. His excitement was warranted, because the specimen turned out to be the first of many australopithecines to be discovered.

Dart described the new specimen soon after its discovery in the February 7, 1925, issue of *Nature*. In the article he suggested that the Taung child, as it came to be known, represented an extinct race of apes intermediate between living anthropoids and man, a "missing link," to use T. H. Huxley's now-famous term. Dart named it a new genus and species, ***Australopithecus africanus.*** The name itself, translating as "southern ape from Africa," first stirred debate. A geologist from

Australopithecus africanus: the first species of *Australopithecus* to be named, based on the type of the Taung child; characterized by humanlike dentition and relatively gracile skull morphology, the species dates to between about 3 million and 2.5 million years ago; represented at other sites in South Africa, and probably also in East Africa.

FIGURE 10–4 Raymond Dart holding the Taung skull, the type fossil of *Australopithecus africanus*.

Oxford wrote that the term was a barbarism, mixing Latin (*"australo-"*) and Greek (*"-pithecus"*) roots in the generic name. This was merely literary criticism, because taxonomic names do not have to be classically or grammatically correct. The real contention, however, lay in Dart's claim of human ancestry for the Taung child. Sir Arthur Keith, perhaps the most highly respected British paleoanthropologist of the day, branded Dart's assessment as "preposterous" in 1925. He considered that the skull showed the essential anatomical features of an ape, with the possible exception of its smaller front teeth. If this suggestion were true, it would have precluded Taung from human ancestry.

The dating of the Taung site has also been a source of continuing controversy. Robert Broom (1867–1951), a South African physician and paleontologist, began a study of the fossil vertebrates from the Taung cave in 1937. He established, on the basis of the evolutionary stages of the fossil mammals contained in the cave deposits, that the date had to be earliest Pleistocene or late Pliocene, a date we now know to be about 1.8 million to 3 million years old.

More recent geological studies (Vogel, 1985; Partridge, 1986) have suggested a date for Taung of only about 1 million years ago. Studies of the monkey fossils at Taung (Delson, 1988), however, suggest a date closer to 2.5 million years ago, and this date seems to accord well with most current assessments.

Further Discoveries of the Australopithecines

After Dart's original 1924 find and the inevitable taxonomic problems associated with a juvenile type specimen (the fossil on which a taxonomic name is based), there was much interest in recovering more australopithecine remains, this time of adults. A number of anatomists had pointed out that juveniles of many higher primates can closely resemble one another, whereas the adult forms are quite divergent.

Robert Broom undertook in 1936 an exploration of the region of northern South Africa, the Transvaal (Figure 10–5). Fossils here are found in *breccia*, a rock-hard substance formed from the debris falling into a cave opening. Broom's techniques were essentially the same as those of the quarrymen who worked in the area—blasting with dynamite. This did not allow a precise mapping of the location of the finds, but it was successful in recovering fossils. Broom managed to find three bone-bearing cave sites in the Transvaal (Sterkfontein, Kromdraai, and Swartkrans) that yielded remains of adult australopithecines, including a complete skull from the Sterkfontein site (from the Afrikaans language, meaning "strong spring"). In the 1940s Dart began work on a fourth cave site, Makapansgat, located about 200 miles to the north of Sterkfontein. After anatomical studies by William King Gregory and Sir Wilfrid LeGros Clark in the 1940s the Taung specimen and the other South African australopithecines were finally considered to be bona fide hominids.

Perhaps the most important discovery from the Sterkfontein site after 30-odd years of nonstop excavations has recently come to light from the oldest (about 3.5 million years old) fossil-bearing deposit known as member 2. Initially, five hominid left-foot bones were rediscovered in various museum boxes by Ron Clarke of the University of Witwatersrand Medical School. Together these bones, and others subsequently found, composed part of what became known as hominid Stw 573 (Figures 10–6 and 10–7). The previously discovered fossils led Clarke and his team to reinvestigate member 2, deposits where they discovered the rest of the skeleton and the skull of a single individual. This was the first discovery of an *in situ* skull and the associated skeleton of an early australopithecine. So far the morphology of the foot bones indicates a more apelike than humanlike pattern, but at this writing the rest of the skeleton is being painstakingly removed from the encasing breccia; any complete diagnosis must await further study (Clarke, 1998).

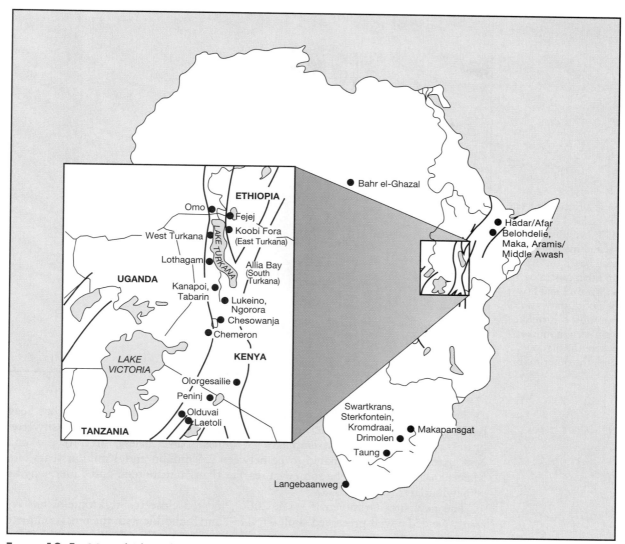

FIGURE 10–5 Map of Africa showing australopithecine fossil sites in East Africa (see detail) and South Africa.

FIGURE 10–6 South African paleoanthropological team led by Ron Clarke (center) has investigated member 2 of the Sterkfontein Caves, initially uncovering foot bones and later a complete skeleton, the first of its kind, of *Australopithecus*. The skeleton is mostly unexcavated.

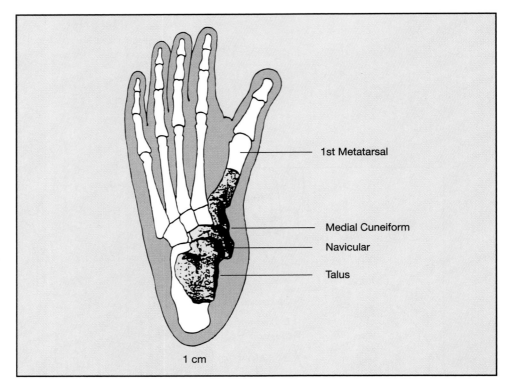

FIGURE 10–7 Reconstructed left foot of the Sterkfontein hominid 573. Lengths of the first and second metatarsals are estimated based on similar bones from other australopithecines (Stw 562 and Stw 89). "Little Foot" shows an apelike opposable toe, unlike the condition seen in modern humans, where the big toe is in line with the other four digits.

- 1st Metatarsal
- Medial Cuneiform
- Navicular
- Talus

1 cm

Dating at the South African cave sites has never been clear, because it has been based on relative ages as determined by the evolutionary stages of the fossil vertebrates contained in the assemblages of bones. Nevertheless, Sterkfontein and Makapansgat can be estimated to be between 2.5 million and 3 million years old. Makapansgat appears to be somewhat earlier than Sterkfontein, and Taung may be somewhat later (Figure 10–8).

The new site, Drimolen (Keyser, 2000), located close to Sterkfontein, has recently yielded a well-preserved skull (DNH 7) and mandible with the most complete dentition thus far found of a robust australopithecine. The skull, assumed to be female, and the mandible, that of a male, demonstrate a greater degree of sexual dimorphism than was previously thought for members of this taxon (Figure 10–9, p. 256). Fossils of *Australopithecus robustus,* which we discuss later in this chapter in more detail, had previously only been known from the nearby sites of Kromdraai and Swartkrans.

Ongoing excavations at Drimolen and other South African sites continue to yield fossil bones. The importance of these sites has been recognized by scientists for decades, and in 1999 they were designated World Heritage localities by the United Nations.

Australopithecine Discoveries from East Africa

Studies aimed at discovering early hominids were pioneered in East Africa in 1932 by French paleoanthropologist Camille Arambourg. Partly as a result of the early hominid discoveries in South Africa, Louis Leakey, an anthropologist trained at Cambridge University in England, became interested in exploring for hominid fossils in East Africa. The son of missionary parents, Leakey grew up in Kenya, and with his wife, archaeologist Mary Leakey, undertook fieldwork at the now-famous site of **Olduvai Gorge,** Tanzania (then Tanganyika) beginning in 1931 (see Figure 10–5). The Leakeys were mostly unsuccessful in discovering early hominids

Australopithecus robustus: robust australopithecines found in cave deposits from South Africa and dated from 2 million to 1 million years ago; most famous representatives were found at the site of Swartkrans, South Africa.

Olduvai Gorge: a site in northern Tanzania yielding remains of robust australopithecines and early *Homo.*

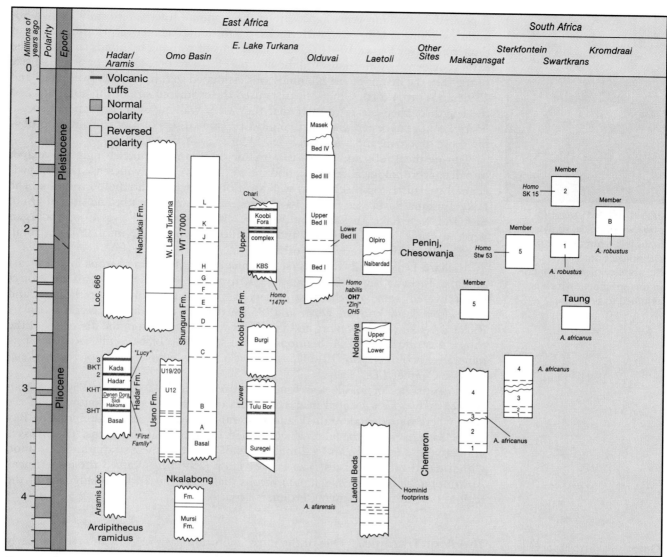

FIGURE 10-8 Chart showing the relative ages of the eastern and southern australopithecine sites. "Polarity" refers to the dated periods of normal and reversed magnetization of the earth's magnetic field through time. "Tuffs" are datable geologic deposits composed of volcanic ash.

until 1959, when Mary Leakey found a complete australopithecine skull. Later, between 1974 and 1979, Mary Leakey turned her energies toward excavations at the site of Laetoli, located to the south of Olduvai.

Laetoli. The first major finds of australopithecines in eastern Africa are at Laetoli, in northern Tanzania (Figure 10–10, p. 257). *Laetoli* is a Maasai word referring to a small flowering shrub that is abundant in the area. Following the discovery of some fragmentary hominid fossils, Mary Leakey began collecting there in 1974. Geochronologist Garniss Curtis of the University of California, Berkeley, used the **potassium-argon method** to date a sample of volcanic ash to 3.7 million years ago. Twenty-four australopithecine fossils are now known from this site.

In 1976 a most remarkable discovery was made in a **tuff** (volcanic ash deposit) at Laetoli. This deposit had preserved footprints of animals living when the ash was

Laetoli: a site in northern Tanzania, south of Olduvai Gorge, where hominids were first found in the 1930s and again in the 1970s; dated to between 3.6 million and 3.8 million years ago.

potassium-argon method: dating technique pioneered by Garniss Curtis that measures the amount of radioactive potassium isotope (K^{40}) to its decay product, argon gas (Ar^{40}), found in rocks of volcanic origin.

tuff: a geological deposit composed of volcanic ash.

FIGURE 10–9 *Australopithecus robustus* skull and mandible from the site of Drimolen, South Africa. Note the absence of a sagittal crest in this specimen, which is assumed to be female.

deposited 3.7 million years ago. Among these animal tracks were trails of two hominids walking side-by-side, with tracks of a third individual overprinting one set of these tracks (see Figure 10–10). These footprints of walking hominids constitute the earliest evidence of bipedalism in the hominid fossil record. On the basis of the size of the feet, the height of the hominids was estimated to have been between 119 and 139 cm (3.9 to 4.6 ft). Other scientists used the estimated size of the hominids and the length of their stride to infer that they were walking at a slow rate of speed. Mary Leakey suggested that the two most prominent sets of footprints were probably those of a male and a female.

During the 1960s and 1970s eastern Africa became an increasingly active area of paleoanthropological research, and the results have greatly increased our knowledge of the australopithecines, as well as of other stages of hominid evolution. The Lake Turkana Basin (see Figure 10–5) contains the australopithecine sites of **Omo,** East and West **Lake Turkana,** and Fejej. F. Clark Howell and Yves Coppens began work at Omo in the late 1960s and continued to work there until 1975. In total, 238 fossil specimens were discovered.

Richard Leakey and Glynn Isaac began collecting fossils and stone artifacts east of Lake Turkana, near Koobi Fora in Kenya. The Koobi Fora Research Project has recovered some of the best-preserved specimens of australopithecines and early *Homo* now known. Work in 1985 on the western side of Lake Turkana by Richard Leakey, Alan Walker, and Frank Brown has resulted in the discovery of the robust australopithecine *A. aethiopicus,* the so-called "Black Skull" because of its mineralized color (Figure 10–11), as well as a nearly complete *Homo erectus* skeleton (see Chapter 11).

A new series of fossils was found by a team led by Meave Leakey and Alan Walker at two sites located near Lake Turkana: Kanapoi to the southwest of the lake, where nine dental, cranial, and postcranial pieces were found; and Allia Bay on the eastern rim of the lake, which yielded 12 additional specimens. These fossils fall between 3.9 million and 4.2 million years, based on their stratigraphic position within dated tuff sequences. The Leakey team (1995) has named these specimens *Australopithecus anamensis* (*anam* means "lake" in the Turkana language of the region) (see the accompanying Frontiers box).

Omo: a site in southern Ethiopia along the lower Omo River, with numerous hominids dating from about 3.4 million to 1 million years ago.

Lake Turkana: hominid sites on both the east and west sides of Lake Turkana (formerly Lake Rudolf), closely associated with Omo and dating to between 4 million and 1.4 million years ago.

Australopithecus aethiopicus: earlier form of robust australopithecines in East Africa dated from 2.6 million to 2.3 million years ago; most famous representative is the Black Skull discovered in 1986 at a site on the western shores of Lake Turkana.

The Afar Triangle. One of the most important eastern African areas for early australopithecines is the Afar Triangle (see Figure 10–6) in northeastern Ethiopia. The broad paleontological significance of the Afar region of Ethiopia was first brought to light by the French geologist Maurice Taieb in the 1960s. Further explorations in the 1970s by Taieb, Donald Johanson, Yves Coppens, and Jon Kalb focused on the **Hadar locality** in the central Afar. Later, in 1981, a multidisciplinary team led by archaeologist J. Desmond Clark undertook a comprehensive survey of the Middle Awash region south of Hadar. For a number of years now Tim White, of the University of California, Berkeley, has been project director, working alongside Berhane Asfaw and other researchers from the National Museum in Addis Ababa.

In 1981 Clark and White's paleontological research team found at the site of Maka, on the eastern side of the Awash River, the first Pliocene-age hominid fossil in the Middle Awash. This specimen, an adolescent, left, proximal femur, was dated by associated faunal remains and is approximately 3.5 million to 4 million years old. In the same year, at the nearby site of Belohdelie, a second hominid was recovered; this one consisted of seven skull fragments, three of which were from an adult, frontal bone. Again on the basis of associated fauna, the Belohdelie fossils are dated at older than 4 million years. Structurally, the femur and skull fragments are similar to their counterparts recovered at Hadar.

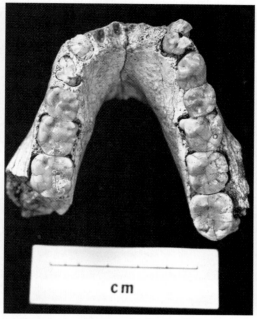
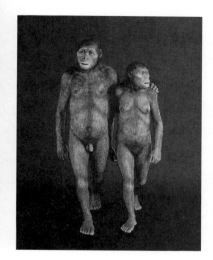

FIGURE 10–10 Laetoli footprint trail (left), mandible of *A. afarensis* (center), and one possible behavioral reconstruction of the Laetoli hominid footprint trail (right).

Explorations of this area in the late 1980s moved to the paleontologically rich Aramis locality on the west bank of the Awash River. The sediments of this region contained several volcanic tuffs, and argon-argon dating indicates a maximum age of 4.4 million years for these fossils.

The most abundant fossil evidence for early australopithecines so far comes from Hadar (Figure 10–12), deposits of which are dated somewhat later in time than Laetoli. These fossils constitute the most complete evidence that anthropologists now have for this period of hominid evolution. Although the fossils were similar in many respects to the South African *Austalopithecus africanus,* together the sample of fossils from Laetoli and Hadar have been combined and used to define a new species, *Australopithecus afarensis* (Johanson, White, and Coppens, 1978).

Hadar: hominid site in northern Ethiopia dating to between 3 million and 3.4 million years ago.

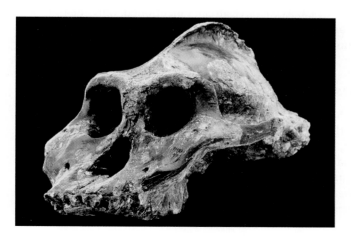

FIGURE 10–11 *Australopithecus aethiopicus* (KNM WT 17000), the oldest known robust australopithecine, from West Turkana, Kenya.

FIGURE 10–12 A view of the Hadar formation in Ethiopia. This area is the most abundant source of australopithecine fossils so far.

INTERPRETATION OF THE EVOLUTIONARY HISTORY

Most paleoanthropologists today are convinced that there are two types of australopithecines: a "gracile" species with a more lightly built skull, termed *Australopithecus africanus* (the earlier East African *A. afarensis* is sometimes included in this category), and a "robust" form with a more heavily built skull, known in South Africa as *Australopithecus robustus* and in eastern Africa as *A. boisei* (Figure 10–13). Most of the anatomical differences between the two australopithecines are related to the very large cheek teeth of the robust australopithecines and the chewing anatomy associated with this adaptation. The gracile forms, by most reckonings, occur earlier in time than the robusts and are considered by most paleoanthropologists to be ancestral, in a broad sense, to the genus *Homo*.

The evolutionary origin of *Australopithecus* is a question that has so far remained unsolved, despite recent discoveries dating up to more than 5 million years ago. Evolutionary relationships hypothesized between Miocene apes (see Chapter 9) and *Australopithecus* cannot at the present time be demonstrated by fossil evidence. This is because there is a gap between 8 million and 4.5 million years ago in the fossil record of hominids. In East Africa, as we have already mentioned, only the fragmentary Lukeino, Lothagam, and Tabarin fossils belong in this time range. These East African fossils constitute insufficient evidence to establish the evolutionary origins of the australopithecines.

Ardipithecus ramidus

The Middle Awash fossil hominids from Aramis, which total more than 90 specimens, represent most of the skeleton and include foot, leg, and pelvic remains. Named as a distinct genus, ***Ardipithecus ramidus*** (*ardi* means "ground" and *ramid* means "root" in the Afar language, thus, "ground ape"; White et al., 1994, 1995) is the most apelike hominid ancestor known (Figure 10–14).

Although the *Ardipithecus* remains are the most primitive from this age found so far, their discoverers insist that the diamond-shaped, blunt canine teeth (less projecting than those of other Miocene hominoids), the shortening of the cranial base, and the shape of the elbow joint are all derived characteristics that point in the

Australopithecus boisei: robust australopithecines found at site in East Africa and dated from 2.4 million to 1.3 million years ago; most famous representatives were found at Olduvai Gorge (*Zinjanthropus*) and East Lake Turkana.

Ardipithecus ramidus: the most primitive species of hominid presently known, dating 4 million to 4.2 million years ago from Aramis, Middle Awash, Ethiopia.

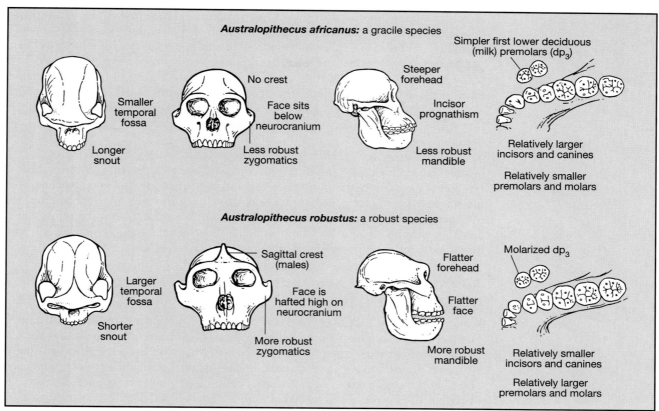

FIGURE 10–13 Comparison of lower teeth, crania, and mandibles of gracile *Australopithecus africanus* and robust *A. robustus*.

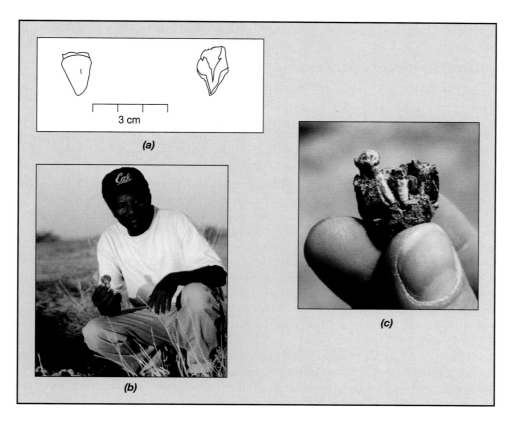

(b)

FIGURE 10–14 (*a*) Side views of upper canine teeth of common chimpanzee (left) and *Ardipithecus*. (*b*) Alemayehu Asfaw, Middle Awash team member, holding upper arm bone of *A. ramidus*. (*c*) Partial mandible of *A. ramidus*.

direction of later hominids. If the known remains of *Ardipithecus* are anatomically hominid, were members of this genus functionally hominid—bipedal—as well? Right now, indirect evidence points in that direction, but the question remains open.

Dental and paleoenvironmental data do give some provocative clues about how and where *Ardipithecus* lived. In contrast to any other known hominid, the enamel layer of the teeth was reportedly thin (refer back to Figure 9–10). If this is not curious enough, the associated fauna, as well as seeds and fossilized wood, indicate that *Ardipithecus*'s habitat was forested, not the savanna-like setting where later hominids were found.

A forest environment for *Ardipithecus* is both confounding and provocative (WoldeGabriel et al., 1994). It is confounding in the sense that, if *Ardipithecus* represents the earliest hominoid ancestor, and if it turns out also to be bipedal, then the selective agents for bipedalism, which have been thought to relate to an open, savannalike setting, may have to be rethought. It is provocative in the sense that it explains why, so far, no hominoid remains older than 4 million years have been found in deposits representing savannalike settings.

Australopithecus anamensis

Next in chronological age are the fossils of *Australopithecus anamensis*, from Kanapoi and Allia Bay, Kenya, dated around 3.8 million to 4 million years ago. The teeth of *A. anamensis* are similar to those of *A. afarensis*, except that the canine of *anamensis* is larger in size and usually more asymmetrical, possessing a long and robust root. The teeth have thicker enamel than those of *Ardipithecus*. The tibia that was recovered at Kanapoi comes from the same (upper) level as did an earlier discovered distal humerus, and it shows bipedal characteristics. Leakey and Walker believe that *A. anamensis* represents one of a number of early emerging, variable hominid species that all were based on the novel bipedal adaptation. Peter Andrews (1995) observes that although all of these so-called species may have been phylogenetically hominids, they seem, ecologically anyway, to be more similar to apes.

Australopithecus afarensis

Australopithesus afarensis at Hadar represents a population of hominids that may have been evolutionarily stable for almost 1 million years. Potassium-argon dates have bracketed the age of the Hadar hominids between 2.8 million and 3.4 million years ago. The first hominid fossils to be discovered at Hadar were a distal thigh bone (femur) and the proximal shin bone (tibia), which fit together to form a knee joint (minus the knee cap). The angle at which the femur joined the tibia in the fossil from Hadar was like a hominid's and unlike an ape's. The femurs in hominids slant downward to the knees, which are quite close together, whereas in apes the femurs are aligned with the long axis of the tibia and the knees are widespread. This was a clear indication that the early australopithecines at Hadar were bipedal, a confirmation of the footprint evidence from Laetoli.

The discoveries at Hadar to date make it one of the most productive of hominid fossil sites. Since 1990, these deposits have yielded more than 330 new specimens. Among the sample, consisting of between 35 and 65 individuals, were the largely complete skeleton from Hadar (Afar) locality AL 288, nicknamed "Lucy" (Figure 10–15), and a concentration of remains of some 13 individuals, nicknamed the "First Family."

In 1993, Yoel Rak found the first pieces of a skull that, when completely collected, turned out to be the most complete cranium thus far discovered in the *afarensis* group. Labeled AL 444-2, the skull is thick-boned, with large canine teeth and heavy cresting, all male characteristics. This skull, according to Bill Kimbel of

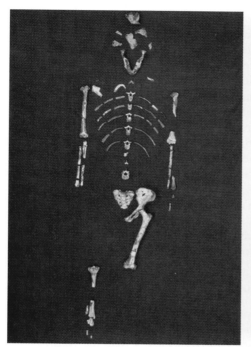

FIGURE 10–15   Left: The partial skeleton of *Australopithecus afarensis* known as "Lucy," from Hadar. Right: Fossil skull AL 444-2 from Hadar. This is the most complete *A. afarensis* skull known to date.

FRONTIERS

The First Saharan Australopithecine

When Raymond Dart reported and named the first australopithecine in 1925, the name he gave it, which means "southern ape," was geographically descriptive and appropriate. But as australopithecine fossils began to be discovered in eastern Africa and even farther north in Ethiopia, the name ceased to be an accurate description of the apparent past range of the subfamily.

In 1996 Michel Brunet of the University of Poitiers in France announced the discovery of a mandible of an australopithecine in the north central African country of Chad, at a site called Bahr el-Ghazal ("river of the gazelle"). This was the first australopithecine site north of the Equator that was not in the East African Rift Valley and the furthest west of any known australopithecine.

The fossil itself was a single mandible, with teeth. It was dated by associated fauna to 3.5 million years

ago, thus about the same age as *Australopithecus afarensis*. At first Brunet and colleagues compared the fossil to this species, but then later they named it a new species, *Australopithecus bahrelghazali*. Today the site lies within the windblown sands of the Sahara Desert, but the fossil species of antelopes, hippos, and pigs preserved with the hominid show that 3.5 million years ago, this area was a well-watered savanna woodland.

What might the skull of *A. bahrelghazali* have looked like? Only future discoveries will answer this question definitively, but, interestingly, a skull of this species may have already been found. Thirty years before Brunet's expedition found the australopithecine mandible, the wife of French paleoanthropologist Yves Coppens kicked over what appeared to be a rock in the same fossil deposits of the Chadian desert. Two hominid eye sockets stared back from a stony face severely worn away by the desert sands. Coppens named the fragmentary skull *Tchadanthropus uxoris* in a

brief report ("*uxoris*" referring to the Latin word for "wife"). With no teeth and the outer several millimeters of its skull sandblasted away, *Tchadanthropus* has remained a tantalizing enigma. The discovery of *A. bahrelghazali* may now have partially solved the mystery of what sort of hominid *Tchadanthropus* was.

A. bahrelghazali is most important because it records the presence of australopithecines in northern Africa during the Pliocene. It is now no longer possible to claim, as Louis Leakey did in 1958, that East Africa alone was the "cradle of mankind." That epithet must now be applied to most of the African continent. Today, only the forested central and western regions of the continent have failed to yield fossil bones of australopithecines.

Some additional information is available on the following Web sites: http://vassun.vassar.edu/~mareed/ evolution/Bahr el Ghazal.html (with photo) and http://www.archeology. org/9603/newsbriefs/hominid.html.

FIGURE 10–16 Sexual dimorphism in *Australopithecus afarensis*, shown in a comparison of female (top) and male (bottom) mandibles.

the Institute of Human Origins, goes a long way toward showing that the Hadar and Laetoli remains represent a single species, with large males and smaller females, rather than two species, as some researchers contend. The size differences are best explained by sexual differences, or dimorphism (Figure 10–16). They represent the same degree of difference one would find in modern apes. However, australopithecine males, although larger than females, did not have proportionately larger canines, an important difference from nonhuman primates. This difference implies that canines had ceased to be used in aggressive display and in male–male competition. The Hadar hominid finds also confirmed estimates. Based on the footprint evidence at Laetoli, the early australopithecines had been small. Lucy, for example, was estimated to have been less than 4 feet tall, although males would have been taller and larger.

In 1994, researchers from the Institute of Human Origins announced the discovery at site 666 of pieces of an upper jaw belonging to the genus *Homo* dating to about 2.33 million years ago. Nearby were found stone tools of the same age, making this one of the oldest associations of fossils and tools thus far discovered.

Hominid Morphology and Behavior

Anthropologists have now carefully compared the East and South African samples of australopithecines. Recent work has shown that the two African groups of early australopithecines (*A. afarensis/anamensis/garhi* from East Africa and *A. africanus* from South Africa) are similar. They both possess relatively large canines, a tendency for nonbicuspid premolars (like apes), a high degree of sexual dimorphism, and a face that is "dished" or depressed in the area around the nasal opening.

Skull structure is the most important criterion for recognizing early, or gracile, *Australopithecus,* because most of the important anatomical and behavioral adaptations of the species are reflected in the skull. Three general adaptations account for cranial form: brain size, erect posture (bipedalism), and use of the teeth.

The relatively enlarged brain gives *A. afarensis* and *A. africanus* a somewhat globular head shape compared with modern apes. This shape is emphasized by the lack of the heavy ridges for muscular attachment, as seen in the ape, the exceptions being the presence of small crests on some specimens of *A. afarensis*. One of the muscles of mastication, the temporalis muscle, which can be felt in the "temple" region, is less developed, particularly in its front part, in *A. africanus* than in *A. afarensis* (see Appendix 1). This muscle attaches to a slight ridge, the temporal line, halfway up the side of the cranial vault in *A. africanus,* most *A. afarensis,* and *Homo.* In gorillas, male chimpanzees, some *A. afarensis,* and robust australopithecines, the temporalis muscles of both sides of the head meet in the midline at the top of the skull, and a heavy ridge of bone is formed, known as the sagittal crest (see Chapter 9).

In general, changes in the structure of the skull and teeth can be used to distinguish the species of *Australopithecus* chronologically. *A. anamensis* (3.5 million to 4.1 million years ago) is the most primitive, with a strongly sloping symphysis of the lower jaw and large canine roots. *A. afarensis* (3 million to 3.6 million years ago) is less primitive, and *A. africanus* (2.6 million to 3 million years ago) shares many derived features with early *Homo,* such as the expanded brain, reduced canine tooth, bicuspid lower third premolars, reduced prognathism of the face, and greater basicranial flexion (Figure 10–17). Many anthropologists believe that *A. afarensis* is the ancestor of *A. africanus. A. anamensis,* if it is a separate species, would then be ancestral to *A. afarensis.* As is discussed in Chapter 11, the earliest members of the genus *Homo* show a number of similarities to "gracile" australopithecines, and this argues for an evolutionary sequence from some species of *Australopithecus.* A number of possible evolutionary sequences exist; for example, *A africanus* to *Homo* has been proposed (McHenry and Berger, 1998).

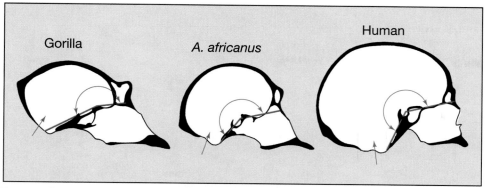

FIGURE 10–17 Skulls of gorilla, *Australopithecus africanus,* and human drawn in midline sections. Curved lines indicate degree of basicranial flexion, which increases from apes to humans. Straight arrows indicate direction and position of the foramen magnum. In humans, the foramen magnum is positioned directly beneath the skull, allowing for an upright spinal column.

Cranial capacity. Since the first discoveries of fossil hominids, studies of fossil **endocasts** (casts of the inside of the cranial cavity) have generated a great deal of interest. The results of these studies, however, have yielded contentious results (Falk, 1992). The cranial capacity of *Australopithecus afarensis* is known to lie between approximately 375 and 425 cubic cm (22.5 to 25.5 cubic in.), and that of *A. africanus* between 400 and 600 cubic cm (24 to 36 cubic in.) roughly equivalent to the brain sizes of modern apes. There is one important difference, however. Body size in gracile *Australopithecus* is smaller than in the modern gorilla or even chimpanzee. *Australopithecus* had a brain-to-body-size ratio larger than that of modern African apes. A relatively larger brain implies that reorganization of neurons had taken place and that australopithecine behavior had become in some respects more complex and elaborate than that of living apes (Figure 10–18). Gracile australopithecine **endocasts** suggest a greater degree of folding and a larger number of convolutions in comparison with living apes.

Facial morphology. The face of *A. afarensis* protrudes less than that of modern apes because the front teeth are smaller. *A. afarensis* and the australopithecines in general have a nose region that is depressed relative to the rest of the face. The functional significance of this "dished face" morphology is related to a relative increase in bone thickness of both sides of the nose and along the cheekbones, which hold the large hominid molars (Rak, 1983). Erect posture in the australopithecines may also have placed a premium on facial reduction for head balance.

Overall, the gracile australopithecine face is *orthognathous,* pushed in under the braincase, in a form similar to that of later hominids. The facial skeleton has moved backward and downward, and the back of the braincase has rotated forward, a process known as **basicranial flexion** (see Figure 10–16). Thus the opening through which the spinal cord enters the brain, the *foramen magnum* (Latin, meaning "great window"), is located halfway between the front and the back of the skull, so that the head is balanced on the vertebral column. In the knuckle-walking apes, the foramen is positioned more posteriorly and its opening is slanted more toward the back of the skull, characteristics related to horizontal posture. Heavy neck muscles hold up and move the head. In australopithecines, a reduced face, basicranial flexion, a centrally placed foramen magnum, and a lack of heavy neck musculature reflect bipedality.

The term **megadont,** meaning "large-toothed," has been applied to the relatively large molars of early hominids as compared with apes. Teeth are the most abundant

endocast: three-dimensional replica of the inside of the brain case, revealing what the exterior of the brain would have looked like.

basicranial flexion: the hinging of the base of the skull and the hard palate together to form a more acute angle; seen in both australopithecine lineages.

megadont: "large-toothed," referring to the relatively large molars of hominids.

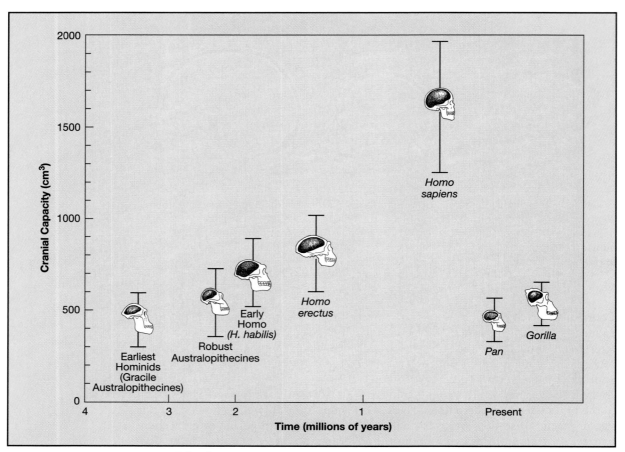

FIGURE 10–18   Cranial capacities of australopithecines compared with extinct and living species of *Homo* and living African apes.

remains of the gracile australopithecines. Their structure parallels that of later hominids of the genus *Homo:* generally large and wide incisors relative to canines, canines functionally similar to incisors, and lower-third premolars that generally do not wear or hone against the back of the upper canines, as they do in apes. In certain aspects, however, australopithecines are more primitive. Their canines are generally larger than those in *Homo,* the lower-third premolar is less "squared" in appearance, the molars are generally longer relative to their width, and they possess a complicated wrinkled ("crenulated") surface pattern. Australopithecines, like all hominids, possess thick enamel on the top surfaces of the molars, a characteristic also shared with some apes, such as the modern orangutan and *Sivapithecus* (see Chapter 9). Thick enamel increases the functional lifetime of the tooth, especially when the diet is abrasive.

Lower limb adaptations.   The pelvic, shoulder girdle, and limb bone remains that have now come to light confirm that the gracile australopithecines were bipeds. There is a difference of opinion about the degree to which they used their upper limbs in locomotion, if at all, and whether *A. afarensis* may have had significant foot and lower limb adaptations for climbing (Susman et al., 1984). Ron Clarke and Phillip Tobias (1995) report on four articulating hominid foot bones originally discovered in 1980 from Sterkfontein, South Africa. Labeled Stw 573 and nicknamed "Little Foot," these fossils are considerably older than the other Sterkfontein fossils (see Figure 10–7). Consisting of a talus, heel, medial cuneiform, and first metatarsal (see Appendix 1), which together make up part of the arch of a left foot, they show human features at the back of the foot but strikingly apelike traits at the front of the foot. The most remarkable of these apelike traits is a great toe that was *divergent,* or opposable, and mobile. According to the discoverers, the Sterkfontein foot bones, possibly as old as 3.5 million years, support the idea of an "evolutionary experimentation" within a wide range of adaptations during the first few million years of hominid evolutionary divergence.

Certainly, the adaptation to bipedalism seems to have differed from that of modern humans. *Australopithecus* had a relatively wider distance from the hip joint to the muscle attachments at the top of the thigh (femur) and a wider flare of the upper crest of the pelvis (the ilium, one of the three components of the pelvis) (Figure 10–19). This provided a wide base of support for the lower limbs in a bipedal stance, as well as strong leverage in lifting the lower limbs during walking. In *Homo* the hip joint has moved closer to the top of the femur and lateral edge of the ilium, in order to expand the birth canal for larger-brained infants. The australopithecine morphology is an efficient, albeit different, bipedal adaptation.

New discoveries of *A. africanus* from member 4 deposits of Sterkfontein reveal several features that are different from other earlier *Australopithecus* species. The new adult material consists of more than 48 fore- and hindlimb specimens and includes an associated partial skeleton, Stw 431. The forelimbs are relatively large but the hindlimbs are much smaller, an apparently primitive morphology resembling more the orangutan pattern than the human one. Thus, from the fossil evidence that we have at present, australopithecine limb proportion and morphology show substanianial variability.

Body size. Overall body size can be estimated from the dimensions of certain fossil bones by comparing them to dimensions of the same bones in known samples of modern humans and living primates whose body weights are known. Estimates

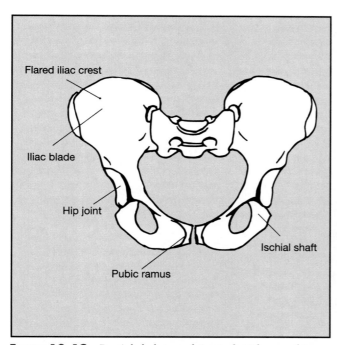
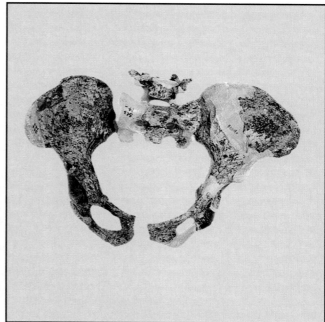

FIGURE 10–19 Partial skeleton of *Australopithecus africanus* STS 14, from Sterkfontein, and reconstructed australopithecine pelvis.

of body size for *A. afarensis* range from approximately 30 to 80 kg (66 to 176 lb) and for *A. africanus* from 30 to 70 kg (66 to 154 lb) (Jungers, 1988).

Paleoecology and Behavior

The paleoecology of *Australopithecus* is reflected in the types of animals and plants and the geological conditions associated with these hominids in fossil deposits. It is important to determine how these remains came to be buried together in order

 **FRONTIERS**

The Earliest Australopithecines and Human Origins

ALAN WALKER

Present-day Lake Turkana in northern Kenya is more than 150 miles (250 kilometers) long and has an area of about 2,500 square mi (6400 km²). Because the lake dominates the local landscape, it is difficult to imagine that the lake was not always present, yet geological evidence clearly shows that for most of the past 4.5 million years, there was no lake. Instead, through most of this period there was only a huge, flat floodplain associated with the proto-Omo River that drained southward from the Ethiopian highlands. The earliest of the several relatively brief lacustrine periods (when a lake was formed), just over 4 million years ago, was associated with sediments that contain the earliest known species of *Australopithecus*.

The first specimen of this species, a single, distal humerus, was collected from the site of Kanapoi, south of Lake Turkana, by a Harvard expedition in the 1960s. Unfortunately, Kanapoi was at the time poorly dated, and determining the fossil's affinities was difficult. Recent expeditions led by Meave Leakey have established new facts about both of these issues. The Kanapoi sediments were laid down by a river that built its delta out into the ancient lake between 4.2 million and 4 million years ago, according to age determinations using the new and quite accurate method of single crystal laser fusion argon-argon analysis. Leakey's expeditions have collected additional fossil teeth, jaws,

cranial parts, and limb bones from Kanapoi, as well as similar fossils from slightly younger sediments (dated to between 3.9 million and 4 million years ago) at Allia Bay, across the modern Lake Turkana from Kanapoi. Leakey and her colleagues named a new species based on the combined Kanapoi/Allia Bay sample. They call it *Australopithecus anamensis*, using the word for "lake" (*anam*) from the Turkana language (Leakey et al., 1995).

To define a new species, biologists must differentiate between the new material and that of older similar species of comparable age. Leakey and her colleagues compared *Australopithecus anamensis* to other known early hominids, namely the more recent *Australopithecus afarensis* from between 3.6 million and 3 million years ago and the slightly older *Ardipithecus ramidus* from about 4.4 million years ago.

This study showed that the new species belongs in the genus *Australopithecus*. First, the enamel on the teeth of the new specimens is thick, as is the enamel on all other australopithecines. Second, *Australopithecus anamensis* shows marked sexual dimorphism in body size, with males being considerably larger than females—another feature found in all species of *Australopithecus*. Finally, *Australopithecus anamensis* is clearly bipedal, as are *afarensis* and other later species. A tibia from Kanapoi shows clear anatomical adaptations that make the knee stable in a bipedal position— adaptations that are lacking in quadrupedal apes. It has an ankle joint that places the foot at a right angle to the long axis of the shin, rather than

being angled closer to the tibia, as in apes. Bipedalism, however, is not the only locomotor adaptation of *Australopithecus anamensis*. A radius of this species, together with the original humerus from Kanapoi, shows that these animals had powerful forelimbs. These facts make it likely that, despite being bipedal, they could still climb effectively and may have spent substantial time in the trees. The new material could not be included in *Australopithecus afarensis*, however, because *anamensis* has retained primitive features that are lacking in *afarensis*. Such features are today known only in African apes.

The new material also differs from *Ardipithecus ramidus* in a number of cranial and dental features, such as the thin enamel on all of the *ramidus* teeth, which contrasts with the thick enamel of *anamensis*. There is at present no published evidence about the locomotor pattern of *ramidus*, but it is found with many forest-dwelling species that suggests a closed habitat. Like *ramidus*, *Australopithecus anamensis* is found with animals that lived in an extensive gallery forest along the ancient rivers or their deltas. For example, there are six species of monkey found at Allia Bay. It is most likely that *anamensis* was also forest dwelling.

Paleoanthropologist and anatomist Alan Walker is professor of anthropology at Pennsylvania State University. He has worked for many years at fossil sites dating from the Miocene to the Pleistocene in East Africa, especially in Kenya.

to understand how they might have been associated in life. Such studies (e.g. Brain, 1981) have shown that hominids in the South African cave sites were probably the remains of carnivore kills (Figure 10–20), whereas East African open-air sites contain hominids that had died under a variety of conditions. Research has shown that *A. afarensis* and *A. africanus* lived in both arid and wetter environments in eastern and southern Africa. Thus, even without the use of stone tools and fire, gracile australopithecines were able to adapt to a variety of African environmental conditions.

In the South African early cave sites, *A. africanus* has been found in association with a high percentage of bush-adapted antelopes, as opposed to grassland-adapted antelopes, indicating a more bush-covered habitat than the same area has today. This paleoecological picture of South Africa is supported by similar reconstructions for the Omo and Hadar sites in Ethiopia. The fauna from Laetoli, however, indicates markedly dry grassland conditions, although surface water, in streams and water holes was present. It is likely that early hominids were dependent on these water sources, because hominids, like many other mammals, need to drink water at least once a day.

On the basis of tooth structure, the diet of the gracile australopithecines was probably omnivorous. Carbon isotope analysis of *A. africanus* shows elevated carbon-13 levels, found in savanna grasses and in the meat of animals that graze on these grasses (Sponheimer and Lee-Thorp, 1999). These results suggest that australopithecines used open-country food resources and ate meat in significant quantities even before they began using stone tools.

Gracile australopithecines seem to have died quite young. It is possible to reconstruct age at death by the wear of the teeth. A study by Alan Mann (1975) on South African australopithecines showed the mean age at death to be a modern human equivalent of 22 years. Mann suggested that australopithecines had a prolonged period of infant dependency, similar to that of modern humans. More recent work, however, on the pattern of dental development and eruption (Bromage and Dean, 1985; Smith, 1986; Conroy and Vannier, 1987) indicates that australopithecines may have had a more apelike, short, and rapid period of growth as infants (Figure 10–21).

Stone tools are not generally associated with fossil remains of the gracile australopithecines. Artifacts are lacking at Laetoli, the early portions of the Omo sequence, and the early hominid-bearing levels at Hadar, Makapansgat, Sterkfontein, and Taung. Only in the Middle Awash, Ethiopia (see Chapter 11), is there an apparent association of tools and hominid remains. Recent discoveries in the Middle Awash at Bouri yielded a skull and partial skeleton named *Australopithecus garhi* (Asfaw et al., 1999), dated at 2.5 million years ago (Figure 10–22). This site also preserves the earliest stone tools and evidence of cut marks on animal bones. So far this evidence suggests that only the latest gracile australopithecines made and used stone tools.

The question of australopithecine tool use is an old one. Dart originally suggested that bone fragments found in Makapansgat were, in fact, tools that australopithecines had used to kill, dismember, and eat animal prey. Dart coined the term *osteodontokeratic* tool culture on the basis of this evidence, because the supposed tools consisted of bone (*osteo-*), tooth (*-donto-*), and horn (*-keratic*). Recent research has shown that much of the damage on fossil bones can be attributed to chewing by hyenas and other carnivores, but some wear and breakage on fossils from the cave of Swartkrans may be attributed to hominid activity. It thus appears that australopithecines may have been tool makers, although their use of stone for this purpose remains improbable, or at least unlikely, on the basis of current evidence.

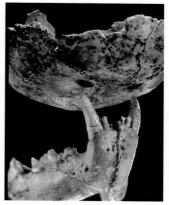

FIGURE 10–20 Leopard mandible and robust australopithecine skull from Swartkrans, showing correspondence between the leopard's canine teeth and holes in the hominid's skull. This individual was eaten by, and probably killed by, a leopard.

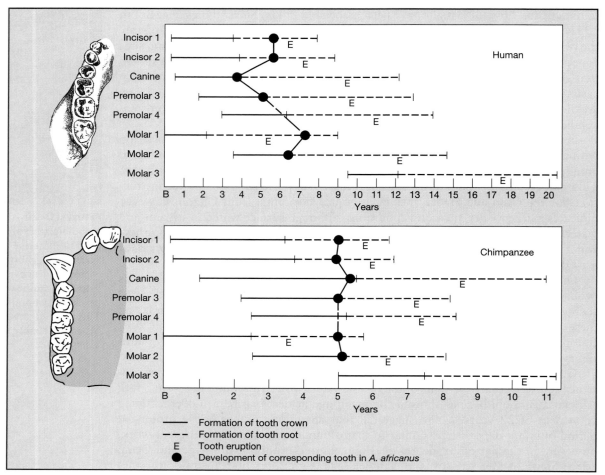

FIGURE 10–21 Dental development in modern humans and chimpanzees, compared to dental development in *Australopithecus africanus*. *A. africanus* had a pattern of dental development that was more similar to that of modern apes than to that of modern humans.

ROBUST AUSTRALOPITHECINES

The robust australopithecines were a group of hominids that is known to have lived in eastern and southern Africa from 2.5 million years ago to about 1 million years ago (see Grine, 1988). Their fossils have not yet been found outside Africa. They were specialized parahuman creatures (Figure 10–23, p. 270), apparently not in modern humans' direct ancestry, but coexistent with early members of the genus *Homo*.

Much of the characteristic robust australopithecine cranial morphology is related to a specialization for heavy mastication. One student of these hominids has termed them "chewing machines." The teeth of these hominids are specialized for high-bite-force grinding. The chewing surfaces of the molars are expanded; premolars are large and molarlike; and the incisors and canines, used for cutting and tearing food, are reduced in size.

Characteristic morphology of the skull includes a sagittal crest along the midline of the skull and heavy cheekbones (zygomatic arches) to support large muscles of mastication. The recently discovered Drimolen skull (see Figure 10–9), however, shows that at least some females lacked a sagittal crest. The face is characteristically

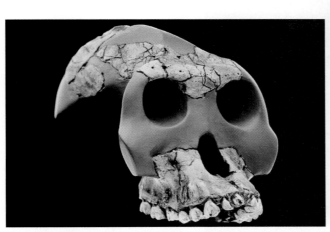  

FIGURE 10–22 Skull of *Australopithecus garhi* from Bouri, Middle Awash, Afar, Ethiopia, dated 2.5 million years ago. The site in which this specimen was found preserves the earliest stone tools and evidence of cut marks on animal remains.

"dished" as in australopithecines generally but is more heavily constructed than in the gracile species to withstand the forces generated in chewing. To lighten the weight of the head, large areas of the skull have developed internal air cells inside the bone. The East African species, *A. boisei,* and the South African *A. robustus* (both sometimes referred to as *Paranthropus*) are similar in all these respects, except that the former appears to be larger and more robust.

From the known cranial endocasts, robust australopithecines apparently possessed brains of an absolute size close to that of the earlier gracile australopithecines. However, because the robust forms probably were of somewhat larger body size, they would have had a relatively smaller brain.

The postcrania of robust australopithecines is poorly known. On the basis of extremity bones and pelvic fragments, the stature of these hominids has been estimated at between 145 and 165 cm (56 to 65 in.) with a weight range of 40 to 90 kg (88 to 198 lb) (Jungers, 1988). The arm may also have been relatively long. Although some foot bones in *A. robustus* suggest a divergent big toe, and thus an apelike form of locomotion, the pelvis and lower limb bones, as well as the central placement of the foramen magnum, strongly suggest well-developed bipedalism.

A number of intriguing paleoanthropological problems still surround the robust australopithecines. According to the dietary hypothesis, one might expect to find these hominids in relatively large numbers in fossil deposits, because herbivores are generally more abundant than omnivores or carnivores in ecological food chains. In fact they occur in virtually the same percentages as the supposedly omnivorous gracile early hominids. The present best estimate of robust australopithecine adaptation is that of a bipedal, hard-object-feeding omnivorous dweller of either woodlands or grasslands within an overall savanna environment.

Another paleoanthropological dilemma associated with the robust australopithecine is ecological niche separation between this hominid and the contemporary *Homo habilis* (see Chapter 11). How could two such species live in the same environment without one eventually ecologically excluding the other? Perhaps tool use was exclusive to *Homo.* Robust australopithecines are found in sites in which primitive (**Oldowan**) stone tools are also found and, in some cases, where *Homo* is lacking. Despite the absence of *Homo* fossils from these sites, they may have left their stone tools there. General opinion seems to lean toward robust australopithecines' lacking the ability to fashion stone tools, but the question is still open.

Oldowan: earliest recognized stone tool tradition associated with the first members of the genus *Homo.* Also called Mode I tools.

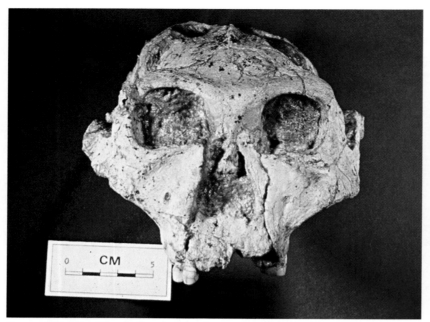

FIGURE 10–23 The skulls of *Australopithecus robustus* (Swartkrans 48, left) and *Australopithecus boisei* (Olduvai Hominid 5, right), two species of robust australopithecines.

For many years it was believed that the phylogenetic origin of the robust australopithecines was from *A. africanus*. Discovery of the more ancient species, *A. aethiopicus* ("Black Skull" KNM WT 17000) at West Lake Turkana, Kenya, dated to 2.5 million years ago, has weakened this interpretation. There is now near overlap in dates for *A. africanus* and *A. aethiopicus,* and this strongly suggests that the ancestry of *A. boisei* is earlier than was originally thought.

Robust australopithecine species seem to persist in Africa until shortly after the appearance of the relatively advanced *Homo erectus* about 1 million years ago (see Chapter 11). Many researchers have suggested that this *Homo* species was able to outcompete the robust australopithecine and thus drove the latter to extinction. As *Homo erectus* increased in size over time, groups required greater food resources and territory, and *H. erectus* were able to physically outcompete robust australopithecines. A second possibility is that ecological change to drier conditions caused the extinction of the robust australopithecines.

RECONSTRUCTING EARLY HOMINID BEHAVIOR

Historical Overview

Historically, three characteristics have been used to emphasize the differences between human and nonhuman primates: *bipedalism;* our *large brain;* and our ability to *communicate symbolically* with language. Using these three characteristics, a number of models of early human behavior emerged to sort out what came first and why these adaptations developed. In this chapter, we discuss bipedalism; we focus on brain size and language in Chapters 11 and 12, respectively.

In *Descent of Man and Selection in Relation to Sex,* Darwin (1871) held that the human brain was the primary feature that initially separated humans from their closest relatives, the African apes. Darwin viewed increased brain size as important in terms of the technological behavior that developed from it. He believed our ancestors became skillful tool makers, producing weapons that allowed the males to become efficient hunters. Darwin did not ignore bipedalism in his model of human evolution, but he held it to be of secondary importance. Darwin believed that bipedalism arose when the ancestral hominid came "to live somewhat less in the trees and more on the ground" as a response to "a change in its manner of procuring subsistence or to a change in the conditions of its native country" (Darwin, 1871:135). Darwin also helped develop the idea of sexually dimorphic behavior. Men were courageous, inventive, and sexually competitive. Females, in his view, leaned more toward the nurturing, housemaking, and reclusive aspects of behavior. Darwin believed selection operated almost exclusively on males, producing larger, more colorful, and stronger individuals than the smaller, more drably ornamented females (as in birds).

New Behavioral Models Emerge: Bipedalism

By the turn of the century, as the number of fossil finds increased, anthropologists created new models of human evolution. These models differed from Darwin's. The fossil discoveries showed that our earliest ancestors possessed brains similar in size to those of living apes but differed from the apes primarily in their bipedal mode of locomotion. Bipedalism, it seemed, was an ancient form of locomotion and, perhaps, the most ancient of all of the hominid anatomical specializations. After the discovery of the Laetoli footprints (refer back to Figure 10–10), there could no longer be any doubt about the matter.

Advantages and costs.   Why did bipedalism become the predominant form of hominid locomotion? Bipedalism certainly was not without costs, because it placed early humans at a disadvantage should they find themselves in the midst of predators they could not outrun. Some argued that hominids could outdistance potential predators, if they had a head start.

Bipedalism provides a selective advantage in other behaviors, such as carrying objects (Hewes, 1964), display or threat behavior (Wescott, 1967), or foraging for widely dispersed food sources (Sigmon, 1971). The most pervasive explanation, however, revolves around the issue of tool use, as stated by S. L. Washburn (1960:9) in his article, "Tools and Human Evolution":

> Some very limited bipedalism left the hands sufficiently free from locomotor functions so that stones or sticks could be carried, played with, and used. The advantage that these objects gave to their users led to more bipedalism and to more efficient tool use.

Washburn and Chet Lancaster's (1968) article entitled "The Evolution of Hunting" depicted men as the active and aggressive procurers of food, defending their families and supplying food by hunting. Women were viewed as dependent, staying close to a home camp, and trading sex for protection and provisioning.

During the 1970s a shift in emphasis away from hunting as the major means of obtaining food was prompted by studies of many nonhuman primates, especially the chimpanzees, and by studies of modern-day hunters and gatherers. Lee, who studied the South African !Kung people, concluded that, on the average, hunting produced only about 35 percent of the group's total food supply, whereas women's gathering activities contributed the rest. These data showed that in most modern hunter-gatherer societies, women are not economically dependent on men for provisioning and most often produce more than men do. Women are also not sedentary. Lee's studies showed that women were away from their base camps for at least as many hours and covered as many miles as the men. At the same time, they often carried infants and other heavy objects (Figure 10–24).

FIGURE 10–24 !Kung women, members of a contemporary hunter-gatherer society, foraging. Women's foraging activites provide the majority of the group's food supply.

Emphasis on foraging.   The matrifocal, matrilineal nature of most nonhuman primate societies also altered ideas about the male role and male associations with females. From this information, new models of early hominid behavior were developed to incorporate female gathering, carrying, and sharing foods with their young, emphasizing the mother–infant bond and kin relationships. In 1971 the first of these revisions appeared in an article entitled "Woman the Gatherer" by Sally Linton. Reciprocal sharing, she believed, occurred first among members of a kin group and was not based on the establishment of sexual bonds or sexual exchange. Where hunting did occur, the first hunters shared food not with sexual partners but with mothers and siblings who had shared food with them. Adrienne Zihlman (1981) stressed that obtaining plant food with tools was the important event that promoted the development of bipedalism, as well as the invention of ways to carry food and/or infants while walking long distances.

Parker and Gibson (1979) developed the concept of *tool-aided extractive foraging,* which focused on behaviors that were designed to benefit offspring. These include maternal food sharing and maternal assistance in obtaining hard-to-get-at or hard-to-process foods, such as nuts, ants, termites, and honey. It was hypothesized that mothers, using tools, extracted and processed foods and then shared this food with young offspring who had not yet developed tool-using behaviors. Gibson (1993) continues, "such food sharing may have selected for communication capacities [and sensorimotor abilities] similar to those of children just learning to talk." This analysis, based on the supposed information-processing abilities of the earliest hominids, suggests that they had diverged from apes by increasing their tool-using, linguistic, and social capabilities. The growing dependence on tool-aided extractive foraging practices, Parker and Gibson believe, was the primary basis for the ape–human split.

Building on these ideas, King (1994) developed a *diachronic* model that viewed tool-aided extractive foraging as important, not only in terms of obtaining difficult-to-get-at foods but also in terms of the *donation of information* from adults to their offspring. She hypothesizes that, the more primates are dependent on tool-aided extractive foraging, the more donated information—teaching—is required to accomplish difficult tasks. This situation selected for greater cognitive abilities; these abilities, in turn, resulted in the ape–human split.

Regardless of whether tool-aided extractive foraging was the important variable in the split of the hominids from the apes, as King (1994:101) remarks, it "is consistent with the suggestion that hominids donated more information than did other primates, and that information donation increased during human evolution." This observation is important for the discussion in Chapter 12 on the evolution of childhood as a stage in the human life cycle.

Parker (1987) claimed that females were "courted" by males with gifts of especially nutritious or hard-to-get foods, such as meat. Bipedal behavior would have had a selective advantage in allowing the females to accurately assess the size of the male, the size of his gift, and the size and tumescence of his genitals. According to Parker, bipedal locomotion arose through sexual selection; it was a part of the male reproductive strategy of "nuptial," or courtship, feeding of estrous females. The model is consistent with some primate field data on pygmy chimpanzees that show males and females sharing food during copulations (Kuroda, 1984).

Environmental change.   The possibility that environmental change had something to do with the emergence of bipedalism has been promoted by several authors. There is good evidence to suggest that about 5.5 million years ago at the close of the Miocene and, later, about 2.5 million years ago, the world grew cooler and major forests gave way to grasslands. During the earlier shift, bipedalism may have arisen as an adaptive response to the need to cover the distances required by larger home ranges in the relatively treeless grasslands (Vrba, 1988). According to this model, a shift to open savanna environments stimulated greater reliance on a bipedal form of locomotion, and this, in turn, may have been related to increased tool use and ultimately the origins of family Hominidae.

Recent studies of forest-living chimpanzees contradict this notion, however. Boesch-Ackermann and Boesch (1994:10–11) compared the behavior of chimpanzees in the Tai Forest with that of chimpanzee populations living in more open environments and showed that "the forest chimpanzees use more tools, make them in more different ways, hunt more frequently and more often in groups, and show more frequent cooperation and food sharing." These authors believe that the environment plays an important role in the evolution of behavior; they do not believe, however, that the open savanna had much to do with the behaviors that, we have come to believe, characterize the early hominids. In addition, they cite new paleoecological studies that suggest that our earliest ancestors, in fact, lived in tropical rain forests (Bailey et al., 1989; Rayner et al., 1993) (Figure 10–25).

The questions of where, when, and why bipedal locomotion arose among primates still remain open. As we saw earlier in this chapter, if *Ardipithecus ramidus*, a forest-dwelling early hominid, proves to be a biped, our current notions of the selective advantage of this form of locomotion in the open savanna environment will have to be revised (Shreeve, 1996).

FIGURE 10–25 Despite the fact that they live in a forested environment, not on the open savanna, bonobos are excellent bipeds, and they often walk bipedally when carrying food. This suggests that food-carrying might have been more important to the development of bipedality than environmental change.

◖ SUMMARY

1. **What characteristics define the hominid family?**
   Hominids are bipedal and relatively large-brained primates, with a less prognathic facial skeleton and relatively smaller canine teeth than apes. The earliest fossil records of hominids occur in Africa at about 4 million years ago. Fragmentary remains earlier in time than this do not allow the origins of the hominids or their exact evolutionary relationships with the living African apes to be determined.

2. **What are the most important sites at which australopithecine remains have been found? What are current beliefs about the evolution and definition of the subfamily?**
   The australopithecines had smaller brains (relatively and absolutely), smaller body sizes, larger teeth, and different hip and lower limb structures, compared

to members of the genus *Homo.* Some eight species of australopithecines are recognized by most paleoanthropologists; they fall into three groups: early, gracile, and robust australopithecines. The first gracile species discovered was *Australopithecus africanus,* by Raymond Dart in 1925 at Taung, South Africa. Mary and Louis Leakey discovered the first East African robust australopithecine, *A. boisei,* in 1959 at Olduvai Gorge, Tanzania. *Ardipithecus ramidus* from the Afar region of Ethiopia is the most primitive australopithecine currently known, and the earliest, dating to 4.3 million to 4.4 million years ago. Early species, *A. anamensis* and *A. afarensis,* dating to 3.9 million to 4.2 million years ago and 2.8 million to 3.4 million years ago, respectively, were possibly descended from *Ardipithecus* and are best known from sites around Lake Turkana, Kenya, and Hadar, Ethiopia. *A. afarensis* was a sexually dimorphic species that may be ancestral to *A. africanus* and the robust australopithecines, *A. aethiopicus, A. boisei,* and *A. robustus.*

3. **Summarize what is known of the structural and ecological characteristics of the robust australopithecines. What is currently believed about their evolutionary relationships with early *Homo* species?**

The robust australopithecines, like the gracile australopithecines, were habitually bipedal, as indicated by the few associated postcranial remains that we have, but their pelves were more widely flaring than in *Homo.* Robust australopithecines are associated with more open woodland and savannalike habitats. Robust australopithecines, which survived to coexist with members of the genus *Homo,* had huge chewing teeth and musculature, suggesting that they had a different dietary specialization.

4. **What selective advantages did bipedalism provide to early hominids? What is the relationship between bipedalism and environmental change?**

Several selective advantages have been proposed. Bipedalism allows hominids to carry objects, to threaten other individuals, and to forage over long distances, as well as to use tools. Bipedalism is particularly important to tool-aided extractive foraging, in which females gather food for offspring. Long periods of dependency allow immature hominids to learn survival and cultural skills from their parents, perhaps contributing to the development of cognitive abilities. It was originally theorized that bipedalism arose as a response to a drier, less forested environment, but recent studies of forest-living chimpanzees, who frequently walk bipedally, put this in doubt.

◀ CRITICAL THINKING QUESTIONS

1. Australopithecines apparently lived only in Africa. Suggest some possible reasons for their absence in Europe and Asia.
2. The australopithecines are the earliest hominids for which we can deduce probable diet. What does this evidence indicate about the basic hominid dietary adaptation?
3. Stone tools are not generally found associated with the early australopithecines. Speculate on tool use in australopithecines for defense and food getting. Is there any evidence for your hypothesis?
4. There are many australopithecine fossils in the Transvaal cave sites of northern South Africa. Do you think the hominids lived in the caves? If not, how did their bones get deposited there?
5. Australopithecine males were substantially larger than females. Using your knowledge of primate behavior, what might this degree of sexual dimorphism suggest about australopithecines' social structure and mating patterns?

◀ INTERNET EXERCISES

Critical Thinking

Origins of Bipedality. This chapter discusses some of the many theories proposed for the evolutionary origin of bipedality. In these exercises, consider these and other theories, and decide which seems to be the best explanation for the development of bipedalism in hominids. Answer the following questions:

1. What benefits does bipedality confer? What drawbacks does it entail?
2. What aspects of the environment, either physical or cultural, encouraged bipedalism in early hominids? Why is bipedalism unique to hominids?
3. What physical and cultural adaptations "came along for the ride" when hominids became bipedal?

Writing Assignment

Major Hominid Sites. For this assignment, research one of the important prehistoric sites discussed in this chapter, such as Laetoli, Sterkfontein, Hadar, or Koobi Fora, Lake Turkana. Present your research in a paper that answers the following questions:

1. Who discovered the site? What were the first discoveries made there?
2. What is the age range of the site? How was the site dated?
3. What is the significance of the site to our current knowledge of human evolution? Is research ongoing? Can further discoveries be expected?

See Companion Web site for Internet links.

MEDIALAB   Finding Lucy

The *Australopithecus afarensis* skeleton known as Lucy is probably the most famous early hominid in the world. Dated to approximately 3.2 million years ago, Lucy was only 1.2 m (4 feet) tall and 19 to 21 years old. At another Hadar site were found the remains of at least 13 other females, males, and children of the same species. *A. afarensis* was a hardy species that survived for more than a million years in harsh and changing environments. In this Web Activity, you will view an interview with Dr. Donald Johanson in which he describes the discovery of Lucy and see footage of East African digs. The text of Chapter 10 describes the Hadar locality where Lucy was found and explains its importance for human paleontology.

WEB ACTIVITY

Hadar, part of the Afar Triangle in northeastern Ethiopia, is one of the most important eastern African areas for early australopithecines. The significance of the Afar region of Ethiopia was first discovered in the 1960s. Explorations in the 1970s focused on the Hadar locality in the central Afar. In 1981, a multidisciplinary team surveyed the Middle Awash region south of Hadar. Work in the area continues today, and discoveries are far from complete. In this activity, you will view contemporary footage of ongoing work.

Activity

1. View the video. How was the discovery of Lucy made? Why was it extraordinary?
2. What specific research methods was Dr. Johanson using when he and his colleagues discovered Lucy?
3. Observe the shots of Dr. Johanson and his colleagues in the field. Who makes up the research team? What facilities are available for the team's working and living arrangements? Describe the site and the camp.

The MediaLab can be found in Chapter 10 on your Companion Web site http://www.prenhall.com/boaz

Dr. Donald Johanson
Institute of Human Origins

THE GENUS *HOMO*

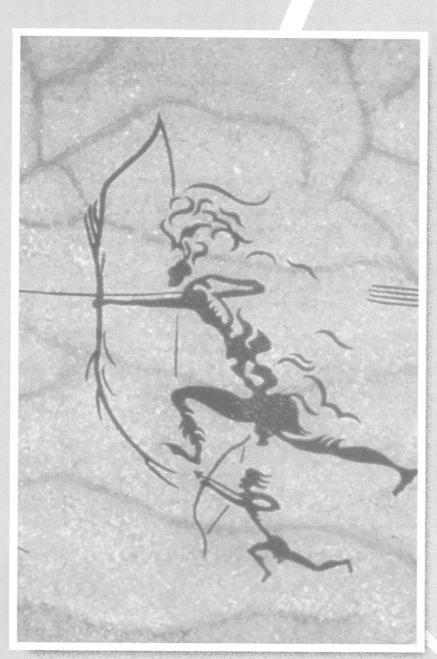

O U T L I N E

After reading this chapter, you should be able to discuss the following questions:

1. What are the major differences between early *Homo* species and australopithecines?
2. When and where did individuals of early *Homo* live? What are the evolutionary relationships of this group to the earlier australopithecines and later species of the genus *Homo*?
3. When and where were the first stone tools made? In addition to tool use, what is known about the cultural adaptations of *Homo* species of the early and middle Pleistocene?
4. When and where did members of the species *Homo erectus* first appear? What does the fossil record tell us about the distribution of *Homo erectus* in terms of time and space?
5. What current theories attempt to explain human language and its origin? How is the structure of the human brain related to language ability?

Experts in the field have generally recognized three species of the genus *Homo*: ***Homo habilis,*** dated from the late Pliocene to the early Pleistocene; ***Homo erectus,*** dated from possibly as early as 1.6 million years ago to 500,000 years ago; and our own species, ***Homo sapiens,*** including large-brained, archaic forms, such as the Neandertals, and moderns, such as ourselves. The various members of the species *Homo sapiens* are discussed in Chapter 12. Some paleoanthropologists now recognize two additional species of early Pleistocene hominid, *H. rudolfensis,* supposedly a contemporary of *habilis,* and *H. ergaster,* a species created to incorporate fossils originally considered to be early *Homo erectus* (about 1.6 million years old). Other groups of fossils, described as *Homo antecessor* followed by *Homo heidelbergensis,* may represent a separate hominid lineage in Africa and Europe contemporary with Asian forms of *Homo erectus* (Table 11–1).

As a group, the genus *Homo* is distinguished from the genus *Australopithecus* by a larger cranial capacity and, thus, a larger brain. Indeed, brain size increases successively from *Homo habilis* to *H. erectus* to *H. sapiens.* Members of the genus *Homo* also have smaller molars; canine teeth shaped more like incisors; and more rounded skulls that generally lack the "dished faces" and cranial crests seen among the australopithecines. Body size increased dramatically in the *Homo* lineage, especially with *Homo erectus.* Archaeological evidence shows that members of the genus *Homo* made stone tools, in probable contrast to most of the australopithecines, who did not.

In this chapter we review the fossil evidence for the emergence and spread of members of the genus *Homo* through to the emergence of the modern species, *H. sapiens.* The timeline for this chapter is presented in Figure 11–1, p. 280.

MAJOR PHYSICAL CHANGES IN EARLY *HOMO*

The Brain

Perhaps the most characteristic trait of *Homo* species is an enlarged brain in relation to body size. Brain size can be relatively accurately predicted from the **endocranial volume,** the space of the brain cavity inside the skull. But this determination is

Homo habilis: earliest generally recognized species of the genus Homo.

Homo erectus: primitive species of the genus Homo, generally considered to have evolved from Homo habilis and to be the ancestor of Homo sapiens.

Homo sapiens: species that includes modern humans as well as archaic Homo sapiens.

endocranial volume: synonymous with cranial capacity; the amount of space inside the skull, occupied in life by the brain and brain coverings.

TABLE 11–1 | Taxonomic Classification of Early Members of the Genus *Homo*

Species	Locality	Specimen Number	Geological Age
Homo habilis	Olduvai Gorge, Tanzania	OH 7	1.8 million years
		OH 8	1.8 million years
		OH 13	1.6 million years
		OH 24	1.9 million years
		OH 62	1.8 million years
	Omo, Ethiopia	L894-1	1.9 million years
	Hadar, Ethiopia	AL 666	2.3 million years
[also classified by some as *Homo rudolfensis*]	East Turkana, Kenya	KNM ER (Kenya National Museum, East Rudolf) 1470	1.9 million years
		KNM ER 1813	1.9 million years
	Uraha, Malawi		2.4 million years
	Sterkfontein, South Africa	STW 53	about 2.0 million years
Early Homo erectus	West Turkana, Kenya	KNM WT 15000 ("Turkana Boy")	1.6 million years
[also classified by some as *Homo ergaster*]	East Turkana, Kenya	KNM ER 3733	1.5 million years
	Swartkrans, South Africa	SK 847	about 1.5 million years
	Modjokerto, Indonesia	Modjokerto 1 "Modjokerto Infant"	about 1.9 million years
	Sangiran, Indonesia	Sangiran Skull IX	about 1.5 million years
	Longgupou, China	—	1.9 million years
	Dmanisi, Georgia	Dmanisi 1 and 2	about 1.6–1.8 million years
Late Homo erectus	Trinil, Java		1.0–0.8 million years
	Lainyamok, Kenya		600,000 years
	Ternifine, Algeria		650,000–450,000 years
	Melka Kunture, Ethiopia		900,000 years
	Salé ⎫		300,000–200,000 years
	Sidi Abderrahman ⎬ Morocco		300,000–200,000 years
	Thomas Quarries ⎭		350,000–240,000 years
	Jian Shi ⎫		300,000–200,000 years
	Zhoukoudian ⎪		500,000–230,000 years
	Hexian ⎬ China		700,000–250,000 years
	Gongwangling [Lantian] ⎪		700,000 years
	Yuanmou ⎭		900,000–500,000 years
	Ceprano, Italy		700,000 years
	Ngandong [Solo] ⎫ Java		46,000–27,000 years
	Sambungmacan ⎭		53,000–27,000 years

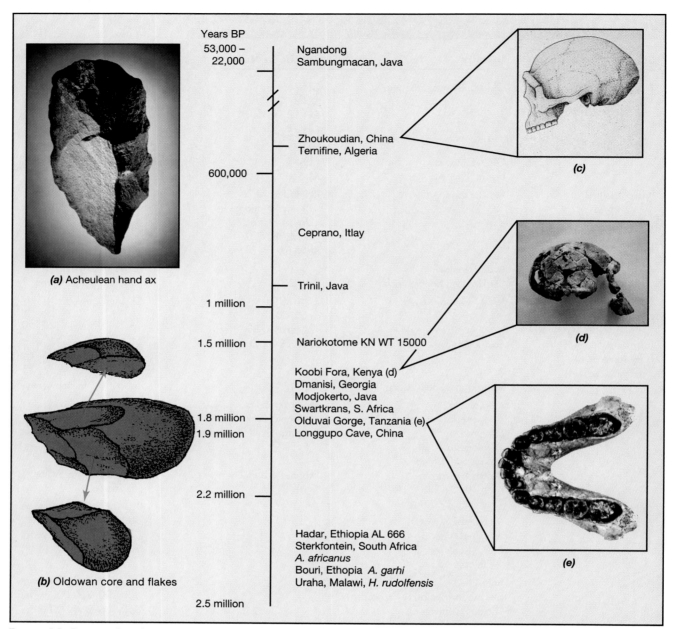

(a) Acheulean hand ax

(b) Oldowan core and flakes

Years BP

53,000 – 22,000   Ngandong Sambungmacan, Java

600,000

Zhoukoudian, China
Ternifine, Algeria

(c)

Ceprano, Itlay

Trinil, Java

1 million

1.5 million   Nariokotome KN WT 15000

(d)

Koobi Fora, Kenya (d)
Dmanisi, Georgia
Modjokerto, Java
Swartkrans, S. Africa
1.8 million   Olduvai Gorge, Tanzania (e)
1.9 million   Longgupo Cave, China

2.2 million

Hadar, Ethiopia AL 666
Sterkfontein, South Africa
A. africanus
Bouri, Ethopia *A. garhi*
Uraha, Malawi, *H. rudolfensis*

(e)

2.5 million

FIGURE 11-1   Timeline for sites and fossils of early *Homo* species.

also somewhat larger than true brain size because of the presence of the membranes that cover the brain (the meninges) and the venous sinuses, which contain blood, between the inside of the skull and the outside of the brain.

The body height and weight of primates exist in a constant relationship to various dimensions of their skeletons. Measuring the size and length of limb bones—such as the human femur (thigh bone)—anthropologists can estimate the body weight and height of fossil hominids. With both brain size and body weight estimates, one can determine the degree of **encephalization**—the size of the brain in relation to body weight. Members of the genus *Homo* have an encephalization quotient higher than that of any australopithecine (Figure 11–2).

encephalization: the process of extreme brain enlargement in the *Homo* lineage.

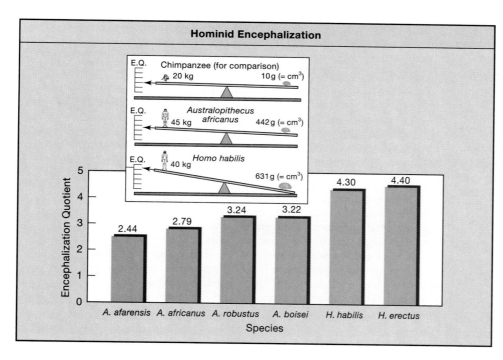

FIGURE 11–2 Hominid cranial capacity, body weight, and encephalization quotients. Encephalization quotient increases steadily from the australopithecines through *Homo*.

The human brain evolved to such a large size and to such complexity because of strong selective forces. Many hypotheses have been advanced to account for this growth. Tool use and increasing cultural and sociobehavioral complexity in the evolving *Homo* lineage have long been thought to be important to selection for an increase in brain size (Washburn, 1960). Cooperative hunting by males has also been implicated. It is now realized, however, that female social cooperation in food getting would have been of equivalent, if not greater, selective importance, because a majority of the daily caloric intake of modern hunter-gatherer groups derives from female-collected food sources (Lee and DeVore, 1968). Other researchers (see Falk, 1990; Foley, 1990; Potts, 1996) have implicated the selective importance of language, ecological parameters, diet, and, recently, the circulatory patterns in the head as a cooling mechanism for an enlarged brain. We consider all of these factors later in this chapter and in Chapter 12.

The Teeth

The teeth as a whole, but particularly the molar teeth, underwent reduction in size in *Homo* compared with the australopithecines (Figure 11–4, p. 282). The molar teeth are more squared in outline, viewed from above, than they are in the australopithecines. The canines are relatively smaller. The third premolar, which in australopithecines tends to be as large as, or larger than, the fourth premolar, is generally relatively smaller in *Homo*.

The grinding teeth, the molars and the premolars, have generally lost their complex enamel wrinkling (crenulation) in *Homo*. Crenulations function to increase the surface area of these teeth in the australopithecines. This would be particularly important in young individuals, whose jaw strength was not as powerful as that of the adults. Reduced tooth size supports to some extent the brain-versus-guts hypothesis of Aiello and Wheeler, in that smaller teeth would be all that would be required to chew a diet of higher-quality food.

Big Brains and Small Guts in Early *Homo:* The Expensive Tissue Hypothesis

Anthropologists Leslie Aiello and Peter Wheeler proposed an innovative idea in 1995 about how the large human brain evolved. Observing that humans, compared to other primates, had large brains, short gastrointestinal tracts, and the same basal metabolic rate as other mammals, they reasoned that there had been a trade-off in human evolution. The gut had decreased in size as the brain had increased. Their argument basically revolves around energy. The human brain uses one-fifth of the body's supply of glucose. The brain has no glucose stores itself and, unlike muscle tissue, cannot metabolize the energy stored in glycogen or fat molecules in the body. When glucose runs out, the brain closes down, and the hominid may lose consciousness and die. But this rarely happens.

How then could early hominids have evolved to maintain their big brains? They could have eaten more energy-rich foods and increased their energy budget, but we know that they didn't do that, because human metabolic rates are not higher than those of other mammals. Nor did they somehow decrease their energy output, because human metabolic rates are not lower than those of other mammals. They could have slept longer hours, thus conserving energy, but this seems unlikely, because most diurnal primates have fairly consistent dawn-to-dusk activity patterns, and natural selection probably didn't select for narcoleptic early *Homo* individuals who dozed when early morning leopards came calling.

Aiello and Wheeler hypothesize that early *Homo* redirected energy to the evolving brain by skimping on the size of other organs, thus conserving the same basal metabolic rate (Figure 11–3). The functions of the heart, liver, and kidneys are too essential to reduce, but the organs of the digestive system—stomach, pancreas, and intestines—are significantly smaller than expected in modern humans. Indirect evidence from the pelvis and rib cage skeleton of Turkana Boy (see Figure 11–7) also suggests that the protuberant abdomen of the australopithecines had become a slender waist by *Homo erectus* (or *Homo ergaster*) times, suggesting that the gut had shrunk.

If we accept that individuals of early *Homo* had a more slender body form and an enlarged brain, but their metabolic rate was unchanged from that of their ancestors, how then did they get enough to eat, considering their significantly smaller stomach and shortened intestines? One possible answer is that they must have changed their diet. The food that they ate must have been higher in calories, lower in fiber, and more easily digestible. We do not yet know the details of this dietary shift to

The Skull and Jaws

The increased size of the brain, around which the skull bones develop during growth, accounts for a higher skull vault in *Homo* than in *Australopithecus* (Figure 11–5). Anthropologists have developed several measurements that express this change, such as height of the skull above the ear opening and the curvature of the frontal bone (frontal angle).

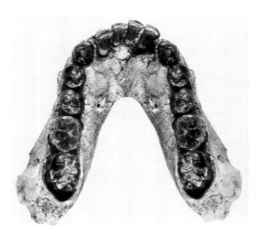
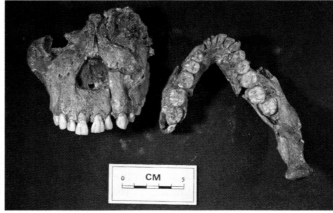

FIGURE 11–4 *Homo habilis* dentition (left), compared with that of *Australopithecus africanus* (right). The two specimens shown are OH 7 and Sts 52.

high-quality foods, but a greater proportion of meat, tubers, insects, honey, or any number of other food items may have played a part. Obtaining foods and processing them external to the body, with stone tools, digging sticks, and perhaps fire, would have also been important.

Aiello and Wheeler named their hypothesis the Expensive Tissue Hypothesis, and they skillfully incorporated anatomical, physiological, paleoanthropological, and primatological data into their analysis. The hypothesis is a synthetic model for appreciating not only isolated parts of anatomy but also the entire anatomy and physiology in human evolution. Aiello and Wheeler have generated a significant amount of new research, making paleoanthropological theorists scramble to tie their own explanations for why the large brain of *Homo* evolved to this new persuasive argument of how it evolved.

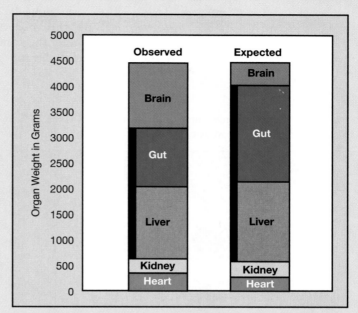

FIGURE 11–3 Left: Actual organ weights in 68 kg (150 lb) humans. Right: Organ weights predicted for a 68 kg (150 lb) human on the basis of typical mammalian organ sizes. The modern human brain is nearly three times larger than would be expected in a typical mammal.

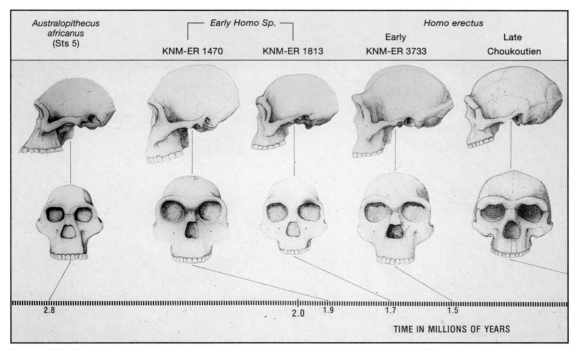

FIGURE 11–5 Side and frontal views of *Australopithecus africanus, Homo habilis,* and *H. erectus.* For *Homo erectus,* both early and later specimens are shown. Note the increased rounding of the skull in the later specimens.

In *Homo* the upper jaw (maxilla) and the lower jaw (the mandible) are decreased in size and bone thickness, because the teeth are decreased in size. Because the dentition is not as large, the muscles that move the teeth are not as heavily developed. Thus in *Homo* the bony face protrudes less (it is less prognathous and more *orthognathous*); the cheekbone (*zygomatic arch*) is smaller; the mandible is lighter in construction; and the temporal lines (where the temporalis muscle attaches to the sides of the skull vault) are reduced in size (Figure 11–6).

FIGURE 11–6   Reconstructed crania of early *Homo* (KNM ER 1470 on the left and KNM ER 1813 on the right), showing some of the major advances over the australopithecines.

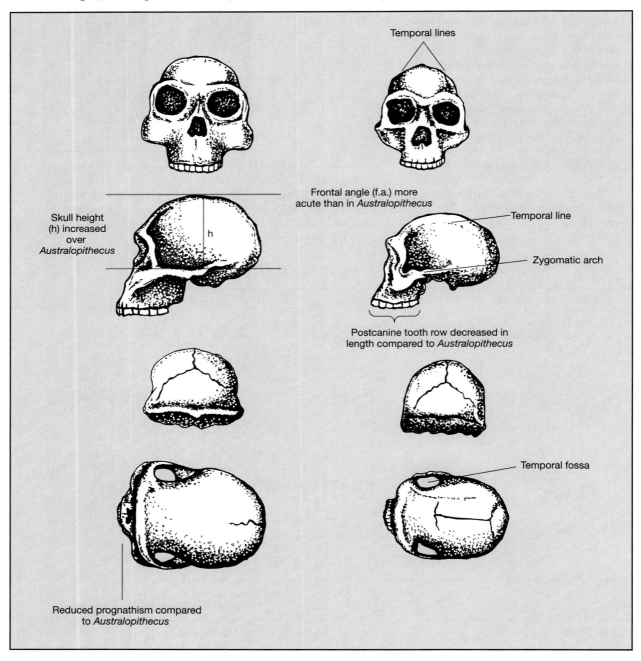

Body Size and Limbs

Body size and weight increased substantially during the evolution of the genus *Homo.* This increase over *Australopithecus africanus* is seen most dramatically in the five-foot-plus (130 cm) reconstructed adult height of the 1.5-million-year-old *Homo erectus* skeleton (KNM WT 15000) from the site of Nariokotome in West Turkana, Kenya (Walker and Leakey, 1993; Figure 11–7). There was a change in relative lengths of limbs. *Homo* is characterized by longer lower limbs (thigh length and leg length), compared to trunk length, and perhaps relatively shorter upper limbs (arm length and forearm length; Figure 11–8).

Increase in lower limb length meant an increased length in *Homo*'s walking stride. This enabled fully bipedal hominids to move more efficiently over greater distances, at the same time attaining greater speeds than those possible, for example, from the bipedal locomotion seen occasionally in the apes, whose lower limbs are shorter. This may have been an important preadaptation for hunting of large animals, which are characteristically "run down" over long distances by modern hunter-gatherers. Larger body size was an advantage in competition for food (in scavenging, hunting, or gathering) with other species and in avoiding predation.

HOMO HABILIS

The earliest species of the genus *Homo* was discovered at Olduvai Gorge in 1960. The species name, *habilis,* was suggested to Louis Leakey by Raymond Dart, and it means "dexterous" or "handy," on the assumption that this species, not the contemporary *Australopithecus boisei,* fashioned the stone tools found at Olduvai Bed I.

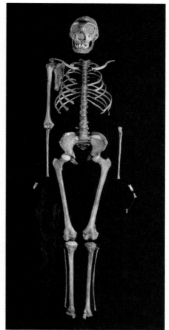

FIGURE 11–7 *Homo erectus* skeleton WT 15000, from Nariokotome, the famous "Turkana Boy." According to Alan Walker, its codiscoverer, this boy was "exceptionally tall for an early hominid . . . and slender of build yet powerful, and stronger than any living human" (Walker and Shipman, 1996:180).

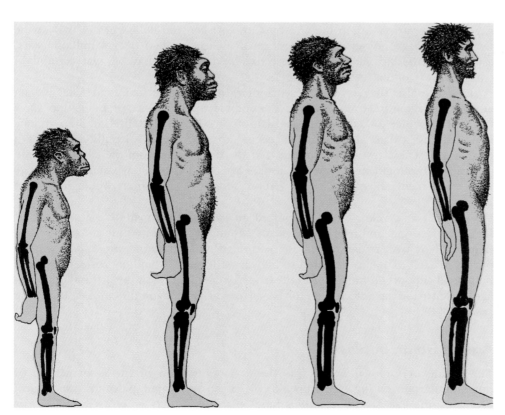

FIGURE 11–8 Relative increase in leg length and relative decrease in arm length from *Australopithecus* to modern *Homo.* For the early hominids there are only three specimens from which an accurate determination of limb length can be made: newly described *A. garhi,* UP 12/1, from Bouri (see Chapter 10); AL 288, from Hadar; and early *H. erectus* WT 15000, from Nariokotome, Kenya.

Since 1964 other specimens of *Homo habilis* have been discovered in Africa—at East Lake Turkana, Kenya; at Uraha, Malawi; at Omo and Hadar in Ethiopia; and at Sterkfontein in South Africa (see Table 11–1 and Figure 11–1). Later work at Olduvai yielded a fragmentary skeleton of *Homo habilis,* Olduvai Hominid 62 (Johanson et al., 1987). This partial skeleton is important, because limb lengths could be estimated from a single individual and thus, the relative lengths of the forelimb and hindlimb were determined for this species. The Uraha mandible, dated to 2.4 million years ago, is currently the oldest evidence for the genus *Homo,* although other fossils from Hadar and Omo are dated at 2.3 million years. *Homo habilis* survived until about 1.6 million to 1.8 million years ago, witnessed by fossil discoveries at Olduvai, Omo, and East Turkana.

It appears from the fossil evidence that *Homo habilis* was relatively larger in body size than were the gracile australopithecines, but apparently *habilis* possessed a more marked degree of sexual dimorphism than later *Homo.* The Olduvai skeleton, OH 62, for example, was a quite small individual, probably a female weighing between 30 and 39 kg (66 to 86 lb). In comparison, the large, probably male members of the species weighed from about 50 kg (110 lb) to possibly more than 90 kg (198 lb). (See, however, McHenry [1988] who contests the notion that *habilis* was larger than gracile australopithecines).

The paleoenvironments at sites where *Homo habilis* has been discovered were open grasslands and partially wooded savannas. Reconstructions are based on the recovery of fossil plant remains and other fauna, such as antelopes, that are commonly associated with savannas. Earlier, australopithecine-bearing sites in the same areas preserve common forest-dwelling species, indicating more wooded environments.

It is still a mystery whether *H. habilis* extended its range outside sub-Saharan Africa. However, a skull of a juvenile hominid found prior to World War II by G. H. R. von Koenigswald at Modjokerto, Java (Indonesia), raises some questions. This fossil, which served as the type specimen for a new species, *Homo modjokertensis,* is exceptionally old for this region. Redating the volcanic material at this site using the argon-argon method by Carl Swisher and colleagues (1994) at the Berkeley Geochronology Center confirmed an earlier date of 1.9 million years, establishing the fact that the Javanese fossil, whatever it may be, was certainly a contemporary of the African *H. habilis.*

Evidence also suggests the presence of early *Homo* on mainland Asia. Huang and his colleagues (1995) reported a mandible from the site of Longgupo Cave (Sichuan Province), China. Paleomagnetic studies (see Appendix 4) and an archaic fauna suggest a date of earliest Pleistocene (approximately 1.8 million years ago) for the site. These researchers report that the discoveries from the cave—hominid dentition, jaw fragments, and stone tools—are comparable in age and morphology with early members of the genus *Homo* and the Oldowan technology of East Africa.

Gabunia and Vekua (1995) reported an early *Homo* mandible at the site of Dmanisi, Georgia, south of the Caucaus Mountains in westernmost Asia. A skull (Figure 11–9) with remarkably close resemblance to African *Homo habilis* was reported in 2000. Dmanisi is dated to between 1.6 and 1.8 million years ago. These finds lend support to the claim that early *Homo* entered Asia by 1.9 million years ago and provide the antecedents for later *Homo erectus* evolution in Asia (Gabunia et al., 2000).

Age of *Homo habilis*

The dating of Olduvai Bed I was the first application of the new method of potassium-argon dating (see Appendix 4) to an important paleoanthropological problem—the age of *Homo habilis* (and *Australopithecus boisei*). Garniss Curtis

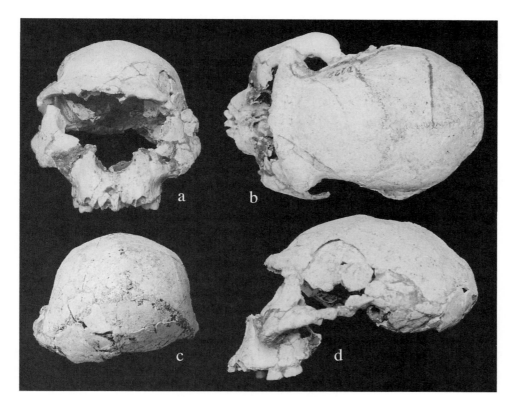

FIGURE 11-9   Frontal, top, back, and left lateral views of the Dmanisi cranium, from the Causcasus of Georgia, westernmost Asia, dated to 1.6 million to 1.8 million years ago. The specimen resembles fossils attributed to *Homo habilis* in Africa.

and J. F. Evernden of the University of California, Berkeley, reported in 1962 a date of 1.73 million years for a basalt, a potassium-rich layer of volcanic material, in Olduvai Bed I. In time, the dating was confirmed by comparisons of fauna and potassium-argon dates from other sites, particularly Omo, and by paleomagnetic dating.

During the 1970s, teams led by Richard Leakey recovered many fossils of individuals belonging to the genus *Homo* from sites on the eastern shore of Lake Turkana. Perhaps the most famous, certainly the most controversial both in terms of its age and classification, was KNM ER 1470 (Figure 11–10). After a hot debate about its age, this important find was dated to about 1.8 million years ago, comparable to the dates earlier determined for fossils found at Olduvai Gorge. Where to place KNM ER 1470 taxonomically remains another matter. Some have placed it among *H. habilis,* whereas others believe that it should be placed in its own species, *rudolfensis.* Most recently a suggestion has been made to include it in a new genus, *Kenyanthropus* (Leakey, 2001; see the Research Highlights box in Chapter 10).

As mentioned earlier, new fossil evidence from sites such as Uraha, Malawi, and Hadar, Ethiopia, has brought the age of the early species of *Homo* back to 2.3 million to 2.4 million years. General consensus now holds that early members of the genus *Homo* may have had their beginnings as early as 2.4 million years ago, and that these species disappeared by about 1.5 million years ago, as more advanced members of the species *Homo erectus* came onto the scene.

Homo habilis and Other Species of Early Homo

A number of paleoanthropologists believe that several species of early *Homo* coexisted (see Table 11–1). One of the species names that has been suggested is *Homo rudolfensis.* Fossils that have been placed in this species are roughly contemporary with those included as *Homo habilis,* about 2 million years old. Fossils of *Homo*

FIGURE 11-10   *Homo habilis* skull, KNM ER 1470, from Koobi Fora, Kenya. This specimen is dated to approximately 1.8 million years ago.

stone artifacts: stones broken or flaked by hominids in order to be used as tools, or unmodified stones found in geological circumstances indicating that hominids carried them and placed them at a site.

rudolfensis are known primarily from deposits located in the Lake Turkana basin and possibly from Malawi (Schrenk et al., 1993). Proponents of the species *Homo rudolfensis* point out that in those designated fossils the face is broader and flatter and the cheek teeth are broader with more complex crowns and thicker enamel than is seen in *H. habilis.* As we have said earlier, so far the best known representative of the *rudolfensis* group is KNM ER 1470 (see Figure 11–6). The few postcranial remains associated with the skull indicate that *rudolfensis* shared some traits with the australopithecines, such as longer hindlimbs, supported by a femur (thigh bone) that attached at the hip joint with a much larger femoral head, than is seen in *H. habilis.*

Although this splitting of the early *Homo* fossils into a number of separate species has received some paleoanthropological support, other experts accept the single group *Homo habilis* as accommodating the variation that is seen in the fossils of early *Homo* (Tobias, 1991). The question, however, remains open.

Later fossils (about 1.5 million years ago), which some have referred to as early *Homo erectus* (Walker and Leakey, 1993), have also been taxonomically split from this taxon into a new species called *Homo ergaster* (Groves and Mazek, 1975). Paleoanthropologist Bernard Wood (1992) describes this new species as consisting of individuals who were large bodied and fully bipedal, distinct from the earlier, smaller, and partially arboreal *Homo habilis.* Other studies (Walker and Leakey, 1993) that have compared the African and Asian fossils have not been able to find consistent differences between *ergaster* and *erectus.* Thus, these researchers contend that the African fossils should remain as they were traditionally placed, in the group *Homo erectus.*

THE FIRST STONE TOOLS

It is likely that early australopithecines, such as *A. africanus,* had developed tool making to some degree, at least to the extent observed in some apes in the wild today. **Stone artifacts**—pieces of rock that by their context or their pattern of breakage indicate deliberate modification—are not usually found in clear association with gracile australopithecines.

Oldowan Stone Tools

The advent of stone tool making is a major event in hominid evolution. It requires a knowledge of rock types (only hard, crystalline rocks make adequate stone tools), the ability to locate source areas for these rocks, an understanding of the properties of rock fracturing (Figure 11–11), and the ability to produce functional tool designs.

FIGURE 11–11 Rock fracturing by early hominids; the making of a core and flakes of early Oldowan stone tools.

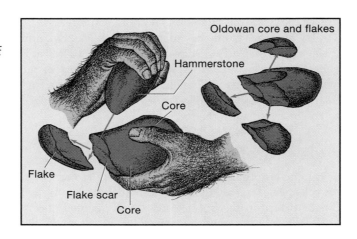

These abilities are far beyond the interest of apes except, as we have observed, in laboratory settings. The earliest evidence for stone tools comes from sites near the Gona River in the Afar region of Ethiopia and is dated to 2.5 million years ago. The tools, now numbering more than 3,000, were recovered by Sileshi Semaw and Jack Harris of Rutgers University. These tools, consisting of Oldowan choppers and flaked cores, named by Mary Leakey after the tools she first described from Olduvai Gorge, are remarkable in that they are at least 100,000 years older than known fossils belonging to the genus *Homo*. Fossils of *Australopithecus garhi* have been found at the near-contemporaneous site of Bouri, but whether this australopithecine species was the stone tool maker remains to be proven by future discoveries.

Mary Leakey has categorized these tools into a number of different types. Basically, however, there are two jobs for which these tools were used—cutting and bashing. Cutting tools were used primarily to dismember carcasses for meat. Research at Olduvai Gorge, Tanzania; Koobi Fora, Kenya; Bouri, Ethiopia; and Senga (Congo, formerly Zaire) has revealed **cut marks** left on animal bones when the muscles were cut off. Bashing tools were used primarily to break open long bones to obtain their fatty marrow. Fatty foods are a particularly valued commodity among modern hunter-gatherers, and the thousands of smashed bone fragments at Olduvai attest to the antiquity of this predilection (Potts, 1988).

Why and how did early *Homo* start using stone tools? Other animals that use stone—apes, sea otters, and certain birds—do so in order to crack open and eat nuts, mussels, eggs, or some other food that is not otherwise accessible to them. Early *Homo* went beyond this, discovering that flaked stone tools can cut—a principle that still underlies many of our food preparation techniques (grating, slicing, paring, blending, chopping, etc.). With the increased cutting-edge surface of a stone flake tool and the force with which it could be used, early *Homo* was able to match the biting and chewing efficiency of much larger and stronger animals with much more impressive dentitions. Another argument for the development of stone tools is that they were used as weapons for protection against predators and for aggressive purposes against other hominids.

Other Aspects of Paleoecology and Behavior

Paleoecology. As was described earlier in this chapter, early members of the genus *Homo* lived in areas of sub-Saharan Africa not remarkably different from the savannas and savanna woodlands that one can still see today in places such as Serengeti, Maasai Mara, and Kruger National Parks. Trees, for fruit and shade, were generally scarcer than in *A. africanus* times. Early *Homo* groups were well integrated into this environment, although they probably competed with robust australopithecines, wild dogs, hyenas, and other carnivores for meat, and with robust australopithecines, baboons, and perhaps some pig species for fruits, vegetables, nuts, and roots. Interestingly, there are no early *Homo* or other hominid fossils that show coexistence with any ape species, implying that species ranges and ecological adaptations of hominids and apes overlapped very little, if at all.

Archaeologists have found evidence that *Homo* butchered and ate hippopotamus, as well as numerous small antelopes and other animals. A major question is whether early *Homo* hunted and killed these animals, or scavenged carcasses left by carnivores, drought, or disease. It is probable that these hominids did not have the technical capabilities to kill animals much larger than themselves. That they did kill each other, however, was brought to light recently by a study on a Sterkfontein fossil, Stw 53. This research revealed stone tool cut marks on the hominid skull, specifically marks on the zygomatic process of the upper jaw. According to researchers, these cut marks represent the disarticulation of the lower jaw rather than a simple defleshing of the jaw's muscle. The postmortem damage inflicted on this individual

cut marks: incisions left on bone as a by-product of skinning or cutting muscle off the bone with stone tools; uniquely characteristic of hominids but sometimes difficult to distinguish from carnivore bite marks or scratch marks made by sand grains.

was the result of saw cuts of a back and forth motion using simple flakes and, consequently, may be the earliest evidence of cannibalism in the genus *Homo* (Pickering, White, and Toth, 1999).

It is also possible that these larger-bodied hominids, finding tree climbing (in whatever available trees there may be in open savanna county) more difficult as a strategy to escape predators, built shelters on the ground. These shelters served as refuges from predators, provided shade during the day, and were warm at night. The earliest such structure has been found in Olduvai Gorge Bed I. It is a circle of large stones that may have served as the groundwork for, presumably, a structure of sticks, branches, or skins.

Foley (1990) has suggested that as home range size increased, perhaps to take advantage of greater foraging or hunting opportunities, so did brain size in the *Homo* lineage. Excavations at Omo and ecological calculations based on body size have given us estimates of early *Homo* population density, around 1.5 individuals per square km (4.5 individuals per square mi) (Boaz, 1979a). We can estimate early *Homo* home range size at about 10.5 square km (approximately 3.8 square mi), and the average number of individuals in a group at about 16, values not unlike those of modern foraging peoples.

Social cooperation.   Other aspects of their behavior we must deduce from analogy to modern hunter-gatherers. The females likely gathered plant foods. Males may have cooperated in hunting for small game and scavenging for meat, an important source of protein. The nuclear family, consisting of a male, one or more females, and their offspring, was possibly the basic social unit. Kinship with others outside the family likely was recognized as a principle that organized the sharing of meat and of other valued food resources, and that regulated alliances both within the group and with other groups. *Homo* groups were probably seminomadic and moved in relation to availability of food and water. Some researchers have suggested that they had a "home base" to which all individuals returned after foraging or hunting and where food was shared (Isaac, 1978).

HOMO IN THE MIDDLE PLEISTOCENE

The middle Pleistocene, which began about 700,000 years ago, was ushered in by a shift in the earth's magnetic pole from a reversed epoch (the Matuyama) to a normal epoch (the Brunhes) (see Appendix 4). Fossils of the middle Pleistocene discovered in China and Java have traditionally been grouped as members of the species *Homo erectus*. Fossils from Africa and Europe, which were at one time considered to be the western counterparts of this same species, are now grouped by many paleoanthropologists as *Homo heidelbergensis*.

The evolutionary trends toward relatively greater cranial capacity, orthognathy, dental reduction, and greater body size that had begun in early *Homo* species continued in their successors. In *Homo erectus,* the skull also began to change to a distinctive form—vault bones became very thick; the area over the eye sockets (supraorbital torus) came to protrude markedly into the brow ridges; the back of the skull (occiput) developed a horizontal ridge, the **occipital torus**; and the area along the sagittal suture became raised into a low prominence, the **sagittal keel**, with flattened areas extending laterally from it (Figure 11–12). Hominids with this distinctive morphology first appeared in Africa about 1.5 million to 1.6 million years ago. As we discussed earlier, they are classified either as *Homo erectus* (Rightmire, 1990) or as *Homo ergaster* (Wood, 1999).

Homo erectus was first discovered at the site of Trinil on the island of Java (Indonesia) by Dutch physician Eugene Dubois in 1891. Dubois discovered a femur

occipital torus: a horizontal raised ridge of bone at the back of the *Homo erectus* skull.

sagittal keel: a low, rounded elevation of bone along the midline of the top of the *Homo erectus* skull.

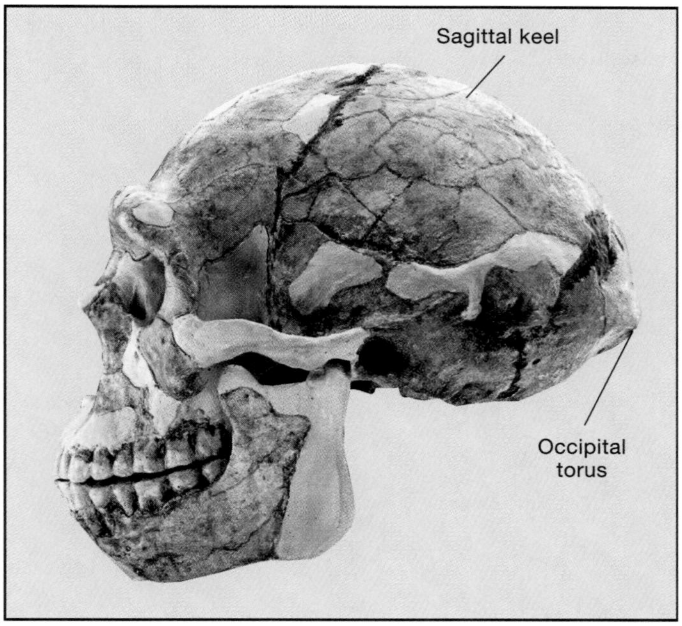

Sagittal keel

Occipital torus

FIGURE 11-12 Reconstruction of the Zhoukoudian *Homo erectus,* showing features typical of this species. Zhoukoudian is dated to 500,000 to 230,000 years ago.

(thigh bone) that had a straight shaft, and he realized from comparative studies of primates that it had to have belonged to a biped. He then found a skull cap with unique anatomy. It was low and thick and had large brow ridges over the eyes. Its face and base were broken away. Dubois believed that the femur and the skull cap belonged together, and he named a new genus and species on that basis: *Pithecanthropus* ("ape–human") *erectus.* The name emphasized the association of a primitive human skull with the advanced trait of human upright walking. The genus *Pithecanthropus* was later abandoned by taxonomists in favor of *Homo.*

The most numerous samples of *H. erectus* fossils were discovered in China, at the cave site of **Zhoukoudian** near Beijing in the 1920s and 1930s. These fossils, popularly known as "Peking Man," were described by Davidson Black and later by Franz Weidenreich. After making casts of the specimens, Weidenreich arranged for the specimens to be sent to the United States for safekeeping at the outbreak of World War II. The Japanese invasion of China occurred after Weidenreich left China. Soon afterward the fossils were packed up and shipped out under the care of a detachment of U.S. Marines who were being evacuated to the coast. There the marines were to be transferred to an American ship and returned to the United States. The marines were captured, however, and the fossils were lost, and although stories abound as to their whereabouts, they have never been recovered.

Zhoukoudian is dated by both radiometric and by **paleomagnetic dating** methods to between 230,000 and 500,000 years ago. New reconstructions of the fossil skulls have been made (Tattersall and Sawyer, 1996) (see Figure 11–12), and the supposed evidence of fire and cannibalism at the site has been reevaluated (see the accompanying Frontiers box).

Paleoecology and Behavior of *Homo erectus*

Members of the genus *Homo* were the first hominid species who are known to have extended their range outside Africa (Figure 11–13). In Asia, the earliest apparent evidence of *Homo* suggests an age of 1.9 million years, for hominid fossils recovered in Java. In Europe, fossil discoveries from Gran Dolino, in the Atapuerco Hills of northern Spain, date the presence of *Homo* there to more than 780,000 years ago, pushing back the date for the occupation of western Europe by at least 300,000

Zhoukoudian: middle Pleistocene cave site of *Homo erectus* near Beijing, China.

paleomagnetic dating: the matching of a sequence of strata with the dated pattern of changes in magnetic orientation through time, thereby dating the sediments.

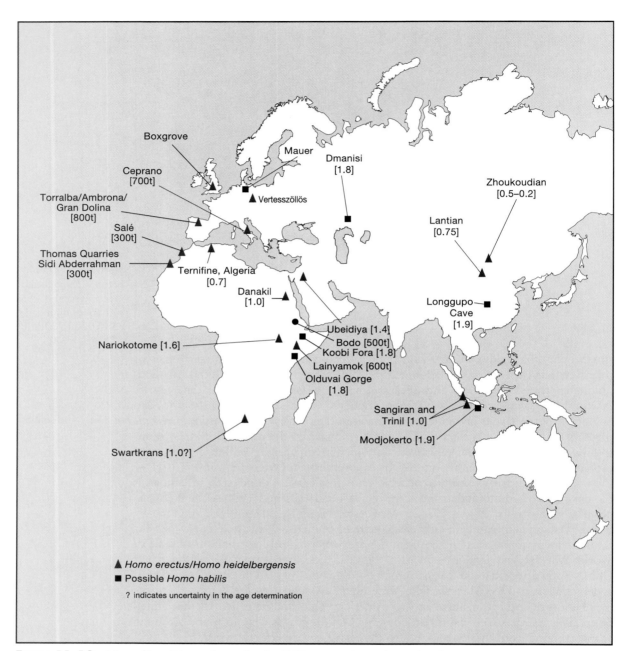

FIGURE 11–13 Map of localities and ages for fossil *Homo* species and associated stone tools. Decimal numbers represent millions of years (i.e., 1.6 = 1,600,000 years). Numbers with a "t" represent thousands of years (i.e., 300t = 300,000). Ages are derived from the use of varying radiometric techniques and biostratigraphic comparisons.

years. Human fossil remains from Gran Dolino consist of a skull and dentition of a boy about 10 to 11 years old, and remains from five other individuals. Descriptions of the youth paint a picture of an individual who possessed both modern and primitive features. The young age of this boy, however, no doubt contributed to some extent to his more modern appearance. It is too early at this point to conclude whether these finds represent yet another species of *Homo* (*H. antecessor*), as claimed by their discoverers, Eudald Carbonell and colleagues (1999), or a western version of *H. erectus*.

FRONTIERS

Zhoukoudian: Neither Hearth nor Home for *Homo erectus*

The fossil remains of *Homo erectus* excavated at the cave site of Zhoukoudian are attributed to more than 40 individuals, one of the largest assemblages of fossil hominids known. Abundant stone tools found at Zhoukoudian showed that these hominids had some form of culture, and a number of archaeologists believed that bone and antlers had been fashioned into their tools as well. The thousands of animal bones found in the cave were naturally attributed to *Homo erectus*'s hunting expertise and culinary refuse, whereas fossil hackberry seeds were put forward as the first paleoanthropological evidence of the vegetarian component of diet. Paleoanthropologists concluded that the hominids lived in the cave where their bones and stone tools were found. In 1975, Chinese paleoanthropologist Chia (Jia) Lan-po published a book whose title succinctly expressed this scenario: "The Cave Home of Peking Man."

Ashes were also found in the sediments at Zhoukoudian, prompting paleoanthropologist Davidson Black to conclude in 1928 that *Homo erectus* had used fire. Some of the ashes, found in vertical patches in the cave wall, looked very much like the remnants of hearths built up over time. A few rare bones showed evidence of burning, and some rocks in the cave were heat-cracked in a way that resembled the rocks around a campfire. This evidence all supported the use of fire for heating and lighting a cold, dark cave, cooking game, and defending against the many large and presumably hungry carnivores of the day. Broken skull bases, split long bones, and possible charring of a hominid bone suggested that *Homo erectus* had also been a cannibal.

Franz Weidenreich (1939) wasn't the first person to toy with the idea of cannibalism, but he went further in its support by suggesting that the brains of some of the individuals found at the Zhoukoudian site had been removed after death through the foramen magnum. Many of these structures were deliberately broken around the edges, supposedly to provide greater access to the brain.

New research is challenging these interpretations of Zhoukoudian. Research by geochemist Stephen Weiner and colleagues (1998), of the Weizmann Institute of Sciences in Israel, indicates that the silica that results from wood-stoked fires is absent from the ashes at Zhoukoudian. The ashes do apparently record some sort of fire in the cave, perhaps the burning of dry guano (from bats or birds) that had accumulated.

And early humans may have set the fires, but it is now clear that the ashes do not record the presence of localized and carefully tended fires, surrounded by stones, used to cook a communal meal and as the focal point of cave life. In short, the ashes at Zhoukoudian are not "hearths" and cannot on present evidence be interpreted in that archaeological context.

New taphonomic research (Boaz and Ciochon, 2001) on the fossils of *Homo erectus* (mostly casts, because the originals have been lost) by Noel Boaz and colleagues show that the very large Pleistocene cave hyena, *Pachycrocuta brevirostris*, could have been responsible for breaking and probably accumulating the early human bones. In fact, the entire cave is reasonably interpreted as a large hyena den, which *Homo erectus* may have visited occasionally to scavenge meat (leaving stone tools and some bone refuse behind), but in which it did not live. And although *Homo erectus* probably did eat their fellow humans from time to time, as cut marks on fossils at other sites indicate, the smashed brain cases and split long bones at Zhoukoudian also fit the pattern of hyena damage. Most of the fossil evidence from Zhoukoudian relates to the dietary behavior of hyenas, not to *Homo erectus*, but research continues at this important site.

Elsewhere in Europe, fossil discoveries confirm the fact that humans had ventured into the region between 800,000 and 900,000 years ago. In 1994 near the Italian town of Ceprano, pieces of a skull that were found associated with chopper tools were dated to this period. According to the Italian paleontologists who discovered and reassembled the skull, its features resemble those of *Homo erectus*, not unexpectedly considering it is a European fossil geographically distinct from the Asian forms, with some distinctive characteristics.

In the same year that the Ceprano fossil was found, British scientists announced the discovery of a tibia, or shin leg bone, as well as hundreds of hand ax tools, from the site of Boxgrove, England. These belong to humans that arrived in Britain some 478,000 to 524,000 years ago. The human remains are more modern looking and the tools are more technologically advanced than those found at Gran Dolina and Ceprano. These sites, and others that have produced tools but not, as yet, hominid remains, demonstrate that from at least 800,000 years ago Europe was continuously occupied by populations of *Homo*.

Ice ages and fire.   Major ice ages began around 900,000 years ago, and the fossil evidence shows that very large carnivores, such as saber-toothed cats and hyenas, were roaming the landscape, which must have made it difficult for humans to survive. As groups pressed into more northern latitudes, they experienced greater seasonal temperature and climatic fluctuations. The colder temperatures likely were important in one of the biggest cultural developments in human history—the control of fire.

The date that hominids first harnessed fire remains an intriguing question. For many years we believed that the earliest evidence of fire—charred bones, pieces of charcoal, and fire-cracked rocks, but not modern humanlike hearths—that was found with *H. erectus* at Zhoukoudian indicated the harnessing of fire. As we pointed out earlier in this chapter, recent studies of the cave's ash levels yielded no silica-rich layers, which would be left by the burning of wood. Wood (as well as grass and leaves) contains silica particles known as *phytoliths,* heat resistant residues that are ubiqui-

FIGURE 11-14   Left: Chinese Acheulean stone tool, one of thousands from the Bose Basin of southern China. Right: Contemporary African Acheulean stone tool. Both are equally refined.

tous in archaeological hearth sites. These results indicate that fire was present in the cave but that its controlled use in hearths was not part of the story (Weiner et al., 1998). Recent excavations at much older sites of Chesowanja and Koobi Fora in Kenya, dated at 1.4 million years ago—that is, about 1 million years earlier than Zhoukoudian—have revealed fire-hardened clay deposits, another indicator of controlled fire use. If this early date for the discovery of fire by humans is upheld by further investigation, early and not late *Homo erectus* would have been responsible.

Acheulean stone tools.   *Homo erectus* was perhaps the first hominid to adapt culturally to forest habitats (Pope, 1988a), making use of bamboo and other nonstone materials. The use of nonstone tools was used to explain why the archaeological record associated with *Homo erectus* in Asia mostly consisted of relatively unsophisticated chopper/chopping tool assemblages, largely lacking the hand axes that are found from this period in Africa and Europe. Recent excavations in the Bose Basin of the Guangxi Zhuang region of southern China, however, has yielded thousands of sophisticated stone tools made about 800,000 years ago (Figure 11–14). This new research casts doubt on the long-standing hypothesis that *Homo erectus* in Asia was less capable culturally of manufacturing stone tools than their contemporaneous African relatives (Yamei et al., 2000). Although the signature piece of the Acheulean, the hand ax, is missing from the Chinese assemblage, to archaeologist Richard Klein of Stanford University, this suggests only that these two separate tool-making traditions had not had recent contact (Yamei et al., 2000).

The stone tools that *H. erectus* did make were technologically more advanced than those of earlier *Homo* species. Beginning archaeology students with practice can generally make Oldowan choppers, but few attain the skill to make an Acheulean hand ax (Figure 11–15), the bifacial stone tool with greatly increased

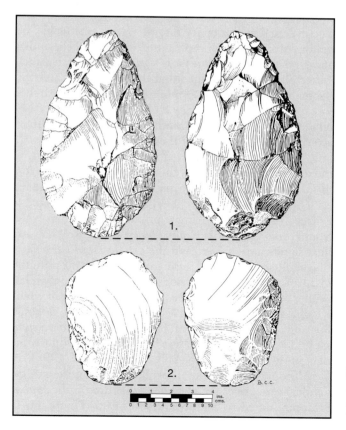

FIGURE 11-15 Top: Acheulean hand ax; bottom: Acheulean cleaver, at about 1 million years ago.

Acheulean: stone tool culture characterized by hand axes, flaked on two sides, thus termed *bifaces.*

cutting edges frequently found associated with *H. erectus.* The assemblages of stone artifacts that include hand axes are referred to by most archaeologists as **Acheulean**, after the site of Saint Acheul in France. The Acheulean assemblage first appears in Africa during Bed II times (1.5 million to 1.2 million years ago) at Olduvai, and it probably evolved from the so-called Developed Oldowan, an advanced type of chopper tradition. Scrapers, flat-edged flaked stone tools, became important during *H. erectus* times, possibly for preparing animal skins for use as clothing.

Social implications.   Using Acheulean tools, *Homo erectus* hunted large animals. The best evidence is at the sites of Torralba and Ambrona in Spain, where hominids successfully hunted and butchered several elephants 500,000 years ago. Hunting large animals has important implications for human behavior. One animal could provide enough meat for a large group, and because it had to be eaten all at once (there was no way to store it), complicated systems of sharing, based on kinship and reciprocity, must have developed. Because hunting large animals was also more dangerous and difficult than catching and killing smaller animals, more complex hunting strategies evolved.

Whether *Homo erectus* could speak is still an open question. Humanlike brain endocasts and the ability to fashion complex stone tools, such as hand axes, have suggested to researchers for some years that *Homo erectus* had the ability to communicate by language. But Ann MacLarnon and colleagues (in Walker and Leakey, 1993) noted in the "Turkana Boy" skeleton from Kenya that the vertebral foramen—the hole through which the spinal cord passes—was significantly smaller than its counterpart in modern humans. These researchers interpreted this anatomical difference to mean that *Homo erectus* had less precise neural control over the breathing muscles needed in humanlike speech. (See the final section in this chapter, "The Evolving Brain and Human Evolution.")

Homo erectus and the Appearance of *Homo sapiens*

The eventual evolutionary fate of *Homo erectus* has been a point of contention for many years. Although most anthropologists believe that *Homo erectus* was broadly ancestral to *Homo sapiens,* a significant minority, including Louis Leakey and Ian Tattersall, have maintained that the species was an extinct side branch and, thus, off the main line leading to *Homo sapiens.* These researchers believe that *H. erectus* was too specialized anatomically to be a direct ancestor of *H. sapiens.* They consider it unlikely that the rounder, thin-boned skull form without heavy brow ridges that characterized early members of the genus *Homo,* such as *H. habilis,* evolved to the long, low, thick, and beetle-browed skull of *Homo erectus,* which then evolved back into the rounder, if much larger, thin-boned skull seen in *Homo sapiens.* But as unlikely as this evolutionary trajectory might seem, an increasing number of fossils support it.

The Buia skull (Figure 11–16) recently discovered in the Danakil Depression of Eritrea, northeastern Africa, provides intriguing evidence of evolutionary change from *Homo erectus* to *Homo sapiens.* The skull has an age of 1 million years and is thus significantly older than the classic *Homo erectus* site of Zhoukoudian, China. The skull shows an interesting combination of primitive and modern features for a fossil of this age. Conclusions, however, remain preliminary, because much of the skull is still embedded in the rock of the deposit in which it was found. The skull has a long, oval-shaped brain case and heavy brow ridges, however, like *Homo erectus.* But unlike the Zhoukoudian fossils (and like *Homo sapiens*), the frontal bone lacks a sagittal keel, and the greatest breadth of the skull is higher up the side of the skull than in the Zhoukoudian skulls (Abbate et al., 1998).

Although the Buia skull probably sits on the *erectus* side of the *erectus–sapiens* divide, there are other specimens that are on the *sapiens* side. The Bodo skull from Ethiopia, dated to about 500,000 years (Figure 11–17), is among the earliest of what we call grade 1 *Homo sapiens.*

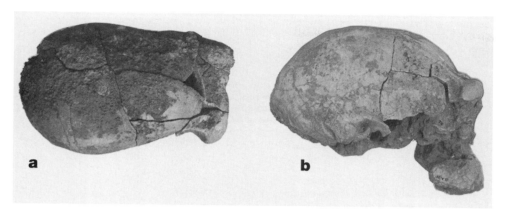

FIGURE 11-16 (a) Anterior and (b) superior views of the Buia cranium, discovered in the Danakil Depression of Eritrea in 1998 and dated to approximately 1 million years ago. The specimen shows a markedly elongated skull and other characteristics that indicate a transitional morphology between *Homo erectus* and *Homo sapiens*.

Increasingly, a number of paleoanthropologists believe that another speciation event occurred after *H. erectus* but before *H. sapiens* and have called this new species *Homo heidelbergensis*. This name, however, is not new. In fact, it was first used to describe a fossilized lower jaw, thought to be pre-Neandertal, that was discovered in 1907 at the site of Mauer, a village near Heidelberg, Germany. The name languished for many years until it was resurrected and expanded to include fossils found throughout the Old World and included in early *Homo sapiens* categories, grades 1 and 2. Consequently, because many researchers believe that *Homo heidelbergensis* holds the key to understanding the ancestry of *Homo sapiens,* many phylogenetic trees have been drawn to reflect these views (Figure 11–18).

Those who prefer to use the name *H. heidelbergensis* rather than *H. erectus* use the following characteristics to distinguish the two species. All would agree that the fossils that are included in *heidelbergensis* originated from *H. erectus* stock about 800,000 years ago in Africa, or, perhaps, western Eurasia. Cranial morphology of the fossils of *heidelbergensis* indicates a large brain, about 1300 cc (50 cubic in.), representing, on average, an approximately 30 percent increase over that of *H. erectus*. Skulls of *heidelbergensis* show a higher cranial vault, and the brow ridges are smaller and separate from one another rather than continuous across the forehead

FIGURE 11-17 Grade 1 archaic *Homo sapiens* skulls from (left to right) Petralona, Greece; Bodo, Ethiopia; and Dali, China. These specimens show *erectus*-like features.

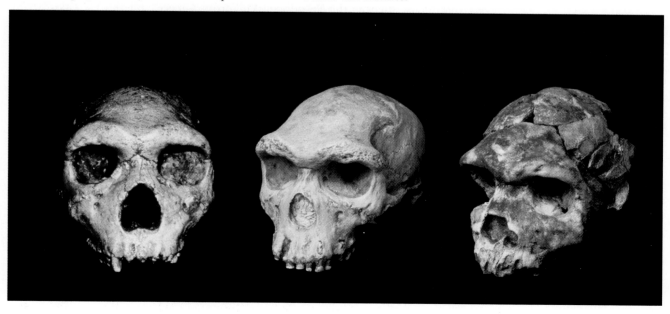

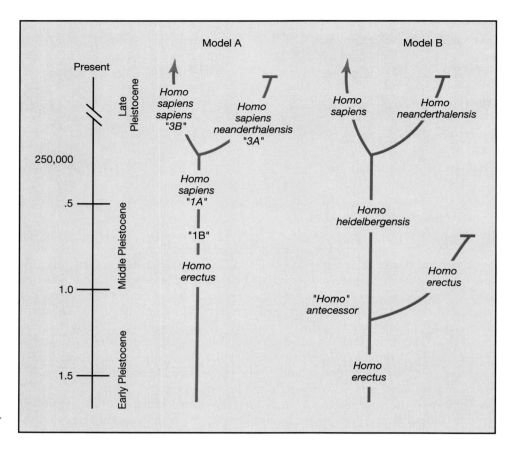

FIGURE 11–18 Two alternative views of mid- to late-Pleistocene human evolution. Model A: *Homo erectus* gives rise to the earliest grade of *H. sapiens,* with a later split that established an isolated population of European/ Middle Eastern Neandertals. Model B: *H. erectus* gives rise to *H. heidelbergensis,* with a later split into two additional species, *H. sapiens* and *H. neanderthalensis. Homo erectus* continues to evolve in parts of Asia until it becomes extinct. One variation of this model includes *H. antecessor* at the base of the *H. heidelbergensis–H. erectus* split.

as seen in *erectus* fossils. The jaws and teeth are generally smaller in size than those of *H. erectus.* One interpretation of the fossil record of this time range is that *H. heidelbergensis* later gave rise to both modern *Homo sapiens,* probably first in Africa, and to the Neandertals of Europe and the Middle East (see Chapter 12).

The transition from *Homo erectus* to *Homo sapiens* seems to have occurred at different times in different parts of the world. As in other human evolutionary transitions, Africa seems to have led the way. Morphologically similar early *Homo sapiens* specimens, such as the Petralona skull from Greece and the Dali skull from China (see Figure 11–17), are known from various parts of the Old World, but they are later in time, dating to around 200,000 years. In Java and the surrounding islands, *Homo erectus* may have lingered on longer than in any other place, possibly because of the isolating effects of the intermittent flooding by rising sea levels. The Ngandong fossils, discovered along the Solo River by G. H. R. von Koenigswald prior to World War II, now dated to only 27,000 to 46,000 years, have many similarities to *Homo erectus.* Some anthropologists classify them as advanced *Homo erectus,* whereas others consider them *erectus*-like *Homo sapiens,* the position that we adopt. Either way, it is clear that the *erectus–sapiens* transition occurred very late in island Southeast Asia.

THE EVOLVING BRAIN AND HUMAN EVOLUTION

The advance of paleoanthropological knowledge of human behavior depends not only on new discoveries of fossil crania and brain endocasts but also on the advancement in knowledge about the workings of the modern human brain. The large size and complexity of the human brain are the most important components of the anatomical and phylogenetic definition of the genus *Homo*. Our knowledge of the evolution of the brain is derived from neurophysiological and anatomical studies of living species and comparative studies of endocasts of fossil species.

Starting about 2 million years ago, some selective advantage resulted in larger brain size, leading to greater intellectual and symbolic abilities. The expansion of the brain was, no doubt, related to a number of factors, including a shift in the way humans procured food. As we have seen, early humans increased their reliance on hunting and effective scavenging of larger game, aided by an increasingly sophisticated technology that produced stone tools. The evolution of large brains, however, was not without its drawbacks and constraints.

Constraints on the Evolution of Large Brains

The radiator hypothesis. As we saw in Chapter 10, structural changes in the pelvis and lower limb were required for habitual bipedalism. In addition, changes in other body structures were required to make this new form of locomotion workable. Dean Falk has promoted the idea that, in the australopithecines, bipedalism was involved in the development of a new means of draining blood from the braincase. In her *radiator hypothesis* of brain evolution, Falk (1992) describes an evolved system in which cerebral blood was drained into an enlarged occipital-marginal sinus (O/M) and, in turn, into the lower vertebral plexus at the base of the skull. According to Falk, this system worked well if the brain was small in size and not overheated by environmental conditions. As a consequence, she believes that the robust australopithecines must have lived in forests rather than out on the hot, open savannas, and that they were limited in terms of brain expansion.

The gracile australopithecines and later members of the genus *Homo*, however, were different. These hominids evolved a "radiator" system of cranial blood drainage, involving a two-way system of emissary veins that passed through small holes in the skull, the emissary foramina. If the temperature of the brain rose, evaporation-cooled blood from the skin could be transferred to the brain; if the brain temperature was at or below body temperature, blood would be drained from the braincase to the vertebral plexus. Selection favored the ever-enlarging brain and an expanding system of emissary veins that kept up with the demands that larger brains would impose. The thermal constraints that had previously kept brain size in check were mostly eliminated by "radiator" cooling of the brains of hominids now able to live on the hot savannas. Consequently, the hominid brain expanded until other constraints, more difficult to overcome anatomically, put the brakes on further enlargement once more.

Narrow birth canal. Perhaps the most difficult obstacle in the way of brain expansion was the simple fact that larger brain size in adult humans meant larger brain size in newborns. Large brain size at birth created problems in the birth process, especially in a hominid whose pelvis, designed for bipedal locomotion, had (relative to a pelvis of a quadruped) a narrow birth canal. The smaller-brained *Australopithecus* probably had no more problems with birth than do chimpanzees (Leutenegger, 1987), because newborn head size was most likely smaller than the opening of the birth canal (Figure 11–19). As the brain enlarged, however, several new factors compensated for a small human birth canal. First, infants were born at increasingly less mature states, which minimized head size; second, the female pelvis changed in shape to maximize the area of the birth canal. Nevertheless, compared with other primates, humans have a small pelvis in relation to neonate head size, and difficult births are the result.

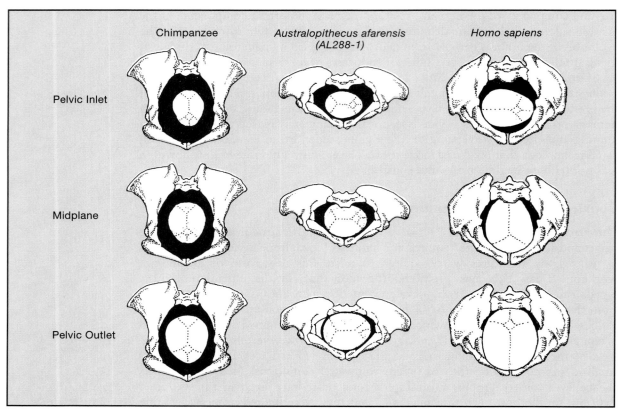

Chimpanzee

Australopithecus afarensis (AL288-1)

Homo sapiens

Pelvic Inlet

Midplane

Pelvic Outlet

FIGURE 11-19   Pelvic size and neonate head size in chimpanzees, *Australopithecus afarensis*, and *Homo sapiens*, showing the very large head of the human neonate.

Although these solutions alleviated some obstetrical problems, they caused others. Because they are born in a relatively undeveloped state, at some point human infants lost the ability to cling to the bodies of their mothers and possessed at birth such poorly developed locomotor skills that much greater effort and care was required from the mother, at least from birth through the first year of life (Figure 11–20). At this point a sexual division of labor may have developed, causing males and females to join together in more stable and longer-term bonds. Modifications of the pelvis involving expansion of the birth canal may also have placed certain limitations on female locomotion, especially on running.

Cerebral Laterality: Two Brains in One

The human neocortex is divided into two cerebral hemispheres (Figure 11–21). Each has somewhat different functions. But what functions do the two hemispheres divide up, and to what degree? Between the hemispheres lies a large tract of fibers, called the **corpus callosum** (Latin, meaning "hard body"), which connects the two halves. Early investigations into the functions of the right and left hemispheres were conducted by Roger Sperry and his colleagues at the California Institute of Technology, who began a series of unique tests on individuals who had "split brains." These patients had histories of *grand mal* epilepsy, a condition that causes a neuroelectrical storm in the brain that disrupts all activity, and had undergone surgical cutting of the corpus callosum. The operation was quite successful not only in reducing the severity of the attacks but also in reducing their frequency in

corpus callosum: the fiber tract connecting across the midline the right and left hemispheres of the brain.

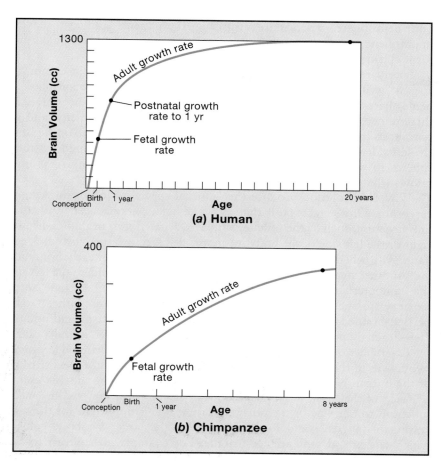

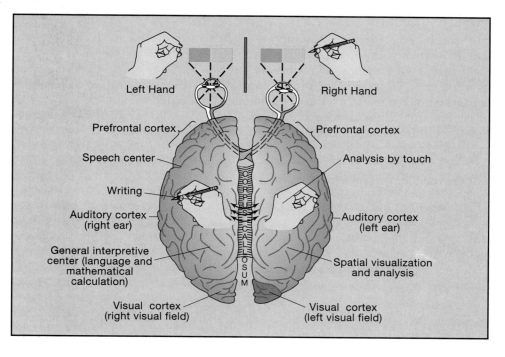

FIGURE 11–20 Brain growth curve in (*a*) humans and (*b*) chimpanzees from conception to adulthood. Differences in the adult growth rates reflect the relative immaturity of human newborns and the "catch up" period of neurological development in the first year of life.

FIGURE 11–21 The human "split brain," showing the cerebral hemispheres and the corpus callosum between them.

both hemispheres. Even more surprising, the patients seemed to have no mental impairment whatsoever. What was a major structure such as the corpus callosum for if cutting it produced no obvious defects?

Sperry received the Nobel Prize in 1981 for his work in demonstrating that speech, writing, and calculation are centered in the left hemisphere. The right hemisphere has a number of capabilities that the left does not have. It can copy three-dimensional diagrams, understand speech, think abstractly, and may be important in the appreciation of music. In general, the right side of the brain controls the left side of the body, and vice versa. The corpus callosum allows the two hemispheres to work together and share information, so that the right brain literally knows what the left brain is doing, and vice versa.

Why did evolution produce this unusual specialization of the two sides of the cerebrum? One suggestion is that only one hemisphere is needed to control a midline structure, such as the tongue. Similarly, *handedness,* or dominance of either the right or the left side of the body for motor tasks, may have evolved, because greater hand skill, whether of the right or the left, was needed in early hominid tool making. Another suggestion is that as the hominid brain expanded, the left side assumed the computerlike capability of calculation and the right became specialized for memory storage. (Current popular thinking that people are either "right-brained" or "left-brained," and that "right-brained" people are artistic and intuitive whereas "left-brained" people are practical and analytical, however, is faulty and simplistic.)

Lateralization, or the development of structural or functional asymmetries in the two halves of the brain, is almost certainly an effect and not a cause of coevolution of the human brain and language. Lateralization is not so much a commitment of one side of the brain to language but rather a segregation of component language functions to one side or the other. The right side is important for the semantic processing of language and for understanding the larger symbolic constructions to which words and sentences contribute. For example, in contrast to simple word meaning, which is lateralized to the left hemisphere, complex ideas, descriptions, narrative, and arguments are processed on the right. Patients with right hemisphere damage have difficulty comprehending the whole of a complex issue.

Language Areas of the Cortex

In 1863 the French physical anthropologist and physician Pierre-Paul Broca announced a discovery based on autopsies of brains of individuals who had lost the ability to speak coherently. In all instances he found that the brain had sustained an injury to the "posterior third of the third frontal convolution." He correctly inferred from this observation that speech ability was localized in this particular part of the brain, now known as **Broca's area** (Figure 11–22). Individuals with damage to this area can utter only short, disjointed fragments of sentences, if they can speak at all. The most surprising aspect of Broca's findings was that the brain injuries affected only the left hemisphere. Broca was one of the first researchers to discover that the cerebral hemispheres have different functions.

In 1874 the German physiologist Karl Wernicke located an area of the temporal lobe that is involved in understanding speech, now known as **Wernicke's area.** Damage to Wernicke's area results in lack of comprehension of both spoken and written language, although the patient can still speak. This area of the brain lies just above the auditory cortex, the part of the temporal lobe that analyzes sound. Like Broca's area, Wernicke's area is bigger on the left side of the brain than on the right side. Interestingly, Wernicke's area is also larger on the left than on the right side in the chimpanzee, which lacks verbal language.

These early successes at locating "language centers" encouraged scientists to look for others. Scientists became convinced that evolution would produce struc-

Broca's area: portion of the cerebral cortex (posterior part of the inferior frontal gyrus, usually on the left side) that is essential for the motor control of speech.

Wernicke's area: portion of the cerebral cortex (parts of the parietal and temporal lobes near the lateral sulcus, usually on the left) that is responsible for understanding and formulating coherent speech.

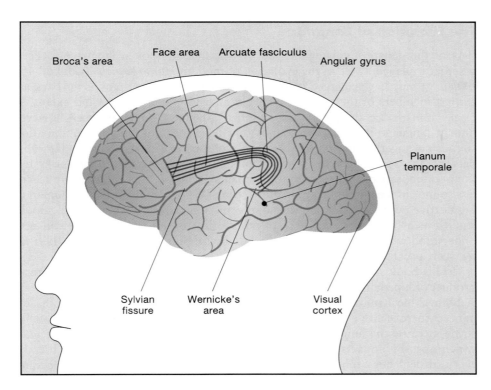

Broca's area
Face area
Arcuate fasciculus
Angular gyrus
Planum temporale
Sylvian fissure
Wernicke's area
Visual cortex

Figure 11–22 Language centers of the brain. Language functions are executed in all major areas of the neocortex. The traditional "centers" are primarily responsible for short-term processing of sensory information, whereas language functions are diffuse.

tural changes in the gross anatomy of the brain, and, if they could find all of the unique structural architecture in the human brain, they might be able to explain language. In the 1960s neuroanatomists thought they had found yet another center for language with the discovery of asymmetries in an area known as the planum temporale (refer to Figure 11–22). In most people the planum temporale is larger on the left side of the brain (although in reality about 25 percent of human brains show no size differences). The planum temporale is believed to be involved in the processing and comprehension of speech and, consequently, to be unique to humans. It is part of the auditory association cortex, with connections to the ear, and it processes sound and sends the information on to other parts of the brain.

Studies by a team led by Patrick Gannon of Mount Sinai Medical School on chimpanzee brains found that in 17 brains examined out of 18, chimpanzees, like most humans, showed size differences in the planum temporale, the left side being larger than the right. Although the function of the planum temporale in chimpanzees is unknown, Terrance Deacon (1997) believes that asymmetry in this area is not likely to be crucial for language. Rather, Gannon's findings support the notion that humans did not evolve new brain structures for language but were able to modify the function of preexisting structures found in other animals.

Today we realize that language functions are executed in all major areas of the neocortex. The traditional "centers" tend to deal with the short-term processing of sensory information, whereas areas progressively farther away function over the long term and with different levels of language integration. For example, there is an integrative progression from parts of words, which are processed in specific areas, to words and phrases, to verbal short-term memory, which is stored in many places in the brain. According to Deacon, symbolic processing, like other aspects of language, is widespread throughout the brain, and this function probably evolved from novel connections rather than from new structures.

The Evolution of Language

Part of the debate involving the first appearance of spoken language focuses on whether it played a role in the evolution of modern *Homo sapiens* (Conkey, 1980). Language may have emerged earlier in human evolution, perhaps as far back as the earliest members of the genus *Homo,* but at what point and to what extent is unclear. Humans use about the same number of sounds as chimpanzees; however, in human language it is not the sounds that have meaning but the combination of sounds put together as words. About the evolution of language, Calvin (1994) ponders the question of how and at what point our ancestors replaced the ape system of "one sound, one meaning" with the human system that uses individually meaningless sounds in meaningful combinations. King (1994:131) believes that human communicative behavior, including social information transfer and language, should be studied as a continuum with that of other primates. Human language can best be understood when compared and contrasted with other forms of information transfer, such as calls and gestures.

In his book *Laughter* (2000), Robert Provine states that speech is a direct byproduct of bipedalism and, thus, an ancient human adaptation. The ability to speak is both a mechanical and neurological issue. In quadrupeds, such as the chimpanzee, there is a one-to-one correlation between breathing pattern and locomotor stride, because the lungs must be fully inflated to add rigidity to the thoracic cage, which absorbs impacts during running. A chimpanzee must take one breath for every stride. They cannot control their breathing independently of their locomotor efforts. As a consequence, articulate speech, a result of exhaling air through the throat, is not possible without major anatomical changes. When hominids stood upright, the thorax was freed of its support function during locomotion, a flexibility that, according to Provine, enabled them to regulate their breathing and, ultimately, to speak. Chimpanzees, in contrast, are unable to manipulate their breathing patterns, limiting them to a simple inhalation–exhalation cycle. Flexible respiratory control made it possible for humans to divide an exhalation into parts and, thus, to speak.

Origins of Modern Language and Speech

Cognitive–neurological perspectives. In 1957, Noam Chomsky of MIT argued that the way in which language develops makes it likely that linguistic ability is innate or instinctual: The brain must have a built-in program, which Chomsky called a *language acquisition device* (LAD), that can put together an inexhaustible array of sentences from a limited number of words. Because individuals often produce sentences that consist of novel combinations of words, it would be difficult to explain such creations solely on the basis of past experiences. He further observed that children before the age of two learn grammatical structure rapidly without any formal training.

More recently, Stephen Pinker (1994), also of MIT, reaffirmed the Chomskian position but disagrees with Chomsky's belief that language abilities emerged as a result of an increase in brain size, passing a crucial threshold with the emergence of modern *Homo sapiens.* Pinker believes that spoken language, in some primitive form, emerged as the result of natural selection early in prehistory. He asserts that the human brain enlarged as a result of the gradual elaboration of language structures and that language provided a survival advantage for early hominids as they developed a hunting and gathering mode of subsistence.

Lynn Schepartz (1993) of the University of Michigan provides some useful definitions of language. First, she notes that language has both internal (cerebral) and external (vocal tract) components. The internal components involve conscious thought that includes "complex mapping and simulation of the world" around us.

The external components are basically behavioral expressions, which include gestures, vocalizations, and articulate speech. **Speech** may be defined as a coordination of activity of both the brain and the vocal apparatus. Spoken language is unique to humans.

speech: the set of verbal sounds used by humans in language.

In determining the origin of language, some believe that it is important to know when humans first gained the ability to name objects. Washburn (1960) believed that the situation that originally led to naming was tool making of a kind more complicated than that performed by chimpanzees. Others believe that some early form of language may have arisen as a more sophisticated system for communicating the location and type of dispersed food or of important individuals, such as close kin. Such vocal communication may also have become more elaborate as a response to the requirements of coordinating individuals in cooperative hunting (Parker and Gibson, 1979; Parker, 1985).

Aiello and Dunbar's (1993) hypothesis, that the size of the brain is the key to understanding cognitive ability and language, is based on a close relationship between relative neocortex size, group size, and the amount of time needed to devote to "social grooming." They believe that group size is limited by the number of relationships that an individual can successfully monitor and that this, in turn, is limited by the relative size of the neocortex. They theorize that hominid group size would have been too great to be sustained by methods of social grooming such as those used by nonhuman primates, and they conclude that language evolved as a binding mechanism for large groups.

Certainly as time went on language would have played a more important role in encoding complex cultural rules. These rules involved ritual, the control and regulation of reproduction, resource distribution, and other rules that ritually transform people's reproductive status through important rites of passage (Hockett and Asher, 1964).

Language and the use of tools. Other attempts to answer the question of language origin use interpretations based on the archaeological record. To what extent can technological ability be correlated with neurological complexity and language? Nick Toth and Kathy Schick caution that technological change results from need and demand. Unlike anatomical change, which often occurs quite slowly, technological development usually proceeds independently at a much faster rate. As Toth and Schick point out, "the challenge is to identify what patterns of material culture in the prehistoric record have implications for intelligence and language" (1993:346).

As we saw earlier in this chapter, the earliest Oldowan stone tools are technologically quite simple, consisting mainly of discarded cores used for flake production. Toth and Schick believe that there is little evidence that early hominid tool makers had a "mental template" for constructing Oldowan tools. Instead, the final shape of the "tool" was probably determined by size, shape, and raw material of the rock being flaked. Wynn (1988) agrees and believes that the construction of Oldowan tools involved only rote learning of a sequence of specific actions that could be transmitted visually.

The Acheulean tool tradition, the second phase of what archaeologists call the **Lower Paleolithic,** presents a different picture. The skills required to make these artifacts are much more sophisticated. Acheulean tool makers had the ability to conceive of a predetermined shape and to construct it. They had the ability to flake and produce a straight cutting edge and, apparently with cultural standardization, they could produce consistently shaped tools (see Figures 11–14 and 11–15). If the Acheulean tool makers had limited or no language skills; their geographic dispersion would have made cultural uniformity difficult. The fact that tools of the Acheulean industry are found throughout the Old World speaks in favor of greater communicative skills in early *Homo.*

Lower Paleolithic: period that featured Oldowan choppers and flakes and Acheulean tools, such as the hand ax.

Do we know when language through speech came about? Certainly the origin of speech is impossible to determine from the fossil record alone, and comparative anatomy of the apes and modern humans has mainly served only to frame the questions that we might ask. Apes have this sort of a brain and vocal apparatus and can't speak, and modern humans show these differences and can speak. To go from point A to point B the vocal apparatus and the brain had to evolve in certain ways.

The process of evolving speech, obviously, was a very gradual one that took place over several hundreds of thousands of years. It may be that the process started when early hominids first began to use stone tools, but the experts can't agree at what point speech is necessary to achieve a certain level of sophistication in tool making.

Some things we do know. The language process did involve changes in the sound producing anatomy of the vocal apparatus. But these changes are ambiguous in terms of what they might tell us about language origins. For example, creating words from sounds is a particular function of the larynx; a low larynx in the throat differentiates modern humans from apes. The position of the larynx, in turn, is related to the flexion of the basicranium, which remained unflexed and apelike, through *Homo erectus*. Tongue musculature and the position of the hyoid bone are also part of the story. In humans the smaller oral cavity and location of the attachment of the tongue musculature enables the tongue to move quickly in the mouth creating the various consonants of speech. In these last two criteria for speech *Homo erectus* joins modern humans and is distinctive from the condition seen in the apes.

As the brain and vocal apparatus evolved in a kind of feedback loop, speech developed gradually. Each small change provided some increased ability and added to an individual's communicative skills. If the evolution of speech, as most experts agree, was a continuum that had no perceptible breaks in it, then only arbitrary decisions will ever allow us to say, "now we spoke."

◖ SUMMARY

1. **What are the major differences between early *Homo* species and the australopithecines?**

   The larger brain is the most characteristic difference that differentiates members of the genus *Homo* from the australopithecines. Most australopithecine brains are no larger than about 550 cc (33 cubic in.) whereas early members of the genus *Homo* show brain sizes well above 600 cc (36 cubic in.). Ratios of brain size to body weight are also significantly different and the encephalization quotient is much higher in *Homo*. The teeth, especially the molars, underwent a reduction in size and lost the more complex crenulations of the occlusal surface. Overall body size and weight increased substantially to modern proportions. Members of the genus *Homo* are characterized by longer, lower limbs and relatively shorter, upper limbs. Increase in lower limb length meant increased length of *Homo*'s walking stride.

2. **When and where did individuals of early *Homo* live? What are the evolutionary relationships of this group to the earlier australopithecines and later species of the genus *Homo*?**

   The earliest members of the genus *Homo* were first described in the species *Homo habilis* from Olduvai Gorge, Tanzania, in the 1960s. Since that time other fossils of *Homo*, perhaps representing different species (such as *rudolfensis*) have been recovered from sites in East Africa dating to about 2 million years ago. The traditional view has been that early members of the genus *Homo* evolved from gracile australopithecine stock about 2.4 million years ago, possibly from the species described as *A. garhi*. This australopithecine species is the only one so far known to have stone tools associated with it. Although it is unclear which species is represented by the fossil evidence found outside of Africa, members of the genus *Homo* have been discovered on the island of Java as early as 1.9 million years ago and elsewhere in Asia by 1.4 million years ago. Possibly members of the species *Homo habilis* by 1.6 million years ago gave rise to larger-brained individuals of the species early *Homo erectus* or *Homo ergaster* by another name.

3. **When and where were the first stone tools made? In addition to tool use, what is known about the cultural adaptations of *Homo* species of the early and middle Pleistocene?**

The earliest evidence for stone tool use comes from Africa, specifically from the site of Gona, Afar, Ethiopia, dated about 2.5 million years ago. These tools are associated with late species of the genus *Australopithecus, A. garhi*. Mary Leakey was one of the first archeologists to categorize the earliest stone tools as Oldowan, primarily consisting of chopper and simple flake type tools. Evidence suggests that early *Homo* built shelters and hunted or scavenged large game animals, such as the hippopotamus. The home range of early *Homo* apparently increased to take advantage of greater foraging or hunting opportunities. Nuclear families may have been the basic social group. Men may have hunted or scavenged, and women may have collected different foodstuffs in an early division of labor. Women's gathering activities, based on analogy to modern hunters and gatherers, may have provided most of the daily nutritional intake for these early humans. Early species of *Homo* probably used fire for many reasons, but the evidence that points to a time or place of the first use of fire in a controlled manner is ambiguous.

4. **When and where did members of the species *Homo erectus* first appear? What does the fossil record tell us about the distribution of *Homo erectus* in terms of time and space?**

According to some researchers, fossils classified as *Homo erectus* are first found in African deposits as early as 1.6 million years ago. Although the taxonomic attribution has not gone unchallenged, and different labels have been given to these fossils (e.g., *Homo ergaster*), they do possess many features that relate them to later individuals of the middle Pleistocene (about 500,000 years ago). By middle Pleistocene times, Asia, at least, was populated by *Homo erectus*, a point of agreement among most experts. Cave sites in China, such as Zhoukoudian, provide many insights into the lives and behavior of these peoples. Hominids appeared in Europe only about 900,000 years ago, later than they did in Asia. These hominids share certain features with Asian *Homo erectus*, and some, such as the fossil remains from Ceprano, Italy, have even been described as *Homo erectus*. Other researchers claim that the differences that can be seen in the European fossils warrant species distinction and classify them as *Homo heidelbergensis*. By about 300,000 to 400,000 years ago, fossils labeled archaic *Homo sapiens* appear and are differentiated in part from the earlier *Homo erectus* by a larger brain (more than 1,200 cc, 72 cubic in.) and changes in cranial shape.

5. **What current theories attempt to explain human language and its origin? How is the structure of the human brain related to language ability?**

The evolution of large brains was not without drawbacks. The advantages that a large brain and increased intelligence provided early *Homo*, however, must have outweighed the disadvantages. Language through speech must have been very important to early *Homo*, increasing their capability to name objects and communicate about events that occurred in the past and those that might happen in the future. The communication systems of the nonhuman primates are not well designed to accomplish this sort of information exchange. The origin of human language may, in some way, be related to the development of a technology more sophisticated than that seen in the modern apes. Stone tool making has been cited by many experts as a critical component that launched hominids into speech. Other experts claim that speech was only possible after the brain and vocal apparatus evolved sufficiently. Experts do not agree, however, at what point this may have happened. Some claim that modern language and speech appeared late in human evolution and was part of complex factors that marked the emergence of modern *Homo sapiens*.

The modern human brain contains a number of important areas that deal with language. Researchers became convinced that evolution produced structural changes in the gross anatomy of the brain and that by understanding this unique cerebral architecture, we might be able to explain language and how it evolved. Today, we realize that language functions are executed in all major areas of the neocortex. The traditional centers deal mainly with the short-term processing of sensory information, whereas other areas function over the long term and with different levels of language integration.

◀ CRITICAL THINKING QUESTIONS

1. The fossil record of the late Pliocene/early Pleistocene suggests that there may have been several species of larger-brained *Homo* and at least one group of robust australopithecine present at the same time in Africa. All of these forms were bipedal in their locomotor adaptations. Generally speaking, under what conditions could all of the hoiminids have existed in the same ecosystem?

2. From the fossil evidence it is apparent that Europe was occupied much later by hominids than was Asia, perhaps by as much as 1 million years. What factors may have accounted for this late dispersal into Europe or, for that matter, an earlier dispersal into Asia?

3. If the ash accumulations at the Zhoukoudian cave do not record the presence of hearths or localized fires, what other possible explanations could there be to explain these deposits?

4. From recent archaeological discoveries in China, it now appears that Asian *Homo erectus* did construct tools of the Acheulean type in the same fashion as did other hominids in Africa and Europe. If two species of hominid coexisted during the middle Pleistocene (*erectus* and *heidelbergensis*), how would you account for the fact they both possessed the same tool culture?

5. What is the advantage, if any, of lateral asymmetry in the human neocortex? Why are certain functions, such as handedness and language, controlled by one side of the neocortex or the other? What advantages might lateralization have provided to our ancestors?

◀ INTERNET EXERCISES

Critical Thinking

Big Brains. Chapter 11 surveyed some of the benefits and costs of the large hominid brain as well as some key brain structures that allow humans to reason and to communicate. For this exercise, attempt to answer the following questions about brain evolution:

1. What circumstances—biological, cultural, or ecological—might have led to the evolution of complex human language?

2. What does it mean to say that the "language centers" of the brain are not solely responsible for language? Is it significant that these same structures exist in non-human primates?
3. What unique human adaptation—for example, bipedality, language, the use of fire—is the most critical to "humanness"? In other words, what, in your opinion, makes us human? Why?

Writing Assignment

Homo erectus. Research one aspect of current knowledge about *Homo erectus,* the first hominid to migrate out of Africa. Write a research paper about one of the following topics or another of your own choosing: culture, body structure, differences among populations, notable fossils, or coexistence with other *Homo* species.

See Companion Web site for Internet links.

The Boxgrove site, in England, has yielded a tibia, or shin leg bone, as well as hundreds of hand ax tools. These belongs to humans who arrived in Britain some 478,000 to 524,000 years ago. The human remains are more modern looking and the tools are more technologically advanced than those found at Gran Dolina and Ceprano. These sites, and others that have produced tools but not, as yet, hominid remains, demonstrate that from at least 800,000 years ago, Europe was continuously occupied by populations of *Homo*.

The Boxgrove site was used for hunting and butchering over tens of thousands of years, beginning at the end of a major glaciation. For much of this time, the climate was similar to that of today, although the fauna was very different. Wild rhinoceros, horses, deer, and bear were abundant.

WEB ACTIVITY

The Quicktime video describes the Boxgrove site and the people who lived there. After viewing it, consider these questions about the people who inhabited this site more than half a million years ago.

Activity

1. Why was this a good area for human activities? What kind of society do these activities imply?
2. What social skills are suggested by the activities carried out at Boxgrove? What cognitive skills?
3. What technological skills are suggested? What implications arise from the fact that technology did not change over tens of thousands of years of occupation?

The MediaLab can be found in Chapter 11 on your Companion Web site http://www.prenhall.com/boaz

HOMO SAPIENS

12

O U T L I N E

After reading this chapter, you should be able to discuss the following questions:

1. What were the key anatomical characteristics of early *Homo sapiens,* including the Neandertals?
2. Describe the key behavioral characteristics of archaic *Homo sapiens* and Neandertals, including tool use and other aspects of culture.
3. What theories account for the appearance of modern humans? What is the most important evidence in favor of each?
4. Describe the physical and cultural features, including tool use and the use of symbols, that distinguish archaic from modern *Homo sapiens.*

As we have seen, *Homo erectus* managed to colonize most of the Old World. Although we are reasonably certain that the earliest *Homo sapiens* superseded *Homo erectus,* the timing, geography, ecological settings, and evolutionary contexts for this replacement are still areas of active research. At least one group of researchers has presented compelling evidence that *Homo erectus* and *Homo sapiens* may have overlapped in places such as Java (Swisher et al., 1996). Did *Homo sapiens* evolve from *Homo erectus* across a broad front worldwide, or did the former evolve from one localized population of *Homo* and spread out to populate the rest of the world, as most of the molecular interpretations now indicate? Was there interbreeding between the immigrants and the resident populations, or were the latter totally replaced?

TABLE 12–1	Important Fossil Discoveries of *Homo sapiens*	
Site, Locality	**Fossil Remains**	**Years Before Present**
***Homo sapiens,* Grade 1 (also classified as *Homo heidelbergensis*)**		
Mauer (Heidelberg), Germany	Mandible	400–700,000
Kabwe (Broken Hill), Zambia	Skull	130–250,000
Bodo, Ethiopia	Skull	600,000
Salé, Morocco	Skull	200–300,000
Dali, China	Skull	180–230,000
Petralona, Greece	Skull	over 230,000
Bilzingsleben, Germany	Skull	230–340,000
Atapuerca, Spain	Various	300,000
***Homo sapiens,* Grade 2 (also classified as *Homo heidelbergensis*)**		
Ndutu, Tanzania	Skull	200–400,000
Steinheim, Germany	Skull	150,000
Narmada, India	Skull	150,000
Saccopastore, Italy	Skull	120,000
Arago, France	Skull	400,000
Swanscombe, England	Partial skull	150,000

The fossil evidence of *Homo sapiens* is much more extensive than that of early *Homo* or of the australopithecines. Many of the later forms of *Homo sapiens* buried their dead, a cultural innovation that accounts for the fact that the fossils are better preserved. In many cases artifacts were placed in graves along with remains, and, as a consequence, many cultural items have been found in direct association with the fossils. This is quite a different situation from the one we encountered in the earlier fossil record, where both tools and fossils were found, but not in the same context, leaving us with the question, who were the tool makers?

Because of a more sophisticated technology, which we describe in detail later in this chapter, *Homo sapiens* came to settle in areas unoccupied by earlier peoples. *Homo sapiens* thus became the most geographically widespread species of any hominid.

The classification of *H. sapiens* is complex. We have organized this information by using a **grade** system for the evolutionary stages of *Homo sapiens*. This system, presented in Table 12–1, allows us to organize the evolving human lineage in terms of morphological complexity. Table 12–1 lists the major fossil specimens for each grade. Each grade is chronologically dated by a variety of techniques (see Appendix 4). The timeline for this chapter is presented in Figure 12–1, and Figure 12–2, p. 315 shows one scheme for possible evolutionary relationships among the recognized species of *Homo* leading up to modern peoples.

grade: level of organization or morphological complexity in an evolving lineage of organisms.

PHYSICAL CHARACTERISTICS OF EARLY *HOMO SAPIENS*

Grade 1

The most primitive representatives of our species, *Homo sapiens* Grade 1, appeared perhaps as early as 700,000 years ago. These fossils are characterized by a rounded skull vault, lacking the sagittal keel and pronounced occipital bun of *H. erectus*

Site, Locality	Fossil Remains	Years Before Present
Homo sapiens, Grade 3A (also classified as H. sapiens neanderthalensis and H. neanderthalensis)		
Neander Valley, Germany	Skull cap/postcrania	100,000
La Chapelle aux Saints, France	Skull/skeleton	50,000
La Ferrassie, France	Skull	70,000
St. Césaire, France	Skull	32–36,000
Shanidar, Iraq	Skeletons	50–70,000
Homo sapiens, Grade 3B (also known as modern Homo sapiens sapiens)		
Omo, Ethiopia	Skulls lacking faces	120,000
Klasies River Mouth, South Africa	Cranial fragments	100,000
Qafzeh, Israel	Skeletons	100,000
Skhul, Israel	Skeletons	90,000

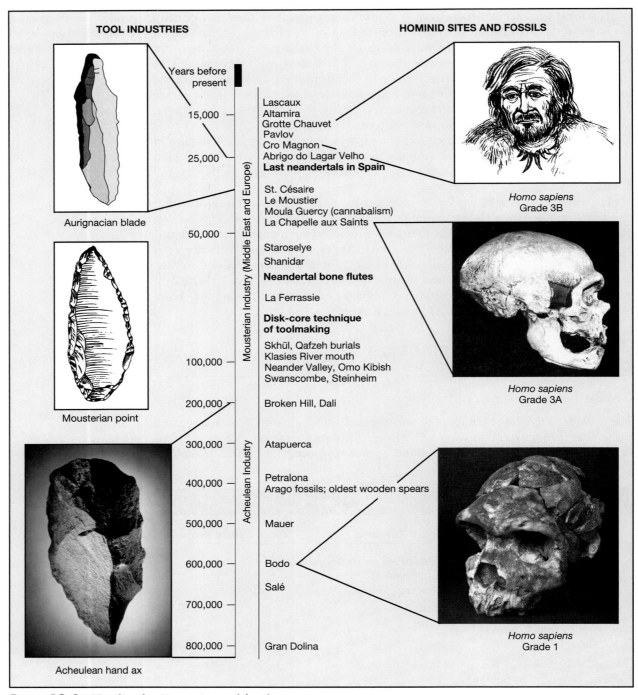

TOOL INDUSTRIES

Aurignacian blade

Mousterian point

Acheulean hand ax

Years before present

15,000

25,000

50,000

100,000

200,000

300,000

400,000

500,000

600,000

700,000

800,000

Mousterian Industry (Middle East and Europe)

Acheulean Industry

Lascaux
Altamira
Grotte Chauvet
Pavlov
Cro Magnon
Abrigo do Lagar Velho
Last neandertals in Spain

St. Césaire
Le Moustier
Moula Guercy (cannabalism)
La Chapelle aux Saints

Staroselye
Shanidar
Neandertal bone flutes

La Ferrassie

**Disk-core technique
of toolmaking**

Skhūl, Qafzeh burials
Klasies River mouth
Neander Valley, Omo Kibish
Swanscombe, Steinheim

Broken Hill, Dali

Atapuerca

Petralona
Arago fossils; oldest wooden spears

Mauer

Bodo

Salé

Gran Dolina

HOMINID SITES AND FOSSILS

Homo sapiens
Grade 3B

Homo sapiens
Grade 3A

Homo sapiens
Grade 1

FIGURE 12–1 Timeline for *Homo* sites and fossils.

(refer back to Figure 11–17). The brow ridges are still prominent, but unlike in *H. erectus,* the ridges are thickest over the medial part of the orbit, and they blend smoothly into the frontal bone behind. The cranial capacity of Grade 1 *Homo sapiens* is greater than that of *Homo erectus,* although both are substantially lower than modern human values (Figure 12–3). The changes in the teeth from *H. erectus* to *H. sapiens* are limited to slight reductions in overall size.

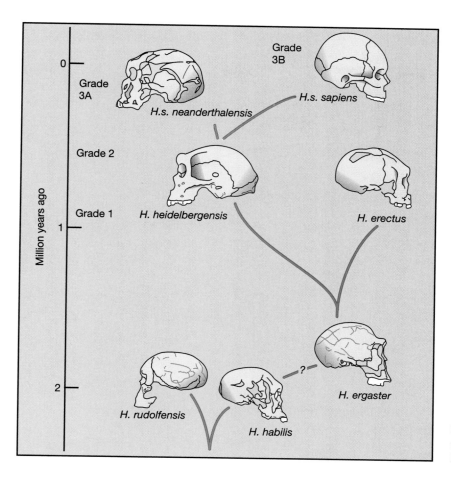

FIGURE 12–2 Possible evolutionary relationships among known species of *Homo*.

Grade 1 *H. sapiens* occurred throughout the Old World, except probably in the northernmost latitudes (Figure 12–4). Broken Hill or Kabwe (Zambia), Bodo (Ethiopia), and Salé (Morocco) have provided ample evidence of earliest *Homo sapiens* in Africa. Petralona (Greece), a mandible from Mauer, near Heidelberg (Germany), skull fragments from Bilzingsleben (Germany), and numerous fossil remains from Gran Dolina, Spain, are among the earliest evidences for *Homo sapiens* in Europe. Numerous fossil remains from Ngangdong (Java) and a skull from Dali (China) attest to earliest *Homo sapiens* in Asia. Some of these fossils, particularly those found in Mauer, Bilzingsleben, and Ngangdong, have also been referred to as different species (*Homo heidelbergensis* for the fossils from Europe and *Homo*

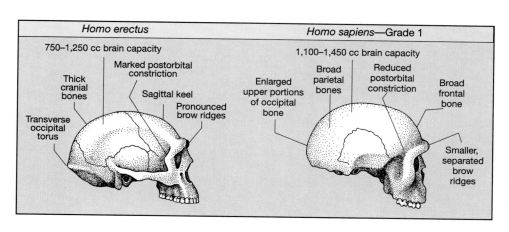

FIGURE 12–3 Comparison of cranial features of *Homo erectus* and *Homo sapiens* Grade 1. *Homo sapiens* Grade 1 is also sometimes referred to as *Homo heidelbergensis*.

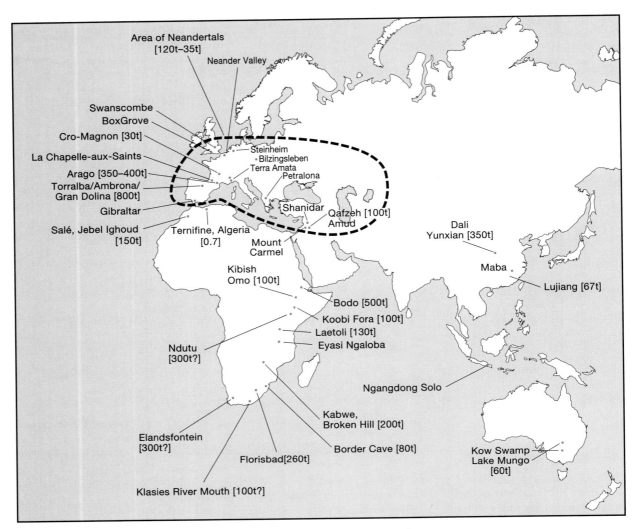

FIGURE 12-4 Map of localities and ages for *Homo sapiens*. Decimal numbers represent millions of years (i.e., 1.6 = 1,600,000 years). Numbers with a "t" represent thousands of years (i.e., 300t = 300,000). Ages are derived from the use of varying radiometric techniques and biostratigraphic comparisons.

erectus for the fossils from Asia). The morphology of these specimens makes a good case for the evolution of *Homo sapiens* from earlier *Homo* populations.

What do the anatomical changes seen in earliest *H. sapiens* mean in terms of changes in behavior or adaptation, and what selective forces led to these changes? One trend is clear: increasing cranial capacity. Selection in the earliest *Homo sapiens* strongly favored greater brain size and, presumably, increased cerebral ability.

Grade 2

Homo sapiens Grade 2 probably ranges in time from approximately 300,000 to somewhat less than 100,000 years ago, although the ages of the fossils in many cases are unclear. The skulls of this grade have lost the *erectus*-like characteristics, and their vaults are higher.

The evidence for these hominids in Europe and Africa is good (refer to Table 12–1 and Figures 12–1 and 12–4). The Saccopastore (Italy), Arago (France)

(Figure 12–5), and Ndutu (Tanzania) specimens are the best representatives, along with two well-studied partial skulls from Swanscombe (England) and Steinheim (Germany). Asia, so far, has yielded few, if any, Grade 2 *H. sapiens* fossils. *H. sapiens* Grade 2 provides a good evolutionary source for modern *Homo sapiens,* both Grade 3A (Neandertal) and Grade 3B (anatomically modern *Homo sapiens*).

Anatomically Modern Humans (Grade 3B)

In 1868, outside of the village of Les Eyzies in the Dordogne region of France, railway workers digging in a hillside uncovered a cache of ancient human bones and tools. The skeletal remains, which belonged to at least three adults and an infant of two or three weeks of age, looked modern, yet the presence of stone tools, perforated nonhuman teeth, and seashells indicated that the remains were of some antiquity. The rock shelter that these workers had dug into carried the name **Cro-Magnon,** and this name has stuck to all western European fossils of nomadic **Upper Paleolithic** peoples who lived somewhere between 35,000 and 10,000 years ago. Since the time of this early discovery of modern peoples, numerous sites from around the world have yielded their fossil remains and artifacts.

Anatomically modern humans (*Homo sapiens sapiens,* Grade 3B) appear around 100,000 or more years ago. Some of the earliest fossil evidence for modern *Homo sapiens* comes from Africa and the Middle East, far earlier than their first appearance in Europe. New dates from Israel indicate that the fossils from the Qafzeh cave near Nazareth are 100,000 years old (Figure 12–6). The more fragmented remains from the Klasies River Mouth caves in South Africa range in time from 120,000 to 90,000 years (Figure 12–7). Fossils found in Asia are also older than those from Europe. At Liujiang, a cave site in southern China, modern human fossil remains have been dated at 67,000 years ago, and at Lake Mungo, southern Australia, new dates indicate that the fossils there are about 60,000 years old. As we piece together the story of the migration of modern *Homo sapiens,* it appears that Europe was one of the last places our species arrived.

How did modern humans differ from earlier or contemporary archaic peoples? Certainly, the bones of *H. sapiens sapiens* are overall less massive than those of earlier peoples or of their contemporaries, the Neandertals (whom we describe later in this chapter). Modern skulls show a shortened base, and the face lacks the heavy brow ridges over the orbits. Instead, the frontal bone ascends vertically, producing a high, straight forehead. The midface is not prognathic, and the teeth do not jut for-

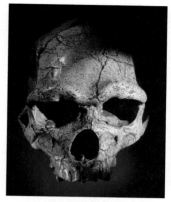

FIGURE 12–5 *Homo sapiens* Grade 2 skull from Arago Cave, France. Some researchers classify this specimen as *H. heidelbergensis.*

Cro-Magnon: cave site in southern France where late Pleistocene anatomically modern humans were first found.

Upper Paleolithic: a series of late Pleistocene cultures typified by a diversification of traditions and stone tools made from blades struck from cores; associated with anatomically modern humans; about 40,000 to 10,000 years ago.

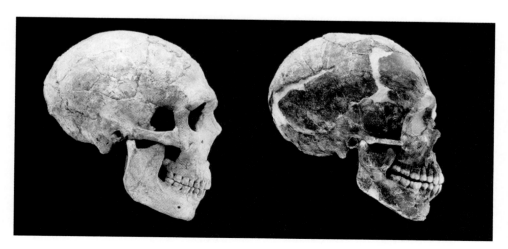

FIGURE 12–6 Fossil evidence documenting anatomical variation in Grade 3 *Homo sapiens.* Left: *H. sapiens sapiens* (Grade 3A) from the site of Qafzeh, in Israel, dated to about 100,000 years ago. Right: *H. sapiens* skull from Jebel Irhoud, Morocco, dated between 125,000 and 90,000 years ago. The Qafzeh skull shows much more modern human anatomy than does the penecontemporaneaus Jebel Irhaud specimen.

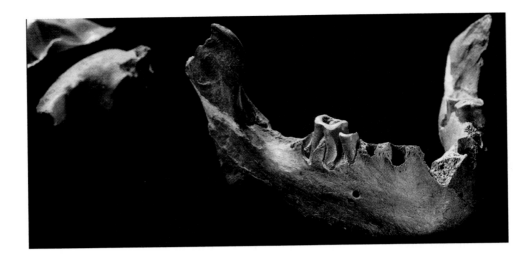

FIGURE 12-7 Mandible from Klasies River, South Africa. This specimen is 90,000 years old.

ward as in the Neandertals (see Figure 12–6). A prominent chin at the front of the lower jaw replaces the receding symphysis typical of earlier peoples, an anatomical response accounted for by smaller teeth and a less prognathic midface. Reconstruction of the postcranial skeleton shows that modern individuals were generally taller than the Neandertals (Figure 12–8).

Geographical expansion continued as the environment changed. The last phases of the last glaciation (sometimes referred to as the Wurm) caused sea levels to drop as much as 350 ft (115 m), exposing landmasses that had previously been under water (Figure 12–9, p. 320). Although land bridges never completely connected Australia to the Southeast Asian mainland, the exposure of much of the bottom of the shallow seas that surround neighboring islands of present day Malaysia and Indonesia increased the area of these land features and made short sea voyages feasible.

It appears that early modern peoples made their way into Australia by boat as early as 60,000 years ago, much earlier than researchers had previously believed. Stone tools discovered at the site of Malakunanja (Arnhem Land, Northern Territory) have been dated to about 55,000 years ago, and the Lake Mungo site has yielded fossil human bones that date to 60,000 years ago. The bones were recovered as part of an elaborate burial that included the use of red ochre powder, a substance that is used in burials elsewhere in the world. Australia had generally been regarded as one of the last places in the Old World that modern humans occupied because of the boat building and navigational skills needed to reach the continent.

Peopling the New World. The Bering Sea between Siberia and Alaska also became a land bridge during these times of expanding ice sheets. This allowed people to spread into the New World at different times between 30,000 and 9,000 years ago along the sea coasts or through ice-free corridors from Alaska and northern Canada down to the more temperate areas of North America. There is evidence that big-game hunters were living in Siberia by 30,000 years ago (Figure 12–10, p. 321). It is evident that groups of these hunters began crossing into the Americas soon after this. They followed herds of now-extinct animals into an area devoid of other humans, apparently much earlier than the first recognized Clovis cultural tradition of 11,000 years ago. Archaeologists previously thought that the fluted stone projectile points that characterize the Clovis culture, first found at a site in Clovis, New Mexico, were evidence of these first immigrants. In recent years, however, a number of well-dated and researched sites have been excavated that are clearly earlier than the Clovis sites. Tools and the remains of mastodons dating to

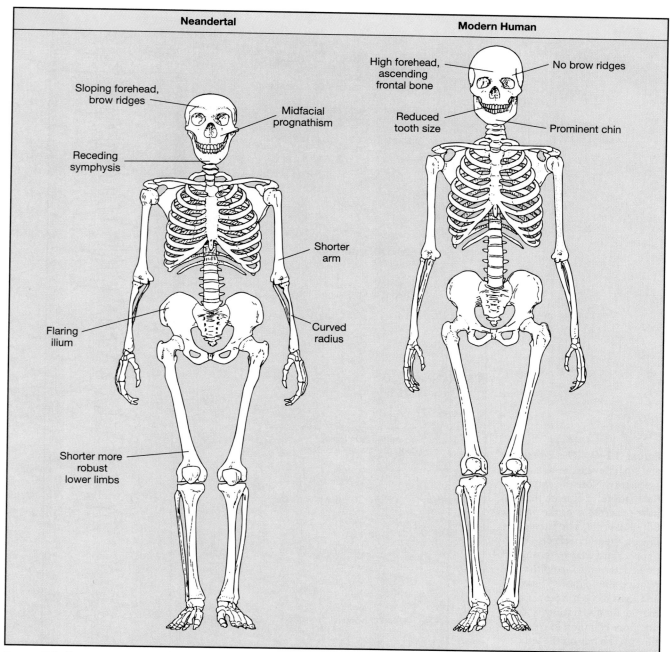

FIGURE 12–8 Comparison of skeletons of Neandertal (reconstructed) and modern *Homo sapiens*. The Neandertals tended to have more robust bones than modern humans, and their limbs tended to be shorter.

13,000 years ago were found in Taima-Taima, Venezuela. An entire village, later covered by a peat bog that preserved stone and wood tools, huts, and mastodon meat, was excavated at Monte Verde, Chile. This important site, located nearly at the tip of South America, was also dated to 13,000 years ago.

Another example of pre-Clovis sites is at Meadowcroft, Pennsylvania, which was studied by archaeologists from the University of Pittsburgh and determined to be between 19,000 and 16,000 years old. It is clear from this evidence that human

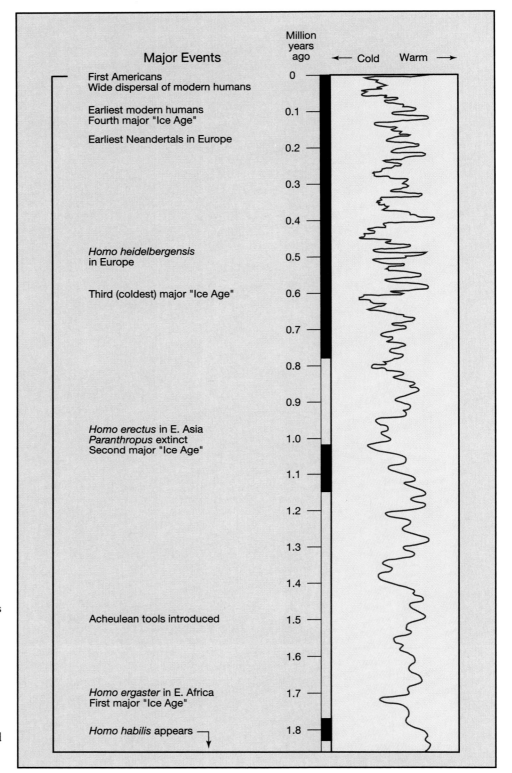

FIGURE 12-9 The ice ages and major events in human prehistory. Note the extreme fluctuations of climate that have occurred over the past 800,000 years. The curved line on the right reflects temperature change through time, determined from the relative abundance of heavy and light oxygen isotopes in marine fossils. (Heavy isotopes are more common in colder times.) The bar on the left represents reversals in the earth's magnetic field: Black segments are periods in which magnetism was like that of today, and white segments are reversed periods, when compasses would have pointed to the South Pole rather than the North Pole.

FIGURE 12-10 Diorama at the American Museum of Natural History reconstructing one of the 15,000-year-old, mammoth-bone huts excavated in Mezhirich, Ukraine. This hut was one of four, each of which was covered by a distinct arrangement of mammoth bones. This hut was built of 17 tons of bones, representing the remains of 95 mammoths, which probably died of natural causes.

occupation of the New World occurred much earlier than previously believed. How much earlier will await the results of work on other sites on both continents.

The Neandertals

By a strange linguistic coincidence, "Neandertal" means "valley of the new man," an appropriate name for the site that provided the first generally recognized human fossil. It was named for Joachim Neumann, a Dusseldorf clergyman and hymn writer of the mid-seventeenth century, who wrote under the name of "Neander," meaning "new man" in Greek. *Tal* (formerly *thal*) is German for "valley."

In 1856, limestone quarrymen found remains of a skeleton, which they thought might be that of a bear, at a cave in the Neandertal. They shoveled the bones out of the cave, losing many pieces in the process, and informed the local schoolmaster, Johannes Fuhlrott, that the bones were there if he chose to collect them. Fuhlrott and an anthropologist from Bonn, Herman Schaafhausen, recognized and described for the first time an extinct human. In 1864, the British anatomist W. B. R. King, deciding that the bones represented a separate species from modern humans,

Migrating Microbes

One of the biggest mysteries in human anthropology is the origin of modern population groups. Who were the original inhabitants of the Americas? Of Australia? Where did they come from, and what language did they speak? Until recently, such questions seemed unanswerable, but innovations in biology are beginning to yield not only intriguing clues but also solid information.

Research on the JC virus, which can be found in the human kidney, revealed some unexpected results for neurotoxicologist Gerald Stoner at the National Institutes of Health. Stoner was studying people with damaged immune systems, in whom the virus sometimes loses DNA in a key regulatory region and transforms itself into a fatal pathogen affecting the brain. During this research,

Stoner discovered the existence of different viral strains. It seems that the DNA of the JC virus in different populations of humans is distinctive and, therefore, could potentially be used to trace the migrations of peoples from one place to another.

The question of origins of New World peoples has generally been considered resolved, because most morphological and genetic studies link New World peoples to those in Asia. On occasion other hypotheses emerge that question this accepted wisdom. Adventurer Thor Hyerdahl of Kon Tiki fame, for example, in the 1950s sailed a balsa raft from South America to the South Pacific in a fruitless attempt to demonstrate that peoples in the New World had their origins in the nomadic seafarers of that region. Studies of the JC virus provide yet additional evidence that this is not so.

Almost every person on earth carries a strain of the JC virus, which was acquired from the parents during childhood. Virologists have identified at least seven major types and nearly two dozen subtypes. The strain of the JC virus that is found in modern Navajo peoples of the American Southwest turns out to be nearly identical to the virus found in a sample of humans living in Tokyo. This viral strain is only somewhat different from that found among the Chamorro, who inhabit the island of Guam in the Pacific Ocean. The Asiatic strain is quite different from those found in peoples of African or European descent. This research further bolsters the theory that peoples of the New World did come from eastern Asia over a land bridge across the Bering Strait, as the archaeological evidence indicates.

named it *Homo neanderthalensis*. Many paleoanthropologists today recognize the **Neandertals** as only a subspecies of *Homo sapiens* and classify them as *Homo sapiens neanderthalensis*.

The Neandertal discovery sparked a scientific controversy unrivaled in length—in a field known for controversy. One side maintained that the fossils documented an extinct species intermediate between humans and apes, and the other maintained that they represented an aberrant, perhaps pathological, modern human. As with most long-standing scientific debates, both sides were partially right and partially wrong. We now know from large numbers of fossil samples that the Neandertals are very similar to modern *H. sapiens* and do not in any meaningful way more closely resemble apes. They are, nevertheless, morphologically distinct and represent an extinct population of *H. sapiens* restricted to Europe and Southwest Asia.

The Neandertals were the first hominids to be recognized as belonging to an ancient population of humanity. When the discovery of the fossil skullcap was made in the Neander Valley, many scientists questioned its relationship to modern humans, and it was only after German anatomist Rudolf Virchow pronounced that the skull belonged to an individual who had suffered from rickets that the furor over the status of Neandertal died down. At least for the moment. Not only did the morphological peculiarities of the skull confuse many of the experts of the time but also no great antiquity of the deposit could be proven. Not until the 1866 fossil discoveries made at a cave site near the village of Spy in Belgium could one say with some certainty that the Neandertals had some antiquity, for found with the human fossils were ancient stone tools and the fossil bones of extinct animals.

With the advent of radiometric dating techniques, the question of the Neandertals' age is much less controversial. The best-dated sites in western and central Europe show that the Neandertals lived in a time range of 100,000 to 28,000

Neandertal: hominid-fossil-bearing cave site in Germany. Fossils representing a late Pleistocene human population in Europe and parts of the Middle East were first used to define the taxon *Homo sapiens neanderthalensis*.

years ago. The oldest Neandertal specimen may be the original fossil found in the Neander Valley, which is now dated at about 100,000 years old. The next candidates for antiquity are the buried remains found at La Ferrassie in France, dated to about 70,000 years ago. New accelerator mass spectrometry radiocarbon dates of about 28,000 years ago for two Croatian (Vindija Locality G1) fossils establish them as the most recent dated Neandertals of the Eurasian distribution of these archaic humans. Perhaps more importantly, the Vindija Cave dates make it clear that the Neandertals had at least 3,000 to 5,000 years of chronological overlap with modern *Homo sapiens,* allowing ample time for various kinds and degrees of contact (Mellars, 1999).

Neandertal anatomy. Although the fossils from Spy and elsewhere in Europe brought to light a rough outline of what Neandertals looked like, it was not until early in the twentieth century that a portrait of the Neandertals could be painted. The discoveries from many new sites in France had brought a wealth of material, and the completeness of the deliberately buried human remains allowed for a reasonable reconstruction of what the Neandertals looked like.

Neandertal anatomy, based on a single old individual from the French site of La Chapelle aux Saints, was first systematically studied between 1911 and 1913 by paleontologist Marcelin Boule. With preconceived notions about these ancient people, Boule pieced the fossils together and, in the process, committed a number of significant errors (Figure 12–11). Fifty years earlier William King wrote down his thoughts on the Neandertal, pronouncing the skull so overwhelmingly apelike that "the thoughts and desires which once dwelt within it never soared beyond those of the brute." In 1863 Thomas Huxley remarked on the original Neandertal fossil in the same manner, describing it as "the most pithecoid of human crania yet discovered." These ideas certainly influenced Boule's thinking about what the Neandertal must have looked like, for in his published monograph of La Chapelle he reconstructs the fossil with an apelike stooping gait and bent-knee posture.

Boule writes unkindly about the Neandertals in almost every respect. He questions their intelligence, fully aware that they possessed brains the same size (larger even!) than modern Europeans. Perhaps they were even mentally retarded. Their bodies were powerfully muscular; no doubt, they were clumsy, thought Boule. The contrast to modern humans was too great. He throws them a bone—inclusion within the genus *Homo* but relegated to a separate and clearly unequal species, *neanderthalensis.* Boule's work was influential, and the Neandertal caricature that he created remained fixed for decades to come.

Our notion of the Neandertals and their daily life has changed dramatically from that of Boule and other scientists of his day. The emphasis now is on the similarities between Neandertals and modern humans, not on the differences, which were overplayed in the past. Today, the Neandertal sample, although not extensive, is represented by individuals of both sexes and of all ages, from infants less than a year old to the elderly. Bones of the entire skeleton are known, and from these we have been able to calculate size ranges for a number of features. Although more males are represented in the sample than females, several body characteristics can be shown to be more sexually dimorphic than is seen in modern humans. For example, based on six male and four female skulls, the average cranial capacity is calculated to be 1,292 cc (77.5 cubic in.) for females and 1,583 cc (95 cubic in.) for males. When the sexes are combined, the mean is 1,410 cc, which is about 6 percent greater than that for modern humans (1,330 cc).

Again combining the data, the height range for the Neandertals is between 4.9 and 5.6 ft (150 to 170 cm), and the range in weight is between 110 and 143 lb (50–65 kg). These last two comparisons are well within the range for modern *Homo sapiens.*

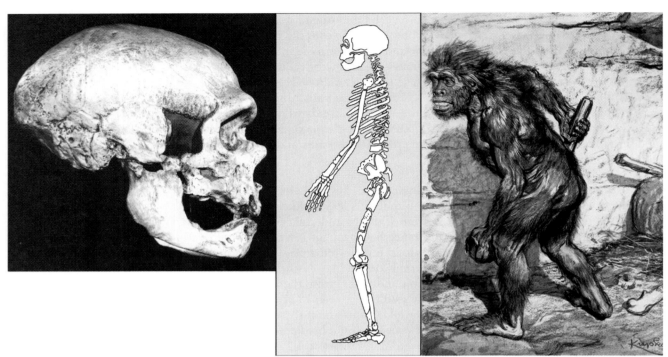

FIGURE 12–11 Early depictions of Neandertals, compared to our modern understanding of these people. (*a*) Skull of a toothless old man from the cave site at La Chapelle aux Saints. (*b*) Boule's 1913 reconstruction of the same individual, with a number of mistakes. Note the stooping posture and bent knees, both incorrect. (*c*) Another incorrect image of a Neandertal, this one by Frantisek Kupka, published in 1909. (*d*) Diorama at the American Museum of Natural History, showing a modern reconstruction of male and female Neandertals. Note the upright postures and strong builds.

midfacial prognathism: forward projection of the bony nose region of the skull; characteristic of Neandertals.

retromolar space: gap to be seen between the last upper molar and the ascending ramus of the mandible when articulated with the skull.

The best-known anatomical trait of Neandertals is their heavy brow ridges (Figure 12–12). The middle portion of the face, around the nasal opening, protrudes greatly in Neandertals (**midfacial prognathism**), and the teeth as a whole are moved forward relative to the skull vault. Because of this anatomical change, there is a gap, called the **retromolar space,** behind the last molar. The forward projection of the face and teeth and the bun-shaped occipital, retained from early *H. sapiens,*

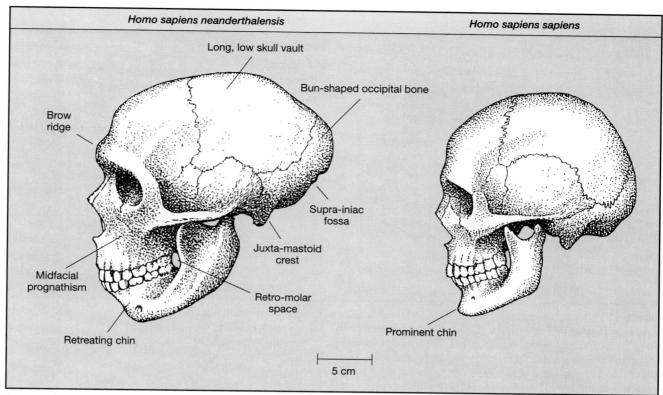

FIGURE 12–12 Comparison of skulls of Neandertal and modern human. Note the characteristic heavy brow ridge, midfacial prognathism, and bun-shaped occipital of the Neandertal.

give the Neandertal skull a low, flat appearance, even though its mean cranial capacity is greater than that of modern humans. The facial skeleton and cheekbones are less strongly constructed and massive than in early *H. sapiens.*

A large, projecting nose with wide openings contributes to the Neandertal's midfacial prognathic appearance. This distinctive nose form was formerly thought to be adaptive in that it enhanced airflow turbulence, thus facilitating heat and moisture exchange. It was argued that the shape and configuration of the nose was an adaptation to the high respiratory demands of a cold, dry climate. Recently, however, Churchill and colleagues (1999) discovered that rather than increasing air turbulence, the anatomy of the Neandertal nose possibly reduced turbulence. This, it was thought, was adaptive, but in a different way, in "decreasing the energetic cost of air transport in active hominids who because of the cold dry air conditions were constrained to nasal ventilation." This debate is important, because it shows that, in one way or another, many of the differences between the Neandertals and modern humans are part of an overall climatic adaptation to the cold environment of glaciated Eurasia.

Boule was right in one instance. The limb bones of the Neandertals do show them to have been powerfully built, stocky individuals, an overall adaptation to the cold climate in which they lived (see Figure 12–8 and Figure 12–11). The Neandertals' distal limbs (lower parts of the arms and legs) were proportionally shorter than those of modern humans. This feature is seen in young adolescents such as the 15- to 16-year-old from the French site of Le Moustier. In addition to shorter arms, the radius is strongly curved. In the shoulder, the Neandertal scapula shows a deep groove for the attachment of the teres minor muscle. When

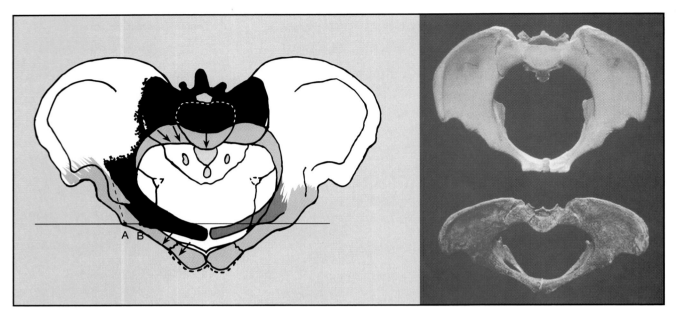

FIGURE 12-13 (*a*) Comparison of the Neandertal pelvic inlet with that of a modern human. This view from above superimposes a modern human male pelvic inlet, shown in black, on that of a Neandertal pelvis, shown in red. The dimensions are about the same, although the shape and position are different. Note the elongated pubic rami, shown at the bottom of the sketch, in the Neandertal pelvis. (*b*) Comparison of the Neandertal pelvis (bottom) with a modern human pelvis. The Neandertal pelvis has broader iliac blades and longer, thinner, pubic rami than the modern pelvis. The hip joint is also positioned more sideways.

this muscle contracts, it counteracts the medial rotational force of very strong arm flexors, thus providing more control of the flexing movement of the arm; this might be important, for example, in throwing objects such as spears.

Neandertals have a unique morphological pattern of the superior pubic ramus, or front of the pelvis (Figure 12–13). The pubic rami are both absolutely and relatively longer and thinner than those found in modern humans. This pelvic feature increases the diameter of the birth canal and may be related to the relatively large head size of Neandertal newborns. In the leg, the femur is robust and possesses a large femoral head. The femoral shaft is cylindrical in cross-section, with a thick cortical bone and a relatively narrow marrow cavity.

Neandertals were most likely geographic variants, a population of *H. sapiens* that differentiated in Europe and Western Asia because of at least partial geographic isolation. Expanded glaciers in northern and mountainous regions and extensive bodies of water formed by glacial melt reduced gene flow during the last two Pleistocene glaciations. Just after 200,000 years ago, the weather in the northern hemisphere began to grow colder. Groups of nomadic hunters following game herds southward had to develop skills in order to survive in this cold climate. At their fullest extent, the glaciers covered more than 30 percent of the world's land surface, compared to only 10 percent today. During the periods of ice advances, Europe was almost entirely icebound.

The penultimate glacial stage, sometimes called the Riss, which began about 186,000 years ago and lasted until 128,000 years ago, was one of the most severe in a long series of glacial advances that began about 700,000 years ago (see Figure 12–9). After 128,000 years ago, warmer periods prevailed once again for a time, and this relief from the cold marked the beginning of the Neandertal occupation of Eurasia. The climate turned colder once again during the last major glacial cycle, which began nearly 17,000 years ago. By 13,000 years ago temperatures were rising and Eurasia once again thawed out, but the ice had left its indelible mark on the landscape and the fauna that survived the cold. It was during the later part of this final glaciation that modern peoples began to slowly replace the Neandertals and other archaic peoples as moderns pushed northward in an expansion of their range.

How Did Modern Humans Come to Look Like This?

There are certainly striking differences in the faces and skulls of modern peoples and the Neandertals. Although the differences are obvious, the reason for the transformation from an archaic morphology to a modern one is not. All modern peoples have ancestors who, for some unexplained reason, eventually lost their primitive facial characteristics: a long, flat skull with big brow ridges and a protruding face.

Daniel Lieberman (2001) of Rutgers University believes he has the answer. Using x-ray images and computed tomography, Lieberman closely exam-ined the size and shape of the sphenoid bone (a bone that makes up part of the side of the skull) in both modern and archaic individuals and found that this bone is 20 to 30 percent shorter in modern peoples than it is in archaics (Figure 12–14). Because the sphenoid is located centrally in the skull (it contacts 17 out of the 22 bones in the skull), it is important in determining the shape and dimensions of the cranium itself. Lieberman believes that the longer sphenoid had been the major factor dictating the long projecting faces of the Neandertals and other archaic humans. A change in the shape of this one bone affects how much the face projects in front of the braincase, and that in turn affects many other aspects of our overall cranial shape and form, such as how large the brow ridges are and how steep the forehead is. The reduction in facial prognathism contributes to the more globular shape of the modern human cranium.

If changing the shape of one bone could result in the remodeling of the whole skull, then the transformation of an archaic skull into a modern one would require the actions of only a few genes at best. Lieberman speculates that a shorter sphenoid is related to a lower position of the larynx, enabling articulate speech and, thus, more effective communication.

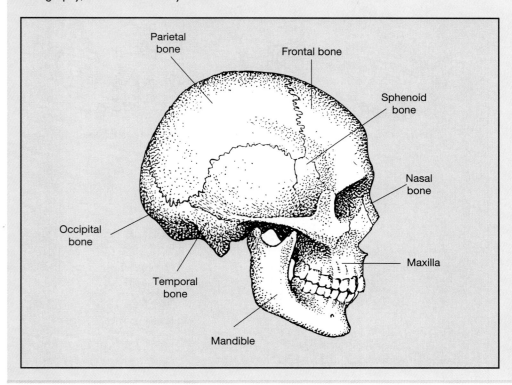

FIGURE 12–14 Position of the lateral part (the greater wing) of the sphenoid bone in a modern human skull.

BEHAVIOR OF EARLY *HOMO SAPIENS*

Tool Use

Early *Homo sapiens* of Grades 1 and 2 used stone tools of the Lower Paleolithic or Old Stone Age. Acheulean hand axes (see Chapter 11) remained a distinguishing component of these cultures, except in Asia, where modified chopping tools or tools made of materials other than stone apparently served similar purposes.

The survival of the Neandertals in the cold northern latitudes of Eurasia was, no doubt, aided by advances in their technological skills. Neandertals are associated with a stone tool industry called the **Mousterian** (Figure 12–15). The Mousterian, in turn, is a part of what archaeologists have called the **Middle Paleolithic,** characterized by new techniques of tool manufacture and by new kinds of stone tools. The Middle Paleolithic followed the Lower Paleolithic, which featured Oldowan choppers and flakes and Acheulean tools, such as the hand ax, which were discussed in the previous chapter.

Dated from about 200,000 to 35,000 years ago, the Middle Paleolithic is roughly comparable to the Middle Stone Age of African prehistory and features technological inventions, such as the **Levallois technique,** used for the production of prepared flakes. This technique marks a great improvement in stone tool technology, because tools could now be made from flakes rather than by shaping heavy cores. Another important technique used extensively by the Neandertals was the use

Mousterian: a Middle Paleolithic stone tool culture characterized by prepared flakes struck off a core; about 250,000 to 40,000 years ago.

Middle Paleolithic: roughly comparable to the Middle Stone Age of African prehistory, featuring technological inventions; about 200,000 to 30,000 years ago.

Levallois technique: technique marking great improvement in stone tool technology; tools were made from flakes rather than by shaping heavy cores.

FIGURE 12–15 Stone tools of the typical Mousterian industry. Flakes were carefully retouched, usually on two sides. Mousterian tools, associated with Neandertals, are part of what archaeologists call the Middle Paleolithic, about 200,000 to 35,000 years before the present.

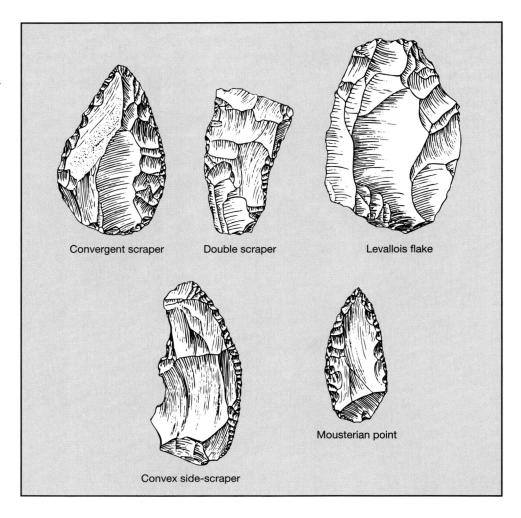

Convergent scraper   Double scraper   Levallois flake

Convex side-scraper   Mousterian point

of the **disc-core.** People of the late Pleistocene began to trim stone cores around the edges to produce disc-shaped cores. From a disc-shaped core, flakes could be knocked off the edges to produce tools. These tools could later be further retouched or trimmed and used for a variety of specialized purposes. The number of different tools was extensive, numbering close to 60 types, as identified by the late French archaeologist Francois Bordes.

Neandertal Behavior Patterns

Neandertals show many cultural traits that we recognize as "human." Burial of the dead (even with flowers, as shown by pollen analysis at Shanidar Cave, Iraq) implies a belief in life after death. The discovery of fossils of old, physically handicapped or virtually toothless Neandertal individuals means that groups to which they belonged cared for and helped to feed them (Figure 12–16; however, see Dettwyler, 1991, for an alternative viewpoint). Special arrangements of bear skulls and deer bones suggest magical hunting rites. A few pieces of crudely polished bone and ivory with scratches indicate the beginnings of artistry. A single tooth with a hole drilled in it, possibly worn as a necklace, and intentional cranial deformation show early ideas of personal adornment and perhaps group identity.

New techniques of research have brought us much closer to understanding the lives of the Neandertals, their patterns of subsistence, and their overall well-being. B. L. Hardy (1997) of Miami University, Ohio, reported on a reanalysis of the stone tools from two Middle Paleolithic sites in the Crimea, Staroselye and Kiik Koba, dated between 60,000 and 40,000 years ago. Microscopic analysis of tools revealed **hafting striations** (marks indicating attachment of stone tools to wooden shafts) and traces of plant tissue, providing good evidence that the stone points were bound to wood shafts and then used, perhaps, as spears. The plant tissue, which consisted of starch grains, may have been the remains of a "glue" used to haft the stone tool to the wooden shaft.

Starchy residue was also found along the working edge of the stone, providing further evidence that the tool may have been used for processing plant food. There is also evidence that these tools served multiple purposes. The tips of many tools show impact striations, indicating their use as projectiles, and mammalian and bird tissue remains show that these hunters were versatile in their choice of prey. Recently, studies (Richards et al., 2000, 2001) of fossil bones of two Neandertals have shown that these humans were skilled hunters who subsisted largely on meat and were by no means the scavengers and vegetarians claimed by many researchers. Chemical analyses of Neandertal skull and jaw bones from the Vindija Cave in Croatia, dated about 28,000 years ago, according to Fred Smith of Northern Illinois University, "proves that European Neandertals were top-level carnivores who lived on a diet of mainly hunted animal meat."

Further examination of Neandertal remains provides information of a different sort. Given the difficult environmental conditions in which the Neandertals lived, how did they fare? Healthwise the Neandertals may have been a lot better off than we previously believed. "The bones were as healthy as those of modern humans" reports Morris Kricum (1999), who studied the x-ray images of the bones of more than 75 Neandertal individuals from sites in Croatia. There is evidence of age-related osteoarthritis and back problems, but the bones show that these Neandertals were not disease-ridden. There is also evidence of injury, but the fractures that did occur healed well. Based on this study, it does not appear that the Neandertals "died off" as a result of dietary deficiencies or other health-related problems.

On the darker side of Neandertal behavior, there is good evidence of warfare. Some Neandertals were apparently wounded or even killed as a result of spearing or blows to the head (see Figure 12–16). Even more grisly is recent proof that some

disc-core: important technique used extensively by Neandertals; involves trimming stone cores around the edges to produce disc-shaped cores from which flakes could be knocked off the edges to produce tools.

hafting striations: marks indicating attachment of stone tools to wooden shafts.

FIGURE 12–16 (*a*) Neandertal specimen from Shanidar, Iran, showing evidence of a healed cranial fracture in the left eye orbit. (*b*) Painting by Richard Schlecht illustrating what some archaeologists believe is evidence that Neandertals took care of elderly and handicapped members of the group. The man in the left foreground is missing part of one arm.

Neandertals were murdered and then butchered and eaten, their remains later disposed of casually. In the French cave site of Moula-Guercy, new evidence for cannibalism provided by Alban Defleur, Tim White, and their colleagues is compelling (Defleur et al., 1999). Research shows that a group of Neandertals systematically defleshed the bones of at least six other individuals, who ranged from adult to juvenile in age, and then broke the bones with a hammerstone and anvil to remove the marrow and brains. In two of the younger individuals the temporalis muscle was cut from the side of the skull and the thigh muscles were removed from the legs. In at least one case the tongue was cut out.

The scattering of the Neandertal remains haphazardly among deer bones, which were also strewn about the cave, scarred with similar cut marks and broken into pieces, makes it seem unlikely that the assemblage results from a mortuary ritual. Cannibalism was reported as part of Neandertal behavior as early as 1899, when excavations at the Croatian site of Krapina brought to light a collection of fragmented bones of 20 or so individuals, both adults and children, some of which possessed cut marks from stone tools. The picture from Krapina remained cloudy, however, because other factors, besides cannibalism, could have accounted for the state of the remains. Excavation technique (dynamite was used to blast apart the deposits) and the possibility that the bones might have been crushed before death as a result of cave roof falls are two alternative possible explanations for the Krapina remains. The evidence from Moula-Guercy, however, removes any doubts that cannibalism was, on occasion, part of Neandertal subsistence.

THE EMERGENCE OF MODERN *HOMO SAPIENS*

Physical Characteristics

Although fragmentary fossil evidence suggests that anatomically modern peoples appeared earlier than 100,000 years ago, abundant fossil evidence of many, mostly complete skeletons of modern individuals, became prevalent only 35,000 years ago throughout the Old World. Anatomically modern humans show many bony features that are less massive than those of archaic forms. The skulls are more rounded, less elongated from front to back, and the forehead is vertically oriented instead of sloping backward as is common in all earlier species (see Figure 12–12). The brow ridges are typically small and not prominent. The presence of a protruding chin characterizes the lower jaw. The base of the cranium is flexed, a condition that some researchers believe is related to the emergence of modern speech and language, and the cranial capacity averages about 1,300 cc (80 cubic in.). Postcranially the limb bones are straighter, less curved, and less robust than seen in the Neandertals, and the pelvis lacks the distinctive long and thin pubic rami of archaic forms (see Figures 12–8 and 12–13).

Origins of Modern Humans

It is generally agreed that hominids belonging to *Homo sapiens* Grades 1 and 2 represent populations ancestral to anatomically modern humans, no matter how they are placed taxonomically. The geological dating and the geographic placement of the sites yielding these fossils, however, as well as the emerging molecular data, have led to three major hypotheses on the origins of modern humans (Stringer, 1990).

The Out-of-Africa Model. The Out-of-Africa Model (Figure 12–17) holds that an African population of anatomically modern *Homo sapiens,* as exemplified by fossils such as those from the Klasies River site in South Africa (see Figure 12–7), appeared early in Africa and migrated into other regions of the Old World about 100,000 years ago. This population spread over the entire Old World and accounts for all the morphological differences seen in the fossil record and in modern humans. This model holds that all the pre-*Homo sapiens sapiens* fossils in Eurasia, such as the Neandertals, were side branches, unrelated to the lineal ancestors of modern human beings, and were either supplanted or wiped out in some way by Cro-Magnon peoples (Tattersall, 1999, 2000).

Studies of mitochondrial DNA (mtDNA) show only small differences in sequences between different modern human populations, especially among Europeans. These data suggest to a number of researchers that modern *Homo sapiens* has a recent origin, without significant genetic contributions from archaic forms of *Homo.*

Recent work by Krings and co-workers (Krings et al., 1997, 1999), investigating mtDNA from a sequence of 378 base pairs in a sample of bone belonging to the original Neander Valley hominid, has shown that it differs considerably from se-

Out-of-Africa Model: evolutionary hypothesis that holds that modern humans evolved first in Africa and then spread out over the rest of the world, displacing or driving to extinction other populations.

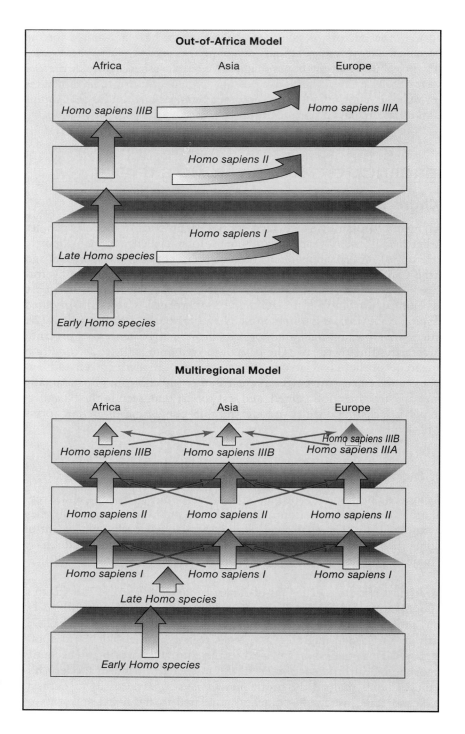

FIGURE 12–17 Two models of *Homo sapiens sapiens* origins.

quences in mtDNA from modern humans. Modern sequences differ from each other by an average of about eight substitutions for the same mtDNA region studied. Chimpanzees and humans differ by an average of 55 substitutions, supporting the notion of a split from a common ancestor about 4 million to 5 million years ago. Recently, Seaman and colleagues (1999) provided some additional comparative data based on sequences of noncoding nuclear DNA. This team found that there are 37 to 55 nucleotide differences between *Pan paniscus* and *Pan troglodytes* and slightly fewer differences (about 27 to 39) between two subspecies of *Gorilla* (*G. g. gorilla* and *G. g. graueri*). These researchers believe that the amount of genetic difference required for two groups to be considered separate species remains an open question. There are 27 sequence differences between modern humans and the Neander Valley hominid, based on the study by Krings and colleagues, indicating a separation between European Neandertals and moderns about 465,000 years ago.

The results from the first mtDNA study were recently replicated using mtDNA extracted from fossils from a cave located in the northern Caucasus, lending additional support to the Out-of-Africa Model (Ovchinnikov et al., 2000). Does this mean that the Neandertals were in fact a different species in the true meaning of the term? Probably not. Whether Neandertals and early modern *Homo sapiens* did interbreed remains an open question. The mtDNA data suggest that if they did interbreed, however, the Neandertal's contribution to the modern gene pool was modest at best.

The Hybridization Model. As we have seen, the Out-of-Africa Model fits the genetic data best but fails to account for some of the apparent morphological continuities that are seen from earlier fossil populations in the same areas. For example, Asian populations today have a high proportion of shovel-shaped incisors, as do Asian *Homo erectus* and archaic *Homo sapiens* in the same region (see Figure 14–2), and modern Europeans have projecting midfacial regions and relatively heavy brows, as do the archaic *Homo sapiens* in that area.

The **Hybridization Model** (Trinkaus and Shipman, 1992) accounts for these morphological continuities by agreeing with the idea that modern human populations migrated out of Africa and replaced archaic peoples they encountered, but that there was gene flow as the immigrants interbred with the residents. Because the population density of the Neandertals was low and the groups were scattered over the cold landscape of western Eurasia, if genetic exchange did occur, then the Neandertals were genetically swamped. That is, few of their genes made it into the pool that characterizes modern peoples. In one sense, they became "extinct" as a distinct population, even though some individuals might have interbred. Clearly, although there are no longer any single individuals who look like the Neandertals in their entirety, certain Neandertal characteristics, such as the heavy brow ridge and facial prognathism, still persist in some modern populations.

The question of interbreeding and hybrids was reopened recently by the announcement of a discovery of an Upper Paleolithic burial at Abrigo do Lagar Velho, in Portugal. The site, dated to 24,500 years ago, yielded the remains of a child who was about four years old. Although Upper Paleolithic artifacts are well known from the region, knowledge about the people who made them is scant, and the child skeleton is important for that reason alone. But the morphology of the child's skeleton is what brought this find to international attention. Portuguese researcher Cidalia Duarte reports that the skeleton presents a mosaic of features, some like the Neandertals and some like modern *Homo sapiens* (Duarte et al., 1999). For example, body proportions resemble those of the Neandertals, whereas pubic bone proportions are more like those of modern peoples.

Paleoanthropological research in the Iberian Peninsula suggests that the Neandertals held on for 5,000 to 10,000 years longer there than they did in the rest of Europe. Are the remains of this four-year-old child evidence of interbreeding between regional Neandertals and migrant modern peoples to southern Iberia? And does this evidence clearly refute strict replacement models of modern human origins, as the Portuguese-led team believes? This remains to be demonstrated with additional skeletal remains, but it does provide food for thought regarding the complexities of the Late Pleistocene emergence of modern humans, and it does enlarge the debate over the role the Neandertals played in the ancestry of modern

Hybridization Model: evolutionary hypothesis that suggests interbreeding between emigrant African populations and resident human populations in other parts of the world.

peoples. If, however, the fossil evidence from Lagar Velho points toward the possibility of interbreeding between some Neandertals and some modern people, Neandertal genetics points in a somewhat different direction.

Some genetic intermixture between Neandertals and early modern peoples could account for the combination of archaic and modern traits seen in modern peoples, especially in Europe. The Hybridization Model, however, is less consistent with results of molecular studies, which show little evidence for genetic intermixture after the divergence from the ancestral *Homo sapiens* population in Africa.

The Multiregional Model. The third model, the **Multiregional Model** (see Figure 12–17), rejects the one-region (African Eden) origin (Wolpoff et al., 2001). Instead, it regards regional ancestral populations of *Homo sapiens* as the major genetic evolutionary pathways to anatomically modern humans. There must have been some genetic interbreeding between regional populations of *Homo sapiens* to have maintained the biological unity of the species and its ability to interbreed. The support for the third model comes primarily from one interpretation of the paleontological record, and its accommodation of much of the available molecular data is poor.

Recent molecular studies. Molecular studies have thrown some light on the timing and place of origin of anatomically modern humans, although consensus on the significance of these findings has yet to be reached. Studies of mitochondrial DNA (Cann et al., 1987; Vigilant et al., 1989) were the first to compare sequence differences in modern human populations. The reasoning behind these studies was that the oldest (most ancient) population of humans should show the greatest amount of genetic difference. What emerged from these studies, popularly known as the "African Eve Hypothesis," consistent with the Out-of-Africa Model, was the knowledge of a basic division in the variability of mtDNA between sub-Saharan African populations and the populations in the rest of the world. It seemed from these studies that the greatest genetic distances (greatest number of sequence differences) in the human species occurred in Africa, with the Khoisan (bushmen) being the population that is most divergent from all other humans. The greatest amount of genetic divergence between these human populations was about 0.6 percent, and based on an estimate of the chimpanzee–human split of 5 million years ago, it was calculated that the common ancestor of modern humans lived in Africa somewhere between 140,000 and 200,000 years ago. Despite a dissenting opinion (Templeton, 1993), these results indicated that Africa was the most likely home for most of the mtDNA genetic diversity of the human species. Because individuals inherit mtDNA only from their mothers, human genetic diversity in mtDNA involves only female lineages, thus giving rise to the label "African Eve" (Figure 12–18).

Other genetic studies supported the Out-of-Africa Model and the conclusions reached by Cann and colleagues. A. M. Bowcock and his group (1994) analyzed polymorphic microsatellite alleles (noncoding parts of the DNA sequence) and discovered that the greatest diversity in these sequences is found in Africa. Similar results have been found using certain regions of the Y chromosome, which is inherited only through the male line. Once again, Africans were shown to have more variation at one locus (coding for the Y Alu polymorphism, YAP) than any other population. From this study it was calculated that the common ancestor of modern humans, an "African Adam," lived about 185,000 years ago.

There have been many criticisms of this research, however, based on technical and theoretical grounds. Researchers who have tried to create alternative ancestor–descendant trees have demonstrated that data entry into the computer that generates the tree affects the way the tree comes out. Different entries of the same data will alter the way the tree looks and can suggest different geographical locations for

Multiregional Model: evolutionary hypothesis that suggests primary continuity from earlier to later human populations in each area of the world, with some gene exchange between populations.

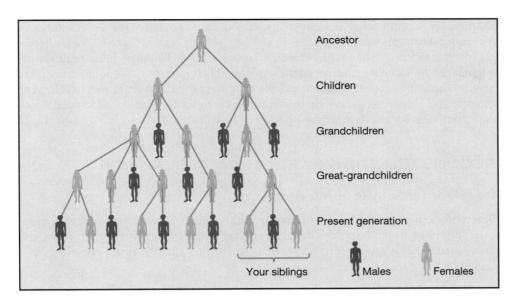

FIGURE 12–18 Mitochondrial DNA is inherited only through female lineages.

the home of "Eve." Perhaps more fundamental is the notion that variation at any given gene site may not accurately reflect a population's movement. It is clear that more studies of more genes are needed (Stoneking, 1993).

Although multiple analyses of mtDNA and the Y chromosome have bolstered the Out-of-Africa Model, the most recently published studies suggest some interesting twists and refinements of the current models. Eugene Harris and Jody Hey (1999) presented evidence that two separate human populations, dating to at least 200,000 years ago, left their genetic legacy in modern peoples. According to this study, one group gave rise to modern Africans and the other group gave rise to all other humans. In this study the researchers compared variations in a gene labeled PDHA1, found on the X chromosome, that codes for a key enzyme in sugar metabolism. The curious thing about this gene is that it is the first one ever found that represents a fixed difference between human populations. At one spot in the sequence, all Africans have one base, whereas all non-Africans have a different base. Although this research does not rule out the Out-of-Africa Model—because both populations might have come from Africa initially—it does suggest the possibility of a multiple ancestry for modern peoples.

In another twist to the origins models, Michael Hammer and Stephen Zegura (1996) showed that a gene on the Y chromosome apparently arose in Asia and then moved back into Africa.

Current hypotheses. Drawing on DNA data, the most recent studies suggest that some modifications to the models are needed. For one, it seems as if the ancestral population numbered only about 2,000 people, a number much smaller than the 10,000 or so people predicted from earlier work. For another, the new data suggest that these people lived between 60,000 and 40,000 years ago, much more recently than thought. This is a scenario now favored by archaeologist Richard Klein (1992), who believes that "a combination of fossil and genetic evidence locates the ancestral population in Africa, and archaeological discoveries imply an initial dispersal out of Africa about 50,000 years ago." Klein makes a distinction between anatomically modern humans and behaviorally modern humans, who are associated with an advanced set of stone tools of the Upper Paleolithic that dates back to 50,000 years or so ago. The key to the transformation from archaic to behaviorally modern humans may be locked in the reorganization of the brain. It may also quite possibly be involved with the development of language. In the final section of this chapter, we discuss what is known about tool use and language development in *Homo sapiens sapiens.*

Interpretation of the fossil record of *Homo sapiens* has now been significantly augmented by the data and perspectives of molecular studies. We look forward to new research into modern human origins that can now draw from paleontological, genetic, and paleoecological data to formulate more sophisticated and more defensible hypotheses for this best-known period of hominid evolution.

RECONSTRUCTING EARLY HUMAN BEHAVIOR

Developments in Tool Making

blades: elongated pieces of stone, parallel-sided and at least twice as long as they are wide, struck off a specifically prepared core.

When modern peoples appear in Europe, so do stone tools made from **blades**, elongated pieces of stone, parallel-sided and at least twice as long as they are wide, and deftly struck off a specifically prepared core (Figure 12–19). From these blades a

FIGURE 12-19 (*a*) Fossilized skull from Cro-Magnon site in France. (*b*) Reconstruction of Cro-Magnon modern *Homo sapiens.* (*c*) Typical Aurignacian tools of the Upper Paleolithic.

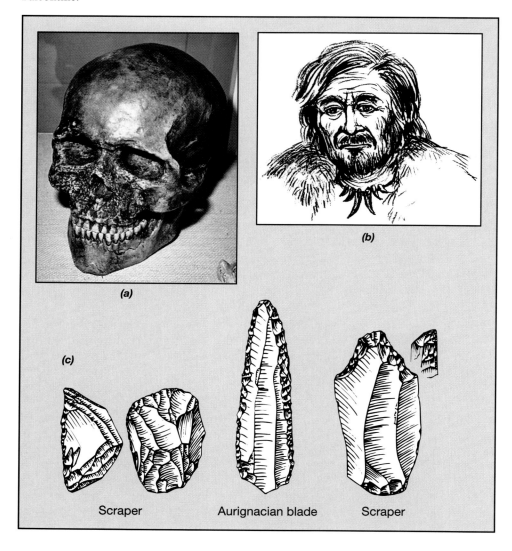

(a)

(b)

(c)

Scraper   Aurignacian blade   Scraper

wide variety of specialized tools could be made, such as the *burin*, a chisel-like tool that had many uses. In addition to this new lithic technology, other materials, such as bone, antler, and ivory, was also artfully shaped into useful items. These tools signal the beginning of the Upper Paleolithic.

There is significant regional variation, however, in tool industries of the Upper Paleolithic, suggesting cultural differences among groups. Although the estimates of time of overlap between Neandertals and modern *Homo sapiens* vary, at least 2,000 or 3,000 years (or about 100 or so generations) is allowed by the most cautious of researchers (Tattersall and Schwartz, 1999). What might have happened during that period of time?

The Chatelperronian and the Aurignacian industries marked the appearance of the Upper Paleolithic in Europe. The finely retouched blade tools of the Aurignacian were innovative. These tools were completely unlike any earlier Middle Paleolithic tool and, therefore, they no doubt were carried into Europe by their manufacturers, who came from elsewhere. Tools of the Chatelperronian industry, in contrast, were probably indigenous inventions from a variant of earlier Mousterian industries, and this probably reflects a pattern of cultural diffusion from modern peoples to the Neandertals.

Although, generally speaking, Mousterian tools are usually associated with archaic peoples and tools of the Upper Paleolithic are found with moderns, it is not always so. For example, two sites in Israel, Qafzeh near Nazareth, and Skhul near Haifa, have been dated to about 90,000 years ago. Here, almost modern fossils were found in association with typical Mousterian implements. In France, by contrast, at the sites of Arcy-sur-Cure and St. Césaire in the Dordogne, typical Neandertal fossils dating to only 34,000 years ago were found in association with tools of the Chatelperronian industry (Figure 12–20). Obviously, the details of the technological shift from Middle to Upper Paleolithic are complex and not fully known at this point.

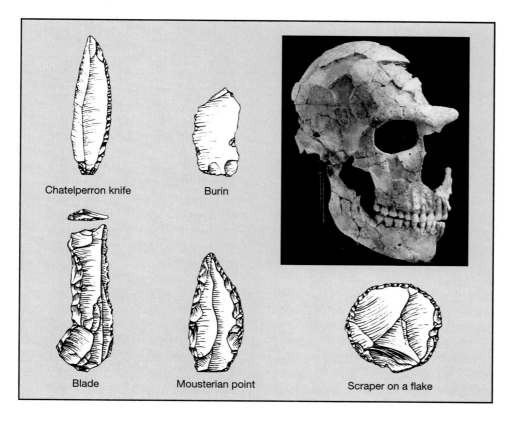

Chatelperron knife   Burin

Blade   Mousterian point   Scraper on a flake

FIGURE 12–20 Neandertal fossil skull from the 34,000-year-old site of St. Césaire, France. Tools associated with the human remains from this site are early Upper Paleolithic, with a strong influence of the earlier Mousterian industry.

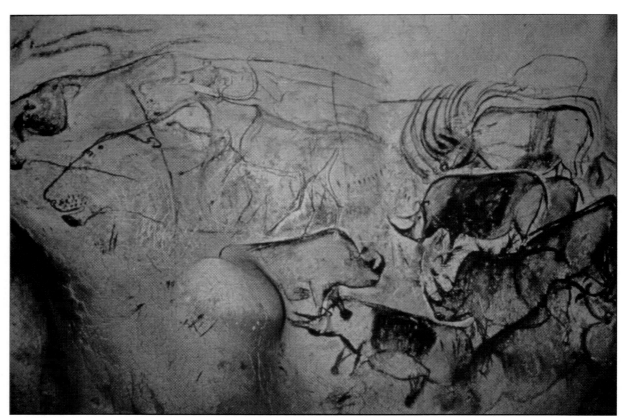

FIGURE 12-21 Painting on the wall of a cave discovered in 1995 in the Vallon Pont D'Arc region of France and dating to approximately 20,000 years ago.

Upper Paleolithic Culture

FIGURE 12-22 An Upper Paleolithic Venus figurine, the Venus of Willendorf (Austria), dating to 27,000 years ago.

Although we may wonder about the details, the Upper Paleolithic transformation must have come about through a transformation of the human brain to its modern state, a process that, no doubt, accounts for many of the cultural advances that accompany modern peoples. For example, modern peoples controlled fire more adeptly than their forebears, constructing stone-lined hearths that generated more heat and in which fires could be banked (insulated to keep them burning). Impressive cave art in the form of paintings and figurines appear (Figures 12–21 and 12–22). Materials from distant sources, such as marine shells and flint, indicate long-distance trading contacts or individual movements. Production of textiles was advanced, indicated by the clothing that adorns many of the Venus figurines (see Figure 12–22). People congregated in relatively large groups (perhaps in response to local food abundance) for part of the year, as indicated by large site sizes, such as Mas d'Azil, in the Pyrenees Mountains between Spain and France.

Our ideas about Upper Paleolithic subsistence have generally revolved around the notion of "man the hunter." Although there is little question that Upper Paleolithic people had the technology to hunt big game, was the meat obtained from hunting their main food source? Abundant evidence of the remains of woolly mammoth and other large-game animals certainly suggests so, but with recent evidence, this picture now seems to be changing. At the Czechoslovakian site of Pavlov, close to the famous site of Dolni Vestonice, which yielded the first of many Venus figurines, archaeologists Olga Soffer and James Adovasio found evidence that points to the significant role women played in obtaining food for the group (see Pringle, 1998). Recovered from this site were small clay fragments, on many of which were impressed on the surface a series of parallel lines. Microscopic analyses of these lines showed them to be a pattern of interlacing fibers, part of a larger weaving. This is the oldest evidence of weaving ever found; the site itself has been dated to about 27,000 years ago. Although the weaving patterns found on different fragments suggest that many styles were used, one pattern reflects a technique that is commonly used to make nets of a secure mesh suitable for capturing small mammals. Although the nets themselves do not prove that women made or even used them in hunting, ethnographic reports of net use by women in modern hunter-gatherer groups suggest that this was a distinct possibility.

How successful was this activity for Upper Paleolithic peoples? At Pavlov, the fossil remains of small game accounts for about 46 percent of the individual animal bones recovered. If Ice Age women collected plants, bird eggs, and shellfish, among other food items, and if they hunted or trapped small game as well, they may have then contributed about 70 percent of all of the calories consumed by members of their group.

Art and Symbolism

Most examples of artwork are unquestionably associated with modern *Homo sapiens,* and they are found relatively late in the record, well after 35,000 years ago. Although it is rare, the evidence for Lower and Middle Paleolithic art, not associated with modern humans, is perhaps more helpful in understanding the origin of language. Although earlier archaic *Homo sapiens* may have lacked the modern ability to verbalize, their conceptual ability, as witnessed in their artwork, supports the notion that they possessed speech to some extent. The oldest example of artwork of this age thus far discovered is a figurine of exaggerated female human form dated to about 230,000 years ago that was excavated from the Acheulean site of Berekhat Ram, Israel (Figure 12–23) (Goren-Inbar, 1986). The earliest burials, which are of Mousterian age, should also be considered as evidence for symbolic behavior, because the human body becomes a symbol once it is provided a burial (Figure 12–24; Schepartz, 1993).

FIGURE 12–23 Acheulean figurine, dated to 230,000 years ago, from Berekhat Ram, Israel.

FIGURE 12–24 Burial of a young woman, with an infant at her feet, from Jebel Qafzeh, Israel. This is one of the earliest known burials of modern *Homo sapiens,* dating to more than 90,000 years ago.

Contemporary with these art forms are examples of objects that were, presumably, used as body ornamentation. This evidence provides additional insight into the evolution of symbolic behavior and speech. Ornamentation is one form of communication (Wobst, 1977). Ornaments name individuals, either their owner or their maker, and shared ornamentation can identify a member of a group (Wiessner, 1990). Alexander Marshack (1989) has offered evidence for body ornamentation beginning with the Lower Paleolithic, believing that as early as 110,000 years ago pierced animal teeth and bone were used as beads or pendants.

Cave art. Upper Paleolithic art is extensive and widespread. Paintings on the walls of caves have been known and studied for decades and have generated competing hypotheses to explain why they were created. Numerous cave art sites are well known (and even re-created for the tourist trade), such as Lascaux Cave in the Dordogne in France and Altamira Cave in northern Spain. These sites come relatively late in the Upper Paleolithic chronology, dating to about 15,000 years or so. In 1994 explorations of a cave in southern France called the Grotte Chauvet, whose entrance had been previously sealed over by landslides, yielded a treasure trove of prehistory. An astonishingly well-preserved collection of wall paintings, more than 300 in number, was found in association with fire hearths, stone tools, and fossil remains of many different animals. In addition to its wealth of cultural information, Grotte Chauvet is important because of its age. Nearly twice the age of other cave art sites, it is dated to more than 30,000 years ago and is now one of the oldest sites of its kind in the world.

The artifacts and paintings in the Grotte have provided us with some new insight into the lives of Upper Paleolithic peoples (Figure 12–25). Although the quality of the art varies, it is equal in its execution to any comparable work elsewhere and later in time. This information provides us with an important time depth to an art form perfected much earlier than we had believed. There are major differences, however, between the art of Grotte Chauvet and that found in more recent sites. For example, at Grotte Chauvet there is a high percentage of depictions of so-called dangerous animals, such as rhinoceros, mammoths, lions, and cave bears. There are at least three times as many rhinoceros painted than in all of the hundreds of other art cave sites.

There are widespread traces and paintings of bears; in fact, the cave itself was occupied by bears, perhaps at the same time the artists were creating their works. Bears may have figured prominently in the myth and ritual of Upper Paleolithic

FIGURE 12–25 Cave art from Grotte Chauvet, France. Unlike most cave art sites, Chauvet depicts a preponderance of "dangerous animals," such as the woolly rhinocerous (left) and the wild bull, *Bos primigenius* (right). Chauvet's rhinos have distinctively rendered ears and a black line around the belly.

peoples, as has also been suggested by some researchers and writers of popular fiction about the early Neandertals (see Jean Auel's *Clan of the Cave Bear* [1980] as an example). In one chamber of the Grotte at least 55 skulls of bears were accumulated, although how they got there is unknown.

The artwork at the Grotte varies in quality. It is possible that the less-expert images were done by young apprentice artists, either guided by older artists or practicing their techniques. The fact that many people may have been in the cave together is attested to by a wall of handprints located at various heights above the cave floor (Figure 12–26). Here, researchers have identified the hands of children and women as well as of men.

The question as to how these people were able to work in a dark cave may have been answered by the presence of fire hearths scattered on the cave floor. One undisturbed hearth was found backed by large pieces of flat, white limestone. The French researchers conclude that, because there were few animal remains nearby, the hearth was not a cooking fire. The floor of the cave was dark, and perhaps the white stones were used as reflectors.

Although many questions were answered by the investigations at Grotte Chauvet, many others were raised. Meg Conkey, archaeologist at the University of California, Berkeley, believes that explaining cave art using only one sort of hypothesis will prove to be very difficult (see Balter, 1999). Chronological and temporal variation in style and subject matter may indicate any number of things—cultural exchange or shifting religious beliefs are only two examples—none of which are conclusive at the moment. It appears from this evidence that the symbolic nature of Upper Paleolithic peoples is a good deal more complex than we have so far imagined.

FIGURE 12–26 Wall of painted handprints, including those of men, women, and children, at Grotte Chauvet.

Sculpture. Wall, or parietal, artworks are not the only items created for unknown purposes by peoples of the Upper Paleolithic. Even more common are portable art pieces. Perhaps of all these types of artifacts the best known are the so-called Venus figurines, named after the ancient Roman goddess of love and beauty. Over the years more than 100 pieces made from bone, stone, antler, ivory, and fired clay have been found. Commonly, there is considerable anatomical detail on the torsos but the heads often lack eyes, mouths, or any facial expressions. Hair, however, may be represented in complex ways (Figure 12–27; see also Figure 12–22).

Evidence of Upper Paleolithic ritual lies in the nature of the raw material from which the Venuses are made. From the Grimaldi Cave in Italy, Venuses were carved from rare material that the artists could have obtained only through trade or distant travel. Some of the figurines were polished and rubbed with red ochre, a material commonly used in burials. One piece was especially interesting to researchers because two figures were portrayed together, their arched bodies facing away from one another, joined at the head, shoulder, and lower limbs. One figure is that of a Venus, whereas the other is an imaginary beast. To some investigators this piece suggests that women played a role in ritual, perhaps acting as shaman. The issues are complex, as was no doubt the behavior of Upper Paleolithic peoples. Glimpses of their reality are offered by their remains, but much is yet to be learned and understood.

The Origins of Speech

Anatomical evidence. Interest in the evolution of cognition, such as sequential thinking and planning, was revived by Binford (1989). Although most recognize that hominid behavior may not have been cognitively structured as it is now, paleoneurologists are in complete agreement that the brains of archaic *Homo sapiens*, especially the Neandertals, were morphologically similar to those of modern humans.

FIGURE 12–27 Clay Venus figurine from the Czechoslovakian site of Dolni Vestonice. This typical female figure emphasizes the large breasts and relatively small waist. The arms and head are nondescript, and few facial features are shown.

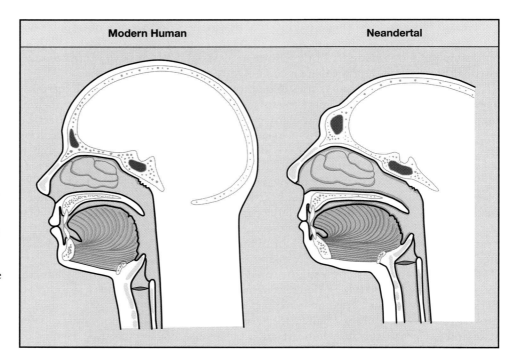

FIGURE 12-28 Comparison of the airway of a Neandertal (right) and a modern human. This reconstruction shows the Neandertal's long palate and tongue, and the higher placement of the larynx. With these key differences, it is unlikely that Neandertals could have produced the range of sounds necessary for modern human speech.

In the early 1970s, Lieberman and Crelin (1971) began pioneering research on vocal tract reconstruction, comparing the shape and position of the tract in modern humans and infants, nonhuman primates, and fossil hominids. They described the supralaryngeal vocal tract of the Neandertal male from La Chapelle and compared it with that of a modern human newborn. In both they found lacking the elongation and bending of the tract that develops later in young juveniles of modern *Homo sapiens.* These authors concluded that the La Chapelle male, like the modern newborn, was limited in his ability to produce some vowels and consonants. They conceded, however, that the brain itself might have been "sufficiently well developed for him to have established a language based on the speech signals at his command" (1971:217) (Figure 12–28).

A number of critical studies of other specimens of archaic *Homo sapiens,* however, indicate that many of these people might have been capable of human speech. Other criticisms were leveled on the basis that the La Chapelle fossil is too pathologically altered to justify any conclusions on speech capabilities (Frayer, 1992) and that errors may have been made in the original reconstruction (Houghton, 1993). Kathleen Gibson of the University of Texas (1994) showed that the range of variation in the shape of modern human vocal tracts is not as limited as previously thought. Certainly, more comparative anatomical work on vocal tracts and the exact relationship of speech to individual variations of shape and position is needed.

Linguistic analysis. Additional insights into the problem of language origins have come from an entirely different area of research—that of linguistic analysis. Johanna Nichols (1994) proposed that the common ancestor of modern languages must be at least 100,000 years old, based on her analysis of grammatical features. She assigned an average age of 5,000 years for each language family and a branching rate of 1.6 languages per family. She concluded that, if there were a single common language, it would take about 100,000 years for it to differentiate into the number of different languages that presently exist.

The varied lines of evidence we have presented show that a relationship exists between language and technology (as evinced through tool manufacture and production of art) that preceded the late arrival of modern *Homo sapiens*. From the evidence at hand, however, the exact links between language and technology remain insufficiently clear to facilitate a completely satisfactory reconstruction of the evolution of language and cognition. Certainly, more information is necessary from many fields, such as neurology, to shed further light on our ancestor's cognitive abilities.

◀ SUMMARY

1. **What were the key anatomical characteristics of early *Homo sapiens*, including the Neandertals?**

The most primitive representatives of *Homo sapiens* (Grade 1) appear as early as 700,000 years ago. The brow ridges are still prominent, but unlike *Homo erectus*, the ridges are thickest over the medial part of the orbit. The cranial capacity has expanded over that of *H. erectus* and evolves to modern size (about 1,300 cc [80 cubic in.]) by the time of the Neandertals. Selection in earliest *Homo sapiens* strongly favored greater brain size and presumably greater cerebral abilities. In later forms the vault of the skull is higher. Tooth size is slightly reduced. The best-known anatomical trait of the Neandertals is the heavy brow ridge. The middle portion of the face around the nasal opening protrudes greatly and the teeth, as a whole, are moved forward relative to the skull vault, creating a gap, the retromolar space behind the last molar. The forward projection of the face and teeth and the bun-shaped occipital give the Neandertal skull a low, flat appearance.

2. **Describe the key behavioral characteristics of archaic *Homo sapiens* and Neandertals, including tool use and other aspects of culture.**

Early *Homo sapiens* used Lower Paleolithic type stone tools such as the Acheulean hand ax. Later *Homo sapiens*, such as the Neandertals, are associated with a stone tool tradition of the Middle Paleolithic, called the Mousterian. These tools show technological innovations, such as the levallois technique used for the production of prepared flakes. Additionally, the disc-core technique was developed to produce flakes that could then be retouched or trimmed to make a number of different tools. Neandertals buried their dead and placed grave goods in the burials that have suggested to some researchers the development of magical hunting rites. Some crude polished bone and ivory artifacts with scratches on them indicate the beginnings of artistry. Microscopic residue analysis of tools reveal hafting of stone points to wood shafts, and chemical analysis of Neandertal bone indicates a high proportion of meat in their diet, and, thus, hunting as a major form of subsistence behavior. Other research shows that the Neandertals were cannibals.

3. **What theories account for the appearance of modern humans? What is the most important evidence in favor of each?**

Three major hypotheses have been constructed to account for the origin of modern *Homo sapiens*. The Out-of-Africa Model holds that an African population of modern *Homo sapiens* appeared early in Africa (100,000 years or more ago) and migrated to other regions of the Old World, arriving finally in Europe about 40,000 years ago. This model states that all of the premodern *Homo sapiens* fossils in Eurasia, such as the Neandertals, were side branches and separate species. This model fits the genetic data, such as the mitochondrial "Eve," but fails to account for some of the apparent morphological continuities that are seen from earlier fossil populations to more recent ones in the same area. The Multiregional Model regards regional ancestral populations of *Homo sapiens* as the major evolutionary pathways to anatomically modern *Homo sapiens*. The model postulates that there must have been interbreeding between regional populations of *Homo sapiens* to have maintained the biological unity of the species. The Hybridization Model accounts for morphological continuities by agreeing with the idea that, although modern humans migrated out of Africa replacing the archaic populations they encountered, there was gene flow as the immigrants interbred with the residents. The resulting genetic intermixture accounts for the combination of archaic and modern traits seen in anatomically modern peoples. This model is less consistent with the molecular interpretations that maintain there is little evidence for genetic intermixture after the divergence from the ancestral *Homo sapiens* populations in Africa.

4. **Describe the physical and cultural features, including tool use and the use of symbols, that distinguish archaic from modern *Homo sapiens*.**

Anatomically modern humans show many bony features that are less massive than those of archaic forms. The skulls are more rounded, less elongated from front to back, and the forehead is vertically oriented instead of sloping backward as is common in all earlier species. The brow ridges are typically small and not prominent. The presence of a protruding chin characterizes the lower jaw. The base of the crania is flexed, a condition that some researchers believe is related to the emergence of modern speech and language, and the cranial capacity averages about 1,300 cc (80 cubic in.). Postcranially, the limb bones are straighter, less curved, and less robust than in the Neandertals.

Most examples of artwork are associated with modern *Homo sapiens*. Although many examples of art are expressed as paintings on the walls of caves, other art forms consist of objects that may have been used as body ornamentation. This evidence provides some insight into the evolution of symbolic behavior and speech, because ornamentation is one form of communication. Another common form of portable art are the "Venus" figurines made from many materials. The varied lines of evidence show that a relationship exists between language and technology (as evinced through tool manufacture and production of art) that preceded the late arrival of modern *Homo sapiens*.

CRITICAL THINKING QUESTIONS

1. It appears from recent discoveries in China that early *Homo* populations possessed cultures that were remarkably similar for hundreds of thousands of years. How do you account for such uniformity over such large geographical distances?

2. There is evidence that *Homo erectus* survived in fairly isolated places in Southeast Asia, such as Java, as recently as 30,000 years ago. How would these people have survived in the face of migrating *Homo sapiens* southward through these islands to Australia as early as 60,000 years ago?

3. From fossil, comparative anatomical, and cultural data, what seems to be the most reasonable explanation now as regards the origin of modern speech?

4. The culture of *Homo sapiens* of the late Pleistocene appears to be fairly uniform: The same technologies produced the same kinds of tools, more or less, throughout Old World populations. In addition, cultural traditions appear to change in similar fashions over time. How is this possible if these human populations represented several different species?

5. The wall or "parietal" art of Upper Paleolithic modern peoples is remarkable in its realism. It is also true that many examples of cave paintings were done in places that are very difficult to access. What factors involving the lives of these people might account for these facts?

◀ INTERNET EXERCISES

Critical Thinking

What Is a Modern Human? This chapter traces the evolution of *Homo sapiens* from the origin of our species through the emergence and early accomplishments of *H. sapiens sapiens*. Based on what you have read so far, and on additional research, define a "modern" human, and indicate when you think modern humans first appeared. Try to answer the following questions:

1. What physical characteristics define modern humans, as opposed to archaic *H. sapiens?* Where and when did these characteristics first appear?
2. What cultural traits define modern humans?
3. How different are you and all the people around you from the first modern humans whom you read about in this chapter? What are the most important differences?
4. How does constructing your own definition of a modern human help you understand the problems that humans face today?

Writing Assignment

The Neandertals. This chapter discusses the stereotypes about Neandertals that have existed since the first specimens of this subspecies were discovered, as well as current ideas about its place in the human family tree. For this exercise, try to answer the following questions about the Neandertals. Present your answers in the form of a research paper.

1. Were the Neandertals a separate species or a subspecies of *H. sapiens?* What evidence supports your conclusion?
2. What were the geographical and chronological limits of the Neandertals? In what ways were they adapted to their environment?
3. Did the Neandertals become extinct, or were they merged into contemporary populations of *H. sapiens sapiens?* What evidence supports your conclusion?

See Companion Web site for Internet links.

Grotte de Chauvet, discovered in 1994, is a complex of painted and engraved chambers dated to around 30,000 B.C. Other dates, some from torch smears on the walls and some from the images themselves, indicate that the site was visited over a period of 6,000 or 7,000 years. The cave was also undoubtedly used as a den by cave bears. This MediaLab gives you a closer look at Grotte de Chauvet. In the activity, we ask you to review what is known about this important site and to speculate on its meaning for the Upper Paleolithic people who created it.

WEB ACTIVITY

The video shows several scenes from the Grotte de Chauvet and describes the site in detail. Your textbook provides several more views of the cave, and several links are provided on the Companion Web site. Use all of this information to consider the following questions.

Activity
1. View the video. Summarize what is known about the cave at this time.
2. What information about the cave complex is still unknown? Of this information, what can be known and what can only be the subject of speculation?
3. Under what ecological and climatic conditions did the cave art of southwest France appear?

The MediaLab can be found in Chapter 12 on your Companion Web site http://www.prenhall.com/boaz

---

THE HOMINOIDS: STUDIES OF APE AND HUMAN BEHAVIOR

As we have seen, the living apes are our closest genetic relatives. Studies in the field and laboratory have shown that this is true behaviorally as well. This means that studying the social behavior of apes can both increase our knowledge of human behavior and help us develop models for understanding human evolution.

As we saw in the three previous chapters, the australopithecines followed later by the early species of *Homo* diverged from a lineage leading to the modern African apes more than 5 million years ago. Since that time, and gradually, brain size in species of the genus *Homo* increased, language evolved, and cultural factors, such as tool use, became more sophisticated. However, we have never lost all of the physical and behavioral factors that link us to our apelike forebears, and the social behavior of modern apes continues to provide us with useful models for understanding human behavior. This chapter reviews ape social behavior and shows how a behavioral continuum model can shed light on universal aspects of human behavior.

There is no single pattern of social organization among the hominoids (Figure 13–1). Field observations have shown that patterns of behavior among the apes are considerably more complex than those observed in the monkeys, and in some cases they are also unpredictable. Long-term field studies on the best known of the apes, the chimpanzees, have shown how complex this behavior can become as patterns emerge and change with varying environmental or social conditions.

13

SOCIAL BEHAVIOR OF APES

The Lesser Apes: The Gibbons and Siamangs

Among the apes, the gibbons and siamangs (the largest of the gibbon species) are the least well-studied in the wild. In one of the first systematic field studies, Clarence Ray Carpenter (1940) studied the gibbons in Malaysia. In his four-month study in 1937 he observed that adult gibbons lived as monogamous pairs, joined by up to four offspring ranging in age from infants to subadults, those animals who are not fully physically mature. Together, the family group occupied space that Carpenter described as a territory. By this he meant that the gibbons defended their home range, sometimes aggressively, against encroachment by other gibbon groups, and, at times, by other species. Gibbon territorial aggression may be directed at neighboring macaque monkeys and even at young orangutans, which gibbons often harass and threaten if they attempt to feed nearby.

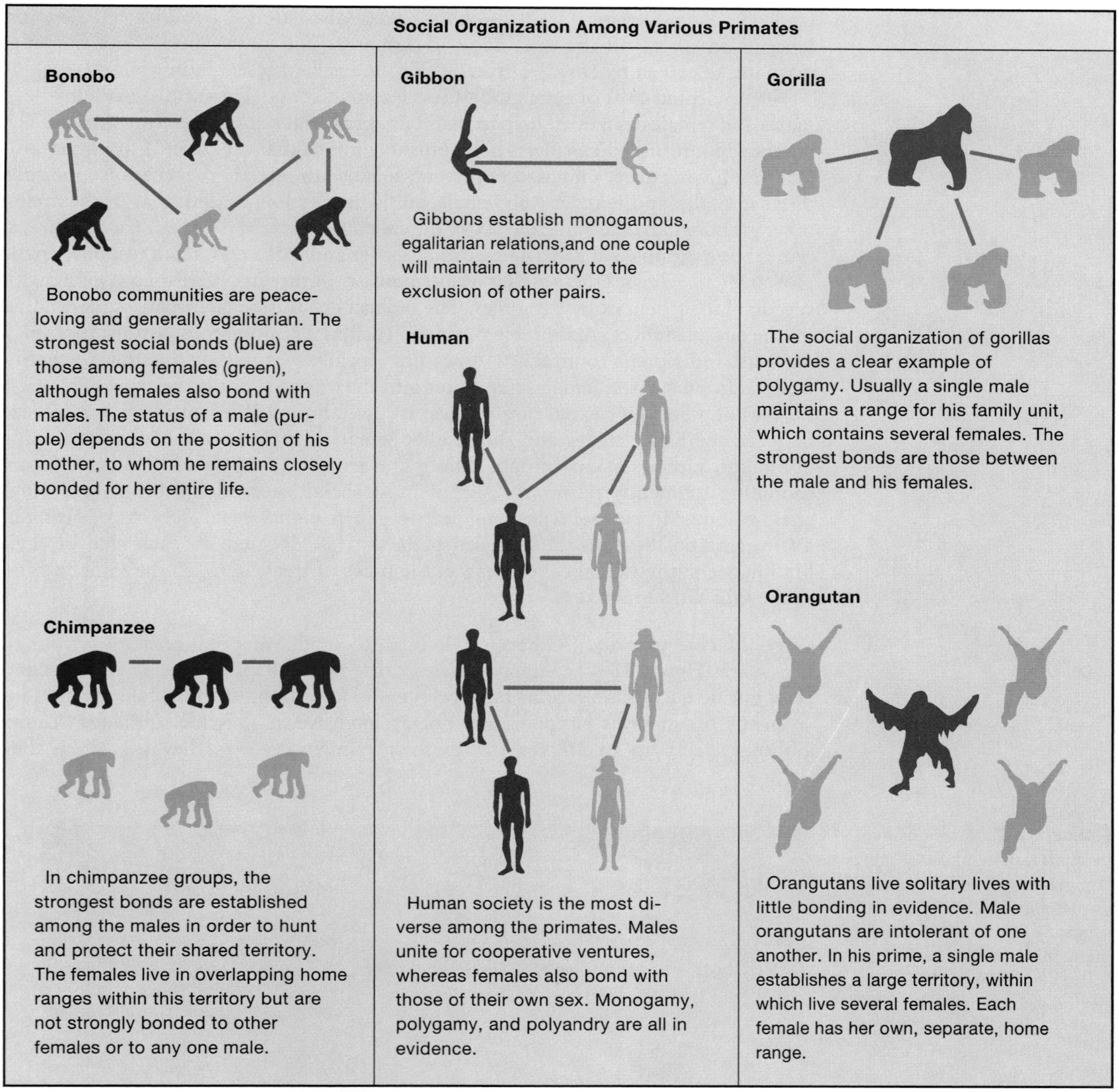

Social Organization Among Various Primates

Bonobo

Bonobo communities are peace-loving and generally egalitarian. The strongest social bonds (blue) are those among females (green), although females also bond with males. The status of a male (purple) depends on the position of his mother, to whom he remains closely bonded for her entire life.

Chimpanzee

In chimpanzee groups, the strongest bonds are established among the males in order to hunt and protect their shared territory. The females live in overlapping home ranges within this territory but are not strongly bonded to other females or to any one male.

Gibbon

Gibbons establish monogamous, egalitarian relations, and one couple will maintain a territory to the exclusion of other pairs.

Human

Human society is the most diverse among the primates. Males unite for cooperative ventures, whereas females also bond with those of their own sex. Monogamy, polygamy, and polyandry are all in evidence.

Gorilla

The social organization of gorillas provides a clear example of polygamy. Usually a single male maintains a range for his family unit, which contains several females. The strongest bonds are those between the male and his females.

Orangutan

Orangutans live solitary lives with little bonding in evidence. Male orangutans are intolerant of one another. In his prime, a single male establishes a large territory, within which live several females. Each female has her own, separate, home range.

FIGURE 13–1 Studies of behavioral organization among the living apes and humans have provided a good deal of insight about the probable traits of our ancestors. This information has allowed biological anthropologists to develop testable hypotheses about the evolution of behavior.

Home range in the wild. In the wild, gibbon groups range over areas of 20 to 40 hectares (ha) (50 to 100 acres) and feed on a variety of foods ranging from small birds to fruits, the latter of which represents about 80 percent of their diets. Carpenter described two unique aspects of gibbon behavior: the formation of a lifelong pair bond between an adult male and an adult female; and unique territorial behavior, characteristically accompanied by loud vocalizations, or calls, that usually occur as part of a morning activity. Both of these were later confirmed in a longer field study by John Ellefson (1968). Gibbons were also studied by Whiten (1982) on Siberut, an island off the west coast of Sumatra. The larger species, the siamang, was later observed by David Chivers (1974) in his field research in Malaysia.

The morning calls of each gibbon species are distinct. These calls, made by both males and females as a duet, help to maintain territorial borders between groups. The absence of morning duets alerts neighboring gibbons that the caller is a solitary animal and helps attract unmated males and females to one another. Because the calls differ in males and females (the female call is usually longer than that of the male), other gibbons can determine the sex of the caller. Frequently, perhaps on a daily basis, two gibbon groups will go to a territorial border and make contact in response to the morning call. The interaction that ensues consists of threats and displays, along with spectacular acrobatics by the males. The intensity of this behavior varies, depending on the circumstances. A valuable resource, such as a fruiting tree, for instance, may motivate individuals to attack without first vocally warning or threatening the intruders. In such cases, females may enter into the fray to support their partners.

Partially because sexual dimorphism is low (about 13 percent difference in size between the larger males and the smaller females), males and females are equally dominant. Either sex can initiate action, and either can displace the other. Mutual grooming frequently occurs as part of most social interactions. Unlike the other apes, gibbons do not build sleeping nests for their night's rest. They sleep, sitting in an upright position on the callused pads that are located on each side of their hindquarters (the ischial callosities), in the forks of trees, in much the same fashion as the Old World monkeys.

Care of the young.   Gibbons give birth to single offspring once every four to five years (Figure 13–2). Siamang males carry their offspring during their second year, but no such observations have been made for gibbon males. Male parental investment for gibbons is apparently not as intensive as it is for siamangs. Young gibbons spend up to 10 years with their families, but as they get older, they

Figure 13–2 Gibbons live in small monogamous families comprised of a mated pair and as many as four dependent offspring at any one time. Siamang males may carry their offspring during the infant's second year after birth.

encounter increased aggression and intolerance, mostly from the same-sex parent. Eventually, the young gibbons are driven to the boundaries of their territory and begin to move independently from their birth group, finally establishing their own home range. When the young gibbons mature, with luck, they form new pair bonds. Gradually, by initiating their morning calls, solitary males and females attract each other, and a new monogamous pair bond develops.

Recent findings. Recent studies of gibbons in the Khao Yai National Park, Thailand, by Thad Bartlett (2000) has revealed a new side to their behavior. Perhaps because the groups of gibbons he studied were used to the presence of people, more open relationships between gibbon groups were revealed. Bartlett discovered that gibbon families were not always hostile to their neighbors, as we had come to believe from earlier studies. He reported that for one family of *Hylobates lar,* as many as 25 percent of their encounters with three other neighbors took place in an affiliative or friendly manner. Mating habits, as well, were not as cut-and-dried as we once believed. Bartlett observed one young male gibbon who left his natal group and joined a neighboring family. He began a courtship with the adult female of the group, began mating with her, and eventually supplanted the older adult male, forcing him out of his own group.

In other research on gibbons, Ryne Palombit (1996) saw one mated female leave her family to join a neighboring widowed male. She stayed with him for several months, mating with him and several other males before she finally returned to her original mate. Certainly, one consequence of this research is the development of a new model of gibbon behavior that focuses on the nonnuclear family: It seems that gibbon mates may come and go, sometimes for good, and the offspring from different unions may grow up together with their mother. In the final analysis, however complicated gibbon behavior turns out to be, it certainly appears to be more interesting than we have thought up to now.

The Orangutan

Some of the first antecdotal information we have of the orangutan (*Pongo pygmaeus*) came from Alfred Russel Wallace, who noted the animal's great strength:

> No animal is strong enough to hurt the *Mawas* (Orangutan), and the only creature he ever fights with is the crocodile. When there is no fruit in the jungle, he goes to seek food on the banks of the river . . . then the crocodile sometimes tries to seize him. He always kills the crocodile by main strength, standing upon it, pulling open its jaws, and ripping up its throat. . . . The *Mawas* is very strong; there is no animal in the jungle so strong as he. (1869:388)

Although they are highly imaginative, Wallace's tales, and those of other travelers, were the only knowledge of the orangutan that people outside of Borneo and Sumatra had for almost a century. Finally, in the late 1960s, David Horr and John MacKinnon (1974) independently initiated the first field studies of the orangutans in Borneo. Later Birute Galdikas (1979) set up her field station at Tanjung Puting Reserve in Borneo and began long-term studies of the behavior and conservation of these wild apes that continue to the present day.

Field studies have shown that adult female orangutans travel nearly exclusively through the middle layers of the forest canopy. Adult males, although also arboreal, possibly because of their larger size, are known to come down to the ground when they travel long distances. Both modes of locomotion, arboreal and terrestrial, are slow going. The areas where orangs live today have been substantially modified by humans, and because of this, present-day orangutan ecology is probably different from what it was when orangutans roamed most of Asia. In Borneo, where most

FIGURE 13–3 (*a*) Adult male orangutan. (*b*) Pregnant female orangutan.

field studies have been undertaken, the lack of nonhuman predators may also be a contributing factor to orangutan behavior. On Borneo, where tigers are absent, orangutans are much more terrestrial than in Sumatra, where tigers have been observed in orangutan home ranges (Galdikas, 1979). MacKinnon (1979) astutely noted that in Sumatra adult males also spend a great deal more time with females and their offspring. This behavior no doubt serves to mitigate the tigers' potential threat as a predator.

Social interaction.   Orangutans are the least gregarious of all the apes (Figure 13–3). The primary units consist of solitary adult males, solitary subadults, and adult females with their young offspring. Larger units occasionally form when two or more primary units aggregate at a common food source, engage in social play (usually involving subadults), or form consort units for reproductive purposes. Social interactions in orangutans tend to increase when preferred fruit trees come into season, producing a temporary abundance of concentrated food.

Despite a temporary concentration of many orangutans in a single area, social interaction in the form of play takes place almost exclusively between juveniles and infants. Encounters between adult males are usually aggressive, and chases and physical fights are common. Physical confrontation between the males, however, may be mediated by natural avoidance, the result of the long call given exclusively by full-grown adults (see Chapter 9). Adult males tolerate **subadult** males, however, and subadult males are rarely aggressive toward each other. An exception to this occurs when a subadult male attempts to copulate with an adult female. If an adult male is at hand to observe the attempt, he will attack and chase off the subadult male.

Interactions among adult female orangutans are relatively rare but generally amicable. Adolescent females are the most sociable of all of the age–sex classes, and they remain so until the birth of their first offspring, when they leave their mothers to form their own mother–infant group. The home range of adult females is between 1.5 and 6 sq km (0.5 to 2.1 sq mi). Adult females occupy overlapping ranges located within the larger adult male ranges. Male residency is generally not permanent, because males often leave particular areas when resident females give birth. Males often stay away for up to several years, returning only when the female resumes her sexual cycling.

Subadult: sexually mature young adult male or female. Subadult males, unlike females, frequently range outside of a mixed sex social group, either independently or with others of their age and status.

TABLE 13–1	Gestation and Interbirth Intervals in Hominoids	
Taxon	**Gestation Length**	**Interbirth Interval**
Gibbon	210 days[a]	2 years[a]
Orangutan	275 days[a]	6–7 years
Chimpanzee	225 days[a]	4.5–7.5 years[b]
Gorilla	251–289 days[a]	4 years[b]
Homo sapiens		
!Kung (Botswana)	266[b]	4–5 years[b]
Hutterites (North America)	266[b]	2 years[b]

[a]Data from Napier and Napier (1967).
[b]Data from Jolly (1985).

Reproduction and care of infants. Unlike chimpanzees, female orangutans show no external signs of ovulation, but they do develop pale labial swelling during their pregnancy. Orangutans tend to mate promiscuously, even though one dominant male's home range tends to overlap that of several females. The relatively large size of each female's home range, in combination with the generally slow locomotion of adults, make it difficult for a single male to defend his entire range and maintain exclusive access to "his" females (Rodman, 1984). When the females are cycling, they prefer the company of adult males and often seek them out. Unescorted females are prone to being raped by subadult males, unless a larger adult male drives them away (Wrangham and Peterson, 1996). Females who are sexually receptive avoid subadult males and resist mating attempts by the subadult males when the females come in contact with the males.

The interbirth intervals in orangutans seem to be among the longest of any primate species. The minimum interval has been reported by Galdikas (1979) to be about five years, with an average span of between six and seven years (Table 13–1).

Mothers and their infants remain together for a number of years. The dispersal of the young away from their mothers begins when the juveniles start to travel and forage independently. Occasionally, older juveniles rejoin their mothers for variable periods of time. Young females probably settle in a home range near their mothers, whereas males disperse over larger distances, competing with other males for home ranges.

The Gorilla

Gorillas (*Gorilla gorilla*) live in relatively stable units of up to 30 animals, consisting of one or more "silverback" males (fully adult males whose hair along the upper back has turned a silver or white color), black-backed subadult males, females, and their immature young (Figure 13–4). Recent reports show that gorillas may also form all-male units that last for at least three years. Subadult males leave their natal groups and travel alone for long periods of time, eventually forming their own mixed-sex troops by taking one or more young females from other groups (Fossey, 1983). Only in rare cases do adult males migrate between established troops.

After the formation of a social unit, females generally remain in that unit, probably because of mutual attraction to the dominant male. Fossey reported that in groups that lose their male—usually, presumably, through death—females do not remain together but rapidly disperse into other groups.

FIGURE 13–4 Adult male gorilla with younger member of the troop.

FIGURE 13–5 Copulatory positions assumed by gorillas.

Daily behavior within the group. Gorillas occupy an average home range of up to 4,000 ha (10,000 acres), which may overlap with the range of a neighboring group. Even with extreme overlapping of ranges and the consequent frequent intergroup contacts, gorillas do not appear to be territorial. The daily routine of slow feeding, play, and resting is usually accomplished over an average distance of only 1 km (.6 mi).

Gorillas often assume a bipedal stance while displaying, chest beating, or charging. The display is initiated by the male, who begins to vocalize with a low "hoot" that gets louder and faster as the display continues. The male may stand bipedally, run about, throw vegetation, slap his chest, and make a violent noise using cupped hands. The sequence may end with the male thumping the ground with one or both palms. However, the gorilla is basically an extremely shy, unobtrusive vegetarian.

Because of their large size and the low nutritional value of their preferred foods, gorillas consume large quantities of leaves, shoots, and the pith of trees. The abundance of food makes for a leisurely pace, and social encounters are conducted in the same relaxed fashion. Fossey (1983) reports infrequent dominance behavior among the group's members, each of whom is ranked hierarchically. The dominant silverback appears to lead the group in its daily activities without quarrel. Play and grooming behavior among the juveniles appear to be relatively infrequent.

The end of the day for a gorilla group finds individuals searching out a suitable spot for retiring for the night. Like chimpanzees, gorillas construct nests of branches and leaves. Most nests, however, are built low in the forest canopy or on the ground. Gorillas usually sleep in different sites each night.

Reproductive behavior. Gorillas apparently have no breeding season. Reproductive behavior in the wild, though infrequent, is varied, with observations not only of dorso-ventral (face-to-rear) mounting but also ventro-ventral (face-to-face) mounting (Figure 13–5). Because of gorillas' large size, the face-to-face position is not dangerous to them. In smaller animals the risk of predation makes the face-to-face position dangerous, because they can less easily disengage themselves and flee. In all-male groups, extensive homosexual interactions, resembling the courtship and mating patterns of the heterosexual troops have been reported (Yamagiwa, 1987).

fusion-fission social organization: social organization based on formation and dissolution of groups.

The Chimpanzee

Although the behavior of chimpanzees (*Pan troglodytes*) largely depends on the specific ecological niche that they inhabit, in general chimpanzees exhibit a **fusion-fission social organization,** in which groups are flexible in size and composition (Badrian and Badrian, 1984). Within many wild groups, small, very temporary subgroups form on the basis of mutual attraction, friendship, and inclination. They forage over a loosely defined but familiar home range (Figure 13–6).

Social interactions.   Unrelated females tend to show little affection toward each other and spend much of their time alone or with their offspring in extensively overlapping home ranges. Males, in contrast, are much more gregarious and at times cooperate in defending communal territory that includes the feeding areas of several females. The social structure of the community depends on male–male bonding, and males often show affiliative behavior toward one another, such as in grooming. Male–male grooming may account for almost 50 percent of all adult interactions (Figure 13–7).

Among the females, cooperative aggression, as well as grooming, accounts for only 10 percent of interactions. Grooming between adult males and females appears to be directly correlated with mating. Female chimpanzees tend to mate with males who spend substantial amounts of time near them grooming or sharing food. Grooming between mothers and sons becomes more reciprocal with age, but sons

FIGURE 13–6   The fusion-fission social organization of chimpanzees. A subgroup of female chimpanzees and their young are foraging and resting away from other group members.

FIGURE 13–7 Two young chimpanzees showing affiliative behavior.

tend to groom their mothers more than the reverse. Grooming is also used by all individuals as an exchange for access to infants, for assistance in alliance formation, and in aggressive behavior.

It is uncommon to observe male chimpanzees, except for a few immature ones, transfer from one community to another. Female chimpanzees at puberty, however, frequently leave their natal group and transfer to other groups (Goodall, 1986). Consequently, the males in a group tend to be more closely related genetically than the females, who may come from many different backgrounds (Tutin and McGinnis, 1981).

Although members of one chimpanzee group may transfer into another, on the whole chimpanzees are frequently intolerant of their neighbors. Although we once thought of chimpanzees as relatively peaceful animals, they can, on occasion, display frightening aggression. Jane Goodall (1986) described one four-year period at her fieldwork site, Gombe, in Tanzania, that was especially violent. Warfare broke out between two groups, and as a result an entire community was annihilated. Goodall's chimpanzees are often territorial, with small units of up to 10 males, females, and young patrolling the periphery of their home range. If these patrols spot groups of nonresident chimpanzees, they may chase or attack them (Figure 13–8).

What made these observations even more chilling is that the incursions of chimpanzees into neighboring territories were deliberate. These were not foraging expeditions; the chimpanzees were not looking for food but for victims. In the case of the Gombe warfare, the adult males of the neighboring Kahama community were attacked and killed one by one, along with some of the females and their young, by the males of the Kasekela group. The remaining females eventually transferred back to the Kasekela community. Recent studies have shown that lethal violence is characteristic of chimpanzees across Africa. Reports from the Mahale Mountains of Tanzania and the Tai National Park of the Ivory Coast tell of episodes of violent behavior that are reminiscent of those at Gombe.

Reproductive behavior. Female chimpanzees exhibit genital swelling during their normal reproductive cycle and also during the early phases of pregnancy. Swelling during pregnancy is accompanied by typical sexually receptive behavior.

When in estrus, females are usually seen moving with one or more adult males. When more than one cycling female is present in a subgroup, their periods of genital swelling often become synchronized, a phenomena known in humans as the *McClintock Effect.* At Gombe, one mother and daughter pair traveled and cycled together and later gave birth within days of each other.

More than 70 percent of the copulations seen in the wild are opportunistic, involving virtually no competition and allowing free choice for either sex. Copulations also occur as part of **consort relationships,** which can last from 3 hours to 50 days, and during which a male monopolizes an estrous female. These constituted less than 25 percent of recorded copulations, however (Tutin and McGinnis, 1981).

For females transferring between groups, sexual receptivity may help to establish bonds with resident males and reduce the immediate danger of aggression. As a consequence, females who transfer typically do so only when they exhibit genital swelling. Establishing bonds with resident males increases male protection of the female and her offspring, reduces aggressive encounters that might adversely affect a pregnancy, and later may reduce the chance of infanticide by the males. Male chimpanzees may use a recent history of social–sexual interactions with females as determinants of whether to attack or to tolerate females and offspring (Hrdy, 1979). Male infants apparently are at greater risk than female infants as victims of male-instigated infanticide. At the Mahale study site, for example, all of the victims were male infants.

Foraging and hunting. Foraging subgroups offer another common pattern of social interaction (Figure 13–8). Subgroups that find an ample food source often pass this information on by hooting and drumming on trees. In nonterritorial groups, any individual, regardless of whether from the caller's group, may respond to these calls and join this temporary gathering. This congregation, described by

consort relationships: pairing off of a female and male for the purposes of mating.

FIGURE 13–8 Chimpanzee foraging involves many types of food. In order for young chimpanzees to know what are appropriate foods to eat, they watch adult animals, often begging for scraps of especially tasty morsels.

FIGURE 13–9 A foraging group of chimpanzees, made up of an extended family.

Reynolds and Reynolds (1965) as a "carnival," has all the earmarks of a large party. Different individuals dash about in highly excited, nonaggressive displays, then finally settle down for a period of intense social interaction, including copulations and grooming (Figure 13–9).

Other unique social behaviors recorded for chimpanzees include cooperative hunting of monkeys, especially *Colobus,* and other small animals by adult males. They often share the kill among themselves and occasionally with other chimpanzees in their group, who may beg, often gesturing with upturned palms (Figure 13–10).

Tool use.   Perhaps the most exciting observations of chimpanzee social behavior concern tool use. The most common tool described by Goodall (1986) is the termite

FIGURE 13–10   Chimpanzee hunting and food sharing behavior in Gombe, Tanzania.

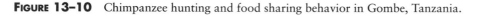

Chimpanzee Hunting Behavior and Human Evolution

CRAIG B. STANFORD

In a forest in Tanzania in East Africa, a group of a dozen chimpanzees is traveling along the forest floor, stopping occasionally to scan the trees overhead for ripe fruit. The group is composed of five adult males, plus several females and their offspring. They reach a tree in which are a group of red colobus monkeys. The male chimpanzees scan the colobus group looking for immature animals or mothers carrying small babies. The colobus, meanwhile, have heard the pant-hoot calls of the chimpanzees approaching and have gathered up their offspring and positioned themselves against a possible attack.

The chimpanzees do indeed attack; the five males—Frodo, Goblin, Freud, Prof, and Wilkie—climb the larger limbs of the tree. They meet the male colobus, who have descended to counterattack. Just in front of me a young colobus attempted to flee the chimpanzees by leaping onto a branch that unfortunately held a male chimpanzee named Atlas. Atlas quickly grabbed the young colobus and dispatched it with a bite to the skull. Within seconds, an estrous female chimpanzee named Trezia ran up to Atlas and begged for meat. Atlas held the colobus carcass away from her; she then turned and presented her sexual swelling to him. They copulated and only then did she receive a share of the meat. An hour later, the last strands of colobus meat, bone, and skin were still being consumed amid occasional outbursts of aggression by individuals who did not receive meat.

Two of the most important and intriguing questions in human evolution are when and why meat became an important part of the diet of our ancestors. The presence of simple stone tools in the fossil record tells us that 2.5 million years ago early hominids were using stone implements to cut the flesh off the bones of large animals that they had either hunted or whose carcasses they had scavenged (Potts, 1988). The pattern of obtaining and processing meat by more recent people has been studied by examining archaeological sites (Steiner and Kuhn, 1992), and also by studying the hunting and meat-eating behavior of modern foraging people, the so-called hunter-gatherers (Kaplan and Hill, 1992).

Modern people and chimpanzees share an estimated 98.5 percent of the DNA sequence, making them more closely related to each other than either is to any other animal species (Ruvolo et al., 1991). Therefore, understanding chimpanzee hunting behavior and ecology may tell us a great deal about the behavior and ecology of those earliest hominids.

After three decades of research on the hunting behavior of chimpanzees at Gombe and elsewhere, we already know a great deal about their predatory patterns. Adult and adolescent males do most of the hunting, making about 90 percent of the kills recorded at Gombe over the past decade. Females also hunt, though more often they receive a share of meat from a male who either captured the meat himself or stole it from the one who did.

Chimpanzees are largely fruit eaters, and meat-eating comprises only about 3 percent of the time they spend eating overall. I estimate that in some years the 45 chimpanzees of the main study community at Gombe kill and consume more than 1,500 lb (about 700 kg) of prey animals of all species. During the peak dry season months, the estimated per capita meat intake is about 65 g (2.3 oz) of meat per day for each adult chimpanzee. This approaches the meat intake by the members of some human foraging societies in the lean months of the year. Chimpanzee dietary strategies may thus approximate those of human hunter-gatherers to a greater degree than we had imagined.

Whether chimpanzee hunters cooperate is a question that has been debated, and the degree of cooperative hunting may differ from one forest to another (Busse, 1978). In the Taï forest in the Ivory Coast, Christophe Boesch has documented highly cooperative hunting behavior and meat-sharing behavior after a kill; the patterns of sharing reward those chimpanzees who participated in the hunt (Boesch, 1994). The highly integrated action by Taï hunters has never been seen at Gombe. In both Gombe and Taï, however, there is a strong positive relationship between the number of hunters and the odds of a successful hunt (Stanford et al., 1994).

This points out the difficulty of interpreting cooperative behavior; even though Gombe hunters do not seem to cooperate, the greater success rate when more hunters are present suggests that some cooperation is occurring.

Did early hominids hunt and eat small and medium-size animals in numbers as large as these? It is quite possible that they did. We know that these earliest hominids were different from chimpanzees in two prominent anatomical features: They had much smaller canine teeth, and they had a lower body adapted for walking on the ground rather than swinging through trees. In spite of lacking the weaponry, such as large canine teeth and tree-climbing adaptations that chimpanzees possess, early hominids probably ate a large number of small and medium-size animals, including monkeys. Chimpanzees do not use their canine teeth to capture adult colobus; rather, they grab the prey and flail it to death on the ground or a tree limb. And once the prey is cornered in an isolated tree crown, group cooperation at driving the monkeys from one hunter to another is quite an efficient killing technique.

In addition to the availability of prey in the trees, there were of course small animals and the young of larger animals to catch opportunistically on the ground. Many researchers now believe that the carcasses of dead animals were an important source of meat for early hominids once they had stone tools to use for removing the flesh from the carcass (Bunn and Kroll, 1986). Wild chimpanzees show little interest in dead animals as a food source, so scavenging may have evolved as an important mode of getting food once hominids began to make and use tools for getting at meat. Before this time, it seems likely that earlier hominids were hunting small mammals as chimpanzee do today, and that the role that hunting played in the early hominids' social lives was probably as complex and political as it is in the social lives of chimpanzees. When we ask when meat became an important part of the human diet, we therefore must look well before the evolutionary split between apes and humans in our own family tree.

Craig B. Stanford is an associate professor of anthropology at the University of Southern California.

FIGURE 13-11 A chimpanzee uses a tunnel probe to extract termites from their nest.

FIGURE 13-12 Adult female chimpanzee cracks open an oil-palm nut using a stone, hammer, and anvil. She reaches to pick up the nut with the right hand while holding the hammer in her left hand. She cracks the nut with her left hand, then she eats the nut with her right hand.

tunnel probe, which is a stick or blade of grass sufficient in size and length to penetrate a termite mound, inviting the resident termites to attack and cling to it (Figure 13–11). The probe is then carefully drawn outward by the chimpanzee and the termites consumed as a tasty meal. Other tools fashioned by chimpanzees include stone and wood hammers used to crack open hard seeds or nuts (Figure 13–12), and bunched-up leaves that act as sponges to retrieve water from caches in trees or otherwise inaccessible small pools. William McGrew summarizes the situation by saying that the material culture of chimpanzees is ubiquitous and diverse. In all populations that have been studied on a long-term basis, the chimpanzees have made and used tools (McGrew, 1998:317), and each population has its own "tool kit" that relates to the special requirements of finding food, acting defensively, grooming, and maintaining social relationships.

Chimpanzee language studies. Chimpanzees are the most outspoken of all the apes, although success in language studies has also been achieved using orangutans, gorillas, and bonobos. The remarkable behavior of the chimpanzee even led some early researchers to believe that, with sufficient training, chimpanzees could be taught to use human language and directly communicate their thoughts to us.

These efforts at teaching chimpanzees and other great apes to speak ultimately failed, primarily because chimpanzees as well as all other nonhuman primates lack the specialized language centers unique to the human neocortex. Efforts were then directed toward teaching chimpanzees some form of hand sign or visual cue language (Figure 13–13). The success of the captive ape nonverbal language studies is partially based on the fact that apes have a large preexisting inventory of signs and gestures, with the capability of learning new ones.

The supposed success of the ape language studies has not been without criticism. Herbert Terrace (1979), reporting results from his own project with a chimpanzee he named Nim, maintained that neither Nim nor the other signing apes were really talking. Rather, they were doing tricks or simple mimicking in order to get what they wanted, usually a food reward. The Lana project, founded by Duane Rumbaugh and Sue Savage-Rumbaugh et al. (1977) at the Yerkes Primate Center, however, provided results that contradicted Terrace's position. The Rumbaughs designed experiments that used a keyboard with more than 100 symbols with which

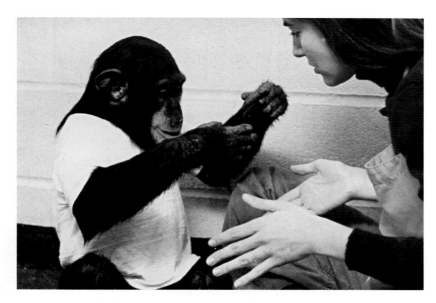

Figure 13–13 Chimpanzee using sign language.

the chimp could respond, and these tests seemed to show that the chimp could formulate some basic rules for grammatical ordering of responses. Apes, it seems, can learn words spontaneously, and they can use them to refer to things that are not present, an ability known as *displacement*. The Rumbaughs claim that chimps can learn words from one another and can talk to one another of things about which the listener does not know. As Sue Savage-Rumbaugh (Savage-Rumbaugh and Lewin, 1994) describes it, apes like humans have language. This is a behavioral domain that is a continuum, not a dichotomy.

The Bonobo

Social structure.   In many ways the overall social structure of the bonobo (*Pan paniscus;* also called "pygmy chimpanzee") reflects an adaptation to feeding in large, predictably abundant food patches. Mixed parties of pygmy chimpanzees, consisting of between 2 and 15 individuals, and including individuals of both sexes and all age classes, are generally larger than those of the common chimpanzee (Figure 13–14). All-male groups of bonobos are rare. In any party of bonobos, one can always find females who are either engaged in sexual activity or nursing offspring. Groups of the common chimpanzee seldom contain both kinds of females. During these frequent group interactions, various behavioral patterns may be seen, such as branch-dragging displays by adult males; female-to-female genital rubbing, which appears to be unique to bonobos; male–male mountings; and heterosexual copulations, initiated by either males or females, that include both the dorso-ventral and ventro-ventral positions (Figure 13–15).

Bonobo social units revolve around a stable core of females who regularly associate with one another and are characterized by high levels of affiliation (Kuroda, 1980). Friendship bonds between individual males and females appear to be quite strong at times, as demonstrated by two individuals cooperating in obtaining food and even sleeping together in the same nest at night. The frequent sexual behavior of the females apparently has resulted in the formation of strong ties between females and males, with the resulting inclination to form stable mixed groups. Although male bonobos show little affection toward one another, they generally show little interest in aggressive interactions outside of dominance rivalry among themselves.

FIGURE 13–14 Bonobo foraging group. Like the common chimpanzee, bonobos eat primarily fruit, pith and leaves as well as an occasional prey such as small mammals, insects, snakes, and fish. Unlike the common chimpanzee, they do not appear to cooperatively hunt or use tools to obtain food.

Reproductive behavior.   Bonobo females have a gestation period of about eight months in length. A mother may nurse her single offspring for up to four years. Because bonobos usually give birth every four and one-half years, they sometimes nurse two infants at once. Bonobos share with humans an extended period of sexual receptivity, which bonobos accomplish by extending also their period of genital swelling. For example, common chimpanzees show a menstrual cycle of approximately 35 days, whereas the bonobos' cycle is nearly 10 days longer. The period of swelling also covers a greater part of the cycle, nearly 75 percent compared to 50 percent of the cycle for the chimpanzee. In bonobo females, even though they are not fertile, sexual swelling reoccurs within the year after they have given birth, adding further to the length of time a female is receptive. Frans de Waal (de Waal and Lanting, 1997:107) summarizes the dramatic difference seen between chimpanzees and bonobos in terms of sexual receptivity: "a chimpanzee female is receptive less than 5 percent of her adult life whereas the bonobo female is so nearly half the time."

Cognitive abilities.   Bonobos show some unique features in their communicative skills. As Savage-Rumbaugh and Lewin (1994) report, some pygmy chimpanzees, especially a male called Kanzi, spontaneously begin to use symbols to communicate with people. Kanzi apparently acquired these symbols by observing his mother working with a researcher. It also seems that Kanzi uses syntax when he communicates by signing. According to Savage-Rumbaugh, some of Kanzi's messages to his human companions display a word order of primitive English.

Bonobos have not been observed to use tools in the wild, either for food gathering or for fighting. Yet laboratory studies have shown that bonobos are exceptional in their powers of observation. Attempts by archaeologists Nicholas Toth and Kathy Schick (Toth et al., 1993; and Schick et al., 1999) to teach Kanzi to make a stone tool proved remarkably successful (Figure 13–16). Stone tool making has been thought to be an exclusively human ability. Although the judgment necessary to calibrate the correct angle and force of impact required to create early humanlike

FIGURE 13–15 Bonobos copulate face to face (ventro-ventrally) in the wild.

stone tools may be beyond bonobo intellectual capacity, Toth's experiments have shown that Kanzi, at least, has the ability to learn to flake stones and to produce a usable tool.

INNATE BEHAVIORS IN HUMANS

Studies of the apes can increase our understanding of early human behavior patterns and the evolution of those patterns toward the modern human condition. Human behavior forms a continuum with ape behavior, and many similarities are the result of shared genes. Tool use, hunting and gathering practices, and bipedal locomotion are behaviors that modern humans share with the apes, though the frequency of these behaviors varies between species. Humans are capable of learning and using symbols, signs, and gestures, but so are the apes, although to a lesser extent.

This section of the chapter concerns the biological and evolutionary basis of human behavior, but we must begin by tempering our remarks and observations. In our search for the evolutionary origins of human social behavior, we are reminded of an important influence on that behavior: culture. Culture is part of the modern human environment; it molds behavior and makes an indelible imprint on each one of us. One can argue that cultural variables have a more immediate influence on behavior than do biological variables. For humans, as for all other species, however, biology forms the template on which behavior is acted out.

Throughout this book we have attempted to show humans as part of the natural world, thus opposing the view that we are a species set apart from it and able to exploit it at whim with little consequence. With this in mind, our review of the biological basis of human behavior returns to an earlier discussion of the concept of the fixed action pattern and the ethological approach to the study of behavior (Chapter 2), because this approach places human behavior firmly within the realm of biology. We begin with examples of genetically controlled human behaviors and advance to a discussion of more complex behaviors.

FIGURE 13–16 Kanzi, a bonobo, making a stone tool.

Fixed Action Patterns

As we saw in Chapter 2, *fixed action patterns* are behaviors that are hard wired into a species: behaviors that all individuals of a species perform instinctively. Many of the clearest human examples of fixed action patterns (FAPs) come from very young infants, because learning, culture, and language can be mostly discounted as factors influencing their behavior and because certain behaviors occur only at certain developmental stages after birth.

Certainly mothers and midwives were able to describe many "instinctual" patterns of behavior in newborns long before these were recognized by behavioral scientists. These neonatal behaviors might include the ability to crawl up the mother's body and find the breast without help, the rhythmic searching movements for the mother's breast, the grasping reflexes of the hands and feet (Figure 13–17), and paddling reactions if the infant is set into water. Newborn infants show FAPs in the first few days of life when their lips are touched, a stimulus that evokes a rhythmic side-to-side movement of the head and opening of the mouth. The movement stops when the infant begins to suckle. This is a programmed "search for the breast" that disappears between six and ten days after birth, when it is commonly replaced by a visually oriented search. However, children may continue to show this behavior occasionally for months—even a two-year-old may do this to find the breast with its eyes closed while sleeping. Programmed crying, homologous to the "lost call" of other mammals, is another FAP in human infants. When the infant is "found," that is, picked up, the crying stops.

As time goes on, infants continue to react innately to certain other stimuli. For example, until the onset of the second month, eye-size spots painted on a square or round two-dimensional surface invariably evoke smiling in the infant. Up to a point, in fact, this schematic representation of the human face does a better job of eliciting smiling than a completely painted and lifelike face. More recent experiments have shown that it makes no difference whether the pair of dots is parallel or vertical or whether in fact there are three dots instead of two. Only one dot by itself fails to evoke infant smiling. In addition to smiling, laughing also appears to arise innately. As a further example, at the age when hearing children begin to babble—one of the initial stages of language development—deaf-born children begin to "babble," or sign with their hands, spontaneously. And the different stages of lan-

FIGURE 13–17 Fixed action patterns in human infants: hand- and foot-grasping reflexes in response to touch.

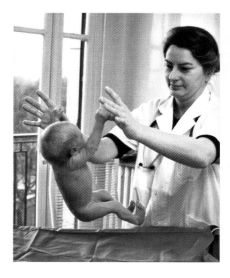
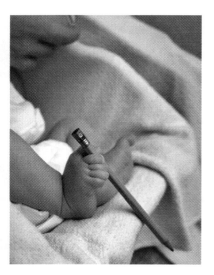

guage development, such as babbling, jargoning, learning words, and production of two-word sentences, follow a similar time sequence in children of all cultures. The same is true of milestones of motor development, such as rolling over, crawling, sitting, standing, walking, and grasping.

No doubt the reason for many behaviors, such as smiling, chuckling, and babbling, can be found by examining the reactions they evoke in the parent. Experiments show that parents, as well as other relatives and even strangers, react very strongly and positively to infants as the infants start to look at them and as their vision focuses on faces that are close to them, a process that begins at birth. Similarly, smiling and laughing reinforce an already very strong mother–infant bond as the child matures. So perhaps some social FAPs have their origin in an infant's need to elicit a mother's attention and affection.

Some FAPs seen in infants exemplify "evolutionary baggage." They are left over from earlier stages of evolution when they were important for survival. For example, when human infants close their fingers and curl their toes around any object that touches their palms or soles, they are probably exhibiting a relic adaptation from clinging onto a furry mother, especially while nursing (see Figure 13–17).

Adult human fixed action patterns are more difficult to define. Evidence suggests, however, that adult behavior has a stronger biological component than many social scientists might admit. Acoustical signals, such as crying, sobbing, or calls for help, have the effect of alarming us, eliciting negative or fearful responses that can be measured by heart rate increases and irregularities in breathing. Olfactory signals, too, can bring very subtle responses that appear to be innate. Women who have lived together in dormitories show a tendency for synchronic menstruation. It appears, however, that ovulation rather than menstruation is the cause of synchronization and that the cause is the hormonal content of urine, perspiration, and saliva passed directly by touch from one individual to another during grooming or through scent from pheromones.

Cross-cultural comparisons provide one indication of shared behavior patterns (Table 13–2). Cultures around the world share characteristics, and individuals within cultures also show consistent forms of behavior. These similarities do not seem to derive from contact between cultures but result from a common biological and psychological substrate. Some examples of these possible adult human FAPs are

TABLE 13–2	**Universal Human Behavioral Characteristics**	
Age-grading	Divination	Community organization
Cosmology	Hospitality	Ethics
Food taboos	Magic	Kin groups
Law	Sexual restrictions	Status differentiation
Ritual	Incest taboos	Dominance-subordination
Symbolization	Defense and/or	Ethnocentrism
Altruism	attachment to territory	Warfare
Self-sacrifice for others	Reification and personification	
Sports	Vengeance	

How many of these human behavioral characteristics do we share with our closest living relatives, the great apes?

From Lopreato (1984).

FIGURE 13-18 Flirting—the prolonged look, looking away and down, reestablishing brief eye contact, and the slight smile—is an example of an adult fixed action pattern.

flirting behavior (Figure 13–18) and greeting behavior (including a very brief upward "flash" of the eyebrows).

Other "Innate" Behaviors

In addition to FAPs, ethologists have discovered other sorts of "innate" behaviors. The first of these is **imprinting,** the formation of a lasting impression during a period of heightened sensitivity to a certain stimulus (see Chapter 3). For example, baby geese need to learn to follow their mother, so they become imprinted to follow any large, moving object that they see within a critical period after hatching. Konrad Lorenz became the "mother" on which a group of goslings became imprinted, because he was the only large moving object around after their hatching. He became the **innate releasing mechanism** that initiated the goslings to follow him as their mother. Human imprinting is much less clear-cut and more subject to interpretation. The best work in this area has been done on mothers and their babies (Klaus and Kennell 1976) and stresses the importance of not separating mother and baby after birth (see Chapter 3 for a detailed discussion of imprinting).

Mammals in general and humans especially have an added level of complexity in their behavior: "logical," or reasoning, ability residing in the large cerebral hemispheres. This part of the brain often overrides innate or even emotional behaviors of the more ancient parts of our brain. An example is our ability to contain our anger in a social situation where an angry or violent response would be inappropriate or even detrimental to our own or another's well-being. This override should not obscure the fact that some part of our brains may be reacting to the world in a different manner than our "thinking" brain. The study of human ethology concentrates on important areas in understanding human behavior—

imprinting: the fixation in an individual of a specific stimulus or set of stimuli during a particular period of sensitivity to learning that stimulus.

innate releasing mechanism: a sensory cue that triggers a certain behavior or set of behaviors in an animal.

Probing the Biology of Emotion and Attachment

In his book *The Expression of Emotions in Man and Animals* (1872), Charles Darwin observed that different species have similar ways of expressing many emotions. New research attempts to map the neural circuits that send the emotional messages that fascinated Darwin. Studies have shown that the amygdala and, perhaps, the prefrontal cortex (which may modulate the emotional activity of the amygdala) have a great deal to do with the emotion of fear. Three new research efforts have provided intriguing clues toward a further understanding of the opposite reactions to fear and avoidance: attachment, bonding, and love.

Rebecca Turner and colleagues (Turner et al., 1999) reported preliminary results of research on the hormone oxytocin, known to be involved in inducing labor and in lactation, and one that can facilitate bonding. Oxytocin levels were measured before, during, and after women in the study sample recalled positive and negative emotional experiences. The results showed that women who were involved in an ongoing committed relationship experienced greater oxytocin increases in response to positive emotions than did single women. Turner further went on to speculate that because oxytocin is released in men and women during sexual orgasm, there is reason to assume that it is also involved in human bonding, because it is responsible for the warm postcoital "glow" of affection rather than the physical sensations of orgasm.

Research by Z. X. Wang and colleagues (1998) provides additional clues to the neurochemical mechanisms behind bonding and attachment. These studies involve the ways the hormone vasopressin affects behavior in different species of rodent. In monogamous, gregarious rodents, such as the prairie vole, vasopressin facilitates affiliation, pair bonding, and paternal care. In solitary polygynous species, such as the montane vole, vasopressin has no effect on social behavior. The key lies in the different patterns of vasopressin receptors in the brain of each species and in the DNA that codes for these receptors. In the social species of vole, there is an additional long DNA sequence; this sequence is missing in solitary species such as the montane vole. This sequence is inserted in the promoter region of the gene, a region thought to be important as an on/off switch regulating the gene's activity. When the vasopressin receptor gene from the social vole was inserted into the DNA of less social mice, a new pattern of receptor expression was created in mouse brains, and the transgenic mice showed an increase in social contact with females, a response not seen in normal mice. These studies show that, at least in rodents, vasopressin can affect changes in social behavior and increase affiliative behavior.

Donatella Marazziti (1999) has made another interesting discovery in her work on obsessive–compulsive disorder (OCD), a condition characterized by compulsions to repeat mundane activities, such as washing one's hands over and over again. She found that there are striking similarities between people who are lovesick and sufferers of OCD. OCD is linked to low levels of the neurotransmitter serotonin, and when Marazziti tested for this chemical in her in-love volunteers, she found that in both groups serotonin levels were about 40 percent less than normal.

Although these studies do not yet show conclusively the exact role brain chemicals play in emotional bonding in humans, the preliminary results are intriguing. As Darwin (1872) concluded more than a century ago, although understanding the origins of emotional expressions remains a great difficulty, it deserves still further attention. Darwin, we are certain, would be pleased to see the extraordinary results science has made in this direction thus far.

including the FAPs, innate dispositions to learn, and innate releasing mechanisms we may have inherited from our ancestors, as well as how our brains are affected by this inheritance.

HUMAN SOCIOBIOLOGY

A number of biologists view *sociobiology* as an important discipline within which scientists can effectively study the evolution of social behavior in animal species. As we saw in Chapter 3, sociobiology is the science of the biological, especially the genetic, basis of social behavior. All mammals rely on learning to some extent. Humans rely on learning more than do chimpanzees but only a little more. Learning among mammals is a matter of degree rather than kind. In comparison with human beings, however, no animal has a spoken language with unlimited possible constructions, nor complex "culture," nor as highly developed and large a cerebral cortex.

How do we relate, then, the findings of sociobiology to human behavior, considering that so much of what we do is apparently learned, affected by personal choice, and subject to change from one situation to the next? Wilson (1996) has suggested three possibilities:

1. Genes merely prescribe the capacity for culture. Therefore, all human behavior is determined by culture.
2. The genotype predisposes humans toward development of certain genetically controlled, species-specific behaviors.
3. Genetic variability still exists, and at least some human behavioral traits have a genetic foundation.

Some researchers would opt for possibility 1. A detailed consideration of human ethology (e.g., Eibl-Eibesfeldt, 1989), however, argues for at least the possibility of 2, because it suggests that there are human species-specific behaviors, and even 3 goes only so far to maintain that some human behaviors have a genetic foundation. Sociobiologists generally do not maintain the extreme position, sometimes imputed to them, that all human behavior is under direct genetic control. It obviously is not.

Sociobiologists have discovered that the degree of relatedness between individuals, thus the percentage of shared genes, can affect certain behaviors. This realization explains both the existence of apparently selfless or altruistic behaviors on the one hand and selfishness and interpersonal competition on the other. Humans throughout the world tend to favor their relatives; furthermore, the higher the degree of relationship, the greater the number of social interactions. If the common substructure of kinship is rooted in biology, then sociobiological theory could predict behaviors that are based on this linkage (Figure 13–19). Napoleon Chagnon (1983), for example, demonstrated that genetic relatedness does play a role in a South American Yanomamö's life, often explaining the basis on which villages split up and fights between village hosts and guests occur.

Human Behavioral Ecology

Human behavioral ecology has become part of the growing field of evolutionary biology. The focus of this more specific research is to view human behavior within its ecological context, and the field shares many of its perspectives with ethology and sociobiology, but there are some important differences (Borgerhoff-Mulder, 1991; Smith, 1992a). As Smith succinctly points out,

> The ethological view of animals enacting "fixed action patterns" was replaced with the view of animals as self-interested strategizers and fitness maximizers—flexible opportunists who could size up any setting they encountered and figure out how to get the most offspring out of it. (SMITH, 1992a:21)

Behavioral ecology has borrowed tools from many disciplines, such as economics and engineering. Thus, decision making under risk and uncertainty, tradeoffs, and **game theory,** to name only a few of the tools used, have become a part of behavioral ecological analysis.

How might a field such as human behavioral ecology help us better understand human behavior? Some of the areas that have interested researchers include the following:

1. *Subsistence strategies:* How do people get food and what are the costs, in terms of energy expenditure and the risks of obtaining it (optimal foraging strategy applied to humans)?
2. *Mating ecology:* In what ways do different ecologies affect one's chances of finding a mate and having offspring?

game theory: the analysis of win–loss combinations in any competitive relationship in order to determine strategy or to predict outcomes of the competition.

FIGURE 13-19   Why do people travel hundreds or even thousands of miles to attend family reunions? Sociobiology tells us that all humans interact more with their relatives than with unrelated people; this innate tendency is the basis for many enjoyable feelings of belonging and togetherness.

3. *Spatial organization:*   How do human groups use the space they live in and how effective are the strategies they use to more efficiently use this space?
4. *Variation in competition and cooperation:*   Why do people sometimes cooperate and sometimes compete to obtain critical resources?

The earliest application of this research involved questions of spatial organization and land use among several hunter-gatherer groups. These studies looked at territoriality in different groups in an attempt to understand why some groups displayed territorial aggression toward their neighbors whereas others did not. This research focused on how different human groups balanced what they conceived to be the projected benefits of exclusive use of their space versus the costs of monitoring and defending that territory (Dyson-Hudson and Smith, 1978).

More recent analysis involving subsistence strategies through **optimal foraging theory** has demonstrated that foragers make choices that yield the highest feasible rate of return from their foraging efforts (in time and energy). Studies of the Ache Indians of Paraguay have shown, for example, that changes in technology (from hunting with bows and arrows to hunting with shotguns) predictably altered the expected return rates for certain prey species (Hill et al., 1987). This simplified picture is complicated by the fact that in humans, unlike other species of animals, prey choice may be ranked in many ways in addition to simple nutritional values.

optimal foraging theory: involves subsistence strategizing; in terms of time and energy, foragers will make choices to maximize the highest feasible rate of return.

FIGURE 13–20 !Kung woman with toddler. Note that the woman is pregnant and her child appears to be three or four years old; a birth interval of about four years has been shown to be optimal for the !Kung people, based on the ecological conditions in which they live.

Human cultural values may rank certain prey higher in accordance with their non-food value (ivory, pelts, etc.), social value (i.e., prestige), or preference as food (taste).

In terms of reproductive strategies, behavioral ecologists consider such topics as maturation rates; age at first and last reproduction; birth spacing; offspring sex ratios; differential treatment of male and female offspring; and variations in mating systems involving monogamy, polygyny, and polyandry. It is in this area that human behavioral ecology most clearly overlaps with sociobiological interests. Early research efforts involved investigations of South African Kalahari !Kung San birth spacing and the idea of self-regulation of fertility. The average birth interval of !Kung mothers is about four years. Richard Lee (1980), who studied these people, argued that the wide birth spacing among foraging !Kung was an adaptation that benefited the mothers by reducing their work effort in terms of transporting and feeding children (Figure 13–20). Later, Blurton-Jones (1987) showed that offspring survival was maximized by 48-month interbirth intervals.

Another foraging population, however, the Hadza, living on the East African savanna, provided quite different data from that of the !Kung. Hadza mothers carry their infants less, allow them to forage independently for their own food, and show a significantly higher fertility. These differences seem to stem from the fact that the !Kung live in an area where the land surface provides for poor distance visibility and a lowered concentration of plant foods for collection by children. Both of these factors, along with differences in nursing frequency and maternal nutritional status, contribute to the !Kung's greater parental vigilance and care per child and, consequently, the increased spacing between births.

Thus far human behavioral ecologists have designed their research efforts to ask and answer simple questions, only to discover that this research involves complex social interactions. A simple matter of prey choice turns out to be connected with gender roles and mating strategies as well as with a decision about who hunts and who stays in camp to reap the benefits brought back by the hunters; optimal birth spacing is interconnected with divisions of labor, parent–offspring relations, and perceived investment. It is difficult to look at ecological adaptations in any social species, especially humans, without considering social processes and cultural transmission.

Culture and Biology

It is apparent from studies of the learning process that the fundamental things that humans do are learned easily. Human speech is a good example of a behavior that is easy for humans to acquire but impossible for our closest living relatives, the apes, to imitate. Expanding this notion more generally, if there is a genetic basis for all human behaviors, it must be related somehow to the ease with which those behaviors are learned. Because human behavior is generally adaptive, specific behavior patterns that provide greater fitness to some individuals must have been selected for in the course of human history. Knowing that at some point in human history different behavior patterns, such as language and tool making, became adaptive to our ancestors, gives us an important perspective. For example, we know that for most of human history we lived in small groups and acted on the basis of our personal relationships to others. This helps explain why most humans find it difficult to live within large groups in urban environments, where kinship usually does not guide social interaction and economic exchange.

The evolutionary perspective on behavior gives us additional insight into behaviors that some social scientists find inappropriate and sometimes deplorable. Aggression, **ethnocentrism**, territoriality, and dominance might be on a list of human behavior patterns that may appear to be dysfunctional. Because aggression appears to be a fundamental characteristic of nearly all animal life, especially in social species, however, it must have a substantial heritable component. In the nonhuman primates, aggressive behavior often leads to the establishment of rank or dominance, which, in turn, provides societal stability to the relationships among individuals. Aggressive behavior is limited, because high-ranking individuals assume a leadership function and are not frequently challenged. Like other animals, humans exhibit distinct territorial behavior. Territoriality and the maintenance of individual space are similar phenomena. Although the exact parameters are culturally defined, we do maintain specific distances between one another.

Human aggression probably functioned much the same in the past. Organized group aggression served a valuable function for defense and territorial spacing in early hominid societies. Organized national sports may be one harmless way for modern-day humans to release these phylogenetically ancient behaviors. In recent years, however, the violence that has accompanied many sports, such as soccer, has removed even these events from the category of "harmless" (Figure 13–21).

Some research has shown that there is a correlation between low levels of the neurotransmitter serotonin and individuals who are prone to violence. As with the nonhuman primates, aggression, or the threat of it, often leads to higher status, and, predictably, in many cases to increased reproductive success. Human males compete for status through whatever means are available to them. Urban street gang members often use violence, or a credible threat, to maintain their reputations. Research on nonhuman primates demonstrates that serotonin levels can be raised or lowered by environmental stimuli.

In their study of vervet monkeys, Lynn Fairbanks and colleagues (2001) have shown that the highest ranking males in a troop have the highest serotonin levels. Low-ranking males show the lowest levels and also tend to be more impulsively aggressive. These studies suggest that serotonin levels increase with an increase in individual dominance rank, and that once high rank is achieved, high levels of serotonin function to maintain high self-esteem in humans (Figure 13–22).

In the view of some researchers, serotonin levels function to regulate self-confidence, depending on feedback from others. High levels of serotonin assist in the maintenance of high social status; low levels, although linked to individuals

ethnocentrism: the pervasive belief present in all cultures that leads individuals to view their own culture as superior to others.

FIGURE 13-21 Organized sports, particularly those that pit nation against nation, may be a relatively harmless substitute for war. However, violence sometimes comes to the surface, as happened at this European soccer game.

who may be more prone to violence, are also likely to discourage other individuals from conspicuously challenging others for fear of punishment. The hypothesis explains observed behavior in low-ranking monkeys whose rage centers in the brain were stimulated through implanted electrodes. These monkeys, rather than attacking other monkeys, as higher-ranking males under the same circumstances would do, would cower by themselves in a remote corner of their laboratory cage.

But what is the significance of the correlation between low levels of serotonin and violent behavior? For low-ranking individuals who find themselves in a situation where the existing social system is not providing adequate rewards, it may pay to circumvent the rules. Low-dominance monkeys often attempt to mate surreptitiously, hiding from the view of dominant males. In the absence of legitimate ways to achieve status, individuals use illegitimate means, and risk-taking increases. It seems, therefore, that low serotonin levels are adaptive in the sense that they prepare individuals to take risks and evade the rules. In humans, this evolutionary explanation suggests that the way to reduce urban violence would be to develop nonviolent means for young men to achieve social status.

Future Prospects

No matter what the sequence of genetic changes that resulted in the behavioral repertoire of modern humans, anthropology has offered many useful perspectives

FIGURE 13–22 Research shows that high-status human males, such as this physician, produce high levels of serotonin, and that this serves to maintain high self-esteem.

toward an understanding of human nature. As we have seen, the behaviors that were once thought to make humans unique from the rest of the animal world, such as tool use, cognitive thought, and language, are, at least in part, shared with other primates. Anthropology has brought us, thus far, toward the realization that we humans, with all our advanced technological skill, still bear the stamp of our earlier

Alienation in Human Societies and Suicide

The genetics of primates, including humans, makes group living both enjoyable and rewarding. There are lots of advantages to living in a group, such as safety, companionship, and increased ability to find resources. Our genetic heritage, however, has restricted our ability to be social. Once a group exceeds a certain size, the members will split into two (or more) smaller ones. Although the maximum number of members in any social group varies somewhat from species to species, in primates the range is usually not large. When this limit has been reached, the group can no longer function as a unit, social organization breaks down, and the inevitable fissioning occurs.

Among nonhuman primates, very large troops exist only in some Japanese macaque monkey societies and in the African forest-living mandrills. Members of the macaque societies stay together primarily for feeding purposes under circumstances of human provisioning. Even though the semblance of troop structure is still apparent, social behavior is unorganized and chaotic, and social interactions are primarily restricted to members of kin subgroups. New observations of mandrills, however, suggest that this is not always the case.

In humans, not belonging to a social group can be as psychologically damaging as being in one that is too large (for example, living in a society whose membership is too large for most interactions to occur on a personal level). As reported in the *British Medical Journal*

(Whitney et al., 1999), people who live in what is called "fragmented" groups, where people interact together for only short periods of time, are usually unmarried, live alone, and are at higher risk of suicide. Psychologists studying these groups found higher rates of suicide than in groups of much lower socioeconomic levels, where financial stresses might reasonably lead to increased suicide levels. In addition, groups where the incidence of social fragmentation increased saw the greatest increases in rates of suicide. Human social behavior clearly has a genetic component, but as with most adaptations it is structured within limits; being outside of any group or being a member of one with too many members can have equally devastating consequences for the individual.

history. As we learn more about ourselves, this fact becomes even more obvious. Distinctions created between ourselves and the rest of the animal world become less evident as research progresses.

◄ SUMMARY

1. **What are the primary types of social organization found among the apes?**
Adult gibbons and siamangs form mated pairs, defend their home ranges, and react aggressively toward other adult pairs and even their own offspring once these have reached a juvenile age.

Unlike gibbons and siamangs, the great apes exhibit various degrees of sexual dimorphism. The larger orangutan adult males defend extensive home ranges that overlap with the smaller ranges of a number of adult females. Female orangutan social organization is usually limited to interactions with close female kin, a mother's younger offspring, and, on occasion, when a female is sexually receptive, an adult male.

Gorillas form stable groups consisting of one or more older "silverback" males, some younger "black-backed" males, females, and other young. Mixed-sex groups apparently remain together because of attraction to the adult "silverback" and often dissolve as a group on the death of that individual.

Chimpanzees display a fission-fusion pattern of social organization where members of a community interact with others on an opportunistic or as-needed basis. Mothers with newborns frequently associate with one another; females in estrus are usually found with adult males. Although female kinship relations are an important component in understanding social interactions, female chimpanzees usually leave their birth group. Chimpanzees are the only nonhuman primate that have been observed in the wild using tools, cooperatively hunting, and engaging in intercommunity warfare.

The bonobos exhibit a higher degree of female affiliation and lower levels of male intratroop display and aggression, compared to common chimpanzees. Bonobos engage in year-round sexual behavior that includes individuals of all ages. This may account for stronger, longer-lasting bonds between males and females, and, consequently, more stable mixed social groups.

2. **What can studies of ape behavior tell us about human behavior? What innate behaviors do humans demonstrate?**
Studies of the apes can increase our understanding of early human behavior patterns and the evolution of those patterns toward the modern human condition. Human behavior forms a continuum with ape behavior, and many similarities are the result of shared genes. Tool use, hunting and gathering practices, and bipedal locomotion are behaviors that modern humans share with the apes, though the frequency of these behaviors varies between species. Apes are capable of learning and using symbols, signs, and gestures.

The most clearly recognizable human behaviors that bear a genetic stamp are the fixed action patterns of infants. Neonatal behaviors include rhythmic searching movements for the mother's breast and grasping reflexes of the hands and feet. Older infants react innately to certain visual stimuli, such as eye-size spots that are painted on a flat surface, which invariably evoke smiling in the infant. Some fixed action patterns are relics of an evolutionary past, such as the clinging reflex, which allowed infants to cling to their mothers' fur. Evidence of adult human fixed action patterns is more difficult to find.

Certain acoustical or olfactory signals, however, have specific effects on individuals that could be considered innate, such as increased heart rates and irregularity in breathing that often occur when people become alarmed. Cross-cultural comparisons of similar behavior patterns show that these similarities, such as flirting behavior, result from a common biological and psychological substrate. Other innate behaviors in humans may be acquired by imprinting, the formation of a lasting impression during a period of heightened sensitivity to certain stimuli, such as mother–infant bonding in the first hour after birth.

3. **What insights have human sociobiology, behavioral ecology, and the study of culture brought to our knowledge of human behavior and human potential?**

Whereas culture provides the framework for almost all human interactions, biology forms the template that limits human behavioral plasticity. Human sociobiology and human behavioral ecology are useful tools in looking at the interface of biology and culture. Sociobiologists do not maintain the extreme position that all human behavior is under direct genetic control. The genetic basis for human behavior, however, is related in some fashion to the ease with which humans learn specific behaviors, such as language on the one hand and ethnocentrism on the other. Human behavioral ecology focuses on human behavior in its ecological context and on humans as self-interested strategizers in the areas of subsistence, mating, spatial organization, and competition and cooperation. The evolutionary perspective gives us additional insight on human behavior. For most of human history we lived in small groups and acted on the basis of our personal relationships with others. This helps explain why humans find it difficult to live within large social groups in modern urban environments.

CRITICAL THINKING QUESTIONS

1. Sexual dimorphism in the apes is variously expressed. In gibbons and siamangs, which are generally monogamous, little sexual dimorphic differences exist. In the great apes, differences in size between the sexes are considerable, and great ape societies may be characterized as promiscuous. How might these facts be useful in providing clues to the sociosexual behavior of early hominids and modern humans? Are we supposed to be monogamous or polygynous?

2. What is the rationale for using behavioral studies of the African great apes as models for understanding early human social behavior rather than studies of, for example, gibbons, which like most humans practice monogamy, or baboons, which live today in the same environments as did our earliest ancestors?

3. What are the limitations in the use of sociobiology in and of itself to help us understand human social behavior?

4. Generally speaking, in the nonhuman primates, aggression maintains the social order and may for that reason be seen as adaptive behavior. Most instances of violence in human societies are disruptive, and violence is, therefore, seen as maladaptive. How would you reconcile these observations?

5. Many aspects of modern human behavior have been linked to causal hormonal factors in the brain. However, living in a social group often alters the prescribed outcome of hormonal influence, as we have seen in experimental situations using nonhuman primates. What might be the applicability of these studies toward an understanding of human behavior?

◀ INTERNET EXERCISES

Critical Thinking

What Is Language? Chapter 13 describes a number of researchers' attempts to teach chimpanzees to use language. Although most primatologists conclude that nonhuman primates cannot learn language in a human sense, others disagree and are continuing to work with chimpanzees and bonobos. For this exercise, research some of these ongoing attempts and decide whether they represent language learning. Consider the following questions:

1. What is human language? To what extent is it based on sounds? On symbols? Do human and nonhuman language form a continuum?
2. What level of language competence have nonhuman primates achieved? What level is typical of human two-year-olds? Ten-year-olds?
3. How do nonhuman primates learn language? How do human infants learn language?

Writing Assignment

Human Universals. The chapter discusses cultural practices that are universal among humans regardless of culture, such as altruism, sports, magic, sexual restrictions, and kin groups (see Table 13–2). Write a paper about some aspect of cultural universals. Choose a particular universal and write about either its manifestation in various cultures around the world or current evidence for the genetic basis of the practice. Be sure to discuss the benefit the practice confers on individual humans and on society in general.

See Companion Web site for Internet links.

MEDIALAB

Violence and Aggression Among Chimpanzees

Chimpanzees in the wild exhibit a wide range of behaviors, depending on the specific ecological niche that they inhabit. In general, chimpanzee groups are flexible in size and composition. And unlike the peaceful bonobo, chimpanzees can exhibit startlingly humanlike forms of aggression.

Recent studies have shown that lethal violence is characteristic of chimpanzees across Africa. Reports from the Mahale Mountains of Tanzania and the Tai National Park of the Ivory Coast tell of episodes of violent behavior. On the video on your Companion Web site, Dr. Jane Goodall describes an especially violent period at Gombe.

WEB ACTIVITY

The chimpanzees of Gombe are often territorial, with small units of up to ten males, females, and young patrolling the periphery of their home range. If these patrols spot groups of nonresident chimpanzees, they may chase or attack them. In the video, Dr. Goodall describes an unusually warlike period at Gombe.

Activity

1. View the video. What is Dr. Goodall's attitude toward the violence she describes?
2. What are the genetic relationships among the chimpanzees in a band? Is there an evolutionary advantage for bands of chimpanzees that attack or destroy other bands?
3. What does the behavior of chimpanzees suggest about human violence and aggression? What does the relatively peaceful behavior of bonobos and gorillas, our two other closely related species, suggest?

The MediaLab can be found in Chapter 13 on your Companion Web site http://www.prenhall.com/boaz

14

HUMAN BIOLOGY AND VARIATION

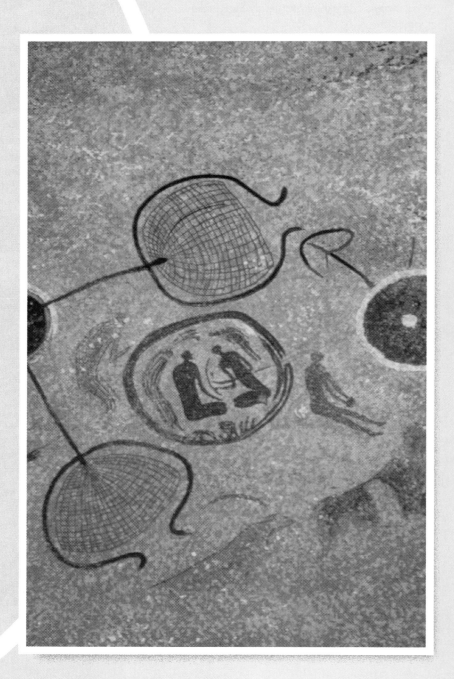

After reading this chapter, you should be able to discuss the following questions:

1. What is phenotypic variation, and how is it measured? What factors increase phenotypic variation?
2. Why is "race" an inadequate way to describe human diversity?
3. Explain the significance of noncoding DNA and neutral mutations.
4. How are polymorphisms, such as hemoglobin S, blood groups, and skin pigmentation, maintained in human populations? How do they benefit individuals?
5. What is known about the influence of genetics on behavior and intelligence?

A random sample of human individuals from any U.S. metropolitan area could show the extent to which we vary worldwide (Figure 14–1). Humans are a morphologically variable species, and part of the reason this variation exists is because members of our species have occupied and still do occupy many diverse habitats. Yet the genetic basis of this variation must be quite small. Human Genome Project research has determined that of the 3 billion base pairs that comprise human DNA, only about 1 percent are functional. This leaves humans with about 30,000 genes, far fewer than earlier estimates of 100,000 or more.

Biochemical evidence shows that humans and chimpanzees differ genetically by only 1 to 2 percent and that this amount of difference was accumulated over a period of probably less than 5 million years. Because the chimpanzee genome probably contains about the same number of genes as the human genome, it has been suggested that the complexity of both species, as well as the differences between them, result from multitasking proteins, not from the number of genes per se. When one considers the small genetic differences that exist between chimpanzees and

FIGURE 14–1 A group of people who show the variety of physical features that are found in the world's many human populations. Based solely on the criterion of physical appearance, biological diversity in humans is substantial. The amount of genetic variation within the entire human species, however, is actually very small.

humans, it is obvious that the human gene pool could not have changed a great deal since the widespread appearance of anatomically modern humans, our Upper Paleolithic hunter-gatherer ancestors, about 35,000 years ago (Eaton, Shostak, and Konner, 1989). The amount of variation within the human species must be considerably less than 1 percent.

Given these facts, why, and to what extent, do modern humans vary from one another, and what are the factors responsible for this variation? Are all of the variable human traits adaptive (caused by natural selection), or do they result from other forces of evolution? In this chapter we review what we know about human variation, attempt to explain this variability at the genetic and phenotypic levels, and discuss the evolutionary framework in which these characteristics have come to exist.

THE NATURE OF HUMAN GENETIC VARIATION

Inherited characteristics are variable at all levels of our biology, down to the genes. These characteristics include features of our external appearance—hair and skin color, facial features, and stature, among others—and of our internal characteristics—our blood types and our abilities to digest or metabolize certain substances. As we saw in earlier chapters, inherited variation results from mutation and from the reshuffling of genes within populations from one generation to the next. We study inherited variation to understand how evolutionary forces have acted and continue to act to produce modern human populations.

There are important patterns to human biological variation. All individuals within a species do not vary equally from one another. Individuals within one family share significant genetic, anatomical, and even behavioral similarities because of their close genetic bonds. There is also a geographic component to variation—individuals drawn from indigenous populations at the far north of Greenland and at the tip of southern Africa will show some degree of difference, although they are still clearly within the same zoological species and subspecies, *Homo sapiens sapiens*. As a rule, the amount of variation between individuals increases with distance: For most traits, the further away from one another two individuals' populations live, the more those individuals tend to differ. Conversely, individuals who live close together within the same population tend to resemble one another both genetically and morphologically. As we saw in Chapter 4, these patterns are the result of and are maintained by the forces of evolution: mutation, selection, migration, and genetic drift.

Populations, however, must pay a price for their variability: genetic load, or the proportional decrease in fitness caused by a variation, relative to the fitness of an optimum genotype (Crow, 1986). Unfavorable genotypes lead to reduced reproductive success and, in some cases, death. Genetic loads may be calculated for all loci, or sites on the chromosomes, and may differ considerably from one another depending on the lethality of the genotypes. In sickle-cell anemia, an example we discussed in Chapter 4 and consider again later in this chapter, the minimum genetic load is calculated based on the deaths caused by the lethal homozygous recessive genotype (about 4 percent of individuals in certain populations). As a rough rule of thumb, a high genetic load usually follows a high degree of genetic variability.

How Variation Is Measured

genetic markers: traits whose genetic causation are known and which can be used in the study of populations.

Biological anthropologists study anatomical variation both quantitatively, in terms of traits that vary in degree; and qualitatively, in terms of traits that are either present or absent. Thus, they collect data on the presence, absence, or frequencies of **genetic markers,** or they collect data on the variations of certain physical characteristics,

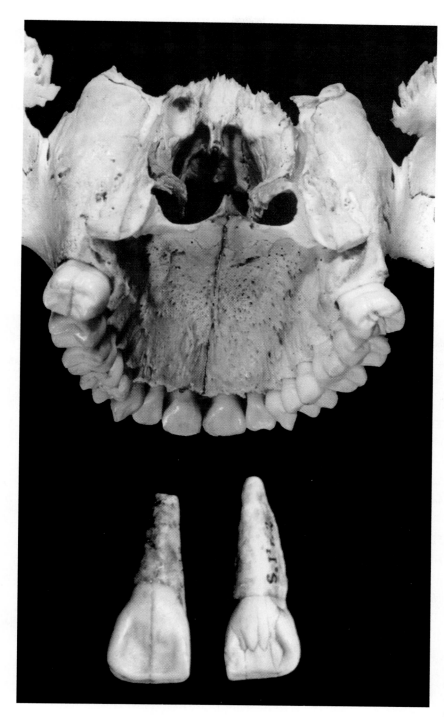

FIGURE 14–2 Top: View of the upper teeth of a modern human (a European) taken from inside the mouth. The inside surface of the middle incisors is smooth, lacking the characteristic indentations seen in the two isolated middle incisors (below). These two teeth are from the *Homo erectus* site of Zhoukoudian in northern China. These so-called shovel-shaped incisors are found more frequently in modern Asian people and their close kin, such as Native Americans, than in other human populations. Shovel-shaped incisors are also found with high frequency in Asian archaic *H. erectus* and *H. sapiens* specimens, suggesting a regional continuation in evolution from Asian *H. erectus* through archaic *H. sapiens* to modern people.

such as fingerprint patterns or height. For example, certain populations have ridges of enamel on the back edges of their upper incisor teeth, a feature known as *shovel-shaped incisors* (Figure 14–2). Moderate to marked shovel-shaped incisors are very common in populations from Asia, including Inuits and Native Americans (Carbonell, 1963). In other populations this trait is found in low frequencies, for example, populations in Africa. In some populations in West Africa frequencies of shovel-shaped incisors reach 10 to 15 percent in adults.

In contrast, quantitative traits, such as body size (from tall to short), head circumference, skin and hair pigmentation (from dark to light), and hair form (from "straight" to "wavy"), vary in all populations. Frequency differences of traits between populations are expressed in terms of differences in mean values of a normal curve. For example, the mean height in one population may be 3.6 cm (1.4 in.) greater than that of another population, yet the entire range of adult height may be found among individuals in each of the two populations.

Most genetic markers are not visible to a human observer. It is not possible to tell whether a person has a particular blood type, for example, within the ABO system (discussed later in this chapter), by looking at his or her external features. The various blood types of this system are found in individuals in all populations, but the types vary in frequency from one population to another. Human populations can be distinguished in part on the basis of these frequencies (Table 14–1). Native American populations, for example, have a very low proportion of B blood types and a relatively high proportion of O blood types (except for members of the Blackfeet tribe, who are mostly AA), compared with most other human populations.

TABLE 14–1 | Worldwide Distribution of Blood Groups[a]

Geographic Area	Sample Size	Blood Type				Allele Frequency		
		O	A	B	AB	A	B	O
Europe								
France	30,810	.42	.45	.09	.04	.29	.07	.67
Italy	11,679	.46	.36	.13	.05	.23	.09	.68
Eastern Europe								
Russia (Leningrad)	54,447	.35	.37	.20	.08	.26	.15	.59
"Armenians" (Russia)	44,632	.29	.50	.13	.08	.35	.11	.54
Asia								
Japan	12,253	.30	.37	.23	.10	.27	.19	.54
Vietnam	114,022	.42	.22	.31	.06	.15	.20	.65
Middle East								
Iran	16,368	.41	.28	.24	.07	.19	.17	.64
Egypt	10,000	.36	.34	.24	.06	.23	.17	.60
Africa								
Nigeria	9,240	.52	.24	.21	.03	.14	.13	.73
Botswana !Kung	114	.70	.25	.03	.02	.15	.02	.83
Pacific Islands								
Hawaii (Natives)	4,670	.41	.53	.04	.02	.33	.03	.64
Easter Island	1,056	.32	.66	.01	.01	.42	.10	.58
Americas (Natives)								
North America (Cherokee)	166	.95	.04	.02	.00	.02	.01	.97
Greenland (Eskimos)	377	.36	.55	.05	.04	.35	.05	.60

[a]Shows from worldwide population samples the frequencies of the ABO blood groups and the frequencies of the A, B, O alleles. Populations with high frequencies of blood type O tend to be peripheral in Europe and Asia, with the highest frequencies reaching nearly 100% among Native Americans. Frequencies of A are higher in Europe and in Native Americans of western North America. The B blood group is almost totally absent from Native American populations. It reaches its highest frequencies in Asia.

From Mourant et al. (1976).

The frequencies of particular alleles among the various blood group systems can support assumed genetic affinity between groups. For example, the suggestion that the gypsies of Hungary originated in India—a suggestion that followed from a linguistic comparison of these two populations—can be supported by the frequency distribution of the ABO blood group system. Care must be exercised, however, in these sorts of analyses. For example, both Blackfeet peoples and Australian Aborigines have high frequencies of the A allele. This fact, alone, would not support a proposition that these two populations are closely related.

The Process of Geographic Isolation

Changing gene frequencies in geographically defined populations is evolution in action, and this change may result in the formation of subspecies. Subspecies, or *races*, created by geographic isolation represent those geographical populations that differ in gene frequencies at particular loci. The creation of subspecies depends on a number of factors (Figure 14–3). These include

1. Partial geographic and partial genetic isolation between populations at any point in time.

FIGURE 14–3   Subspecies, or "races," of savanna baboons. Hybrid zones exist between the different baboon populations, blurring distinctions between groups at geographical boundaries. Baboon "races" evolved as a result of geographical isolation.

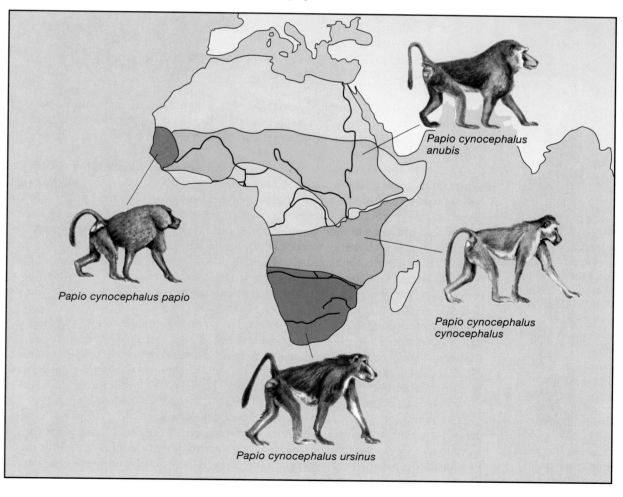

Papio cynocephalus anubis

Papio cynocephalus papio

Papio cynocephalus cynocephalus

Papio cynocephalus ursinus

2. The amount of time during which gene flow has been reduced between two populations.

3. Mutations that occur and spread in one population but not in another.

Although we do not recognize subspecies differences in modern human populations, the forces of geographic isolation on human populations in the past have contributed to the establishment of variability that can be measured today. New laboratory techniques allow us to compare different individuals within a population and to compare differences between populations. We can quantify these differences. At the DNA level, where the base pairs can be directly sequenced, the average individual is somewhat less than 1 percent different in sequence from any other randomly chosen individual. Because there are about 3 billion base pairs in the human haploid genome, however, this 1 percent difference represents thousands of different genetic combinations. If we compare individuals and populations, it appears that up to 80 percent of all variation in humans is found *within* any one population, and that only 20 percent of the variation represents differences *between* populations. This means that any given person is likely to differ more, on a genetic level, from individuals within his or her own population than that individual differs from a person from another population on the other side of the globe.

There are no single features of modern populations that clearly set one group off from the next. At best, we can only characterize a population in terms of a suite of frequencies of morphological and genetic traits that can be statistically related to the origin of that population in a geographical location. As we see in the next section, in today's human populations, the results of migration make any definition of "race" meaningless.

EARLY STUDIES OF HUMAN VARIATION: THE CONCEPT OF "RACE"

Darwin showed that inherited variation was a key element in natural selection. Scientists interested in human evolution thus began in the nineteenth century to study human variation and to interpret variation in evolutionary terms. The first attempts were clumsy.

The prevailing theoretical and philosophical debate concerning human origins before and around Darwin's time was between supporters of the single origin (**monogenism**) and of the many origins (**polygenism**) of the human species. Debate centered on whether the differences seen in modern populations were of such a degree that different human populations should be considered separate species, or whether populations were varieties of the same species all stemming from a single origin. Those who emphasized the differences, such as the early American anthropologist Samuel G. Morton of Philadelphia (1839), were strong proponents of polygenism. Polygenists supported the clear-cut separation of the major human populations, usually into separate species.

Monogenists emphasized the similarities among populations and pointed out that all individuals of the different groups could interbreed. Monogenism had the support of Western Christian doctrine, because it upheld the single origin of humanity, in accordance with the book of Genesis. Major proponents of monogenism were Johann Friedrich Blumenbach and Erasmus Darwin, the grandfather of Charles Darwin (see Chapter 2).

The initial ideas about human races were developed around a series of "types," defined by morphological or metric features of body, head, facial, or hair forms. If an individual possessed the one or two characteristics considered essential for inclusion in that type, then that was the type or race to which he or she was assigned. There are several problems with this typological approach. First, there is little provi-

monogenism: in the history of anthropology, relating to a single or unitary origin of the human species, connoting that all human populations were part of one species; an early point of agreement between the Church and Darwinism.

polygenism: in the history of anthropology, relating to a multiple origin of the human species, connoting that different populations were different species; used by some to defend slavery and by others to justify colonial mistreatment of indigenous peoples.

sion for variability. And second, there is no provision for cases that are on the ends of the distributions of populations—for example, an individual who has as parents members of two different populations.

Unfortunately, anthropology has been involved since its inception in the study of "race." Blumenbach studied the variations in cranial forms in living human groups and categorized them into five major "races," which he termed *Caucasian, Mongolian, Malayan, Ethiopian,* and *American* (see Chapter 1, Figure 1–6). Foreshadowing modern population biology, however, Blumenbach stressed that his division of the human species was arbitrary, because, as he stated, "One variety does so sensibly pass into the other that you cannot mark out the limits between them." The tradition of categorizing "races" was followed by numerous other researchers and continued as recently as 1962 (Coon).

The concept of the biological species, as defined by Linneaus more than 300 years ago (see Chapter 4), took into account the idea that species were reproductively isolated from one another; in other words, members of different species could not interbreed to produce fertile offspring. A species under these conditions was definable, and the characteristics that made it unique from all other species could be listed and compared. Later, when researchers had to consider the existence of species that had no living members, both those that had become extinct with no issue and those that had evolved into different species, the definition of species became complicated, but the ability to interbreed, as far as it could be determined, still figured prominently in it. Species were viewed as immutable and static.

In contrast, in biology "race" is a dynamic concept, one in which change and variability are important features. As Figure 14–3 showed, within species, members of different subspecies or "races" become different from one another as a result of geographical isolation, but they are not so different that they become incapable of interbreeding. As a consequence, the gene pool from which members of such populations draw changes every generation, as a result of interbreeding, microevolution in response to changing environmental circumstances, and unique mutations. Some of these situations result in different gene pools becoming more similar, as in the case of interbreeding, whereas others result in gene pools becoming more different, as in the case of mutations. In either case, the gene pool remains continually in flux. Population movement and adaptive evolutionary change may create different morphological patterns, but by their very nature, they are definable only at a single time and particular place. Among humans it is not possible to define "races" in any meaningful way, because any definition that attempts to do that, from Blumenbach onward, implies a static quality that simply does not exist.

Biology and Culture

There has been a long-standing historical confusion in anthropology concerning the relationship between biology and culture; it is a confusion that is manifested in everyday life and language as well. For example, if you were to apply for a job with the federal government, the application form might ask you to check your "ethnic affiliation" or "ethnicity." One of the purposes of this question is to determine how many individuals from different populations are hired by the agency, in keeping with the government's fair and equal employment policies. But is the question the agency is asking eliciting the information it wants? The term *ethnicity* really refers to sociocultural identity that may vary independently from one's biological background.

The categories used by the U.S. government are based on a number of different, and not necessarily equivalent, factors. Attempts are often made to compare apples and oranges. For example, these categories may include such terms as *Hispanic,* largely a language-based term, referring to Spanish speakers who may differ in their physical appearance; *African American* and *Asian American,* geographically based terms that can relate to real population affinities; *Native American,* which can refer to a wide

0

array of geographic populations of broadly Asian affinities ranging from South America to Alaska to the Pacific Islands; *white,* a purely descriptive grouping based on skin color; or *Caucasian,* an old term referring to a European "type" from eastern Europe.

Other widely used terms, such as *Jewish* and *Muslim,* have a clearly religious connection. But what do these terms connote? Should Jews and Muslims be considered to belong to the same ethnic group because they share a common original language? Or should they be considered to be two ethnic groups because they have different religions, Judaism and Islam, respectively? Or are they both? What about a population that has a distinguishing physical characteristic, such as the small stature of the Central African Mbuti (pygmies), but that is not linguistically distinct, instead speaking the languages of their Bantu neighbors? What about two populations, such as the Hopi and Navajo, that are physically very similar but have quite different languages and cultural adaptations to the same environment? There are no straightforward answers to these questions, although it is clear that biological categories (a population genetics issue) and cultural categories (issues of ethnicity and ethnic groups) should be decoupled from one another, because they can vary independently.

Although positive benefits may result from the use of ethnic categories, far-reaching, negative effects are just as common. **Racism** is that set of beliefs and behaviors that uses culturally defined categories, based on a few phenotypic traits, to discriminate against people. Discrimination may occur in such disparate areas as social mores, religious doctrine, educational planning, public health policy, and medical practice, among others (Shipman, 1994). Therefore, we prefer to avoid terms such as *race* and *ethnic group* when discussing humans and their biology, and instead to use the term *population* instead. As we discuss, populations exhibit differences in frequencies of some alleles that can help us trace our human history.

Tracing Relationships Among Human Populations

Genetic studies have now added substantially to our understanding of human population variability. The reconstruction of gene lineages in some ways parallels the use of discrete anatomical markers in deciphering the history of human variation, although new molecular studies have not supported the outdated human racial divisions based on morphology. Mitochondrial DNA (mtDNA) studies have been at the forefront of this research. Cann (1988) and colleagues have surveyed worldwide mtDNA diversity and analyzed the data in terms of patterns of genetic relationships. They suggest that the major division in human populations lies at a split between Eurasian and African populations. The degree of genetic polymorphism—diversity—in Africa is five times that in the rest of the world's populations. Using these data and the criterion of genetic distance, the category, "Africans," would have to be broken up into a number of separate populations. To emphasize the differences that exist between African populations and the rest of the world, mtDNA data have shown that an individual with English ancestors is more similar genetically to an individual with Japanese ancestors than are two individuals drawn from any two of contiguous African populations.

racism: a policy or opinion that unfairly generalizes real or perceived characteristics of a specific ethnic group, population, or "race" to every member of that group, and that may be used to deny resources or fair and equal treatment to an individual on the basis of membership in that group.

GENETIC ORIGINS OF VARIATION

Work in molecular biology and anthropology is changing our understanding of the interrelationships among human populations and the source of the tremendous variation seen in human populations. In this section, we describe some of the ways genetic variability may be introduced into populations, starting at the DNA level.

Although variability has been found in a number of different loci, often the reasons behind it have been elusive. The problem of understanding genetic variability is compounded by the fact that we now recognize that variability exists in sections in noncoding DNA as well as in coding DNA. *Noncoding DNA*—DNA that does not code for polypeptide chains—is not usually subject to tests of fitness by natural selection. Most polymorphic patterns (variations) found in noncoding DNA exist as a result of chance processes and genetic drift. The fact that these noncoding units change over time at predictable rates (a consequence of change by chance rather than by selection), however, makes them extremely useful in phylogenetic studies, both long term (millions of years) and short term (several generations), depending on the section of noncoding DNA studied.

We begin this discussion with the noncoding loci of nuclear DNA.

Noncoding DNA Sequences

Noncoding sections of the DNA molecule consist of short runs of nucleotides repeated in tandem, perhaps thousands of times. These repetitive noncoding DNA segments constitute more than one-third of the human genome and are important sources of mutations on which natural selection operates. Such segments may have originated as retroviral elements that integrated themselves randomly into the host's genome but now appear to be inactive. These segments are replicated every time the DNA replicates.

Tandem repeats of DNA sequences, those structured one after the other, have been found scattered throughout the human genome. The size of the repeating units range from two base pairs (for example, CA) to 20,000 base pairs. Repetitive sequences may be found in special locations, such as in and around the centromere of the chromosome. These are generally shorter than 200 base pairs. Another type of repetitive sequence is the hexamer, TTAGGG, which is repeated in tandem between 5,000 and 10,000 times at the ends of the chromosomes. Natural selection may have conserved this repeat element because of the role it plays in maintaining chromosome length.

One other characteristic of these segments is that they are or were *transposable*: They can move from one place to another within the genome. Transposable DNA segments have the potential to remodel genomes and to ease the movement of genetic material. These segments, popularly called "jumping genes," range in length from 50 base pairs to 10,000 base pairs. Because there are so many of these jumping genes, they have a high potential of introducing harmful mutations to the coding section of the genome. Potential damage is minimized by peculiarities of jumping genes. First, most transposable segments are no longer jumping genes—they merely represent jumps that occurred in the past. Second, the small percentage of transposable segments that do "jump" to new locations often avoid active gene sites. Third, some jumpers are active only in the organism's germ cells, and in these cases damage to the body or somatic cells is avoided.

Thus, although the potential for damage is substantial, some jumpers can and may have in the past contributed beneficially as mutations to the evolution and survival of species. For example, an important part of the vertebrate immune system apparently resulted from a transposable segment called RAG that played a critical role early in vertebrate evolution.

There are two major classes of transposable, repetitive DNA, which differ from one another in length: short interspersed elements (SINES) and long interspersed elements (LINES).

Short interspersed elements. *Short interspersed elements (SINES)* are short segments of DNA, of which the *Alu family* is the most common. Alus are named after the restriction enzyme Alu I, which acts to break apart most Alu elements. It is estimated that about 500,000 Alu elements are dispersed throughout the human genome, representing about 5 percent of the total DNA (Stoneking et al., 1997).

Most Alus are about 300 base pairs in length, and can be divided into different subfamilies that underwent extensive changes in their positions in the DNA at different periods of primate evolution. Because of their very slow rate of change, the presence or absence of a particular Alu in specific evolutionary lineages can be used to calculate the date of divergence of the lineages. For example, because it is found in all primate lineages, we can tell that the Alu IV subfamily probably originated about 60 million years ago.

Unlike the Alu elements, *microsatellite DNA* is highly polymorphic—in other words, there are different repeat sequences in different individuals. Microsatellite DNA evolves rapidly: The rate has been determined by laboratory observation to be about 1 mutation per 1,000 gametes. Although this rate is high, microsatellite changes are rare events over periods of a few generations, even in large families. These loci can therefore be used as relatively stable markers of recent human family trees.

Microsatellite DNA segments are composed of between 15 and 100 tandem repeats of one, two, or three base sequences, for example AAAAAA or CACACA. These repeats are known as *simple sequence repeats,* or SSRs. The CA repeat occurs once in approximately every 30,000 base pairs throughout the human lineage.

Long interspersed elements.   *Long interspersed elements (LINES)* are longer segments within the human genome. The most predominant human LINE, LI, is about 6.4 million base pairs in length. DNA segments called *minisatellites* are composed of long tandemly repeated units, lined up like boxcars. Each identical sequence, or repeat unit, is between 10 and 40 base pairs in length. In humans, many minisatellites have been discovered. Each one occurs from 1 to 50 times throughout the genome. The greater the number of polymorphisms and the higher the rate of heterozygosity, the more useful minisatellite DNA can be in resolving issues of recent human migration history and, perhaps, even the issue of the origin of modern *Homo sapiens* (Harding, 1992).

Coding DNA: Neutral Mutations

Neutral mutations are mutations that are neither harmful nor beneficial, but that modify the DNA sequences that code for polypeptides and thus build proteins. Neutral mutations are sources of variation in coding DNA, the part of the DNA that makes up the genes. They contribute to the formation of genetic polymorphisms in human populations. The spread of neutral mutations within populations is the result of genetic drift, as we saw in Chapter 4. In Chapter 4, we showed how two selectively neutral alleles may coexist over a considerable period of time, when there is no apparent advantage of one allele over the other. The frequency of the resulting polymorphic genotypes varies over time only by chance.

Several known variable phenotypes might fall into the category of neutrality, because none has been demonstrated to affect individual fitness. The first example involves the excretion of a substance called **methanethiol,** found in some human foods. Probably a single dominant allele controls the excretion of methanethiol once it has entered the body's system, usually after an individual has eaten asparagus. One estimate of the frequency of this allele in an English population is 0.23 (23 in 100). Carriers of this allele can be identified because of the strong odor of their urine after they eat asparagus. Other individuals, in contrast, who are homozygous for the recessive allele, can eat as much as a pound of asparagus without any detectable odor in their urine. Studies have not confirmed any differential selective advantage for these genotypes.

A second example involves the enzyme betamin, which controls the breakdown of the red pigment betacyanin, commonly found in beets. This enzyme is manufac-

methanethiol: a chemical breakdown product of asparagus with a detectable odor, excreted in urine by carriers who possess the dominant allele.

Controlling AIDS Through Genetic Research

D.R. Davies and colleagues (Davies et al., 2000) described the three-dimensional structure of an enzyme that allows a transposable DNA segment in a bacterium to "jump" from one part of the DNA to another (Figure 14–4). Their team's findings may be extremely useful to AIDS researchers, because HIV-1 uses a process similar to DNA transposition to insert itself into human DNA. Thus, this research may enable scientists to find a way to prevent HIV infection.

A group of enzymes called *transposases* make transposition possible, and these enzymes are remarkably similar to enzymes called *integrases* that, in retroviruses such as HIV, facilitate the transposition of their DNA into human DNA. By discovering the three-dimensional structure of the enzyme, the researchers were able to see how the enzyme and DNA interact. To control HIV, pharmaceutical firms are studying compounds that can inhibit HIV-1 integrase activity; consequently, researchers now have a model system that will assist them in achieving this goal.

New research also shows how, before transposition, one copy of the transposase binds to a specific region at one end of the transposon (the segment that will be transposed) and a second copy binds to an identical region at the opposite end. Neither enzyme can cut DNA at the site it attaches to until a loop DNA segment forms at the place where the ends of each enzyme come together and attach to themselves. The architecture of the resulting DNA–enzyme complex positions each enzyme so it can cleave the opposite ends of the transposable segment of DNA from its original position on the DNA lineup. The free-floating DNA–enzyme complex can then move freely before it reinserts itself into a new location.

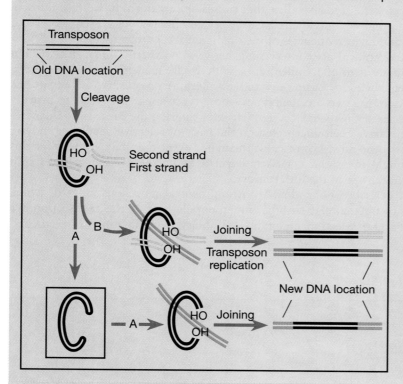

FIGURE 14–4 Transposon jumping: A transposon (black) embedded in an old DNA location (orange) moves to a new DNA location (red) through one of two pathways. Both pathways (A and B) include two identical reaction steps: (1) the cleavage of the first strand at each DNA end and (2) the joining of this to a new DNA site. Cut-and-paste transposons (pathway A) cleave both strands at each end of the element before the joining step. Inset: Organization of the "hairpin" intermediate of the transposase-DNA complex. Each end of the mobile element DNA (black) is locked in place through contacts with both transposase subunits (red and orange).

tured only by individuals who possess the dominant allele. Homozygous recessive individuals do not produce the enzyme. As a consequence, when these individuals eat moderate amounts of beets, their urine turns red because of the presence of the pigment. In a sample taken in England, the frequency of the recessive allele is about 0.31. There is no known selective advantage in the ability to excrete betacyanin or, for that matter, to break it down in the first place.

A third example that is also under genetic control involves the ability to taste different substances. R. J. Williams, a biochemist, investigated taste sensitivity for a number of substances and found that individuals had different "taste profiles," or responses to the different substances used (Williams, 1951). For example, whereas 251 individuals said that sugar tasted sweet, 21 unrelated individuals reported a bitter taste. Identical twins usually agreed in their responses, indicating the genetic basis for differences in one's ability to taste. Neutral genetic markers such as these are useful in studying population movements and gene flow, because their frequencies will not be affected by selection.

Clines.   Gradients in allele frequencies are known as *clines.* For example, we can speak of a cline in skin color from southern Italy to northern Italy gradually getting lighter as one goes north. Likewise, there is a cline of the B allele of the ABO blood group system, from Asia, where the allele is common, toward Europe, with the allele gradually becoming more rare (see Table 14–1). The reason for the cline in the first case may be natural selection, and in the second case, population migration patterns.

A particularly good example of a cline in human populations is the incidence of **cerumen,** or ear wax, types in Eurasia (Figure 14–5). In northern China, 96 percent of the population has dry cerumen (that is, "nonsticky" ear wax). These individuals are homozygous for the recessive allele that causes dry cerumen. In western Europe, more than 90 percent of individuals have "wet" cerumen, a very different type of ear wax, indicating high frequencies of the dominant wet cerumen allele.

Over the geographical area intervening between northern China and western Europe there is a gradient of cerumen types, with dry frequencies increasing west to east and wet frequencies increasing east to west. Because no selective advantage has been determined for the two cerumen types—both types apparently serve to provide a protective barrier against small foreign particles entering the ear canal—their frequency variations have been interpreted on the basis of selective neutrality and are indicative of past gene flow. Historically, the major event that may account for this cline is the Mongol invasion, a mass movement of northern Asian peoples into western Asia and Europe in the fifth century.

This section described noncoding DNA and neutral mutations, both of which are useful ways of tracing relationships among populations. In the next section, we consider how natural selection maintains variability in populations through bal-

cerumen: ear wax; a waxy or dry secretion of glands located in the external ear canal.

FIGURE 14–5   An example of a cline: allele frequencies of dry cerumen (ear wax) from Asia to Europe.

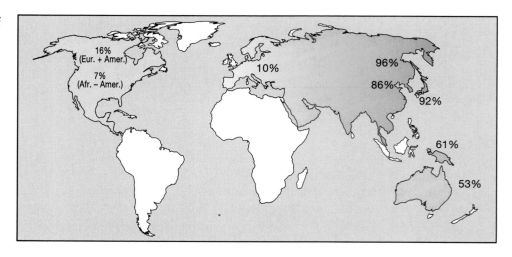

anced polymorphisms. We also consider how potentially harmful alleles can be maintained in a population under specific circumstances.

HOW NATURAL SELECTION MAINTAINS HUMAN VARIATION

The Example of Malaria

Sickle-cell trait.   Although biological anthropologists and geneticists have documented much variation in human populations, under many circumstances they have been unable to ascertain either the selective advantages or the evolutionary forces that produce the variation. In those cases where we have determined the reason for variability, large fitness differences among individuals within the study population usually exist. Such a situation exists for sickle-cell hemoglobin. In this example, individuals who are heterozygous for the sickle-cell trait (who carry the mutant allele for the beta chain of hemoglobin, HbAHbS) have protection against **malaria.**

Hospital data demonstrate that patients with normal hemoglobin (HbAHbA) can be infected with the malarial parasite, after being bitten by certain species of mosquito that carry the parasite, 20 percent more frequently than those individuals who are heterozygous for sickle-cell trait. In one West African hospital, out of 1,013 heterozygotes, 132, or only about 13 percent, had heavy parasite infestation, whereas out of 2,858 normal homozygous individuals, 955, or about 33 percent, had the same degree of parasitic infection. This means that the sickle-cell gene, in the heterozygous state, carries considerable selective advantage in a malarial environment. Sickle-cell frequencies do vary in clinal fashion, depending on the degree to which malaria is present in an environment throughout the year. For example, in regions where the rainy season is only three months long, malaria is less of a threat than in regions where the rainy season lasts six months, because the mosquitoes that carry the parasite and require water to lay their eggs in would also have shorter breeding seasons.

Death caused by malaria for normal homozygous individuals is, however, considerably more likely to occur than for the heterozygous individuals, because the malarial parasite cannot reproduce well in red blood cells that contain some sickle-beta-hemoglobin chains. This situation is referred to as a *balanced polymorphism:* because selection favors the heterozygote genotype, it maintains a balance in the frequencies of the homozygote genotypes (Figure 14–6).

malaria: from the Italian, meaning "bad air," from the original, mistaken belief that the disease was air borne; often fatal disease caused by a protozoan infecting the red blood cells and transmitted from one carrier to another by the bite of a female *Anopheles* mosquito; symptoms include chills, sweating, fever, vomiting, diarrhea, and convulsions.

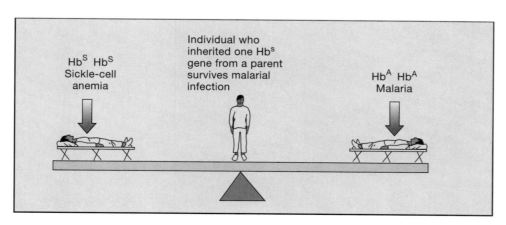

Hb^S Hb^S
Sickle-cell
anemia

Individual who
inherited one Hb^s
gene from a parent
survives malarial
infection

Hb^A Hb^A
Malaria

FIGURE 14–6   Schematic depiction of the balanced polymorphism that exists between sickle-cell anemia (left), malaria (right), and the heterozygote sickle-cell gene carrier, who is protected against malaria (center).

Malaria is an extremely prevalent infectious disease worldwide, second only to HIV (Figure 14–7). Malaria was probably a major cause of death throughout human history and still accounts for more than 1.5 million deaths each year. In addition to the death rate from malaria, there is a significant genetic load resulting from the deaths of individuals who are homozygous recessive for the sickle-cell gene. A high genetic load suggests that the genetic accommodation between humans and the malarial parasite is a relatively recent one. About 4 percent of the population dies because of the lethal homozygous mutant combination (HbSHbS) so that about 32 percent of the population can be protected from the effects of malaria. The 4 percent death rate per generation is a significant genetic load. Natural selection over time should favor possible alternative solutions that reduce genetic load if such variations exist in the gene pool. An "ideal" solution would be a single-locus protection against malarial infection that is not detrimental to individuals homozygous for the mutant gene.

Adaptation through evolution can occur only when a population has sufficient variability. Mutations, the source of population variability, do not occur because they are needed. Rather, the process of mutation is continuous and random. As the environmental situation changes, some mutations will, by chance, turn out to be adaptive. Given the relative infrequency, however, of mutations and the finite nature of populations (there are only so many individuals in any given species), we would not expect to find the same adaptation in two different populations. Throughout the world many human populations have been exposed to malaria, and genetic adaptations to malaria are varied. In Africa, for example, the adaptation of highest frequency is sickle-cell hemoglobin (Hb^s). In Southeast Asia a different mutant (Hb^e) works to protect individuals from malaria. Hb^e, however, is much less lethal than Hb^s when in the homozygous state.

Hb^s, Hb^e, and a third allele, Hb^c, are found in fairly large areas of the world at heterozygote frequencies of 10 to 30 percent, the highest in populations in tropical Africa and in a few locations around the Mediterranean and in India. In addition to these, at least three other variants exist whose local heterozygote frequencies may reach 50 percent. It is interesting to note that the structural differences between hemoglobin variants A, S, and C consist of one amino acid substitution at position 6

FIGURE 14–7 Malarial areas of the world, and frequencies of the Hb^s (sickle-cell) allele. Higher frequencies of Hb^s correspond to higher incidences of both malaria and sickle-cell anemia.

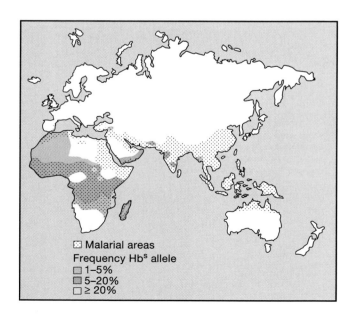

in the beta chain of the hemoglobin molecule. Glutamic acid appears at this position in "normal" (A) hemoglobin, valine in the variant (S), and lysine in variant (C).

G6PD deficiency.   In areas where Hb^s and Hb^c both occur, the frequency of Hb^s is lower than that of Hb^c. Predictably, the Hb^c allele, with its higher degree of fitness (lower genetic load in the homozygous recessive genotype), is spreading. Time is the important ingredient. Over time, natural selection will weed out the more lethal genotypes in favor of those that are less lethal. Given the opportunity, selection will operate on alternative mutations. A further way for natural selection to lower the genetic load on a population involves shifting genetic protection from a single-locus to a two-locus (or more) mechanism (Figure 14–8). Substantiating this prediction, we again look at West African and Mediterranean populations that carry other specific alleles whose frequencies correlate with the presence of malaria. At one of these loci, alleles produce the enzyme **G6PD** (glucose-6-phosphate dehydrogenase), which is important in red blood cell metabolism. Where the frequency of Hb^s is high, the mutant forms of the G6PD gene, leading to deficiency in the enzyme, are also found (Greene, 1993).

Thalassemia.   Under ordinary conditions, carriers of one of the G6PD deficiency alleles exhibit no abnormal effects. Only if a carrier is administered an antimalarial drug will he or she develop anemia. Anemia will also occur if a carrier eats the bean of the fava plant, *Vicia faba,* or comes into contact with the plant's pollen. The disease caused by G6PD deficiency and brought on by the fava bean is commonly known as "favism" and is characterized by fever, abdominal pain, anemia, and coma. It was originally found chiefly in Italy and was associated with long-term diets of the raw bean. G6PD deficiency is now known to be widespread in populations exposed in the past to malarial infection. In Israel, for example, among Kurdish Jews, the frequency of the G6PD-deficiency alleles may reach higher than 60 percent. The relationship between G6PD and malaria demonstrates how natural selection acts in some human populations in a different way from that involving the sickle-cell allele. By responding to malaria through the development of a defense that affects red blood cell metabolism, individuals are protected against the parasite's lethal effects by reducing its ability to reproduce in the red blood cell.

G6PD: glucose-6-phosphate dehydrogenase, an enzyme necessary for red blood cell metabolism; G6PD deficiency is caused by recessive genes and can result in the disease favism.

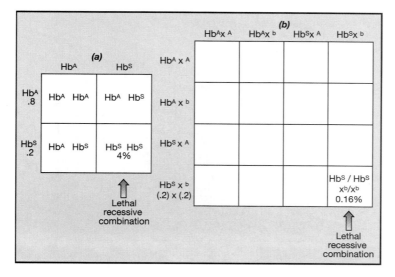

FIGURE 14–8 Natural selection works to reduce genetic load. (*a*) The genetic load for the Hb^s homozygous recessive condition is calculated to be 4 percent, because the genotype is nearly always fatal in non-Western societies. (*b*) Over time, natural selection can act to reduce the genetic load by incorporating the protective advantage of a second polymorphism. In this example, a hypothetical gene (X), with two alleles, A and B, reduces the genetic load from 4 to 0.16 percent.

The third locus that has been associated with malaria also contains alleles that are concerned with the synthesis of the polypeptide chains that make up the hemoglobin molecule. Individuals who have one of the alleles for beta-**thalassemia** have defective hemoglobin because of the partial suppression of the formation of the normal beta-chain. As a consequence, these individuals may be anemic. On mainland Italy the frequency of the heterozygotes for beta-thalassemia reaches 20 percent, and in some Sardinian populations it approaches 40 percent. The high frequencies of these genotypes in many populations, and the frequent severity of the anemia, suggest that natural selection should be reducing these frequencies through differential fitness. That this has not occurred is again good evidence of natural selection at work. We presume that the counteracting selection is for protection against malaria, and as with sickle-cell hemoglobin and G6PD deficiency, a lowered efficiency of red blood cell activity and metabolism apparently slows the reproduction of the malarial parasite. The frequencies of the anemia-producing alleles vary like those of the Hb^s allele, being higher in areas where malaria is present.

A study of the relationships among malaria, beta-thalassemia, and G6PD-deficiency alleles was undertaken in Sardinia. Here the frequency of the alleles was correlated with altitude, the interpretation being that the higher the altitude, the lower the incidence of malaria, because at the higher elevations fewer mosquitos that carry the parasite are found. There are fewer mosquitoes at higher altitudes primarily because of the lack of places (open, still water) mosquitoes need to breed (Figure 14–9). The prediction borne out by this study was that, as the effects of malaria on the human population diminished, the incidence of malaria-related alleles would also decrease in frequency.

The complicated example of malaria illustrates the interaction between disease, genetics, and natural selection. A heterogeneous group of genetic variants of various red cell components (including hemoglobin S, beta-thalassemia, and G6PD deficiency) all appear to impart an increased fitness in malarial environments, the end

thalassemia: from the Greek, meaning "sea blood," in reference to the blood's dilute nature; genetic disorders affecting hemoglobin metabolism that can range from negligible clinical effects to fatal anemia.

FIGURE 14–9 Incidence (average frequency) of G6PD deficiency and the thalassemia trait among villagers on the island of Sardinia. Incidence of both traits is lowest at high altitudes, away from coastal areas where malaria is endemic.

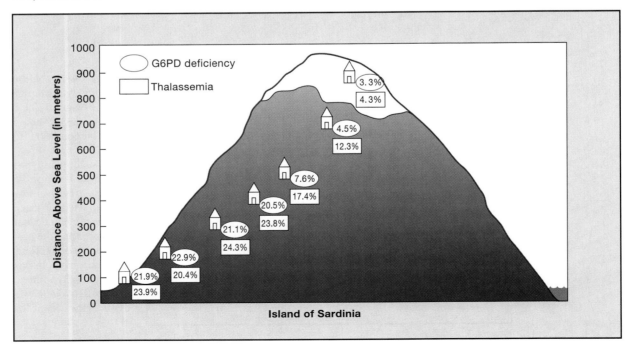

result of which is the production of a common phenotype, one in which the red cell environment is less favorable for the malarial parasite to survive and reproduce.

Blood Group Polymorphisms

ABO blood groups. The idea of transfusing the blood of one individual into that of another dates back several centuries. As early as the seventeenth century, blood transfusions were attempted, but the patients often died. The question of why some patients survived transfusion was not correctly answered until 1900. K. Landsteiner discovered in that year what ultimately became one of the most widely known genetic systems, the **ABO blood group.** Individuals may have an A, B, AB, or O blood type. The genotypes for these types are AA or AO, BB or BO, AB, and OO, respectively.

The ABO system was the first of many blood groups to be discovered (Table 14–2), and the reason that it was first is relatively simple. Blood group variations depend

ABO blood group: blood group system discovered by Landsteiner in 1900 defined by agglutination (clotting) reactions of red blood cells to natural anti-A and anti-B antibodies. Blood type A reacts to only anti-A, type B reacts only to anti-B, type AB reacts to both, and type O reacts to neither.

TABLE 14–2	Human Blood Group Systems and Antigens
Blood Group System	**Antigens**
ABO	A, A_1, B
H	H
I	I, i, I^T, I^D, I^F
MN	M, N, S, s, U, Cl^a, Far, He, Hill, Hu, M^A, M^C, M^e, M^g, M_1, Mi^a, Mt^a, Mur, M^v, Ny^a, Ri^a, S^B, Sj, St^a, Sul, Tm, U^B, Vr, Vw, N^A, Z
P	P1, P2 (Tj^a), P3 (P^k)
Rh	Rh1 (D, Rh_o), Rh2 (C, rh'), Rh3 (E, rh''), Rh4 (c' hr'), Rh5 (e, hr''), Rh6 (f, ce, hr), Rh7 (Ce, rh_i), Rh8 (C^w, rh^{w1}), Rh9 (C^x, rh^x), Rh10 (V, ce^s, hr^v), Rh11 (E^w, rh^{w2}), Rh12 (G, rh^G), Rh13 (Rh^A), Rh14 (Rh^B), Rh15 (Rh^C), Rh16 (Rh^D), Rh17 (Hr_o), Rh18 (Hr), Rh19 (hr^s), Rh20 (VS, e^s), Rh21 (C^G), Rh22 (CE), Rh23 (D^w), Rh24 (E^T), Rh26, Rh27 (cE), Rh28 (hr^H), Rh29 (RH), Rh30 (Go^a), Rh31 (hr^B), Rh32, Rh33
Lutheran	Lu^a (Lu1), Lu^b (Lu2), Lu^{ab} (Lu3), Lu4, Lu5, Lu6, Lu7, Lu8, Lu9, Lu10, Lu11, Lu12, Lu13, Lu14 (Sw^a)
Kell	K1 (K), K2 (k), K3 (Kp^a), K4 (Kp^b), K5 (Ku), K6 (Js^a), K7 (Js^b), K8 (kw), K9 (KL), K10 ($U1^a$), K11, K12, K13, K14, K15, K16
Lewis	Le^a (Le1), Le^b (Le2), Le^x, Le^{ab}(Le3), Mag (Le4), Le^c (Le5), Le^d
Duffy	Fy^a (Fy1), Fy^b (Fy2), Fy^{ab} (Fy3), Fy4
Kidd	Jk^a (Jk1), Jk^b (Jk2), Jk^{ab} (Jk3)
Cartwright	Yt^a, Yt^b
Xg	Xg^a
Dombrock	Do^a, Do^b
Auberger	Au^a
Cost-Sterling	Cs^a, Yk^a
Wright	Wr^a, Wr^b
Diego	Di^a, Di^b
Vel	Vel 1, Vel 2
Sciana	Sm, Bu^a
Bg	Bg^a, Bg^b, Bg^c, Ho, Ho-like, Ot, Sto, DBG (similar to HL-A7 of lymphocytes)
Gerbich	Ge1, Ge2, Ge3 (anti-Ge1 = M.Y.; anti-Ge1,2 = Ge; anti-Ge1,2,3 = Yus)
Coltan	Co^a, Co^b
Stoltzfus	Sf^a

From *Dorland's Medical Dictionary.* Saunders, Philadelphia (1974).

on differences in the chemical structure of complex molecules that make up the membrane of the red blood cell. A large proportion of the surface of the red blood cell is devoted to antigens of the ABO system. An *antigen* is an identifiable chemical structure within a blood group system that is specified by certain alleles. For example, individuals who do not have the A allele will not produce an A antigen on the surface of the red blood cells but will possess a preexisting, natural antibody to A. An *antibody* is an immunoglobulin molecule with a specific amino acid sequence evoked by the presence of a specific antigen. Thus, individuals who lack the B antigen but possess the A antigen also possess anti-B.

The ABO system differs from the other 22 known blood group systems, such as the **Rh blood group,** in an important way: In these other systems, antibodies are not initially present if certain system antigens are absent. Antibodies to specific antigens are manufactured only if foreign antigens are introduced, as, for example, by transfusion. Because of this difference, the reaction to foreign antigens of the ABO system is immediate, whereas in the other systems, reactions may be delayed. In short, the ABO system was discovered first because it is the first to respond to foreign substances.

When incompatible blood is mixed together, a reaction occurs between the antigens present on the surface of the red blood cells that are introduced and the antibodies to them, which are present in the blood of the recipient. The antibody makes the foreign red blood cells clump together in clots. These clots are capable of blocking small blood vessels, often with fatal results.

Frequencies of the different blood groups have been shown to vary geographically (refer back to Table 14–1). How might natural selection have played a role in the origins of this variation?

Hemolytic incompatibility in newborns.   When we look carefully at the data, we see that blood group polymorphisms cannot be completely explained by the forces of chance and genetic drift. One clue explaining blood group polymorphisms comes from their great antiquity. Antigens for the ABO system, for example, have been found to exist in all mammals and even in birds. The fact that polymorphisms still exist after such vast amounts of time demands the explanation that these polymorphisms must be balanced. Yet for a balanced situation to exist, some selective advantages must be found for the heterozygotes. In the case of the Rh system and some other blood groups systems, however, the opposite has been found to be true. Heterozygotes are at a disadvantage in examples that involve **hemolytic incompatibility** between the mother and her fetus for both the ABO system and, especially, the Rh system (Figure 14–10).

Until quite recently, heterozygous fetuses [AO or BO, or Dd(Rh+)] were at direct risk for spontaneous miscarriage, a risk that increased as the mother conceived succeeding offspring. The blood group data, therefore, present a considerable paradox. The existence of multiple alleles can be explained only by a balanced polymorphism, yet the supposedly favored heterozygote may be fatally at peril.

Rh incompatibility occurs in a pregnancy in which the fetus is an Rh+ (Dd) heterozygote and the mother is Rh− (dd) (see Figure 14–10). Because of the nature of the placental membrane, D antigens on the red blood cells of the offspring may cross over into the blood supply of the mother during the birth of the first child. Because the mother has no D alleles, her immune system responds by manufacturing an antibody to them, anti-D, which functions, as many antibodies do, to agglutinate (clump) the foreign D antigens and remove them from her system. Red blood cells can occasionally cross the placental barrier from fetus to mother, and the maternal anti-D antibodies occasionally travel from mother to offspring. If enough maternal anti-D is transferred to the fetus, it can cause hemolytic disease, a situation where fetal red blood cells carrying the D antigen are clumped together causing fatal clotting in the circulatory system.

Rh blood group: a complex system of blood antigens originally discovered by Landsteiner and Weiner in 1940 using blood from the rhesus monkey, which lent the first two letters of its name to the system. Rh antigens are controlled by a number of different alleles yielding many different phenotypes.

hemolytic incompatibility: destruction of red blood cells caused by the action of antibodies, resulting in release of hemoglobin into the plasma.

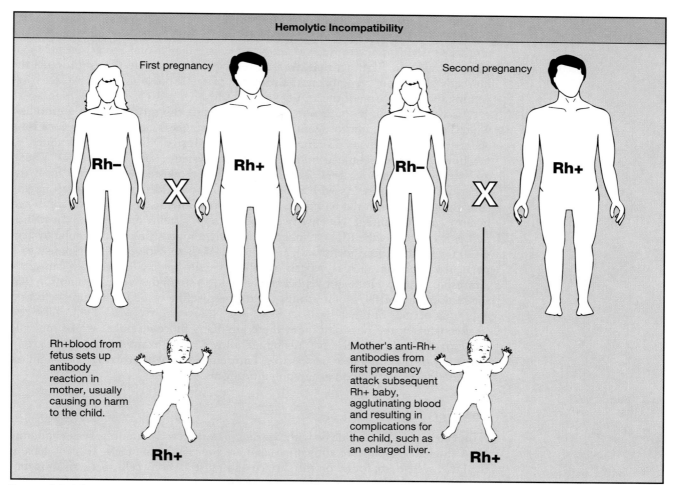

Hemolytic Incompatibility

First pregnancy

Rh–   X   Rh+

Rh+blood from
fetus sets up
antibody
reaction in
mother, usually
causing no harm
to the child.

Rh+

Second pregnancy

Rh–   X   Rh+

Mother's anti-Rh+
antibodies from
first pregnancy
attack subsequent
Rh+ baby,
agglutinating blood
and resulting in
complications for
the child, such as
an enlarged liver.

Rh+

FIGURE 14–10   Mechanism of hemolytic incompatibility between mother and fetus.

As Figure 14–10 shows, a mother's first pregnancy is generally a safe one, with respect to hemolytic disease. Under normal conditions, no blood passes directly between the fetus and mother. But about the time of birth, fetal red blood cells can transfer between the fetus and mother, at which time the mother's immune system begins to produce anti-D antibodies. In subsequent pregnancies, residual anti-D antibodies can have a cumulative effect and do serious harm to the fetus.

If the child dies of hemolytic disease, usually right after birth, its two alleles, D and d, are lost to the population gene pool. If a balanced polymorphism favoring the heterozygote genotype did not exist, and each of the alleles (D and d) were of equal fitness, chance processes alone would lead to the loss over time of one or the other. In the Rh example, hemolytic incompatibility clearly selects against the heterozygote, yet both D and d alleles remain in the gene pool. That this is true is a puzzle for human geneticists. The case of double incompatibility between the Rh and ABO blood groups may shed some light on the solution.

Like the Rh system, the ABO system also provides situations in which hemolytic incompatibility may result in the fetus. In fact, all ABO phenotypes are potentially incompatible if the fetus possesses an antigen that the mother does not. Cohen (1970a, 1970b), supporting earlier work, showed how maternal-fetal pairs who were doubly incompatible for both ABO and Rh had less risk of fetal death than those in which the fetus was incompatible only for one system or the other. We do not know why this is the case.

The protective effect of double incompatibility for the Rh system is better understood. Apparently, antibodies to A or B, which may normally circulate in the mother's system, attack those fetal red blood cells if they manage to get into the maternal circulation. The fact that the fetal red blood cells are destroyed prevents the mother's body from recognizing the presence of the D allele in the first place, preventing the production of the anti-D antibody.

As we have said, blood group antigens stimulate the production of antibodies, which, in turn, function to eliminate foreign substances, including disease-causing agents, from an individual's circulatory system. Most of the studies attempted so far, however, have examined individual antigen systems, such as the ABO system, and studied the various gene frequencies as if they existed in isolation from the other antigen systems. As with malaria, several independent systems, each having something to do with the blood environment, may interact to produce a combined heterozygote advantage. Twenty-two blood group systems have now been identified. Some, such as the Rh system, contain many antigens (in this particular system 47 antigens have been identified). If each one of these evolved as a response to a particular situation, such as malaria, we should easily be able to identify a causal relationship. That we have not yet been able to do so strengthens our assumption that the multiplicity of the blood groups themselves are the results of natural selection over long periods of time.

Recognizing the possibility that there are many more instances where multiple incompatibility has a selective advantage allows us to examine the blood group frequency data from a new perspective. Future research will probably shed light on the remainder of the blood group polymorphisms.

The HLA System

If the blood groups provide us with puzzling paradoxes, the immune system and the **HLA** (human lymphocyte antigen) system are even more complex. The antigens of the HLA system are found on the surface of almost all body cells, perhaps most importantly on the *leukocytes* (Greek, meaning "white cells"), the white blood cells. These antigens protect the body from foreign substances by recognizing and eliminating them. These antigens are coded on chromosome 6 at seven closely linked loci: A, B, C, D, Dr, Dq, and Dp. Additional loci and the Ir genes, which control the immune response by determining the level of antibody response, are also found near the HLA loci.

At least 23 alleles (or antigens) have been discovered at the A locus, 47 at B, 8 at C, 19 at D, 16 at Dr, 3 at Dq, and 6 at Dp. In combinations of two, these allelic systems produce an enormous number of genotypes, certainly more than all of the known red blood cell group systems put together. Some of the allelic combinations are found in all human populations; others are restricted to specific geographical groups. Some interesting correlations have been discovered, for example, linking HLA B8 and intolerance to gluten, a protein contained in wheat and barley. Apparently, the frequency of this allele in European populations is related to the length of time peoples have engaged in agriculture. The frequency of gluten intolerance is lowest in those groups that adopted agriculture early in their history and highest in those that adopted agriculture more recently.

Inherited differences in HLA antigens are medically important in situations where the tissue of one individual is grafted onto that of another. The rejection of the graft, referred to as *tissue incompatibility*, is less severe if the antigens of the host and those of the donor are identical or closely related. The complex of antigens found in the blood groups and **histocompatibility** of HLA systems may well be responses to various disease-causing agents. It is certainly a sophisticated and complex system that has been evolving for a long time, and, in theory, the complexity of these systems would be the practical and anticipated result of natural selection.

HLA: human lymphocyte antigen system; a white blood cell antigen system important in the immune response.

histocompatibilty: immunologic similarity or identity of tissues; used in referring to tissues appropriate for grafting in medical procedures.

Lactose Intolerance

The kinds of foods that we eat today, such as bread cereals and dairy products, developed late in human history. Domestication of plants and animals occurred only some 10,000 years ago, and our modern diet is mainly the result of this agricultural revolution (see Chapter 15). The diets of our hunter-gatherer ancestors no doubt emphasized wild plant foods, supplemented by some meat and marrow and no dairy foods once children had been weaned. Although the agricultural revolution came about in many cultures of the world more or less simultaneously, specific cultures adapted to new foods in different ways. Tolerance of lactose, a sugar found in milk, is one example of how people from different geographic regions adapt differently to new diets (Table 14–3). The U.S. government learned this lesson the hard way when agencies responsible for foreign-aid programs discovered that food shipments of powdered milk to needy countries were being destroyed, or in some cases used to whitewash houses, by the people it was meant to feed (Figure 14–11). In cow's milk, lactose amounts to 4 to 5 percent of the total volume, but in powdered or condensed milk, it may be as high as 15 to 38 percent.

For milk sugar to be digestible, the enzyme *lactase* is needed to break down lactose to its component sugars, glucose and galactose. Although nearly all mammals, including humans, produce lactase at birth, enzyme production falls off sharply, later in childhood and probably stops before puberty in most humans. Most adults in the world are lactose intolerant. Therefore, when they consumed milk products that were shipped as food aid, they suffered from diarrhea and stomach cramps. To individuals already weakened by hunger, these additional problems could be life threatening.

The evolutionary significance of lactase deficiency might be viewed in terms of the ways different populations use milk products (Holden and Mace, 1997). As a way of avoiding spoilage, some people ferment their raw milk, producing from it yogurt and cheese. In both these foods lactose may already be broken down into its component sugars before ingestion. Not all cheeses, however, are low in lactose; it depends on the specific type of cheese and how it is processed. In some European groups where dairy farming has a long history, people of all ages drink raw milk. Thus, selection pressures may have favored the production of the enzyme throughout adult life, allowing these populations to use an available food source.

FIGURE 14–11 Well-intentioned relief shipments of powdered milk only exacerbated the health problems of many starving, lactose-intolerant Biafrans.

TABLE 14–3	Lactose Intolerance in Human Populations (percentages)				
European Derived		**African Derived**		**Asian Derived**	
Swedish	4	Ibos	99	Thai	97–100
Swiss	12	Bantus	90	Inuit	72–88
European/ Americans	2–19	African/ Americans	70–77	Asian/ Americans	95–100
				Native Americans	58–67

The percentage of lactose intolerant individuals in select human populations. Low frequencies of lactose intolerance are correlated with extensive diary farming as an important mode of subsistence in European and European derived populations; among the Fulani of Africa, a group of nomadic cattle herders whose diets also contain large quantities of raw milk; and some Indian populations.

From Molnar, 1998:133.

Skin Pigmentation

Biology of skin color.   Unlike the genetics of lactase production, the anatomy, physiology, and genetics of the skin and its coloration are complex and have been under a variety of selective pressures for millions of years, even before humans first left their African homeland. The skin is composed of two layers, an outer *epidermis* and an inner *dermis*. The coloration of the lower levels of the epidermis is what determines skin color. Coloration, on a light to dark scale, depends mainly on the presence of the pigment **melanin.** *Melanocytes,* cells found in the lower layers of the epidermis, produce this dark pigment; actual skin color depends on how active the melanocytes are in producing melanin, because the number and density of these cells are the same in light- and dark-skinned individuals. Hemoglobin, carotene (yellow–red pigment molecules), and the thickness of the skin itself all contribute to skin color.

Additionally, one environmental factor affecting skin coloration is the sun's ultraviolet (UV) radiation. The red color of a sunburn, the body's first response to excessive UV light in most people, is the result of a concentration of hemoglobin near the skin's surface. A suntan, the body's usual second response to UV light, can also darken any color skin by stimulating the production of additional melanin. Even very dark-skinned individuals will "tan" in response to UV exposure.

The genetics of skin color are not completely understood. Most researchers believe that, rather than a single locus of a major gene, many loci and their multiple alleles work in combination to determine a person's pigmentation. One of the most common misconceptions about "race" concerns skin pigmentation. The lay public, in particular, often confuses race with skin color, as in the terms "white race," "people of color," and "black race." Skin color is, indeed, a very noticeable anatomical characteristic of inherited human variation. However, it is not in itself a reliable indicator of population affinities. For example, Africans, the Dravidians of southern India, and native Australians, among others, all have darkly pigmented skin, but otherwise they share no close genetic affinities. They are more closely related to geographically close lightly pigmented populations than to one another. This suggests that variations in skin pigmentation are adaptive and have been under strong selective forces throughout human evolutionary history. To understand the variation in human skin color we must investigate its adaptive significance.

Adaptive significance of skin color.   Human skin serves in a general adaptive sense to regulate the penetration of UV light. In the lower latitudes (areas near the equator that experience intense UV radiation), pigmented epidermal skin prevents the carcinogenic portion of the sun's radiation, particularly the B-range ultraviolet light (UVB), from reaching the dermis. This prevents sunburn and, eventually, skin cancer from developing. However, UV-induced skin cancers generally occur late in life and rarely affect an individual's reproductive success. Thus, although avoiding skin cancer is a benefit to the individual, this benefit is not important in terms of natural selection, because it has little effect on reproductive fitness.

The question of why lightly pigmented skin evolved is not so clearly answered. We do know that sunlight, in addition to producing harmful effects on the human body in excessive amounts, also has beneficial effects. Vitamin D is produced in the skin and subcutaneous tissue when light penetrates and is absorbed there. It is necessary for the absorption of calcium. Although vitamin D can also be eaten in the form of fish or fortified milk (if individuals in the population are lactose tolerant), experimental results indicate that most of the body's vitamin D derives from sunlight (Cardinali and Wurtman, 1975). In the extreme northern and southern latitudes, however, there may not be sufficient UVB throughout the year to produce adequate amounts of vitamin D in the skin. Humans are able to live in these regions only as a consequence of diets that are high in vitamin D.

melanin: from the Greek, meaning "black"; a dark brown or black pigment that occurs in the skin, eyes, and hair.

If vitamin D is insufficient during growth, and a calcium deficiency results as a consequence, a condition known as **rickets** develops. In this disease the lower limbs become bowed outward and the pelvic bones are deformed, because the bones lack sufficient calcium. The fossil record shows that rickets was evident in some of the Neandertals in Ice Age northern Europe. Although rickets may have been present in ancient populations, however, Robins (1991) has claimed that the disease is one more closely associated with urbanization—thus it is a disease of civilization, not one particularly worrisome to our Paleolithic ancestors. Bearing this all in mind, researchers believe that a more lightly pigmented skin is advantageous to individuals who live in regions of reduced solar radiation. These researchers explain the distribution of skin pigmentation on the basis of vitamin D requirements for individuals living in different environmental conditions.

Others found fault with the vitamin D model, arguing that dark pigmented skin could produce adequate levels of the vitamin as far north as the Arctic Circle even if only 10.5 percent of the body surface was exposed on some regular basis. Researchers further pointed out that rickets is rare in North American Indians, even though they are darker skinned than Europeans who live at comparable latitudes (Beadle, 1977).

Nina Jablonski and G. Chaplin (1999) took a new look at yet another explanation for the evolution of human skin pigmentation. They argue that in individuals who live under conditions of high UVB intensity throughout most of the year, dark skin pigmentation protects against UV-induced destruction of folate, a metabolite essential for the normal development of the neural tube in embryos and also for normal spermatogenesis in adult males. Unlike skin cancer, the regulation of folate levels and the role folate plays in embryonic development and male fertility can be directly related to individual fitness, and for these reasons, increased concentrations of melanin would be adaptive. These researchers also claim that dark pigmentation prevents UVB-induced injury to sweat glands, essential for thermoregulation. Dark skin pigmentation would then be a required part of the mechanism of thermoregulation of the brain and, thus, was probably an ancient adaptation for early hominids.

Clearly, skin color has adaptive value for people living under different environmental conditions. Nevertheless, the picture is clouded by many factors that may have contributed to the overall pattern of skin color distribution of modern peoples.

rickets: from the Old English, meaning "twisted," a disease caused by deficiency of calcium and characterized by the symptoms of poor calcification of bones, skeletal deformities, disturbance of growth, and generalized muscular weakness.

Gene Variability and Athletic Performance

As the 30,000 or so genes of the human genome have been decoded, more and more of who we are and what we can do is being illuminated. Dr. Hugh Montgomery of the Centre for Cardiovascular Genetics at London's Rayne Institute led a study that involved variants of the angiotensin-converting enzyme (ACE) gene (Williams et al., 2000). The enzyme that is encoded at this locus is active in skeletal muscle. There are, so far, two known alleles for this gene, one of which has 287 more base pairs than the other. In the English population sampled, the frequency of the homozygous short allele was 25 percent, 50 percent of the population was heterozygous, and another 25 percent was homozygous for the long allele.

Preliminary research shows that the long allele results in lower enzyme activity. People who carry the long allele have enhanced endurance and greater muscle efficiency, which gives them an athletic edge over heterozygotes and those whose genotype has only the short allele. A study of British army recruits demonstrated training-related differential changes in the mechanical efficiency of skeletal muscle between those who were homozygous for the long allele and those of other genotypes, as measured by energy used per unit power output.

The evolutionary significance of this variability has yet to be assessed. Studies of the frequencies of the two alleles in worldwide populations might provide some clues as to why this variation exists in the first place. The results might somehow relate to differences observed in human locomotor abilities.

We can be confident, however, that skin color is a product of natural selection and not a characteristic that can be or should be used as a criterion to delimit one specific population of people from another.

Evidence for human migrations. Knowing this, can the distribution of human skin color today tell us anything about how long it took to produce such variability in the first place? C. Loring Brace believes that the spread of modern peoples into the New World and into Australia provides us with appropriate test cases (Brace et al., 1999). As we saw in Chapter 12, the late Pleistocene spread of peoples of Asiatic descent throughout the New World was a rapid event—it took, perhaps, as little as 15,000 years for people to move from the eastern end of the Bering land bridge in Alaska to within 10 degrees of Antarctica. In this instance there are no significant differences in skin pigmentation over this entire range—Native Americans of all latitudes have similar skin pigmentation.

In the case of Australia, which modern peoples have inhabited for about 50,000 years, there is a slight skin color gradient from north to south—northerners, who live closer to the Equator, have darker skin than southerners. Brace concludes that based on these examples, it would have taken at least 200,000 years of "in situ residence at the latitude of London, Berlin, and Kiev to have produced the degree of pigment characteristic of the people who continue to live there today" (1999:96). This would explain why the indigenous peoples of North America are darker skinned than Europeans, even though they live at the same latitude—they have occupied the continent for only a short period of time.

GENETIC INFLUENCE ON BEHAVIORAL VARIATION

Although human behavior has as its primary component culture, or the patterned learned behavior adopted as a result of living and growing up in a society (Figure 14–12), many human behaviors also have a direct genetic basis. Among the

FIGURE 14–12 One of the many ways in which the next generation becomes enculturated, or learn the culture into which it has been born.

mammals, primates show the highest amounts of behavioral variability, and humans show the highest level among primates. How much of this variability is because of the responsiveness of culture and learning, and how much is because of genetic variation, has been examined by examining behavioral differences between groups where cultural and genetic influences can be minimized. For example, studies of behavioral differences between males and females in the same culture, coupled with a functional interpretation of hormonal differences in behavior, attempt to relate behavior to biological sex differences. Studies of identical twins, who share the same genes but may have different cultural experiences as they mature, have also provided important insights into the interplay of genetics and culture in behavior.

Sex Differences

Part of the folklore of any human culture consists of stories describing behavioral differences. Of these, those stories that describe differences between men and women are probably the most common. For example, before the advent of empiricism, Aristotle thought that men had more teeth than women. It would have been simple for Aristotle to open up the mouths of a number of men and women and count their teeth, but he never did. Similarly, the idea that men are more intelligent than women has been shown in scientific studies to be wrong, but for centuries this idea remained in place. It was not until 1920, for example, that U.S. society held women to be competent to vote. In many countries of the world, women's suffrage has yet to come to pass.

The most recent work on sex differences in intelligence supports the contention that the two sexes do not, on the whole, differ greatly in average IQ. They do differ, however, in certain components of IQ. The best recognized of these is that men outscore women on most tests of *spatial IQ*, a component of IQ that measures such abilities as copying geometric figures and mentally rotating complex figures. Both biological and cultural explanations have been advanced to explain this fact, but neither, as yet, is conclusive (MacKintosh, 1998).

Alcoholism. A widespread folk belief is that men can consume more alcohol with less effect than can women. This is one folk tale, however, that does contain some truth. On average, women are smaller than men, and, as a result, they are usually more affected than men after consuming the same amount of alcohol. This observation, though, fails to explain the fact that when men and women of equal size drink the same quantities of alcohol, most women tend to get intoxicated more rapidly. Although cultural rules that indicate how men and women are expected to act if they drink might explain some of the folk observations, researchers wondered if there might not be a biological explanation as well. Women, as it turns out, produce far less of a crucial enzyme in the lining of their gastric tract than do men (Frezza et al., 1990).

This enzyme, alcohol dehydrogenase (ADH), breaks down alcohol, reducing the amount that gets into the bloodstream. Because of the reduced amount of the enzyme, women absorbed about 30 percent more alcohol than men in one study (Figure 14–13). Further studies have shown that men who are alcoholics have gastric alcohol dehydrogenase that is only half as active as that found in nonalcoholic men, but alcoholic women show almost no enzyme activity at all, which probably explains why alcoholic women suffer more heavily from liver damage than do alcoholic men (Yoshida et al., 1991). For the sample studied (Italian men and women), this research showed that significant variation in alcohol metabolism in the gastric tract occurred between the sexes. But the story is more complicated than this.

Research on gastric alcohol dehydrogenase activity in different populations showed variability, but of a different nature. Studies of individuals in Asia tell us that gastric enzyme activity for both males and females is undetectable. In addition, Asians commonly possess an allele that changes the metabolic pathway of alcohol in the bloodstream, producing an external reaction: reddening of the skin. In most

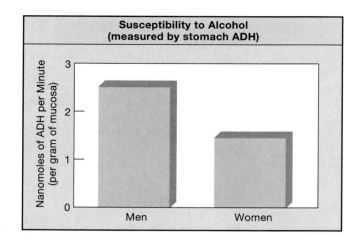

Susceptibility to Alcohol
(measured by stomach ADH)

FIGURE 14-13 Production of alcohol dehydrogenase (ADH) after consumption of alcohol in men and women. Stomach ADH production is approximately 30 percent higher in men than in women.

Asians there is no gastric "first pass" protection at all from alcohol entering the blood stream, adding another twist to the story.

If that weren't enough, this tale spills over from one that seemed to be a purely human concern into one involving our closest living relatives, the nonhuman primates. An attempt to determine the extent of gastric alcohol dehydrogenase activity in baboons (Algar et al., 1992) demonstrated that a "first pass" situation did exist. So at least one kind of Old World monkey (a cercopithecine) showed similar biochemistry to humans. A follow-up study (Almquist et al., unpublished) showed that the same sexual difference in gastric activity as is seen in some human populations is also present in macaque monkeys.

We have no clear-cut explanations for these observations as yet. Some ethnographic observations, however, may provide additional pieces to the puzzle. Undoubtedly, one of the oldest intoxicants used by humans is alcohol. As with most other intoxicants and hallucinogens, cultural studies suggest that its ingestion generally falls within the realm of male behavior and outside the realm of what is considered to be proper female behavior (Mandelbaum, 1965:282). In hunting and gathering societies, as well as in peasant/agricultural societies, drug or alcohol use is usually culturally prohibited for women of childbearing years (Saunders, 1980:67), intoxication being known to have important negative reproductive consequences both pre- and postnatally. Evidence from a number of cultures, in contrast, shows that this prohibition may be suspended for postmenopausal women (women beyond the age of childbearing). If we could demonstrate that for a considerable time regular alcohol use was predominantly a male activity, we might conclude that selection was operating to provide some protection against what clearly is a poison to the system. The genetics of this protection would be what it seems to be—sexually dimorphic.

But what of those human populations that do not show "first pass" sexual dimorphism? Here the answer probably lies in the limited spread of viticulture (grape production and wine making) into Asia, to modest consumption of alcohol from any source by Asians, and to the fact that Asian populations preferred alternative intoxicants. And the nonhuman primates? Here the data on alcohol metabolism is incomplete; not enough species have been studied. The data we have so far are not inconsistent with what we know about the diets of the cercopithecines—they are fruit eaters when they can get it, and much of the ripest fruit is well fermented, with a high alcohol level as a result of sugar conversion. Some monkeys do get drunk (K. Milton, personal communication). Males, who are usually able to dominate the feeding patches, may, as a consequence, ingest more fruit that contains alcohol than females.

These hypotheses need to be fine-tuned through future research on both the feeding behavior of different nonhuman primate species and on biochemical assays of gastric tissue in diverse groups, such as the colobines, in which fruit plays a very minor role in their diets. Certainly, more work needs to be done before the evolutionary implications of these observations can be understood. Research, so far, does show that an evolutionary perspective can be useful in generating new models of understanding variability.

Heredity and Environment

Studies of identical (monozygotic) twins who have been reared apart provide one of the simplest and most powerful methods for disentangling the influence of environmental and genetic factors on human characteristics and their variable expression (Figure 14–14). The published report of The Minnesota Study of Twins Reared Apart (Bouchard et al., 1990) offers a basis for understanding the contributions of genetics versus environmental influences.

The total variance between any two individuals for a given trait is composed of variance caused by genetic differences plus variance caused by environmental factors. In the twin study, for traits such as IQ, or **intelligence quotient,** variance caused by genetic factors was approximately 70 percent of the total. These findings do not imply that traits such as IQ cannot be enhanced. The Bouchard study did not define or limit what might conceivably be achieved in an optimal environment, but it did indicate that in the broad middle class of an industrial society, two-thirds of the observed variances of IQ can be traced to genetic variation.

Researchers have found that IQ can be improved or reduced by many factors, such as how parents talk to their infants, the availability and quality of early daycare programs, and the overall amount of schooling an individual receives. This suggests that even a factor as highly heritable as intelligence may be malleable through early intervention. For example, children with Down Syndrome (a syndrome caused by a chromosomal abnormality and resulting in physical symptoms and mental retardation) who receive early childhood intervention (from birth) usually achieve a state of mild mental retardation or borderline low to normal IQ (about 70 IQ). This is a huge contrast to children born in times past with Down Syndrome, who were typically raised in institutions and assumed to be uneducable. Those adults mostly cannot speak or read and are typically classified as severely

intelligence quotient: a score on a standardized psychological test designed in Western Europe and North America to measure an individual's aggregate capacity to act purposefully, think rationally, and deal effectively with the environment.

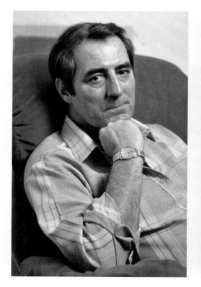

FIGURE 14–14 Identical twins studied in the Minnesota Study. These men were separated at birth and reared apart from each other; the similarities between them are striking.

retarded with IQs of about 20, a 50-point difference from children who received early intervention. Other studies have consistently shown that the substitution of infant formula for breast feeding lowers IQ by 5 to 8 points, which is about the same result expected from moderate lead poisoning. Prenatal cocaine use also lowers IQ by an average of 3 points (K. Dettwyler, personal communication, 2000).

Studies of how environmental influences affect IQ have examined the development of language and have provided some of this new evidence. For example, we know that vocabulary is an important component of IQ tests, and new research shows that a strong positive correlation exists between talkative mothers and the vocabulary of their infants, a correlation that is apparent as early as 26 months of age. Children of the most talkative mothers had vocabularies more than four times as large as the vocabularies of children of the quietest mothers. This same relationship extended to the use of complex sentences. It is clear that lots of sensory stimulation by parents in the early years can have a long-term impact on their children's IQ.

In another study, preschool intervention had dramatic results. By the time children were three years old, those who attended preschool exhibited average IQs of about 101, more than 17 points higher than the average IQs of a control group of children who did not attend a preschool. Follow-up reports indicate that the effects are long-lasting: the children in the preschool group still maintained a 5-point lead over controls at 15 years of age.

Other studies have shown that later schooling is also important in forming and maintaining IQ. The IQs of children born to migrant parents, for example, declined, because they missed more and more school. It is estimated that each year of schooling can raise IQs by about 3.5 points. At present it is likely that given the genetics of any individual, IQ can be affected by experiential contributing factors.

Race, Social Class, and IQ

The heritability of intelligence has been difficult to predict, because the actual genetic basis of intelligence is not well understood. (For that matter, there is disagreement about what "intelligence" is and of what aptitudes it is comprised.) The Minnesota Twin Study may provide us with one estimation of heritability, but we must consider a number of other factors before we can apply the data from specific individuals to whole populations.

What is intelligence and how has it been measured? From a biological point of view we might consider intelligence as a manifestation of the innate intellectual

The Flynn Effect

Political scientist James Flynn (1987) of the University of Otago in New Zealand has documented a rise of about 20 IQ points in every 30-year generation in 20 countries. This trend has been obscured by the fact that the major IQ test developers change the norms of their tests every 15 to 20 years, resetting the mean to 100. What Flynn's data mean is that, if everyone who took an IQ test today was scored using the norms set 50 years ago, more than 90 percent of them would be classified as geniuses, with IQ scores higher than 130. Similarly, if our parents' or grandparents' IQ scores, obtained 50 years ago, were measured against today's norms, more than 90 percent of them would be labeled "mildly mentally retarded" with IQs lower than 70. Biological factors, such as better nutrition, could underlie the Flynn Effect, but genetic changes occur much too slowly to account for it. Schooling is the primary suspect, because the average length of schooling has significantly increased from less than eight years in the 1920s to more than 13 years in today's educational system.

capacity of the brain (Birdsell, 1981). Innate intelligence, however, cannot yet be defined in precise genetic terms. Psychologists have usually examined intelligence by testing such skills as memory, problem solving, ability to synthesize information, and motivation (more difficult to measure). Some psychologists have listed up to 120 components of intelligence (Bodmer and Cavalli-Sforza, 1976).

Intelligence is usually measured by administering a standardized test to an individual and then scoring that test. One common intelligence test is the well-known Stanford-Binet IQ test. IQ is calculated by measuring a person's "mental age" based on the test score and dividing it by his or her chronological age. The test sets the average response at 100, with the range for average intelligence falling between 90 and 110. Because the test supposedly measures a number of abilities, individuals often score differently on the various test sections. Furthermore, throughout an individual's lifespan, IQ can change by as much as 30 points.

One question that has been investigated by many researchers for many years concerns the range of intelligence for different populations. Is there any evidence to suggest that whole groups of people fall below (or rise above) some hypothetical worldwide average?

In the United States the most controversial aspect of IQ testing has been a fairly consistent and large body of data that suggests the average IQ of African Americans to be about 15 points below that of white Americans. In a number of cases, educators and others have attributed these differences to genetics. This contention, however, is rejected by most anthropologists and evolutionary biologists. A number of tests have confirmed their stance. If white Americans on the average were more intelligent than African Americans and the difference were due to genetics, African Americans with a high degree of European admixture should do better on IQ tests than African Americans who do not have a high degree of European admixture. They do not. In addition, test scores achieved by northern "blacks" are consistently higher than those achieved by southern whites as groups.

In a parallel case, Japanese children from a socioeconomically disadvantaged group, the Buraku-min, scored an average of 16 points below other Japanese children, roughly comparable to the difference between white Americans and African Americans. Yet there is no way to distinguish the Buraku-min as a group from other Japanese except by their place of birth or current residence. Such examples indicate that "intelligence," as measured by standardized tests, has a strong environmental component (Birdsell, 1981:386–387).

There are other population differences in IQ scores. For example, Chinese and Japanese students often achieve higher scores than white students on spatial IQ and on other nonverbal tests. As yet there is no evidence to indicate whether such differences are environmental or genetic in origin.

One of the most exhaustive studies on the subject of "race" and IQ was published by Arthur Jensen (1998), an educational psychologist at the University of California, Berkeley. Jensen has been in the fray for years (Jensen, 1969, 1980) because of his assertion that the 15-point difference between average IQ scores for African Americans and American whites is primarily the result of genetic factors. Criticisms of Jensen's latest effort alleges that he erred in the construction of his study sample, leading to an invalid treatment of the data. The 15-point IQ gap between his two sample populations, which he believes he has demonstrated, may in fact be only a statistical artifact (Jorion, 1999).

Besides problems in methodology, other environmental factors affecting IQ scores—diet, disease, educational quality, and social class—must somehow figure into the formula that determines IQ. If whole groups of people are affected by the same factors, IQ scores will also likely be affected; a poor environment will produce lower IQs for all. IQ tests in and of themselves can only attempt to measure the intelligence of people with some common cultural background. To measure the average intelligence of African peasants, for example, based on the results of standardized U.S. IQ tests would be foolish. It is likely, for example, that people who have grown up in a traditional farming economy know a great deal more about plants and animals than do residents of a U.S. city, but that does not make either group more "intelligent" than the other. To obtain a meaningful measure of the difference in intelligence between members of two different groups is difficult, because no one yet has constructed a "culture-free" IQ test.

A Final Word About Variability

Whatever the ancient origins and adaptive significances of genetic variability, variation has pervasive and important repercussions in our society. A human species whose early members did not vary much genetically with respect to cognitive and motivational attributes, and whose members were uniformly average by current standards, would have created a very different society from the one we know. Modern society, the result of the contributions of individuals who belong to a much more variable gene pool than in the past, not only augments the influence of genotype on behavioral variability but also permits this variability to contribute reciprocally to the rapid pace of cultural change.

◖ SUMMARY

1. **What is phenotypic variation, and how is it measured? What factors increase phenotypic variation?**
   Humans are one of the most biologically variable of the animal species, a fact that reflects the wide range of environments and habitats in which people live. Biological anthropologists measure this variability both quantitatively, as in stature and weight, and qualitatively, as in the presence or absence of the shovel-shaped incisor. Although the level of heterozygosity (between 10 and 15 percent) at loci among individuals within a population is only slightly lower than the differences seen between individuals from different populations, variation shows a geographical component that is the result of evolution. Generally, the amount of variation between individuals increases with distance: The farther away individuals' populations are, the more those individuals tend to differ. The primary factors that may increase genetic differences are selection and genetic drift.

2. **Why is "race" an inadequate way to describe human diversity?**
   Local, geographically defined populations of humans are sometimes termed "races." "Race," however, is a term that has been frequently misused and is not synonymous with "ethnic group." Although geographically isolated populations develop their own unique characteristics by mutation, genetic drift, and natural selection, the continual genetic exchange that occurs between populations makes it impossible to define human "races." It is also not scientifically useful to do so. Modern genetic studies show that some traditionally measured characteristics, such as skin color, are not good guides to population affinities.

3. **Explain the significance of noncoding DNA and neutral mutations.**
   Certain mutations in coding DNA that may arise in individuals and spread by chance probably have no discernible selective advantage but can help scientists establish relationships among populations. Such examples include the variable excretion of methanethiol. By definition, noncoding DNA is neutral and, therefore, not subject to natural selection. These sections of DNA, however, are also polymorphic and can be used in the same way as neutral mutations in coding DNA to trace population migrations and relatedness.

4. **How are polymorphisms, such as hemoglobin S, blood groups, and skin pigmentation, maintained in human populations? How do they benefit individuals?**

Variable conditions, such as sickle-cell anemia, provide heterozygotes in malarial areas of the world with an increased ability to resist the disease. The spread of these mutations is the result of natural selection and migration. Much of the variability in human populations is not so clearly understood, yet a selective advantage for heterozygotes (a balanced polymorphic situation) must be present to account for the enormous numbers of combinations of alleles, such as among the blood groups and the HLA system. Variations in skin color are maintained in populations as a result of selection in different environmental settings that most probably relate to the intensity of ultraviolet light from the sun at different latitudes. The genetics of skin pigmentation are unclear, and factors relating to the synthesis of vitamin D in the skin and the regulation of folate may be important determinants of skin color variation.

5. **What is known about the influence of genetics on behavior and intelligence?**

There may be considerable genetic influence on behavioral variation, as well as on morphological and physiological variation. The former is an area where twin studies have been useful, especially in understanding the inheritance of intelligence. No convincing evidence, however, exists for genetic differences in intelligence between human populations.

In other areas, such as in studies of alcoholism, an understanding of variation coupled with an evolutionary perspective has generated new models of understanding these conditions in terms of the prevalence of variation and its distribution in different populations.

CRITICAL THINKING QUESTIONS

1. Biologically speaking, races are the result of genetic isolation and the first step in the process that leads to speciation. What factors have prevented different populations of humans from becoming different subspecies or, for that matter, species?
2. If race is a concept that defies definition, what use does it still have, if any, in our understanding of human evolution and variability?
3. What major factors have contributed to the fact that we are mostly at a loss to explain genetic variability in the blood group and HLA systems?
4. Why are most phenotypic characteristics, such as skin color, poor indicators of the place of geographic origin of any individual? What characteristics might be more useful indicators of geographic origin?
5. "Race" and intelligence continue to be part of the debate about the meaning of performance differences between individuals from different populations. With our understanding of human genetics and evolutionary principles, why hasn't the question of population differences in intelligence been resolved?

INTERNET EXERCISES

Critical Thinking

Exploring Human Diversity. This chapter describes some of the ways that individuals and populations vary. In this exercise, you will focus on a worldwide research project whose goal is to explore the diversity and underlying unity of the entire human genome, the Human Genome Diversity Project. After accessing the appropriate Web sites and investigating both the given sites and their links, write a paper that answers the following questions:

1. What is the difference between the Human Genome Diversity Project (HGDP) and the Human Genome Project? What are the goals, methods, and purpose of each project?
2. How does the HGDP differentiate between human groups? How does it define a population? What are the implications of these definitions?

Writing Assignment

What Is "Race"? Your textbook explores the idea of "race" and concludes that this concept is a contentious one in terms of explaining human diversity. In this exercise, define "race" in your own words. Write an essay in which you try to answer the following questions:

1. What characteristics are usually included in definitions of race? Are these characteristics meaningful ones in terms of human variation?
2. What is the ultimate source of human diversity and variation?
3. What importance does society place on "racial" grouping and on ethnic diversity? How do the government and private organizations use information about "race" and ethnicity? What is the importance of this information?

See Companion Web site for Internet links.

The Case of the Balanced Polymorphism

The topic of this chapter was human variation. Although biological anthropologists and geneticists have documented much variation in human populations, under many circumstances they have been unable to ascertain either the selective advantages or the evolutionary forces that produce the variation. In those cases in which we have determined the reason for variability, large fitness differences among individuals within the study population usually exist. As we saw, such a situation occurs for sickle-cell hemoglobin. In this example, individuals who are heterozygous for the sickle-cell trait have protection against malaria. We also saw that the sickle-cell trait is just one balanced polymorphism that gives a degree of protection against malaria.

WEB ACTIVITY

The animation provided on the Web site is a basic Punnett square, familiar to anyone who has ever taken a biology

course. Use it to consider the implications of this balanced polymorphism on human populations.

Activity
1. View the animation. What genotypes does it assume for the parents? How would the chance of an offspring inheriting the heterozygous condition change if one parent had a different genotype? Both parents?
2. Must the heterozygous condition be maintained in the population at a relatively high level in order for the mutation to confer benefits? Why or why not?
3. Suppose sickle-cell trait were a dominant trait rather than a recessive one. Could it still be a balanced polymorphism?

This MediaLab can be found in Chapter 14 on your Companion Web site http://www.prenhall.com/boaz

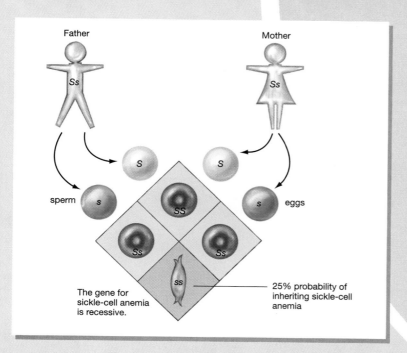

Father Mother

sperm

eggs

SS

Ss

Ss

ss

The gene for sickle-cell anemia is recessive.

25% probability of inheriting sickle-cell anemia

15

THE HUMAN LIFE CYCLE: HUMAN BIOLOGY, GROWTH, AND ADAPTABILITY

After reading this chapter, you should be able to discuss the following questions:

1. What insights have human growth studies shed on stages of human growth; the relationship between growth and evolution; and genetic, hormonal, and environmental influences on growth?
2. How does the human body adjust to changes in climate, light levels, altitude, and diet?
3. What pressures does modern urban life place on human biology and adaptation?

Throughout this book, we have seen how populations genetically adapt to changing environmental conditions over time. This is evolution, a long-term response involving changes in the genetic makeup of a population. As a result of evolution, the human organism is a compendium of physiological and morphological adaptations. Some of these basic adaptations are very old, extending back to early vertebrate and even prevertebrate ancestors (see Chapter 5). Others have much more recent evolutionary origins.

We have already seen that individuals in a population vary genetically from one another (see Chapters 4 and 14). Variability in gene pools offers the possibility that some individuals will be successful under different or changing environmental situations. The **genetic plasticity** of a species is the degree to which individuals can survive under increasingly diverse environmental situations, and the different ways that individuals respond to changing environmental circumstances are measures of this plasticity.

The ability of an individual to adapt to different environmental conditions, and the relation of this ability to the evolution and biology of the population, is called **adaptability.** This term refers also to an individual's reaction to changes in environmental conditions, and it includes any biochemical, physiological, or behavioral response that improves the individual's ability to function. Throughout an individual's life cycle, a dynamic interaction exists between environment and physiology, and this interaction is the subject of this chapter.

Within the genetic limits of any species, each individual can, in varying degrees, make short-term changes in his or her physiology in response to specific environmental situations. At high altitudes, for example, the body's response to **hypoxia** (a lowered percentage of oxygen in the air) is to increase both respiration and heart rate. This response increases both blood flow and the amount of oxygen that can be carried in a dissolved state in the blood.

We begin this chapter on adaptability with a survey of human growth and development. The study of growth is important from at least two different perspectives. First, as J. M. Tanner (1989), the British growth specialist, put it, growth is a mirror of the condition of society. Growth rates and development respond to the environmental conditions that surround an individual during his or her life. Less than optimal environmental conditions can limit the realization of the genetic potential of an individual. For example, a child who is subject to a period of malnutrition may not reach his or her full potential height.

Second, the study of growth provides important clues toward an understanding of evolution. As J. M. Tanner (1989:339) explained, "The study of growth is important in elucidating the mechanisms of evolution, for the evolution of morpho-

genetic plasticity: ability of a developing organism to alter its form and function in conformity with demands of the immediate environment.

adaptability: range of physiological and anatomical changes and adjustments allowed by a species' adaptation.

hypoxia: condition of reduced oxygen supply to tissues despite adequate blood supply.

logical characters necessarily comes about through alterations in the inherited pattern of growth and development."

HUMAN GROWTH STUDIES

The process by which human beings increase in physical size is termed *growth*. *Development,* however, refers to increases in complexity of function (for example, as an infant's motor skills develop, the infant becomes able to lift the head independently, then to roll over, then to crawl, and eventually to walk). As we discuss in greater detail later in the chapter, the term *development* is often used synonymously with "maturation" and "differentiation." Most physical growth ends by the age of 20 to 25 in modern humans.

The study of human growth is a broad field and one to which biological anthropologists and human biologists have made and continue to make significant contributions. J. M. Tanner suggests in *A History of the Study of Human Growth* (1981) that there were three main themes in the development of the field.

First, there have been social motivations for growth studies. Investigations of the physical and physiological development of children began, for example, in Britain in response to the child labor reform movement during the nineteenth century. At this time, eruption of the second molar, which commonly occurs at age 12, began to be taken as a sign that a child had reached puberty and was old enough to work. The second molar became known as the "factory molar."

Second, some studies of growth are motivated by medical concerns, such as early studies that monitored the physical and developmental progress of children. For example, in the late 1890s, Franz Boas, an American anthropologist, undertook large-scale anthropometric studies of American schoolchildren in order to establish for the U.S. Department of Education standards for weight and height at each

FRONTIERS

Evolutionary Considerations of Human Growth

Robert Martin (1996) has argued that modern human growth patterns of the brain and body become necessary once adult brain size reaches about 850 cc (51 cubic in.). At this point, the size of the pelvic outlet of recent fossil hominids and modern peoples does not allow for sufficient fetal growth to accommodate the development of what will become the large adult brain. According to Barry Bogin (1998), at this point in evolutionary history, the modern human pattern of growth, one of rapid postnatal brain growth and slow body growth, is required to reach adult brain size.

For *Australopithecus afarensis,* who shared an adult brain size of about 400 cc (24 cubic in.) with modern chimpanzees, postnatal growth consisted of

the typical mammalian pattern of infant, juvenile, and adult stages. If this pattern of growth characterized early hominids, the expansion of the adult brain size from *Australopithecus* forward must have constrained the size of early *Homo* populations. Among chimpanzees, for example, population growth is currently equal to zero, because of an interbirth interval somewhere around 5.5 years. For populations to expand, extending the infancy stage or the birth interval for early *Homo* would not have been a realistic option to support further brain growth, but the addition of a short childhood stage might have been, because most children no longer nurse and can be cared for by others.

Further brain expansion in *Homo erectus* to 850 to 900 cc (51 to 54 cubic in.) requires a humanlike pattern of brain

and body growth—that is, the period of childhood is extended and the more dependent infancy stage is decreased. The resulting reproductive advantage could explain how *H. erectus* populations expanded in size and geographic range beyond that of earlier hominids. Hominids with brain sizes from 1,100 cc and up to those of modern *H. sapiens* are characterized by growth patterns of increasingly longer periods of childhood and the addition of a new stage of adolescence. The latter stage also continues to increase to the modern average length of anywhere from four years to about eight years. According to Bogin, the more technologically adept early *H. sapiens* were, the more likely they were to require an adolescent stage of development, during which they learned the skills they needed to become successful adult members of their societies.

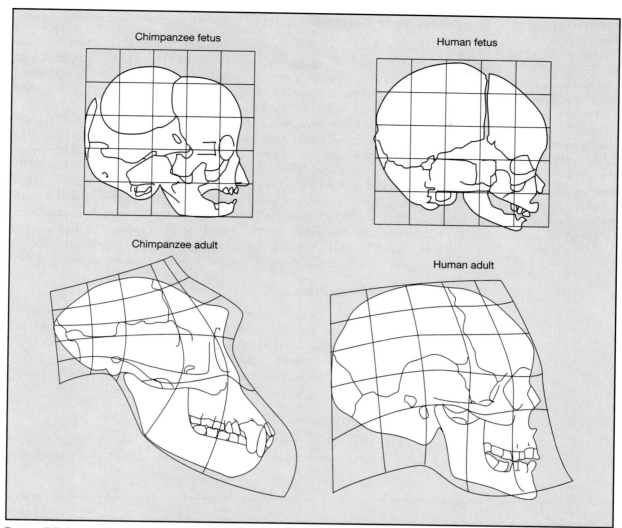

Figure 15–1 Comparison of (left) fetal and adult chimpanzee skulls to (right) fetal and adult human skulls. Superimposed on the outlines of the skulls are transformation grids, which show relative growth patterns. The relative amount of distortion in the grid lines that overlie the adult skulls indicates the relative amount of growth of different parts of the skull.

chronological age. Other such studies are those related to nutritional requirements for normal growth, the effects of environment on growth, and medical aspects of growth and its abnormalities.

Third, evolutionary studies of growth are prompted by a desire to understand the interaction between growth and the evolutionary biology of the human species. For example, comparing the rates of growth between closely related species can provide important insight into the different biology of each (Figure 15–1). Brain growth rate in humans is different from that in the apes. The accelerated fetal brain growth rate in humans continues postnatally to about one year of age. In the apes, the rate at which the postnatal brain grows slows immediately after birth. This is in part due to the extension of childhood years in humans relative to chimpanzees as well as a reflection of the birth process. In humans, birth may be a difficult process, as large-headed newborns exceed the normal dimensions of the mother's birth canal. Such a situation at birth demands the smallest possible head size (and, thus, brain size). The accelerated rate of postnatal brain growth is a way by which humans, less developed at birth, "catch up" with the comparably aged apes.

development: embryological differentiation of organs and tissues; sometimes considered the earliest stage of growth.

interstitial growth: growth by new cell formation throughout the mass of a structure, tissue, or organ.

appositional growth: growth by adding of layers at a specific point or plane.

anthropometry: the techniques of physical anthropologists used to measure the human body.

How Growth Is Defined

Growth is usually distinguished from **development**, a process that occurs from embryonic stages through early adulthood and consists of the differentiation of various tissues and body parts. *Growth* has sometimes been defined as "increase in size," *development* as "increase in tissue diversity." Here, both growth and development are considered as components of the same continuous process.

Growth takes place in several ways. The most common pattern is an increase in the number of cells. Soft body structures, such as the brain or muscles, develop by **interstitial growth,** where cells proliferate from many centers within the structure. Muscle tissue represents a unique pattern of growth in that fibers are formed by the fusion of several cells, which means that each fiber has more than one nucleus. Hard or rigid structures, however, such as bones or teeth, develop by **appositional growth,** the laying down of new layers on top of those already formed. Counting these layers can tell us how old an individual is or was. Growth does not proceed at the same rate in all tissues (Figure 15–2). Indeed, differential growth, defined as the relative growth rates between two structures, is an important way of distinguishing among species.

How Growth Is Measured

Biological anthropologists, also known as *auxologists,* measure growth and other physical attributes of living humans using instruments designed for the purpose. **Anthropometry** is the subfield involved with the measurement of the human body. As in the study of skeletal remains, a number of somatological landmarks (Figure 15–3) have been defined for the living body. These serve to standardize measurements and comparisons among human groups and among individuals.

The Seven Stages of Human Growth

Traditionally, four stages of growth and development have been defined for mammalian species. These are *prenatal/gestation stage,* which lasts from conception to

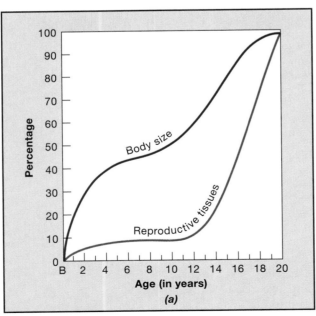
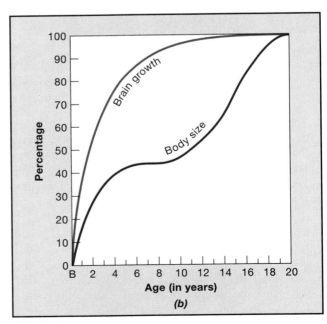

FIGURE 15–2 Relative growth rates of reproductive tissues (*a*) and brain size (*b*), compared with overall body size. The brain develops most rapidly before age two; the reproductive tissues develop most rapidly during adolescence.

birth; *infancy,* from birth to the eruption of the first permanent tooth (for humans this is the first lower molar, which erupts at five to six years of age); *juvenile,* from eruption of the first permanent tooth to eruption of the last tooth (in humans this is the third molar, which erupts at 15 to 25 years of age; and *adulthood,* from the eruption of the last permanent teeth to death.

Recently Barry Bogin (1995, 1998) adds to this list three additional stages that he claims are unique to humans. In his scheme he lists seven stages of growth: **embryonic,** which takes place before birth, and during which there is rapid growth and differentiation in function of various tissues; **infancy, childhood, juvenile,** and **adolescence,** during which a balance between growth and differentiation of tissue functions exists; **adulthood,** when the primary activity is the steady replacement of cells; and **old age,** when the rate of cell death is greater than the rate of replacement. In the nonhuman primates the relative length of the stages of growth and development remains relatively constant throughout the order (Figure 15–4). As the life span increases, every stage of life is extended; for example, both gestation and infancy are longer. This lengthening of every stage of the life span is correlated with adult body size: larger primates live longer. Humans have the longest life span of the primates and the longest periods of growth and development.

Bogin has characterized each of the early stages with both biological and behavioral features. Infancy is defined as that period when the individual is nourished almost exclusively by the mother's milk. This stage ends with weaning, which, he

embryonic: that period of growth prior to birth, especially weeks three through eight; growth during the last six months of gestation is sometimes referred to as fetal growth.

infancy: earliest stage of postpartum growth, extending from birth to the time of first permanent molars.

childhood: period of growth from weaning to the attainment of adult brain size.

juvenile: period of growth between eruption of first and last permanent teeth.

adolescence: period of growth between puberty and the attainment of full adult stature.

adulthood: period from after the eruption of the last permanent teeth to death.

old age: subperiod of adulthood typified by a greater rate of cell death than replacement.

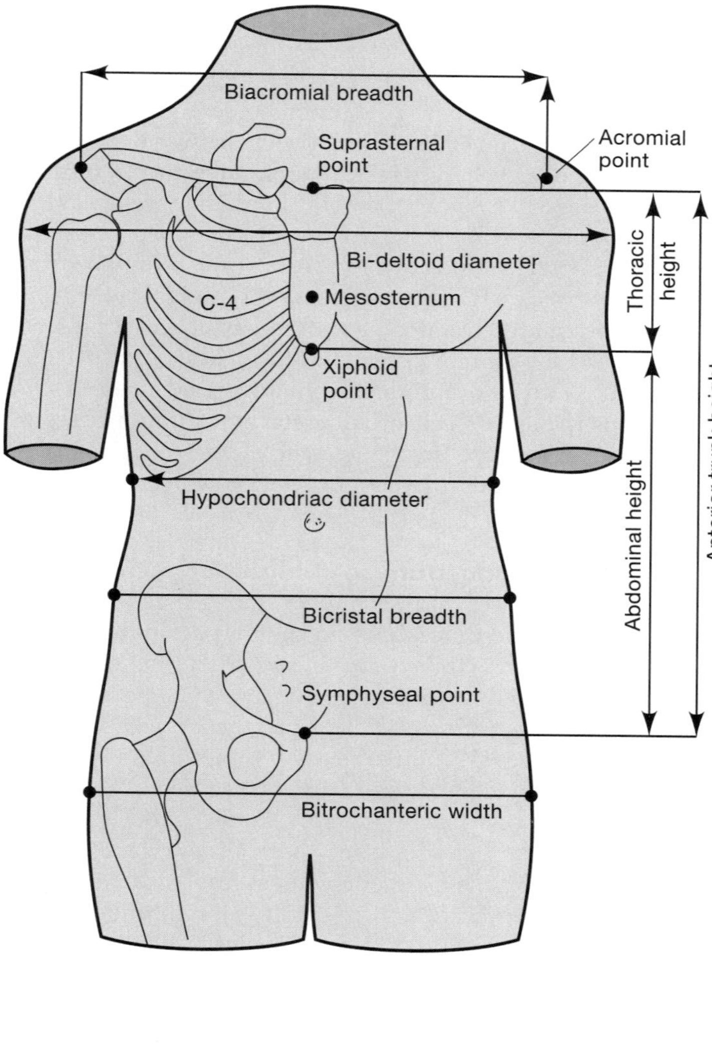

FIGURE 15–3 Somatological landmarks used in measurement and assessment of growth. Landmarks, which are central to anthropometry, are defined as anatomical points from which particular dimensions are measured. The landmark defines the measurement and allows it to be replicated by other researchers.

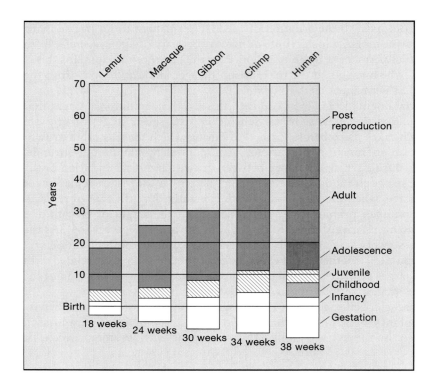

FIGURE 15–4 Comparative life stages in humans and other primates. Note the progressive prolongation of the life stages in the higher primates, from monkeys to humans.

claims, in preindustrialized societies occurs at about three years of age. Childhood is a period of continued dependency, characterized by reliance on others for feeding and protection. It ends when the brain has reached adult weight, about six to seven years of age. The juvenile period occurs between the end of childhood and the beginning of puberty. In the United States, puberty may begin as early as age 10 (with an average age of 12.6 years), and for boys about two years later. Puberty, from the Latin, *pubertas,* which refers to the age of the appearance of pubic hair, now commonly refers to the period at which the sex organs (in boys, the testes, prostate gland, and seminal vesicles; in girls, the uterus and vagina) suddenly enlarge.

Postpubescent accelerated growth in height and weight and the development of secondary sexual characteristics mark the adolescent stage. This stage ends when adult stature and full reproductive maturity are reached, though in many human populations the attainment of adult stature does not necessarily coincide with full reproductive maturity. On the average, adolescence ends, and maturity or adulthood begins, by about 19 years of age for women and 21 to 25 years of age for men, although these ages vary.

The unique human pattern: Childhood. According to Bogin, the human pattern of growth after birth is unique among the mammals. Several stages, such as childhood and adolescence, have no counterpart in the growth patterns of other animals. For the largest-brained member of the primates, the relatively slow physical growth of childhood holds several advantages. It extends the period of brain development and provides time for the development of technical as well as social skills. In addition, Bogin (1995:53) believes that childhood should also be viewed as involving a feeding adaptation: During this stage, a child may be provisioned with food by kin other than the mother. In Bogin's model this adaptation is significant, because it allows the mother time to care more intensely for her most recent offspring, assured that the older one will be cared for by others.

Evolutionarily speaking, there might be a reproductive advantage to humans in shortening the length of infancy by inserting childhood between the end of infancy

TABLE 15–1	Comparative Fertility in Three Human Groups and the Chimpanzee			
	Chimpanzee	!Kung (Botswana)	Agta (Philippines)	Ache (Paraguay)
Menarche (age in years)	8.8	16.6	17.1	14.3
Age at first birth (years)	14	19.9	20.1	18.5
Birth spacing (years)	5.6	4.1	3.05	3.2
Fertility rate (average number of children)	2.0	4.7	—	—
Average reproductive lifespan (years)	25–30	36	—	—

Data from Smith (1992a).

and the juvenile period. The childhood stage frees the mother from nursing and the impediments that continuous nursing places on ovulation. This assumes, of course, that the reduced fertility caused by lactational amenorrhea (cessation of mestruation while nursing) only ends when a woman ceases to nurse. Especially in well-nourished mothers, this subfecundity may end well before the end of nursing. It is quite possible for a mother to become pregnant and have another child while still nursing the older child, and then tandem nurse the two. But human females do have a potentially shorter interval between births of offspring, an adaptation that might offer a reproductive advantage over the closely related apes (Table 15–1). The reduction of the birth spacing interval enables humans to produce more offspring compared with apes.

The adolescent growth spurt. The stage of human adolescence is also unique among the primates because it is marked by a rapid acceleration in growth of the skeleton that accompanies the onset of sexual maturation (Figure 15–5). Growth seems to seek a target, rather than to proceed according to a strict schedule. If growth that would normally have occurred at a certain age is delayed because of poor nutrition or illness, when conditions improve there may be a rapid period of growth to "catch up." This aspect of growth is termed **canalization,** because there are certain channels or paths that it will follow. For normal and healthy individuals this growth spurt at its peak averages 9 to 10.3 cm (3.5 to 4 in.) per year in boys and 7.1 to 9.0 cm (2.8 to 3.5 in.) per year in girls (Tanner and Whitehouse, 1976). This growth spurt is mostly responsible for the average 12.6 cm (5 in.) height difference between males and females. Of course, males do have two more years, on average, of slow childhood growth before the spurt, and they also tend to have longer and more intense growth spurts, additional factors to be considered when considering height differences between males and females. The timing of adolescent growth is different for males and females (see Figure 15–5). Females complete the growth spurt before becoming fertile. Males, however, begin the growth spurt after they have begun to produce sperm.

Stunting in growth that begins in infancy may result in short adults, and about one-third of the world's children are somewhat more than two standard deviations below U.S. standards in height. Recent studies provide some evidence that spontaneous catch-up in height can occur, if the environment is somehow enriched,

canalization: regulatory forces that hold the processes of development in predetermined channels.

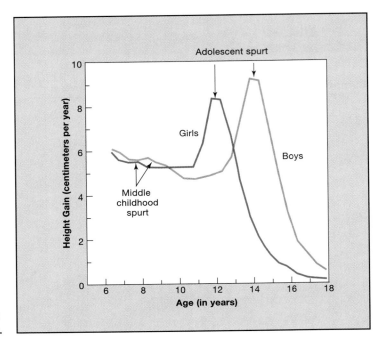

FIGURE 15–5 Growth spurts in height for girls and for boys.

although children from the lowest socioeconomic levels never reach normal standards. Still, no studies have researched the effects of providing optimum nutrition to chronically stunted children, so we don't yet know the potential for catch-up in most groups of stunted children.

Unsuspected growth-encouraging nutrients may well be missing in many populations of the world. For example, in the United States, it was discovered that the addition of zinc to the diets of some children led to substantial increases in height growth in girls. Unfortunately, we do not yet know the dietary requirements for either normal or catch-up growth in height, although these are under study. Thus, the question remains somewhat open as to whether a deficit in early nutrition permanently affects individuals in terms of a growth "scar," or whether catch-up is inevitable given a change in their circumstances.

The adolescent growth spurt occurs in one form or another in all modern human populations, but when did this spurt come into play in human evolution? Holly Smith (1989) carefully studied the KNM WT 15000 skeleton, the "Turkana Boy," that was recovered from 1.6-million-year-old sediments of West Lake Turkana, Kenya (see Figure 11–7). As was described in Chapter 11, the Turkana boy was probably less than 11 years old at the time of his death. According to Smith, the boy's skeleton was highly advanced developmentally at this stage, thus he would not have experienced a later "adolescent growth spurt" had he lived through his teenage years. In other words, considering that the human lineage is about 6 million years old, the growth spurt may be a relatively recent development.

For many girls around the world, adolescence is correlated with menarche, which occurs at about the age of 12.5 years, on average, usually followed by a period of one to three years of subfecundity. Females also usually do not attain adult pelvic inlet size until 17 to 18 years, because the pelvis has its own pattern of growth, which is slower than that of the reproductive tract. Taking everything into account, a female may not reach adult reproductive maturity until about the age of 20 to 24 years. Younger mothers face higher risks of miscarriage, and in the United States they are twice as likely to give birth to babies of lower-than-average birth weight.

The pattern of development for boys differs from that of girls; boys become fecund at an early age. Early seminal fluids often contain very few sperm, however, and becoming fully fecund is a process that takes several years for males, just as it does for females. Boys attain adult size and the physical appearance of adult males after they become fecund. The median age for any sperm production is about 13.4 years, yet cross-cultural evidence shows that few males are successful as fathers until they reach an age somewhere in their twenties. In the United States, for example, statistics report that only 4 percent of all births are fathered by men younger than 20 years old. The survival advantage of adolescence for boys, Bogin claims, is that, with increasing blood testosterone levels, they become more interested in adult activities and begin to behave more like adult males, while at the same time continuing to look like boys.

Bogin summarizes his argument for the adaptive value of adolescence with the following: Though they are still subfecund, adolescent girls are perceived by adults as adults, and this maximizes their ability to learn female adult social roles. Boys, however, are sexually mature while they learn male adult social roles, but they are not perceived as adults. The advantage to the adolescent growth spurt is that this unique style of social and cultural learning can occur.

Genetic and Hormonal Control of Growth

Genetic messages for growth are mediated by the secretions of the *endocrine glands* (Figure 15–6). Several secretions of endocrine glands, known as *hormones*, are important for growth in human beings. The most important of these is **somatotropin,** or growth hormone, which is secreted by the **pituitary gland** located at the base of the brain. Growth hormone is secreted episodically, and secretion may be affected

somatotropin: hormone of the anterior lobe of the pituitary that promotes body growth, fat mobilization, and inhibition of glucose utilization.

pituitary gland: endocrine gland at the base of the cerebral cortex.

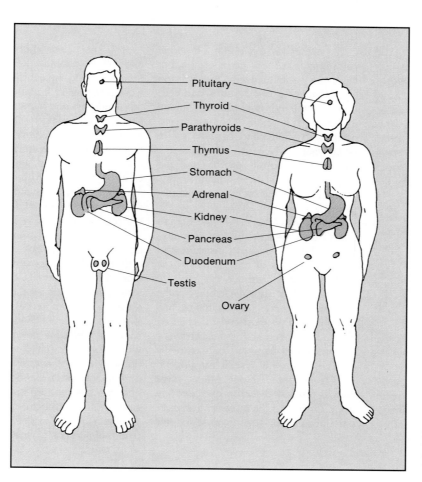

Pituitary
Thyroid
Parathyroids
Thymus
Stomach
Adrenal
Kidney
Pancreas
Duodenum
Testis
Ovary

FIGURE 15–6 Endocrine glands in the human body. Hormones can also be produced by other organs in the body.

hypothalamus: part of the ancient forebrain; located below the thalamus at the base of the brain's third ventricle; important in autonomic nervous system functions, such as endocrine gland activity.

thyroid hormone: also known as thyroxine, an iodine-containing hormone secreted by the thyroid gland and important in regulating the rate of tissue metabolism.

by a number of factors, including stress and exercise. The actual secretion of the growth hormone is regulated by the **hypothalamus.**

Thyroid hormone, secreted by the thyroid gland in the neck, is also important in growth from birth through adolescence. The lack of either of these hormones in sufficient quantities will result in retardation of growth and small size. The artificial administering of growth hormones and their chemical substitutes (steroids) enhances muscle development in athletes, but it also leads to *hypertrophy,* or excessive development, and damage to certain internal organs, especially the liver. At adolescence, gonadal hormones (from the ovaries in the female and from the testes in the male), particularly *testosterone* (an androgen) in the male and estrogen in the female, are added to the already-present pituitary and thyroid hormones. Secretion of androgen usually begins several years before puberty.

Growth and Development: A Guide to Evolutionary History

The study of growth is one important way biologists shed light on how evolution works. There is a general correspondence in the stages of a species' embryological growth and the major stages of its phylogenetic history. This is not surprising. Evolution used the structural blueprint at hand to adapt to new conditions. As evolution has proceeded, the end results of development and growth of species through

Shortcomings of the Bogin Model

Controversy about the interpretation of data and disagreement with conclusions reached by others are not unusual occurrences in science. The nature of science is to debate. Katherine Dettwyler offers some insights into the study of growth and development and some criticisms of the Bogin model. According to Dettwyler,

Around the world there are no cultures in which children are nourished "almost exclusively" by their mother's milk to the age of three years. Most children begin eating foods other than their mother's milk by four to six months of age, some earlier and some later, but the vast majority of children are eating substantial solids by 12 months of age.

Dettwyler states that breast milk can continue to be a major part of the diet for several more years.

The age of weaning in preindustrial societies varies. The mean of the average age of weaning in different societies, taken from survey data of 64 "traditional" societies published by

C. S. Ford in 1964 is about 2.8 years. The range is 2.5 to 7 years of age, but there are societies where the average age of weaning is 4.5 years, and children in some industrial societies nursed as long as 8 years. The underlying norm for breastfeeding is about six to seven years, which coincides with the end of major brain growth and the eruption of the first permanent teeth—the end of infancy as it is traditionally defined.

Dettwyler further counters Bogin's ideas about feeding children by pointing out that anyone can provide solid food for a child at any age. There is "nothing magic" about the age of three years that says the mother is the only one who can provide for a child until this age; in most cultures children during the second half of their first year eat foods that are part of the family food resources, not specifically supplied by the mother. Likewise, many other people provide childcare and feed the baby. Often, it is the three- to five-year-old sibling who is responsible for this task.

It is not clear that shorter birth intervals are adaptive. With many pregnancies during the course of a lifetime, women can suffer from maternal depletion syndrome and higher mortality. For example, according to the genealogies of the nineteenth century in the United States, many women started having babies at age 16, and subsequently had children every one to three years until the mother had 10 or more children by the age of 36 years. At this point mothers often died along with one or two of their youngest offspring. This is not adaptive. Certainly, one consequence of a shortened birth space is higher child morbidity and mortality. For example, a woman might have 14 children, but only six survive. Compare this to the woman who had only eight children during the same reproductive period as the first woman but whose children all survive. In addition to the other costs of a shortened birth space and, thus, shorter durations of breast feeding, are lowered IQs and emotional loss associated with the fact that the mother does not breast feed for a normal duration of time.

time have changed dramatically (refer back to Figure 15–1), but the early stages of differentiation have been much more conservative. For this reason the embryos of sharks, chickens, dogs, and humans are all similar, but as growth proceeds the species-specific pattern becomes clearly expressed. Brains in human embryos, for example, shows relatively more growth than brains in embryos of other species at the same level of development. Nevertheless, the *sequence* in which structures develop reflects to some degree the sequence in which they evolved. This principle can be of use when paleontologists attempt to determine the "primitive" or "derived" nature of anatomical traits. The embryological development of the horse, for example, clearly shows that its single-toed foot develops from a five-toed appendage, a conclusion well-documented in the fossil record.

One of the ways in which evolution produces species differences is by altering growth patterns—that is, by slowing, accelerating, or truncating the growth of certain parts of the body relative to others. Generally, species that are far removed phylogenetically from one another diverge in their patterns of growth early in their developmental histories. More closely related species diverge in growth patterns much later. The later stages of growth have been the foci of evolutionary changes that separate humans from our closest primate relatives. The evolutionary changes in rates of growth are termed **heterochrony** (McKinney and McNamara, 1991).

There are two categories of heterochrony. The first alters growth patterns by slowing the growth of certain parts of the body while normal sexual development proceeds. This results in an adult of the new species looking like the juvenile form of the ancestral species. This juvenilization is known as **pedomorphosis.**

Pedomorphosis is important in human evolution, because it explains many specific human anatomical traits. Adult humans resemble juvenile nonhuman primates in many characteristics (see Figure 15–1). Like infants of other species, adult humans have relatively large heads, the head is flexed toward the ventrum of the body, and there is a relatively high retention of body fat. There are likely a number of selective reasons for these pedomorphic characteristics in humans. No doubt large brain size (accounting for a large head), bipedalism (accounting for balanced or "flexed" head position), regulation of temperature (relating to hairlessness allowing effective sweating), and long-term energy storage (accounting for fat retention) all play a role in the selection for pedomorphic characteristics.

The second category of heterochrony is **peromorphosis,** or adultification of body form. Evolution can produce species differences by continuing growth for a longer period of time, accelerating development in some of the life stages, or adding additional stages to the end of the life cycle of descendant species. An example of peromorphosis in human evolution is the growth of the relatively long lower limbs.

Secular Trends in Growth and Maturation

Better health, resulting from the eradication of some infectious diseases and overall improved nutrition, has allowed certain populations to achieve more of their genetic potential for growth and to attain that growth at earlier chronological ages. In many countries we have, over time, observed increases in height and weight and a decrease in the age of menarche. Because these trends are not always confined to the upper-economic segment of a population, we deduce that a better balance in diet, with the regular consumption of essential minerals and vitamins, must certainly be more important than some single factor increase, such as calories. We study **secular trends,** those that we observe from one generation to the next, to understand the effects, over time, of nutrition, socioeconomic factors, and general health conditions on the growth and maturity in populations.

heterochrony: Greek, meaning "different time"; refers to the changes in rate of growth characteristic of species' evolutionary divergence from an ancestral species.

pedomorphosis: the retention of a juvenile stage in some part of a descendant species' morphology or behavior, in comparison with its ancestral species.

peromorphosis: the extension of growth or "adultification" of some part of the morphology or behavior of a descendant species, in comparison with its ancestral species.

secular trends: trends in growth or morphological characteristics that are attributable to changing environmental factors, such as nutrition and disease, and not to genetic adaptation.

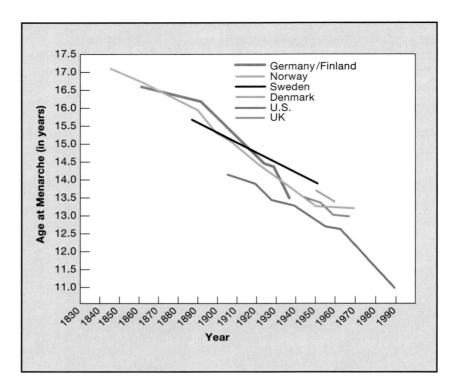

FIGURE 15-7 Secular trend in decreased age of menarche in Western Europe and North America.

In Western Europe and North America, studies have demonstrated several important trends. J. M. Tanner (1989) has shown that there was a decrease in the age of menarche in these regions: from average ages of between 15 and nearly 17 years in the 1800s to 12.5 to 14.5 years in the 1940s (Figure 15-7). Women in advantaged socioeconomic conditions, however, experience menarche 12 to 18 months earlier than poor women. This is primarily because of the generally better level of nutrition in the advantaged group. Studies have shown that when lean body mass (LBM) has reached a critical point, menarche will occur. The ratio of subcutaneous body fat to lean body mass prior to puberty is about 1 to 5. At menarche this ratio increases to about 1 to 3.

In one of the classic studies of human growth, Franz Boas measured the stature and head diameters of European immigrants to the United States and then compared them with the same measurements of their children, who were born and reared in the United States. He found that stature in the children was somewhat higher than that in their European parents and that head diameters were larger as well. At the same time, secular trends were observed in European American males who lived in North America. At all ages, males living in the 1960s were taller than their counterparts living in 1880 (Figure 15-8).

Growth and Development in Different Human Groups

In most populations around the world, given a good diet and health, individuals will grow to be quite similar in body size and structure to individuals in modern U.S. populations. In other populations, however, the genetic messages for growth may differ. For example, anatomist A. Abbie (1977) found that Australian Aborigines showed growth curves similar to Europeans' up to the age of five to six years. After that point, the length of the lower limbs in aborigine children increased rapidly. Adult aborigines have, on average, longer legs than do Europeans and are in this respect similar to many African adults, with the exception of the Central African Efe,

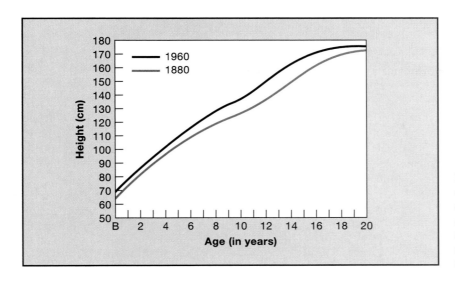

FIGURE 15-8 Comparison of stature in American-born children of European descent and earlier populations of the same heritage. Over time, adult height increased by as much as 5 cm (2 in.).

Baka, and Mbuti populations. Similar patterns also emerge when comparisons between individuals of European and African descent are made (Figure 15–9).

Differences caused by environment. Bogin, Wall, and MacVean (1992) studied two ethnic groups in Guatemala: Mayas and members of a higher-socioeconomic group called *ladinos*. Mayan children are on average shorter than ladino children of the same age. Is this difference caused by genetic differences or by

FIGURE 15-9 (*a*) Africans and Australian aborigines have longer legs compared to Europeans, relative to sitting height. (*b*) Olympic 400 m (1200 ft) runners: comparison of physiques of two individuals, European (left) and African (right), both having the same sitting height. The African runner clearly has longer legs.

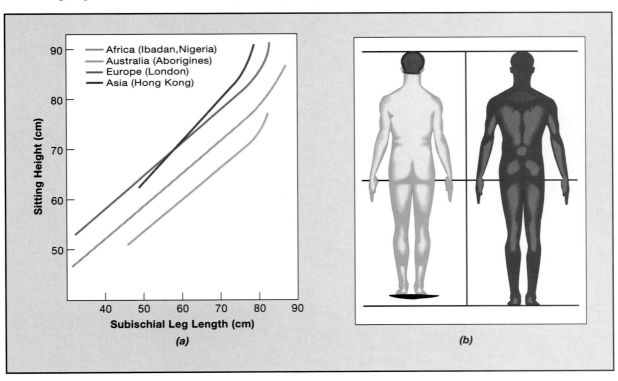

nutritional and environmental differences? The mean difference in height between Mayan and ladino boys is established during childhood and maintained without significant change during adolescence. Girls of the two groups, however, established differences in mean height during childhood that increased during adolescence, and Mayan girls, in addition to having a shorter adolescent period than that of the *ladinas,* had a slower rate of growth at all ages. In contrast to the Mayan boys, Mayan girls do not show a delay in maturation. From many studies it seems that girls in general possess genetics that override or "buffer" some environmental effects on adolescent growth. As a consequence, Mayan girls appear to proceed through adolescence more in accordance with genetically determined timing for development than Mayan boys.

Although genetics may play a greater role in the timing of growth in girls than in boys, this is not necessarily a useful explanation for the differences between the two ethnic groups of children. When we compare the Mayan and ladino study with others in which poor nutrition and health are environmental factors, similar patterns of difference emerge. Data from rural India and Gambia reveal boys who, like the Mayans, show slower growth velocities and longer periods of growth during childhood and adolescence and end up significantly shorter in stature than cohorts who are better nourished and healthier. In a study of infants in Kenya from age zero to six months, maternal nutritional status was an important predictor of the infants' anthropometric measurements at birth. Maternal hemoglobin levels were particularly associated with infant weight and head circumference (Bhargava, 2000).

Studies of secular trends in Mayan children living in Florida and Los Angeles have shown that these immigrants are significantly taller and heavier than Mayan children living in Guatemala. Although they are still shorter, on the average, than African American or Mexican American children living in the United States, they appear to be in the process of a trend leading to increased stature. The average increase of 5.5 cm (2.2 in.) in height for Mayan children reared in the United States is substantial. This illustrates clearly the fact that socioeconomic improvement and better emotional health is an important factor influencing growth, and that the greater the deprivation, the greater the effect on growth potential.

Recent studies of the growth of grade-school children living in poverty in the United States (Crooks, 1999) confirm the correlation among deprivation, growth potential, and general health. In a sample of children who lived in eastern Kentucky, more than one-fifth were below the U.S. norm for height, and 9.1 percent showed stunting. One-third of the children were overweight and 13 percent were obese. More girls than boys were stunted in growth, whereas more boys than girls tended to be obese. According to Crooks, explanations for low height are probably found in the socioeconomic level of the family, a situation found in many developing countries around the world. Obesity, in contrast, might best be explained in terms of community economics and infrastructure, where limited opportunities exist for school-sponsored, organized exercise.

Differences caused by genetics. A case in which genetics overrides environment is that of the Efe of eastern Congo (formerly Zaire; Figure 15–10), studied by Bailey (1991). The Efe are among the smallest of modern humans: Males average 1.42 m (4 ft 8 in.) and females average 1.35 m (4 ft 5 in.). Efe babies at birth are smaller than babies born to a neighboring group, the Lese, even though nutritional and environmental factors are similar. Efe show slower growth throughout childhood and a slower peak velocity of growth at adolescence. Their small body size has evolved through natural selection, possibly for greater heat dissipation in their hot, humid environment.

Tanner (1989) makes an important distinction between the nutritional effects on rate of growth during development and those affecting the adult condition. He

FIGURE 15–10 The Efe of eastern Congo are among the smallest of modern peoples. Efe males average 1.42 m (4 ft 8 in.) in height, and females average 1.35 m (4 ft 5 in.).

observes that nutrition appears to affect rate first: Growth slowdowns occur in undernourished children (along with the young of animals in general). This regulation of growth is an important accommodation among animals to counter the uncertainties of the food supply; that is, as a conservation method, slowdowns are periods waiting better times for growth optimization.

Responses to Modernization and the Urban Environment

Living in modern urban environments has put other kinds of stresses on human populations. Changes in diet, in the routine of physical activity, in stress levels, and in lifestyle may all, in various ways, affect human biology. Any of these factors may have the immediate effect of increasing blood pressure, which can contribute to many health problems, such as heart disease and stroke (Figure 15–11). There also may be longer-term consequences that affect growth.

Urban life is a relatively recent cultural phenomenon in human evolutionary history. Until 1950, much of the world's population still lived as peasant farmers in small social groups, much as humans have done since the agricultural revolution about 10,000 years or so ago. Urban life created both environmental and social situations that have considerably modified our earlier lifestyles. Although improvements in health and nutrition have allowed individuals in many populations to reach more of their genetic potential for growth, urban environments have exacted a price.

To give one example, although the majority of the world's societies permit some use of tobacco and alcohol, consumption has been overwhelmingly reserved for males; however, urban environments allow the relaxation of these cultural rules and sometimes allow women of childbearing years to drink and smoke. Both tobacco and alcohol use are clearly responsible for poor fetal health and slower prenatal growth: The average birth weight of children born to women who smoke is less than that of children born to women who do not smoke. Although there is medical controversy as to just how much alcohol pregnant women can safely consume, even small amounts in early pregnancy can cause fetal alcohol syndrome. This condition may result in newborns who have overall small body size, small heads with possible facial deformities, organ disorders, possibly lowered IQ, and reduced impulse control.

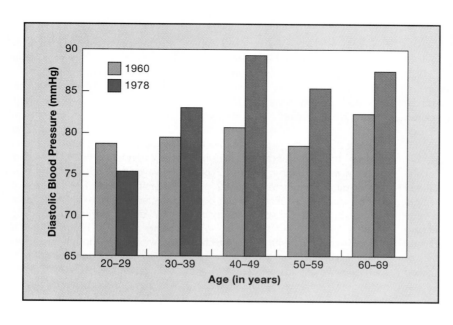

FIGURE 15–11 One example of the effects of modernization on male diastolic blood pressure, from a study done in the Gilbert Islands, South Pacific, during a time of rapid modernization. After modernization occurs, diastolic blood pressure tends to increase with age, where before it had remained largely constant.

Psychological stress also has been proven to affect growth. Infants and children who have been exposed to continual emotional stress from family breakups, among other factors, show reduced growth patterns. Psychological stress may contribute to a reduced appetite and difficulty sleeping. We know, for example, that growth hormones are commonly secreted into the bloodstream during the first few hours of sleep. If the normal level of growth hormone is reduced as a consequence of disturbed sleep, overall growth may be reduced.

Certainly, urban societies, as opposed to traditional ones, have greater levels of many different kinds of pollution. For example, some decreases in average height may be attributable to the presence of toxic waste and noise. In a study of Japanese children who lived close to Osaka International Airport, Schell and Ando (1991) concluded that their observations of shorter than average height in their sample could be attributed to noise pollution and psychological stress generated by continual noise, which creates disturbed sleep patterns and reduced secretions of growth hormones.

HUMAN ADAPTABILITY TO THE ENVIRONMENT

Human attributes came about by adaptation to a certain set of environmental conditions (hot, dry, terrestrial) and a certain ecological niche (large terrestrial home range, omnivorous, and culture-bearing), yet they allow the human species to be extremely adaptable throughout a range of modern environments. By understanding the limits of human adaptability and how adaptation to the environment takes place, we can understand much of the essence of human biology.

Individual humans respond physiologically to changes in many different environmental conditions, such as heat, cold, and pollution. It seems, however, that whereas humans adapt to a wide range of climates, climate apparently has little effect on development. For example, studies show that for well-nourished girls the age of menarche is not perceptibly affected by major climatic differences. Girls in Nigeria average 13.3 years of age at menarche, whereas Inuit girls average 13.8 years of age. Compare this to the average 13.2 years of age for girls raised in

How Disease Affects Growth: The Case of HIV

Children's growth is impaired in as many as 80 percent of the cases of symptomatic HIV infection. Compared with the values obtained from same-age healthy children, a child with HIV infection often appears "normal" but younger by several years than he or she really is. This "failure to thrive," defined as an abnormally slow rate of weight gain and growth, may result from three possible causes: reduced energy intake; intestinal malabsorption; and increased metabolism leading to a catabolic, or degrading, state of body function (Guarino, 1998).

Energy intake may be reduced either by oral or esophageal infections, swallowing problems, or inadequate nutrition as a consequence of poverty. The intestine is a frequent target in HIV infection, and intestinal dysfunctions relate to growth failure. Somewhere between 20 and 50 percent of infected children have dysfunctional intestinal tracts. In these children, some 32 percent of all carbohydrates and 62 percent of iron that is taken into the body are not digested or absorbed by the intestine.

Most children with HIV infection show a reversal of the normal response to weight loss: Instead of the metabolism decreasing, it increases,

resulting in a catabolic state that may be associated with fever, infection, neuroendocrine abnormalities, or chronic inflammation. All of these conditions, together with a reduced energy intake, are responsible for growth failure in children with HIV infection. The use of genetically engineered human-derived recombinant growth hormone (GH), however, has proven to be effective in reversing body-weight loss in HIV-infected adults. With the availability of new antiretroviral drugs, progress is being made in reducing the effect of growth failure, and in a growing number of cases, these therapies are providing children with AIDS with longer life spans and a better quality of life.

Southeast Asia, who, like girls in Nigeria, grow up in hot climates where temperatures frequently reach 45° C (113° F). All three of these groups also closely approximate the age of menarche of European girls (Tanner, 1989:146).

Human adaptability to changing environmental conditions consists of genetically shaped responses within the range that is characteristic of the species' adaptation, as determined by natural selection (see Chapters 2, 3, and 4). Within their range of adaptive responses individuals react to changes in their environment in three different ways:

1. **Acclimatization** is accommodation over a period of weeks or years to environmental conditions. Acclimatizing to living in high mountains is an example.
2. **Acclimation** is a short-term (minutes to weeks) physiological response to changed environmental conditions. Individuals acclimate over several days to new time zones, as in "jet lag." Light-skinned individuals acclimate to increased exposure to sunlight by tanning. Increased heart rate with exercise and increased metabolism in cold weather are other examples.
3. **Habituation** is an even shorter-term accommodation to a temporary environmental stimulus. Tuning out the monotonous sound of an air-conditioner during a lecture is an example. Individuals within populations, as well as entire populations, may differ in their thresholds and responses to stimuli.

Heat and Cold

Body size and climate. During the nineteenth century, observations of mammalian body size showed that size could be correlated with climatic variation. C. Bergmann in 1847 formalized these observations as a rule when he observed that "within a polytypic warm-blooded species, the body size of the subspecies usually increases with decreasing mean temperature of its habitat." In other words, low temperature is associated with large body size. Much later, in the early 1950s, D. F. Roberts studied the relationships of mean annual temperature and mean weight of adult males in different populations and established the validity of Bergmann's Rule to humans. Today we know that many factors can have an effect on weight, not the least of which is diet. For example, in some tropical populations, individuals on average have developed heavy body weights. The Samoans have the heaviest average body weight worldwide.

Bergmann's Rule is based on physical laws that govern heat loss or retention. A small animal has a relatively large surface area compared to its body mass. Its body therefore acts as a radiator transferring internal body heat to the surrounding air. As an animal's body size increases, its surface area becomes relatively smaller, as does the amount of body heat it transfers to the air. In fact, if body shape remains the same, a standard mathematical relationship exists: As body size increases, body surface area increases by the surface area squared, but body mass (weight) increases by the mass cubed. Thus, by simply getting larger and exposing relatively less surface area, individuals conserve body heat in colder climates.

The Efe of Central Africa, the southern African Khoisan, and the Semang of Borneo, all living in relatively hot regions, have relatively large surface area to body mass ratios, compared to populations that live in colder climates, such as the Inuit (Newman, 1975). In general children of all populations are more "heat-adapted" because they have relatively greater surface areas and adults are more "cold-adapted" because they have relatively greater mass.

In 1877 Allen formulated another rule noting that "in warm-blooded species the relative size of exposed portions of the body decreases with the decrease of mean temperature." Allen's Rule predicts that cold-adapted species should have relatively shorter appendages and hot-adapted species should have relatively longer

acclimatization: physiological adaptation over a period from weeks to years that may have some morphological effect, but that is not passed on genetically.

acclimation: physiological adaptation over a period from minutes to weeks.

habituation: neurophysiological mechanism for "tuning out" unwanted stimuli, an accommodation that takes only a few minutes.

appendages. This generalization seems to hold up better than the one for overall body size. Polar bears, for example have shorter ears than grizzlies, which in turn have shorter ears than black bears, which live in temperate climates. In humans the longer limbs that characterize some African populations and the shorter limbs of the Inuit are the two extremes.

Physiological responses to heat and cold constitute human **thermoregulation,** an important part of human adaptation. Humans have a tropical origin, a fact demonstrated not only by the fossil record but also by human biology. No other indication of this origin is stronger than the range of temperature at which human beings achieve thermal equilibrium—that is, the ambient temperature at which we neither gain nor lose heat. This temperature for a naked adult at rest is approximately 25° C (77° F), depending on humidity.

Loss of body heat.   There are four ways in which body heat is lost. Of these four, *sweat evaporation* is the most important in hot environments, because the body can monitor the process by altering the production of sweat from its two million or more **sweat glands** depending on the internal and external temperature. Once sweating starts, either because of exercise or increasing temperature, the temperature of the skin is maintained at between 35° C and 39° C (95° F and 102° F).

Varying quantities of heat may be lost by *radiation* when, as a result of vasodilation (dilation of small blood vessels), increased amounts of blood circulate near the skin surface. The surface blood vessels dilate when heat loss is required and constrict when heat needs to be retained by the body. In cool environments, radiation accounts for a greater percentage of heat loss from the skin than do other factors, such as evaporation, combined. A small amount of heat loss may occur as a result of *conduction.* In this case, heat exchange occurs as a result of physical contact with another object. In people, heat may be lost, for example, as a result of contact with clothing. Heat may also be lost or gained by *convection.* Convection is heat exchange as a result of movement of air molecules as heat flows from warm objects to cooler ones. For instance, cool air from a fan that passes over the body promotes body heat loss by convection and by increasing the rate of evaporation.

When internal body temperature decreases, the body produces more heat by muscular contraction (shivering), by increasing the body's metabolic rate, and by **vasoconstriction** (contraction of small blood vessels near the skin's surface). An even older physiological response to cold is "goose bumps." This is a reflex that makes the hair on our skin stand up, increasing the insulating effect of fur (even though fur has disappeared from the hominid body).

If the temperature continues to drop, a "warming response" can be seen in individuals of Native American populations, especially among the Inuit, and to a lesser extent in individuals of European populations: The hands or feet become vasodilated to increase circulation and raise the temperature of the extremity. Individuals of African descent show the most continuous vasoconstriction and the lowest average rewarming response among individuals of other populations. This response to cold seems to be a genetically controlled part of thermoregulatory physiology that has evolved in cold-adapted populations of the Northern Hemisphere.

Light and Solar Radiation

As our species has moved into temperate habitats and become increasingly urbanized, our relationships to light have changed in three major ways: The spectrum of light has been altered, the level of radiation is different, and the number of hours per day that an individual is exposed to artificial light as opposed to natural light has increased dramatically. The **pineal body** at the base of the brain (where the

thermoregulation: controlling the body's temperature by a number of physiological and behavioral means.

eccrine or sweat glands: glands that excrete a watery liquid over much of the surface area of the head, face, neck, and body during heat stress.

vasoconstriction: the contraction of small blood vessels next to the skin's surface; a response to cold.

pineal body: small cone-shaped part of the brain located below the corpus callosum; synthesizes the hormone melatonin, which is important in mediating estrus cycling in mammals; and reacts to ambient light in the environment.

French philosopher Descartes thought the soul was located) controls daily rhythms relating to light and dark (Cardinali and Wurtman, 1975). The original human adaptation to light was undoubtedly tropical, with day length virtually the same all year long. But as hominids expanded into increasingly northern and southern latitudes, they had to adapt to changing day lengths. As yet, the details of this adaptation are poorly understood. But we have ample evidence that when days shorten or lengthen with the seasons, humans can suffer emotional changes. Light therapy, in which an individual is subjected to bright, intense light, has been found to be an effective treatment for some conditions, such as symptoms of depression in night-shift workers resulting from light deprivation. Furthermore, modern urban people living in temperate climates worldwide spend much of their lives indoors, particularly in the winter months. This alters not only the amount of light received but also the spectrum and intensity.

High Altitude

The high altitude habitations found in Asia, Africa, and South America present a multistress environment to the millions of people who live there. Living at altitudes greater than about 3,000 m (9,840 ft) above sea level causes a number of physiological changes. Biological anthropologists have studied these changes in order to learn how rapidly nonacclimated individuals can adapt to the low oxygen levels (*hypoxia*) found at high altitudes. For visitors to these altitudes, the immediate response to hypoxia is increased breathing and heart rate. Although this response increases partial oxygen pressure in the lungs and, at the same time, blood flow, it also contributes to difficulty in sleeping and to bouts of hyper- and hypoventilation.

A longer-term physiological response to low oxygen pressure is the reduction, somewhere from 20 to 30 percent, in the amount of oxygen that the body can absorb. As a consequence, work capacity for high altitude visitors is diminished. Studies suggest, however, that individuals who grow up in high altitudes acclimatize themselves and have oxygen consumption and work capacity measurements close to those of individuals born at sea level (Frisancho, 1975). Acclimatization to high altitudes and to the decreased amounts of oxygen in the air results in increases in lung volume, hemoglobin count, and the percentage of the volume of blood that is occupied by cells. In the latter case, for example, red blood cells become more highly concentrated.

Although hypoxia is the primary stress factor in high altitude environments, there are others, such as high solar radiation, cold, aridity, rough terrain, and a limited nutritional base. A recent study of children living in Tibet showed that although they are generally smaller than children of more well-off parents living in lower altitudes, even at altitudes of 3,200 m (10,500 ft), size is probably more a result of nutrition than hypoxia. Data from this study (Weitz et al., 2000) do not offer any support for the hypothesis that hypoxia at altitudes above 3,200 m affects body size. The study did note, however, that male adults at 4,300 m (14,100 ft) have narrower, shallower thoraxes than males at lower altitudes. Whether these measurable differences are functionally significant remains uncertain.

Nutritional and Dietary Aspects of Adaptation

Humans are omnivores and have eaten a very wide range of plant and animal foods, minimally prepared before it was eaten, for many millions of years (Harding and Teleki, 1981; Table 15–2). Ancestral humans, like today's hunter-gatherer groups, still have a diet that is composed primarily of plant foods, low in fat and high in fiber. This adaptation confers a large degree of dietary adaptability, but it has its limits.

	Grams[2]	Percent Total Energy
Protein	250	33
Animal	190	
Vegetable	60	
Fat	70	21
Animal	30	
Vegetable	40	
Carbohydrate	340	46
Total Fiber	150	
	1,130	100

TABLE 15-2 | **Daily Diet of Preagricultural Humans[1]**

[1] Based on an average modern human hunter-gatherer diet of 3,000 kilocalories, composed of 35% meat and 65% plant foods.
[2] Represents weight less water content. Weight of actual ingested food is 2,250 g (5 lb.). Equivalent food weight for same energy in modern American diet is 3 lb.

From Eaton et al. (1988).

With the advent of fire and cultural food preparation techniques, the potential range of edible foods expanded and made the overall diet more nutritious. Or did it? Newman (1975) suggested that as a result of the early hominid reliance on animal meat, the body lost the ability to synthesize several important amino acids. Although hominids lost the ability to synthesize some amino acids, they were not at a selective disadvantage, because their diets supplied these essential nutrients. However, during the Neolithic Revolution, that period of time about 10,000 years ago when farming and village life became predominant and the food supply more stable, the overall human diet may have become less nutritious because of a dependence on single plant food staples. For example, in the Middle East agriculturalists came to depend on wheat and barley for much of their diet. A similar problem exists in some cultures today, such as those in which dependence on rice or manioc has led to malnutrition and even nutritional diseases.

Jared Diamond (1992), physiologist at the University of California, Los Angeles, describes studies of a diabetes epidemic on the Pacific island of Nauru and points out other problems when changes in diet occur. Only a few generations ago, the 5,000 or so Micronesians living on this island had a lifestyle that depended on fishing and subsistence farming. The discovery of phosphate deposits, and the substantial income that mining this substance produced, however, dramatically changed the Nauruans' energetic way of life. Now virtually all food is imported, the caloric intake is more than double the norms set by the nearby Australians, and obesity is practically universal. Noninsulin-dependent diabetes mellitus (NIDDM), which, prior to 1950, was unknown in this population, now affects almost two-thirds of adults by the age of 55 to 64 years, contributing to most nonaccidental deaths and to one of the world's shortest life spans.

Unfortunately, this example is not uncommon among developing peoples in other parts of the world. It is the extent of the problem on Nauru that is remarkable. Studies, however, show that the epidemic may have passed its peak, though not because of a decline in the environmental risk factors. Rather, it appears that natural selection has reduced the percentage of individuals who are genetically predisposed to NIDDM. Because it often occurs in women during their peak reproductive years, NIDDM results in increased incidence of stillbirth. As a consequence, over a few generations the number of islanders who possessed the NIDDM genotype has been reduced.

This question remains to be answered: If NIDDM represents a major world health problem (50 million diabetics are estimated in China and India alone), then why is the genotype so common? One hypothesis, proposed by J. V. Neel (1962), has been labeled the **thrifty genotype**. Neel suggested that whenever the daily food supply becomes sparse and varies unpredictably in amount, the individuals with an advantage would be those who, during times when food is plentiful, could convert most of their ingested calories into fat through quick insulin release. Because these calories will be stored instead of immediately burned, they can be drawn on during times when food is scarce. Under such circumstances the NIDDM genotype would be advantageous, but it would lose its advantage in individuals recently introduced to modern high-calorie diets and sedentary lifestyles. As Boyd Eaton, Marjorie Shostak, and Melvin Konner (1988:159) conclude,

> Our bodies today simply haven't "learned" that there is no longer an advantage to carrying extra weight. We are still essentially Late Paleolithic hunters and gatherers, and our appetite-control centers continue to operate as if the food surplus may come to a crashing halt at any time. We persist in storing up against that eventuality and, because the shortages fail to materialize, we become obese. Fat people . . . are stocking up for a famine that never comes.

MODERN LIFE AND HUMAN EVOLUTION

As we have seen, for 90 percent of our evolutionary history we have lived in tropical environments, in small groups of related individuals, eating for the most part low-sugar, high-fiber foods, and leading physically demanding lives. In modern industrialized contexts, where humans lead sedentary lives; use formulas instead of breast feeding; and eat highly processed foods that are high in sugar, salt, and saturated fats, people suffer from "diseases of civilization" that are virtually unknown among hunter-gatherers (Table 15–3). Among these are **hypertension** and the related problems of heart attack, cancer, gastric ulcers, and stress-related disorders. Studies also show among urban dwellers an increase in blood pressure and **serum cholesterol**

thrifty genotype: adaptation of storing "excess calories" as fat, and then burning them during periods of famine or scarcity of food.

hypertension: persistently high blood pressure; above 140 mm Hg systolic (contraction) and 90 mm Hg diastolic (dilation) pressures of the heart.

serum cholesterol: cholesterol is a lipid (fat), deriving from animal products in the diet, that when in high concentrations in the blood serum is associated with lesions and plaque buildup in arteries.

TABLE 15–3	**Leading Causes of Death in the United States, 1997**

"Diseases of civilization" are in **bold** type.

1. **Heart disease**
2. **Cancer**
3. **Cerebrovascular disease (stroke)**
4. **Bronchitis, emphysema, asthma**
5. **Pneumonia and influenza**
6. **Diabetes**
7. Accidents
8. Alzheimer's Disease
9. **Kidney disease**
10. **Septicemia**

From: National Center for Health Statistics (NCHS) annual mortality tapes.

TABLE 15–4	Serum Cholesterol Values in Human Hunter-Gatherer Groups
Population	**Average Serum Cholesterol Value**
Hadza (Tanzania)	110
Eskimos (Canada)	141
San (Botswana)	120
Aborigines (Australia)	139
Pygmies (Congo)	106
Caucasians (United States)	210

From Eaton et al. (1989).

levels (Table 15–4) and a tendency for blood pressure to increase with age. In contrast, traditional populations show lower blood pressure and no tendency for blood pressure to increase with age (Little and Baker, 1988). In an attempt to counter some of the deleterious effects of civilized life, the "Paleolithic prescription" calls for the return, within modern technological limits, to many of the practices of diet and exertion employed by our ancestors.

Overpopulation

As we have seen, hunter-gatherer groups have relatively low fertility rates, and our Paleolithic ancestors never faced the problems of overpopulation (Figure 15–12). Quite the contrary. Rather than curbing the birthrate, societies, until recently, attempted to maximize child production and minimize infant and childhood mortality. Between 1650 and 1850, the world's population more than doubled, from half a billion to 1.2 billion. In the next 100 years, it more than doubled again, to 2.5 billion. Today, some 6 billion people live on the earth, and every 10 seconds another 27 people are born. Many projections have been made as to the number of people the planet will have to support in the future. Some are more bleak than others.

FIGURE 15–12 World population growth and growth estimates. Branches represent projected growth, given no change in the current world birthrate. Other predictions are less ominous. Some projections show that world population will peak at about 10.6 billion by 2050 and then decline, as fertility rates drop below replacement levels, to about 1.7 children per woman.

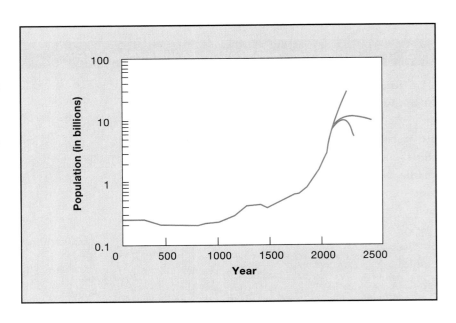

Obesity and the Modern Human Diet

Recent reports from an environmental research group, Worldwatch Institute, describe a growing problem for many individuals of the world's developed nations: obesity. In fact, for the first time in history there may be as many people overweight, perhaps as many as 1.1 billion, as there are underfed. Obesity, however, isn't necessarily an indication of improved diets, better health, or an overall better world economy. In fact, the opposite seems to be true.

In developing countries it is often the people of wealth who are overweight, whereas the vast majority of poor individuals remain undernourished. In contrast, the opposite seems to be true in the United States. The better educated rich tend to maintain an appropriate weight and eat healthier diets, whereas the poor suffer from obesity as a result of a diet of relatively inexpensive and fat-laden "fast food." In the United States, 55 percent of the population is overweight, and one in four adults is considered to be obese. A preponderance of overweight adults characterizes many of the world's richest urban nations, such as Britain and Germany. In comparison, 56 percent of the adults in Bangladesh are underweight. The report shows that both the overweight in wealthy nations and the underweight in poor nations live in situations where sickness, disability, and shortened life expectancy are the rule rather than the exception.

Almost all projections show that the world population will hit nearly 10.6 billion people by 2050 or so, but after that, many factors could help determine whether the human population increases further. By 2150 world population size could be anywhere from as few as 3.8 billion to as many as 27 billion people.

The difference between these two projections is the number of children borne by each woman, or the **total fertility rate (TFR)**. Currently the worldwide average TFR is about 3.3 children and declining. If rates continue to drop to about 2.0 children per woman, then the population will stabilize at 10.8 billion by 2150. If the average stops declining and remains at 2.6 children, the population will quadruple to 27 billion, but if it falls to 1.6 children, then the population will shrink to 3.6 billion by 2150.

What factors will account for these differences? One possible reason for a worldwide downward trend in fertility rates is an increase in education for women. Additionally, as more people leave rural areas for cities, family size is projected to decrease, because large families are not assets for urban dwellers. Also, urban women have more opportunities available to them from advances in modern medicine to plan their families than rural women have, more, at least, than has been the case in the past.

Today, the world population problem poses a new challenge to human adaptability and may force significant changes still only vaguely contemplated by modern peoples. The one-child policy in China, even though morally repugnant to some, may be a preview of things to come in many societies.

There are other, less dramatic, possibilities for change. Our diet, as we have seen, is a mixture of plant and animal foods. Whether we hunted or scavenged, animal proteins have been a necessary component of our diet, because they are relatively complete in their contents of essential amino acids. Even today in many parts of the world animal protein is almost the only way to secure a complete and balanced pattern of amino acids in a diet consisting predominantly of plant foods. Conditions of overpopulation require a hard look at land use, however, because they make us view the domesticated animal as a competitor to humans. Cropland produces 10 to 20 times the amount of human food that we can obtain from animals grazing on the same land (Almquist, 1969).

All of our food originates in plants; the animal is only a converter. What has kept animals in use as converters? Originally, they were valuable for locating and converting food items that humans could not, or would not, consume, such as

total fertility rate (TFR): population-wide average number of children a woman who lives to the end of her reproductive years gives birth to and who survive to adulthood.

seeds, roots, and wild grasses. Today, however, under the conditions of the modern feed lot, where animals consume supplemental food that humans could use, animal food is an ever-increasing luxury. Today, human diets that are centered around meat are an inefficient use of resources, because the animal has to be fed before it is fed to people. For example, before a pig reaches slaughtering weight, it consumes about 600 lb (270 kg) of corn and 100 lb (45 kg) of soybean meal. The meat yield of the pig provides about 2,200 daily calories for about 50 days for one person. Eating the corn and the soybean meal directly, the same person would have enough food for more than 500 days! Furthermore, with the advances in genetic engineering, plant varieties can be developed that are no longer deficient in particular amino acids.

Our knowledge of nutrition can help to improve our efficiency in how we use plant food. Protein blending, adding soybeans (which contain a surplus of lysine) to corn, and supplementing this mixture with a synthetic methionine (lacking in soybeans) would produce an adequate diet. Technologically, as the world population situation becomes more critical, we can gradually shift to a diet predominantly derived from plants. Although such an adaptation will pose no physiological problem, such changes will inevitably be strongly culturally challenged by our traditional eating patterns and may become acceptable only after no alternative exists.

The crowded, noisy, and generally "artificial" conditions of modern urban life are very recent environments in which humans live. The consequences to human biology and psychology are profound, though they are still not fully understood. Yet cities, being cultural entities, are environments that can be changed if necessary to better fit human adaptations evolved over millions of years.

◀ SUMMARY

1. **What insights have human growth studies shed on stages of human growth; the relationship between growth and evolution; and genetic, hormonal, and environmental influences on growth?**

   Growth patterns in all species are, to a certain extent, reflections of their evolutionary history. The prolonged period of human adolescence, coupled with a delayed maturation of the brain, are important adaptations for extended learning. The rapid catch-up period of growth in the first year after birth advances the human newborn to the same stage of locomotor ability achieved soon after birth by the smaller-brained but less dependent apes. In addition to evolutionary concerns, the study of growth patterns provides a measure of how well a population is adapted to its environment. Poor nutrition, pollution, stress, and a number of sociological factors, such as family size, can slow growth and prevent individuals from reaching their genetic potential of adult stature.

2. **How does the human body adjust to changes in climate, light levels, altitude, and diet?**

   Humans have adapted to a wide range of environments, even though for millions of years our ancestors were primarily a tropical species. In the course of this adaptation, humans have evolved unique ways of coping with diverse climates by thermoregulation: sweating to cool down the body and vasoconstriction of the extremities to maintain heat. Those living in high altitudes are acclimatized to low oxygen levels by producing more red blood cells. The fact that humans are especially physiologically malleable has allowed us to explore and survive in Arctic as well as tropical climates. Humans have a varied diet, but it is clear that there are limits to our adaptability to consume too much of any particular food.

3. **What pressures does modern urban life place on human biology and adaptation?**

   Perhaps the most telling limitations of our diet come from studies of "modern" diseases of the heart and arteries, those related to high blood pressure and diabetes. Modern lifestyles that incorporate high sugar, salt, and saturated fats, coupled with a lack of exercise, have proved to be a deadly combination. Modern medicine is investigating the consequences of our urban adaptation, and some practitioners have suggested a "Paleolithic prescription" that recommends a return to many of the practices of diet and exercise that characterized the lifestyles of our preagricultural ancestors.

◀ CRITICAL THINKING QUESTIONS

1. If adaptability is defined as an individual's reaction to change in environmental conditions, in what way could change of this sort be described as Lamarckian in nature? What limits would you place on this argument?
2. "Catch-up" is a term used in this chapter to describe different aspects of growth, both as a long-term human adaptation and as an aspect of short-term adaptability. What does this mean?
3. Describe several of the ways nutrition plays a role in human growth. What are some of the consequences of poor nutrition on growth, especially for the young?
4. The "Paleolithic prescription" has been described as the cure-all for some of the problems humans face as part of the process of urbanization. Provide several examples of how this might be true.

◀ INTERNET EXERCISES

Critical Thinking

The Paleolithic Diet. Chapter 15 describes the type of diet our hominid ancestors might have eaten. Recently, a variety of individuals—some scientists, some not—have claimed that the so-called Paleolithic diet can prevent the illnesses of civilization. In this exercise, you will research the Paleolithic diet and evaluate it critically. Try to answer the following questions:

1. What is the Paleolithic diet? On what research about early humans is this dietary prescription based? How does the Paleolithic diet differ from current nutritional guidelines?
2. Does the Paleolithic diet represent the most current thinking about the human ancestral environment? Why or why not?
3. What health benefits do proponents of the Paleolithic diet claim? What evidence backs up these claims?

Writing Assignment

Hunter-Gatherer Groups. The text uses living hunter-gatherer groups as a context for discussing aspects of human biological adaptation, such as diet. For this exercise, find out more about such cultures. Research one of the groups mentioned in the text—the !Kung, the Efe, the Hadza—or another group from a different part of the world, such as the Amazon or Malaysia. Try to answer the following questions:

1. In what kinds of social groups do the people live? How large are these groups?
2. What is the basis of their diet? What foods are supplied by men? By women?
3. How often do women bear children? How many children does the average woman bear in her lifetime? Who cares for the children?

See Companion Web site for Internet links.

In this book, we saw that humans evolved in the context of a certain set of environmental conditions (hot, dry, terrestrial) and a certain ecological niche (large terrestrial home range, omnivorous, and culture-bearing). In Chapter 15, we saw that these characteristics allow the human species to be extremely adaptable throughout a range of modern environments. By understanding the limits of human adaptability and how adaptation to the environment takes place, we can understand much more of the essence of human biology.

Human adaptability to changing environmental conditions consists of genetically shaped responses within the range that is characteristic of the species' adaptation, as determined by natural selection. Within their range of adaptive responses, individuals react to changes in their environment through acclimatization, acclimation, and habituation. Humans also make cultural adaptations that allow them to live in particular environments.

WEB ACTIVITY

The Inukiak Eskimos who live along the Arctic coast of Alaska have adapted to one of the harshest climates on earth. The video "The Story of Nanukalaq" displays many of the physical and cultural adaptations these people have made to the Arctic environment.

Activity

1. View the video. Based on the physical characteristics you observe and the discussion of adaptation to cold in Chapter 15, describe the physical adaptations of the Inukiak people to their environment. Speculate on how these adaptations came about.
2. What cultural adaptations enable the Inukiak Eskimos to live in the Arctic? Describe some of the cultural patterns you see in the video.
3. Explain how culture and evolution work together to enable humans to adapt to harsh environmental conditions.

The MediaLab can be found in Chapter 15 on your Companion Web site http://www.prenhall.com/boaz

HUMANS IN EVOLUTIONARY PERSPECTIVE: APPLIED BIOLOGICAL ANTHROPOLOGY

O U T L I N E

After reading this chapter, you should be able to discuss the following questions:

1. What are the goals of applied biological anthropology, and what human traits and aspects of the human condition does the discipline consider?
2. What insights does biomedical anthropology shed on common human diseases?
3. What are the goals and methods of forensic anthropology?
4. What does evolutionary biology suggest about the needs of people in a modern, urbanized world?

The subject of human evolution has excited both the public and scientific imaginations for many years. But the application of biological anthropological knowledge has lagged behind the intellectual popularity of the subject. Although many professional and lay people alike know about, and are fascinated with, fossils such as "Lucy" and the Neandertals, they may wonder whether these dusty relics of our evolutionary past have any relevance to our current life and problems. There are signs that this attitude is now changing. As we saw in Chapter 15, knowledge of our evolutionary history and of our hominid ancestors can teach us a tremendous amount about our daily lives.

As the perspective of evolutionary biology has pervaded both the natural and social sciences, so also has it affected such applied areas as medicine, psychotherapy, education, and conservation. We begin this chapter with a discussion of the basis for applying biological anthropology to the modern human condition.

PREMISES AND GOALS OF APPLIED BIOLOGICAL ANTHROPOLOGY

Although applied biological anthropology is still developing into a distinct discipline, biological anthropologists have been active in practical applications of their research for many years. For example, one of the most prominent nineteenth-century German biological anthropologists, Rudolf Virchow (Figure 16–1), founded the public health service in Berlin. And the great French anthropologist Paul Broca made many contributions to the medical treatment of brain disorders. In the twentieth century the list of applications of biological anthropological research was diverse and wide ranging, from designing the dimensions of fighter plane cockpits, to assisting in the apprehension of criminals, to urban planning. This chapter discusses the major areas of applied biological anthropology, keeping in mind that the field is a dynamic one and new applications are being developed every year.

Definition

Biological anthropology becomes **applied biological anthropology** when it focuses on solving practical problems of human well-being. For example, applied anthropological research on the incidence of disease in a certain population will generally differ from a public health project in **epidemiology** by investigating biological parameters, rather than simply whether patients survived or died.

Anthropologists bring an approach that includes a broad comparative perspective on the human biological response to the environment. They may look at, in

applied biological anthropology: use of the method and theory of biological anthropology to solve problems or address questions of practical significance.

epidemiology: study of the geographic distribution, spread, and control of disease.

FIGURE 16–1 Rudolph Virchow, one of the first applied physical anthropologists, founded the public health service in Berlin in the late 1800s.

addition to the manifestations of the disease in question, birth weights of babies, growth rates of children, and many other biological parameters that often escape medical attention. Applied biological anthropologists use an evolutionary approach in considering the overall human adaptive response. They work within the contexts of evolution, culture, and environments.

Anthropology is a population-based biological science, and, unlike medicine, it does not focus on the individual (Figure 16–2). Its conclusions may be statistical,

FIGURE 16–2 Difference in approach between traditional medicine and biological anthropology. Traditional medicine focuses on the individual, whereas biological anthropology considers the individual in the context of the population. For example, traditional medicine might consider a sports injury as a problem to be fixed, perhaps by replacement of a worn out joint. Biological anthropology would seek to understand the problem in terms of the structural evolution of the human body. Solutions might include strengthening exercises or a change in the training regimen to enhance strong muscles and avoid overstraining weak ones.

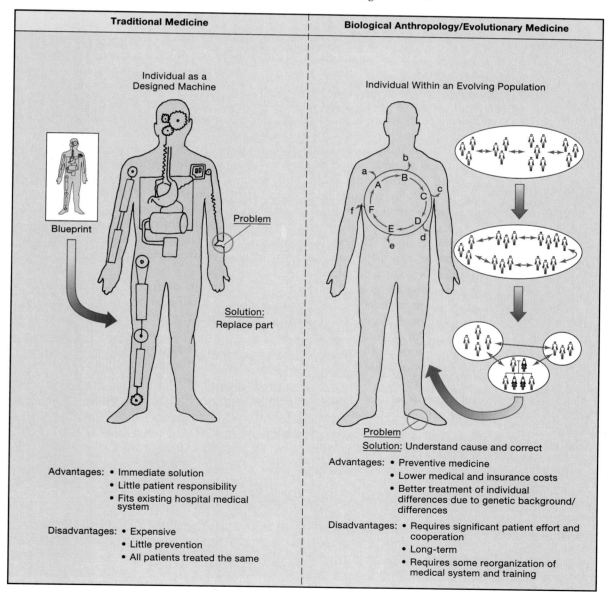

and its statements are probabilistic. One example of the importance of the use of anthropological data is the following. A six-month-old child is brought in for his medical checkup, and the examining nurse notes that he seems to have an enlarged head. A second appointment is made for the child with a growth specialist, who measures the child's head and compares his measurements with population based statistics on head size for infants of the age. The specialist finds that the child is in the 95th percentile for children his age; that is, only 5 out of 100 children would have heads as large as his at his age. The specialist recommends further tests, including a brain scan, a procedure the parents are hesitant to have performed.

At this point a biological anthropologist enters the picture and is able to show, by reference to other statistical data, that the child's head dimensions are the same, in proportion to the general population, as those of his parents. The anthropologist cannot make an individual diagnosis but can show that the child's head dimensions are within the "normal" population limits of growth. After consultation with their child's physician, the parents decide against a brain scan.

Human Adaptation and the Modern Environment

Human beings are remarkably adaptable, as we saw in Chapter 15. But there are limits to this adaptability. Obviously, people cannot live underwater or in outer space without the aid of technology. But are there less obvious examples of a lack of fit between human beings and their environment? The answer is a definite yes, and for those of us living in the technologically complex Western world, many of the examples of this lack of fit are close to home.

The conflict between the conditions of the modern world and basic human adaptations is known as the **Discordance Hypothesis.** *Discordance* means being at odds with something: In this case, our modern lifestyles and urban environment are at odds with our genetic heritage. As Boyd Eaton (Eaton et al., 1988:39) put it, "that the vast majority of our genes are ancient in origin means that nearly all our biodiversity and physiology are fine-tuned to conditions of life that existed before 10,000 years ago." The evolutionary perspective that applied biological anthropology provides can help people bring their living environment into closer congruence with their biological adaptation as human beings.

Underlying the goal of concordance (the opposite of *discordance*) is the realization that natural selection has produced, through millions of years of evolution, a good fit between human adaptive capabilities and the environment, as these have coevolved. An evolutionary perspective indicates that human beings are the product of a long process of change that has produced a certain way of solving problems and getting work done. A static machine metaphor for human adaptation has been replaced by the more complex idea of a **feedback system** that has been selected for over immense spans of time and under many different circumstances. Like the proverbial auto mechanic who ignores the directions and ends up with a few pieces left over from the engine just reassembled, scientists who ignore the overall evolutionary context of human biology and behavior may well find that their solutions to human problems are less than optimal.

Goals of Applied Biological Anthropology

One of the important goals of applied biological anthropology is to construct explanatory frameworks, within evolutionary and environmental contexts, for the many physical and behavioral traits of the human species. These explanatory frameworks are scientific hypotheses and, therefore, must be testable. For example, an applied biological anthropologist might hypothesize that knee injuries are very

Discordance Hypothesis: theory that human biology and behavior, as shaped by evolution, are at odds with modern human environments.

feedback system: in information theory, the concept that change in one step of a loop will affect a subsequent step that will in turn affect the starting point.

common among athletes, because early in the evolutionary history of the knee joint arboreal climbing was important, and stresses on the knee were different millions of years ago than they are today. These are broad goals, and they will certainly be applied much more widely in the future of this still-new discipline.

EVOLUTIONARY MEDICINE

Evolutionary medicine, sometimes also termed *Darwinian medicine* (Williams and Nesse, 1991; Stearns, 1998), is the field that specifically relates knowledge of human biology and evolution to medical research and treatment of disease. But until recently the connection between biological anthropology and medicine was viewed as largely static. Using the machine metaphor again, anthropologists and anatomists were seen as necessary for describing the parts, but only the physicians, the master engineers, knew how to put them together. Medicine was concerned with the machinelike functioning of genes and cells, not with the overall functioning of the organism.

New initiatives in evolutionary medicine, however, have begun to influence traditional medicine. Evolutionary medicine is the study and treatment of the causes, distributions, and cultural correlates of disease within a framework of evolution by natural selection. It is one of the most important new areas of applied biological anthropology and holds particular relevance to people's everyday lives. The following case studies represent the range of issues dealt with by anthropologists and physicians who work in evolutionary medicine.

Sudden Infant Death Syndrome

Anthropologist James McKenna (McKenna et al., 1990) was, by training, an expert in nonhuman primate mother–infant behavior when he became interested in the problem of human **Sudden Infant Death Syndrome** (SIDS). SIDS, also known as "crib death," is the leading cause of death of very young infants in the United States. Standard medical research has failed to find either a cause or a cure for the syndrome. McKenna believed that the practice, very unusual from an evolutionary and nonhuman primate standpoint, of isolating young infants in a crib away from the parents had something to do with the problem. He undertook extensive studies of other cultures in which there are standard parent–infant "cosleeping" arrangements and of other primates where infants and mothers sleep together (Figure 16–3), and he found that SIDS did not occur.

evolutionary medicine: the application of evolutionary principles and deductions from biological anthropology to the practice of medicine; also termed *Darwinian medicine.*

Sudden Infant Death Syndrome: "crib death"; sudden and unexpected death of apparently healthy infants, usually between three weeks and five months of age.

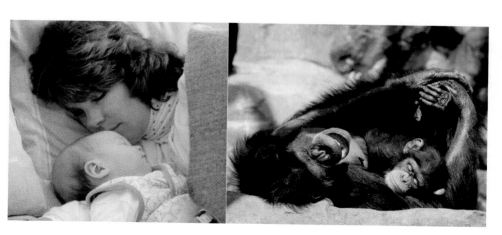

FIGURE 16–3 Cosleeping is widespread among both nonhuman primates and among humans of many different cultures.

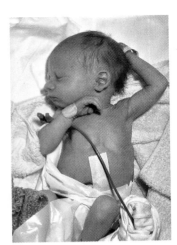

FIGURE 16–4 Infant with neonatal jaundice.

In association with medical researchers, McKenna then began to investigate the neurological development of infants who died of SIDS. This research strongly implied that these infants were neurologically not yet fully capable of breathing on their own during sleep, and needed the external stimulation, or pacemaker effect, of nearby maternal breathing and heartbeat (McKenna et al., 1990). It appears that cosleeping infants respond to their mothers' movements and sleep less deeply. During periods of uninterrupted deep sleep, an infant is more likely to stop breathing than at other times. The mother's constant jostling significantly reduces this risk. McKenna's evolutionary approach has provided alternatives to research efforts that have focused on finding elusive viruses or hidden trauma as a cause of the innumerable infant deaths resulting from SIDS.

Neonatal Jaundice

Newborn babies may develop a yellowish cast to the skin (Figure 16–4), similar to that of jaundiced adults, between the second and fifth days after birth. Adult jaundice is a condition in which the pigment known as **bilirubin**, formed from hemoglobin during normal destruction of the red blood cells, builds up in the body, as a result either of impaired liver function or of a lack of enzymes that convert bilirubin to other products that can be excreted. Neonatal jaundice is also caused by an elevated amount of bilirubin and has been explained as being a result of a still-immature and not fully functioning liver. Traditionally, it was treated primarily by phototherapy, the application of bright light, which oxidizes the excess bilirubin and makes the yellowish pigmentation disappear. One evolutionary explanation for this treatment was that early hominids lived outdoors and newborn babies would normally have been exposed to significantly greater amounts of light than modern indoor-living babies receive.

Two biomedical anthropologists, John Brett and Susan Niemeyer (1990), questioned this treatment and also the medical reasons for it. They contended that the presence of bilirubin enabled a newborn's body to rid itself of **free radicals,** highly reactive oxygen molecules that can damage developing tissues, particularly the brain. While the baby was in its mother's uterus, her bloodstream and immune system removed these and other harmful substances. Excess bilirubin, contend Brett and Niemeyer, is an excellent method that evolution has developed for protecting a baby's first few days in its own oxygen-rich environment before its own immune system begins to function adequately.

Coping with the "Diseases of Civilization"

At the same time that Western medical researchers were making advances in understanding the genetic mechanisms of diseases and their more effective treatment, biological anthropologists, studying the health and physiology of non-Western peoples, discovered that the very diseases that Western medical practitioners considered an intrinsic, genetically coded part of human biology do not appear among hunter-gatherer peoples (see Chapter 15). Such maladies as cancer, stroke, heart attack, and diabetes, termed *diseases of civilization* (see Table 15–3) by Eaton and colleagues (1989), are rare. Instead, trauma, parasites, and infectious diseases are the major killers of non-Western peoples. Another important discovery was that individuals in hunter-gatherer groups (and, by extension, early hominids), if they survived the high mortality period of early childhood, lived remarkably healthy lives and had excellent chances of living to advanced ages. The conclusion from this research was, then, that there must be something about the environments or lifestyles of Westerners that caused these diseases, at the same time that Western sanitation, antibiotics, and immunizations reduced mortality in infancy and childhood relative to the higher rates seen in nonindustrial agricultural populations.

bilirubin: a bile pigment from the liver that results from the breakdown of hemoglobin in red blood cells; bilirubin normally circulates in the blood in a complex with albumin but can increase in certain pathological conditions such as hepatitis.

free radicals: highly reactive "active" molecules of oxygen (mainly O_2^-) formed from the breakdown of oxygen molecules in the body.

 **FRONTIERS**

Evolutionary Medicine

S. BOYD EATON, M.D.

In prestigious universities around the world, theoretical physicists are attempting to find a modern day Holy Grail. They want to unravel basic relationships between the four fundamental, natural forces—gravity, electromagnetism, and the strong and weak forces of atomic nuclei—with the ultimate aim of integrating these into a "unified field theory." A Nobel Prize awaits this achievement, which will rank with the discoveries of Newton and Einstein.

On a less exalted plane, evolutionary medical theory attempts to unify or integrate important disciplines related to health care: genetics, epidemiology, pathophysiology, and disease prevention. Genetics deals with the building blocks basic to all biomedical science. Epidemiology studies disease distribution: For example, why breast cancers are more common in Boston than in Tokyo. Pathophysiology seeks to explain disease mechanisms: Just how does an elevated serum cholesterol level lead to atherosclerosis? And, of course, disease prevention is dedicated to finding lifeways that can delay or forestall indefinitely the development of serious illnesses. Evolutionary theory is central to all these endeavors and provides a conceptual framework that facilitates the interrelationship of each to the others.

Health status reflects the interaction of genetic makeup (for individuals) or the gene pool (for populations) with lifestyle factors:

Genes + Lifestyle = Health Status

When viewed as an equation, our gene pool represents the constant, over time, because humans living in the twentieth-first century are less than 0.005 percent different, genetically, from their preagricultural ancestors of 10,000 years ago. In contrast, lifestyle factors can change drastically in only a generation or two; therefore, they represent the equation's variable element.

Members of recently studied gatherer-hunter societies, present-day surrogates for our Late Paleolithic ancestors, have low cholesterol levels and their diets provide ample amounts of antioxidant vitamins. In contrast, the "new" (in evolutionary terms) life circumstances of affluent Americans show elevated average serum cholesterol concentrations and reduced antioxidant intake. Pathophysiologically, this phenomenon results in greater production of oxidized cholesterol (specifically, oxidized low density lipoprotein cholesterol, or LDL); it is this material, which accumulates within developing atherosclerotic plaques, that leads ultimately to hardening of the arteries, heart attacks, and strokes.

Epidemiological studies increasingly link breast cancer incidence to reproductive events. Early menarche, delayed first birth, failure to breast-feed, lower parity (number of births), and late menopause are all significant risk factors. In each instance, the reproductive experience of women in Western nations heightens susceptibility: Compared with foragers, Americans experience menarche earlier, are older at first birth, breast-feed far less, have fewer babies, and experience menopause later. The experience of Japanese women is closer to that of foragers than is that of Americans, hence the epidemiological findings (higher incidence of breast cancer in Boston than in Tokyo) might have been anticipated.

In the light of evolutionary medical theory, health promotion recommendations should reflect the life circumstances of our ancestors, either directly, as for diet and exercise, or indirectly, as for reproductive factors. Early first birth and increased parity would be socioeconomically disadvantageous for most women, but fortunately the hormonal correlates of these factors can be recreated independently by endocrinological manipulation (in much the same way that oral contraceptives facilitate birth control), thereby substantially increasing women's resistance to carcinogenesis.

Western medical practice historically has been oriented toward diagnosis and treatment of disease. Now, as economic considerations exert ever more influence on the health care system, we must place more emphasis on the importance of health promotion activities. The American public, however, has become somewhat disenchanted with the conflicting results of epidemiological studies and with advice about diet and exercise that seems to fluctuate as capriciously as the stock market. The unifying influence of evolutionary medical theory can combat this jaundiced view by providing a consistent, rational framework for health promotion recommendations, a logic for ordering research priorities, and a compelling incentive for individual preventive activities.

The scientific impact of evolutionary medicine pales beside that expected from the unified field theory of physics, but its effect on health care costs, and, more importantly, on the well-being of people, will nevertheless be profound.

S. Boyd Eaton, M.D., Adjunct Professor of Anthropology at Emory University, is a pioneer in the development of evolutionary medicine.

Obesity and the human ecology of fat deposition. Recent medical surveys indicate that some 20 to 30 percent of Americans are overweight (defined as being 20 percent or more above the "normal" mean weight for their height). Although strong societal and medical forces encourage individuals to moderate food intake, increase exercise, and reduce body weight, obesity continues to be a major health problem. It contributes directly or indirectly to heart disease, high blood pressure (hypertension), diabetes, and musculoskeletal problems ranging from back pain to flat feet.

There are four types of fat in the human body, defined on the basis of their locations and how they are metabolized:

1. *Brown fat* is found mainly in babies and young children and functions to protect them from hypothermia. It exists mostly on the back between the shoulder blades.
2. *Subcutaneous fat* occurs over almost the whole body but is found especially in the abdominal region and in the female breasts. It is directly related to "excess nutrition" built up during times of plenty. It serves as a long-term reservoir of energy and is metabolized during periods of famine or starvation.
3. *Hip/thigh fat* is found predominantly in adult females and presents a different metabolic pattern than the more generally distributed subcutaneous fat. Hip/thigh fat serves solely as an energy reservoir for pregnancy and lactation; even in cases of near starvation, females who are not pregnant or nursing do not metabolize this energy reservoir.
4. *Intra-abdominal fat* occurs inside the abdominal cavity, especially in a structure that drapes from the stomach known as the greater omentum. Males have a predominance of this type of fat, which is metabolized the most rapidly of all the types of fat. It is a short-term energy reservoir that may have evolved to assist males in the short-term fasting that accompanied hunting. In modern humans, this fat deposit is associated with increased risk of heart disease.

Except for brown fat, human fat deposits are an adaptation for storing energy in a seasonal round of feast or famine, the "thrifty genotype" (see Chapter 15). In hunter-gatherer societies, which live in seasonal environments, individuals build up their fat reserves in the wet season of the year when food is plentiful and use them during the dry season when food is scarce. The percentage of fat in the body fluctuates from about 10 to 15 percent in men and about 20 to 30 percent in women (Eaton et al., 1989:63). Today, most people living in the Western world have no season of scarcity, and thus the fat reserves that build up in the body remain there unless exercise or moderation of food intake (dieting) takes place.

Obesity contributes to high blood pressure by creating an internal physiological environment in which cholesterol builds up and plaque is deposited on the inside walls of arteries, which constricts their diameters (Figure 16–5). The heart must pump harder to push the blood through these constricted arteries. When the arteries of the heart itself become constricted or occluded, the heart muscle can no longer get adequate oxygen for its work and a heart attack results.

Diverticulitis. Over millions of years, hominids have evolved eating patterns that are related to the "feast or famine" seasonal round. Ancient diets had a high proportion of roughage—fibrous fruits and plant material that was low in energy but filling—and relatively small amounts of high-calorie animal fat and sugar. Nevertheless, natural selection ensured that hominids craved sweets and fats, for dietary balance and for energy. Similar cravings occur with certain important minerals, particularly salt. Potato chips and pizza, both loaded with fat and salt, are excellent examples of what early hominids, not knowing any better, might have imagined as ideal foods. Not only does excess dietary fat contribute to heart disease, as noted previously, and excess sodium (versus potassium) raise blood pressure, but these "junk foods" also lack the fiber that early hominid foods had.

For millions of years our ancestors consumed large amounts of crude dietary fiber. Their diets consisted largely of fruits, roots, seeds, and other vegetable foods. As a result, the human large bowel functions properly only with a relatively large volume of fiber waste material moving through it, which is pushed on by waves of

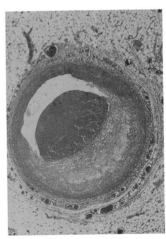

FIGURE 16–5 View of inside of artery showing buildup of plaque, which causes high blood pressure and, in turn, contributes to heart disease.

muscular contraction. Modern processed foods, which contain low-fiber content and which make up much of the diet of some people, do not produce enough waste bulk for effective bowel functioning. Consequently, intestinal muscles contract with greater force, creating higher pressures within the bowel in order to move along smaller volumes of waste. Higher bowel pressure can produce herniation of the bowel lining at weak points in the muscular wall, forming *diverticula*, pouchlike protrusions through the colon wall (Figure 16–6). When these become infected and inflamed, a serious disease known as diverticulitis results. **Diverticulitis** is a common bowel disorder that affects nearly one-half of all people in the United States over the age of 50, and it can be mostly avoided by eating a "Paleolithic" diet high in fiber and plant roughage.

Breast cancer. Eaton and colleagues (1994) have implicated the late onset of first pregnancies in Western women and the high proportion of reproductive time they spend nonpregnant and nonlactating as the primary contributing factors to breast cancer. In a comparative study of Asian and American women, Eaton noted that early onset of menarche, late menopause, fewer children born, and lower frequency of suckling infants all positively correlate with higher incidences of breast cancer. Mechanisms for this correlation are still under study, but it appears that either high or varyingly fluctuating levels of estrogen may be related. Unlike the situation found among many Western urban women, the common reproductive cycle among women in agricultural societies, and probably among our ancestors, is marked by a late onset of menarche, irregular and infrequent menstruation, more children, longer periods of lactation, and earlier menopause, all of which contribute to lower levels of estrogen throughout a woman's life span.

Human Populations, Infectious Diseases, and Parasites

The most significant agent of natural selection for any population is disease, which has produced most of the polymorphic variation that is found in gene pools. (We saw the evolutionary effects of endemic disease when we studied the relationship between malaria and sickle-cell anemia and Tay-Sachs disease and tuberculosis in Chapter 4.) Devastating plagues have spread recurrently through human populations, causing the deaths of tens of thousands of people. Although the exact numbers of individuals who died is unknown, the European Black Death of the mid-fourteenth century killed from 30 to 90 percent of those infected. Researchers have estimated that about one-third of Europe's population died during this epidemic of bubonic plague.

Genetic resistance to HIV. As of June 2000, according to the World Health Organization, the worldwide epidemic caused by HIV had killed 18.8 million people, and an estimated 34.3 million were living with HIV or AIDS. In 1999, 5.4 million people were newly infected with HIV, and 2.9 million people died from the infection. An effective medical strategy to develop a cure that would prevent HIV replication in infected people has proven elusive. The ability of HIV to mutate has made a vaccine approach difficult, because any vaccine can attack only a single type of virus, and vaccines are mostly ineffective against viruses that can change their outer protein coats quickly. Curiously enough, an evolutionary approach to finding a cure or preventative measure for HIV infection has not been among the popular strategies employed—until recently. A number of significant pieces of information have helped change the direction that new research has taken.

Fact 1: Over a period of many years, through the painstaking collection of blood samples, it has been discovered that a number of high-risk people (that is,

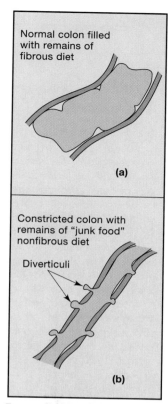

FIGURE 16–6   Cross-section of human colon with (*a*) normal fibrous diet and (*b*) junk-food diet resulting in the formation of diverticuli.

diverticulitis: inflammation of an outpocketing of the wall of the large intestine.

FRONTIERS

Prediction and Evolutionary Theory: Influenza A

Darwin viewed his theory of evolution by natural selection as primarily useful in understanding the past. How did the innumerable life forms come to be? His idea of descent from a common ancestor was one answer to this perplexing problem. Darwin paid scant attention to the possibility that his evolutionary principles could be used to predict future events. In fact, most evolutionary biologists have denied that the theory of evolution had any predictive value at all.

Modern evolutionary biology, through analyses of genetic relationships among species (also called *phylogenetic analyses*), has altered this view. In fact, theorists argue, the primary importance in biology of phylogenetic trees is that they make the field predictive. In chemistry, the periodic table of elements allows chemists to make predictions about reactions between elements. In biology, phylogenetic trees are constructed to predict where characteristics that have already evolved in one species might appear in another

species where they have not yet been observed. A team of biologists lead by R. M. Bush (1999) has now shown how phylogenetic analyses can be used to make predictions about the evolutionary course of future life forms. We specifically consider the case of the human influenza A virus. From a medical point of view, this evolutionary model could be extremely useful in predicting which new strains of flu virus might appear each year and thus in preparing vaccines in advance to protect against those strains.

The human influenza virus differs from many other kinds of viruses in that, although many different strains may appear at any time, most of them do not survive to contribute to future influenza diversity. Instead, usually only one strain survives from one year to the next. This strain in turn gives rise to future strains, from which, again, only one strain survives. Bush and his colleagues (1999) discovered that the most likely strain to survive is the one that possesses the most changes among the 18 amino acids that make up a protein called *hemagglutin*. Hemagglutin is one of two proteins that comprise the large

spikes located on the surface of the virus. These spikes are important because in the human body they are foreign antigens, and a person who develops antibodies to them is more likely to resist infection by this particular viral strain. The less varied the spike is structurally, the more rapid is an effective immune response. Therefore, the most successful viral strains, those that thwart, at least for a while, the body's immune system, are those with the more altered amino acids making up this protein. Being able to identify which of the many viral strains possess the most altered amino acid sequence allows researchers to predict which is more likely to give rise to future strains of the virus.

Evolutionary biologist David Hillis (1999:1867) sums up the implications of this discovery, "Evolution isn't something that just happened in the past, evolution can be observed in the present, and in some cases can be used to predict the future.... School boards and science educators need to understand this simple fact. If students don't learn about evolution, they can't possibly understand modern biology or medicine."

---

intravenous drug users, homosexuals, and heterosexuals who engaged in anal intercourse, among others) never became infected with HIV.

Fact 2: Substances secreted by **CD8 lymphocytes** suppress the replication of HIV. These substances turn out to be members of a poorly known class of hormonelike molecules called *chemokines,* which are thought to help cause inflammation, among other things. As part of their overall function, they bind to a chemokine receptor, called **CCR5,** found on the surface of a **CD4 cell,** the primary initial target of HIV. When chemokines bind to their receptors they block HIV from doing the same thing, thus preventing HIV from entering the CD4 cell and replicating within it (Figure 16–7).

Fact 3: In some individuals, the gene that codes for the CCR5 receptor protein is defective, and in some cases the protein produced is so badly misshapen that the CD4 cell destroys it before it can become a surface feature on the CD4 cell wall.

Fact 4: Without the CCR5 receptor, HIV cannot penetrate the CD4 cell and, therefore, cannot replicate.

These facts led researchers to the discovery that, indeed, there is a defective chemokine receptor gene, and that about 1 in 100 Caucasian Americans is homozygous for the defective gene. These people are immune to HIV infection. In addition, about one in five individuals are heterozygous, and, apparently, heterozygous individuals stay healthy two to three years longer than infected individuals who are homozygous nondefective.

CD8 lymphocytes: one of two classes of T-cells within the immune system; the primary job of the CD8 cell is to kill foreign substances such as viruses, thus the label "killer" T-cells.

CCR5: specific receptor site found on CD4 cells; receptor sites are surface features on cell membranes where different chemical substances bind.

CD4 cells: regulatory or "helper" T-cells; assist in the production of antibodies or in the action of the "killer" CD8 cells.

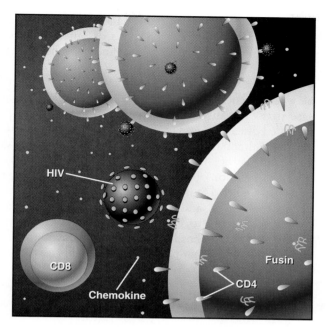

FIGURE 16-7   Immunity to HIV in some individuals is achieved by the blocking of CD4 receptor sites with hormonelike proteins called chemokines that are produced by CD8 cells.

From what we know about other epidemics and the presence of genes that offer protection against disease, one could predict that in the case of HIV, natural selection might have offered an opportunity for resistance. Based on the high numbers of individuals who carry the defective chemokine receptor gene, however, it is apparent that the mutation that causes this condition could not have arisen recently and spread opportunistically as a result of HIV. Many researchers argue that the initial spread of the defective gene may have been the result of an ancient epidemic as many as 100,000 years ago in Caucasian populations. The survivors of that epidemic carried the defective gene, resulting in its commonplace occurrence in modern populations. But for this gene to remain common for so long, natural selection must have somehow been operating in its favor. What the selective advantage of this mutant allele was before HIV is a mystery to be solved.

What about other populations? People of African and Asian descent may also have their own unique genetic protection against HIV. There are uninfected African and Asian high-risk people, and they don't carry the defective chemokine receptor gene. The prediction from the perspective of evolutionary medicine is that there may be other human resistance genes. The recent discoveries of HIV-resistant individuals and the chemokine defective receptor gene must surely be only a small part of a bigger picture.

Evolutionary approaches to treatment.   Evolutionary medicine has also contributed to a better understanding of the response of the human body to disease. Williams and Nesse (1991), for example, note that the increased body temperature (**fever**) that frequently accompanies infectious disease is actually adaptively beneficial, because it creates an internal environment in which enzymes can work faster and bacteria can be killed more effectively. The standard medical practice of reducing fever, thus, may actually work against the patient's best interests. Children with chicken pox whose low-grade fevers were lowered actually recovered from the disease more slowly than children whose fevers were untreated (Ewald, 1994).

Populations of some hunter-gatherers have exceedingly high levels of parasite loads in their bodies, as was probably the case throughout most of our evolutionary history. The Mbuti of Congo, for example, have elevated white blood cell counts

fever: elevation of body temperature above normal; in disease, caused by the body's reaction to infection by microorganisms.

bilharzia: infection by the parasitic blood fluke *Schistosoma*, which lays its eggs in the liver; leads to liver and occasionally kidney damage; also known as *schistosomiasis*.

cholera: infectious disease caused by the bacterium *Vibrio cholerae* and spread usually by contaminated drinking water; symptoms include severe diarrhea, dehydration, shock, and kidney failure.

cystic fibrosis: hereditary disease of children and young adults affecting the lungs, pancreas, and other exocrine glands.

and widespread prevalence of malaria, **bilharzia,** and other parasites. Indications are that the relative parasite loads of our ancestors were high, and we probably have a number of genetically defined defense mechanisms as holdovers of our adapting to these loads.

Another discovery demonstrates this same type of coevolutionary relationship between a genetic defense and a disease. This is the case of **cholera,** a bacterial disease that can cause death by dehydration though diarrhea, and **cystic fibrosis,** an inherited disease caused by a recessive gene in a homozygous condition that results in chronic pulmonary disease, pancreatic and other glandular failures, and death. Cystic fibrosis is the "most common, fatal, homozygous recessive disorder of the Caucasian population" (Gabriel et al., 1994:107). Today median survival is 28 years of age. In the United States among people of European ancestry, 5 percent of individuals carry one gene, and 1 in 2,400 live births are homozygous and affected with the disease (compared to 1 in 17,000 live births among African Americans). Why the gene is so common has been a mystery. Research with genetically engineered strains of mice has shown that people with cystic fibrosis are immune to the toxins produced

Evolution of the Primate Immune System

It remains unclear how the body's immune system decides, among the diversity of possible responses, to react to various bacteria, viruses, and parasites. The type of immune response to mount and the strength are two of the many issues that remain unanswered. Discussions of these issues often revolve around the costs and benefits of maintaining any particular type of immune system. In the laboratory, for example, in a number of species, artificial selection for an increased ability to resist pathogens is associated with a decrease in overall fitness. Vertebrates possess an adaptive immune system in which different types of cells carry a wide variety of antibody receptors that can recognize an almost unlimited range of foreign antigens. If this type of immune system is costly in a Darwinian sense, then natural selection should favor enhanced resistance to pathogens only when necessary. This observation led Charles Nunn and colleagues (Nunn et al., 2000) to pose the following questions: Is investment in immune protection greater in species that are exposed to a larger number of pathogens, and do the kinds of pathogens make a

difference in terms of the degree of immune response?

Nunn's team believes that their research has proven that investment in immune protection is greater in at-risk individuals based on 41 primate species that they investigated. Baseline white blood cell counts were gathered from individual nonhuman primates, and it was discovered that total white blood cell counts are higher in promiscuous species than in monogamous ones. For example, white blood cell counts were high in the Barbary macaque, a species whose females may mate with up to 10 males a day during estrus. White blood cells counts were correspondingly low in gibbons, a species whose females are mostly monogamous and mate infrequently.

These results showed that the greatest investment in immune defenses were made by nonhuman primates that were most at risk of sexually transmitted diseases. In contrast, the research showed that there is no evidence of higher white blood cell counts associated with greater exposure to ordinary infectious diseases, because the counts did not correlate with group size or population densities of the animals studied. These researchers argued that monogamous species find it too costly to maintain the

slightly higher white blood cell counts typical of their promiscuous relatives. Sexually transmitted diseases are widespread in nature, cause chronic rather than acute infections, and result in substantial reductions in fitness through sterility.

With the supposition that greater frequency of sexual contact leads to an increased risk of contracting an STD, Nunn's team found that the levels of all three kinds of white blood cells, neutrophils, lymphocytes, and monocytes, were elevated in promiscuous species. Curiously, these cells have very different functions. One question, among many, is why there are higher numbers of lymphocytes in promiscuous primates, if it is the lymphocyte's diversity and capacity to make an effective memory response, rather than its overall numbers, that determines the effectiveness of the immune response and the outcome of infection?

This and other questions aside, however, if the hypothesis bears out, it might help explain why humans, basically a monogamous primate species, are susceptible to all kinds of sexually transmitted diseases, whereas chimpanzees, our closest living relative and a highly promiscuous species, are not.

by the cholera bacterium. These individuals of course die of cystic fibrosis, but heterozygotes, individuals who carry one copy of the gene, are protected from the cholera toxin at a 50 percent level. Because cholera must have taken a heavy toll in the evolutionary past of European populations, a balanced polymorphism exists, and we can explain through this evolutionary mechanism the high percentage of cystic fibrosis genes in the population (see Chapter 14 for other examples of balanced polymorphisms).

Structural Problems

A number of medical problems that beset human beings are traceable to our bipedal stance and locomotion, a relatively recent adaptation in evolutionary terms. And as body size has increased in human evolution and obesity in modern Westerners becomes more common, some of these problems have become more severe.

The human foot. Our feet have many problems that are related to our ancestors' climbing heritage. Basically, the ape foot is a grasping organ, which evolved for holding on to branches by using a divergent toe, and supporting the body weight in a vertical position with the foot inverted (sole facing inward). The human foot, in contrast, is a rigid supporting organ that, although built on the basic ape plan, supports the body's weight with the sole of the foot flat on the ground. The **longitudinal arch** in the human foot is an important component of our ability to stride and "toe-off" in walking and is a feature lacking in the ape foot. The human great toe, brought into line with the other toes, plays an important role in stabilizing the longitudinal arch. However, if it diverges away and is mobile, like an ape's foot, flat feet result (Figure 16–8). When body weight in a standing human presses down, a rolled in, or *pronated*, foot results. This condition can cause foot pain from the excessive muscle effort needed to compensate for the lack of skeletal and joint support.

The knee. The knee joint is another rather fragile part of the human body, as runners and football players will readily admit. This fragility is also a residue of our quadrupedal heritage. All joints have a functional trade-off between strength and mobility. The knee is a quite mobile, very shallow joint formed between the distal end of the femur and the flat top of the tibia. It is rimmed with an up-lipped cartilage ring known as the **meniscus,** and the knee cap, or *patella,* in front

longitudinal arch: the upwardly arched structure composed of bones and connecting ligaments on the medial side of the human foot.

meniscus: from the Latin, meaning "lens"; the cartilage rimming the articular surface of the tibia at the knee joint and which forms a basin for the articular end of the femur.

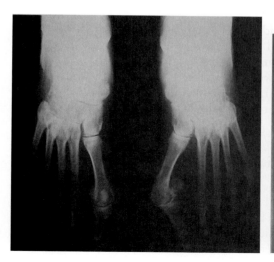
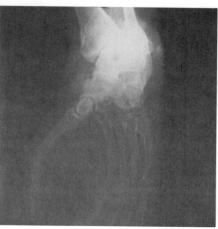

FIGURE 16–8 Left: x-rays showing divergence of the big toe (first metatarsal and hallux) in the human foot. This condition leads to flat feet. Compare with the normal condition in the gorilla foot (right).

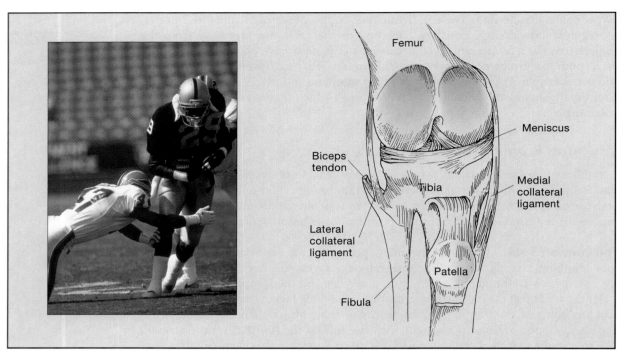

FIGURE 16–9   Bone and ligament structure of the human knee, showing the stronger structures on the lateral side. Inset: side tackle in football, which commonly results in tearing of medial collateral ligament.

(Figure 16–9). The evolutionary heritage of our knee joints comes from our ancestors' ability to flex and extend this joint through a wide range of movement while supporting the weight of the body with a grasping foot. Thus, the lateral (outside) ligaments that support the knee joint are the strongest, exactly the opposite to the force administered in football tackles to the lateral side of the knee. The knee is similarly not adapted to the vertical forces resulting from long-distance running, which is exercise that can result in ligament and meniscus tears and pain. Fortunately, running with cushioned shoes can help alleviate this problem.

FORENSIC ANTHROPOLOGY

Forensic anthropology is the applied side of that branch of biological anthropology known as *skeletal biology*, also termed osteology. It is the study of human skeletal remains for the purpose of solving crimes and for personal identification (Ubelaker, 1995). Forensic anthropologists collaborate extensively with law enforcement officers, the military, international human rights organizations, and medical examiners' offices. Not surprisingly, forensic anthropology is the largest applied subdiscipline of biological anthropology.

Facial and Dental Reconstruction

Perhaps the oldest and best known, but also most problematic, aspect of forensic anthropology is facial reconstruction. Facial reconstruction has not been as widely considered in forensic anthropology as have other characteristics, such as stature or sex determination, because of its arbitrariness. Many attempts have shown that one skull can lead to markedly different facial reconstructions, depending on the

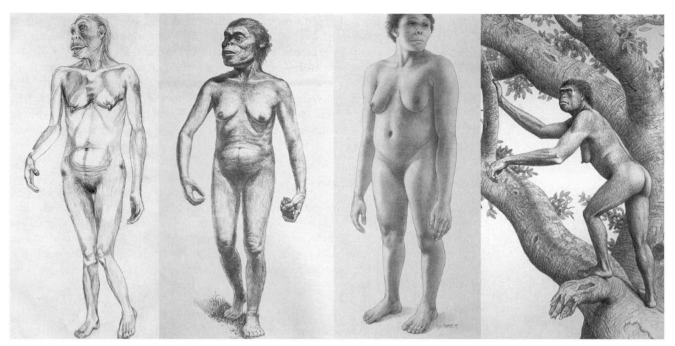

FIGURE 16–10 The National Geographic Society commissioned four different artists to sketch a 2-million-year-old female *Homo habilis* from the same set of bones. The figure shows the four remarkably different drawings the artists produced. This exercise demonstrates that there is no single correct way to reconstruct the appearance of a living individual from a set of bones.

sculptor. This fact was clearly demonstrated by a recent exercise in the reconstruction of the face and body of one of our ancestors (Figure 16–10). Today one of the leading experts in this field is John Gurche.

Although the skull can provide a means of developing a general outline of the face, and average tissue thicknesses can provide some indications of soft-part anatomy (Figure 16–11), many of the facial features that are critical to personal identification leave no marks on the skull. Nevertheless, facial reconstruction may be used when all else fails. Ubelaker (1995) suggests that facial reproduction be used only to inform the public through the media that the remains of a person of that general appearance have been recovered. This publicity may lead to further developments in

FIGURE 16–11 One skull, two stages of its forensic reconstruction, and a photograph of the living individual. Forensic reconstruction often proves unreliable, because many facial features leave no trace on the skull.

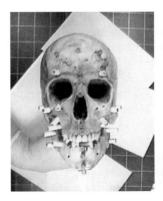
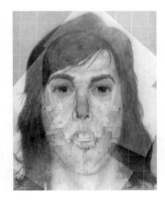

solving a case. Occasionally, a photograph of a missing individual may be matched with a skull by a process of overlaying the images in a computer, controlling for orientation and exact measurements (Ubelaker and O'Donnell, 1992).

Teeth are particularly useful in identifying individuals, because of their idiosyncratic nature and because they can be matched to dental records. A telltale gap between the front teeth proved the single most important determining factor in forensic anthropologist Clyde Snow's positive identification of the Nazi SS officer Josef Mengele, the Auschwitz "Angel of Death," from a skull exhumed in Brazil (Joyce and Stover, 1991).

Skeletal Reconstructions

Forensic anthropologists use many clues evident on bones to determine the identification and history of a skeleton. Using standard osteological techniques, specialists can determine sex, age, stature, individual characteristics, and population affinities if the remains are complete enough. Any remnants of clothes associated with the bones can give valuable clues as to weight and height.

Cause of Death

Forensic anthropologists categorize most trauma that they can detect in bony remains to (1) gunshot wounds, (2) blunt force trauma, or (3) sharp force trauma. These types of damage are readily identified in broad outline, but the details can be bedeviling. For example, if a skeleton shows both gunshot and blunt force trauma, which injury caused death? And can anthropologists be confident enough of their conclusions to testify in court in cases where their expert testimony may be critical in determining the guilt or innocence of a defendant? These and similar questions make forensic anthropology a challenging subdiscipline of applied biological anthropology (Iscan and Kennedy, 1989).

Human Rights Investigations

As challenging as identifying individual criminal cases may be for forensic anthropologists, identifying the victims of state-sponsored human rights abuses can be even more so. Joyce and Stover (1991) describe the long-term work of Clyde Snow and the Argentine Forensic Anthropology Team in unearthing and identifying the remains of thousands of "the Disappeared," who were mainly young political dissenters who were detained, tortured, and executed without trial by the military junta that ruled Argentina in the late 1970s. Risking death threats and overcoming bureaucratic obstacles, Snow and his team succeeded in focusing attention on and investigating a number of the execution-style murders of more than 9,000 individuals who had been missing. Working with the courts, Snow's forensic team excavated cemeteries (Figure 16–12) and correlated medical and dental records of persons reported missing with exhumed skeletons. To gain an estimate of the magnitude of the problem, they gathered cemetery records throughout Argentina that showed that after the 1976 military coup, the numbers of anonymous burials rose drastically in those cemeteries located near prisons and detention centers. Absolute numbers of anonymous burials rose dramatically between 1976 and 1977, the height of the military's repression. There was a demographic shift as well. Before the coup most of the anonymous burials had been of destitute men older than 35 years of age. The percentage of individuals between the ages of 21 and 35 buried in unmarked graves rose from 15 percent before 1976 to 56 percent after the coup (Joyce and Stover, 1991:260–261). These figures and statistics provided irrefutable evidence of the thousands of the Argentinian "Disappeared" who would, in the main, never be identified further.

Figure 16–12 Excavation of anonymous graves in the Avellaneda Cemetery, Buenos Aires, for the Argentine Team for Forensic Anthropology, 1988.

Molecular forensic anthropology also contributed to the resolution of the human problems associated with the Argentinian Disappeared. In 1984, Mary-Claire King, a geneticist at the University of California, Berkeley, developed a genetic screening test for determining the relatedness of grandparents to missing children. King and her Argentinian collaborator Ana Maria Di Lonardo used the HLA (human lymphocyte antigen) proteins for testing grandpaternity and grandmaternity (Di Lonardo et al., 1984). This was necessary because, when the government death squads abducted and executed political opponents, they also abducted their victims' children, whom they adopted out to Argentinians who were in favor with the government. In one case, King and Di Lonardo took small blood samples from an eight-year-old girl suspected of being the child of a Disappeared couple, along with samples from the couple's parents (the girl's grandparents). Although a retired police chief and his wife claimed the child to be their biological daughter, the HLA tests conclusively proved the girl to be the granddaughter of the Disappeared's parents. Consequently, the courts awarded custody to her maternal grandmother.

 **FRONTIERS**

Evolution of Nonlife Through Nanotechnology

Darwin considered evolution by natural selection a process that took place only in living things. During Darwin's time, technology interfered with this process in only one, rather simple way: through selective breeding. One tinkered with characteristics, such as a dog's coat color or a cow's milk production, and consequently, with the genes that controlled them, but outside of varieties within a species, nothing new was ever produced. Modern technology goes far beyond what Darwin might have imagined, yet his evolutionary principles may still prove to be very important to the design and application of new products.

Back in 1959 theoretical physicist Richard Feynman suggested that it would be possible one day to build machines so small that they would consist of only a few thousand atoms (the term *nanotechnology* comes from *nanometer*, or one-billionth of a meter; for comparison, a typical virus is about 100 nanometers in width). The promise of this new technology is to create machines that could be used to construct anything, using molecules or even atoms as building blocks. Today, by recombining DNA from different species, genetic engineers have already put some of this theory into practice. For example, bacterial cells with recombinant DNA are used to construct medically useful hormones.

This type of nanotechnology, however, is limited to the tasks that cells already do. Goals of future research involve producing entities that are designed to accomplish any task. *Nanobots*, independent entities produced through nanotechnology, would accomplish the work. For example, nanobots could be placed in the human blood stream, programmed to seek out cholesterol deposits on vessel walls, and disassemble them. How would these nanobots work? Their "brains" might consist of DNA that is programmed to provide instructions for specific work. Tiny "fingers" could be made using nanotubes, hairlike carbon molecules, discovered in 1991, that are 100 times as strong as steel. These "fingers" could manipulate molecules in certain ways based on information provided by the nanobots' DNA "brains."

To accomplish complicated tasks, or to search for enough raw material for such tasks, billions, perhaps trillions, of nanobots would be needed. The only practical way to create nanobots in such numbers would be to have them create more of themselves. Nanotechnologists want to design nanobots that can do two things: (1) carry out their primary tasks and (2) build perfect replicas of themselves. At this point old theory becomes pertinent to new

technology. What if the nanobots don't stop replicating and, instead, become cancerlike runaway growths on a host the nanobot was designed to help. Certainly, there are ways to overcome this technological glitch; technologists could design nanobots to operate only under certain conditions, such as within a very narrow range of temperature. This trait would also halt their unwanted spread from one host to another. Nanobots could be programmed to stop reproducing before too many of them are produced or to self-destruct after a specified number of generations.

The problem that concerns nanotechnologists is mutation. For example, through chance mutation the self-destruct code may be lost in the process of replication, which might produce a mutant strain of nanobots. Already possessing the ability to avoid the host's own immune system, these rogue self-replicators would be favored by selection, so they would produce more offspring and become more numerous than the original variety—in the classic Darwinian definition of fitness. In this hypothetical scenario the nanobots ultimately kill off their creators, who then join the multitude of species that have become extinct. Worrisome as this scenario might be, the real worry to evolutionary biologists is slightly different: Although they don't dismiss the danger, nanotechnologists really believe they can handle it.

HUMAN ECOLOGY AND QUALITY OF LIFE

As biological anthropology succeeds in defining the limits of human adaptation, opportunities to design better and more evolutionarily consistent living arrangements will increase. Environmental pollution has become a major factor in lowering the standard of living for millions of people in the modern world. Increased noise pollution near busy airports leads to decreased birth weights in babies (Schell, 1991) and only recently, with modern medicine and nutrition, have secular trends in body size approached those of our Paleolithic hunter-gatherer ancestors (see Chapter 15). Nevertheless, the many substances foreign to our biological adaptations that are now common in our drinking water, in the foods we eat, and in the air we breathe create an environment that is hostile to human health and survival. Ridding our environment of these disease-causing substances while ensuring an adequate supply of food and energy to a growing world population is a major challenge for the entire human species.

Anthropologist Lionel Tiger argued in his 1992 book *The Pursuit of Pleasure* that all humans have some fundamental entitlements to certain aspects of the environment that are basically "normal" and therefore "pleasurable." If we accept this premise, and its implication that society and governments should accept the challenge of fostering such environments, then much needs to be done. If, for example, Tiger is correct that expansive views of trees and bodies of water are "psychopleasures" born of human evolutionary adaptation over millions of years, then how do dwellers in urban glass towers, surrounded on all sides by similar towers, meet this need? And what about people who live in squalid urban slums? If having an open fire with its warm glow, heat, and smoky smell are also evolutionary entitlements, how is the equally pressing need for clean air in our urban centers satisfied?

As more and more people are born and inhabit the earth, more and more crowding and interaction become inevitable. The scale of the world's population of more than 6 billion people is simply incomprehensible to a hominid who evolved in a context in which groups of between 25 and 150 people were his or her entire lifelong social environment (Allman, 1994). The myriad social and economic problems that beset the modern city–state—from racism to poverty to homelessness to unemployment to crime to bureaucratic inefficiency—are possibly symptoms of this discordance between human evolution and modern human living conditions. Modern urban environments need to mimic the small groups, the intimate settings, and the natural and unpolluted surroundings of our ancestors. Such a utopian solution is clearly very far off, but one thing remains certain. It will be easier to change our surroundings to fit our adaptation than to change our adaptation to fit surroundings that are outside the limits passed on to us from our ancestors.

◀ SUMMARY

1. **What are the goals of applied biological anthropology, and what human traits and aspects of the human condition does the discipline consider?**
Biological anthropology as a research field has many developing areas of application. The primary goal of applied biological anthropology may be said to be solving practical problems of human well-being. The Discordance Hypothesis explains the conflict between the environmental conditions of our evolutionary past and the current, culturally based conditions under which we live. A goal of applied biological anthropology in medicine is to seek concordance between environmental conditions and human biology. Applied biological anthropology uses an adaptationist paradigm, which accepts that there are adaptive and evolutionary reasons for most structures and functions of the human body.

2. **What insights does biomedical anthropology shed on common human diseases?**

Biomedical anthropology relates knowledge of human biology and evolution to medicine. One of its most active new areas is evolutionary medicine, which is the study and treatment of the causes, distributions, and cultural correlates of disease within a framework of evolution by natural selection. Some of the diseases studied by biological anthropologists include SIDS (Sudden Infant Death Syndrome), neonatal jaundice, "diseases of civilization," obesity, diverticulitis, and breast cancer. Infectious diseases, such as AIDS, also can be understood in evolutionary terms. This understanding, which integrates population biology and genetics, helps us prevent and cope with the diseases. Balanced polymorphisms can explain a number of previously confusing human maladies, such as sickle-cell disease and cystic fibrosis. A number of structural problems, such as flat feet and knee pain, are traceable to our bipedal mode of locomotion.

3. **What are the goals and methods of forensic anthropology?**

Forensic anthropologists using skeletons can determine sex, age, stature, individual characteristics, population affinities, and whether trauma was involved in a death. This information can be used to help ascertain cause of death in legal cases and identify missing persons in human rights investigations.

4. **What does evolutionary biology suggest about the needs of people in a modern, urbanized world?**

An appreciation of our evolutionary history and adaptations to our past environments will help us design appropriate living situations for ourselves today and for our descendants.

◀ CRITICAL THINKING QUESTIONS

1. There is intense interest among the general public and nutritionists alike in the ideal human diet—one that satisfies human dietary requirements, tastes good, and is nutritious. Review the evolutionary history of primates and hominids as discussed in this text and, using the principles of evolutionary medicine, suggest some guiding principles.

2. If what we "like,"—what we take pleasure in—evolved alongside our anatomy and physiology, why is it that many things we like to eat are not good for us?

3. A number of biological anthropologists who study living nonhuman primates believe that these species, or at least those most closely related to human beings, should have the same ethical and legal rights as people and should be protected by governments from murder, mistreatment, and unfair confinement. What do you think? How would laboratory research using primates be affected?

4. Forensic anthropologists are becoming increasingly active in international investigations of human rights abuses and crimes against humanity. Many of the cases of genocide that forensic anthropologists investigate are motivated by ethnic hatred and racism. In addition to uncovering evidence of crimes, do scientists have a moral responsibility to educate local people about human biological variation and cultural diversity?

◀ INTERNET EXERCISES

Critical Thinking

SIDS. The chapter suggests an evolutionary explanation for SIDS (Sudden Infant Death Syndrome), as well as a preventive measure based on childcare habits of people in many societies. For this exercise, evaluate this evolutionary approach against the standard Western medical explanation and preventive measures for SIDS. Consider the following:

1. What is known about the causes of SIDS? What is the standard approach to prevention?
2. What evidence suggests that an evolutionary approach would be effective? What additional evidence is needed for the effectiveness of this approach to be proven?

Writing Assignment

Forensic Anthropology. The chapter details parts of the world, such as Argentina, where forensic anthropologists have investigated human rights violations. Unfortunately, such incidents continue to happen, most recently in the Balkans. Choose a part of the world where human rights violations are occurring at the present time and research the role of forensic anthropologists in discovering the criminals and identifying the victims. Write a brief research paper about your findings.

See Companion Web site for Internet links.

Cystic fibrosis (CF) is an inherited disease caused by a recessive gene in homozygous condition that results in chronic pulmonary disease, pancreatic and other glandular failures, and death. Cystic fibrosis is the most common, fatal, homozygous recessive disorder of the Caucasian population. Today median survival is still only 28 years of age. In the United States among people of European ancestry, 5 percent of individuals carry one gene, and 1 in 2,400 live births is homozygous and affected with the disease.

Why the gene is so common has been a mystery. Research has shown that people with cystic fibrosis are immune to the toxins produced by the cholera bacterium. These individuals, of course, die of cystic fibrosis, but heterozygotes, who carry only one copy of the gene, are protected from the cholera toxin at a 50 percent level. Because cholera took a heavy toll on European populations in the evolutionary past, a balanced polymorphism exists.Thus, the evolutionary mechanism explains the high percentage of cystic fibrosis genes in the population.

WEB ACTIVITY

Gene therapy involves the insertion of a single gene from one organism into another organism. In the case of gene therapy for CF, the gene is inserted into a common virus that infects respiratory tissue, the adenovirus. As the QuickTime video explains, this treatment shows some promise for individuals who inherit this otherwise fatal disease.

Activity
1. View the video. What parts of the body does CF affect?
2. Why was the adenovirus chosen for gene therapy for CF?
3. Given that cholera is no longer common among European populations, would you expect the balanced polymorphism to change over the evolutionary future of these peoples? What type of change would you expect, and what would be the mechanism of this change?

The MediaLab can be found in Chapter 16 on your Companion Web site http://www.prenhall.com/boaz

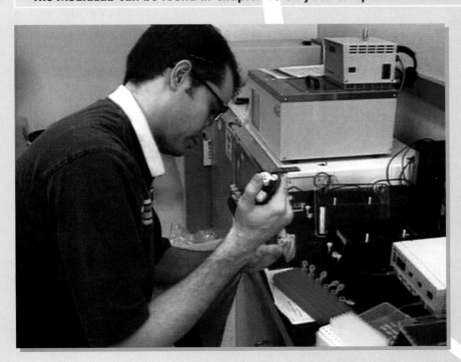

THE LANGUAGE OF BIOLOGICAL ANTHROPOLOGY: HUMAN ANATOMY

Finding one's way around the structures in the human body requires an understanding of some navigational terms. First, we must "pin down" the body. Anatomists have done this by defining **anatomical position,** a standard placement of the human body standing erect with head looking forward, arms at the side with palms facing forward, and feet flat on the ground facing forward. The front part of the body is termed **anterior** or **ventral** ("belly"). The back part of the body is termed **posterior** or **dorsal** ("back"). And upper and lower parts of the body are called **superior** and **inferior,** respectively. Anatomical structures are always defined in reference to anatomical position. For example, we would say that an acrobat's chin is inferior to the forehead even though the acrobat might be swinging upside down from a trapeze. When discussing limbs, **proximal** refers to a part near the center of the body, and **distal** refers to a part farther away from the body.

Anatomical position for nonhuman animals differs somewhat from that of humans. Because four-footed animals normally do not stand erect, their anatomical position is defined as facing forward with all four feet on the ground. Anterior, posterior, inferior, and superior, then, are defined in the context of this orientation. In comparative anatomy, unlike human anatomy, ventral is synonymous with inferior, and dorsal is synonymous with superior. This system of terminology is also used in describing the brain.

Planes in the body are also important to understand and visualize. A **median** (or **midsagittal**) **plane** cuts the body in half lengthwise, into right and left halves. **Sagittal** planes cut the body parallel to the left or right of the median plane. A **transverse plane** cuts the body in half crosswise, at a right angle to the long axis of the body. And a **coronal plane** cuts the body into ventral and dorsal halves.

Orientation and description of teeth also has its own terminology. We can think of a set of teeth as a triangle, with the apex at the front of the mouth. A direction along the tooth row toward this apex is termed **mesial,** and a direction away from the apex is termed **distal.** The sides of teeth are termed **lingual** if they are on the side facing the tongue, and **labial** (for front teeth facing the lips) or **buccal** (for teeth facing the cheeks).

Basic Movements

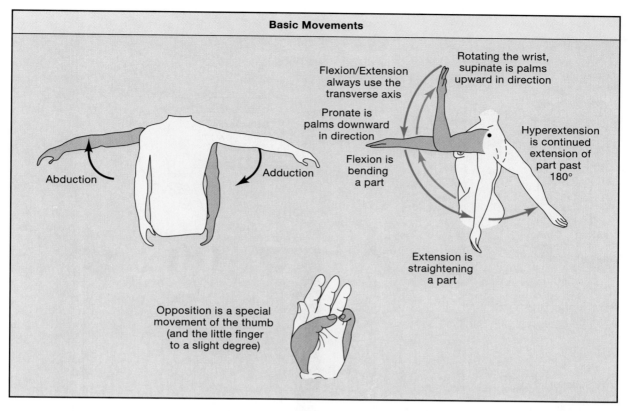

Flexion/Extension always use the transverse axis

Pronate is palms downward in direction

Flexion is bending a part

Rotating the wrist, supinate is palms upward in direction

Hyperextension is continued extension of part past 180°

Extension is straightening a part

Abduction

Adduction

Opposition is a special movement of the thumb (and the little finger to a slight degree)

Mammalian Tooth

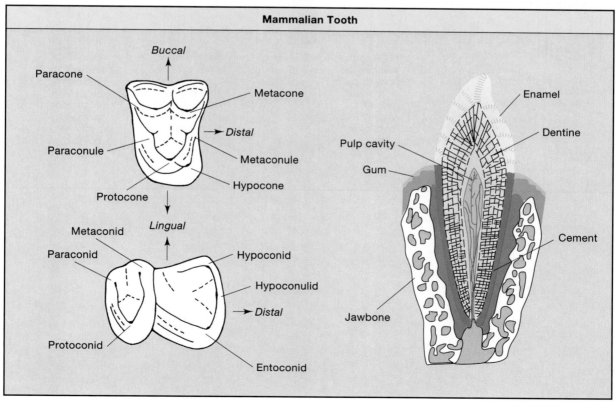

Buccal

Paracone

Metacone

Paraconule

Distal

Metaconule

Protocone

Hypocone

Lingual

Metaconid

Paraconid

Hypoconid

Hypoconulid

Distal

Protoconid

Entoconid

Enamel

Dentine

Pulp cavity

Gum

Cement

Jawbone

Planes and Orientations

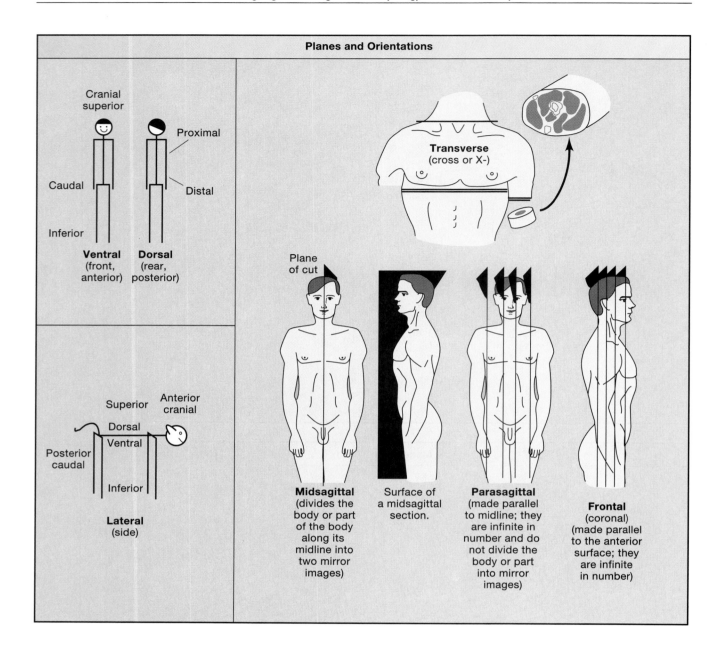

Bones

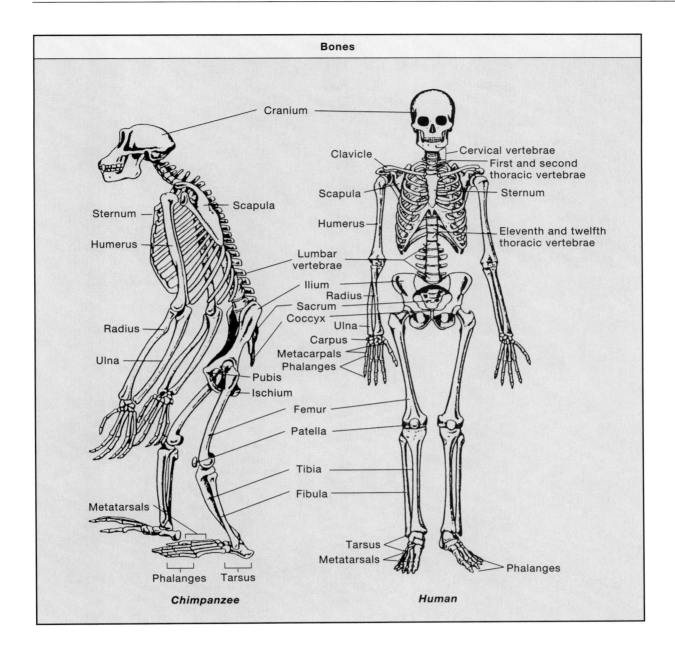

Cranium

Clavicle

Cervical vertebrae

First and second thoracic vertebrae

Scapula

Sternum

Humerus

Eleventh and twelfth thoracic vertebrae

Sternum

Scapula

Humerus

Lumbar vertebrae

Ilium

Radius

Radius

Sacrum

Coccyx

Ulna

Ulna

Carpus

Metacarpals

Phalanges

Pubis

Ischium

Femur

Patella

Tibia

Fibula

Metatarsals

Tarsus

Metatarsals

Phalanges

Phalanges   Tarsus

Chimpanzee

Human

The Brain

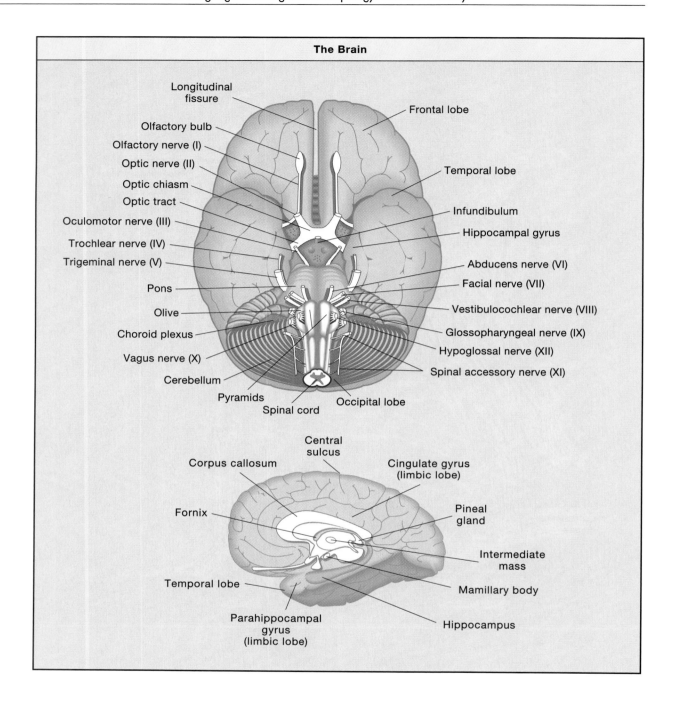

THE LANGUAGE OF BIOLOGICAL ANTHROPOLOGY: GEOLOGY

The geological time scale provides an important way to describe how old and in what time context ancient organisms lived. The largest categories of time in the geological time scale are termed **eras.** Eras are divided into **periods.** For the most recent two periods of geological time, there are also smaller divisions known as **epochs.** As methods of determining the absolute ages of fossil sites have improved, so have our ideas of the age limits of the various time boundaries been refined. These boundaries are shown in the accompanying table.

Geological Terminology

Time (millions of years ago)	Era	Period	Epoch	Etymology
	Cenozoic	Quaternary	Holocene (Recent)	"entirely recent"
0.01			Pleistocene	"most recent"
1.8		Tertiary	Pliocene	"more recent"
5.5			Miocene	"less recent"
24			Oligocene	"scanty recent"
34			Eocene	"dawn recent"
54			Paleocene	"ancient recent"
65	Mesozoic	Cretaceous		"chalk-bearing"
145		Jurassic		from Jura Mts., Switzerland
215		Triassic		"three-parts"
245	Paleozoic	Permian		from region in eastern Russia
290		Carboniferous		"carbon-bearing"
360		Devonian		from Devon, England
410		Silurian		from Welsh tribe of Siluria
440		Ordovician		from Welsh tribe of Ordovices
505		Cambrian		from Cambria, Wales
545	Precambrian	Ediacaran		from Ediacara, Australia

THE LANGUAGE OF BIOLOGICAL ANTHROPOLOGY: BIOLOGY AND TAXONOMY

The scientific discipline that studies naming is termed **taxonomy.** Although the naming of new species and the renaming of old species continually keeps classificatory schemes changing, scientists need to agree on the definition of the animal species and higher categories to which reference is being made. A formal taxonomic name at any level is known as a **taxon.**

All biological species are formally classified by a **binomial** system, under which they are assigned two, usually Latin, names. The first of these names, used alone, is the **genus.** Both names used together designate the **species** to which the animal is assigned.

Zoological classification is *hierarchical,* that is, organized in levels, one under another. In practice, the International Code of Zoological Nomenclature establishes the rules of taxonomy for animal species. There are many rules, but, basically, the code says that names that were proposed first for a species always have *priority* over names proposed later. There must be a clearly designated type specimen with a description of the characteristics that distinguish its species from other closely related species. The classification can be somewhat arbitrary. For example, it does not matter if we call ourselves *Homo sapiens sapiens* or *Gorilla gorilla beringei* as long as everyone understands what group of animals is being referred to. Most classifications attempt to strike a balance between current taxonomic usage and recent findings in both paleontological and molecular realms. The full taxonomic classification of the human species, along with other living primates, is presented on the following page; common names of each classification are given in parentheses.

Kingdom Animalia (Animals)

  Phylum Chordata (Chordates)

    Subphylum Vertebrata (Vertebrates)

      Class Mammalia (Mammals)

        Subclass Eutheria (Placental Mammals)

          Order Primates (Primates)

            Suborder Prosimii (Prosimians)

              Infraorder Lemuroidea (Lemuroids)

                Family Cheirogalidae (Dwarf and Mouse Lemurs)

                Family Daubentoniidae (Aye-aye)

                Family Galagidae (Bushbaby)

                Family Indridae (Indri and Sifaka)

                Family Lemuridae (Lemur)

                Family Lepilemuridae (Sportive Lemur)

                Family Lorisidae (Potto and Loris)

              Infraorder Tarsioidea (Tarsioids)

                Family Tarsiidae (Tarsier)

            Suborder Anthropoidea (Anthropoids)

              Infraorder Platyrrhini (New World Monkeys)

                Subfamily Pitheciinae (*Pithecia, Chiropotes, Cacajao*)

                Subfamily Callicebinae (Titi monkeys)

                Subfamily Aotinae (owl monkeys)

                Subfamily Atelinae (spider monkeys, howler monkeys, woolly monkeys)

                Subfamily Cebinae (capuchin monkeys, squirrel monkeys)

                Subfamily Callitrichinae (tamarins and marmosets)

              Infraorder Catarrhini ("Old World Primate")

                Superfamily Cercopithecoidea (Old World Monkey)

                  Family Cercopithecidae (Cercopithecids)

                  Subfamily Cercopithecinae (cercopithecines)

                  Subfamily Colobinae (Colobus, langurs)

                Superfamily Hominoidea (Apes, Humans, and Intermediates)

                Family Pongidae (Orangutan)

                Family Gorillidae (Gorilla)

                Family Panidae (Chimpanzee and Bonobo, or Pygmy Chimpanzee)

                Family Hominidae (Hominid)

                  Subfamily Australopithecinae (australopithecines)

                  Subfamily Homininae (Hominine)

                    Genus *Homo* (Human, "Man")

                    Species *Homo* sapiens (Human, "Man")

                      Subspecies *Homo sapiens sapiens* (Human, sometimes "anatomically modern human")

DATING METHODS IN PALEOANTHROPOLOGY

relative framework: relative dating; using comparative methods, such as stratigraphic position or fauna, to determine whether a fossil, artifact, or site is younger or older than other fossils, artifacts, or sites.

R1 date: determination that a fossil or artifact is contemporaneous with the sediments in which it is buried. The analysis of the florine content in bones buried together is one way to establish contemporaniety.

R2 date: determination of the relative age of a site in relation to its stratigraphic position in a local "rock" sequence (e.g., Bed I within the stratigraphy of Olduvai Gorge).

R3 date: determination of the relative age of a site in relation to its stratigraphic position in a regional "rock" sequence (e.g., the stratigraphic units of Olduvai Gorge within the framework of stratigraphy of East Africa).

biostratigraphy: establishing a sequence through time of faunal units ("zones"), which are characterized by the presence of specific fossil species.

rock stratigraphy: "lithostratigraphy"; establishing a sequence through time of sedimentary, volcanic, or other units characterized by their geological consistency (e.g., Bed I, as a rock unit within the Olduvai Gorge stratigraphic sequence). Rock units may be described in a hierarchical manner from larger to smaller, such as formation, member, bed.

RELATIVE DATING TECHNIQUES

In his book *Frameworks for Dating Fossil Man* (1969), Kenneth Oakley described two ways in which the age of things could be estimated: relative and absolute (now called chronometric) dating methods. The **relative framework** involves ways in which materials can be placed in the context of their surroundings and dated as either older than or younger than something else. Knowing that a specimen is older or younger than another specimen is important in determining evolutionary sequences. Oakley established four levels of relative dates, termed R1 through R4, based on how the date is determined.

R1 Dates

Oakley's **R1 date** establishes the fact that any material found in a deposit is contemporary with, or belongs to, the deposit in which it is found. For example, tests on fossil bones for an R1 date include fluorine and uranium analyses and nitrogen analysis. Both fluorine and uranium accumulate as a fossil ages, and nitrogen levels generally diminish with age. Therefore, if all bones found in the same deposit show the same amount of fluorine, which animals absorb from local ground water, it may be determined that they are all of the same age and belong to that particular paleoenvironment. R1 dates are particularly useful for showing that materials actually come from a particular site. For example, if a firm R1 date had been established at the beginning of the Piltdown discoveries, the fraud would have been detected at once rather than 40 years later when Oakley and others revisited these famous forgeries.

R2 and R3 Dates

Oakley's **R2** and **R3 dates** attempt to link the primary site with known stratigraphic units in the local and regional area. The dates are commonly established with biostratigraphic and rock-stratigraphic analyses. **Biostratigraphy** deals with fossils of specific animal species found in one deposit of a known age that can be used to date deposits of an unknown age containing the same species (Figure A–1, p. 470). Biostratigraphy is based on the assumption that individuals of the same species lived at about the same time. Biostratigraphy is based on the establishment of faunal zones, which paleoanthropologists use in determining relative ages of deposits and fossils. For instance, the australopithecine cave sites in South Africa have been mostly dated using biostratigraphic means.

    Rock stratigraphy involves the character and sequence of rock layers or strata. Character analysis includes the composition and the arrangement of the rocks in the strata. The sequence of the strata usually can be determined using the **principle of superposition,** which states that in any undisturbed strata, the older, earlier deposited strata underlie the younger, more recently deposited strata. In many cases, however, faulting or discontinuities in the exposures make superpositional relationships unclear, and other means, such as tephrostratigraphy (discussed later), are used for purposes of correlation.

R4 Date

Oakley's **R4 date** involves a comparison of morphological features that one fossil shares with another fossil of known age. For example, it is tempting to estimate the age of fossils found in deposits of unknown age that morphologically resemble *Homo erectus* based on time spans of dated fossils of that species. The difficulty in obtaining a date by morphological means, however, involves the fact that similar morphologies may persist over long periods of time and are thus not always in synchrony.

Other Correlation-Based Methods of Relative Dating

Tephrostratigraphy.   **Tephrostratigraphy** details the record of explosive volcanism. Products of volcanic eruptions include ash and pumice and are collectively referred to as *tephra*. The glass component of most of these products contains a geochemical "fingerprint" that is unique to a particular eruption. By identifying characteristic geochemical signatures from widely spaced localities, geologists can correlate stratigraphic sequences in cases where materials for absolute dating are absent. Relative sequences and ties to dated localities can, thus, be established. The uniqueness of the geochemical fingerprint is a result of the complex magnetic history of the tephra, which produces the slightly different percentages of elemental components such as silicon, aluminum, and iron. Miscorrelation is perhaps the most serious problem that affects the accuracy of the tephrostratigraphic dates, because geochemical signatures can be misleading and apparent similarities do not always reflect valid correlations.

Correlations to tephra found interspersed in deep sea cores have provided a stratigraphic link between terrestrial and marine records, permitting correlations of isotopic and biostratigraphic records from the oceans to land. The best example of the use of tephrostratigraphy in paleoanthropology involves the Plio-Pleistocene deposits in the Turkana Basin in Kenya and Ethiopia (see Chapter 10). There, the technique proved effective in resolving the stratigraphic complexity of the Koobi Fora region and the controversy involving the age of the KBS tuff (Feibel, 1999).

Amino acid racemization.   Every amino acid can occur in two different forms, which are mirror images of one another. Almost all amino acids display what is known as the L configuration; the D configuration is its mirror image. After the death of an organism, the D/L ratio slowly changes from near zero to one. This is called the **racemization process.** Temperature is the most important control of the conversion rate, and because the temperature history over thousands of years of any organic materials can never be completely known, it is difficult to produce a reliable chronometric age from the D/L ratio. Because samples from the same site must share the same temperature history, however, relative ages can be determined at any particular locality. For relative dates to be reliable, analyses comparing one site to another should be performed on similar material of the same species. This technique is potentially useful for samples whose ages run from several years to several million years, depending on the amino acid analyzed.

Paleomagnetism.   **Paleomagnetism** dating is based on the history of the earth's ancient magnetic field, which can be determined through the analyses of iron-rich rocks and sediments that preserve the magnetizations (Kappleman, 1993). Results of analysis provide the direction of the earth's magnetic field at the time and place of the deposition of the rocks. At various times throughout the earth's history, the

principle of superposition: one of Charles Lyell's geological rules, holding that lower or deeper "rock" units in a sequence are older than "rock" units found higher up in the same sequence. For example, Bed I, Olduvai Gorge is supposedly older than Bed IV because of its position in the Olduvai sequence.

R4 date: establishing the relative age of a fossil or artifact by its appearance (morphology) in comparison to similar fossils or artifacts of known age from established relative sequences.

tephrostratigraphy: establishing a relative sequence of volcanic events (by superposition) and determining the geochemical "fingerprint" of each volcanic eruption in a stratigraphic sequence. New volcanic material may be placed within the sequence based on its individual "fingerprint."

racemization process: change in the ratio of D configuration to its mirror image, L, of various amino acids on the death of an organism. This conversion occurs at a steady rate and is affected mainly by the external temperatures to which the remains are subjected.

paleomagnetism: past fluctuations preserved in rocks of the intensity and direction of the earth's magnetic field establish a relative sequence of the earth's normal and reversed epochs.

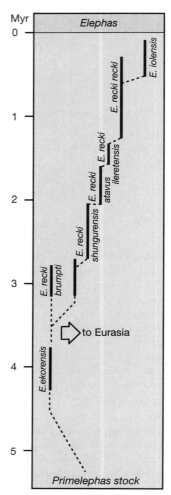

FIGURE A-1 Biostratigraphy of fossil genera of elephants, *Elephas,* in Africa from 4 million years to the present.

geomagnetic field has reversed its polarity. This means that during certain time periods, magnetic north was directed to the south pole instead of to the north. A stratigraphic record of polarity (*magnetostratigraphy*) is composed of alternating zones of normal (north to north) and reverse polarity (Figure A–2).

The discovery of paleomagnetic reversals was made about 35 years ago, and a well-documented geomagnetic reversal time scale (GRTS) has been constructed. For site correlation to be accurate, some independently derived age must be obtained for at least one stratum in order to correlate the site polarity record with the GRTS. The possibility of magnetozones being missing from a stratigraphic sequence is one serious limitation of the use of paleomagnetism as a dating tool, because intervals of nondeposition are usually the rule rather than the exception in terrestrial strata. Care must be taken to preserve the original sample orientation, and heating of the sample to more than 550°C (1022°F) must have occurred to erase previous magnetization. Paleomagnetism is almost the only useful dating method in sedimentary strata that lack volcanic or other materials suitable for radioisotopic dating. This proved to be the case in obtaining dates for the australopithecine cave deposits in South Africa and in the dating of the hominid cave site of Gran Dolina (Atapuerca, Spain) to older than 780,000 years (see Chapters 10 and 11), because these sediments lie in the Matuyama reversed polarity period, or *chron.*

FIGURE A-2 A portion of the magnetostratigraphic time scale showing major intervals of normal (in green) and of reverse (in gold) polarity. Polarity chrons, "epochs" (e.g. Brunhes) are named (on left) as well as subchrons (e.g., Jaramillo) (on right). The most recent system of polarity nomenclature defines polarity chrons and subchrons with the chron definitions and numbers following from the numbered magnetic anomaly profiles. The letters *n* or *r* are appended to chron subdivisions to denote zones of normal and reversed polarity. Subchrons are further subdivided by a number and letter in order from youngest to oldest.

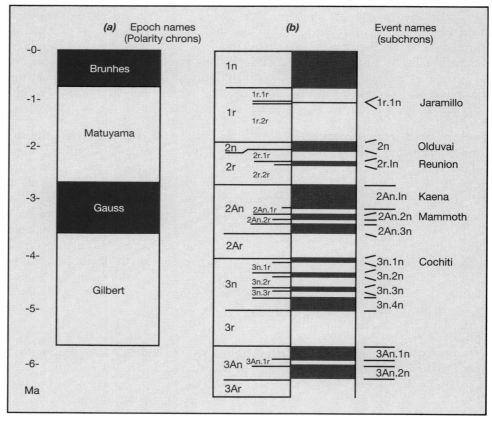

CHRONOMETRIC DATING

Oakley labeled his second framework the *absolute chronology*. The term *absolute* has been mostly replaced by the term **chronometric,** meaning measurement of time. This term was changed because all dates have a probability of error based on limitations inherent in the dating method. Therefore, dates are never "absolute" (Ludwig and Renne, 2000).

Classes of Chronometric Dates

Oakley's **A1** date is derived from the specimen itself, for example, a date may be obtained from bone by carbon-14 dating or from tooth enamel by electron spin resonance (both techniques are discussed later). An **A2** or **A3** date is obtained from analysis of material that surrounds the specimen at the site locality itself, or from material at another site that can be correlated to the site locality. For example, volcanic material can be dated using the 40Ar/39Ar method (discussed later) to date sediments in which hominid fossils are buried. An **A4** date is derived from extrapolations of dates obtained from unrelated strata, by correlations made possible using other methods. For example, deep sea core dates can, at times, be used to date land strata, given the appropriate use of correlative methods such as tephrostratigraphy. Figure A–3 reviews some of the chronometric dating methods and their usefulness in terms of dating various material.

Chronometric Dating Methods

Radiocarbon dating. Radiocarbon dating, which uses the radioactive decay of carbon-14 (14C), was first developed in 1949 by Willard Libby from the University of Chicago. Dating of organic material is based on the production of radioactive 14C in the upper atmosphere from the bombardment of nitrogen-14 by neutrons produced by cosmic rays. Living organisms take in 14C, in the form of $14CO^2$, along with other molecules, when they breathe. Although 14C that is taken in decays while the organism is alive, at death the exchange of 14C with the atmosphere ceases, and the 14C content, which is about 59 billion atoms per g (2.1 billion atoms/oz) of carbon, decays without replenishment. The **half-life** of 14C, or the time it takes for the original amount of the material to reduce by one-half, is 5,730 years. The number of 14C atoms can be measured directly using accelerator mass spectrometry (AMS).

Carbon-14 dating requires that several assumptions be true. First, the number of 14C atoms per g must be both known and constant over time. Second, the number of 14C atoms must represent only the remaining 14C atoms from the specimen itself, because contamination of the sample with younger organic material is the single biggest error factor of this method. For samples older than 40,000 years, fewer than 1 percent of the original number of 14C atoms remain, and it is, therefore, almost impossible to guarantee that contamination of samples this old has not occurred. Samples that may be used for radiocarbon dating include any material that is less than 40,000 years old and that was once part of a living organism, such as wood, paper, charcoal, and bone (Taylor, 1996).

Potassium/Argon and 40Ar/39Ar dating. Potassium argon (K/Ar) was among the earliest quantitative methods applied to dating materials of paleoanthropological interest. This method is based on measuring both the parent (40K) and the daughter (40Ar) of the natural radioactive decay of 40K, calculating age based on a well-defined half-life of 1.250 billion years. Early applications by Curtis and Evernden (1962) to dating volcanic deposits at Olduvai Gorge doubled the known time scale of human evolution from about 1 million to 2 million years.

chronometric: "measurement of time," establishment by a variety of methods of the age of an object or site in years before present. For example, by K/Ar dating, the age of Bed I Olduvai Gorge is 1.8 million years.

A1: chronometric dating of the age of an object, such as carbon-14 dating of bone or charcoal.

A2: chronometric dating of the age of the deposit in which an object is determined to be contemporaneous, such as K/Ar dating of volcanic material near or in which an object is found. For example, *Homo habilis* is thought to be about 1.8 million years old, because it is found in Bed I Olduvai Gorge dated to that age by K/Ar dating.

A3: chronometric dating of the age of a correlated deposit to a deposit in which an object is found.

A4: chronometric dating of the age of a deposit, such as one from a deep sea core that can be related in some manner to a terrestrial deposit in which an object is found.

radiocarbon dating: carbon-14 dating, a radioactive isotope of carbon that is formed in the atmosphere and is absorbed as carbon dioxide by living things until their death. The amount of carbon-14 remaining in the organic object since its death determines the object's age.

half-life: the time it takes for any radioactive substance (isotope) to decay to half of its original amount. For example, it takes 5,730 years for any amount of carbon-14 to decay to one-half of that amount.

potassium-argon: radioactive decay of potassium 40 to the stable (nonradioactive) element argon. In volcanic material this decay can be measured and the age of the rock determined. Argon39/ argon40 is a variant of this technique where the ratio of the amounts of these isotopes of argon are measured to determine the age of the volcanic rock that contains them.

The 40Ar/39Ar method has now largely supplanted the K/Ar method, because it offers many advantages in terms of both accuracy and precision (Deino et al., 1998). The newer method is among the most precise dating methods available, with errors of .5 percent or less in time ranges from 100,000 to 10,000,000 years. There is no practical older age limit for the method, and materials less than 2,000 years old have been dated with 10 percent accuracy. One of the advantages of this method over the older K/Ar method is that it can date contaminated tuffs and altered rocks by accounting for either the loss of radiogenic 40Ar or the inheritance of 40Ar derived from physical contamination with older material, both factors that contribute to error in the K/Ar method.

Samples to be dated are first irradiated in a nuclear reactor to convert 39K to 39Ar. The amount of 39Ar produced is proportional to the amount of 40K in the sample. 39Ar, thus, serves as a proxy for 40K. The advantage of this method is that it avoids having to analyze the quantities of potassium and argon by separate techniques, thus eliminating one potential source of error, because both 39Ar and 40Ar are quantified in the same experiment. Although the 40Ar/39Ar method has proven to be extremely useful to paleoanthropology, one of its first applications, the dating of the KBS tuff at Koobi Fora, Lake Turkana, Kenya, yielded an incorrect age (2.5 million instead of 1.9 million years), which set off a decade-long controversy that was only resolved by using other methods and more precision in obtaining the samples that were analyzed.

Both K/Ar and 40Ar/39Ar are most useful for dating volcanic rocks and minerals. This is also the methods' chief weakness. Such minerals are useful because they begin to accumulate 40Ar only after cooling from the high temperature of volcanic eruptions, in which all of their original 40Ar is lost in the molten state. A2 dating of fossils depends largely on the existence of datable volcanic materials in direct stratigraphic position to them. Fossils found bracketed between two volcanic layers may be dated by estimating the time it look to lay down the intervening strata. As

FIGURE A-3 Different chronometric dating methods and their limitations as to the extent of time these methods can usefully date objects or material. For example, radiocarbon (C14) is useful as a chronometric method only back as far as 40,000 years ago, whereas potassium-argon (K/Ar) has the potential to date material related to the origins of the earth, about 4.5 billion years ago.

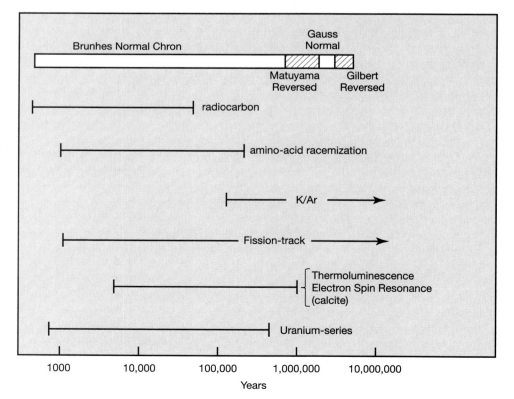

stratigraphic distance increases, dating accuracy depends on an accurate assessment of sedimentation rate. Luckily, the East African fossil record occurs in a region that was active volcanically, and that volcanic material, which consists of ash and lava flows, punctuates the stratigraphic sequences that have yielded the fossil remains. In contrast, australopithecine fossils from South Africa are only known from cave deposits devoid of volcanic material. Thus, these are poorly dated.

Uranium-series dating. Uranium-series dating comprises several different methods, all relying on the build up or decay of one or more of the radioactive daughter isotopes of uranium. Because of the length of the half-life of many of these isotopes, only one method of radioactive decay, 230Th/234U, has contributed substantially to paleoanthropological dating. 234U has a half-life of 245,000 years and 230Th has a half-life of 75,000 years. Uranium (U), unlike thorium (Th), is highly soluble in water; as a result, precipitated minerals, such as calcium carbonate, contain significant amounts of uranium but no thorium. Over approximately 300,000 to 500,000 years, radioactive decay causes 234U to change to 230Th. Measurement of the relative abundance of each of these isotopes during this period provides a chronometric age of the sample. This method assumes that during the life of the sample it has not gained or lost uranium or thorium except by decay.

This method offers a high degree of precision and accuracy, because few other assumptions are needed to account for contributing sources of error that could affect a date. Fossils from the Chinese site of Danjing were dated at 550,000 years from associated carbonate flowstones. The main weakness of this method is the narrow range of suitable materials that can be used for dating. Carbonates from once-living organisms, such as mollusk shells, are unsuitable, because the initial uranium content is generally very low.

***Radiation damage dating methods* (trapped charge methods).** The three methods outlined here are all based on the spontaneous decay of a parent isotope that leaves some sort of structural damage in the host material. The **fission-track dating** method uses the decay of 238U by fission into daughter isotopes of variable mass that leaves "tracks," or trails, of structural damage in its mineral host. Fission tracks may be erased over time, particularly if the material is heated. The long half-life of 238U of 8.2×10^{15} years (8.22 quadrillion years) requires large concentrations of uranium in order to generate track densities that can be counted reliably. This requirement is met in such minerals as zircon and volcanic glass. Many problems arise in the counting process, however, such as subjectivity in being able to recognize tracks from fission events of other decays, such as those that involve another isotope of uranium, 235U. For high-precision geochronology, the fission track method is rarely the method of choice, because most of the applicable materials that can be dated by this method are volcanic rocks that can be dated by 40Ar/39Ar methods. Fission track can provide corroborative dates that are used to resolve a dispute, such as the one that was generated over the age of the KBS tuff at Koobi Fora. In this case the fission-track date supported the more recent date of the tuff of 1.9 million years.

Luminescence dating relies on the measurement of light emitted from the crystal defects when material is heated (*thermoluminescence*) or stimulated using infrared or visible light. The zero age time of the material is taken to be when the material was last strongly heated. This might be when a piece of pottery was fired or when volcanic action produced an ash. The age range of this method, depending on the material used, is from 10,000 to several hundreds of thousands of years. There are multiple problems involving the luminescence method, such as the incomplete emptying of the luminescence centers of trapped electrons on heating the material, which makes it a method of low precision and has an error of ± 10 percent. This

uranium-series dating: decay of thorium 230 to uranium 234 is the most useful of all the uranium radioactive decays in paleoanthropological studies because of the half-life of thorium 230 of 245,000 years. The measure of the ratio of these two radioactive isotopes in material, such as shell, determines the age of the material.

radiation damage dating methods: methods that can rely on the effects of natural radiation on objects over time to dislodge electrons from their normal orbits in atoms. In different ways, either directly or indirectly, the number of dislodged electrons are measured, and with the assumption that the larger this number of dislodged electrons is the older the object is, thus, a determination of the age of the object can be made.

fission-track dating: radiation damage dating method that relies on the effects of radioactive decay of uranium 238 found within certain minerals of different daughter isotopes. The decay of uranium leaves "tracks," or trails, of structural damage in the host material. The greater the number of these tracks, the older the material is.

luminescence dating: chronometric dating by measuring the amount of light (luminescence) that is emitted from an object, such as pottery, after it has been heated. Heating the object will release trapped electrons present as the result of exposure to external radiation from impurities in the material. The greater the luminescence, the older the object.

method also removes the age information from the sample, so that a procedure can only be performed once (Feathers, 1996).

Electron spin resonance (ESR) dating is similar in concept to luminescence dating except that it extends to older ages (up to 1 million years) and has other methodological advantages. An ESR measurement, unlike a luminescence measurement, may be performed repeatedly on the same sample. Ikeya first applied ESR spectrometry as a dating method in 1975. The method allows age estimates of minerals that have been precipitated, such as those found in tooth enamel. The basis for ESR dating is that a sample records all of the radioactivity from the time it is formed until the time that it is measured. After the death of the animal, its teeth may be buried, at which time the tooth enamel starts to record the radioactivity of the environment that surrounds it. These radioactive elements emit high-energy particles and rays that damage the material with which they interact. Radiation knocks off negatively charged electrons from atoms, changing them from a ground state to a higher-energy state. This leaves positively charged "holes" in the ground state, which, after a short time, are refilled by electrons returning to the ground state. Because all minerals contain impurities that can trap electrons, however, some do not return to their ground state, and these can be measured, either by heating the mineral or by ESR spectroscopy. The number of trapped electrons in the mineral is, in part, a result of the duration of radiation exposure and, thus, of age (Grun, 1993).

The advantage of ESR dating is that a wide variety of materials can be used, including shells, burnt flint artifacts, teeth, and bone. Because of many uncertainties, including estimating radiation dose and buildup of the ESR signal with dose, however, the method by itself is not highly precise; errors are common in the range of 15 to 30 percent. By obtaining corresponding dates using the 230Th/U method that could validate the uranium-uptake history assumed for the ESR dates of the same material, one can add precision to the date determined by ESR. This strategy was successfully used by McDermott and colleagues (1993) to validate ESR dates of several Israeli sites that contain Neandertal and early-modern hominid fossils.

electron spin resonance (ESR) dating: after the death of an individual, the enamel in the teeth records the radioactivity of the deposit in which they are buried. Electrons of atoms in the enamel may be dislodged from their orbits by radioactivity and trapped in "holes" or impurities found in the enamel. The number of trapped electrons, which increase at a steady rate, determines the age of the specimen.

GLOSSARY

A1: chronometric dating of the age of an object, such as carbon-14 dating of bone or charcoal.

A2: chronometric dating of the age of the deposit in which an object is determined to be contemporaneous, such as K/Ar dating of volcanic material near or in which an object is found. For example, *Homo habilis* is thought to be about 1.8 million years old, because it is found in Bed I Olduvai Gorge dated to that age by K/Ar dating.

A3: chronometric dating of the age of a correlated deposit to a deposit in which an object is found.

A4: chronometric dating of the age of a deposit, such as one from a deep sea core that can be related in some manner to a terrestrial deposit in which an object is found.

ABO blood group: blood group system discovered by Landsteiner in 1900 defined by agglutination (clotting) reactions of red blood cells to natural anti-A and anti-B antibodies. Blood type A reacts to only anti-A, type B reacts only to anti-B, type AB reacts to both, and type O reacts to neither.

acclimation: physiological adaptation over a period from minutes to weeks.

acclimatization: physiological adaptation over a period from weeks to years that may have some morphological effect, but that is not passed on genetically.

Acheulean: stone tool culture characterized by hand axes, flaked on two sides, thus termed *bifaces*.

adapoids: lemurlike fossil prosimians of the Eocene age.

adaptability: range of physiological and anatomical changes and adjustments allowed by a species' adaptation.

adaptability: the range of physiological and behavioral responses that an individual can make to adjust to environmental changes.

adaptation: biological change effected by evolution to accommodate populations to different environmental conditions.

adolescence: period of growth between puberty and the attainment of full adult stature.

adulthood: period from after the eruption of the last permanent teeth to death.

agonistic: behavior that appears in aggressive encounters.

allele: alternate form of a gene.

allopatric speciation: formation of new species over time as a result of geographic isolation between members of an original single species.

allopatric: two species or populations that live in distinct geographical ranges that do not overlap. Contact at the boundaries of two population may result in the formation of hybrid groups.

amniote egg: an egg characteristic of the reptiles that could be laid and developed out of water.

Amphibia: vertebrate class that includes frogs, salamanders, and extinct species living much of their lives on land but whose reproduction remains tied to water.

analogy: two characters are similar because of adaptation for similar functions.

anthropoids: "higher" primates, including monkeys, apes, and humans.

anthropology: the study of humankind.

anthropometry: the techniques of physical anthropologists used to measure the human body.

apomorphy: in cladistic terminology, a newly arisen or derived trait used in systematics.

applied biological anthropology: use of the method and theory of biological anthropology to solve problems or address questions of practical significance.

appositional growth: growth by adding of layers at a specific point or plane.

archaeology: the anthropological study of past cultures, their social adaptations, and their lifeways by use of preserved artifacts and features.

Ardipithecus ramidus: the most primitive species of hominid presently known, dating 4 million to 4.2 million years ago from Aramis, Middle Awash, Ethiopia.

assort: the independent separation of pairs of genes on one chromosome from pairs of genes on other chromosomes; also known as Mendel's Second Law of Independent Assortment.

Australopithecines: small-brained, bipedal members of an early genus of the family Hominidae; flourished from the early Pliocene (about 4 million years ago) to early Pleistocene (1 million years ago) and was replaced by members of the genus *Homo*.

Australopithecus aethiopicus: earlier form of robust australopithecines in East Africa dated from 2.6 million to 2.3 million years ago; most famous representative is the Black Skull discovered in 1986 at a site on the western shores of Lake Turkana.

Australopithecus afarensis: gracile species of *Australopithecus* found at sites in East Africa and dated from 4 million to 2.5 million years ago; most famous representatives of this taxon are "Lucy" from Hadar, Ethiopia, and the Laetoli footprints in Tanzania.

Australopithecus africanus: the first species of *Australopithecus* to be named, based on the type of the Taung child; characterized by humanlike dentition and relatively gracile skull morphology, the species dates to between about 3 million and 2.5 million years ago; represented at other sites in South Africa, and probably also in East Africa.

Australopithecus anamensis: new species of *Australopithecus* discovered at two sites around Lake Turkana, described in 1995 by Meave Leakey and Alan Walker, and dated to 4.0 million years ago.

Australopithecus boisei: robust australopithecines found at site in East Africa and dated from 2.4 million to 1.3 million years ago; most famous representatives were found at Olduvai Gorge (*Zinjanthropus*) and East Lake Turkana.

Australopithecus robustus: robust australopithecines found in cave deposits from South Africa and dated from 2 million to 1 million years ago; most famous representatives were found at the site of Swartkrans, South Africa.

autosomes: referring to chromosomes other than the sex (X and Y) chromosomes.

basal ganglia: structures in the forebrain of vertebrates that form part of the R-Complex.

basicranial flexion: the hinging of the base of the skull and the hard palate together to form a more acute angle; seen in both australopithecine lineages.

behavior: patterns of animal activity over time.

bilharzia: infection by the parasitic blood fluke *Schistosoma,* which lays its eggs in the liver; leads to liver and occasionally kidney damage; also known as *schistosomiasis.*

bilirubin: a bile pigment from the liver that results from the breakdown of hemoglobin in red blood cells; bilirubin normally circulates in the blood in a complex with albumin but can increase in certain pathological conditions such as hepatitis.

bilophodont: two-lophed tooth. Characteristic occlusal surface pattern of Old World monkeys where the mesial two cusps and the distal two cusps, respectively, are each connected by a loph.

bimaturism: phenomenon of physically distinct morphs of adult males, males that have developed the full set of secondary sex characteristics and those that have not.

biological anthropology: the study of human evolution, biology, variation, and adaptation (also known as physical anthropology).

biostratigraphy: establishing a sequence through time of faunal units ("zones"), which are characterized by the presence of specific fossil species.

blades: elongated pieces of stone, parallel-sided and at least twice as long as they are wide, struck off a specifically prepared core.

blending inheritance: the mixing in equal halves of the contributions of parents in their offspring.

bonobo: *Pan paniscus,* a species (?) of chimpanzee distinct in some morphological ways, but not reproductively isolated, from the common chimpanzee, *Pan troglodytes,* and living in a different, nonoverlapping range—the Central Congo (formerly Zaire) forest basin; also termed the "pygmy chimpanzee."

brachiation: arboreal locomotion in the apes where progression below branches is accomplished by using elongated forelimbs only; "arm-swinging."

Broca's area: portion of the cerebral cortex (posterior part of the inferior frontal gyrus, usually on the left side) that is essential for the motor control of speech.

bunodont: the surface or occlusal anatomy of the cheek teeth where the cusps are rounded in shape and low in height.

Callitrichinae: subfamily of marmosets and tamarins.

canalization: regulatory forces that hold the processes of development in predetermined channels.

cartilage bone: bone formed by development from cartilage and growth at epiphyses, characteristic of vertebrate limb bones.

cartilage: supporting tissue more elastic and flexible than bone (e.g., the "gristle" in meat).

catarrhines: primates of the Old World, including monkeys, apes, and humans.

catastrophism: theory that earth history is explicable in terms of violent and sudden cataclysms that destroyed most living species, after which a new set of creations established new species.

CCR5: specific receptor site found on CD4 cells; receptor sites are surface features on cell membranes where different chemical substances bind.

CD4 cells: regulatory or "helper" T-cells; assist in the production of antibodies or in the action of the "killer" CD8 cells.

CD8 lymphocytes: one of two classes of T-cells within the immune system; the primary job of the CD8 cell is to kill foreign substances such as virusus, thus the label "killer" T-cells.

Cebidae: family of New World monkeys.

Cercopithecines: subfamily of Old World monkeys with generally omnivorous or graminivorous diets.

cerumen: ear wax; a waxy or dry secretion of glands located in the external ear canal.

childhood: period of growth from weaning to the attainment of adult brain size.

cholera: infectious disease caused by the bacterium *Vibrio cholerae* and spread usually by contaminated drinking water; symptoms include severe diarrhea, dehydration, shock, and kidney failure.

chordates: animals with a notochord and a dorsal nerve cord.

chromosomes: structures composed of folded DNA found in the nuclei of the cells of eukaryotic organisms.

chronometric: "measurement of time," establishment by a variety of methods of the age of an object or site in years before present. For example, by K/Ar dating, the age of Bed I Olduvai Gorge is 1.8 million years.

cingulum: a "belt" (from Latin), referring to a raised ridge of enamel encircling a tooth crown.

cladistics: the common term for the study of the phylogenetic relationships among a group of related animals by reference to only derived traits shared in common.

cladogram: branching diagram showing relative relationships among taxonomic groups of animals; not to be confused with a phylogenetic tree, which postulates ancestor–descendant relationships.

cline: a gradient of genotypes or phenotypes over a geographic range.

codons: three-unit bases of DNA that code for one of 20 amino acids or that code for a stop or termination of translation of that particular segment of DNA.

collector bias: the selection choices that an individual makes in assembling a collection of specimens.

colobines: subfamily of Old World monkeys, leaf-eating and mostly arboreal.

communication: transmission of information by sensory means.

consort relationships: pairing off of a female and male for the purposes of mating.

convergence: the evolution of similar traits in two distantly related animals, such as similar streamlined body form for swimming in dolphins and sharks.

corpus callosum: the fiber tract connecting across the midline the right and left hemispheres of the brain.

Cro-Magnon: cave site in southern France where late Pleistocene anatomically modern humans were first found.

crossing-over: the exchange of genes between paired chromosomes during cell duplication.

cultural anthropology: the anthropological study of human societies, their belief systems, their cultural adaptations, and their social behavior.

culture: learned aspects of behavior passed on from one generation to the next in human societies.

cut marks: incisions left on bone as a by-product of skinning or cutting muscle off the bone with stone tools; uniquely characteristic of hominids but sometimes difficult to distinguish from carnivore bite marks or scratch marks made by sand grains.

cystic fibrosis: hereditary disease of children and young adults affecting the lungs, pancreas, and other exocrine glands.

deduction: inferring conclusions about particular instances from general or universal premises.

deductive reasoning: the process whereby observed facts are gathered and then explained by a plausible hypothesis.

development: embryological differentiation of organs and tissues; sometimes considered the earliest stage of growth.

diploid: having two sets of chromosomes, as normally found in the somatic cells of higher organisms.

directional selection: selection that acts to move the mean of a population in one particular direction.

disc-core: important technique used extensively by Neandertals; involves trimming stone cores around the edges to produce disc-shaped cores from which flakes could be knocked off the edges to produce tools.

Discordance Hypothesis: theory that human biology and behavior, as shaped by evolution, are at odds with modern human environments.

diverticulitis: inflammation of an outpocketing of the wall of the large intestine.

DNA hybridization: method of assessing genetic relationships by splitting and "reannealing" strands of DNA from different species.

DNA: double-chain molecule that contains the genetic code.

dominance rank: the relative hierarchical position of an individual in a social group.

dryopithecid: family of middle Miocene hominoids found mostly in Europe.

Early Divergence Hypothesis: hypothesis that postulates an ancient evolutionary split (more than 15 million years ago) of African apes and humans from a common ancestor.

eccrine or sweat glands: glands that excrete a watery liquid over much of the surface area of the head, face, neck, and body during heat stress.

ecological niche: the ecological space to which a species is adapted, including its habitat, diet, and behavior.

ecology: the science that studies the biological relationships between species and their environment.

effective population size: a measure of the number of individuals of reproductive age in a population and the variance in the number of gametes that each individual produces.

electron spin resonance (ESR) dating: after the death of an individual the enamel in the teeth records the radioactivity of the deposit in which they are buried. Electrons of atoms in the enamel may be dislodged from their orbits by radioactivity and trapped in "holes" or impurities found in the enamel. The number of trapped electrons, which increase at a steady rate, determines the age of the specimen.

embryonic: that period of growth prior to birth, especially weeks three through eight; growth during the last six months of gestation is sometimes referred to as fetal growth.

encephalization: the process of extreme brain enlargement in the *Homo* lineage.

endocast: three-dimensional replica of the inside of the brain case, revealing what the exterior of the brain would have looked like.

endocranial volume: synonymous with cranial capacity; the amount of space inside the skull, occupied in life by the brain and brain coverings.

endothermy: the maintenance of constant body temperature; "warm-blooded."

enzymes: polypeptides that catalyze or accelerate chemical reactions.

epidemiology: study of the geographic distribution, spread, and control of disease.

epistasis: gene masking the effect of a nonallelic gene.

estrus: the period within the female reproductive cycle that usually corresponds to ovulation and where the female may engage in sexual activity.

ethnocentrism: the pervasive belief present in all cultures that leads individuals to view their own culture as superior to others.

ethology: the biological study of animal behavior that deals with species-specific or genetically linked behavior.

eukaryotes: organisms that have a nucleus containing DNA in their cells.

evolution by natural selection: Darwin and Wallace's theory that inherited variability results in the differential survival of individuals and in their ability to contribute to offspring in succeeding generations.

evolutionary medicine: the application of evolutionary principles and deductions from biological anthropology to the practice of medicine; also termed *Darwinian medicine*.

exon: the expressed segment of a gene, separated from other exons by introns.

exoskeleton: hard and inflexible outer covering of the body of invertebrate animals, such as insects and crustaceans.

family: a taxonomic grouping of similar genera.

feedback system: in information theory, the concept that change in one step of a loop will affect a subsequent step that will in turn affect the starting point.

fever: elevation of body temperature above normal; in disease, caused by the body's reaction to infection by microorganisms.

fibrinopeptide: blood protein related to blood clotting.

field studies: in primatology, studies of species in their natural habitat, uninfluenced or influenced to a minor degree by interactions with humans.

fission-track dating: radiation damage dating method that relies on the effects of radioactive decay of uranium 238 found within certain minerals of different daughter isotopes. The decay of uranium leaves "tracks," or trails, of structural damage in the host material. The greater the number of these tracks, the older the material is.

fitness: the extent to which the genes of an individual survive in its descendants.

fixed action pattern (FAP): behaviors that are form-constant; appear spontaneously during development; are characteristic of all members of the species; cannot be unlearned; and are released or caused by a particular stimulus, external environmental condition or internal physiological environment, of the animal.

foraging strategies: behavior patterns that result in the discovery and procurement of food.

fossils: remains of animals and plants preserved in the ground.

founder effect: type of genetic drift caused by sampling a small amount of genetic variation from the original population in a group of individuals colonizing a new area.

free radicals: highly reactive "active" molecules of oxygen (mainly O_2^-) formed from the breakdown of oxygen molecules in the body.

fusion-fission social organization: social organization based on formation and dissolution of groups.

G6PD: glucose-6-phosphate dehydrogenase, an enzyme necessary for red blood cell metabolism; G6PD deficiency is caused by recessive genes and can result in the disease favism.

game theory: the analysis of win–loss combinations in any competitive relationship in order to determine strategy or to predict outcomes of the competition.

genes: units of the material of inheritance, now known to be sequences of DNA.

genetic drift: allele frequency changes caused by chance effects, not affected by selection; most common in small population sizes.

genetic markers: traits whose genetic causation are known and which can be used in the study of populations.

genetic mutation: heritable change in the genetic material, located in the sex cells, that brings about a change in phenotype.

genetic plasticity: ability of a developing organism to alter its form and function in conformity with demands of the immediate environment.

genetic polymorphism: the existence of two or more genetic variants within a population; can be a **balanced polymorphism** when selection favors the heterozygotes, as in sickle-cell anemia.

genetics: the study of heredity and variation.

genotype: the genetic composition of an organism, as compared to phenotype, the manifestation of its genes.

genus: a taxonomic grouping of similar species.

globin: a protein of hemoglobin that is found inside red blood cells.

grade: level of organization or morphological complexity in an evolving lineage of organisms.

grooming behavior: slow systematic picking through the hair of another individual to remove foreign matter; important in primate social interactions.

habituation: neurophysiological mechanism for "tuning out" unwanted stimuli, an accommodation that takes only a few minutes.

Hadar: hominid site in northern Ethiopia dating to between 3 million and 3.4 million years ago.

hafting striations: marks indicating attachment of stone tools to wooden shafts.

half-life: the time it takes for any radioactive substance (isotope) to decay to half of its original amount. For example, it takes 5,730 years for any amount of carbon-14 to decay to one-half of that amount.

haploid: having a single set of chromosomes, as found in the sex cells or gametes of higher organisms.

haplorhines: taxonomic grouping that includes the living tarsiers and their direct ancestors.

Hardy-Weinberg equilibrium: hypothetical condition in which there is no selection or other forces of evolution acting on a population and in which gene and genotype frequencies stay the same from one generation to the next. For two alleles at one locus, alleles p + alleles $q = 100\%$.

harem species: in primatology, species characterized by social groupings of one dominant male and a number of females and their young.

hemolytic incompatibility: destruction of red blood cells caused by the action of antibodies, resulting in release of hemoglobin into the plasma.

heterochrony: Greek, meaning "different time"; refers to the changes in rate of growth characteristic of species' evolutionary divergence from an ancestral species.

heterodonty: the condition of possessing teeth differentiated for different functions; contrasted with the homodont dentition of many reptiles, such as living crocodiles.

heterozygous: bearing two different alleles at a genetic locus.

histocompatibilty: immunologic similarity or identity of tissues; used in referring to tissues appropriate for grafting in medical procedures.

HLA: human lymphocycte antigen system; a white blood cell antigen system important in the immune response.

holotype: the single specimen on which a taxonomic name is based.

home range: the area that a group or population inhabits and ranges over, the boundaries of which, unlike a territory, are not defended.

Hominidae: the zoological family in which humans and their more recent fossil antecedents are classified; bipedal hominoids with increased brain-to-body-size ratio.

Hominidae: the zoological family to which living humans and their bipedal relatives, all now extinct, belong.

hominoids: modern apes, modern humans, and their immediate ancestors.

hominoids: taxonomic superfamily to which the apes and people and their immediate ancestors belong.

Homo erectus: primitive species of the genus *Homo,* generally considered to have evolved from *Homo habilis* and to be the ancestor of *Homo sapiens.*

Homo habilis: earliest generally recognized species of the genus *Homo.*

Homo sapiens: species that includes modern humans as well as archaic *Homo sapiens.*

homologous: similar because of common descent or common inheritance.

homoplasty: similarity of two characters because of parallel evolution (adaptation to similar environments) without a common ancestor.

homozygous: bearing two identical alleles at a genetic locus.

hormone: a chemical substance produced by an organ or structure of the body that acts on or affects another distinct organ or structure.

human biology: the branch of biological anthropology that studies human physiology and adaptation.

Hybridization Model: evolutionary hypothesis that suggests interbreeding between emigrant African populations and resident human populations in other parts of the world.

hypertension: persistently high blood pressure; above 140 mm Hg systolic (contraction) and 90 mm Hg diastolic (dilation) pressures of the heart.

hypothalamus: part of the ancient forebrain; located below the thalamus at the base of the brain's third ventricle; important in autonomic nervous system functions, such as endocrine gland activity.

hypothesis: an explanation of a set of observations that can be disproved or falsified by additional observations or facts.

hypoxia: condition of reduced oxygen supply to tissues despite adequate blood supply.

imitative: relating to information gained through observing other individuals and not through one's own experience.

imprinting: the fixation in an individual of a specific stimulus or set of stimuli during a particular period of sensitivity to learning that stimulus.

inbreeding: the increased incidence of mating within a population that results in an increase in homozygosity within the population.

inclusive fitness: the sum of an individual's reproductive success and that of its relatives, in proportion to their percentage of shared genes.

inductive scientific method: inferring a generalized conclusion from particular instances.

infancy: earliest stage of postpartum growth, extending from birth to the time of first permanent molars.

infanticide: killing of infants.

innate releasing mechanism: a sensory cue that triggers a certain behavior or set of behaviors in an animal.

intelligence quotient: a score on a standardized psychological test designed in Western Europe and North America to measure an individual's aggregate capacity to act purposefully, think rationally, and deal effectively with the environment.

interstitial growth: growth by new cell formation throughout the mass of a structure, tissue, or organ.

intron: noncoding sequence of DNA that is not transcribed by the m-RNA.

ischial callosity: the callused pads that cover the ischial tuberosity in all Old World monkeys and gibbons. This pad is used primarily for sitting for long periods usually while the animal sleeps.

juvenile: period of growth between eruption of first and last permanent teeth.

karyotype: identified and numbered arrangement of chromosomes.

knuckle walking: a unique form of quadrupedal locomotion observed only in the African apes. Specialized anatomical adaptations in the wrist and hand allow the upper body weight to be supported on the dorsal surface of the middle phalanges while the rest of the weight is supported by the plantar surfaces of the feet.

laboratory studies: in primatology, controlled studies of captive primates.

labyrinthodonts: extinct, predatory amphibians of the Carboniferous period, some of whom were ancestral to the first reptiles.

lactation: in mammals the period following birth of offspring, during which time the offspring receive breast milk from the mother.

Laetoli: a site in northern Tanzania, south of Olduvai Gorge, where hominids were first found in the 1930s and again in the 1970s; dated to between 3.6 million and 3.8 million years ago.

Lake Turkana: hominid sites on both the east and west sides of Lake Turkana (formerly Lake Rudolf), closely associated with Omo and dating to between 4 million and 1.4 million years ago.

laryngeal sacs: the larynx or "voice box" is expanded, creating a resonating chamber used in the production of loud vocalizations. Characteristic of howler monkeys of South America, and the siamangs and orangutans of Southeast Asia.

Late Divergence Hypothesis: a hypothesis that postulates a recent evolutionary split (5 million to less than 15 million years ago) of the African apes and humans from a common ancestor.

learn: to remember information or an experience and retain for use in future behavior.

Levallois technique: technique marking great improvement in stone tool technology; tools were made from flakes rather than by shaping heavy cores.

life history strategies: behavioral decisions that each animal in a species must make to acquire food, avoid predators, and find mates. These decisions may increase inclusive fitness and, thus, vary the reproductive success of different individuals.

limbic system: an adaptation of the primarily olfactory part of the forebrain, important in sexual and maternal behavior.

linguistics: the anthropological study of languages, their diversity and connections, and the interaction of language and culture in society.

linkage: the tendency of genes to be inherited together because of their location and proximity to one another on one chromosome.

locomotion: means of moving about.

locus: a "place" on a chromosome or segment of DNA where a gene is located.

longitudinal arch: the upwardly arched structure composed of bones and connecting ligaments on the medial side of the human foot.

loph: a crest of enamel on the occlusal surface of the dentition.

Lower Paleolithic: period that featured Oldowan choppers and flakes and Acheulean tools, such as the hand ax.

luminescence dating: chronometric dating by measuring the amount of light (luminescence) that is emitted from an object, such as pottery, after it has been heated. Heating the object will release trapped electrons present as the result of exposure to external radiation from impurities in the material. The greater the luminescence, the older the object.

macroevolution: large-scale change at the level of new species, genera, and higher-level taxa.

malaria: from the Italian, meaning "bad air," from the original, mistaken belief that the disease was air borne; often fatal disease caused by a protozoan infecting the red blood cells and transmitted from one carrier to another by the bite of a female *Anopheles* mosquito; symptoms include chills, sweating, fever, vomiting, diarrhea, and convulsions.

mandible: the lower jaw of mammals, composed of a fusion of the reptile dentary and articular bones.

marsupials: pouched mammals.

megadont: "large-toothed," referring to the relatively large molars of hominids.

meiosis: the process whereby eukaryote sex cells halve their DNA for combination with the sex cells of another individual.

melanin: from the Greek, meaning "black"; a dark brown or black pigment that occurs in the skin, eyes, and hair.

membrane bone: bone formed by development from a connective tissue membrane, characteristic of vertebrate skull bones.

meniscus: from the Latin, meaning "lens"; the cartilage rimming the articular surface of the tibia at the knee joint and which forms a basin for the articular end of the femur.

menstruation: monthly, cyclic shedding of the lining of the uterus by nonpregnant female primates, particularly noticeable in humans.

metabolic rate: the rate at which energy is expended in all the chemical reactions in an animal's cells and tissues.

methanethiol: a chemical breakdown product of asparagus with a detectable odor, excreted in urine by carriers who possess the dominant allele.

microevolution: small-scale, within-species evolutionary change.

microfauna: the smallest members of a fauna, commonly small mammals, such as rodents, insectivores, and prosimian primates.

Middle Paleolithic: roughly comparable to the Middle Stone Age of African prehistory, featuring technological inventions; about 200,000 to 30,000 years ago.

midfacial prognathism: forward projection of the bony nose region of the skull; characteristic of Neandertals.

migration: the movement of a reproductively active individual into a population from a distant population, thus bringing new genes into that population.

mitochondria: organelles within the cell with their own DNA that carry on energy metabolism for the cell.

mitochondrial DNA: the DNA within the mitochondria, abbreviated as mtDNA; mtDNA evolves approximately 10 times faster than the DNA in the cell nucleus.

mitosis: the replication of the DNA during splitting of a cell and migration of each duplicated portion to a new cell.

monogamous: referring to one male–one female pair bonding.

monogenism: in the history of anthropology, relating to a single or unitary origin of the human species, connoting that all human populations were part of one species; an early point of agreement between the Church and Darwinism.

morphology: the study of the form and anatomy of physical structures in the bodies of living or once living organisms.

motor cortex: the part of the cerebral cortex located in the precentral gyrus that controls voluntary movements of the body.

Mousterian: a Middle Paleolithic stone tool culture characterized by prepared flakes struck off a core; about 250,000 to 40,000 years ago.

multimale groups: in reference to primate social organization, groups of primates where a number of males of various dominance rank live together in the same group.

Multiregional Model: evolutionary hypothesis that suggests primary continuity from earlier to later human populations in each area of the world, with some gene exchange between populations.

muscles of mastication: muscles of the jaw, primarily the temporalis and masseter, that provide the power in chewing.

mutation: any novel genetic change that may affect both genes and chromosomes. Such changes are spontaneous and random in occurrence. Mutations are the source of all variability in populations, and, if they occur in the sex cells usually during the formation of gametes, they hold the possibility of altering the phenotypes in succeeding generations.

natal residents: residents of a group that were born in the group.

natural selection: the process of differential reproduction whereby individuals who are well adapted to their environment will be "favored," that is, they will pass on more of their heritable attributes to the next generation than other, less well-adapted individuals.

naturalistic fieldwork: the study of primates in their natural environment.

Neandertal: hominid-fossil-bearing cave site in Germany. Fossils representing a late Pleistocene human population in Europe and parts of the Middle East were first used to define the taxon *Homo sapiens neanderthalensis*.

negative assortative mating: individuals who bear little resemblance to one another mate more frequently than would be expected by chance.

neocortex: the evolutionary "new" part of the cerebral cortex, characteristic of mammals.

neo-Darwinism: the combined theory of evolution by natural selection and modern genetics.

neurocranium: that part of the skull holding the brain.

neutral mutation: mutation that is not acted on by selection; it does not affect the fitness of an organism in a particular environment. Neutral mutations accumulate at a more or less constant rate over time.

observational learning: learning by seeing and hearing.

occipital torus: a horizontal raised ridge of bone at the back of the *Homo erectus* skull.

old age: subperiod of adulthood typified by a greater rate of cell death than replacement.

Oldowan: earliest recognized stone tool tradition associated with the first members of the genus *Homo*. Also called Mode I tools.

Olduvai Gorge: a site in northern Tanzania yielding remains of robust australopithecines and early *Homo*.

oligopithecids: Oligocene anthropoids whose affinities to later hominoid primates remains obscure.

Omo: a site in southern Ethiopia along the lower Omo River, with numerous hominids dating from about 3.4 million to 1 million years ago.

omomyoids: tarsierlike prosimians, among the earliest haplorhines of the Eocene age.

opposable thumb: a central primate characteristic that contributes to the prehensility of the hands and feet and the mode of locomotion, climbing by grasping.

optimal foraging theory: a predictive theory based on food-getting behavior selected to balance a group's needs to find food against the costs of getting it; involves subsistence strategizing; in terms of time and energy, foragers will make choices to maximize the highest feasible rate of return.

orthogenesis: mistaken view of evolutionary change always proceeding in a "straight-line," directed course.

ovulation: release of a mature egg cell from the female's ovary, after which it can be fertilized by a male sperm cell.

Out-of-Africa Model: evolutionary hypothesis that holds that modern humans evolved first in Africa and then spread out over the rest of the world, displacing or driving to extinction other populations.

paleoanthropology: the study of the physical characteristics, evolution, and behavior of fossil humans and their relatives, incorporating parts of biological anthropology and archaeology.

paleomagnetic dating: the matching of a sequence of strata with the dated pattern of changes in magnetic orientation through time, thereby dating the sediments.

paleomagnetism: past fluctuations preserved in rocks of the intensity and direction of the earth's magnetic field establish a relative sequence of the earth's normal and reversed epochs.

paradigm: a framework for understanding and interpreting observations.

parallelism: the evolution of similar traits in two closely related species, such as elongated hind legs for jumping in two small rodent species.

parapithecids: Oligocene anthropoids, the most primitive of the known species from Fayum, Egypt.

paratypes: a group of specimens on which a taxonomic name is based.

pedomorphosis: the retention of a juvenile stage in some part of a descendant species' morphology or behavior, in comparison with its ancestral species.

perineal: relating to the area between the anus and the external genitalia, the perineum.

peromorphosis: the extension of growth or "adultification" of some part of the morphology or behavior of a descendant species, in comparison with its ancestral species.

phenotype: an organism's appearance, a result of genetic and environmental factors.

pheromones: hormones that produce their effect by the sense of smell.

phyletic gradualism: term used to characterize Darwin's idea of evolutionary rate; slow, gradual change over long periods of time.

phylogeny: the study of evolutionary relationships of organisms.

pineal body: small cone-shaped part of the brain located below the corpus callosum; synthesizes the hormone melatonin, which is important in mediating estrus cycling in mammals; and reacts to ambient light in the environment.

pituitary gland: endocrine gland at the base of the cerebral cortex.

placentals: evolved mammals with very efficient reproductive systems, which include the placenta, a structure that provides the developing embryo with well-oxygenated blood and food, and that takes away carbon dioxide and waste.

placoderms: early fish with biting jaws.

platyrrhines: New World monkeys.

play: behavior that is not directed toward any clearly defined end result, such as food getting, and which is frequently characteristic of young mammals.

plesiadapiforms: archaic primates of the Paleocene and Early Eocene epochs (also called plesiadapoids).

pliopithecid: medium-size, folivorous hominoids known from the middle-late Miocene of Eurasia.

polygenic: a trait controlled by the interaction of genes at more than one locus.

polygenism: in the history of anthropology, relating to a multiple origin of the human species, connoting that different populations were different species; used by some to defend slavery and by others to justify colonial mistreatment of indigenous peoples.

polypeptide chain: a molecule consisting of a long chain of amino acids joined together by peptide bonds.

population: a geographically localized group of individuals in a species that more likely share a common gene pool among themselves than with other individuals in the species.

positive assortative mating: positive correlation between partners in some character. Individuals who resemble one another mate more frequently than would be expected by chance.

potassium-argon: radioactive decay of potassium 40 to the stable (nonradioactive) element argon. In volcanic material this decay can be measured and the age of the rock determined. Argon39/argon40 is a variant of this technique where the ratio of the amounts of these isotopes of argon are measured to determine the age of the volcanic rock that contains them.

potassium-argon method: dating technique pioneered by Garniss Curtis that measures the amount of radioactive potassium isotope (K^{40}) to its decay product, argon gas (Ar^{40}), found in rocks of volcanic origin.

predation rate: frequency of killing and eating of individuals of a prey species by predator species living in the same environment.

primate: the order of mammals that includes living and extinct monkeys, apes, and humans, as well as more primitive taxa.

primates: the zoological order of mammals that includes living and extinct monkeys, apes, and humans, as well as more primitive taxa.

primatologists: scientists who study primates, usually primate behavior and ecology.

principle of superposition: one of Charles Lyell's geological rules, holding that lower or deeper "rock" units in a sequence are older than "rock" units found higher up in the same sequence. For example, Bed I, Olduvai Gorge is supposedly older than Bed IV because of its position in the Olduvai sequence.

proconsulids: family of early Miocene hominids known mostly from sites in eastern Africa.

prognathic: forward jutting, as in the jaws of many primates, primarily as a result of large canine teeth.

prokaryotes: organisms such as bacteria that lack a differentiated cell nucleus.

promiscuity: sexual relations with a number of partners.

propliopithecids: the largest anthropoid (catarrhine) primates from the Oligocene of Egypt, sometimes considered the earliest hominoids.

prosimians: primates typified by small body size and frequently nocturnal adaptations in the living forms.

punctuated equilibrium: term coined by Stephen J. Gould and Niles Eldredge to characterize evolution typified by long periods of little or no change (stasis) interrupted by bursts of rapid change (punctuational events).

quantum evolution: term coined by George Gaylord Simpson to describe stepwise evolutionary change.

quantum theory of heredity: passing of traits as clear-cut quantifiable units not subject to subdivision; characteristic of Mendelian genetics.

racemization process: change in the ratio of D configuration to its mirror image, L, of various amino acids on the death of an organism. This conversion occurs at a steady rate and is affected mainly by the external temperatures to which the remains are subjected.

racism: a policy or opinion that unfairly generalizes real or perceived characteristics of a specific ethnic group, population, or "race" to every member of that group, and that may be used to deny resources or fair and equal treatment to an individual on the basis of membership in that group.

radiation damage dating methods: methods that can rely on the effects of natural radiation on objects over time to dislodge electrons from their normal orbits in atoms. In different ways, either directly or indirectly, the number of dislodged electrons are measured, and with the assumption that the larger this number of dislodged electrons is the older the object is, thus, a determination of the age of the object can be made.

radiocarbon dating: carbon-14 dating, a radioactive isotope of carbon that is formed in the atmosphere and is absorbed as carbon dioxide by living things until their death. The amount of carbon-14 remaining in the organic object since its death determines the object's age.

random mating: mate choice among individuals in a population without regard to phenotype or genotype (also known as panmixis).

R-Complex: the most primitive part of the triune brain model of Paul MacLean; the site that controls certain ritualistic, stereotypical, and social communication behaviors.

R1 date: determination that a fossil or artifact is contemporaneous with the sediments in which it is buried. The analysis of the florine content in bones buried together is one way to establish contemporaneity.

R2 date: determination of the relative age of a site in relation to its stratigraphic position in a local "rock" sequence (e.g., Bed I within the stratigraphy of Olduvai Gorge).

R3 date: determination of the relative age of a site in relation to its stratigraphic position in a regional "rock" sequence (e.g., the stratigraphic units of Olduvai Gorge within the framework of stratigraphy of East Africa).

R4 date: establishing the relative age of a fossil or artifact by its appearance (morphology) in comparison to similar fossils or artifacts of known age from established relative sequences.

relative framework: relative dating; using comparative methods, such as stratigraphic position or fauna, to determine whether a fossil, artifact, or site is younger or older than other fossils, artifacts, or sites.

replication: a duplication process requiring copying from a template, in this case the DNA molecule.

reproductive fitness: relative reproductive success of certain individuals over others as measured by survival of offspring into adulthood in a particular environment; the ability of one genotype to produce more offspring relative to this ability in other genotypes in the same environment.

retromolar space: gap to be seen between the last upper molar and the ascending ramus of the mandible when articulated with the skull.

Rh blood group: a complex system of blood antigens originally discovered by Landsteiner and Weiner in 1940 using blood from the rhesus monkey, which lent the first two letters of its name to the system. Rh antigens are controlled by a number of different alleles yielding many different phenotypes.

rickets: from the Old English, meaning "twisted," a disease caused by deficiency of calcium and characterized by the symptoms of poor calcification of bones, skeletal deformities, disturbance of growth, and generalized muscular weakness.

RNA: ribonucleic acid, a molecule similar to DNA except that uracil (U) replaces thymine (T) as one of its four bases; the hereditary material in some viruses, but in most organisms a molecule that helps translate the structure of DNA into the structure of protein molecules.

rock stratigraphy: "lithostratigraphy"; establishing a sequence through time of sedimentary, volcanic, or other units characterized by their geological consistency (e.g., Bed I, as a rock unit within the Olduvai Gorge stratigraphic sequence). Rock units may be described in a hierarchical manner from larger to smaller, such as formation, member, bed.

sagittal crest: crest of bone that develops as some large primates, as well as other mammals, age. The result of an ever-enlarging temporalis muscle that covers the walls of small braincases.

sagittal keel: a low, rounded elevation of bone along the midline of the top of the *Homo erectus* skull.

sarcopterygians: lobe-finned fish capable of some support of the body on land.

sectorial: literally "cutting," first lower premolar of apes and some monkeys, a unicuspid tooth whose forward edge shears against the back edge of the occluding upper canine, honing it to sharpness.

secular trends: trends in growth or morphological characteristics that are attributable to changing environmental factors, such as nutrition and disease, and not to genetic adaptation.

segregation: the separation of recessive and dominant alleles during reproduction, allowing maintenance of their separate identities and later full expression of their traits; sometimes referred to as Mendel's First Law of Segregation.

semi–free-ranging studies: in primatology, the study of primate groups that are in some way affected by or are dependent on humans, yet live more or less "normal" social lives.

sensory cortex: the part of the cerebral cortex located in the postcentral gyrus that senses touch, temperature, and pain on all parts of the body.

serum cholesterol: cholesterol is a lipid (fat), deriving from animal products in the diet, that when in high concentrations in the blood serum is associated with lesions and plaque buildup in arteries.

sexual dimorphism: the evolution of two sexes whose adult members can differ from one another substantially in their external morphology.

sexual reproduction: reproduction resulting from the exchange of genetic material between two parent organisms.

sexual selection: selection through male–male competition or female choice in which certain characteristics evolve that confer a reproductive advantage on the individual that possesses them.

sivapithecid: family of middle to late Miocene hominoids found mostly in Asia. Species of this group may be ancestral to the modern orangutan.

social behavior: actions and interactions of animals within groups.

sociobiology: evolutionary study of social behavior emphasizing relative reproductive success of individuals, including their inclusive fitness within a population.

socioecology: evolutionary study of social behavior emphasizing the adaptation of species to their environment and ecological conditions.

somatic mutation: nonheritable change in the genetic material of the cells of the body.

somatotropin: hormone of the anterior lobe of the pituitary that promotes body growth, fat mobilization, and inhibition of glucose utilization.

special creation: the nonevolutionary theory associated with catastrophism that held that totally new species, unrelated to prior species, were created after extinctions.

speciation: the splitting of one species into two or more species over time (cladogenesis) or the change of an earlier species in a lineage to a new, later one.

species: an actually or potentially interbreeding group of organisms in nature.

speech: the set of verbal sounds used by humans in language.

stereoscopic vision: the ability to perceive depth by virtue of the fact that the fields of vision of each eye partially overlap, thus giving the brain information sufficient to reconstruct an accurate impression of depth or distance.

sternal glands: scent-producing glands of the chest common in many prosimians and the anthropoids such as the orangutan. The scent is used in territorial display and marking.

stone artifacts: stones broken or flaked by hominids in order to be used as tools, or unmodified stones found in geological circumstances indicating that hominids carried them and placed them at a site.

strepsirhines: taxonomic grouping of lemurlike prosimians, both living and extinct.

subadult: sexually mature young adult male or female. Subadult males, unlike females, frequently range outside of a mixed sex social group, either independently or with others of their age and status.

subspecies: a geographically defined population within a species, the individuals of which tend to share certain physical and genetic traits but who are nevertheless infertile with other members of the species; a race.

Sudden Infant Death Syndrome: "crib death"; sudden and unexpected death of apparently healthy infants, usually between three weeks and five months of age.

suspensory: positional behavior; ability of hominoids to hang (from branches) using one or both fully extended forelimbs.

symbiosis: the theory that formerly free living primitive organisms came together to form a single organism capable of metabolism and reproduction as a unit.

sympatric speciation: formation of new species over time as a result of ecological isolation between members of an original single species who occupied the same ecosystem within their geographic range.

sympatric: two species or populations whose geographical home ranges overlap.

systematics: the science of classifying and organizing organisms.

taphonomy: the paleontological study of burial processes leading to the formation and preservation of fossils.

taxonomy: the science of naming different organisms.

tephrostratigraphy: establishing a relative sequence of volcanic events (by superposition) and determining the geochemical "fingerprint" of each volcanic eruption in a stratigraphic sequence. New volcanic material may be placed within the sequence based on its individual "fingerprint."

thalassemia: from the Greek, meaning "sea blood," in reference to the blood's dilute nature; genetic disorders affecting hemoglobin metabolism that can range from negligible clinical effects to fatal anemia.

theory: usually a set of hypotheses that withstands attempts at disproof and continues to successfully explain observations as they are made, thus gaining scientific support over time.

therapsid: mammal-like reptile with a skull opening behind the eye and with differentiated teeth.

thermoregulation: controlling the body's temperature by a number of physiological and behavioral means.

thrifty genotype: adaptation of storing "excess calories" as fat, and then burning them during periods of famine or scarcity of food.

thyroid hormone: also known as thyroxine, an iodine-containing hormone secreted by the thyroid gland and important in regulating the rate of tissue metabolism.

tissue: literally meaning "woven;" in anatomy referring to an aggregate of cells of the same type, which form a structural unit of the body.

total fertility rate (TFR): population-wide average number of children a woman who lives to the end of her reproductive years gives birth to and who survive to adulthood.

transcription: transfer of genetic information encoded in a DNA sequence to an RNA message.

transformation: incorporation of another cell's DNA into a cell's own DNA structure.

translation: synthesis of a polypeptide chain from an RNA genetic message.

triune brain: the division of the human brain by Paul MacLean into three broad divisions based on phylogenetic and functional patterns.

tuff: a geological deposit composed of volcanic ash.

typology: idealist definition of an entire group by reference to a type that tends to ignore variation from that ideal.

uniformitarianism: principle that processes observable today can account for past events in geological history.

Upper Paleolithic: a series of late Pleistocene cultures typified by a diversification of traditions and stone tools made from blades struck from cores; associated with anatomically modern humans; about 40,000 to 10,000 years ago.

uranium-series dating: decay of thorium 230 to uranium 234 is the most useful of all the uranium radioactive decays in paleoanthropological studies because of the half-life of thorium 230 of 245,000 years. The measure of the ratio of these two radioactive isotopes in material, such as shell, determines the age of the material.

variation: the range of differences in physical or genetic makeup across, within, and between populations of individuals of the same species.

vasoconstriction: the contraction of small blood vessels next to the skin's surface; a response to cold.

ventro-ventral position: two individuals facing each other with bodies in contact.

vertebrates: animals with backbones and segmented body plans.

vertical clinging: a type of posture and locomotion characteristic of many strepsirhines in which these primates, clinging to vertical supports, move by leaping between the supports.

vertical clinging and leaping: the method of locomotion characteristic of many living prosimians, and inferred to have been a method of locomotion in some early primates.

victoriapithecids: earliest fossil Old World monkeys of the Miocene, ancestral to later cercopithecids and colobines.

Wernicke's area: portion of the cerebral cortex (parts of the parietal and temporal lobes near the lateral sulcus, usually on the left) that is responsible for understanding and formulating coherent speech.

Y-5 pattern: cusp pattern on hominoid cheek teeth. Lower molars have an expanded talonid basin surrounded by five rounded cusps.

Zhoukoudian: middle Pleistocene cave site of *Homo erectus* near Beijing, China.

REFERENCES

Abbate, E., Albianelli, A., Azzaroli, A., Benvenuti, M., Tesfamarian, B., Bruni, P., Cipriani, N., et al. (1998). A one-million-year-old *Homo* cranium from the Danakil (Afar) depression of Eritrea. *Nature* **393**:458–460.

Abbie, A. A. (1977). Multidisciplinary studies on Australian Aborigines. In *Human Adaptability: A History and Compendium of Research in the International Biological Programme* (K. J. Collins and J. S. Weiner, eds.), pp. 37–39. Taylor and Francis, LTD., London.

Aiello, L. C., and Dunbar, R. I. M. (1993). Neocortex size, group size, and the evolution of language. *Curr. Anthropol.* **34**:184–193.

Aiello, L. C., and Wheeler, P. (1995). The expensive-tissue hypothesis. *Current Anthropol.* **36**:199–221.

Alexander, R. D. (1974). The evolution of social behavior. *Ann. Rev. Ecol. Syst.* **5**:324–384.

Algar, E. M., et al. (1992). Gastric ADH in the baboon: Purifications and properties of high K enzyme consistent with a role in first pass alcohol metabolism. *Alcoholism: Clin. Exp. Res.* **16**:922–927.

Allman, W. F. (1994). *The Stone Age Present.* Simon & Schuster, New York.

Almquist, H. J. (1969). The future of animals as food producers. *Proc. West. Poul. Dis. Conf.*, 18th, University of California, Davis, 1969.

Andrews, P. (1987). Aspects of hominoid phylogeny. In *Molecules and Morphology in Evolution: Conflict and Compromise* (C. Patterson, ed.), pp. 23–53. Cambridge Univ. Press, Cambridge, UK.

Andrews, P. (1995). Ecological apes and ancestors. *Nature (London)* **376**:555–556.

Andrews, P., and Cronin, J. E. (1982). The relationships of Sivapithecus and Ramapithecus and the evolution of the Orangutan. *Nature (London)* **297**:541–546.

Asfaw, B., White, T. D., Lovejoy, O. C., Latimer, B., Simpson, S., and Suwa, G. (1999) *Australopithecus garhi*: A new species of early hominid from Ethiopia. *Science* **284**:629–635.

Auel, J. (1980). *Clan of the Cave Bear.* Crown, New York.

Badrian, A., and Badrian, N. (1984). Group composition and social structure of Pan paniscus in the Lomako Forest, Zaire. In *The Pygmy Chimpanzee: Evolutionary Biology and Behavior* (R. Susman, ed.), pp. 325–346. Plenum, New York.

Bailey, R., Head, G., Jenike, M., Owen, B., Rechtmann, R., and Zechenter, E. (1989). Hunting and gathering in tropical rain forest: Is it possible? *Am. Anthropol.* **91**:59–82.

Bailey, R. C. (1991). The comparative growth of Efe pygmies and African farmers from birth to age 5 years. *Ann. Hum. Biol.* **18**:113–120.

Balter, M. (1999). New light on the oldest art. *Science* **283**:920–922.

Bartlett, T. Q. (2000). Range size and territoriality among white-handed gibbons (Hylobates lar) in Khao Yai National Park, Thailand. *Amer. J. Phys. Anthropol., Suppl.* **30**:103-104.

Bartlett, T. Q. (2001). Extra-group copulations by sub-adult gibbons: Implications for understanding gibbon social organization. *American Journal of Physical Anthropology Suppl.* **30**:36.

Beadle, P. C. (1977). The epidermal biosynthesis of cholecalciferol (vitamin D3). *Photochem. Protobiol.* **25**:519–527.

Beard, K. C., and Wang, J. (1995). The first Asian Plesiadapoids (Mammalia: Primatomorpha). *Ann. Carnegie Mus.* **64**(1):1–33.

Begun, D. R. (1992). Miocene fossil hominids and the chimp-human clade. *Science* **257**:1929–1933.

Benefit, B., and McCrossin, M. (1993). New Kenyapithecus postcrania and other primate fossils from Moboko Island, Kenya. *Am. J. Phys. Anthropol. (Suppl.)* **16**:55–56.

Bergmann, C. (1847). Über die Verhältnisse der Wärmeökonomie des Thiere zu ihrer Grösse. *Göttlinger Studien* **3**:595–708.

Bhargava, A. (2000). Modeling the effects of maternal nutritional status and socioeconomic variables on the anthropometric and psychological indicators of Kenya infants from age 0 to 6 months. *Amer. J. Phys. Anthropol.* **111**:89–104.

Biegert, J. (1963). The evolution of characteristics of the skull, hands, and feet for primate taxonomy. In *Classification and Human Evolution* (S. L. Washburn, ed.), pp. 116–145. Aldine, Chicago.

Binford, L. (1989). *Debating Archeology.* Academic Press, New York.

Birdsell, J. B. (1981). *Human Evolution: An Introduction of the New Physical Anthropology.* Houghton-Mifflin, Boston.

Blakemore, C. (1977). *Mechanics of the Mind.* Cambridge University Press, Cambridge, UK.

Blurton-Jones, N. (1987). Bushmen birth spacing: Direct tests of some simple predictions. *Ethol. Sociobiol.* **8**:183–203.

Boaz, N. T. (1977). Paleoecology of early Hominidae in Africa. *Kroeber Anthropol. Soc. Pap.* **50**:37–62.

Boaz, N. T. (1979). Early hominid population densities: New estimates. *Science* **206**:592–595.

Boaz, N. T. (1985). Early hominid paleoecology in the Omo basin, Ethiopia. In *L'Environnement des Hominidés au Plio-Pléistocène, Fondation Singer-Polignac*, pp. 283–312. Masson, Paris.

Boaz, N. T. (1988). Status of *Australopithecus afarensis*. *Yearb. Phys. Anthropol.* **31**:85–113.

Boaz, N. T. (1993). *Quarry. Closing in on the Missing Link.* Free Press, New York.

Boaz, N. T., Ciochon, R. L., Xu, Q., and Liu, J. (2000). Large mammalian carnivores as a taphonomic factor in the bone accumulation at Zhoukoudian. *Acta Anthropoligica Sinica Suppl.* **19**:224–234.

Bodmer, W. F., and Cavalli-Sforza, L. L. (1976). *Genetics, Evolution and Man.* Freeman, San Francisco.

Boesch, C. (1994). Hunting strategies of Gombe and Tai chimpanzees. In *Chimpanzee Cultures* (W. C. McGrew, F. B. M. de Waal, R. W. Wrangham, and P. Heltner, eds.), pp. 77–92. Harvard Univ. Press, Cambridge, MA.

Boesch-Ackermann, H., and Boesch, C. (1994). Hominization in the rainforest: The chimpanzee's piece of the puzzle. *Evol. Anthropol.* **3**:9–16.

Bogin, B. (1995). Growth and development: Recent evolutionary and biocultural research. In *Biological Anthropology: The State of the Science* (N. T. Boaz and L. D. Wolfe, eds.), pp. 49–70. International Institute for Human Evolutionary Research, Bend, OR.

Bogin, B. (1998). Human growth from an evolutionary perspective. In *The Cambridge Encyclopedia of Human Growth and Development* (S. L. Ulijaszek, F. E. Johnston, and M. A. Preece, eds.), pp. 104–105. Cambridge University Press, Cambridge, UK.

Bogin, B., Wall, M., and MacVean, R. (1992). Longitudinal analysis of adolescent growth of Ladino and Mayan school children in Guatemala: Effects of environment and sex. *Am. J. Phys. Anthropol.* **89**:447–457.

Borgerhoff Mulder, M. (1991). Human behavioral ecology. In *Behavioral Ecology: An Evolutionary Approach*, 3rd ed. (J. R. Krebs and N. B. Davies, eds.), pp. 69–98. Blackwell, Oxford.

Bouchard, T. J., Lykken, D. T., McGue, M., Segal, N. L., and Tellegen, A. (1990). Sources of human psychological differences: The Minnesota study of twins reared apart. *Science* 250:223–228.

Bowcock, A. M., Ruiz-Linares, A., Tomfohrde, J., Minch, E., Kidd, J. R., and Cavalli-Sforza, L. L. (1994). High resolution of human evolutionary trees with polymorphic microsatellites. *Nature (London)* 368:455–457.

Bown, T. M., Kraus, M. J., Wing, S. L., Fleagle, J. G., Tiffany, D., Simons, E. L., and Vondra, C. F. (1982). The Fayum primate forest revisited. *J. Hum. Evol.* 11:603–632.

Brace, C. L., Henneberg, M., and Relethford, J. H. (1999). Skin color as an index of timing of human evolution. *Amer. J. Phys. Anthropol. (Suppl.)* 28:95–96.

Brain, C. K. (1981) *The Hunters or the Hunted: An Introduction to African Cave Taphonomy.* University of Chicago Press, Chicago, IL.

Brett, J., and Niemeyer, S. (1990). Neonatal jaundice: A disorder of transition or adaptive process. *Med. Anthropol. Q.* 4:149–161.

Bromage, T. G., and Dean, M. C. (1985). Re-evaluation of the age of death of immature fossil hominids. *Nature (London)* 317:525–527.

Brunet, M., Beauvilain, A., Coppens, Y., Heintz, E., Montaye, A. H. E., and Pilbeam, D. (1996). Australopithecus bahrelghazali, une nouvelle espece d'hominide ancien de la region de Koro Toro (Tchad). *C.R. Acad. Sci. Paris* 322, Serie iia: 907–913.

Buffon, G. L., Compte de. (1767). *Nomenclature des Singes. Histoire Naturelle Générale et Particulaire.* Imprimerie Royale, Paris.

Bunn, H. R., and Kroll, E. M. (1986). Systematic butchery by Plio/Pleistocene hominids at Olduvai Gorge, Tanzania. *Current Anthropol.* 27:431–452.

Bush, R. M., Bender, C. M., Subbarao, K., Cox, H. J., and Fitch, W. M. (1999). Predictive evolution. *Science* 286:1921.

Busse, C. (1978). Do chimpanzees hunt cooperatively? *Am. Naturalist* 112:767–770.

Butler, A. B., and Hodos, W. (1996). *Comparative Vertebrate Neuroanatomy: Evolution and Adaptation.* John Wiley and Sons, New York.

Calvin, W. H. (1994). The emergence of intelligence. *Sci. Am.* October: 101–107.

Cann, R. L. (1988). DNA and human origins. *Ann. Rev. Anthropol.* 17:127–143.

Cann, R. L., Stoneking, M., and Wilson, A. C. (1987). Mitochondrial DNA and human evolution. *Nature (London)* 325:31–36.

Carbonell, E., de Castro, J., and Arsuaga, J. (1999). Preface: The site of Gran Dolina. *J. Human Evol.* 37:309–311. Other articles pertaining to this site follow in this issue.

Carbonell, V. M. (1963). Variations in the frequency of shovel-shaped incisors in different populations. In *Dental Anthropology* (D. R. Brothwell, ed.), pp. 211–234. Pergamon, Elmsford, NY.

Cardinali, D. P., and Wurtman, R. J. (1975). Methods for assessing the biological activity of the mammalian pineal organ. *Methods Enzymol.* 39:376–397.

Carpenter, C. R. (1934). A field study of the behavior and social relations of the howling monkey (Alouatta palliata). *Comp. Psychol. Monogr.* 10:1–168.

Carpenter, C. R. (1940). A field study in Siam of the behavior and social relations of the gibbon (Hylobates lar). *Comp. Psychol. Monogr.* 16:1–212.

Carpenter, C. R. (1942). Sexual behavior of free-ranging rhesus monkeys, Macaca mulatta. *Comp. Psychol. Monogr.* 33:113–142.

Cartmill, M. (1982). Basic primatology and prosimian evolution. In *A History of American Physical Anthropology, 1930–1980* (F. Spencer, ed.), pp. 147–186. Academic Press, New York.

Cavalli-Sforza, L., and Edwards, M. (1967). Phylogenetic analysis: Models and estimation procedures. *Amer. J. Human Genetics,* 19:233–257.

Chagnon, N. (1983). *Yanomamo: The Fierce People,* 3rd ed. Holt, Rinehart and Winston, New York.

Chaimanee, Y., Suteethorn, V., Jaeger, J. J., and Ducrocq, S. (1997). A new late Eocene anthropoid from Thailand. *Nature* 385:429–431.

Chapman, C. A., Fedigan, L. M., Fedigan, L., and Chapman, L. J. (1989). Post-weaning resource competition and sex ratios in spider monkeys. *Oikos* 54:315–319.

Charles-Dominique, C. (1977). *Ecology and Behavior of Nocturnal Primates.* Columbia Univ. Press, New York.

Churchill, S. E., Shackelford, L. L., Georgi, J. N., and Black, M. T. (1999). Airflow dynamics in the Neandertal nose. *J. Human Evol.* 36:A5.

Chomsky, N. (1957). *Syntactic Structures,* Ser. Janna Linguaram No. 11. 's-Gravenhage, Mouton.

Chia, L.-P. (1975). *The Cave Home of Peking Man.* Foreign Languages Press, Beijing.

Cichon, R. L., and Holroyd, P. A. (1994). The Asian origin of Anthropoidea revisited. In *Anthropoid Origins* (J. G. Fleagle and R. F. Kay, eds.), pp. 143–162. Plenum, New York.

Clarke, R. J. (1998). First ever discovery of a well-preserved skull and associated skeleton of *Australopithecus. S. Afr. J. Sci.* 94:460–463.

Clarke, R. J., and Tobias, P. V. (1995). Sterkfontein member 2 foot bones of the oldest South African hominid. *Science* 269:521–524.

Clutton-Brock, T. H., and Harvey, P. H. (1977). Primate ecology and social organization. *J. Zool.* 183:1–39.

Cohen, B. H. (1970a). ABO and Rh incompatibility. I. Fetal and neonatal mortality with ABO and Rh incompatibility: Some new interpretations. *Am. J. Hum. Genet.* 22:412–440.

Cohen, B. H. (1970b). ABO and Rh incompatibility. II. Is there a dual interaction in combined ABO and Rh incompatibility? *Am. J. Hum. Genet.* 22:441–452.

Conkey, M. (1980). The identification of prehistoric hunter-gatherer aggregation sites: The case of Altamira. *Curr. Anthropol.* 21:609–629.

Conroy, G. C. (1990). *Primate Evolution.* Norton, New York.

Conroy, G. C., Pickford, M., Senut, B., et al. (1992a). Otavipithecus namibiensis, first Miocene hominoid from Southern Africa. *Nature* 356:144–148.

Conroy, G. C., Pickford, M., Senut, B., VanCouvering, J., and Mein, P. (1992b). The Otavi Mountain land of Namibia yields Southern Africa's first Miocene hominoid. *Res. and Expl.* 8:492–494.

Conroy, G. C., Senut, B., Gommery, D., Pickford, M., and Mein, P. (1996). Brief communication: New primate remains from the Miocene of Namibia, Southern Africa. *Am. J. Phys. Anthropol.* 99:487–492.

Conroy, G. C., and Vannier, M. W. (1987). Dental development of the Taung skull from computerized tomography. *Nature (London)* 329:625–627.

Coon, C. (1962). *Origin of Races.* Knopf, New York.

Crompton, R. H. (1995). Visual predation, habitat structure, and the ancestral primate niche. In *Creatures of the Dark: The Nocturnal Prosimians* (L. Alterman, G. H. Doyle, and M. K. Izard, eds.), pp. 11–30. Plenum, New York.

Cronin, J. E. (1983). Apes, humans and molecular clocks: A reappraisal. In *New Interpretations of Ape and Human Ancestry* (R. Ciochon and R. Corruccini, eds.), pp. 115–150. Plenum, New York.

Cronin, H. (1992). Sexual selection: Historical perspectives. In *Keywords in Evolutionary Biology* (E. F. Keller and E. A. Lloyd, eds.), pp. 286–293. Harvard University Press, Cambridge, MA.

Crook, J. H., and Gartlan, J. S. (1966). Evolution of primate societies. *Nature* 210:1200–1203.

Crooks, D. L. (1999). Child growth and nutritional status in a high-poverty community in eastern Kentucky. *Amer. J. Phys. Anthropol.* 109:129–142.

Curtis, G. H., and Evernden, J. P. (1962). Age of basalt underlying Bed I, Olduvai. *Nature* 194:610–612.

Dart, R. A. (1925). *Australopithecus africanus:* The man-ape of South Africa. *Nature (London)* 115:195–199.

Darwin, C. R. (1839). *Journal of Researches into the Geology and Natural History of the Various Countries Visited by H. M. S. Beagle.* Colburn, London.

Darwin, C. R. (1859). *The Origin of Species by Natural Selection.* Murray, London.

Darwin, C. R. (1871). *The Descent of Man and Selection with Respect to Sex.* Murray, London.

Darwin, C. (1872). *The Expression of the Emotions in Man and Animals.* Reprinted in 1965. University of Chicago Press, Chicago.

Darwin, C. R. (1958). *The Autobiography of Charles Darwin and Selected Letters,* edited by Francis Darwin (1892). Dover Publications, Mineola, NY.

Davies, D. R., Goryshin, I. Y., Reznikoff, W. S., and Rayment, I. (2000). Three-dimensional structure of the Tn5 synaptic transposition intermediate. *Science* 289:77–85.

Dawkins, R. (1989). *The Selfish Gene,* 2nd ed. Oxford Univ. Press, Oxford, UK.

Deacon, T. (1997). *The Symbolic Species: The Co-Evolution of Language and the Brain.* W. W. Norton, New York.

Defleur, A., White, T. D., Valensi, P., Slimak, L., and Cregut-Bonnoure, E. (1999). Neanderthal cannibalism at Moula-Guercy, Ardeche, France. *Science* 286:128-131.

Deino, A. L., Renne, P. R., Swisher, C. C., III. (1998). 40Ar/39/AR dating in paleoanthropology and archeology. *Evol. Anthropol.* 6:63–75.

Delgado, R. A., Jr., and Van Schaik, C. P. (2000). The behavioral ecology and conservation of the orangutan (*Pongo pygmaeus*): A tale of two islands. *Evol. Anthropol.* 9:201–218.

Delson, E. (1988). Chronology of South African australopith site units. In *Evolutionary History of the "Robust" Australopithecines* (F. E. Grine, ed.), pp. 317–324. de Gruyter, New York.

Dettwyler, K. (1991). Can Paleopathology provide evidence for "compassion"? *Amer. J. Phys. Anthropol.* 84:375–384.

DeVore, I., and Washburn, S. L. (1963). Baboon ecology and human evolution. In *African Ecology and Human Evolution* (F. C. Howell and F. Bourliere, eds.), pp. 335–367. Aldine, Chicago.

De Waal, F. B. M., and Lanting, F. (1997). *Bonobos: The Forgotten Ape.* University of California Press, Berkeley.

Diamond, J. (1991). Curse and blessing of the ghetto. *Discover* 12(March): 60–65.

Diamond, J. M. (1992). Diabetes running wild. *Nature* 357:362–363.

Di Lonardo, A. M., Darlu, P., Baur, M., et al. (1984). Human genetics and human rights: Identifying the families of kidnapped children. *Am. J. Forensic Med. Pathol.* 5:339–347.

Disotell, T. (1996). The phylogeny of Old World monkeys. *Evol. Anthropol.* 5:18–24.

Disteche, C. M. (1999). Escapees on the X chromosome. *Proc. Natl. Acad. Sci.* 96:14180–14182.

Dixon, A. F. (1981). *The Natural History of the Gorilla.* Columbia Univ. Press, New York.

Dobzhansky, T. (1937). *Genetics and Origin of Species.* Columbia Univ. Press, New York.

Dolhinow, J. P. (1995). The common languar of north India. In *Primate Behavior Field Stuides of Monkeys and Apes* (J. Devore, ed.), pp. 197–249. Holt, Rinehart and Winston, New York.

Dolhinow, P. C., and Taff, M. A. (1993). Rivalry, resolution and the individual. Cooperation among male langur monkeys. In *Milestones in Human Evolution* (A. J. Almquist and J. A. Manyak, eds.), pp. 75–92. Waveland Press, Prospect Heights, IL.

Doran, D. M., and Hunt, K. D. (1994). The comparative locomotor behavior of chimpanzees and bonobos: Species and habitat differences. In *Chimpanzee Cultures* (R. Wrangham, W. McGrew, F. deWaal, and P. Heltne, eds.), pp. 93–108. Harvard Univ. Press, Cambridge, MA.

Drea, C. M., and Wallen, K. (1999). Low status monkeys "play dumb" when learning in mixed social groups. *Proc. Natl. Acad. Sci.* 96(22): 12965–12969.

Duarte, C., Mauricio, J., Pettitt, P. B., Souto, P., Trinkaus, E., van der Plicht, H., and Zilhao, J. (1999). The early Upper Paleolithic human skeleton from the Abrigo do Lagar Velho (Portugal) and modern human emergence in Iberia. *Proc. Natl. Acad. Sci. USA* 96:7604–7609.

Duboule, D. (ed.). (1994). *Guidebook to the Homebox Genes.* Oxford Univ. Press, Oxford, UK.

DuMond, F. V., and Hutchinson, T. C. (1967). Squirrel monkey reproduction: The "fatted" male phenomenon and season spermatogenesis. *Science* 158:1067–1070.

Dunbar, R. I. M. (1986). The social ecology of gelada baboons. In *Ecological Aspects of Social Evolution: Birds and Mammals* (D. I. Rubenstein and R. W. Wrangham, eds.). Princeton Univ. Press, Princeton, NJ.

Dunbar, R. I. M. (1992). Neocortex size as a constraint on group size in primates. *J. Hum. Evol.* 20:469–493.

Dyson-Hudson, R., and Smith, E. A. (1978). Human territoriality: An ecological reassessment. *Am. Anthropol.* 80:21–41.

Eaton, S. B., Konner, M., and Shostack, M. (1988). *The Paleolithic Prescription: A Program of Diet and Exercise and a Design for Living.* Harper & Row, New York.

Eaton, S. B., Pike, M. C., Short, R. V., Lee, N. C., Trussell, J., Hatcher, R. A., Wood, J. W., Worthman, C. M., Blurton Jones, N. G., Konner, M. J., Hill, K. R., Bailey, R., Hurtado, A. M. (1994). Women's reproductive concerns in evolutionary context. *Quart. Rev. Biol.* 69:353–367.

Eaton, S. B., Shostak, M., and Konner, M. (1989). *The Paleolithic Prescription: A Program of Diet and Exercise and a Design for Living.* Harper & Row, New York.

Eibl-Eibesfeldt, I. (1975). *Ethology: The Biology of Behavior.* Holt, Rinehart and Winston, New York.

Eibl-Eibesfeldt, I. (1989). *Human Ethology.* de Gruyter, New York.

Eisenberg, J. F., Muckerhirn, N. A., and Rudran, R. (1972). The relation between ecology and social structure in primates. *Science* 176:863–874.

Eldredge, N. (2000). *The Triumph of Evolution and the Failure of Creationism.* W. H. Freeman, New York.

Ellefson, J. O. (1968). Territorial behavior in the comon white-handed gibbon, *Hylobates lar* Linn. In *Primates: Studies in Adaptation and Variability* (P. C. Jay, ed.), pp. 180–199. Holt, Rinehart and Winston, New York.

Ewald, P. (1994). *Evolution of Infectious Diseases.* Oxford Univ. Press, London.

Fairbanks, L. A. (1988). Vervet monkey grandmothers: Interactions with infant offspring. *Int. J. Primatol.* 9:425–441.

Fairbanks, L. A., Melega, W. P., Jorgensen, M. J., et al. (2001). Social impulsivity inversely associated with CSF5-HJAA and fluoxetine exposure in vervet monkeys. *Neuropsychopharmacol.* 24(4): 370–378.

Falk, D. (1990). Brain evolution in *Homo*: The "radiator" theory. *Behav. Brain Sci.* **13**:333–381.

Falk, D. (1992) *Braindance.* Henry Holt, New York.

Feathers, J. K. (1996). Luminescence dating and modern human origins. *Evol. Anthropol.* **5**:25–36.

Feibel, C. (1999). Tephrostratigraphy and geological context in paleoanthropology. *Evol. Anthropol.* **8**:87–100.

Fisher, P. E., Russell, D. A., Stoskopf, M. K., Barrick, R. E., Hammer, M., and Kuzmitz, A. A. (2000). Cardiovascular evidence for an intermediate or higher metabolic rate in an Ornithischian dinosaur. *Science* **288**:503–505.

Fisher, R. A. (1918). The correlations between relatives on the supposition of Mendelian Inheritance. *Transactions of the Royal Society of Edinburgh* **52**:399–433.

Foley, R. (1990). The causes of brain enlargement in human evolution. *Behav. Brain Sci.* **13**:354–356.

Ford, C. S. (1964). *A Comparative Study of Human Reproduction.* Taplinger, New York.

Fossey, D. (1983). *Gorillas in the Mist.* Houghton-Mifflin, Boston.

Frayer, D. W. (1992). The persistence of Neanderthal features in post-Neanderthal Europeans. In *Continuity or Replacement?* (G. Brauer and F. H. Smith, eds.), pp. 179–188. A A Balkema, Rotterdam.

Frezza, M., et al. (1990). High blood alcohol levels in women. The role of decreased gastric alcohol dehydrogenase activity and first pass metabolism. *New Engl. J. of Med.* **322**:95–99.

Frisancho, A. R. (1975). Functional adaptation to high hypoxia. *Science* **187**:313–319.

Gabriel, S. E., Brigman, K. N., Koller, B. H., Boucher, R. C., and Smuts, M. J. (1994). Cystic fibrosis heterozygote resistance to cholera toxin in the cystic fibrosis mouse model. *Science* **266**:107–109.

Gaburnia, L., et al. (2000). Earliest Pleistocene hominid cranial remains from Dmanisi, Republic of Georgia: Taxonomy, geological setting, and age. *Science* **288**:1019–1025.

Galdikas, B. (1979). Orangutan adaptation at Tanjung Puting Reserve: Mating and ecology. In *The Great Apes* (D. A. Hamburg and E. R. McCown, eds.), pp. 195–233. Benjamin/Cummings, Menlo Park, CA.

Gannon, P. J., and Kheck, N. M. (1999). Primate brain "language" area evolution: Anatomy of Heschl's gyrus and planum temporale in hominids, hylobatids and macaques and of planum temporale in Pan troglodytes. *Amer. J. Phys. Anthropol. Suppl.* **28**:132–133.

Gebo, D., MacLatchy, L., Kityo, R., Deino, A., Kingston, J., and Pilbeam, D. R. (1997). A hominoid genus from the early Miocene of Uganda. *Science* **276**:401–404.

Gebo, D. L. (1989). Locomotor and phylogenetic considerations in anthropoid evolution. *J. Hum. Evol.* **18**:201–233.

Gibson, K. R. (1993). Tool use, language and social behavior in relationship to information processing capacities. In *Tools, Language and Cognition in Human Evolution* (K. R. Gibson and T. Ingold, eds.), pp. 251–269. Cambridge University Press, Cambridge, UK.

Gibson, K. R. (1994). Continuity theories of human language origins versus the Lieberman model. *Language and Communication* **14**:97–114.

Goldschmidt, R. B. (1940). *The Material Bais of Evolution.* Yale University Press, New Haven, CT.

Goodall, J. (1986). *The Chimpanzees of Gombe.* Harvard University (Belknap Press), Cambridge, MA.

Goodman, M. (1961). The role of immunochemical differences in the phyletic development of human behavior. *Hum. Biol.* **33**:131–162.

Goodman, M. (1962). Evolution of the immunologic species specificity of human serum proteins. *Hum. Biol.* **34**:105–150.

Goodman, M. (1973). The chronicle of primate phylogeny continued in proteins. *Symp. Zool. Soc. London* **33**:339–375.

Gordon, T. P., Rose, R. W., Grady, C. L., and Bernstein, I. S. (1979). Effects of increased testosterone secretion on the behavior of adult male rhesus living in a social group. *Folia Primatol.* **32**: 149–160.

Goren-Inbar, N. (1986). A figurine from the Acheulean site of Berekhat Rom. *Mitakufat Haeven* **19**:7–12.

Gould, S. J., and Eldredge, N. (1993). Punctuated equilibrium comes of age. *Nature* **366**:223–227.

Grant, V. (1991). *The Evolutionary Process: A Critical Study of Evolutionary Theory,* 2nd ed. Columbia University Press, NY.

Greene, L. S. (1993). G6PD deficiency as protection against falciparum Malaria: An epidemiologic critique of population and experimental studies. *Yearb. Phys. Anthropol.* **36**:153–178.

Greenfield, L. O. (1980). Late divergence hypothesis. *Am. J. Phys. Anthropol.* **52**:351–365.

Gregory, W. K. (1927). Dawn man or ape? *Sci. Am.* **83**:230–232.

Gregory, W. K., and Hellman, M. (1926). The dentition of Dryopithecus and the origin of man. *Am. Mus. Anthropol. Pap.* **28**:1–123.

Grine, F. E. (ed.). (1988). *Evolutionary History of the "Robust" Australopithecines.* de Gruyter, New York.

Groce, N. E., and Whiting, J. W. (1985). *Everyone Here Spoke Sign Language: Hereditary Deafness on Martha's Vineyard.* Harvard Univ. Press, Cambridge, MA.

Groves, C. P., and Mazek, V. (1975). An approach to the taxonomy of the Hominidae: Gracile Villafranchian hominids of Africa. *Cas. Mineral. Geol.* **20**:225–247.

Guarino, A. (1998). HIV and growth. *Cambridge Encyclopedia of Human Growth and Development,* pp. 338–340. Cambridge University Press, Cambridge, UK.

Gunn, R. (1993). Electron spin resonance dating in paleoanthropology. *Evol. Anthropol.* **2**:172–181.

Gutin, J. (1992). Why bother? *Discover* (June):34–39.

Hafleigh, A. S., and Williams, C. A., Jr. (1966). Antigenic correspondence of serum albumins among the primates. *Science* **151**:1530–1535.

Hall, K. R. L., and Devore, J. (1965). *Baboon Social Behavior* (I. DeVore, ed.), pp. 53–110. Holt, Rinehart and Winston, New York.

Hamburg, D. A. (1963). Emotions in the perspective of human evolution. In *Expression of the Emotions in Man* (P. H. Knapp, ed.), p. 313. International Universities Press, New York.

Hamilton, W. D. (1963). The evolution of altruistic behavior. *Am. Nat.* **97**:357–366.

Hamilton, W. D. (1971). Selection of selfish or altruistic behaviors in some extreme models. In *Man and Beast: Comparative Social Behavior* (J. Eisenberg and W. Dillon, eds.), pp. 59–91. Smithsonian Institution Press, Washington, DC.

Hammer, M., and Zegura, S. (1996). The role of the Y chromosome in human evolutionary studies. *Evol. Anthropol.* **5**:116–134.

Harding, R. M. (1992). VNTR's in review. *Evol. Anthropol.* **1**(2):62–71.

Harding, R. M., and Teleki, G. (eds.). (1981). *Omnivorous Primates. Gathering and Hunting in Human Evolution.* Columbia Univ. Press, New York.

Hardy, B. L. (1997). Evidence for plant exploitation at the middle Paleolithic site of Starosel'e, Crimea. *J. Human Evol.* **32**:A7–A8.

Harris, E., and Hey, J. (1999). X chromosome evidence for ancient human histories. *Proc. Natl. Acad. Sci.* **96**:3320–3324.

Harrison, T. (1986). A reassessment of the phylogenetic relationships of Oreopithecus bambolii Gervais. *J. Hum. Evol.* **15**:541–583.

Hausfater, G. (1976). Predatory behavior of yellow baboons. *Behaviour* **56**:44–68.

Henneberg, M., and Thackeray, J. F. (1995). A single-lineage hypothesis of hominid evolution. *Evol. Theory* **11**:31–38.

Hennig, W. (1966). *Phylogenetic Systematics*. U. of Illinois Press, Urbana.

Herschel, J. F. W. (1831). *A Preliminary Discourse on the Study of Natural Philosophy*. Carey and Lea, Philadelphia.

Hewes, G. W. (1964). Hominid bipedalism: Independent evidence for food carrying theory. *Science* **146**:416–418.

Hill, A., and Ward, S. (1988). Origin of the Hominidae: The record of African large hominoid evolution between 14 my and 4 my. *Yearb. Phys. Anthropol.* **31**:49–83.

Hill, K., Kaplan, H., Hawkes, K., and Hurtado, A. M. (1987). Foraging decisions among Ache hunter-gatherers: New data and implications for optimal foraging models. *Ethol. Sociobiol.* **8**:1–36.

Hillis, D. M. (1999). Predictive evolution. *Science* **286**:1866–1867.

Hockett, C., and Ascher, R. (1964). The human revolution. *Curr. Anthropol.* **5**:135–168.

Hoffstetter, R., and Lavocat, R. (1970). Découverte dans le Déséadier de Bolivie de genres pentalophodontes appuyant les affinités africaines de rougeurs caviomorphes. *C. R. Acad Sci.* **271**:172–175.

Holden, C., and Mace, R. (1997). Phylogenetic analyis of the evolution of lactose digestion in adults. *Hum. Biol.* **69**:605–628.

Hooeger, J. E., and Strick, P. L. (1993). Multiple outlet channels in the basal ganglia. *Science* **259**:819–821.

Horai, S., et al. (1995). Recent African origin of modern humans revealed by complete sequences of hominoid mitochondrial DNAs. *Proc. Nat. Acad. Sci.* **92**:532–536.

Houghton, P. (1993). Neandertal supralaryngeal vocal tract. *Am. J. Phys. Anthropol.* **90**:139–146.

Hrdy, S. B. (1977). *The Langurs of Abu*. Harvard Univ. Press, Cambridge, MA.

Hrdy, S. B., Janson, C., and Van Schaik, C. (1995). Infanticide: Let's not throw out the baby with the bath water. *Evol. Anthropol.* **3**:151–154.

Huang W., Ciochon, R., Gu Y., Larick, R., Fang Q., Schwarcz, H., Yonge, C., de Vos, J., and Rink, W. (1995). Early *Homo* and associated artifacts from Asia. *Nature* **378**:275–278.

Hull, D. L. (1973). *Darwin and His Critics: The Reception of Darwin's Theory of Evolution by the Scientific Community*. Harvard University Press, Cambridge, MA.

Hurst, L. (1999). Why are there only two sexes? Oral presentation at the Festival of Science, Sheffield, England, September.

Isaac, G. L. (1978). The food sharing behavior of protohuman hominids. *Sci. Am.* **238**:90–109.

Isbell, L. A. (1991). Contest and scramble competition: Patterns of female aggression and ranging behavior among primates. *Behav. Ecol.* **2**:143–155.

Iscan, M. Y., and Kennedy, K. A. R. (1989). *Reconstruction of Life from the Skeleton*. Alan R. Liss, New York.

Jablonski, N. G., and Chaplin, G. (1999). The evolution of human skin pigmentation. *Amer. J. Phys. Anthropol. Suppl.* **28**:159.

Jensen, A. (1969). How much can we boost IQ and scholastic achievement? *Harv. Educ. Rev.* **39**:1–123.

Jensen, A. (1980). *Bias in Mental Testing*. Free Press, New York.

Jensen, A. R. (1998). *The g Factor: The Science of Mental Ability*. Praeger, Westport, CT.

Jisaka, M., Kawanaka, M., Sugiyama, H., Takegawa, K., Huffman, M. A., Ohigashi, H., and Koshimizu, K. (1992). Antischistosomal activities of sesquiterpene lactones and steroid glucosides from *Vernonia amygdalina*, possibly used by wild chimpanzees against parasite-related diseases. *Biosci., Biotech., and Biochem.* **56**:845–846.

Johanson, D. C., Masao, F. T., Eck, G. G., White, T. D., Walter, R. C., Kimbel, W. H., Asfaw, B., Manega, P., Ndessokia, P., and Suwa, G. (1987). New partial skeleton of *Homo habilis* from Olduvai Gorge, Tanzania. *Nature (London)* **327**:205–209.

Johanson, D. C., White, T. D., and Coppens, Y. (1978). A new species of the genus Australopithecus (Primates: Hominidae) from the Pliocene of eastern Africa. *Kirtlandia* **28**:1–14.

Jolly, A. (1966). *Lemur Behavior: Madagascar Field Study*. Univ. of Chicago Press, Chicago.

Jolly, A. (1985). *The Evolution of Primate Behavior*, 2nd ed. Macmillan, New York.

Jorion, P. (1999). Intelligence and race: The house of cards. Book review of Jensen's on Intelligence-g-fctor. *Psycoloquy* **10**(64).

Joyce, C., and Stover, E. (1991). *Witnesses from the Grave: The Stories Bones Tell*. Ballantine Books, New York.

Jungers, W. L. (1988). New estimates of body size in australopithecines. In *Evolutionary History of the "Robust" Australopithecines* (F. E. Grine, ed.), pp. 115–125. de Gruyter, New York.

Kaplan, H., and Hill, K. R. (1992). The evolutionary ecology of food acquisition. In *Evolutionary Ecology and Human Behavior* (E. A. Smith and B. Winterhalder, eds.), pp. 167–202. de Gruyter, New York.

Kappelman, J. (1993). The attraction of paleomagnetism. *Evol. Anthropol.* **2**:89–994.

Kawamura, S. (1959). The process of sub-culture propagation among Japanese macaques. *Primates* **2**:43–60.

Keith, A. (1896). An introduction to the study of the anthropoid apes. *Nat. Sci.* **9**:316–326, 372–379.

Keith, A. (1899). On the chimpanzees and their relationship to the gorilla. *Proc. Zool. Soc. London*, pp. 296–312.

Kelley, J. (1987). Species recognition and sexual dimorphism in Proconsul and Rangwapithecus. *J. Hum. Evol.* **15**:461–495.

Kelley, J. (1998). Noncompetitive replacement of apes by monkeys in the late Miocene of Eurasia. *Amer. J. Phys. Anthropol (Supp.)* **26**:137–138.

Kelley, S. E. (1994). Viral pathogens and the advantage of sex in the perennial grass *Anthoxanthum odoratum*. *Philosophical Transactions of the Royal Society of London B* **346** (1317):295–302.

Kettlewell, H. B. D. (1973). *The Evolution of Melanism*. Clarendon Press, Oxford, UK.

Keyser, A. W. (2000). The Drimolen skull: The most complete australopithecine cranium and mandible to date. *S. Afr. J. Sci.* **96**:189–192.

King, B. (1994). *The Information Continuum: Evolution of Social Information Transfer in Monkeys, Apes, and Hominids*. SAR Press, Santa Fe, NM.

King, M.-C., and Wilson, A. C. (1975). Evolution at two levels in humans and chimpanzees. *Science* **188**:107–116.

Klaus, M., and Kennell, J. (1976). *Maternal-Infant Bonding. The Impact of Early Separation or Loss on Family Development*. C. V. Mosby, St Louis, MO.

Klein, R. (1989). *The Human Career*. Univ. of Chicago Press, Chicago.

Klein, R. G. (1992). The archeology of modern humans. *Evol. Anthropol.* **1**:1–5.

Kricum, M. (1999). Neanderthals may have been healthy. Reported in the *Daily News* (Philadelphia) by Associated Press writer Joann Loviglio, September 26.

Krings, M., Geisert, H., Schmitz, R.-W., Krainitzki, H., and Paabo, S. (1999). DNA sequence of the mitochondrial hypervariable region II from the Neandertal type specimen. *Proc. Natl. Acad. Sci. USA* **96**:5581–5585.

Krings, M., Stone, A., Schmitz, R.-W., Krainitzki, H., Stoneking, M., and Paabo, S. (1997). Neandertal DNA sequences and the origin of modern humans. *Cell* **90**:19–30.

Krings, M., Stone, A., Schmitz, R. W., Krainitzki, H., Stoneking, M., and Paabo, S. (1997). Neandertal DNA sequences and the origin of modern humans. *Cell* **90**:19–30.

Kummer, H., and Kurt, F. (1963). Social units of a free-living population of hamadryas baboons. *Folia Primat.* 1:4–19.

Kuroda, S. (1980). Social behavior of the pygmy chimpanzee. *Primates* 21:181–197.

Kuroda, S. (1984). Interaction over food among pygmy chimpanzees. In *The Pygmy Chimpanzee: Evolutionary Biology and Behavior* (R. Susman, ed.), pp. 301–324. Plenum, New York.

Kurtén, B. (1972). *Not From the Apes*. Pantheon Books, New York.

Lahn, B. T., and Page, D. C. (1997). Functional coherence of the human Y chromosome. *Science* 278:675–680.

Lartet, E. (1856). Note sur un grand singe fossile qui se rattache au groupe des singes supérieurs. *C. R. Hebd. Seances Acad. Sci.* 43:219–223.

Leakey, M. G., Feibel, C. S., McDougal, I., and Walker, A. (1995). New four-million-year-old hominid species from Kanapoi and Allia Bay, Kenya. *Nature (London)* 376:565–571.

Leakey, M. G., Spoor, F., Brown, G. H., Gathogo, P., Kiarie, C., Leakey, L. and McDougall, I. (2001). New hominin genus from eastern Africa shows diverse middle Pliocene lineages. *Nature* 210:433–440.

Lee, R. B. (1980). Lactation, ovulation, infanticide, and women's work: A study of hunter-gatherer population regulation. In *Biosocial Mechanisms of Population Regulation* (M. Cohen, R. Malpass, and H. Klein, eds.), pp. 321–348. Yale Univ. Press, New Haven, CT.

Lee. R. B. and DeVore, I. (eds.). (1968). *Man the Hunter*. Aldine, Chicago.

LeGros Clark, W. E. (1964). *The Fossil Evidence for Human Evolution*. Univ. of Chicago Press, Chicago.

Leutenegger, W. (1987). Neonatal brain size and neurocranial dimensions in Pliocene hominids: Implications for obstetrics. *J. Hum. Evol.* 16:291–296.

Lewontin, R. C. (1972). The apportionment of human diversity. In *Evolutionary Biology* (T. Dobzhansky, ed.), Vol. 6, pp. 381–398. Plenum, New York.

Lieberman, D. (2001). Another face in our family tree. *Nature (London)* 410:419–420.

Lieberman, L., and Kirk, R. (1996). The trial of Darwin is over: Religious voices for evolution and the "fairness" doctrine. *Creation/Evolution* 16:1–9.

Lieberman, P., and Crelin, E. S. (1971). On the speech of Neanderthal man. *Linquistic Inquiry* 11:203–222.

Linton, S. (1971). Woman the gatherer: Male bias in anthropology. In *Women in Perspective: A Guide for Cross-Cultural Studies* (S. Jacobs, ed.), pp. 9–21. Univ. of Illinois Press, Urbana.

Little, M. A., and Baker, R. T. (1988). Migration and adaptation. In *Biological Aspects of Human Migration* (C. G. N. Mascie-Taylor and G. W. Lasker, eds.), pp. 167–215. Cambridge University Press, Cambridge, UK.

Lopreato, J. (1984). *Human Nature and Biocultural Evolution*. Allen and Unwin, London.

Lorenz, K. (1965a). *On Aggression*. Harcourt, Brace, New York.

Lorenz, K. (1965b). *Evolution and Modification of Behavior*. University of Chicago Press, Chicago.

Loy, J. (1987). The sexual behavior of African monkeys and the question of estrus. In *Comparative Behavior of African Monkeys* (E. Zucker, ed.), pp. 175–195. Alan R. Liss, New York.

Loy, J. (1992). Behavioral dynamics among primates: An overview. *Perspect. Primate Biol.* 4:79–94.

Ludwig, K. R., and Renne, P. R. (2000). Geochronology on the paleoanthropological time scale. *Evol. Anthropol.* 9:101–110.

Lyell, C. (1830–1833). *Principles of Geology*. John Murray, London.

McDermott, F., Grun, R., Stringer, C. B., Hawkseworth, C. J. (1993). Mass-spectrometric U-series dates for Israeli Neanderthal/early modern hominid sites. *Nature (London)* 363:252–255.

McHenry, H. M. (1984). The common ancestor: A study of the postcranium of *Pan paniscus, Australopithecus* and other hominids. In *The Pygmy Chimpanzee: Evolutionary Biology and Behavior* (R. Susman, ed.), pp. 201–230. Plenum, New York.

McHenry, H. M., and Berger, L. (1998). Body proportions in *Australopithecus afarensis* and *A. Africanus* and the origin of the genus *Homo*. *J. Human Evol.* 35:1–22.

MacKinnin, J. (1974). *In Search of the Red Ape*. Holt, Rinehart and Winston, New York.

McKinney, M. L., and McNamara, K. J. (1991). *Heterochrony: The Evolution of Ontogeny*. Plenum Press, New York.

MacLean, P. D. (1990). *The Triune Brain in Human Evolution*. Plenum, New York.

Malina, R. M. (1975). *Growth and Development*. Burgess, Minneapolis, MN.

Malthus, T. R. (1798). An essay on the principle of population as it affects the future improvement of society. Reprinted in 1960 *On Population* (G. Himmelfarb, ed.). Random House Modern Library, New York.

Mandelbaum, D. C. (1965). Alcohol and culture. *Curr. Anthropol.* 6:281–293.

Mann, A. (1975). *Some Paleodemographic Aspects of the South African Australopithecines*. University of Pennsylvania Publications in Anthropology, Vol. 1. 171 pp. Philadelphia.

Marazziti, D., Akiskal, H. S., Rossi, A., et al. (1999). Alteration of the platelet serotonin transporter in romantic love. *Psychol. Med.* 29(3):741–745.

Margulis, L., and Sagan, D. (1986). *Origins of Sex: Three Billion Years of Genetic Recombination*. Yale Univ. Press, New Haven, CT.

Marler, P. (1973). A comparison of vocalizations of red-tailed monkeys and blue monkeys, *Cercopithecus ascanius* and *C. mitis,* in Uganda. *Z. Tierpsychol.* 33:223–247.

Marshack, A. (1989). Evolution of the human capacity: Symbolic evidence. *Yearb. Phys. Anthropol.* 32:1–34.

Martin, R. D. (1968). Towards a new definition of primates. *Man* 3(3):377–401.

Martin, R. D. (1983). Human brain evolution in an ecological context. Fifty-second James Arthur Lecture. American Museum of Natural History, New York.

Martin, R. D. (1996). Scaling of the mammalian brain. The maternal energy hypothesis. *New Physiol. Sci.* 11:149–156.

Martini, F. H., and Timmons, J. J. (1995). *Human Anatomy*. Prentice Hall, Upper Saddle River, NJ.

Mayr, E. (1963). *Animal Species and Evolution*. Harvard Univ. Press, Cambridge, MA.

McGrew, W. C. (1988). Parental division of infant care-taking varies with family composition in cotton-topped tamarins. *Anim. Behav.* 36:285–286.

McGrew, W. (1992). *Chimpanzee Material Culture*. Cambridge Univ. Press, New York.

McGrew, W. (1998). Culture in the nonhuman primates. *Annual Rev. Anthropol.* 27:301–328.

McHenry, H. M. (1988). New estimates of body weight in early hominids and their significance to encephalization and megadontia in "robust" australopithecines. In *Evolutionary History of the "Robust" Australopithecines* (F. E. Grine, ed.), pp. 133–148. de Gruyter, New York.

McHenry, J., and Berger, L. (1998). Body proportions in *Australopithecus afarensis* and *A. Africanus* and the origin of the genus. *Homo. J. Human Evol.* 35:1–22.

McKenna, J., Mosko, S., Dungy, C., and McAninch, J. (1990). Sleep and arousal patterns of co-sleeping human mother-infant pairs: A preliminary physiological study with implications for the study of sudden infant death syndrome. *Am. J. Phys. Anthropol.* 83:331–347.

MacKintosh, J. J. (1998). *IQ and Human Intelligence.* Oxford Univ. Press, Oxford, UK.

Mellars, P. (1999). "Acculturation," "co-existence" and the end of the Neanderthals. *J. Human Evol.* 36:A13.

Michod, R. (1997). What good is sex? *The Sciences* 37:42–46.

Mitani, M. (1992). Preliminary results of the studies on wild western lowland gorillas and other sympatic diurnal primates in the Ndoki Forest, northern Congo. In *Topics in Primatology*, Vol. 2 (Itoigawa et al., eds.), pp. 215–224. University of Tokyo Press, Tokyo.

Molnar, S. (1998). *Human Variation: Races, Types and Ethnic Groups,* 4th ed. Prentice Hall, Upper Saddle River, NJ.

Morbeck, M. E. (1979). Forelimb use and positional adaptation in Colobus guereza: Integration of behavioral and anatomical data. In *Environment, Behavior and Morphology: Dynamic Interactions in Primates* (M. Morbeck, H. Preuschoft, and N. Gomberg, eds.), pp. 95–118. Fischer, New York.

Morbeck, M. E. (1983). Miocene hominoid discoveries from Rudabánya: Implications from the post-cranial skeleton. In *New Interpretations of Ape and Human Ancestry* (R. Ciochon and R. Corruccini, eds.), pp. 369–404. Plenum Press, New York.

Morwood, M. J., Aziz, F., O'Sullivan, P., Nasruddin, Hobbs, D. R., and Raza, A. (1999). Archaeological and palaeontological research in central Flores, East Indonesia: Results of fieldwork 1997–98. *Antiquity* 73:273–286.

Morwood, M. J., O'Sullivan, P., Aziz, F., and Raza, A. (1998). Fission track age of stone tools and fossils on the east Indonesian island of Flores. *Nature* 392 (12 March): 173–176.

Moya-Sola, S., Kohler, M., and Rook, L. (1999). Evidence of himinid-like precision grip capability in the hand of the Miocene ape Oreopithecus. *Proc. Natl. acad. Scie. USA* 96:313–317.

Mourant, A. E., Kopec, A. C., and Domaniewska-Sobczak, K. (1976). *The Distribution of the Human Blood Groups and Other Polymorphisms.* Oxford Univ. Press, London.

Mueller, A. (1995). Duetting in the titi monkey Callicelous cupreus. *Neotrop. Primates* 3(1):18–19.

Napier, J. R., and Napier, P. (1967). *Handbook of Living Primates.* Academic Press, New York.

Napier, J. R., and Walker, A. (1967). Vertical clinging and leaping: A newly recognized category of locomotor behavior in primates. *Folia Primatol.* 6:204–219.

Neel, J. V. (1962). Diabetes mellitus: A "Thrifty" Genotype rendered detrimental by "progress." *Am. J. Hum. Genet.* 14:353–362.

Newman, R. W. (1970). Why man is such a sweaty and thirsty naked animal: A speculative review. *Hum. Biol.* 42:12–27.

Newman, R. W. (1975). Human adaptation to heat. In *Physiological Anthropology* (A. Damon, ed.), pp. 80–92. Oxford University Press, New York.

Nichols, J. (1994, February). Paper presented at the annual meeting of the American Association for the Advancement of Science, February. San Francisco.

Nunn, C. L., Gittleman, J. L., and Antonovics, J. (2000). Promiscuity and the primate immune system. *Science* 290:1168–1170.

Oakley, K. P. (1969). *Frameworks for Dating Fossil Man,* 3rd ed. Weidenfeld and Nicolson, London.

Ovchinnikov, I. V., et al. (2000). Ancient mtDNA. *Nature* 404:490–493.

Owen, R. (1859). *On the Classification and Geographical Distribution of the Mammalia.* Parker, London.

Palombit, R. A. (1996). Pair bonds in monogamous apes: A comparison of the siamang Hylobates syndactylus and the white-handed gibbon Hylobates lar. *Behaviour* 133:321–356.

Parker, S. T. (1985). A social-technological model for the evolution of language. *Curr. Anthropol.* 27:671–639.

Parker, S. T. (1987). A sexual selection model for hominid evolution. *Hum. Evol.* 2:235–253.

Parker, S. T., and Gibson, K. R. (1979). A developmental model for the evolution of language and intelligence in early hominids. *Behav. Brain Sci.* 2:367–408.

Partridge, T. (1986). Paleoecology of the Pliocene and lower Pleistocene hominids of southern Africa: How good is the chronological and paleoenvironmental evidence? *S. Afr. J. Sci.* 82:80–83.

Petter, J. J. (1965). The Lemurs of Madagascar. In *Primate Behavior* (I. DeVore, ed.), pp. 292–319. Holt, Rinehart and Winston, New York.

Pickering, T. R., White, T. D., and Toth, N. (1999). Stone tool cut marks on Stw 53, an early hominid from Sterkfontein, South Africa. Abstract Paleoanthropology Society Annual Meeting. *J. Hum. Evol.* 36:A17.

Pickford, M., Senut, B., Ssemmanda, I., Elepu, D., and Obwona, P. (1988). Premiers résultats de la mission de l'Uganda. Palaeontology expedition à Nkondo (Pliocene du Bassin du Lac Albert, Ouganda). *C. R. Acad. Sci.* Ser. 2 306:315–320.

Pilbeam, D. R. (1972). *The Ascent of Man.* Macmillan, New York.

Pilbeam, D. R. (1978). Rearranging our family tree. *Hum. Nat.* 1(6):38–45.

Pilbeam, D. R. (1980). Major trends in human evolution. In *Current Argument on Early Man* (L. Konigsson, ed.), pp. 261–285. Pergamon, Oxford.

Pilbeam, D. R. (1986). The origin of Homo sapiens: The fossil evidence. In *Major Topics in Primate and Human Evolution* (B. Wood, L. Martin, and P. Andrews, eds.), pp. 331–338. Cambridge Univ. Press, Cambridge, UK.

Pilbeam, D. R. (1996). Genetic and morphological records of the Hominoidea and hominid origins: A synthesis. *Molec. Phylogenet. Evol.* 5:155–168.

Pilbeam, D. R., Rose, M. D., Badgley, C., et al. (1980). *Miocene Hominoids from Pakistan.* Postilla No. 181. Yale Peabody Museum, New Haven, CT.

Pilgrim, G. E. (1915). New Siwalik primates and their bearing on the questions of evolution of man and the Anthropoidea. *Rec. Geol. Surv. India* 45:1–74.

Pinker, S. (1994). *The Language Instinct.* William Morrow, New York.

Pope, G. G. (1988). Recent advances in Far Eastern paleoanthropology. *Annual Rev. Anthropol.* 17:43–77.

Potts, R. (1988). *Early Hominid Activities at Olduvai.* de Gruyter, New York.

Pringle, H. (1998). New women of the ice age. *Discover* 19(4):62–69.

Provine, R. (2000) *Laughter: A Scientific Investigation.* Viking Press, New York.

Pusey, A. E., and Parker, C. (1987). Dispersal and philopatry. In *Primate Societies* (B. Smuts, D. Cheney, R. Seyfarth, T. Struhsaker, and R. Wrangham, eds.). Univ. of Chicago Press, Chicago.

Pusey, A., Williams, J., and Goodall, J. (1997). The influence of dominance rank on the reproductive success of female chimpanzees. *Science* 277:828–831.

Rae, T. C. (1999). Mosaic evolution in the origin of the Moninoidea. *Folia Primatol.* 70:125–135.

Rak, Y. (1983). *The Australopithecine Face.* Academic Press, Orlando, FL.

Rasmussen, D. T. (1990). Primate origins: Lessons from a neotropical marsupial. *Am. J. Primatol.* 22:263–277.

Rayner, R. J., Moon, B. P., and Masters, J. C. (1993). The Makapansgat australopithecine environment. *J. Hum. Evol.* 24:219–231.

Read, A. F., and Allen, J. E. (2000). The economics of immunity. *Science* 290:1104–1105.

Rendall, D., Cheney, D. L., and Seyfarth, R. M. (2000). Proximate factors mediating "contact" calls in adult female baboons (Papio cynocephalus ursinus) and their infants. J. Comp. Psychol. 114(1).

Reynolds, V., and Reynolds, F. (1965). Chimpanzees of the Budongo Forest. In Primate Behavior (I. DeVore, ed.), pp. 368–424. Holt, Rinehart and Winston, New York.

Richard, A. F. (1985a). Primates in Nature. Freeman, New York.

Richard, A. F. (1985b). Social boundaries in a Malagasy prosimian, the sifaka (Propithecus verreauxi). Intl. J. Primatol. 6:553–568.

Richards, M. P., Pettitt, P. B., Trinkaus, E., Smith, F. H., Paunovic, M., and Karavanic, I. (2000). Neanderthal diet at Vindija and Neanderthal predation: The evidence from stable isotopes. Proc. Natl. Acad. Sci. USA 97:7663–7666.

Richards, M. P., Pettitt, P. B., Stiner, M. C., and Trinkaus, E. (2001). Stable isotope evidence for increasing dietary breadth in the European mid-Upper Paleolithic. Proc. Natl. Acad. Sci. USA 98:6528–6532.

Richmond, B., and Strait, D. S. (2000). Evidence that humans evolved from a knucle-walking ancestor. Nature 404:382–385.

Robins, A. H. (1991). Biological Perspectives on Human Pigmentation. Cambridge Univ. Press, Cambridge, UK.

Robinson, J. G. (1986). Seasonal variation in the use of time and space by the wedge-capped capuchin monkey, Cebus olivaceus: Implications for foraging theory. Smithsonian Contrib. Zool. 432:1–60.

Robinson, J. T. (1963). Adaptive radiation in the australopithecines and the origin of man. In African Ecology and Human Evolution (F. C. Howell and F. Bourliere, eds.), pp. 385–416. Aldine, Chicago.

Rodman, P. S. (1984). Foraging and social systems of orangutans and chimpanzees. In Adaptations for Foraging in Nonhuman Primates (P. S. Rodman and J. G. H. Cant, eds.), pp. 134–160. Columbia University Press, New York.

Rodman, P. S. (1988). Resources and group size of primates. In The Ecology of Social Behavior (C. N. Slobodchikoff, ed.), pp. 83–108. Academic Press, San Diego, CA.

Romer, A. S. (1971). Vertebrate Paleontology. Univ. of Chicago Press, Chicago.

Rowell, T. E. (1993). Reification of social systems. Evol. Anthropol. 2:135–137.

Ruvolo, M. E. (1994). Molecular evolutionary processes and conflicting gene trees: The hominoid case. American Journal of Physical Anthropology 94:89–113.

Ruvolo, M. (1997). Genetic diversity in hominoid Primates. Ann. Rev. Anthropol. 26:515–540.

Ruvolo, M., Disotell, T. R., Allard, M. W., Brown, W. M., and Honeycutt, R. L. (1991). Resolution of the African hominoid trichotomy by use of a mitochondrial gene sequence. Proc. Natl. Acad. Sci. 88:1570–1574.

Sarich, V. M., and Wilson, A. C. (1967). Immunological time scale for hominid evolution. Science 158:1200–1203.

Saunders, B. (1980). Psychological aspects of women and alcohol. In Women and Alchol. Camberwell Council on Alcoholism (ed.), pp. 67–100. Tavistock, New York.

Sauther, M. L., Sussman, R. W., and Gould, L. (1999). The socioecology of the ringtailed lemur: Thirty-five years of research. Evol. Anthropol. 8:120–132.

Savage-Rumbaugh, S., and Lewin, R. (1994). Kanzi, the Ape at the Brink of the Human Mind. Wiley, New York.

Schaller, G. B. (1963). The Mountain Gorilla: Ecology and Behavior. Univ. of Chicago Press, Chicago.

Schell, L. M. (1991). Pollution and human growth: Lead, noise, polychlorobiphenyl compounds, and toxic wastes. In Applications of Biological Anthropology to Human Affairs (C. G. N. Mascie-Taylor and G. W. Lasker, eds.), pp. 83–116. Cambridge Univ. Press, Cambridge, UK.

Schell, L. M., and Y. Ando. (1991). Postnatal growth of children in relation to noise from Osaka International airport. J. Sound Vibration 151:371–382.

Schepartz, L. A. (1993). Language and modern human origins. Yearb. Phys. Anthropol. 36:91–126.

Schick, K. D., Toth, N., Garufi, G., Savage-Rumbaugh, E. S., Rumbaugh, D., and Sevcik, R. (1999). Continuing investigations into the stone tool-making and tool-using capabilities of a bonobo (Pan paniscus). J. Archeol. Sci. 26:821–832.

Schrenk, F., Bromage, T. G., Betzler, C. G., Ring, U., and Juwayayi, Y. M. (1993). Oldest Homo and Pilocene biogeography of the Malawi Rift. Nature 365:833–836.

Schultz, A. H. (1924). Growth studies on primates bearing upon man's evolution. Am. J. Phys. Anthropol. 7:149–164.

Schultz, A. H. (1936). Characters common to higher primates and characters specific to man. Q. Rev. Biol. 11:259–283, 425–455.

Schultz, A. H. (1969). The Life of Primates. Weidenfels & Nicolson, London.

Schwartz, E. (1934). On the local races of the chimpanzee. Ann. Mag. Nat. Hist. [10] 13:576–583.

Seaman, M. I., Deinard, A. S., and Kidd, K. K. (1999). Incongruence between mitochondrial and nuclear DNA estimates of divergence between Gorilla subspecies. Amer. J. Phys. Anthropl. Suppl. 28:247.

Senut, B., et al. (2001). Compte Rendu Acad. Sci. 332:137–144.

Seyfarth, R. M., Cheney, D. L., and Marler, P. (1980). Monkey responses to three different alarm calls: Evidence of predator classification and semantic communication. Science 210: 801–803.

Shellis, R., Beynon, A., Reid, D., and Hiiemae, K. (1998). Variations in molar enamel thickness among primates. J. Hum. Evol. 35:507–522.

Shipman, P. (1994). The Evolution of Racism. Simon & Schuster, New York.

Shreeve, J. (1996). Sunset on the Savanna. Why do we walk? Discover 17:116–125.

Sibley, C. G., and Ahlquist, J. E. (1987). DNA hybridization evidence of hominoid phylogeny: Results from an expanded data set. J. Mol. Evol. 26:99–121.

Sibley, C. G., Comstock, J. A., and Ahlquist, J. E. (1990). DNA hybridization evidence of hominoid phylogeny: A reanalysis of the data. J. Mol. Evol. 30:202–236.

Sige, B., Jaeger, J. J., Sudre, J., and Vianey-Liaud, M. (1990). Altiatlasius koulchii n. gen. et sp., Primate Omomyidae du Paleocene superieur du Maroc, et les origenes des euprimates. Palaeontographica Abt. A 214:31–56.

Sigmon, B. A. (1971). Bipedal behavior and the emergence of erect posture in Man. Am. J. Phys. Anthropol. 34:55–60.

Simons, E. L. (1990). Discovery of the oldest known anthropoidean skull from the Paleogene of Egypt. Science 247:1567–1569.

Simons, E. L., and Pilbeam, D. R. (1965). Preliminary revision of the Dryopithecinae (Pongidae, Anthropoidea). Folia Primatol. 3:81–152.

Simons, E. L., and Rasmussen, D. T. (1994). A whole new world of ancestors: Eocene anthropoideans from Africa. Evol. Anthropol. 3:128–138.

Simons, E. L., and Rasmussen, D. T. (1996). Skull of Catopithecus browni, an early Tertialry catarrhine. Amer. J. Phys. Anthropol. 100:261–292.

Simpson, G. G. (1944). Tempo and Mode in Evolution. Columbia University Press, New York.

Simpson, G. G. (1953). The Major Features of Evolution. Simon & Schuster, New York.

Small, M. F. (1989). MS monkey. Nat. Hist., January:10–12.

Smith, B. H. (1986). Dental developments in Australopithecus and early Homo. Nature (London) 323:327–330.

Smith, B. H. (1989). Growth and development and its significance for early hominid behavior. *Ossa* 14:63–96.

Smith, E. A. (1992a). Human behavioral ecology. I. *Evol. Anthropol.* 1:20–25.

Smith, E. A. (1992b). Human behavioral ecology. II. *Evol. Anthropol.* 1:50–55.

Smith, H. M. (1960). *Evolution of Chordate Structure.* Holt, Rinehart and Winston, New York.

Smith, J. Maynard (1978). *The Evolution of Sex.* Cambridge Univ. Press, Cambridge, UK.

Smuts, B. (1987). What are friends for? *Nat. Hist.* 92:36–45.

Sober, E. (ed.). (1984). *Conceptual Issues in Evolutionary Biology: An Anthology.* MIT Press, Cambridge, MA.

Southwick, C. H., and Smith, R. B. (1986). The growth of primate field studies. *Comp. Primate Biol.* 2A:173–191.

Sponheimer, M., and Lee-Thorp, J. A. (1999). Isotopic evidence for the diet of an early hominid, *Australopithecus africanus. Science* 283:368–370.

Stanford, C. B., Wallis, J., Mpongo, E., and Goodall, J. (1994). Hunting decisions in wild chimpanzees. *Animal Behav.* 131:1–20.

Stearns, S. (ed.). (1998). *Evolution in Health and Disease.* Oxford University Press, Oxford, England.

Stokes, W. L. (1988). *Essentials of Earth History.* Prentice Hall, Englewood Cliffs, NJ.

Stoneking, M. (1993). DNA and recent human evolution. *Evol. Anthropol.* 2:60–73.

Stoneking, M., Fontins, J. J., Clifford, S. L., et al. (1997). Alu insertion polymorphisms and human evolution: Evidence for a larger population size in Africa. *Genome Res.* 7 (11):1061–1071.

Stiner, M. C., and Kuhn, S. L. (1992). Subsistence, technology, and adaptive variation in middle Paleolithic Italy. *Amer. Anthropol.* 94:306–339.

Stringer, C. B. (1990). The emergence of modern humans. *Sci. Am.* 263:98–104.

Sussman, R. W. (1991). Primate origins and the evolution of angiosperms. *Am. J. Primatol.* 23:209–223.

Susman, R. W., and Garber, P. A. (1987). A new interpretation of the social organization and mating system of the Callitrichidae. *Int. J. Primatol.* 8:73–92.

Sussman, R. L. (1988). Hand of Paranthropus robustus from Member I, Swartkrans: Fossil evidence for tool behavior. *Science* 240:781–784.

Sussman, R. L., Stern, J., Jr., and Jungers, W. (1984). Arboreality and bipedality in the Hadar hominids. *Folia Primatol.* 43:113–156.

Swisher, C. C., III, Curtis, G. H., Jacob, T., Getty, A. G., Suprijo, A., and Widiasmoro. (1994). Age of the earliest known hominids in Java, Indonesia. *Science* 263:1118–1121.

Swisher, C. C., III, Rink, W. J., Anton, S. C., Schwarcz, H. P., Curtis, G. H., Suprijo, A., and Widiasmoro. (1996). Latest *Homo erectus* in Java: Potential contemporaneity with *Homo sapiens. Science* 274:1870–1874.

Szalay, F. S. (1972). Paleobiology of the earliest primates. In *The Functional and Evolutionary Biology of Primates* (R. H. Tuttle, ed.), pp. 3–35. Aldine, Chicago.

Tague, R., and Lovejoy, O. C. (1986). The obstetric pelvis of A.L. 288-1 (Lucy). *J. Hum. Evol.* 15:237–255.

Tanner, J. M. (1964). *The Physique of the Olympic Athlete.* George Allen and Unwin, London.

Tanner, J. M. (1981). *A History of the Study of Human Growth.* Cambridge Univ. Press, Cambridge, UK.

Tanner, J. M. (1989). *Foetus into Man,* rev. and enlarged ed. Harvard Univ. Press, Cambridge, MA.

Tanner, J. M., and Whitehouse, R. H. (1976). Clinical longitudinal standards for height, weight, height velocity and weight velocity and the stages of puberty. *Arch. Disease in Childhood* 51:170–179.

Tattersall, I. (1999). *The Last Neanderthal.* Westview Press, Boulder, CO.

Tattersall, I. (2000). Once we were not alone. *Sci. Amer.* 282(1): 56–62.

Tattersall, I., and Sawyer, G. J. (1996). The skull of "Sinanthropus" from Zhoukoudian, China: A new reconstruction. *J. Human Evol.* 31:311–314.

Tattersall, I., and Schwartz, J. H. (1999). Hominids and hybrids: The place of neanderthals in human evolution. *Proc. Natl. Acad. Sci. USA* 96:7117–7119.

Taylor, R. E. (1996). Radiocarbon dating: The continuing revolution. *Evol. Anthropol.* 4:169–181.

Templeton, A. R. (1993). The "Eve" hypothesis: A genetic critique and reanalysis. *Am. Anthropol.* 95:51–72.

Terbough, J. T. (1985). The ecology of Amazonian primates. In *Key Environments: Amazonia* (G. Prance and T. Lovejoy, eds.), pp. 284–304. Pergamon, New York.

Terrace, H. (1979). How Nim Chimpsky changed my mind. *Psychol. Today,* November: 65–76.

Tiger, L. (1992). *The Pursuit of Pleasure.* Little, Brown, Boston.

Tobias, P. V. (1991). *The Skulls, Endocasts, and Teeth of Homo habilis. Olduvai Gorge,* Vol. 4. Cambridge Univ. Press, Cambridge, UK.

Toth, N. (1985). Archaeological evidence for preferential right-handedness in the lower and middle Pleistocene, and its possible implications. *J. Hum. Evol.* 14:607–614.

Toth, N. (1987). The first technology. *Sci. Am.* 256:112–121.

Toth, N., and Schick, K. D. (1993). Early stone industries and inferences regarding language and cognition. In *Tools, Language and Cognition in Human Evolution* (K. Gibson and T. Ingold, eds.), pp. 346–362. Cambridge Univ. Press, Cambridge, UK.

Toth, N., Schick, K. D., Savage-Rumbaugh, E. S., Sevcik, R. A., and D. M. Rumbaugh. (1993). *Pan* the tool-maker: Investigations into the stone tool-making and tool-using capabilities of a bonobo *(Pan paniscus). J. Archeol. Sci.* 20:81–91.

Trinkaus, E., and Shipman, P. (1992). *The Neanderthals: Of Skeletons, Scientists and Scandal.* Vintage Books, New York.

Trivers, R. L. (1972). Parental investment and sexual selection. In *Sexual Selection and the Descent of Man* (B. Campbell, ed.). Aldine, Chicago.

Turner, R. A., Altemus, M., Enos, T., et al. (1999). Preliminary research on plasma oxytocin in normal cycling women. Investigating emotion and interpersonal distress. *Psychiatry* 66(2): 97–113.

Tutin, C., and McGinnis, P. (1981). Sexuality of the chimpanzee in the wild. In *Reproductive Biology of the Great Apes: Comparative and Biomedical Perspectives* (C. Graham, ed.), pp. 239–264. Academic Press, New York.

Tuttle, R. H. (1967). Knucklewalking and the evolution of hominoid hands. *Am. J. Phys. Anthropol.* 26:171–206.

Tuttle, R. H. (1975). Parallelism, brachiation, and hominid phylogeny. In *The Phylogeny of the Primates* (W. Luckett and F. S. Szalay, eds.), pp. 447–480. Plenum, New York.

Tyson, E. (1699). *Orang-Outang, sive Homo sylvestris: Or; The Anatomy of a Pygmie Compared With That of Monkey, an Ape, and a Man.* Bennet, London.

Ubelaker, D. H. (1995). Latest developments in skeletal biology and forensic anthropology. In *Biological Anthropology: The State of the Science* (N. T. Boaz and L. D. Wolfe, eds.), pp. 91–106. International Institute for Human Evolutionary Research, Bend, OR.

Ubelaker, D. H., and O'Donnell, G. (1992). Computer-assisted facial reconstruction. *J. Forensic Sci.* 37:155–162.

Van Shaik, C. P. (1983). Why are diurnal primates living in groups? *Behaviour* 87:120–143.

Van Schaik, C. P., and Dunbar, R. I. M. (1990). The evolution of monogram in large primates: A new hypothesis and some crucial tests. *Behaviour* 115:30–62.

Vigilant, L., Pennington, R., Harpending, H., Kocher, T. D., and Wilson, A. C. (1989). Mitochondrial DNA sequences in single hairs from a southern African population. *Proc. Natl. Acad. Sci. U.S.A.* **86**:9350–9354.

Vogel, J. C. (1985). Further attempts at dating the Taung tufas. In *Hominid Evolution: Past, Present, and Future* (P. V. Tobias, ed.), pp. 189–194. Alan R. Liss, New York.

Vrba, E. S. (1988). Late Pliocene climatic events and hominid and hominid evolution. In *Evolutionary History of the "Robust" Australopithecines* (F. Grine, ed.), pp. 405–426. de Gruyter, New York.

Vrba, E. S. (1994). An hypothesis of heterochrony in response to climatic cooling and its relevance to early hominid evolution. In *Integrative Paths to the Past* (R. Corruccini and R. Ciochon, eds.), pp. 345–376. Prentice Hall, Upper Saddle River, NJ.

Wade, M. J. (1978). A critical review of the models of group selection. *Q. Rev. Biol.* **53**:101–114.

Walker, A. (1967). Locomotor adaptations in living and fossil Madagascar lemurs. Ph.D. Dissertation, University of London.

Walker, A. (1993). The origin of the genus Homo. In *The Origin and Evolution of Humans and Humanness* (D. T. Rasmussen, ed.), pp. 29–47. Jones & Bartlett, Boston.

Walker, A. and Shipman, P. (1996). *The Wisdom of the Bones.* Knopf, New York.

Walker, A., Zimmerman, M., and Leakey, R. (1981). A possible case of hypervitaminosis A in Homo erectus. *Nature (London)* **296**:248–250.

Walker, A. C., and Leakey, R. E. F. (eds.). (1993). *The Nariokotome Homo erectus Skeleton.* Harvard University Press, Cambridge, MA.

Wallace, A. R. (1869). *The Malay Archipelago.* Macmillan, London.

Wang, Z. X., Young, L. J., DeVries, G. J., et al. (1998). Voles and vasopressin: A review of molecular, cellular, and behavioral studies of pair-bonding and paternal behaviors. *Prog. Brain Res.* **119**:483–499.

Ward, C. V., Leakey, M. G., Brown, B., Brown, F., Harris, J., and Wlker, A. (1999). South Turkwell: A new Pliocene hominid site in Kenya. *J. Hum. Evol.* **36**:69–95.

Ward, P., and Zahavi, A. (1973). The importance of certain assemblages of birds as "information-centres" for food-finding. *Ibis* **115**(4):517–534.

Ward, S., Brown, B., Hill, A., Kelley, J., and Downs, W. (1999) Equatorius: A new hominoid genus from the middle Miocene of Kenya. *Science* **285**:1382–1386.

Washburn, S. L. (1960). Tools and human evolution. *Sci. Am.* **203**:63–75.

Washburn, S. L. (1963). Behavior and human evolution. In *Classification and Human Evolution* (S. L. Washburn, ed.), pp. 190–203. Aldine, Chicago.

Washburn, S. L., and Harding, R. S. O. (1975). Evolution and human nature. In *American Handbook of Psychiatry,* 2nd ed. Vol. 6, Chapter 1:3–13.

Washburn, S. L., and Lancaster, C. S. (1968). The evolution of hunting. In *Man the Hunter* (R. Lee and I. DeVore, eds.), pp. 292–303. Aldine, Chicago.

Washburn, S. L., and Moore, R. (1980). *Ape into Human,* 2nd ed. Little, Brown, Boston.

Watson, J. D. (1970). *Molecular Biology of the Gene,* 2nd ed. Benjamin, Menlo Park, CA.

Watts, D. P. (1989). Infanticide in mountain gorillas: New cases and a reconsideration of the evidence. *Ethology* **81**:1–18.

Weiner, S., Xu, Q., Goldberg, P., Liu, J., and Bar-Yosef, O. (1998). Evidence for the use of fire at Zhoukoudian, China. *Science* **281**:251–253.

Weitz, C. A., Garruto, R. M., Chen-Ting, C., Ji-Chuan, L., Rui-Ling, L., and Xing, H.. (2000). Growth of Qinghai Tibetans living at three difference high altitudes. *Amer. J. Phys. Anthropol.* **111**:69–88.

Wescott, R. W. (1967). The exhibitionistic origin of human bipedalism. *Man* **2**:630.

Westenberg, K. (1999). From fins to feet. *Natl. Geogr. Mag.,* 114–127.

White, T. D., Suwa, G., and Asfaw, B. (1994). Australopithecus ramidus, a new species of early hominid from Aramis, Ethiopia. *Nature (London)* **371**:306–312.

Whitney, E., Gunnell, D., Dorling, D., et al. (1999). Ecological study of social fragmentation, poverty and suicide. *Brit. Med. J.* **319**(7216):1034–1037.

Whitten, T. (1982). *The Gibbons of Siberut.* J. M. Dent, London, UK

Wiessner, P. (1990). Is there a unity to style? In *Uses of Style in Archeology* (M. Conkey and C. Hasdorf, eds.), pp. 105–112. Cambridge Univ. Press, Cambridge, UK.

Williams, A. G., Rayson, M. P., Jubb, M., World, M., Woods, D. R., Hayward, M., Martin, J., Humphries, S. E., and Montgomery, H. E. (2000). Psysiology: The ACE gene and muscle performance. *Nature (London)* **403**:614.

Williams, G. C. (1966). *Adaptation and Natural Selection.* Princeton Univ. Press, Princeton, NJ.

Williams, G. C., and Nesse, R. M. (1991). The dawn of Darwinian medicine. *Q. Rev. Biol.* **66**:1–22.

Williams, R. J. (1951). Biochemical Institute Studies. IV. Individual metabolic patterns and human disease: An exploratory study utilizing predominantly paper chromatographic methods. *Univ. Tex. Publ.* **5109**:7–21.

Wilson, E. O. (1975). *Sociobiology: The New Synthesis.* Harvard Univ. Press, Cambridge, MA.

Wilson, E. O. (1996). Culture as a biological product. In *Search of Nature,* pp. 107–126. Island Press, Washington, DC.

Winchester, A. M. (1972). *Genetics: A Survey of the Principles of Heredity,* 4th ed. Houghton-Mifflin, Boston.

Wobst, H. M. (1977). Stylistic behavior and information exchange. In *For the Director: Research Essays in Honor of James B. Griffin* (C. E. Cleland, ed.). Anthropol Pap. No. 61, pp. 317–342. Ann Arbor Museum of Anthropology, Ann Arbor, MI.

WoldeGabriel, G., White, T. D., Suwa, G., Renne, P., deHeinzelin, J., Hart, W. K., and Helken, G. (1994). Ecological and temporal placement of early Pliocene hominids of Aramis, Ethiopia. *Nature* **371**:330–333.

Wolfe, L. D. (1981). Display behavior of three troops of Japanese monkeys. *Primates* **22**:24–32.

Wolpoff, M. H., Hawks, J., Frayer, D. W., and Huntley, K. (2001). Modern human ancestry at the periphery: A test of the replacement theory. *Science* **291**:293–297.

Wood, B. (1999). The human genus. *Science* **284**:65–71.

Wood, B. A. (1992). Taxonomy and evolutionary relationships of Homo erectus. Cour. Forschungsint, Senckenberg, Frankfurt, Germany.

Wrangham, R. W. (1980). An ecological model of female-bonded primate groups. *Behaviour* **75**:262–300.

Wrangham, R. W. (1983). Ultimate factors determining social structure. In *Primate Social Relationships: An Integrated Approach* (R. Hinde, ed.), pp. 255–262. Blackwell, Oxford.

Wrangham, R. W. (1987). Evolution of social structure. In *Primate Societies* (B. B. Smuts, D. L. Cheny, R. M. Seyfarth, R. W. Wrangham, and T. T. Struhsaker, eds.), pp. 282–296. Univ. of Chicago Press, Chicago.

Wrangham, R. W., McGrew, W., deWaal, F., and Heltne, P. (eds.). (1994). *Chimpanzee Cultures.* Harvard Univ. Press, Cambridge, MA.

Wrangham, R., and Peterson, D. (1996). *Demonic Males, Apes and the Origin of Human Violence.* Houghton Mifflin, New York.

Wright, K. (1990). Cradle of mutation. *Discover* **11**(9):22–23.

Wynn, I. (1988). Tools and the evolution of human intelligence. In *Machiavellian Intelligence* (R. Byrne and A. Whiten, eds), pp. 271–284. Oxford Univ. Press (Clarendon), Oxford.

Yamagiwa, J. (1987). Intra- and inter-group interactions of an all-male group of Virunga Mountain gorillas. *Primates* **28**:1–30.

Yamei, H., Potts, R., Baoyin, T., Zhengtang, G., Deino, A., Wei, W., Clark, J., Guangmao, X., and Weiwen, H. (2000). Mid Pleistocene Acheulean-like stone technology of the Bose Basin, South China. *Science* **287**:1622–1626.

Yoder, A. (1997). Back to the future: A synthesis of strepsirhine systematics. *Evol. Anthropol.* **6**:11–22.

Yoshida, A., Hsu, I. C., and Yasunami, M. 1991. Genetics of human alcohol-metabolizing enzymes. *Proc. Nucl. Acid Res. Mol. Biol.* **40**:255–287.

Zihlman, A., Cronin, J. E., Cramer, D. L., and Sarich, V. M. (1978). Pygmy chimpanzee as a possible prototype for the common ancestor of humans, chimpanzees, and gorillas. *Nature* **275**: 744–746.

Zimmer, C. (1999). Fossil offers a glimpse into mammal's past. *Science* **283**:1989–1990.

Zuckerman, S. (1932). *The Social Life of Monkeys and Apes.* Routledge & Kegan Paul, London.

CHAPTER 1: CO Berna Villiers; **1-1** Christian Jegou/Publiphoto/ Photo Researchers, Inc.; **1-3** Anthro-Photo File; **1-4** Rikard Lama/ Liaison Agency, Inc.; **1-6** (left) The Granger Collection (right) Blumenbach, Jo. Frid. *De Generis Humani Varietate Nativa.* Editio terti. Gottingae: Fandenhoek et Ruprecht, 1795. Reprinted in *The Anthropological Treatises of Johann Friedrich Blumenbach,* translated and edited by Thomas Bendyshe. Burndy Library/Dibner Institute for the History of Science and Technology, Cambridge, Massachusetts; **1-7** Michael Nichols/NGS Image Collection; **1-9** CORBIS; **1-10** Illustration from C. J. Lumsden and E. O. Wilson, *Promethean Fire* (Harvard University Press, 1983). Reprinted with permission. Chromosome comparison reprinted with permission from *Science* **208**:1145, fig. 2. Copyright 1980 American Association for the Advancement of Science; **1-11** Michael Nichols/NGS Image Collection; **1-13** Dr. Gerhard Storch/Forschungsinstit ut Senckenberg; **1-14, 1-17** From *Phylogeneny Reconstruction in Paleontology* by Robert M. Schroch, pp. 188, 173, copyright © 1986 Van Nostrand Reinhold; **1-18** The mapping data were produced by the Chromosome 22 Mapping Group at the Sanger Centre and were obtained from the World Wide Web at *http://www.sanger.ac.uk/HGP/Chr22;* **1-19** © The Natural History Museum, London.

CHAPTER 2: CO Berna Villiers **2-1, 2-2** Culver Pictures, Inc.; **2-4** North Wind Picture Archives; **2-5** Brian Yarvin/Photo Researchers, Inc.; **2-6** James L. Amos/NGS Image Collection; **2-7** (top) Kenneth W. Fink/Photo Researchers, Inc. (bottom) Frans Lanting/Photo Researcher, Inc.; **2-8** *Population Genetics and Evolution* by Mettler/ Gregg/Schaffer, © 1969. Reprinted by permission of Pearson Education, Inc. Upper Saddle River, NJ; **2-9** (top) Leonard Lee Rue III/ Animals Animals/Earth Scenes (bottom) Neg./Transparency no. 35948. Courtesy Dept. of Library Services, American Museum of Natural History; **2-10** (left) Corbis/Stock Market (right) Margot Conte/Animals Animals/Earth Scenes; **2-11** LOC/Science Source/ Photo Researchers, Inc.; **2-14** O. Alamany & E. Vicens/CORBIS; **2-15** (left) Tom McHugh/Photo Researchers, Inc. (right) Michael Kevin Daly /Corbis/Stock Market; **2-16** Joe M. Macedonia, Indiana University; **2-17** Hulton/Archive; **2-18** (left) Frans Lanting/Minden Pictures (center) Stan Osolinski/Stone (right) Joseph M. Macedonia.

CHAPTER 3: CO Berna Villiers; **3-1** Hulton/Archive; **3-2** Reprinted with permission of Pearson Education, Inc. Upper Saddle River, NJ 07458; **3-3** Rosalind Franklin/Science Source/Photo Researchers, Inc.; **3-4** Biophoto Associates/Science Source/Photo Researchers, Inc.; **3-8** *The Processing of RNA* by James E. Darnell Jr., illustration by Jerome Kul, copyright 1983 from Scienctific American, Inc. 249(1):94. Reprinted with permission of the illustrator. **3-10** Andrew H. Knoll, Harvard University; **3-11** Adapted from R. J. Huskey, University of Virginia; **3-12** From *Essentials of Anatomy and Physiology* by Frederic Martini and Edwin F. Bartholomew. Reprinted by permission of Pearson Education Inc. Upper Saddle River, NJ 07458; **3-13** Reprinted with permission of Pearson Education, Inc. Upper Saddle River, NJ 07458; **3-14a** Reprinted with permission of Pearson Education, Inc. Upper Saddle River, NJ 07458; **3-14b** From *Concepts of Genetics,* 5/e by Klug/Cummings. Reprinted with permission of Pearson Education, Inc. Upper Saddle River, NJ 07458.

CHAPTER 4: CO Berna Villiers; **4-2** From *Genetics: A Human Concern* by Sutton, H. Eldon. © 1985. Reprinted with permission of Pearson Education, Inc. Upper Saddle River, NJ 07458; **4-4** W. Stansfield, *Genetics,* 1969, McGraw Hill, reproduced with per-

mission of The McGraw-Hill Companies; **4-6** VU/Stanley Flegler/ Visuals Unlimited; **4-7** David Barritt/Liaison Agency, Inc.; **4-8** Ian Worpole © 1990. Reprinted with permission of Discover Magazine; **4-9** M. W. Tweedle/Photo Researchers, Inc.; **4-11** From *Population Genetics and Evolution* by Mettler/Gregg/Schaffer, © 1969. Reprinted with permission of Pearson Education, Inc. Upper Saddle River, NJ 07458; **4-12** Figure from *Biological Evolution* by Peter Price, copyright © 1966 by Saunders College Publishing, reproduced by permission of the publisher.

CHAPTER 5: CO Berna Villiers; **5-1** Kenneth Eward/NGS Image Collection; **5-4** (left) Robert & Linda Mitchell Photography (right) Larry S. Roberts/Visuals Unlimited; **5-5** From *The Anatomical Primer,* by permission of the author, D. A. Langebartel; **5-6** *Human Anatomy* by Martini, Frederic, © 1995. Reprinted by permission of Pearson Education, Inc. Upper Saddle River, NJ 07458; **5-8** (a) From Monroe W. Strickberger, *Evolution,* 2000 Jones and Bartlett Publishers, Sudbury, MA. *www.jbpub.com.* Reprinted with permission (b) Figure adapted from *Biological Evolution* by Peter Price, copyright © 1996 by Saunders College Publishing, reproduced by permission of the publisher; **5-9** (left and right) Jonathan Blair/NGS Image Collection; **5-11** *Evolution of the Vertebrates,* E. H. Colbert and M. Morales. copyright © 1991 John Wiley and Sons. This material is used by permission of John Wiley & Sons, Inc.; **5-12** (bottom left) Cabisco/Visuals Unlimited (bottom right) Petit Format/Nestle/ Science Source/Photo Researchers, Inc.; **5-15** Mark A. Klingler/The Carnegie Museum of Natural History; **5-17** Rod Williams/Bruce Coleman, Inc.; **5-19** After Romer; **5-20** (a,b) From Monroe W. Strickberger, *Evolution,* 2000 Jones and Bartlett Publishers, Sudbury, MA. *www.jbpub.com.* Reprinted with permission. (c) *Essentials of Anatomy and Physiology* by Frederic Martini and Edwin F. Bartholomew. Reprinted by permission of Pearson Education, Inc. Upper Saddle River, NJ 07458; **5-23** *Essentials of Anatomy and Physiology* by Frederic Martini and Edwin F. Bartholomew. Reprinted by permission of Pearson Education, Inc. Upper Saddle River, NJ 07458; **5-24** (left) Wayne Lynch/DRK Photo (right) McGuire/Anthro-Photo File.

CHAPTER 6: CO Berna Villiers; **6-1** From *Primate Adaptation and Evolution* by J. G. Fleagle. Copyright © 1988 Academic Press. Reprinted with permission. Illustrations by Kim Reed-Deemer, Northern Illinois University; **6-2** Figure from "Skeleton of Mesopithecus" in *Primate Adaptation and Evolution,* Second Edition by John Fleagle, copyright © 1999 by Academic Press, reproduced by permission of the publisher; **6-3** Figure from "Primate Locomotor Categories" in *Primate Adaptation and Evolution* by John G. Fleagle, copyright © 1988 by Academic Press, reproduced by permission of the publisher; **6-4** (a) Figure from "Reconstruction of Plesiadapis" in *Primate Adaptation and Evolution* by John G. Fleagle, copyright © 1988 by Academic Press, reproduced by permission of the publisher; **6-5** From Ian Tattersall, *The Human Odyssey,* 1993. Reprinted with permission; **6-7** Jean-Philippe Varin/JACANA/Photo Researchers, Inc.; **6-8** Napier and Walker, *Folia Primatologica.* Copyright © 1967 by S. Karger AG, Basel. Reprinted with permission; **6-12** *Yearbook of Physical Anthropology* 38:199-238, 1995, E. L. Simons. Reprinted with permission; **6-13** © 1985 David L. Brill. David L. Brill/Brill Atlanta; **6-14** Figure from "Evolutionary Relationships Among Early Anthropoids" in *Primate Adaptation and Evolution,* Second Edition by John G. Fleagle, copyright © 1999 by Academic Press, reproduced by permission of the publisher; **6-15** (left) From Steven M. Stanley, *Earth and Life through Time*, W. H. Freeman (right) Richard F. Kay; **6-16** Elwyn L. Simons, Duke University; **6-17** Figure from "Morphological Differences in the New World and Old World Monkeys" in *Primate Adaptation and Evolution* by John G. Fleagle, copyright © 1988 by Academic Press, reproduced by permission of the publisher; **6-18** Figure from "Evolutionary Relationship of New World Monkeys" in *Primate Adaptation and Evolution* by John G. Fleagle, copyright © 1988 by Academic Press, reproduced by permission of the publisher; **6-19** Figure from "Map—Monkey Dispersal" in *Primate Adaptation and Evolution* by John G. Fleagle, copyright © 1988 by Academic Press, reproduced by permission of the publisher.

CHAPTER 7: CO Erich Lessing/Art Resources, NY; **7-1** Figure from *Primate Adaptation and Evolution,* Second Edition by John G. Fleagle, copyright © 1999 by Academic Press, reproduced by permission of the publisher; **7-2** David Haring/Peter Arnold, Inc.; **7-3** Figure from *Primate Adaptation and Evolution,* Second Edition by John G. Fleagle, copyright © 1999 by Academic Press, reproduced by permission of the publisher; **7-4** Figure from *Primate Adaptation and Evolution,* Second Edition by John G. Fleagle, copyright © 1999 by Academic Press, reproduced by permission of the publisher; **7-5** Figure from *Primate Adaptation and Evolution,* Second Edition by John G. Fleagle, copyright © 1999 by Academic Press, reproduced by permission of the publisher; **7-6** Figure from *Primate Adaptation and Evolution,* Second Edition by John G. Fleagle, copyright © 1999 by Academic Press, reproduced by permission of the publisher; **7-7** Kevin Schafer/CORBIS; **7-8** Figure from *Primate Adaptation and Evolution,* Second Edition by John G. Fleagle, copyright © 1999 by Academic Press, reproduced by permission of the publisher; **7-9** Figure from *Primate Adaptation and Evolution,* Second Edition by John G. Fleagle, copyright © 1999 by Academic Press, reproduced by permission of the publisher; **7-10** Art Wolfe, Inc.; **7-11** Figure from *Primate Adaptation and Evolution,* Second Edition by John G. Fleagle, copyright © 1999 by Academic Press, reproduced by permission of the publisher; **7-12** Andrew L. Young/Photo Researchers, Inc.; **7-14** Claus Meyer/Minden Pictures; **7-15** Rolano Seitre/Bios/Peter Arnold, Inc.; **7-16** Robert W. Madden/NGS Image Collection; **7-17** Tim Davis/Photo Researchers, Inc.; **7-18** Figure from *Primate Adaptation and Evolution,* Second Edition by John G. Fleagle, copyright © 1999 by Academic Press, reproduced by permission of the publisher; **7-19** Figure from *Primate Adaptation and Evolution,* by John G. Fleagle, copyright © 1988 by Academic Press, reproduced by permission of the publisher; **7-20** Art Wolfe/Stone; **7-21** Charles Philip Cangialosi/CORBIS; **7-22** Gerald Lacz/Peter Arnold, Inc.; **7-23** Rob & Ann Simpson/Simpson's Nature Photography; **7-24** Figure from *Primate Adaptation and Evolution,* Second Edition by John G. Fleagle, copyright © 1999 by Academic Press, reproduced by permission of the publisher; **7-25** Dieter & Mary Plage/Bruce Coleman, Inc.; **7-26** Robert Hynes/NGS Image Collection; **7-28** From *Human Anatomy* by Martini, Frederic, © 1995. Reprinted by permission of Pearson Education, Upper Saddle River, NJ 07458; **7-29** Figure from *Primate Adaptation and Evolution,* by John G. Fleagle, copyright © 1988 by Academic Press, reproduced by permission of the publisher; **7-30** Art Wolfe, Inc.; **7-31** Renee Lynn/Photo Researchers, Inc.; **7-32** Joe McDonald/Visuals Unlimited; **7-33** Art Wolfe, Inc.; **7-34** Copyright © Zoological Society of San Diego, San Diego, California, U.S.A. All right reserved; **7-35** Bruce Coleman, Inc.; **7-36** Gerry Ellis/ENP Images; **7-37** Jim Moore/Anthro-Photo File; **7-38** R. Van Nostrand/Photo Researchers, Inc.; **7-39** Frans Lanting/Minden Pictures.

CHAPTER 8: CO Berna Villiers; **8-1** Art Wolfe/Stone; **8-2** (top) Anthro-Photo File (bottom) Frans Lanting/Minden Pictures; **8-3** N. DeVore/Anthro-Photo File; **8-4** Figure from *Primate Adaptation and Evolution,* by John G. Fleagle, copyright © 1988 by Academic

Press, reproduced by permission of the publisher; **8-5** Frans Lanting/Minden Pictures; **8-6** Dr. M. S. Mayilvahnan/Tropical Trannies; **8-7** (top) Annie Griffiths Belt/NGS Image Collection (bottom) Frans Lanting/Minden Pictures; **8-8** From *Primate in Nature* by Richard. Copyright © 1985 by Freeman and Company. Used with permission; **8-9** Irven DeVore/Anthro-Photo File; **8-10** Photo by Frans de Waal; courtesy Living Links Center for the Advanced Study of Human and Ape Evolution, Emory University; **8-11** Martin Rogers/Stock Boston; **8-12** Barbara Smuts/Anthro-Photo File; **8-13** Bruce Coleman, Inc.; **8-14** R. Wrangham/Anthro-Photo File; **8-15** Figure from *Primate Behavior: Field Studies of Monkeys and Apes* by Irven DeVore. Copyright © 1965 by Holt, Rinehart and Winston and renewed 1993 by Irven DeVore, reproduced by permission of the publisher; **8-16** Peter Veit/DRK Photo; **8-17** K. & K. Ammann/Bruce Coleman, Inc.; **8-18** Photo by Frans de Waal; courtesy Living Links Center for the Advanced Study of Human and Ape Evolution, Emory University; **8-19** Frans Lanting/Minden Pictures; **8-20** Photo by Frans de Waal; courtesy Living Links Center for the Advanced Study of Human and Ape Evolution, Emory University; **8-21** Paul Simonds; **8-22** Photo by Frans de Waal; courtesy Living Links Center for the Advanced Study of Human and Ape Evolution, Emory University; **8-23** Photo by Frans de Waal; courtesy Living Links Center for the Advanced Study of Human and Ape Evolution, Emory University.

CHAPTER 9: CO Berna Villiers; **9-1** Figure from "Apes and Humans" in *Primate Adaptation and Evolution* by John G. Fleagle, copyright © 1988 by Academic Press, reproduced by permission of the publisher; **9-3** From *Yearbook of Physical Anthropology* by David Begun, 1994, reproduced with permission of the author; **9-7** Walker/Pickford, *New Interpretations of Ape and Human Ancestry.* copyright © 1983 by Kluwer Academic/Plenum Publishers. Reprinted with permission; **9-9** Photos courtesy of Glenn Conroy, Washington University, St. Louis; **9-11** Philbeam/Institute of Human Origins; **9-12** Begun et al., *Function, Phylogeny, and Fossils.* Copyright © 1997 by Kluwer Academic/Plenum Publishers. Reprinted with permission; **9-13** Figure from *Primate Adaptation and Evolution,* Second Edition by John G. Fleagle, copyright © 1999 by Academic Press, reproduced by permission of the publisher; **9-14** From *Human Evolution,* 3d Ed. By R. Lewin, p. 118. © 1993. Reprinted by permission of Blackwell Science, Inc.; **9-15** With permission, from the *Annual Review of Anthropology,* Volume 26 © 1997 by Annual Reviews *www.AnnualReviews.org.*

CHAPTER 10: CO Berna Villiers; **10-1** Meave Leaky, Fred Spoor/Kenya National Museum; **10-2** Noel T. Boaz; **10-4** David Brill/David L. Brill Photography/Brill Atlanta; **10-5** Adapted from *Encyclopedia of Human Evolution & Prehistory* by Ian Tattersall. Eric Delson, John Van Couvering. Copyright © 1988. Reprinted with permission; **10-6** AFP/CORBIS; **10-9** Kenneth Garrett/NGS Image Collection; **10-10** (left) John Reader/Science Photo Library/Photo Researchers, Inc. (center) Noel T. Boaz (right) Photo by D. Finnin/C. Chesek. Courtesy Dept. of Library Services, American Museum of Natural History; **10-11** National Museums of Kenya, Nairobi. © 1995 David L. Brill. David L. Brill/Brill Atlanta; **10-12** Nanci Kahn/Institute of Human Origins; **10-13** Figure in *Primate Adaptation and Evolution,* by John G. Fleagle, copyright © 1988 by Academic Press, reproduced by permission of the publisher; **10-14** (b) © 1994 Tim D. White/Brill Atlanta (c) National Museums of Kenya, Nairobi. © 1995 David L. Brill. David L. Brill/Brill Atlanta; **10-15** (left) Institute of Human Origins (right) Institute of Human Origins, Arizona State University; **10-16** W. H. Kimbel/Institute of Human Origins; **10-19** (right) John Reader/Science Photo Library/Photo Researchers, Inc.; **10-20** David L. Brill/David L. Brill Photography/Brill Atlanta; **10-22** (left) Original housed in National Museum of Ethiopia, Addis Ababa. © 1999 David L. Brill/Brill Atlanta (center) National Museum of Ethiopia, Addis Ababa. © 1999 David L. Brill/Brill Atlanta (right)

National Museum of Ethiopia, Addis Ababa. © 1999 David L. Brill/Brill Atlanta; **10-23** (left) K. Cannon-Bonventure/Anthro-Photo File (right) David L. Brill/David L. Brill Photography/Brill Atlanta; **10-24** M. Shostak/Anthro-Photo File; **10-25** Frans Lanting/ Minden Pictures.

CHAPTER 11: CO Berna Villiers; **11-1** (a) © John Reader/Photo Researchers, Inc. (c) Noel T. Boaz (d) Noel T. Boaz (e) Philip V. Tobia, Medical School, University of the Witwatersrand, Johannesburg, South Africa; **11-2** Reprinted with permission from Frederick E. Grine, Editor. *Evolutionary History of the "Robust" Australopithecines* (New York: Aldine de Gruyter). Copyright © 1988 Aldine de Gruyter and Elisabeth S. Vrba, "An Hypothesis of Heterochrony in Response to Climatic Cooling . . ." in *Integrative Paths to the Past*, Corrucini/Ciochon eds., ©1994, p. 366. Reprinted by permission of Prentice Hall, Upper Saddle River, New Jersey 07458; **11-3** Aiello, Leslie C. and Peter Wheeler, "The Expensive-Tissue Hypothesis," *Current Anthropology* 36:199-221, copyright 1995 by The University of Chicago Press. Reprinted with permission; **11-4** (left) Philip V. Tobia, Medical School, University of the Witwatersrand, Johannesburg, South Africa (right) K. Cannon-Bonventure/Anthro-Photo File; **11-5** Noel T. Boaz; **11-7** National Museums of Kenya, Nairobi. © Davie L. Brill. David L. Brill/Brill Atlanta; **11-9** Courtesy University of Florida @ Gainesville; **11-10** Noel T. Boaz; **11-12** American Museum of Natural History. © 1996 David L. Brill/Brill Atlanta; **11-14** R. Potts/Smithsonian National Museum of Natural History/Smithsonian Institution; **11-15** Reprinted with permission of J. Desmond Clark, Professor Emeritus of Anthropology. University of California, Berkeley; **11-16** From *Nature* 393:459. Courtesy of Professor Ernesto Abbate; **11-17** (left) Paris Pavlakis, Ph.D., University of Ioannina, Greece (center) Photo by Willard Whitson. Courtesy the Library, American Museum of Natural History (right) Courtesy of and copyright by Eric Delson; **11-19** *Ancestors: The Hard Evidence*, E. Delson. Copyright © 1985 Allan R. Liss. This material is used by permissin of John Wiley & Sons, Inc.; **11-21** *Human Anatomy* by Marini/Timmons, © 1997. Reprinted by permision of Pearson Education, Upper Saddle River, NJ 07458; **11-22** Reprinted with permission of the Estate of Bunji Tagawa.

CHAPTER 12: CO Berna Villiers; **12-4** From *Human Evolution*, 3rd Ed. By R. Lewin, p. 152. © 1993. Reprined by permission of Blackwell Science, Inc.; **12-5** Kenneth Garrett/NGS Image Collection; **12-6** Israel Antiquities Authority, Rockefeller Museum. © 1995 David L. Brill. David L. Brill/Brill Atlanta; **12-7** Kenneth Garrett Photography; **12-8** Illustration by Diana Salles in Ian Tattersall, *The Last Neanderthal*, Westview Press, 1999. Reprinted with permission; **12-9** From Ian Tattersall, *The Human Odyssey*, 1993. Reprinted withpermission; **12-10** Neg./Transparency no. 4938(9). (Photo by D. Finnin/C. Chesek). Courtesy Dept. of Library Services, American Museum of Natural History; **12-11** (top, left) Negative number 327424. Photo by Rota. Courtesy the Library, Americn Museum of Natural History (top right) © Chris Hellier/CORBIS (bottom) Neg. Transparency no. 4937(6). (Photo by J. Beckett/C. Chesek). Courtesy Dept. of Library Services, American Museum of Natural History; **12-13** (left) Courtesy Yoel Rak, Department of Anatomy—Tel Aviv University (right) Dr. Owen Lovejoy, Kent State University. © 1994 David L. Brill. David L. Brill/Brill Atlanta; **12-16** (left) Erik Trinkaus, Washington University (right) Richard Schlecht/NGS Image Collection; **12-19** © François Bordes, *The Old Stone Age*, copyright © 1977, reproduced with permission of The McGraw-Hill Companies, Inc.; **12-20** (photo) Laboratoire d'Anthropologie, University de Bordeaux I. © 1985 David L. Brill. David L. Brill/Brill Atlanta; **12-21** Liaison Agency, Inc.; **12-22** © Archivo Iconografico, S. A./CORBIS; **12-23** Institute of Human Origins, Arizona State University; **12-24** Kenneth Garrett/NGS Image Collection; **12-25** (left) © Archivo Iconografico, S. A./CORBIS (right) © Gianni Dagli

Orti/CORBIS; **12-26** Kenneth Garrett/NGS Image Collection; **12-27** Ira Block/NGS Image Collection; **12-28** Illustration by Diana Salles in Ian Tattersall, *The Last Neanderthal*, Westview Press, 1999. Reprinted with permission.

CHAPTER 13: CO Berna Villiers; **13-1** Reprinted with permission from Laurie Grace; **13-2** PhotoDisc, Inc.; **13-3** (left) Manoj Shah/Stone (right) Timothy Laman/NGS Image Collection; **13-4** Tom McHugh/Photo Researchers, Inc.; **13-5** Schaller, George, *The Mountain Gorilla*. Copyright © 1963. Reprinted with permission; **13-6** Michael Nichols/NGS Image Collection; **13-7** Renee Lynn/Stone; **13-8** Hulton/Archive; **13-9** Michael Nichols/NGS Image Collection; **13-10** (left) Wrangham/Anthro-Photo File (right) Nancy Nicolson/ Anthro-Photo File; **13-11** Peter Davey/Bruce Coleman, Inc.; **13-12** Michael Nichols/NGS Image Collection; **13-13** Terrace/Anthro-Photo File; **13-14** Frans Lanting/Minden Pictures; **13-15** Frans Lanting/ Minden Pictures; **13-16** Rose A. Sevcik/Shelly Williams, Georgia State University; **13-17** (left) Petit Format/J. Da Cunha/Photo Researchers, Inc. (right) Suzanne Szasz/Photo Researchers, Inc.; **13-18** Irenaus Eibl-Eibesfeldt, Max Planck Institute for Behavioral Physiology, Andech, Germany; **13-19** Bob Daemmrich/The Image Works; **13-20** Anthro-Photo File; **13-21** Hulton/Archive; **13-22** Blair Seitz/ Science Source/Photo Researchers, Inc.

CHAPTER 14: CO Berna Villiers; **14-1** Bill Losh/FPG International LLC; **14-2** Alan Mann/University of Pennsylvania Museum of Archaeology and Anthropology; **14-3** From *Primates in Nature* by Richard. Copyright © 1985 by Freeman and Company. Used with permission; **14-4** Reprinted with permission from "Transposon 'Jumping'" by Davies et al. from *Science*, **289**, 11, fig. 1. Copyright 2000 American Association for the Advancement of Science; **14-11** UPI/CORBIS; **14-12** © Adam Woolfitt/CORBIS; **14-14** D. Gorton/Time Inc., NJ.

CHAPTER 15: CO Berna Villiers; **15-1** Bogin, Barry, *Patterns of Human Growth*. Copyright © 1988 by Cambridge University Press. Reprinted with the permission of Cambridge University Press; **15-3** From George Oliver, *Practical Anthropology*. Copyright © 1969. Courtesy of Charles C. Thomas Publisher, Ltd., Springfield, Illinois; **15-4** Reprinted with permission from Lovejoy, "The Origins of Man," *Science* 211, 342, fig. 1. Copyright 1997 American Association for the Advancement of Science; **15-5** Tanner, J. M. (1962). "Growth at adolescnce: with a general consideration of the effects of heredity and environmental factors upon growth and maturation from birth to maturity." *Human Growth*, 2/e, Blackwell Scientific Publications, Oxford. Reprinted with permission; **15-6** Barret/Abramoff/Kumaran/Millington, *Biology*, © 1986, p. 382. Reprinted by permission of Prentice Hall, Upper Saddle River, NJ 07458; **15-10** Peacock/Anthro-Photo File; **15-12** Reprinted with permission from J. Cohen, "Population Growth and Earth's Human Carrying Capacity," from *Science*, **269**, 341, fig. 1. Copyright © 1995 American Association for the Advancement of Science.

CHAPTER 16 CO Berna Villiers; **16-1** National Archives and Records Administration; **16-3** (left) James Sugar/Black Star (right) Tom McHugh/Photo Researchers, Inc.; **16-4** James Stevenson/Science Photo Library/Photo Researchers, Inc.; **16-5** Biophoto Associates/Photo Researchers, Inc.; **16-7** John Karapelou/© 1987. Reprinted with permission of Discover Magazine; **16-8** Dr. Melissa McDonnell; **16-9** (left) Long Photography, Inc.; **16-10** (left) Sloan Portia/NGS Image Collection (left center) Kazuhiko Sano/NGS Image Collection (right center) John Daugherty/NGS Image Collection (right) Mauricio Anton/NGS Image Collection; **16-11** Gene O'Donnell/Federal Bureau of Investigation; **16-12** Equipo Argentino de Antropologia Forense/EAAF archives.

APPENDIX 4 Figures from Richard Klein, *The Human Career: Human Biological and Cultural Origins*, 1989, pp. 10 and 23.